Quick Search

The most common way to search West HR Advisor is to enter a search in the *Quick Search* text box. For example, to run a search on *Military Leave*, simply type **Military Leave** in the text box, then click **Go**.

Note: For information about the sources and authors used in HR Advisor, click **About HR Advisor**.

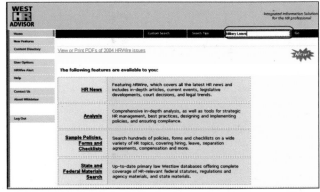

Custom Search

Use the Custom Search feature to limit your search to one or two publications, to search by state, or to use advanced searching techniques. This search for *co-worker harassment* limits the search to News and Analysis sources.

Finding Sample Forms, Policies, and Checklists

Select **Checklists** or **Forms and Policies** from the Home page to search hundreds of forms and policies.

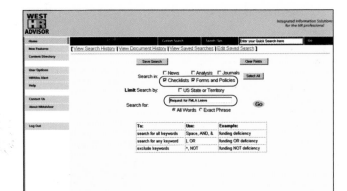

Viewing and Saving Your Search Results

Within your search result, you can click the arrows at the bottom of the page to select the document for which you want to view or browse the full contents.

Click **Save Search** to save your search results for later viewing. You can also set up an Alert to have your search run in the future and have the results e-mailed to you.

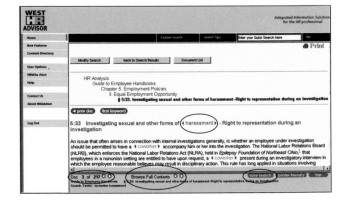

Human Resource Management

Eleventh Edition

Robert L. Mathis
University of Nebraska at Omaha

John H. Jackson
University of Wyoming

THOMSON
™
SOUTH-WESTERN

Australia · Canada · Mexico · Singapore · Spain · United Kingdom · United States

Human Resource Management, 11e
Robert L. Mathis, John H. Jackson

VP/Editorial Director:
Jack W. Calhoun

VP/Editor-in-Chief:
Dave Shaut

Executive Editor:
John Szilagyi

Senior Developmental Editor:
Mardell Toomey

Marketing Manager:
Jacquelyn Carrillo

Senior Production Editor:
Deanna Quinn

Technology Project Editor:
Kristen Meere

Manufacturing Coordinator:
Diane Lohman

Production House:
Graphic World, Inc.

Printer:
R.R. Donnelley
Willard, Ohio

Art Director:
Anne Marie Rekow

Cover and Internal Designer:
Anne Marie Rekow

Cover Images:
© Photodisc

Web Coordinator:
Karen Schaffer

For permission to use material
from this text or product, submit
a request online at
http://www.thomsonrights.com.

For more information
contact South-Western,
5191 Natorp Boulevard,
Mason, Ohio 45040.
Or you can visit our Internet site
at: http://www.swlearning.com

TO

Jo Ann Mathis
who manages me

R. D. and M. M. Jackson
who were successful managers of people for many years

1) TOP Four problems

2) Make SIX connections

3) 6 steps implement
to improve — don't
have to come from
your chapters
(other chapters/common
sense)

Contents in Brief

SIX-PACK

STILL TOGETHER

COMFORTABLY NUMB

THE WHO Break-Away Team

The WHO

TOP 4 ORG'L ISSUES

MINIMUM SIX Connectors EXPlain Concept How relates to office Space

v

Contents

SECTION 3

TRAINING AND DEVELOPING HUMAN RESOURCES 261

SECTION 4

COMPENSATING HUMAN RESOURCES 361

S E C T I O N   5

EMPLOYEE RELATIONS 457

Contents

Preface

The authors of this book are extremely pleased with the success of *Human Resource Management.* This book is the leader both in the academic market for human resource (HR) texts and in the market for HR professionals who are pursuing professional certification. Our approach in revising each edition of this book is simple. We extensively review the academic and practitioner literature published since the last revision and incorporate it into this latest edition. In this way, readers can be certain that they are getting the most up-to-date HR content possible. Furthermore, we ask academics and practitioners, both those who use this book and those who do not, to provide us with formal input on the previous edition and what coverage should be added, deleted, or changed. We have always been receptive to input from our reviewers and have used their observations and good ideas.

You now have in your hands the end result of this careful and thorough process: the eleventh edition of Mathis and Jackson's *Human Resource Management.* Be assured that it remains the most current, comprehensive resource in the HR field for both academic and professional use.

THE ELEVENTH EDITION

The eleventh edition has been significantly changed to reflect the challenges facing HR management as they evolve. In addition to the new research content, this edition has other useful additions that are worth noting, as follows:

HR Metrics

The value of HR management activities increasingly has to be justified to executives in organizations by using financial and other data. To identify ways to respond to these pressures, the eleventh edition includes a feature in most chapters called "HR Metrics" that identifies how different HR management activities are being measured. A special metrics icon ⦀⦀⦀⦀ is used to identify this content.

Technology Transforming HR

A new feature, Technology Transforming HR, focuses on how technology is being used to change how HR activities are performed. This feature is found in all chapters and serves as both a preview of how HR will be changing and a source of information on specific approaches currently being used.

Global Coverage

Rather than having a separate chapter on global HR management as in the past, the coverage of global issues has been integrated throughout the various chapters. This integration is a reflection of the current business environment, in which most organizations face global competition. Consequently, HR issues and practices are becoming more transnational in nature. In the chapters, global material is indicated with a small global icon ⬤ and highlighted in the HR Globally boxed feature.

Human Resource Management, Eleventh Edition Web Site

At a Web site dedicated to the eleventh edition, instructors and students will find useful tools and additional resources to enrich and extend textbook presentations. Instructors will find downloadable ancillary materials. Students and other readers can locate other resources, such as quick links to a number of useful items, at *http://mathis.swlearning.com.*

Included on the Web site are listings of HR literature, resources, and important organizations. Also, the Web site contains Web addresses for a variety of electronic newsletters from some leading consulting firms that provide HR content. Accessing these newsletters provides timely information on current HR events, court decisions, studies, and other areas. Links to job boards and salary survey sources are available as well.

Internet

The Internet has become a valuable tool for HR professionals and affects a number of HR activities. To incorporate Internet links, this edition has several features. For example, throughout the text the "Logging On" feature identifies Web sites that contain useful sources of HR information in specific content areas. Each of these links contains a specific World Wide Web address active at the publication time of this text. Also, where appropriate, an expanded number of references from Web addresses are cited in the chapter notes.

West Thomson HR Advisor on the Web

An additional resource in the eleventh edition is the West Thomson HR Advisor on the Web. As an industry leader in providing information to HR professionals, West Thomson produces and sells HR Advisor to thousands of HR practitioners. Through a cooperative arrangement and at no additional cost, every instructor and purchaser of the new text will receive an individualized access code to all of the HR Advisor content. Instructions for gaining access are printed on the inside front cover of each copy of the eleventh edition.

HR Advisor readers will be able to access current analyses of HR issues, view sample HR policies in more than 70 areas, obtain compliance guidelines, download numerous sample HR forms, and review background details on many topics that expand or supplement the coverage in the book. To tie in the West content throughout the book, all chapters contain as a margin feature specific item notations and directions for linking to the HR Advisor content in the designated area.

ORGANIZATION OF THE ELEVENTH EDITION

The organization of the eleventh edition reflects important changes from the previous edition. The following overview highlights some of the significant content and changes made.

HR's Strategic Contribution to Organizational Effectiveness

This text stresses how HR professionals and the activities they direct contribute to the strategic business success of organizations. The first chapter looks at the roles of HR management, particularly the importance of the *strategic* role of HR management, and how it is being affected by HR technology. The competencies for careers in HR also are discussed. Chapter 2 addresses the strategic factors affecting HR, strategic HR planning, and how to evaluate the effectiveness of HR management.

Individual Performance and Employee Retention

In the competitive world of today, organizations need individuals who perform well and remain as employees. Chapter 3 contains extensive content on employee retention. No other general HR text provides comparable in-depth coverage of retention.

Equal Employment and Affirmative Action

Chapters 4 and 5 cover equal employment opportunity (EEO). As suggested by reviewers, Chapter 4 addresses the various laws, regulations, and court decisions that determine the legal framework of EEO. Because the issues of diversity and equal employment are so closely linked, Chapter 5 looks at various aspects of implementing equal employment, such as affirmative action, sexual harassment, age discrimination, and other issues. That chapter concludes with a discussion of diversity and the importance of managing diversity as a critical part of HR management.

Staffing the Organization

Chapter 6 describes job design issues that have an impact on organizations and the people working in them. Based on job design, the chapter then provides useful coverage of job analysis and various approaches to and methods of job analysis.

Chapter 7 focuses on recruiting in various labor markets. It discusses the difficulties of recruiting employees with rare skills—and new methods to attract individuals with rare skills. The chapter contains considerable content on Internet recruiting and the evaluation of recruiting efforts. An expansion of the well-regarded coverage on selection in Chapter 8 encompasses the selection strategy choices that management must make. The revised discussion of psychological testing and interviewing approaches and techniques reflects current research and practices in HR management.

Training and HR Development

Chapter 9 discusses the strategic role training plays in organizations and how training must be linked to business strategies and organizational competitiveness. Specific content on adult learning and newer training design and delivery means is provided. As the text addresses the growing use of *e-learning,* it discusses both the contributions and problems associated with Web-based training. Chapter 10 on HR development looks at the means organizations use to expand the capabilities of their human resources. The chapter contains content on succession planning and why it is a growing focus of HR management.

Performance Management

Chapter 11 expands the material on identifying and measuring employee performance, including additional information on the numerous approaches used. The chapter emphasizes performance management and the role of the performance appraisal process in enhancing the performance of human resources in organizations.

Compensating Human Resources

Compensation of human resources covers pay, incentives, and benefits. Chapters 12 and 13 include information on approaches such as broadbanding and competency-based pay to augment the well-regarded coverage of base compensation, pay-for-performance, and variable-pay programs already in those chapters. Chapter 14 highlights the growing concerns of the cost of benefits, which face HR professionals and organizations, with specific new content that discusses consumer-driven health-care programs.

Employee Relations

The discussion of employee relations addresses several areas, including health, safety, and security. The coverage in Chapter 15 identifies current health and safety issues and OSHA compliance requirements. The chapter also provides new content on the prevention of workplace violence and the importance of workplace security. The various issues associated with employee rights and discipline, such as employment-at-will, privacy rights, and substance abuse, have been expanded in Chapter 16. It also looks at such emerging issues as electronic monitoring, privacy, e-mail, and other employee-rights issues affected by technology.

Union-Management Relations

The changing role of unions in the U.S. economy is discussed in Chapter 17. In addition to covering the basic laws and regulations governing union management relations in the United States, the chapter discusses reasons for the declining percentage of workers in unions and the challenges facing both unions and management. It concludes with coverage of collective bargaining and grievance management.

CHAPTER FEATURES

Each chapter begins with specific learning objectives. Next, the "HR Headline" feature contains an example of a contemporary HR problem, situation, or practice in an actual organization to more fully illustrate a concept presented in the chapter. Each chapter also includes at least one "HR Perspective," a feature that highlights HR management examples, ethical issues, and research studies. Additionally, many chapters contain another feature, "HR Practice," which presents suggestions on how to handle specific HR issues or situations. Both the "West Group" and the "Logging On" features provide links to additional material beyond the text content. New to this edition, the "HR Globally" feature points out special international HR concerns, and the "Technology Transforming HR" feature illustrates how technological advances are affecting HR.

Following a point-by-point summary, the review and discussion questions provide critical thinking queries. At the end of every chapter, a case presents a real-life HR problem or situation using actual organizations as examples. An addition to the eleventh edition is the inclusion of a Supplemental Case, which describes typical HR problems faced in organizations. These supplemental cases are available on the Web site for the book, *http://mathis.swlearning.com.* Finally, reference notes cite sources used in the chapter, with particular attention given to the inclusion of the most current references and research possible. About 90% of all references are new or updated from the previous edition, which makes this book the most current text available.

SUPPLEMENTS

Instructor's Manual with Video Guide
0-324-28963-4

The instructor's manual represents one of the most exciting and useful instructor's aids available. Comprehensive teaching materials, including chapter overviews, chapter outlines, instructor's notes, and suggested answers to end-of-chapter Review and Application Questions and "Learning Review" questions are provided for every chapter. The video guide describes the content in the video segments that is available to help integrate individual chapter content through current, interesting examples.

Test Bank
0-324-28968-5

The eleventh edition test bank is significantly revised and upgraded from previous editions. The test bank contains more than 1,500 test questions prepared by Janelle Dozier. Multiple-choice, true/false, and essay questions are provided for every chapter. Answers are cross-referenced to pages within the text so that it is easy to pinpoint where relevant material is found. When the answer to a true/false questions is "false," feedback is provided to underscore the reason why. New to this edition are questions identified by type, such as definition, application, and analytical and critical reasoning.

ExamView
0-324-28969-3

ExamView contains all of the questions in the printed test bank. This program is an easy-to-use test creation software compatible with Microsoft Windows. Instructors can add or edit questions, instructions, and answers. Questions may be selected by previewing them on screen, selecting them randomly, or selecting them by number. Instructors can also create quizzes online whether over the Internet, a local area network (LAN), or a wide area network (WAN).

Instructor's Resource CD
0-324-28962-6

The Instructor's Resource CD includes the instructor's manual, test bank, and ExamView. In addition, it includes a comprehensive set of full-color PowerPoint presentation slides, prepared by Charlie Cook of the University of West Alabama.

PowerPoint Slide Presentation

Instructor's PowerPoint slides are available on both the Instructor's Resource CD and on a password protected Instructor's Web site. Approximately 400 slides are included.

Transparency Acetates
0-324-28965-0

Prepared in conjunction with the instructor's manual, a full-color set of 50 transparency acetates is also available to instructors to enhance classroom presentations.

Video
0-324-28966-9

A brand new video collection features companies with innovative HR practices, many of which have been recognized for their excellence in HR practices. Both small and large companies are featured in the videos, and all video content is closely tied to concepts within the text.

Student Resource Guide
0-324-28961-8

Designed from a student's perspective by Tonya Elliott, a certified HR professional, this useful study guide provides aids that students need to maximize results in the classroom and on exams, and, ultimately in the practice of HR. Chapter objectives and chapter outlines aid students in reviewing for exams. Study questions include matching (10–15 per chapter), true/false (15 per chapter), idea completion (5 per chapter), multiple choice (20–25 per chapter), and essay questions (3 per chapter). Answer keys are provided for immediate feedback to reinforce learning.

Please visit our product support Web site *http://mathis.swlearning.com,* which offers additional instructional and learning tools to complement our text.

Human Resource Management West HR Advisor

This Web-based learning resource provides practical information, policy guidelines, and other useful information that is valuable to both instructors and students. As an industry leader in providing information to HR professionals, West produces and sells HR Advisor to thousands of HR practitioners.

Through a cooperative arrangement at no cost, every instructor and individual purchasing a new text will receive an individualized access code to all of the HR Advisor content on a special Web site. Details are printed on the inside the front cover of each copy of the eleventh edition. The HR Advisor readers will be able to read current analyses of HR issues, view sample HR policies in more than 70 areas, obtain compliance instructions, download numerous sample HR forms, and review background details on many topics that expand or supplement the coverage in the eleventh edition. To tie in the West HR Advisor content throughout the book, all chapters contain specific item notations as a margin feature, and directions for linking to the HR Advisor content in the designated area.

ACKNOWLEDGMENTS

The success of edition after edition of *Human Resource Management* can largely be attributed to our reviewers who have generously offered both suggestions for improvements and new ideas for the text. The eleventh edition reviewers whom we would like to sincerely thank include:

John Cote
Baker College

Robert Mitchell Crocker
Stephen F. Austin State University

Barbara R. Dastoor
Nova Southeastern University

Janice S. Gates
Western Illinois University

Kathleen Fenninger
KMJ Consulting

Darrin Kass
Bloomsburg University

Donna Ledgerwood
University of North Texas

Jonathan S. Monat
California State University

Matt Newby
Heald College

Stephanie Narvell
Wilmington College

Sharon L. Segrest
California State University, Fullerton

Tom Stone
Oklahoma State

Chris Turpin
Virginia Eye Institute

Philip E. Varca
University of Wyoming

Fraya Wagner-Marsh
Eastern Michigan University

David Wheeler
Robert Morris University

Finally, some leading HR professionals provided ideas and assistance. Appreciation is specifically expressed to Nicholas Dayan and Kathleen McCumber.

Those involved in changing messy scrawls into printed ideas deserve special recognition. At the top of that list is Jo Ann Mathis, whose guidance and diligence made this book better. Others who assisted with many critical details include Carolyn Foster and our copyeditor, Cheryl Drivdahl.

The authors thank John Szilagyi, Executive Editor, and Mardell Toomey, Senior Developmental Editor, for their guidance and involvement. We also appreciate the support of our Senior Production Editor, Deanna Quinn, whose efforts contributed significantly to making the final product appealing.

The authors feel confident that this edition will continue as the standard for the HR field. We believe it offers a relevant and interesting look at HR management, and we are optimistic that those who use the book will agree.

Robert L. Mathis, SPHR
Omaha, Nebraska

John H. Jackson
Laramie, Wyoming

Dr. Robert L. Mathis

Dr. Robert Mathis is Professor of Management at the University of Nebraska at Omaha (UNO). Born and raised in Texas, he received a B.B.A. and M.B.A. from Texas Tech University and a Ph.D. in Management and Organization from the University of Colorado. At UNO he has received the University's "Excellence in Teaching" award.

Dr. Mathis has co-authored several books and has published numerous articles covering a variety of topics over the last 25 years. Dr. Mathis also has held numerous national offices in the Society for Human Resource Management and in other professional organizations, including the Academy of Management. He has served as President of the Human Resource Certification Institute (HRCI) and is certified as a Senior Professional in Human Resources (SPHR) by HRCI.

He has had extensive consulting experiences with organizations of all sizes and in a variety of areas. Firms assisted have been in telecommunications, telemarketing, financial, manufacturing, retail, health-care, and utility industries. He has extensive specialized consulting experience in establishing or revising compensation plans for small- and medium-sized firms. Internationally, Dr. Mathis has consulting and training experience with organizations in Australia, Lithuania, Romania, Moldova, and Taiwan.

Dr. John H. Jackson

Dr. John H. Jackson is Professor of Management at the University of Wyoming. Born in Alaska, he received his B.B.A. and M.B.A. from Texas Tech University. He then worked in the telecommunications industry in human resources management for several years. After leaving that industry, he completed his doctoral studies at the University of Colorado and received his Ph.D. in Management and Organization.

During his academic career, Dr. Jackson has authored four other college texts and over 50 articles and papers, including those appearing in *Academy of Management Review, Journal of Management, Human Resources Management,* and *Human Resources Planning.* He has consulted widely with a variety of organizations on HR and management development matters. During the past several years, Dr. Jackson has served as an expert witness in a number of HR-related cases.

At the University of Wyoming, he has served three terms as Department Head in the Department of Management and Marketing. Dr. Jackson has received the top teaching award at Wyoming and was one of the first to work with two-way interactive television for MBA students in the state. He has served on the boards of directors of the Wyoming Business Council and the Wyoming Workforce Development Council. In addition to teaching, Dr. Jackson is president of Silverwood Ranches, Inc.

Human Resource Management

Eleventh Edition

Nature of Human Resource Management

Changing Nature of Human Resource Management

After you have read this chapter, you should be able to:

- Define HR management and identify the seven categories of HR activities.

- Discuss three challenges facing HR today.

- Describe how the major roles of HR management are being transformed.

- Identify the purposes and uses of HR technology.

- Discuss why ethical issues affect HR management.

- Explain the key competencies needed by HR professionals and why certification is important.

What Do HR Managers Do?

The reality of what HR managers do on a weekly basis varies significantly from what is typically reported in academic and media sources. Here is some of what an HR manager in a 700-employee firm dealt with during one week:

* Resolved an employee complaint about "offensive" pictures being shown by a co-worker
* Met with the CEO to plan compensation budgets for the following year
* Met with an outside lawyer regarding a racial discrimination complaint by a former employee who had been terminated because of performance problems
* Negotiated with the provider of health-care insurance benefits to bring a projected 22% increase in premiums down to a 14% increase
* Reviewed an employee performance appraisal with a supervisor and discussed how to communicate both positive feedback and problem areas

* Advised an executive on the process for terminating a sales manager whose sales performance and management efforts were significantly below the sales goals set
* Addressed a manager's report of an employee's accessing pornographic Web sites on his company computer
* Chaired an employee recognition luncheon
* Discussed an employee succession plan for the Customer Operations Division, consisting of 400 employees
* Discussed with the other members of the Executive Leadership Team (the CEO, the CFO, and Division Heads) an employee staffing plan for the following year and ways to reduce employee turnover

Many other topics were part of this HR manager's job that week. However, that list illustrates one fact: "there are a wide range of issues that are part of the regular work in HR management."

"It's very obvious to the CEO whether you get it or not. If you only understand the HR part of the business, there won't be much rapport."

—Nancy Anderson

Nature of Human Resource Management

Human Resource (HR) management
The direction of organizational systems to ensure that human talent is used effectively and efficiently to accomplish organizational goals.

As a field, Human Resource (HR) management is undergoing significant transformation. **Human Resource (HR) management** is the direction of organizational systems to ensure that human talent is used effectively and efficiently to accomplish organizational goals. Whether employees are in a big company with 10,000 positions or a small non-profit agency with 10 positions, those employees must be recruited, selected, trained, and managed. They also must be compensated, and many will be given benefits of some type, which means that an appropriate and legal compensation system is needed. In an environment in which

Figure 1-1	*HR Management Activities*

Effective
what is appropriate

Efficiently utilization of Time

Global

Environmental

Technological

Strategic HR Management
* HR planning
* HR measurement
* HR technology

Employee and Labor Relations
* Employee rights and privacy
* HR policies
* Union/management relations

Equal Employment Opportunity
* Compliance
* Diversity
* Affirmative action

Cultural/Geographic

HR ACTIVITIES

Health, Safety, and Security
* Health and wellness
* Safety
* Security

Staffing
* Job analysis
* Recruiting
* Selection

Economic

Compensation and Benefits
* Wage/salary Administration
* Incentives
* Benefits

HR Development
* Orientation
* Training
* Employee development
* Career planning
* Performance management

Political

Legal

Social

▭ **External environment**

the workforce keeps changing, laws and the needs of employers change too. Therefore, HR management activities continue to change and evolve.

HR Activities

HR management is composed of seven interlinked activities taking place within organizations, as depicted in Figure 1-1. Additionally, external forces—legal, economic, technological, global, environmental, cultural/geographic, political, and social—significantly affect HR activities and how they are designed, managed, and changed.

THOMSON
★
™
WEST

HR FUNCTIONS
Lists activities within each HR function.
Custom Search:
☑ CHECKLISTS
Exact Phrase: HR functions and activities

Global Forces and HR Management HR management truly is becoming transnational as organizations compete globally. For instance, in the past few years, the international outsourcing of U.S. jobs to India, the Philippines, China, and other countries has become a significant political concern. Also, the worldwide growth of global firms such as Toyota and SAP means that management must consider transnational concerns in all HR activities. In this book, global content is integrated throughout all the chapters, rather than being isolated into a separate chapter. The global content is highlighted by a special global icon as the following seven HR activities are discussed.

Strategic HR Management To anticipate and respond to the HR changes facing organizations, strategic HR management has grown in importance. As part of maintaining organizational competitiveness, *HR effectiveness* must be increased through the use of *HR metrics.* One key to increasing HR effectiveness is using *HR technology.* Many organizations have *HR management systems (HRMSs),* which use information technology to provide managers and employees with more accurate and timely information on HR programs and activities. Through *HR planning,* managers attempt to anticipate forces that will influence the future supply of and demand for employees. An additional strategic HR concern is the *motivation* and *retention* of employees. All these topics are discussed in Chapters 2 and 3.

Equal Employment Opportunity *Compliance* with equal employment opportunity (EEO) laws and regulations affects all other HR activities and is integral to HR management. The *diversity* of a multi-cultural and global workforce is creating more challenges for HR professionals and all managers. For instance, HR plans must ensure sufficient availability of a diversity of individuals to meet *affirmative action* requirements. The nature of EEO and diversity management is discussed in Chapters 4 and 5.

Staffing The aim of staffing is to provide an adequate supply of qualified individuals to fill jobs in an organization. By studying what workers do, *job analysis* lays the foundation for the staffing function. Then both *job descriptions* and *job specifications* can be prepared to use when *recruiting* applicants for job openings. The *selection* process is concerned with choosing qualified individuals to fill jobs in the organization. Staffing activities are discussed in Chapters 6, 7, and 8.

HR Development Beginning with the *orientation* of new employees, HR development includes different types of *job-skill training.* Also, *development* of all employees, including supervisors and managers, is necessary to prepare organizations for future challenges. *Career planning* identifies paths and activities for individual employees as they develop within the organization. Assessing how employees perform their jobs is the focus of *performance management.* Activities associated with HR development are examined in Chapters 9, 10, and 11.

Compensation and Benefits Compensation in the form of *pay, incentives,* and *benefits* rewards people for performing organizational work. Employers must develop and refine their basic *wage and salary* systems. Also, the use of *incentive programs* such as gainsharing and productivity rewards is growing. The rapid increase in the costs of benefits, especially health-care benefits, will continue to be a major issue. Compensation, variable pay, and benefits activities are all discussed in Chapters 12, 13, and 14.

Health, Safety, and Security Ensuring the physical and mental health and safety of employees is vital. The Occupational Safety and Health Act of 1970 (OSHA) has made organizations more responsive to concerns for *safety* through a focus on reducing work-related illnesses, accidents, and injuries. Through a broader focus on *health,* HR management can use *employee assistance programs (EAPs)* to help employees with substance abuse and other problems and thereby retain otherwise satisfactory employees. *Health promotion* programs that encourage healthy employee lifestyles are becoming more widespread. Also, workplace *security* has grown in importance. Health, safety, and security activities are examined in Chapter 15.

Employee and Labor Relations The relationship between managers and their employees must be handled effectively if both the employees and the organization are to prosper together. Whether or not some of the employees are represented by a union, *employee rights* must be addressed. It is important to develop, communicate, and update HR *policies and procedures* so that managers and employees alike know what is expected. In some organizations, *union/ management relations* must be addressed as well. Activities associated with employee and labor/management relations are discussed in Chapters 16 and 17.

HR in Organizations

In a real sense, *every* manager in an organization is an HR manager. Sales managers, head nurses, drafting supervisors, college deans, and accounting supervisors all engage in HR management, and their effectiveness depends in part on the success of organizational HR systems. However, it is unrealistic to expect a nursing supervisor or an engineering manager to know about the nuances of equal employment regulations, or how to design and administer a compensation and benefits system. For that reason, larger organizations frequently have people in an HR department who specialize in these activities.

Smaller Organizations and HR Management In the U.S. and worldwide, the number of small businesses continues to grow. According to data from the U.S. Small Business Administration (SBA), small businesses employ over 50% of all private-sector employees and generate 60% to 80% of all net new jobs each year.[1]

In surveys by the SBA, the issues identified as the greatest concerns in small organizations are consistently: (1) shortages of qualified workers, (2) increasing costs of benefits, (3) rising taxes, and (4) compliance with government regulations. Notice that three of the top four concerns have an HR focus, especially when governmental compliance with wage/hour, safety, equal employment, and other regulations are considered.

As a result, for many smaller organizations HR issues are often significant. But not every organization is able to maintain an HR department. In a company with an owner and only three employees, the owner usually takes care of HR issues. As an organization grows, often a clerical employee is added to handle payroll, benefits, and required HR record keeping. If new employees are hired, supervisors and managers usually do the recruiting, selecting, and training. These HR activities reduce the time that supervisors and managers have to focus on operations, sales and marketing, accounting, and other business areas. At 80 to 100 employees, an organization typically needs to designate a person to specialize in HR management. Other HR jobs are added as the company gets even larger.

Cooperation of HR with Operating Managers Cooperation between operating managers, such as those in sales and manufacturing, and HR staff is necessary for HR efforts to succeed. In many cases, the HR professionals and staff members design processes and systems that the operating managers must help implement. The exact division of labor between HR and other departments varies from organization to organization. Figure 1-2 shows how various training and development activities are handled in organizations, according to surveys conducted by the Bureau of National Affairs.

Throughout this book, figures labeled Typical Division of HR Responsibilities illustrate how HR responsibilities in various areas are typically divided in organizations having specialized HR departments. The first such figure, 1-3, shows

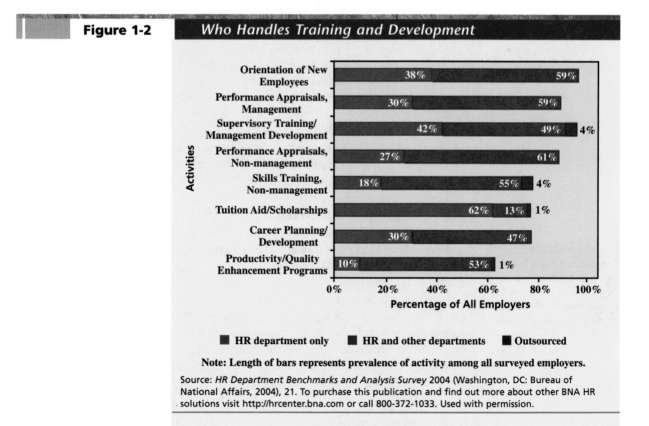

Figure 1-2

Who Handles Training and Development

Activities (Percentage of All Employers):

- Orientation of New Employees: 38%, 59%
- Performance Appraisals, Management: 30%, 59%
- Supervisory Training/Management Development: 42%, 49%, 4%
- Performance Appraisals, Non-management: 27%, 61%
- Skills Training, Non-management: 18%, 55%, 4%
- Tuition Aid/Scholarships: 62%, 13%, 1%
- Career Planning/Development: 30%, 47%
- Productivity/Quality Enhancement Programs: 10%, 53%, 1%

■ HR department only ■ HR and other departments ■ Outsourced

Note: Length of bars represents prevalence of activity among all surveyed employers.

Source: *HR Department Benchmarks and Analysis Survey* 2004 (Washington, DC: Bureau of National Affairs, 2004), 21. To purchase this publication and find out more about other BNA HR solutions visit http://hrcenter.bna.com or call 800-372-1033. Used with permission.

Figure 1-3	Typical Division of HR Responsibilities: Training

HR Unit	Managers
◆ Prepares skill-training materials ◆ Coordinates training efforts ◆ Conducts or arranges for off-the-job training ◆ Coordinates career plans and employee development efforts ◆ Provides input and expertise for organizational development	◆ Provide technical information ◆ Monitor training needs ◆ Conduct and monitor continuing on-the-job training ◆ Continually discuss employees' growth and future potential ◆ Participate in organizational change

how the responsibilities for training might be divided between the HR department and operating managers in an organization.

MANAGEMENT OF HUMAN CAPITAL IN ORGANIZATIONS

Organizations must manage four types of assets:

◆ *Physical:* Buildings, land, furniture, computers, vehicles, equipment, etc.
◆ *Financial:* Cash, financial resources, stocks, financial securities, etc.
◆ *Intangible:* Specialized research capabilities, patents, information systems, designs, operating processes, etc.
◆ *Human:* Individuals with talents, capabilities, experience, professional expertise, relationships, etc.

All these assets are crucial in varying degrees. However, the human assets are the "glue" that holds all the other assets together and guides their use to achieve organizational goals and results.[2] Certainly, the cashiers, stockers, supervisors, and other employees at Home Depot or the doctors, nurses, receptionists, technical professionals, and other employees at a hospital allow all the other assets of their organization to be used to provide customer or patient services. By recognizing the importance of human assets, organizations are increasingly emphasizing human capital.

Human Capital and HR

Human capital is not the people in organizations—it is what those people bring and contribute to organizational success.[3] **Human capital** is the collective value of the capabilities, knowledge, skills, life experiences, and motivation of an organizational workforce.

Sometimes it is called *intellectual capital* to reflect the thinking, knowledge, creativity, and decision making that people in organizations contribute. For example, firms with high intellectual capital may have technical and research employees who create new biomedical devices, formulate pharmaceuticals that can be patented, and develop new software for specialized uses. All these organizational contributions indicate the value of human capital.

Human capital
The collective value of the capabilities, knowledge, skills, life experiences, and motivation of an organizational workforce.

|||||| **Measuring the Value of Human Capital** The value of human resources in organizations can be seen in various ways. One is sheer costs. In some

industries, such as the hospitality industry, employee costs exceed 60% of total operating costs. Various studies have found that an average of 60% to 70% of total company expenditures are related to human resources today, compared with about 38% in 1992.[4]

Increasingly, organizations are recognizing the strategic value of their human assets.[5] With that recognition comes an increasing need to measure how the value of their human capital is changing.[6] This focus on human capital, much like that on other capital resources such as finances, has led to greater interactions between HR leaders and Chief Financial Officers (CFOs). One study by Mercer, a global consulting firm, found that most CFOs see human capital as a key factor in creating value for shareholders. However, only 16% have calculated the return on human capital investments.[7] The measurement of human capital is discussed more in Chapter 2.

Human Resources as a Core Competency

The development and implementation of specific organizational strategies must be based on the areas of strength in an organization. Referred to as *core competencies,* those strengths are the foundation for creating a competitive advantage for an organization. A **core competency** is a unique capability that creates high value and differentiates an organization from its competition.

Core competency
A unique capability that creates high value and differentiates an organization from its competition.

Certainly, many organizations have stated that their human resources differentiate them from their competitors and are a key determinant of competitive advantage.[8] Studies also have documented that HR practices help create competitive advantages.[9] Organizations as widely diverse as FedEx, Nordstrom, and Dell Computer have focused on human resources as having special strategic value for the organization.

Some ways that organizations make human resources a core competency are attracting and retaining employees with unique professional and technical capabilities, investing in the training and development of those employees, and compensating them in ways that retain them and keep them competitive with their counterparts in other organizations. For example, small community banks have picked up numerous small- and medium-sized commercial loan customers because the banks emphasize that their customers can deal with the same employees directly every time, rather than having to call an automated service center in another state. The focus is on developing their human resources to give them a competitive advantage as they face significant HR challenges.

▌ HR MANAGEMENT CHALLENGES

The environment faced by organizations and their managers is a challenging one. A force affecting the management of human resources is the *globalization of business,* as shown in such areas as international outsourcing and global competitive pressures. Significant changes in *economic forces* and the rapid growth in *technology* have changed how people work. *Changing demographics* in the workforce are significantly affecting HR management, particularly with the increase in the diversity of employees and the aging of the workforce in many countries. All of these factors are combining to put more *cost pressures* on organizations. Consequently, employers in many industries have reduced the number of jobs and employees as part of *organizational restructuring.* A look at some of these challenges follows.

HR *Globally*

The Costs of International Outsourcing

It has been estimated that during the past few years almost 600,000 U.S. jobs have been "transferred" to foreign locations, in low-wage countries such as China, Mexico, the Philippines, Thailand, India, Romania, and Bangladesh. According to forecasts by Forrester Research, the greatest number of those jobs has been in computer technology and office/customer support.

The primary reason for these shifts is to save on labor costs. To illustrate, a Java computer programmer with a college degree is paid about $5,000 a year in India, but $60,000 a year in the U.S. The average yearly pay of financial analysts who have MBAs and are fluent in English is $15,000 to $20,000 in Bulgaria, Argentina, and India, compared with $100,000 or more in the U.S. Less-skilled employees of customer call centers who are fluent in English average $150 a month in China, whereas comparable U.S. employees make about $2,000 a month.

Even more troublesome for U.S. workers is the projection by Forrester Research that in the next decade, 3.3 million jobs will be moved out of the U.S. Projections also suggest that at least a million or more jobs will be internationally outsourced from Great Britain, France, Germany, Sweden,

and other European countries to lower-wage countries. Estimates are that numerous jobs in areas such as computers, sales, architecture, legal services, and life sciences will migrate to low-wage countries.

Despite the huge cost savings obtained by international outsourcing, the loss of U.S. jobs is leading to significant concerns by U.S. employers, politicians, and customers. Various legislative proposals have been made to address those concerns, and numerous media reports continue to highlight the international outsourcing trend.

There are also concerns about the quality of the customer service provided by individuals who are not familiar with U.S. or European cultures, even if they are fluent in various languages. These concerns have led some U.S. firms to move customer service operations back to the U.S., even though costs are higher there. Nevertheless, international outsourcing will continue—for example, IBM has indicated that thousands of software jobs are being moved to India. A comment by an IBM executive illustrates the conflicts: "One of the challenges that we deal with every day is trying to balance the business needs versus impact on people."[10]

Globalization of Business

The internationalization of business has proceeded at a rapid pace. Many U.S. firms, both large and small, receive a substantial portion of their profits and sales from other countries. Firms such as Coca-Cola, Exxon, Mobil, Microsoft, Ford, and General Electric derive half or more of total sales and profits outside the United States. The reverse is also true. For example, Toyota, based in Japan, is growing its market share and number of jobs in the U.S., and North American sales provide 70% of its profits worldwide.[11] Also, Toyota, Honda, Nissan, and other Japanese automobile manufacturers, electronics firms, and suppliers have established operations in the U.S.

The globalization of business has shifted from trade and investment to the integration of global operations, management, and strategic alliances, which has significantly affected the management of human resources. One illustration is about international outsourcing, as the HR Globally indicates. Whenever international outsourcing occurs, HR management should be involved to ensure the appropriate consideration of various laws, cultural factors, and other issues.[12]

Global Security and Terrorism Another global challenge for international employers is the threat of terrorism. The events of September 11, 2001, changed the world for the U.S. and other countries. Firms around the world have had to develop terror response and security plans. International firms, such as oil companies, have dramatically increased security for both operations and employees. Terrorist threats and incidents have significantly affected airlines, travel companies, construction firms, and even retailers such as McDonalds. HR management must respond to such concerns as part of transnational operations.

Economic and Technological Changes

Economic and technological changes have altered several occupational and employment patterns in the United States. Several of these changes are discussed next.

Occupational Shifts A major change is the shift of jobs from manufacturing and agriculture to service and telecommunications. In general, the U.S. economy has become predominately a service economy, and that shift is expected to continue. Over 80% of U.S. jobs are in service industries, and most new jobs created by the year 2010 will also be in services.[13] Projections of growth in some jobs and decline in others illustrate the shifts occurring in the U.S. economy. Figure 1-4 lists occupations that are expected to experience the greatest growth in percentage and numbers for the period ending in 2010. Most of the fastest-growing occupations percentage-wise are related to information technology and health care. The anticipated increase in technology jobs is due to the rapid growth of information technology, such as databases, systems design and analysis, and desktop publishing, while the growth in health-care jobs is due to the demands of an aging population. In contrast, many of the fastest-growing jobs in terms of numbers are in lower-skilled service fields.

Workforce Availability and Quality Concerns Many parts of the United States face significant workforce shortages that exist due to an inadequate supply of workers with the skills needed to perform the jobs being added. It is not that there are too few people—only that there are too few with the skills being demanded. For instance, a study of U.S. manufacturing firms revealed that about 80% of them have been experiencing a moderate to serious shortage of qualified

Figure 1-4	Fastest Growing Jobs to 2010		
Percentage Increase in Jobs		**Increase in Job Numbers**	
Computer software engineers	100%	Food-service / fast food workers	673,000
Computer support specialists	97%	Customer service representatives	631,000
Network administrators	82%	Registered nurses	561,000
Personal / home care aides	62%	Retail salespersons	510,000
Physicians assistants	53%	Computer support specialists	490,000
Medical records technicians	49%	Cashiers	474,000
Information systems managers	48%	Security guards	391,000
Physical/occupational therapists	46%	General/operating managers	363,000
Fitness trainers	40%	Nurses aides	323,000
		Post-secondary teachers	315,000
		Home health aides	291,000

Source: U.S. Bureau of Labor Statistics, *www.bls.gov.*

workers. The primary reasons were shifting demographics, the negative image of the manufacturing industry, and inadequately educated U.S. workers.[14]

Even though more Americans are graduating from high school (84% over age 25 have high school diplomas) and from college (almost 26% over age 25 now have college degrees), employers are concerned about the preparation and specific skills of new graduates. Comparisons of international test results show that students in the U.S. perform slightly above average in math and science, but *well behind* students in some other directly competitive nations.[15] Also, graduates with degrees in computers, engineering, and the health sciences remain in short supply relative to the demand for them. That is another reason why international outsourcing has grown. Unless major improvements are made to U.S. educational systems, its employers will be unable to find enough qualified workers for the growing number of skilled jobs of all types.

Growth in Contingent Workforce "Contingent workers" (temporary workers, independent contractors, leased employees, and part-timers) represent more than 20% of the U.S. workforce. Many employers operate with a core group of regular employees who have critical skills, and then expand and shrink the workforce through the use of contingent workers.

The use of contingent workers has grown for many reasons. A significant one is that many contingent workers are paid less and/or receive fewer benefits than regular employees. Omitting contingent workers from health-care benefits saves some firms 20% to 40% in labor costs. Another reason for the increased use of contingent workers is that doing so may reduce legal liability for employers. As more and more employment-related lawsuits are filed, some employers have become more wary about adding regular full-time employees. By using contract workers, employers reduce the number of legal issues they face regarding selection, discrimination, benefits, discipline, and termination.

Technological Shifts and the Internet Globalization and economic shifts have been accelerated by technological changes, with the Internet being a primary driver. The explosive growth in information technology and in the use of the Internet has driven changes in jobs and organizations of all sizes. For employees and managers, technology means always being "available." Cell phones, wireless networks for laptop computers, and personal digital organizers allow many workers to be always "on call." Technology is also enabling more people to work from home, at nights and weekends, which is resulting in more weekly hours worked and more stress on balancing work and personal lives.

Organizations have had to deal with the management of "virtual employees," who may not be working on-site, and of employees and vendors in other countries. They have also had to develop human resource policies regarding electronic sexual harassment and inappropriate Internet usage, among other day-to-day issues introduced by technology. But organizations have taken advantage of technology to establish e-learning programs whereby employees can access training programs through Web-based systems. Many HR management practices, such as employee benefits enrollment, performance appraisal documentation, job posting, and recruiting, have become Web based. These and many other examples illustrate how technological advances and the Internet are changing how HR management activities are performed.

Workforce Demographics and Diversity

The U.S. workforce has been changing dramatically. It is more diverse racially and ethnically, more women are in it than ever before, and the average age of its members is now considerably older. As a result of these demographic shifts, HR management in organizations has had to adapt to a more varied labor force both externally and internally.

Racial/Ethnic Diversity Racial and ethnic minorities account for a growing percentage of the overall labor force, with the percentage of Hispanics equal to or greater than the percentage of African Americans. Immigrants will continue to expand that growth. An increasing number of individuals characterize themselves as *multi-racial,* suggesting that the American "melting pot" is blurring racial and ethnic identities.

Racial/ethnic diversity has created greater cultural diversity as well, because of its accompanying differences in traditions, languages, religious practices, etc. For example, global events since 2001 have increased employers' attention to individuals who are Muslim, and more awareness and accommodation for Islamic religious beliefs and practices have become a common concern.

Women in the Workforce Women constitute about 47% of the workforce in the U.S. and 43% in Europe.[16] Many women workers are single, separated, divorced, or widowed, and therefore are "primary" income earners. Many women who are married have spouses who are also employed. A growing number of households in the U.S. include "domestic partners," who are committed to each other though not married and who may be of the same or the opposite sex.[17]

For many workers in the United States, balancing the demands of family and work is a significant challenge. Although that balancing has always been a concern, the increased number of working women and dual-career couples has resulted in greater tensions for many workers, both male and female. Employers have had to respond to work/family concerns in order to retain employees. Responses have included greater use of flexible hours, job sharing, the establishment of child-care referral services or on-site child-care facilities, and more flexible leave programs.

Aging Workforce In many economically developed countries, the population is aging, resulting in a significantly aging workforce.[18] In the U.S., over the next decade, a significant number of experienced employees will be retiring, changing to part-time, or otherwise shifting their employment. Replacing the experience and talents of longer-service workers is a growing challenge facing employers in all industries.

Overall, the growing diversity and aging of the workforce are creating more tensions and a greater likelihood of individuals filing employment discrimination complaints against employers. Therefore employers are having to devote more time and effort to ensuring that non-discriminatory policies and practices are followed. Training on diversity issues and the effective management of diversity issues in organizations are getting more attention.

Organizational Cost Pressures and Restructuring

An overriding theme facing managers and organizations is to operate in a "cost-less" mode, which means continually looking for ways to reduce costs of all types—financial, operations, equipment, and labor. Pressures from global competitors have forced many U.S. firms to close facilities, use international outsourcing, adapt their management practices, increase productivity, and decrease labor costs in order to become more competitive. The growth of information technology, particularly that linked to the Internet, has influenced the number, location, and required capabilities of employees.

One familiar example is Wal-Mart, the giant retailer, whose corporate philosophy is providing the lowest prices to customers. As a result, Wal-Mart has driven its vendors and suppliers to reduce their costs. One result has been for suppliers to manufacture their goods overseas by using cheaper labor rates. Another consequence has been for many suppliers to cut jobs and close factories that were not as cost-efficient and productive as foreign competitors. So while Wal-Mart has grown, and Wal-Mart's customers have gotten lower prices, many suppliers and other retailers have had to follow the "cost-less" strategy.[19]

To respond to the cost pressures, many organizations have restructured to become more competitive. Also, firms in the same industries have completed mergers and acquisitions (M&As) to ensure greater global competitiveness.

As part of organizational changes, many organizations have "rightsized" by: (1) eliminating layers of managers, (2) closing facilities, (3) merging with other organizations, and (4) outplacing workers. To improve productivity, quality, and service while also reducing costs, they are re-designing jobs and affecting people. One of the challenges that HR management faces with organizational restructuring is dealing with the human consequences of change. The human cost associated with downsizing has been much discussed in the popular press: increased workloads and a "survivor's mentality" for those who remain; loss of employee and customer loyalty; unmet cost-savings; and ultimately, increased turnover of the remaining employees.

These organizational shifts have caused some organizations to reduce the number of employees, while at the same time scrambling to attract and retain employees with different capabilities than were previously needed. To respond to organizational cost pressures and restructurings, as well as the other HR challenges it faces, HR management has had to transform the roles it plays in organizations.

HR MANAGEMENT ROLES

Several roles can be fulfilled by HR management. The nature and extent of these roles depends on both what upper management wants HR management to do and what competencies the HR staff have demonstrated. Three roles are typically identified for HR:

- *Administrative:* Focusing on HR clerical administration and recordkeeping
- *Operational and Employee Advocate:* Managing most HR activities and serving as employee "champion"
- *Strategic:* Becoming a contributor to organizational results and the "keeper" of organizational ethics

The administrative role has been the dominant part of HR. However, as Figure 1-5 indicates, a significant transformation in HR is occurring. The HR pyramid is having to be turned upside down, so that significantly less HR time and fewer HR staff are used for clerical administration. Notice in Figure 1-5 that the per-

Figure 1-5

Changing Roles of HR Management

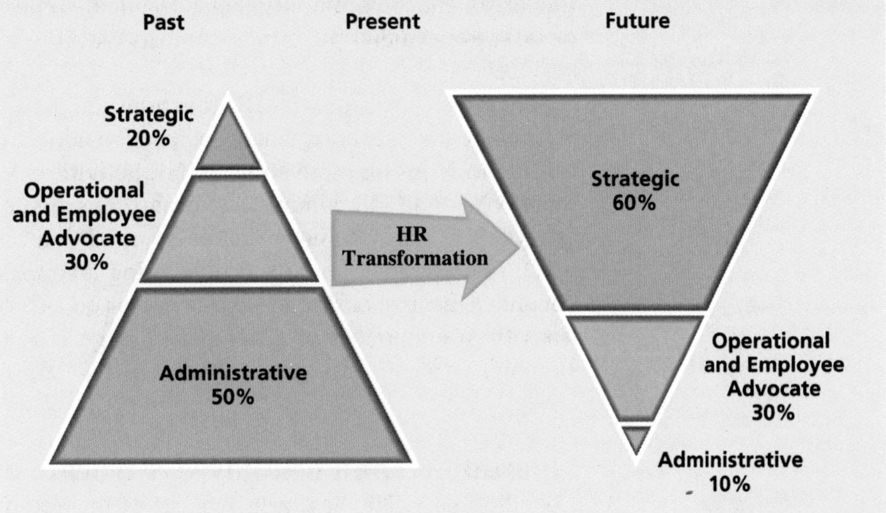

Note: Example percentages are based on various surveys.

centage of emphasis on the operational and employee advocate role is remaining constant. The greatest shift is for HR to devote more emphasis to strategic HR management. A study by Towers-Perrin, a large consulting firm, found that HR is being pressured to change because of four critical business issues identified by senior HR managers: cost-reduction pressures, business restructuring, broadscale downsizing/layoffs, and globalization of business.[20] A look at each of the roles of HR and how they are being transformed follows.

Administrative Role of HR

The administrative role of HR management has been heavily oriented to processing and record keeping. However, this role has given HR management in some organizations the reputation of being staffed by paper shufflers who primarily tell managers and employees what cannot be done. If limited to the administrative role, HR staff are seen primarily as clerical and lower-level administrative contributors to the organization. Two major shifts driving the transformation of the administrative role are greater use of technology and outsourcing.

Technology Transforming HR To improve the administrative efficiency of HR and responsiveness of HR to employees and managers, more HR functions are becoming available electronically or are being done on the Internet. Web-based technology is reducing the amount of HR administrative time and staff needed. Technology is being used in all HR activities, from employment application and employee benefits enrollment to e-learning using Internet-based resources. Later in this chapter there is more discussion on the nature, types, and uses of HR technology.

Outsourcing of HR Increasingly, many HR administrative functions are being outsourced. A recent survey found that about 50% of all HR work is being outsourced, and HR outsourcing revenues for vendors have jumped $15 billion in just two years. According to various surveys by outsourcing firms, the areas most commonly outsourced are employee assistance/counseling, pension/retirement planning, benefits administration, training, and payroll services.[21]

The primary reasons why HR functions are outsourced is to save money on HR staffing, to take advantage of specialized vendor expertise and technology, and to be able to focus on more strategic HR activities. As a result, it is forecasted that up to 65% of all HR administrative staff jobs are or will be eliminated in the next few years. These jobs are being outsourced to firms both in the U.S. and worldwide. For example, a major firm offering administrative services for retirement benefits is using a customer service center on a Caribbean island to answer questions from employees of a number of large U.S. firms. Estimates are that outsourcing arrangements such as that will save employers 30% or more on labor costs.[22]

Operational and Employee Advocate Role for HR

Traditionally, HR has been viewed as the "employee advocate" in organizations. As the voice for employee concerns, HR professionals traditionally have been seen as "company morale officers" who do not understand the business realities of the organizations and do not contribute measurably to the strategic success of the business. Despite this view, someone must be the "champion" for employees and employee issues.

HR professionals spend considerable time on HR "crisis management" dealing with employee problems that are both work and non-work related. Employee advocacy helps ensure fair and equitable treatment for employees regardless of personal background or circumstances. Sometimes the HR advocate role may create conflict with operating managers. However, that role is important to make the organization a better place to work. In addition, without the advocate role, employers would face even more lawsuits and regulatory complaints than they do now.

The operational role requires HR professionals to identify and implement needed programs and policies in the organization, in cooperation with operating managers. This role traditionally includes many of the HR activities mentioned earlier in the chapter. HR implements plans suggested by or developed with other managers, as well as those identified by HR professionals. Even though priorities may change as labor markets and economic shifts occur, the operational HR role emphasizes support for executives, managers, and employees when addressing and resolving HR problems and issues.

Operational activities are tactical in nature. Compliance with equal employment opportunity and other laws are ensured, employment applications are processed, current openings are filled through interviews, supervisors are trained, safety problems are resolved, and wages and salaries are administered. These efforts require coordinating the management of HR activities with actions of managers and supervisors throughout organizations.

Managers' and employees' impressions of HR are driven directly by how those individuals experience the benefits and services that HR provides. Unfortunately, operating managers hold a less positive view of HR than might be desired. In a survey by Watson Wyatt, about one-third of managers rated HR as performing well, while 24% rated HR as performing poorly. The remaining managers rated HR as "average" in meeting managerial needs.[23]

HR DEPARTMENT ORGANIZATION CHART Depicts options for different HR department organizations.
Custom Search:
☑ ANALYSIS
Exact Phrase: Structuring the HR department

Figure 1-6

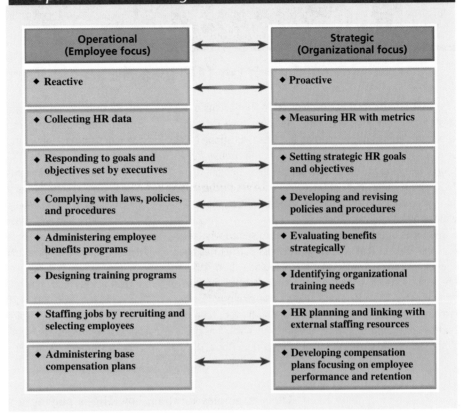

Figure 1-6 — Operational to Strategic Transformation of HR

Strategic Role for HR

Differences between the operational and strategic approaches in a number of HR areas exist.[24] As shown in Figure 1-6, the strategic HR role requires that HR professionals be pro-active in addressing business realities and focus on future HR needs, such as workforce planning, compensation strategies, and demonstrating the value of HR to top management.

Many executives, managers, and HR professionals increasingly see the need for HR management to become a greater strategic contributor to the "business" success of organizations. Even organizations that are not-for-profit, such as governmental and social service entities, must manage their human resources in a "business-oriented" manner.

"Contributing at the Table" The role of HR as a *strategic business partner* is often described as "having a seat at the table," and contributing to the strategic directions and success of the organization. This role means partnering with the Chief Financial Officers (CFOs) and meeting the expectations of the Chief Executive Officer (CEOs). For instance, at Target, the major retailer, HR is accountable for workforce planning, staffing, and employee retention, all of which affect customer service in Target stores.[25]

LOGGING ON...

HR Executive
This Web site focuses on strategic issues for HR and includes news and success stories for key HR decision-makers.
www.workindex.com/ hrexecutive

Research on HR as a Strategic Partner

Significant attention has been given to HR becoming a strategic partner in organizations. However, the extent to which that transition is occurring has been questioned. Research by Lawler and Mohrman published in *Human Resource Planning* provides some perspectives. Beginning in 1995 and continuing every three years, the researchers have surveyed senior HR executives in large U.S. firms, most of which have global operations.

The focus of the tri-annual surveys is to see to what extent the role of HR as a strategic business partner has been changing. However, somewhat discouragingly, from 1995 to the latest survey, HR spent only about 23% of its time on its strategic role. The operational role as a service provider has remained relatively constant at about one-third of time spent. Rather surprisingly, the administrative role has declined only slightly over the same time period. About 40% of

the HR respondents indicated that they function as full strategic business partners, up from 29% in 1995. Most of the remaining responses indicated some strategic HR involvement.

To provide further insights, Lawler and Mohrman compared how HR contributes to organizations where it is a full strategic partner and where it is not. As would be expected, the "strategic players" place more emphasis on planning, organizational design, and other broader HR activities. Also, their firms have made much greater use of technology and HR information systems.

Overall, this study illustrates that HR is moving toward being more strategic. But the movement is occurring somewhat more slowly than might be expected, despite a large number of articles and seminars on the need for HR to become a strategic partner.[26]

Other examples illustrate how HR is playing a significant strategic role. At BASF, a global chemical firm with 89,000 employees, HR is in charge of a corporate restructuring plan to save $250 million annually and reduce staffing costs by 30% over a four-year period. At a much smaller firm, Wegman's Food Markets in New York, HR is focusing on controlling benefits costs by educating employees about increasing their use of generic drugs, which has cut the firm's prescription drug costs while preserving benefits for employees.[27] However, as described in the HR Perspective, even though this role of HR is recognized, many organizations still need to make significant progress toward fulfilling it. Some examples of areas of strategic contributions by HR are as follows:

- Evaluating mergers and acquisitions for organizational "compatibility," structural changes, and staffing needs
- Conducting workforce planning to anticipate the retirement of employees at all levels and workforce expansion identified in organizational strategic plans
- Leading site selection efforts for new facilities, or transferring operations to international outsourcing locations
- Instituting HR management systems to reduce administrative time and staff
- Working with executives to develop a revised sales compensation and incentives plan as new products/services are rolled out to customers.

Collaborative HR
The process of HR professionals from several different organizations working jointly to address shared business problems.

Collaborative HR Increasingly, organizations are implementing new approaches to improve the efficiency and effectiveness of HR management. **Collaborative HR,** the process of HR professionals from several different organizations jointly working to address shared business problems, is becoming more prevalent. In this approach, a number of different firms from various industries collaborate on sharing HR resources with other firms in a collaborative group.

Usually these firms are from different industries, so that no competitive conflicts arise. The employers in the group participate in research related to employee engagement and turnover issues. This sharing of information and programs allows each firm to benefit from the expertise of other firms, without having the time and expense of developing some of their own HR practices. For example, Union Pacific Railroad (UPRR) has taken the collaborative approach with a number of other firms, such as Ford Motor Company, to exchange information and ideas related to employee turnover assessment and retention practices. UPRR has other unique collaborative efforts with organizations such as Duke Energy, Deere and Company, and 3M.[28]

HR TECHNOLOGY

The use of information technology of all types is transforming the various roles of HR management. Over the past decade, firms have developed and implemented information systems to simplify use of vast amounts of HR data.

Human resource management system (HRMS)
An integrated system providing information used by HR management in decision making.

Greater use of technology has led to organizational use of a **human resource management system (HRMS),** which is an integrated system providing information used by HR management in decision making. The HRMS terminology emphasizes that making HR decisions, not just building databases, is the primary reason for compiling data in an information system. The use of HR technology has grown rapidly in the past decade as "workforce technologies" are used to transform the way HR delivers its activities.[29]

Purposes of an HRMS

An HRMS serves two major purposes in organizations. One relates to administrative and operational efficiency, the other to effectiveness. The first purpose of an HRMS is to improve the efficiency with which data on employees and HR activities are compiled. Many HR activities can be performed more efficiently and more quickly and with less paperwork if automated. One survey of about 200 companies found a 60% decline in HR administrative work when employees were given self-service access to HR through Web-based systems.[30]

The second purpose of an HRMS is more strategic and is related to HR planning. Having accessible data enables HR planning and managerial decision making to be based to a greater degree on information rather than relying on managerial perceptions and intuition. One study found that 47% of the surveyed firms use HR technology to help with strategic HR planning and particularly with attracting and retaining human resource talent.[31] The Technology Transforming HR discussion on the next page illustrates how an HRMS at a small law firm has paid off.

The final stage of implementing an HRMS is *HR work flow.* In this stage, not only can the users access information and input changes, the system will now guide the users through all the steps of the transaction. An increasing number of firms have HRMSs that allow employees access to Web-based 401(k) information, and employees and managers are able to make changes to their own data without the assistance of an HR professional.

Price Law Group

Organizations of all sizes are using HR technology to transform how HR activities are performed. One example is Price Law Group, a California firm with 11 offices and 110 employees. Until recently, most of the HR files and records at Price were maintained manually, although some limited efforts to use Microsoft Excel had been tried. But then the HR Manager and executives at Price recognized that an integrated HRMS was needed.

After various software packages had been researched, an HRMS was selected. Because it had been integrated with the payroll database, the new system allows both HR and the firm's operating managers better access to employee compensation and benefits data. The system is used for HR applications such as company benefits coverage for employees, employee attendance data, and scheduling of employee performance reviews. It has been estimated that use of the HRMS has saved at least $10,000 in benefits premiums. Also, the system has freed up time for the HR Manager and the Operations Manager to focus on more strategic HR planning issues, because less time is needed for maintaining and processing HR administrative tasks.[32]

Uses of an HRMS

An HRMS has many uses in an organization. The most basic is the automation of payroll and benefits activities. Another common use of HRMS is tracking EEO / affirmative action activities. Beyond those basic applications, the use of Web-based information systems has allowed the HR unit in organizations to become more administratively efficient and to deal with more strategic and longer-term HR planning issues. Web-based systems include these:

- *Bulletin boards:* Information on personnel policies, job postings, and training materials can be accessed by employees globally.
- *Data access:* Linked to databases, an extranet or an intranet allows employees to access benefits information such as sick leave usage or 401(k) balances. This frees up time for HR staff members who previously spent considerable time answering routine employee inquiries.
- *Employee self-service:* Many HR technology uses enable employees to access and update their own personnel records, change or enroll in employee benefits plans, and respond to employment opportunities in other locations. Obviously, maintaining security is critical when the employee self-service option is available.
- *Extended linkage:* Integrating an HRMS allows the databases of vendors of HR services and an employer to be linked so that data can be exchanged electronically. Also, employees can communicate directly from throughout the world to submit and retrieve personnel details, take on-line training courses, and provide complete career planning data.

The greater use of HRMS technologies is affecting how HR activities are performed in may ways. To illustrate, Coca-Cola has a Web-based employee self-service program for its worldwide staff in over 200 countries. Employees can go on-line to access and change their personal data, enroll in or change benefits programs, and prepare for performance reviews. The employee self-service system is available in various languages, and reflects country and cultural differences.[33] Such self-service HRMSs are estimated to reduce HR administrative transaction costs by 43%.[34] Additional examples of how various HR activities are being transformed by technology will be presented throughout the chapters of this text.

ETHICS AND HR MANAGEMENT

Closely linked with the strategic role of HR is the way HR management professionals influence the organizational ethics practiced by executives, managers, and employees. On the strategic level, organizations with high ethical standards are more likely to meet long-term strategic objectives and profit goals. Organizations that are seen as operating with integrity are viewed more positively by individuals in the community and in industrywide, as well as by consumers and employees.[35] That positive view often translates into bottom-line financial results and the ability to attract and retain human resources.

The need for great attention to ethics has grown in the past few years, as evidenced by the corporate scandals in the U.S. at Enron, WorldCom, Tyco, numerous financial and investment firms, and other organizations. Ethical problems at Parmalat (an Italian-based food company), Credit Lyonnais (a French financial firm), and other companies illustrate that ethical lapses are not problems just in the United States.

Ethics and Global Differences

Differences in legal, political, and cultural values and practices in different countries often raise ethical issues for global employers. Those employers also must comply with their home-country laws. The U.S. and some Western European countries have laws regarding the conduct of firms based domestically. For example, the Foreign Corrupt Practices Act (FCPA) prohibits U.S. firms from engaging in bribery and other practices in foreign countries that would be illegal in the United States. However, competing firms from certain other countries are not bound by similar restrictions, which may create competitive disadvantages for U.S. and European firms.[36]

The impact of those laws often requires global managers to draw some fine ethical distinctions between bribery and gift-giving, particularly given differences in business practices in various Asian and Eastern European countries.[37] Two examples illustrate typical ethical dilemmas:

- Many global firms have found that establishing or expanding operations in some Asian, African, and Latin American countries is much easier if the global firm arranges for the children of key government officials to be admitted to and receive scholarships from colleges and universities in the United States or Great Britain. Without this "sponsorship," the global firms often face endless delays in obtaining the necessary government agency approvals for its operations.
- In some Eastern European and Asian countries, obtaining a new telephone line in less than three months requires making a cash payment, referred to as an "expediting charge," to the local manager of the telephone office. All parties to the deal know that the manager personally will retain the cash, but a telephone is essential for doing business internationally.

These and other situations reflect how different legal, political, and cultural factors in other countries can lead to ethical conflicts for global managers. Some global firms have established guidelines and policies to reduce the payments of bribes, but even those efforts do not provide detailed guidance on handling the situations that can arise.

HR's Role in Organizational Ethics

Organizations that are seen as ethical in the way they operate have longer-term success. Because people in organizations are ones making ethical decisions on a daily basis, HR management plays a key role as the "keeper and voice" of organizational ethics. All managers, including HR managers, must deal with ethical issues and be sensitive to how they interplay with HR activities.[38] To help HR professionals deal with ethical issues, the Society for Human Resource Management (SHRM) has developed a code of ethics for its members. There are a number of different views about the importance of HR in ensuring that ethical practices, justice, and fairness are present throughout HR practices.[39] Figure 1-7 identifies some of the most frequent areas of ethical misconduct involving HR activities.[40]

Ethical issues pose fundamental questions about fairness, justice, truthfulness, and social responsibility. Ethics deals with what "ought" to be done. Just complying with the laws does not guarantee ethical behavior. Laws and regulations cannot cover every situation executives, managers, and employees will face. Instead of relying on laws, people must be guided by values and personal behavior "codes," including the following two questions:

◆ Does the behavior or result meet all applicable *laws, regulations, and government codes*?

◆ Does the behavior or result meet both *organizational standards* and *professional standards* of ethical behavior?

Figure 1-7	Examples of Ethical Misconduct in HR Activities
Types of Misconduct	**Examples of Employee, Supervisor, and Managerial Behavior**
Compensation	◆ Misrepresenting hours and time worked ◆ Falsifying expense reports ◆ Personal bias in performance appraisals and pay increases ◆ Inappropriate overtime classifications
Employee Relations	◆ Employees lying to supervisors ◆ Executives/managers providing false information to public, customers, and vendors ◆ Personal gains/gifts from vendors ◆ Misusing/stealing organizational assets and supplies ◆ Intentionally violating safety/health regulations
Staffing and Equal Employment	◆ Favoritism in hiring and promotion ◆ Sexual harassment ◆ Sex, race, and age discrimination in hiring, discipline, and termination

How UPS Delivers Ethics and Corporate Integrity

With all the reports of corporate scandals in the past several years, one company whose name has not appeared in them is UPS, a transportation and logistics firm. The "Big Brown" company, as UPS is also called, sees ethics as a primary part of achieving competitive advantage with customers, as well as an aid in attracting and retaining employees at all levels. Lea Soupta, Senior Vice President of HR, and her staff are key in ensuring that UPS has ethical practices throughout the firm's worldwide operations. The company has underscored the importance of HR by placing Soupta on its Board of Directors.

UPS has taken a number of actions to, as it says, "lead with integrity." A detailed code-of-conduct manual is given to and reviewed with all employees. The manual includes specific examples of ethical situations that employees may face and how to respond to them. The manual itself is updated regularly, and the code of conduct is reinforced annually through training sessions and communications.

Additionally, UPS contracts with an external firm to provide a hotline for receiving confidential calls on ethical problems. The vendor notes the information and sends it to a special compliance department at UPS where investigations and follow-up are handled. Regular summaries of the hotline reports are presented to department managers and senior executives. Annually, managers complete a "conduct code" report that asks specific questions about ethical problems that have arisen during the year. In summary, an emphasis on ensuring corporate integrity and ethical behavior permeates UPS, and HR plays both strategic and operational roles in delivering on ethics at UPS.[41]

Ethical Behavior and Organizational Culture

Organizational culture
The shared values and beliefs in an organization.

Numerous writers on business ethics consistently stress that the primary determinant of ethical behavior is **organizational culture,** which is the shared values and beliefs in an organization. Basically, organizational culture is "how things are done here." Every organization has a culture, and that culture influences how executives, managers, and employees act in making organizational decisions. For example, the more common it is for employees to lie about why they missed work in order to use sick leave, the more likely it is that employees will adopt that behavior. Or, if meeting objectives and financial targets is stressed, regardless of how the desired results are obtained, then it should not be a surprise when executives and managers fudge numbers or falsify cost records. The financial scandals in many firms in recent years illustrate the consequences of an "anything goes" organizational culture. However, a positive ethical culture exists in many organizations, as the HR Perspective describes.

HR plays a key role in ensuring ethical behavior in organizations. One survey revealed that the number of employees reporting ethical misconduct has grown in the past few years, primarily because of the corporate scandals from several years earlier.[42] When the following four elements of ethics programs exist, ethical behavior is likely to occur:[43]

- A written code of ethics and standards of conduct
- Training on ethical behavior for all executives, managers, and employees
- Means for employees to obtain advice on ethical situations they face, often provided by HR
- Systems for confidential reporting of ethical misconduct or questionable behavior

Yet, having all those elements may not prevent individual managers or executives from engaging in or failing to report unethical behavior. Even HR staff members may be reluctant to report ethics concerns, primarily because of fears that doing so may affect their current and future employment. Specific ethical issues that have created difficulty in the HR area include the following:

♦ How much information on a problem employee should be given to or withheld from another potential employer?

♦ Should an employment manager check credit agency or law enforcement records on applicants without informing them?

♦ What obligations are owed a long-term employee who has become an ineffective performer because of changes in the job skills required?

♦ What impact should an employee's off-the-job lifestyle have on promotion decisions if on-the-job work performance has been satisfactory?

♦ Should employees who smoke be forced to stop smoking on the job when new no-smoking restrictions are implemented by the employer? Also, should an employer be allowed to reject a job applicant solely on the basis of off-the-job smoking?

♦ Should an otherwise qualified applicant be refused employment because the applicant's dependent child has major health problems that would significantly raise the employer's insurance costs?

♦ How should co-workers' "right to know" be balanced with individual privacy rights when a worker discloses he or she has AIDS, Hepatitis C, or other serious communicable diseases?

A broad study of ethics is philosophical, complex, and beyond the scope of this book. The intent here is to highlight ethical aspects of HR management. Various ethical issues in HR management are highlighted throughout the text as well.

▌▌ HR MANAGEMENT COMPETENCIES AND CAREERS

As HR management becomes more complex, greater demands are placed on individuals who make HR their career specialty. Even readers of this book who do not become HR managers and professionals will find it useful to know about the competencies required for effective HR management.

HR Competencies

The transformation of HR toward being more strategic has implications for the competencies needed by HR professionals. To identify those competencies, the University of Michigan (UM) and the Society for Human Resource Management (SHRM) recently conducted a cooperative study. Data were gathered over a fifteen-year period, and then a specific study was completed with 7,000 HR professionals and other executives and managers. The results of the studies have been summarized to identify five basic sets of HR competencies.[44] One useful product of the UM/SHRM study is the development of an HR competency self-assessment, which individual HR professionals can complete in order to identify.[45] The five areas of HR competencies are described briefly as follows:

♦ *Strategic contribution:* The key competency that HR needs to fulfill its strategic role is the ability to be a strategic contributor to organizational success. That means that HR must focus on the long-term implications of HR issues.

- *Business knowledge:* HR professionals must have business knowledge of the organization and its strategies if they are to contribute strategically. They must understand the financial, technological, and other facets of the industry and the organization.[46]
- *HR delivery:* The HR activities must be delivered effectively and efficiently in ways that meet the needs of both the organization and its employees.
- *HR technology:* Technology, particularly information systems and Web-based resources, have become a significant part of HR management today. HR professionals must develop the abilities needed to work effectively with various dimensions of an HRMS.
- *Personal credibility:* HR professionals must have credibility personally and professionally. That means they must develop effective internal relationships with individual executives, employees, managers, and supervisors. Also, HR professionals must establish personal and professional credibility in various external relationships.

HR Generalist
A person who has responsibility for performing a variety of HR activities.

HR Specialist
A person who has in-depth knowledge and expertise in a limited area of HR.

HR Management as a Career Field

There are a variety of jobs within the HR career field, ranging from executive to clerical. As an employer grows large enough to need someone to focus primarily on HR activities, the role of the **HR generalist** emerges—that is, a person who has responsibility for performing a variety of HR activities. Further growth leads to the addition of **HR specialists,** or individuals who have in-depth knowledge and expertise in limited areas of HR. Figure 1-8 shows the most common areas of HR specialists, with benefits being the most prevalent.

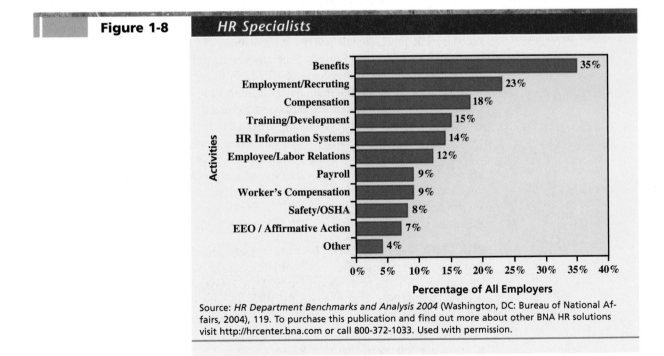

Figure 1-8   *HR Specialists*

Source: *HR Department Benchmarks and Analysis 2004* (Washington, DC: Bureau of National Affairs, 2004), 119. To purchase this publication and find out more about other BNA HR solutions visit http://hrcenter.bna.com or call 800-372-1033. Used with permission.

HR jobs can be found in both corporate headquarters and field/subsidiary operations. A compensation analyst or HR director might be found at a corporate headquarters. An employment manager for an auto parts manufacturing plant and a European HR manager for a global food company are examples of field and subsidiary HR professionals. The two types of jobs have different career appeals and challenges.[47]

Compensation and Career Outlook Compensation levels for HR jobs vary by industry, company size, and geography. As would be expected, pay generally increases with company size, although it may vary significantly due to differences in job responsibilities in small, medium, and large firms. Many HR executives and managers are eligible for short- and long-term incentives.[48]

Regarding career outlook, the number of jobs in the HR field is expected to remain relatively flat over the next several years, primarily due to employers outsourcing HR responsibilities to vendors and other entities. The need for HR generalists and specialists will grow somewhat as a result of retirement and job shifts. However, an abundant supply of qualified candidates for HR jobs is expected. Consequently, entry into the field likely will be very competitive and compensation levels may not increase significantly for entry-level HR jobs. Certain specialists, such as those in compensation or HR information technology, will have greater opportunities than will training or employment specialists.

HR Professionalism and Certification

The idea that "liking to work with people" is the major qualification necessary for success in HR is one of the greatest myths about the field. Depending on the job, HR professionals may need considerable knowledge about employment regulations, finance, tax law, statistics, and information systems. In most cases, they also need extensive knowledge about specific HR activities.

LOGGING ON...

Human Resource Certification Institute
This site lists information on the HRCI certification process.
www.hrci.org

Professional Involvement and Development The broad range of issues faced by HR professionals has made involvement in professional associations and organizations important. For HR generalists, the largest organization is the Society for Human Resource Management (SHRM). Public-sector HR professionals tend to be concentrated in the International Personnel Management Association (IPMA). Other major specialized HR organizations include the International Association for Human Resource Information Management (IHRIM), the World at Work Association, and the American Society for Training and Development (ASTD).

One of the characteristics of a professional field is having a means to certify the knowledge and competence of members of the profession. The CPA for accountants and the CLU for life insurance underwriters are examples. The most well-known certification programs for HR generalists are administered by the Human Resource Certification Institute (HRCI), which is affiliated with SHRM.

PHR/SPHR Certification The most widely known HR certifications are the Professional in Human Resources (PHR) and the Senior Professional in Human Resources (SPHR), both sponsored by HRCI. Over 50,000 HR professionals are certified as PHR or SPHR. Annually, thousands of individuals take the certification exams. HRCI also sponsors a Global Professional in Human Resources (GPHR) certification. Eligibility requirements for PHR, SPHR, and GPHR certification are shown in Figure 1-9. Appendix A identifies test specifications and knowledge areas covered by the PHR and SPHR. Additionally, those who want

Figure 1-9   *HR Certification*

The Human Resource Certification Institute offers three types of professional certifications for HR generalists.

PHR Certification	SPHR or GPHR Certification
◆ Complete at least 2 years of exempt-level (professional) HR experience (recommended: 2–4 years). ◆ Pass the PHR certification exam. ◆ Students may take and pass exam, and receive certification after 2 years of experience.	◆ Complete at least 2 years of exempt-level (professional) HR experience (recommended: 6–8 years). ◆ Pass the SPHR or GPHR exam.

Details on these certifications are available from the Human Resources Certification Institute, *www.hrci.org*.

to succeed in the field must update their knowledge continually. One way of staying current on HR is to tap information available from the list in Appendix B.

GPHR Certification Beginning in 2004, HRCI established a certification for global HR professionals. The addition of global certification recognizes the growth in HR responsibilities in organizations throughout the world. The global outline addresses HR content for those with HR responsibilities in multiple countries. The subject areas for the global certification are as follows:

- Strategic international HR management
- Organizational effectiveness and employee development
- Global staffing
- International assignment management
- Global compensation and benefits
- International employee relations and regulations

Other HR Certifications Increasingly, employers hiring or promoting HR professionals are requesting certification as a "plus." HR professionals feel that HR certification gives them more credibility with corporate peers and senior managers. Additional certification programs for HR specialists and generalists are sponsored by various organizations. For specialists, some well-known programs include the following:

- Certified Compensation Professional (CCP), sponsored by the World at Work Association
- Certified Employee Benefits Specialist (CEBS), sponsored by the International Foundation of Employee Benefits Plans
- Certified Benefits Professional (CBP), sponsored by the WorldatWork Association
- Certified Performance Technologist (CPT), co-sponsored by the American Society for Training & Development and the International Society for Performance Improvement

- Certified Safety Professional (CSP), sponsored by the Board of Certified Safety Professionals
- Occupational Health and Safety Technologist (OHST), given by the American Board of Industrial Hygiene and the Board of Certified Safety Professionals
- Certified Professional Outsourcing, provided by New York University and the Human Resource Outsourcing Association[49]

SUMMARY

- HR management is the direction of organizational systems to ensure that human talent is used effectively and efficiently to accomplish organizational goals.
- HR management activities can be grouped as follows: strategic HR management; equal employment opportunity; staffing; HR development; compensation and benefits; health, safety, and security; and employee and labor relations.
- All organizations need HR management, but larger ones are more likely to have a specialized HR function.
- There are four types of assets in organizations: physical, financial, intangible, and human.
- Human assets should be seen as human capital, which is the collective value of the capabilities, knowledge, skills, life experiences, and motivation of an organizational workforce.
- Four major HR challenges faced by managers and organizations now and in the future are the globalization of business, economic and technological changes, workforce demographics and diversity, and organizational cost pressures and restructuring.

- HR management must fulfill three roles: (1) administrative, (2) operational and employee advocate, and (3) strategic.
- HR roles are being transformed by technology, outsourcing, and the need for HR to become a more strategic contributor.
- HR technology in the form of Human Resource Management Systems (HRMS) helps improve administrative efficiencies and expand information for strategic HR planning.
- An HRMS can be designed and implemented in several ways.
- Ethical behavior is crucial in HR management, and HR professionals regularly face a number of HR ethical issues.
- The five areas of competencies needed by HR professionals are strategic contribution, business knowledge, HR delivery, HR technology, and personal credibility.
- Current knowledge about HR management is required for professionals in the HR career field, and professional certification has grown in importance for HR generalists and specialists.

REVIEW AND APPLICATION QUESTIONS

1. Why is it important for HR management to transform from being primarily administrative and operational to becoming a more strategic contributor?
2. Describe how economic and workforce changes are affecting organizations in which you have worked, and give specific examples of how these changes should be addressed.
3. Assume you are an HR Director with a staff of seven people. A departmental objective is for all staff members to become professionally certified

within a year. Using Internet resources of associations listed in Appendix B, develop a table that identifies six to eight certifications that could be obtained by your staff members, and show the following details for each certification:
- Name of sponsoring organization
- Name and types of certification
- Addresses for relevant Web sites containing more information
- Experience and education requirements
- Nature of certification process

To check your knowledge of the chapter, review the following. (Answers after the supplemental case.) For more questions, see the Study Guide.

1. The aim of _____ is to provide an adequate supply of appropriately qualified individuals to fill jobs in an organization.
   a. diversity assessment and training
   b. staffing
   c. HR planning and analysis
   d. human resource development
2. Recruiting and selecting employees for current openings is an example of the _____ role of human resource management activities.
   a. operational
   b. administrative
   c. global
   d. strategic

3. Approximately _____% of U.S. jobs are in the service industry.
   a. 60
   b. 70
   c. 80
   d. 90
4. For HR generalists, the largest professional HR organization is the _____.
   a. International Personnel Management Association (IPMA)
   b. American Society for Training and Development (ASTD)
   c. Human Resource Certification Institute (HRCI)
   d. Society for Human Resource Management (SHRM)

CASE
HR CONTRIBUTES AT SYSCO

Many people in the U.S. are not familiar with SYSCO, but they see its results because SYSCO is the largest food services and distribution company with almost $24 billion in annual sales. SYSCO supplies food products to customers in restaurants, hotels, supermarkets, hospitals, and other companies. In a firm the size of SYSCO with over 40,000 employees, HR management is making significant contributions to organizational success. As an indication of this success, SYSCO received the Optimas award for general HR Excellence from *Workforce Magazine.*

Beginning several years ago, the need to revitalize HR activities was recognized by both executives and senior HR staff members. At the time, the SYSCO operating regions had administered many of their own HR practices. To bring change to HR corporate-wide, while preserving the entrepreneurial independence of the regions, a "market-driven" HR approach was developed. In this approach, corporate HR identified ways it could assist regional operations, and then developed programs and services that met regional needs. However, unlike in many other

corporations where corporate HR programs would be "mandated" to operating units, SYSCO took a different approach. Key to market-driven HR is that managers in the regional operations must be convinced to "buy" the corporate HR services. For example, if a supervisory training program is developed by corporate HR, regional managers decide if they want to use the program for supervisory training in their regions.

Another part of creating HR as market driven was the establishment by corporate HR of a Virtual Resource Center (VRC) to provide services to managers and employees. A key aspect of the VRC is use of HR technology to gather extensive data on HR activities and provide that data to operating managers. One source of data is workplace climate surveys of employees. Using the survey data, HR developed initiatives to increase safety, which reduced workers' compensation claims by 30%, resulting in savings of $10 million per year.

Another problem that SYSCO had was high turnover rates of night shift warehouse workers. Recruiting these workers has been a constant challenge for SYSCO and other distribution firms. By implementing a variety of programs and services, based on employee and managerial input from the surveys, the retention rate for these warehouse employees has been increased by 20%, resulting in savings of $15 million per year. These savings are due to reduced time and money spent recruiting, selecting, and training new employees. Also, employees with more experience are more productive and more knowledgeable about SYSCO operations and products.

Another area where HR has contributed is with truck and delivery drivers. Data gathered through the VRC has been used to revise base pay and incentive programs, increase driver retention rates, and improve driver safety records. Additionally, customer satisfaction rates increased and delivery expenses declined.

All of these changes illustrate that HR efforts at SYSCO have been paying off for the company, managers, and employees. But as the value of HR efforts is recognized by more managers, HR's role at SYSCO is likely to continue growing and changing.[50]

Questions

1. How does the market-driven approach illustrate that HR has strategic, operational, and administrative roles at SYSCO?

2. Discuss what types of HR changes could have affected reductions in workers' compensation expenses, employee turnover, and increases in customer satisfaction.

SUPPLEMENTAL CASE: Phillips Furniture

This case describes a small company that has grown large enough to need a full-time HR person. You have been selected to be the HR Manager, and you have to decide what HR activities are needed and the role HR is to play. (For the case, go to **http://mathis.swlearning.com.**)

Learning Review Answers: 1. b 2. a 3. c 4. d

NOTES

1. *Small Business by the Numbers* and other reports from the U.S. Small Business Administration, *www.sba.gov.*

2. Lisa M. Aldisent, *Valuing People! How Human Capital Can Be Your Strongest Asset* (Chicago: Dearborn Trade Publishing, 2002).

3. For a useful overview of human capital, see Leslie A. Weatherly, "Human Capital—The Elusive Asset," *SHRM Research Quarterly,* March 2003.

4. Bassi, "Human Capital Advantage: Developing Metrics for the Knowledge Era," Spring 2001 *www.linezine.com;* and Ramona D'Zinkowski, "The Measurement and Management of Intellectual Capital," *Management Accounting,* 78 (2000), 32–36.

5. Robert S. Kaplan and David P. Norton, "Measuring the Strategic Readiness of Intangible Assets," *Harvard Business Review,* February 2004, 52–60.

6. Alan P. Brache, "Managing Human Capabilities," *Journal of Organizational Excellence,* 22 (2003), 61.

7. *Human Capital Management: The CFO's Perspective* (New York: Mercer Human Resource Consulting, 2003).

8. Richard Finn, "Human-Capital Management (HCM)," *Human Resource Management International Digest,* 11 (2003), 2.

9. Christopher J. Collins and Kevin D. Clark, "Strategic Human Resource Practices, Top Management Team Social Networks, and Firm Performance," *Academy of Management Journal,* 46 (2003), 740–751.

10. Adapted from data at Forrester Research (*www.forrester.com*); Stephanie Armour and Michelle Kessler, "USA's New Money-Saving Export: White Collar Jobs," *USA Today,* August 5, 2003, 1B; Pete Engardio, Aaron Bernstein, and Manjeet Kripalani, "Is Your Job Next?" *Business Week,* February 2003, 50–60; and Maureen Minehan, "Offshore Outsourcing Stirs Controversy," *Global Perspectives,* July 2003.

11. Alex Taylor III, "The Americanization of Toyota," *Fortune,* December 8, 2003.

12. Andy Meisler, "Think Globally, Act Rationally," *Workforce Management,* January, 2004, 40–45.

13. U.S. Bureau of Labor Statistics, 2004, *www.census.gov.*

14. *Keeping America Competitive: How a Talent Shortage Threatens U.S. Manufacturing* (Washington, DC: National Association of Manufacturers, 2003).

15. *Education at a Glance* (Paris: Organization for Economic Cooperation and Development, 2003).

16. "Europe Looking to Women for Declining Work Force," *Omaha World-Herald,* December 22, 2003, D1.

17. U.S. Census Bureau, *Current Population Survey, www.census.gov.*

18. Jean-Phillipe Cotis, "Population Ageing, Facing the Challenge," *OECD Observer,* September, 2003.

19. Charles Fishman, "The Wal-Mart You Don't Know," *Fast Company,* December 2003, 68.

20. *Tough Times, Tougher HR* (New York: Towers-Perrin, 2003).

21. "Internal HR: Outsourcing Growth," *Workforce Management,* December 2003, 89; and Beth McConnell, "Small Majority of Companies Outsource Some HR Duties," *HR News,* August 14, 2003, *http://www.shrm.org/hrnews.*

22. Bruce Shutan, "Wave of the Future," *Human Resource Executive,* July 2003, 26–30.

23. Allen Halcrow, "A 360-Degree View of HR," *Workforce,* June 2002, 28–34.

24. Dina M. Cox and Channing H. Cox, "At the Table," *Workspan,* November 2003, 21–23.

25. Barbara Parus, "HR: From Paper Pusher to Strategic Partner," *Workspan,* November 2003, 26–29.

26. Based on Edward E. Lawler III and Susan A. Mohrman, "HR as a Strategic Partner: What Does It Take to Make It Happen?" *Human Resource Planning,* 26 (2003), 15–28.

27. Theresa Minton-Eversole, "HR Must Forge Partnerships . . .," *HR News,* October 10, 2003, *www.shrm.org/hrnews.*

28. Based on information provided by Jamie Herbert, SPHR, Omaha, Nebraska, 2004.

29. The authors acknowledge the assistance of Tim Kitely, Christine Lange, and Sanjeev Tina in providing research and content suggestions on HR technology.

30. *HR on the Web: The Investment Is Paying Off* (New York: Towers-Perrin, 2003).

31. "The Evolution of Workforce Technologies," *Trend Watcher,* January 23, 2004.

32. Based on "Acentis Streamlines Price Law Group's HR," *Human Resource Executive,* November 2002, 48.

33. Kristen B. Frasch, "Coca-Cola Talent Leader Shares Story of a Self-Service 'Soft Sell,'" October 13, 2003, *www.workindex.com.*

34. "Cedar Workforce Technologies Survey," December 1, 2003, *www.thecedargroup.com.*

35. "Managing with Soul: Combining Corporate Integrity with the Bottom Line," November 14, 2003, *www.workindex.com.*

36. Jakob Svensson, "Who Must Pay Bribes and How Much? Evidence from a Cross-Section of Firms," *Quarterly Journal of Economics,* 118 (2003), 207.

37. Claire D'Souza, "An Inference of Gift-Giving Within Asian Business Culture," *Asia Pacific Journal of Marketing and Logistics,* 15 (2003), 27–39.

38. For a more in-depth discussion of HR ethical issues, see Linda Gravett, *HRM Ethics: Perspectives for a New Millennium* (Cincinnati: Atomic Dog Publishing, 2003).

39. Michelle R. Greenwood, "Ethics and HRM: A Review and Conceptual Analysis," *Journal of Business Ethics,* March 2002, 261–279.

40. "Survey Examines Relationship Between HR and Ethics," *HR News, www.shrm.org/hrnews*; other surveys; and personal interviews with selected HR professionals.

41. Adapted from Richard Stolz, "What HR Will Stand For," *Human Resource Executive,* January 2003, 20–28.

42. *National Business Ethics Survey* (Washington, DC: Ethics Resource Center, 2003).

43. Margaret M. Clark, "Corporate Ethics Programs Make a Difference, but Not the Only Difference," *HR Magazine,* July 2003, 36.

44. The summarization of the five competencies is based on Wayne Brockbank and Dave Ulrich, *Competencies for the New HR Guidebook* (Alexandria, VA: Society for Human Resource Management, 2003).

45. For details, see *The HR Competency Self-Assessment,* available at *www.shrm.org/competencies.*

46. Shari Caudron, "HR Is Dead, Long Live HR," *Workforce,* January 2003, 26–30.

47. Susan J. Wells, "The Path Taken," *HR Magazine,* July 2003, 50–54.

48. Annually, SHRM and Mercer Human Resource Consultants do a compensation survey of HR jobs. For details see *Human Resource Management Positions,* part of the Mercer Benchmark Database at *www.shrm.org* or *www.mercer.com.*

49. Glenn Davidson, "Who Knows This Stuff?" *HRO Today,* December 2003, 62.

50. Based on Patrick J. Kiger, "HR Proves Its Value," *Workforce,* March 2002, 28–33.

CHAPTER 2

Strategic HR Management and Planning

After you have read this chapter, you should be able to:

- ◆ Explain strategic HR management and how it is linked to organizational strategies.

- ◆ Describe how legal, political, cultural, and economic factors affect global HR management.

- ◆ Discuss four dimensions of organizational effectiveness and how HR contributes to each.

- ◆ Define HR planning and outline the HR planning process.

- ◆ Discuss several ways of managing a surplus of human resources.

- ◆ Identify why HR metrics must consider both strategic and operational HR measures.

HR *Headline*

Measurement of HR Is Crucial to Strategic Success

Many executives and operating managers recognize the importance of HR but have concerns about the lack of quantifiable measures of HR efforts. Various surveys have found that over half of executives and 80% of operating managers see HR management as critical to their organizations. However, those surveyed indicate that HR activities are not being evaluated adequately, using specific quantifiers measures similar to those used for activities performed in other departments.

The greatest way of showing that HR management is strategic is to present better data on the financial effects of HR programs. HR expenses represent about 60% or more of the total expenses in many firms. But justification for those expenditures and documentation of the value added by HR is lacking.

Fortunately, a growing number of HR professionals have responded to these concerns and are developing HR metrics to provide hard data on the strategic and operational contributions of HR management. One example of how HR measurement has been helpful is seen at Verizon, the large telecommunications firm. Several years ago Verizon began using 17 questions to evaluate HR activities as part of a "balanced scorecard" process. Questions look at factors such as talent availability, turnover reduction and retention plans, HR service delivery, and the firm's return on investment on its people expenditures. These evaluation efforts continue to give Verizon a better understanding of the cost/benefit payoffs of its HR efforts, and how well these efforts contribute to attainment of Verizon's strategic and operational goals.[1]

"We spend hundreds of millions of dollars a year on employees. Human resources is the biggest investment we have."

—*Sarah Meyerrose*

Effective management of all resources, including human resources, is significant in determining longer-term organizational success. The extent to which organizations reach established strategic goals and objectives results in organizational effectiveness. Many organizations are becoming increasingly aware that human resources often contribute to a competitive advantage.

NATURE OF STRATEGIC HR MANAGEMENT

Strategic HR management
Use of employees to gain or keep a competitive advantage, resulting in greater organizational effectiveness.

Strategic HR management refers to the use of employees to gain or keep a competitive advantage, resulting in greater organizational effectiveness. Figure 2-1 shows the factors that affect strategic HR management. Because business strategies affect HR plans and policies, consideration of human resource issues should be part of the strategy formulation process. It may be important to identify competitive advantage opportunities that fit the existing employees or to assess strategic alternatives given the current capabilities of organizational human resources. HR managers should be scanning the environment to pinpoint what workforce skills are and are not available. HR professionals also should be able to estimate lead times for adjusting to labor shortages or surpluses. In summary, HR should be involved in implementing strategies that affect and are affected by human resources.

As an example, the organizational success of Dell Computer is strongly linked to strategic use of human resources by the firm. A technical service representative at Dell has significant specialized product knowledge, information systems

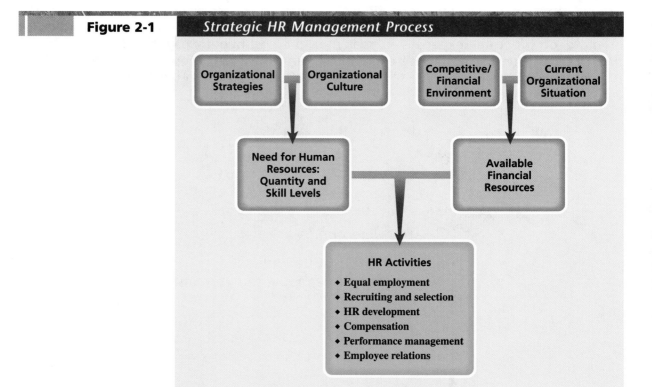

Figure 2-1 · *Strategic HR Management Process*

Organizational Strategies

Organizational Culture

Competitive/ Financial Environment

Current Organizational Situation

Need for Human Resources: Quantity and Skill Levels

Available Financial Resources

HR Activities
- Equal employment
- Recruiting and selection
- HR development
- Compensation
- Performance management
- Employee relations

technical expertise, problem-solving skills, and customer interaction and communication abilities. The value of Dell's human resources is demonstrated daily to its customers and has been a major contributor to Dell's growth and success. The human resources Dell uses are located at customer service centers in India and at other facilities throughout the world. One challenge facing Dell and other transnational companies is keeping and expanding human resources. Some operations and jobs have been moved from the U.S. to India, the Philippines, Poland, and other developing countries where pay levels are significantly lower for comparably qualified individuals. But these moves have been part of Dell's overall successful corporate business strategies.

Linkage of Organizational and HR Strategies

There should be a close relationship between organizational strategy and HR strategy. Two basic types of organizational strategies can be identified: *cost-leadership* and *differentiation*. A company like Wal-Mart follows a cost-leadership strategy, and firms like Intel or Microsoft follow a differentiation strategy. A cost-leadership strategy approaches competition on the basis of low price and high quality of product or service. The differentiation strategy is more appropriate in a more dynamic environment characterized by rapid change, and requires continually finding new products and new markets. The two strategies may not be mutually exclusive; it is possible for an organization to pursue one strategy with some products or services, and the other strategy with other products or services.

A cost-leadership strategy may require an organization to "build" its own employees to fit its specialized needs. This approach needs a longer HR planning horizon. When specific skills are necessary for a new market or product, it may be more difficult to develop them quickly internally. A differentiation strategy is more responsive, meaning that HR planning is likely to have a shorter time frame. Also, this type of approach makes greater use of external sources, such as the acquisition of another company with specialized employees, to staff the organization. With the globalization of business, many organizations must succeed throughout the world.

GLOBAL COMPETITIVENESS AND STRATEGIC HR

The globalization of business has meant that more organizations operate in multiple countries or have foreign operational links to international suppliers, vendors, and outsourced contributors. Rapid growth of international outsourcing also indicates the linkage between global competitiveness and HR management.

Types of Global Organizations

A growing number of organizations that operate in only one country have recognized the need to develop more global operations. As they broaden their operations worldwide, organizations may pass through three stages.

Importing and exporting
Buying and selling goods and services with organizations in other countries.

Importing and Exporting The first phase of international interaction consists of **importing and exporting.** Here, an organization begins buying and selling goods and services with organizations in other countries. Generally, HR activities are not affected except for travel policies for those going abroad.

Multi-national enterprise (MNE)
Organization that has operating units located in foreign countries.

Global organization
Firm that has corporate units in a number of countries that are integrated to operate worldwide.

Multi-National Enterprises As firms develop and expand, they identify opportunities to begin operating in other countries. A **multi-national enterprise (MNE)** is an organization that has operating units located in foreign countries. As the MNE expands, it hires workers from the countries in which it has operations. Because laws and regulations in those countries likely differ from those in the home country, the HR professionals in the parent organization must become knowledgeable about each country in which the MNE operates and must know how to adapt staffing, training, compensation, health and safety, and labor relations.

Global Organization An MNE can be thought of as an international firm, in that it operates in various countries, but each foreign business unit is operated separately. In contrast, a **global organization** has corporate units in a number of countries that are integrated to operate as one organization worldwide. All managers and employees in global organizations need a global "mindset."[2] HR management in truly global organizations moves people, especially key managers and professionals, throughout the world. Individuals who speak several languages fluently are highly valued, and they will move among divisions and countries as they assume more responsibilities and experience career growth.

Having a global HR mindset means looking at HR issues from a global perspective, using ideas and resources throughout the world, and ensuring openness to other cultures and ideas.[3] This global mindset requires consideration of a number of factors, including legal, political, cultural, and economic forces that significantly affect the competitiveness of organizations and global HR management.

Global Legal and Political Factors

Firms in the U.S., Europe, and elsewhere are accustomed to relatively stable political and legal systems. However, many nations function under turbulent and varied legal and political systems. Therefore, HR-related laws vary in character and stability. Compliance with laws on wages, benefits, union relations, worker privacy, workplace safety, and others illustrate the importance of HR management when operating transnationally. As a result, it is crucial for HR professionals to conduct a comprehensive review of the political environment and employment laws before beginning operations in a country. The role and nature of labor unions also should be a part of that review.

Global Cultural Factors

Culture
Societal forces affecting the values, beliefs, and actions of a distinct group of people.

Cultural forces represent another important concern affecting international HR management. **Culture** is composed of societal forces affecting the values, beliefs, and actions of a distinct group of people. Cultural differences certainly exist between nations, and significant cultural differences also exist within countries. One has only to look at the conflicts caused by religion or ethnicity in Africa, the Middle East, and other parts of the world to see the importance of culture in international organizations. Convincing individuals from different religious, ethnic, or tribal backgrounds to work together in a global firm may be difficult in some parts of the world.

One widely used way to classify and compare cultures was developed by Geert Hofstede, a Dutch scholar and researcher. Hofstede conducted research on more than 100,000 IBM employees in 53 countries, and he defined five dimensions useful in identifying and comparing cultures. A review of each of those dimensions follows.[4]

Power distance
Dimension of culture that refers to the inequality among the people of a nation.

Power Distance The cultural dimension of **power distance** refers to the inequality among the people of a nation. In countries such as Canada, the Netherlands, and the United States, there is less inequality than in countries such as France, Mexico, and Brazil. As power distance scores increase, status and authority differences between superiors and subordinates decrease. One way in which differences on this dimension affect HR activities is that the reactions to management authority differ among cultures. Countries like the Netherlands and the United States may use more employee participation in decision making, while countries like Mexico and Brazil use a more autocratic approach to managing.

Individualism
Dimension of culture that refers to the extent to which people in a country prefer to act as individuals instead of members of groups.

Individualism Another dimension of culture identified by Hofstede is **individualism,** which is the extent to which people in a country prefer to act as individuals instead of members of groups. On this dimension, people in some Asian countries tend to focus less on individual interests and more on group interests, whereas those in the United States are more individualistic. These differences imply that more collective action and less individual competition are likely in countries that de-emphasize individualism.

Masculinity/femininity
Dimension of culture that refers to the degree to which "masculine" values prevail over "feminine" values.

Masculinity/Femininity The cultural dimension **masculinity/femininity** refers to the degree to which "masculine" values prevail over "feminine" values. Masculine values identified by Hofstede were assertiveness, performance orientation, success, and competitiveness; feminine values included quality of life, close personal relationships, and caring. Respondents from Japan had the most masculine values, while those from the Netherlands had more feminine values. Differences on this dimension may be tied to the role of women in the culture. Consider the different roles of women and the variations in what is "acceptable" for women in the United States, Saudi Arabia, Japan, and Mexico. These differences suggest how this dimension might affect the assignment of women managers to jobs in those countries.

Uncertainty avoidance
Dimension of culture that refers to the preference of people in a country for structured rather than unstructured situations.

Uncertainty Avoidance The dimension of **uncertainty avoidance** refers to the preference of people in a country for structured rather than unstructured situations. Nations focusing on avoiding uncertainty, such as Japan and France, tend to be more resistant to change. In contrast, people in places such as the United States and Great Britain tend to have more "business energy" and to be more flexible.

A logical use of differences in this factor is to anticipate how people in different countries will react to changes instituted in organizations. In more flexible cultures, what is less certain may be considered more intriguing and challenging, which may lead to greater entrepreneurship and risk taking than in the more "rigid" countries.

Long-term orientation
Dimension of culture that refers to the preference of people in a country for long-term values as opposed to short-term values.

Long-Term Orientation Developed a decade after the original studies, the dimension of **long-term orientation** refers to the preference of people in a country for long-term values, emphasize the future, as opposed to short-term values, which focus on the present and the past. Long-term values include thrift and persistence, while short-term values include respect for tradition and fulfillment of social obligations. A long-term orientation was more present in Japan and India, while a short-term orientation tended to be held by people in the United States and France.

Differences in many other facets of culture could be discussed. But it is enough to note that international HR managers and professionals must recognize that cultural dimensions differ from country to country and even within countries. Therefore, the HR activities appropriate in one culture or country may have to be altered to fit appropriately into another culture or country.

Global Economic Factors

Economic factors are linked to political, legal, and cultural issues, and different countries have different economic systems. In many developed countries, especially in Europe, employment restrictions and wage levels are high. The differences between labor costs in the U.S. compared with those in Germany and Norway are significant. Figure 2-2 shows the differences in manufacturing unit labor costs in various countries. As a result of these differences, many U.S. and European firms are moving jobs to lower-wage countries, such as Romania, China, and Thailand.

Critics of globalization cite the extremely low wage rates paid by the international firms and the substandard working conditions that exist in some underde-

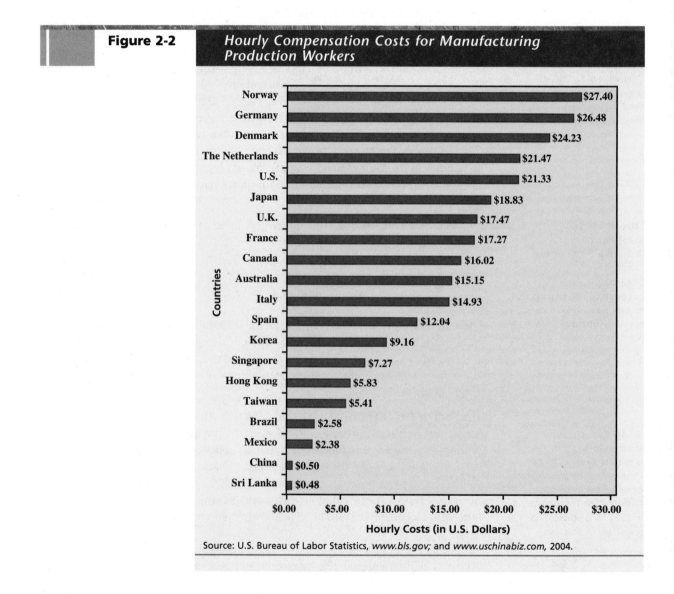

Figure 2-2

Hourly Compensation Costs for Manufacturing Production Workers

Source: U.S. Bureau of Labor Statistics, *www.bls.gov*; and *www.uschinabiz.com*, 2004.

veloped countries. Examples include Cambodians making $40 a month sewing garments for U.S. retailers, and workers in many Chinese toy manufacturing firms earning $1 a day. Various advocacy groups have accused Nike, Adidas, Levi Strauss, Liz Claiborne, and other global firms of being "sweatshop employers."

Global employers counter that even though the wage rates in some countries are low, their employees often receive higher wages and better working conditions than exist in the local countries. Also, many employees in the host countries now have jobs, which allows them to improve their living standards.

Global Economic Interdependence There is a high level of economic interdependence among the economies of various countries. To take advantage of this interdependence, firms have established operations throughout the world, formed joint ventures, or merged with firms in other countries.

The development of a number of regional trade and political alliances also contribute to globalization. One well-known alliance is the North American Free Trade Agreement (NAFTA), negotiated by Canada, Mexico, and the United States. Its impact on U.S. employers and jobs has been a continuing source of debate.[5] In Western Europe, efforts over several decades led to the creation of the European Union (EU) and the introduction of the Euro currency. The EU has also established labor and other standards, and their adoption by individual EU countries has led to greater similarity of HR practices in EU-based firms and foreign firms operating in the EU.

Global Productivity and Strategic HR Management Increases in national wage levels (the cost of paying employees) without increases in national productivity lead to inflation, which results in an increase in costs and a decrease in purchasing power. Also, lower rates of productivity make for higher labor costs and a less competitive position for the products and services of a nation in the world marketplace. That is why global productivity issues are closely linked to organizational effectiveness and performance.[6] HR is (or should be) involved with all the global challenges by identifying how it can aid in increasing organizational productivity, help deal effectively with global issues and foreign competition, and enhance innovativeness in the organization. This kind of thinking is indicative of strategic HR management.

■ ORGANIZATIONAL EFFECTIVENESS AND STRATEGIC HR MANAGEMENT

Every organization has a mission that identifies its reasons for existence. To fulfill its mission, the organization must have goals and objectives to achieve. For example, a hospital exists to provide health care services. To meet its mission, the hospital must set specific targets and state desired results. One target that the hospital may wish to meet is an 80% average occupancy rate (that is, 400 of its 500 beds occupied on the average day) so that it receives enough income to pay for its building debt, equipment, employees, and other expenses.

Effectiveness for organizations is defined as the extent to which goals have been met. Organizational effectiveness can be identified using a number of different approaches.[7] **Efficiency** is the degree to which operations are done in an economical manner. Efficiency can also be thought of as a short-term measure that compares inputs and costs directly against outputs and benefits. Organizations must be able to achieve their goals within the constraints of limited resources. For example, providing on-site child care for all employees might help

Effectiveness
The extent to which goals have been met.
Efficiency
The degree to which operations are done in an economical manner.

an employer achieve the goal of reducing turnover, but the costs of operating the child-care center could be too high, so the center would not be established.

Conversely, an action that improves efficiency may not be effective in the long run. For instance, a large bank cut staff and closed branches to reduce costs. Over the following year, organizational productivity decreased, customer dissatisfaction increased, 15% of customers closed their accounts, and turnover of the remaining employees increased significantly. Thus, the staff cuts did not contribute to organizational effectiveness, even though they resulted in some short-term cost savings.

HR management plays a significant strategic role. In organizations where there are identifiable HR "strengths," organizational effectiveness is enhanced.[8] Strategic HR management plays a significant role in several dimensions of organizational effectiveness. Four prominent ones are these:

- Organizational productivity
- Financial contributions
- Service and quality
- Organizational culture

Organizational Productivity and HR Efforts

The more productive an organization, the better its competitive advantage because the costs to produce its goods and services are lower. Better productivity does not necessarily mean more production; perhaps fewer people (or less money or time) are used to produce the same amount. In its most basic sense, **productivity** is a measure of the quantity and quality of work done, considering the cost of the resources used. A useful way to measure the productivity of a workforce is to determine the total cost of people required for each unit of output. For example, a retailer may measure productivity as a ratio of employee payroll and benefits to sales, or a bank may compare the number and dollar amount of loans made to the number of loan officers employed. This provides a metric of productivity per loan officer.

A useful way of measuring HR productivity of human resources is to consider **unit labor cost,** which is computed by dividing the average cost of workers by their average levels of output. Using unit labor costs, one can see that paying relatively high wages still can result in a firm being economically competitive if high productivity levels are achieved. Low unit labor costs can be a basis for a strategy focusing on human resources. Productivity and unit labor costs can be evaluated at the global, country, organizational, or individual level.

Improving Organizational Productivity Productivity at the organizational level ultimately affects profitability and competitiveness in a for-profit organization, and total costs in a not-for-profit organization. Perhaps none of the resources used for productivity in organizations are so closely scrutinized as human resources. Many strategic HR management efforts are designed to affect organizational productivity, as Figure 2-3 indicates.

- *Organizational restructuring* involves eliminating layers of management and changing reporting relationships, as well as cutting staff through downsizing, layoffs, and early retirement buyout programs. HR usually plays a key role in all these efforts.
- *Re-designing work* often involves having fewer employees who work longer hours and perform multiple job tasks. It may also involve replacing workers

Productivity
Measure of the quantity and quality of work done, considering the cost of the resources used.

Unit labor cost
Computed by dividing the average cost of workers by their average levels of output.

Figure 2-3   *Approaches to Improving Organizational Productivity*

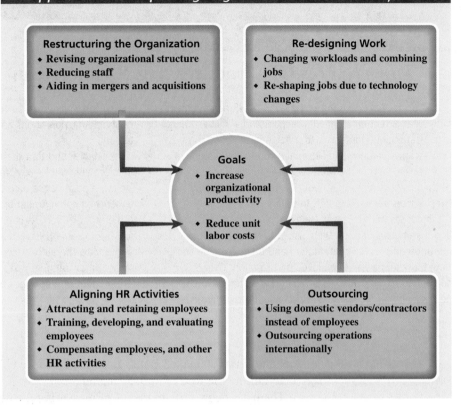

with capital equipment or making them more efficient by use of technology or new processes.

◆ *Aligning HR activities* means making HR efforts consistent with organizational efforts to improve productivity. This alignment includes ensuring that staffing, training and development, performance management, compensation, and other HR activities all contribute to organizational effectiveness.

◆ *Outsourcing analyses and assistance* involves HR in conducting cost-benefit analyses to justify outsourcing, negotiating with outsourcing vendors, ensuring that contractors domestically and internationally are operating legally and appropriately, and linking the organization's employees to the outsourcing firm's employees.

Organizational Effectiveness and Financial Contributions of HR

A second aspect of organizational effectiveness relates to HR management being a financial contributor. During the past several years, HR management has given significant attention to linking more effectively with financial executives, including Chief Financial Officers (CFO).[9] The purpose of this linkage has been to make certain that HR is a financial contributor to organizational effectiveness. CFOs are constantly looking at the return on investment (ROI) of all resources and expenditures in organizations, including the ROI of human expenditures. Two firms that are well known for determining the ROI of HR are Dow Chemi-

Research on HR Practices and Business Unit Performance

One of the key questions at the heart of HR management is to what extent different HR practices and activities affect organizational performance. To provide insight on this question, Wright, Gardner, and Moynihan conducted a study of 50 business units in the food service industry. Because each of the business units operated relatively independently, the HR practices varied from unit to unit.

Employees in three areas (salespeople, delivery drivers, and warehouse workers) were asked to complete surveys about organizational commitment and their views on selection, training, pay, and employee participation. Over 5,000 completed surveys were returned and used for research analyses. The authors also had access to data on business unit performance, such as worker compensation costs, quality, shrinkage, operations and payroll expenses, and profitability.

The study found that there is a definite link between HR practices and employee commitment to the organization. The more positive the employees' views of HR practices, the higher their commitment to remaining with and contributing to the organization. As important, there was a strong relationship of some HR practices to operating expenses and profitability. The authors concluded that HR practices do impact organizational performance, with the organizational commitment of employees being a significant factor.[10]

cal and First Tennessee Bank. Both have invested significant time and effort in determining the ROI of human capital.[11]

There are many different ways of measuring the financial contributions of HR, and many difficulties associated with doing so. For example, if a firm invests $20,000 for a supervisory training program, what does it gain in lower worker compensation costs, lower legal costs, higher employee productivity, and lower employee turnover? Or if it introduces new HR management system software that costs $800,000, what will it save in reduced staffing, lowered response times, and other factors? Questions such as these illustrate that HR must be able to provide financial justification for its activities. Later in this chapter, the discussion of HR metrics will highlight some specific HR measurement approaches.

Often HR is seen by CFOs and others as a "cost center," but that view is changing as HR professionals demonstrate their financial contributions. As the HR Perspective indicates, HR practices do affect the performance of business units.

Customer Service and Quality Linked to HR Strategies

In addition to productivity, customer service and quality significantly affect organizational effectiveness. Having all employees focus on customers contributes significantly to achieving organizational goals and maintaining a competitive advantage.[12] In many organizations, service quality is greatly influenced by the individual employees who interact with customers.[13] For instance, organizations with high turnover rates of employees quitting their jobs have seen slow sales growth.[14] It seems customers see continuity of customer service representatives as important in making sales decisions.

Unfortunately, overall customer satisfaction with sales quality has declined in the United States and other countries.[15] One example from several years ago illustrates the importance of service excellence. Within the first six months after being hired, a new CEO at Home Depot directed that labor costs and staffing in the company stores be reduced. As a result, a significant number of customers complained about not being able to find employees to help them, having to wait a long time to check out, and encountering shortages of merchandise on shelves. At the same time, Lowe's, a major competitor, expanded staff and advertised its "customer service" emphasis. The result was that Lowe's sales and profitability grew significantly, while Home Depot's results flattened. After a year, the Home Depot CEO admitted that the "cost-cutting" approach had created customer problems and significantly affected the performance of the firm. Since then, Home Depot has added staff and taken steps to repair its customer service image.

Quality Delivering high-quality services and/or products can significantly influence organizational effectiveness. Whether producing automobiles, as General Motors and Toyota do, or providing cellular phone service, as Verizon and Cingular Wireless do, a firm must consider how well its products and services meet customer needs. Therefore, many organizations such as General Electric and Johnson & Johnson have emphasized efforts to enhance quality. The thrust of all these programs is to get tasks done right and efficiently, so that quality services are delivered the first time, every time. The problems with quality that some U.S. auto manufacturers have had, compared with other firms such as Toyota and Honda, illustrate the important effect of quality on sales, revenue, costs, and ultimately organizational effectiveness. Attempts to improve quality have worked better for some organizations than for others.[16]

Organizational Culture and Organizational Effectiveness

The shared values and beliefs in an organization is the **organizational culture.** Managers definitely must consider the culture of the organization, because otherwise excellent strategies can be negated by a culture incompatible with those strategies.[17] Further, the culture of the organization, as viewed by the people in it, affects attraction and retention of competent employees. Numerous examples can be given of key technical, professional, and administrative employees leaving firms because of corporate cultures that seem to devalue people and create barriers to the use of individual capabilities. What is evident in many organizations is that HR management strategies and practices are central to organizational cultures, and thus organizational effectiveness.[18] Certainly, large firms as different as Southwest Airlines, Intuit, Yahoo!, Dell Computer, Marriott International, and Lowe's have used HR to create organizational cultures that are seen positively by employees, customers, and others.

Therefore, organizational culture should be seen as the "climate" of the organization that employees, managers, customers, and others experience. This culture affects service and quality, organizational productivity, and financial results. Alignment of the organizational culture and HR management efforts impacts customer satisfaction, employee retention, and, ultimately, organizational effectiveness. This alignment requires giving significant attention to HR planning.

▓▓ HUMAN RESOURCE PLANNING

The competitive strategies and objectives of an organization are the foundation for **human resource (HR) planning,** which is the process of analyzing and identifying the need for and availability of human resources so that the organization

Figure 2-4 | *Purpose of HR Planning*

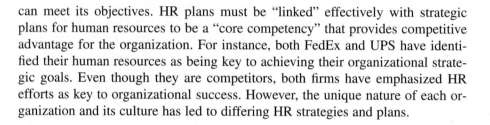

can meet its objectives. HR plans must be "linked" effectively with strategic plans for human resources to be a "core competency" that provides competitive advantage for the organization. For instance, both FedEx and UPS have identified their human resources as being key to achieving their organizational strategic goals. Even though they are competitors, both firms have emphasized HR efforts as key to organizational success. However, the unique nature of each organization and its culture has led to differing HR strategies and plans.

Purpose of Strategic HR Planning

The focus of HR planning, as shown in Figure 2-4, is to have the *right number of human resources,* with the *right capabilities,* at the *right times,* and in the *right places.* In HR planning, an organization must consider the availability of and allocation of people to jobs over long periods of time, not just for the next month or even the next year.

This level of planning requires knowledge of strategic expansions or reductions in operations and any technological changes that may affect the organization. To illustrate, Walgreen, the large retail chain, has had an aggressive expansion plan for the past several years. Each new Walgreen's store must be staffed with pharmacists, managers, and customer service employees. For this firm, one of the biggest pressures is ensuring that enough pharmacists are available—a challenge that has resulted from a continuing shortage of graduates in pharmacy as well as from Walgreen's retail service setting, which requires pharmacists to work different hours and face different demands than those in hospitals and clinics. Therefore, HR planning at Walgreen's has had to identify how and where to find enough pharmacists to fill openings caused by turnover and retirement, as well as to staff all the new stores.[19]

This example also illustrates that HR planning must identify the knowledge, skills, abilities, experience, and other characteristics affecting the capabilities of employees for current and future jobs. It must consider changes in those capabilities as well. For instance, southwestern U.S. cities increasingly need multilingual police and fire officers to meet the needs of the growing number of citizens who are Hispanic, Sudanese, Vietnamese, and other ethnic groups for whom English may not be widely used. Forecasting specific language capabilities and identifying means for enhancing the language skills of existing police and fire officers, as well as hiring a more diverse workforce, are part of successful HR planning for those cities.

HR PLANNING
Provides an overview of
key steps in HR
planning.
Custom Search:
☑ ANALYSIS
Exact Phrase: Virtues of
HR planning

Additionally, as part of analyses, HR plans can be made for shifting employees within the organization, laying off employees or otherwise cutting back the number of employees, retraining present employees, or increasing the number of employees in certain areas. Factors to consider include the current employees' knowledge, skills, and abilities in the organization and the expected vacancies resulting from retirements, promotions, transfers, and discharges. In summary, doing HR planning right requires significant time and effort by HR professionals working with executives and managers.

HR Planning Responsibilities

In most organizations that do HR planning, the top HR executive and subordinate staff specialists have most of the responsibilities for this planning. However, as Figure 2-5 indicates, other managers must provide information for the HR specialists to analyze. In turn, those other managers need to receive data from the HR unit. Because top managers are responsible for overall strategic planning, they usually ask the HR unit to project the human resources needed to implement overall organizational goals.

Small Businesses and HR Planning

The need for HR planning in larger organizations is clear because if some formal adjustments to changes are not made, people or even entire divisions might be working at cross-purposes with the rest of the company. In a smaller business, even though the owner/manager knows on a daily basis what is happening and what should be done, planning is still important. Perhaps the most difficult area for HR planning in small businesses is family matters and succession.[20]

Particular difficulties arise when a growing business is passed from one generation to another, resulting in a mix of family and non-family employees. Key to a successful transition is having a clear HR plan. In small businesses, such a plan includes incorporating key non-family members in HR planning efforts, because non-family members often have important capabilities and expertise that family members do not possess.[21] Planning for the attraction and retention of these "outsiders" may be vital to the future success of smaller organizations.[22] Small businesses, depending on how small they are, may use the HR planning process that

Figure 2-5	*Typical Division of HR Responsibilities: HR Planning*

HR Unit	**Managers**
• Participates in strategic planning process for entire organization • Identifies HR strategies • Designs data systems for HR planning • Compiles and analyzes data from managers on staffing needs • Implements HR plan as approved by top management	• Identify supply-and-demand needs for each division/department • Review/discuss HR planning information with HR specialists • Integrate HR plan with departmental plans • Monitor HR plan to identify changes needed • Review employee succession plans associated with HR plan

Figure 2-6   *HR Planning Process*

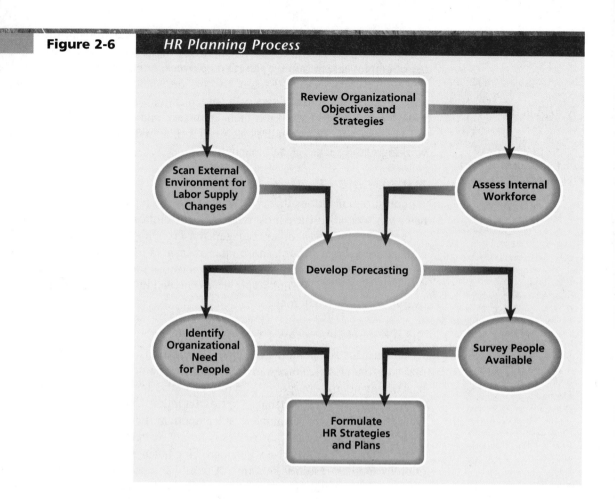

follows, but in very small organizations, the process is much more intuitive and is often done entirely by the top executives, who often are family members.

HR Planning Process

The steps in the HR planning process are shown in Figure 2-6. Notice that the HR planning process begins with considering the organizational objectives and strategies. Then HR needs and supply sources must be analyzed both externally and internally, and forecasts must be developed. Key to assessing internal human resources is having solid information accessible through a human resource management system (HRMS).

Once the assessments are complete, forecasts must be developed to identify the relationship between supply and demand for human resources. Management then formulates HR strategies and plans to address imbalances, both short term and long term.

HR Strategies
Means used to anticipate and manage the supply of and demand for human resources.

HR strategies are means used to anticipate and manage the supply of and demand for human resources. These strategies provide overall direction for the ways HR activities will be designed and managed. Finally, specific HR plans are developed to provide more specific direction for the management of HR activities. The most telling evidence of successful HR planning is a consistent alignment of the availabilities and capabilities of human resources with the needs of the organization over a period of time.

▌▌ SCANNING THE EXTERNAL ENVIRONMENT

Environmental scanning
Process of studying the environment of the organization to pinpoint opportunities and threats.

At the heart of strategic planning is **environmental scanning,** a process of studying the environment of the organization to pinpoint opportunities and threats. The external environment especially affects HR planning because each organization must draw from the same labor market that supplies all other employers. Indeed, one measure of organizational effectiveness is the ability of an organization to compete for a sufficient supply of human resources with the appropriate capabilities. All elements of the external environment—government influences, economic conditions, geographic and competition issues, and workforce changes—must be part of the scanning process.

Government Influences

An expanding and often bewildering array of government regulations affect the labor supply and therefore HR planning. As a result, HR planning must be done by individuals who understand the legal requirements of various government regulations. For example, firms operating globally may need to know that in France, the government has changed the length of the workweek from 39 to 35 hours. Also, the European Union has the Working Time Directive, which states that European workers should be limited to a maximum of 48 hours a week.

In the U.S. and other countries, tax legislation at local, state, and federal levels also affects HR planning. Pension provisions and Social Security legislation may change retirement patterns and funding options. Elimination or expansion of tax benefits for job-training expenses might alter some job-training activities associated with workforce expansions. Employee benefits may be affected significantly by tax law changes. Tax credits for employee day care and financial aid for education may influence employer practices in recruiting and retaining certain workers. In summary, an organization must consider a wide variety of government policies, regulations, and laws during the HR planning process.

Economic Conditions

The general business cycle of economic recessions and economic booms also affects HR planning. Factors such as interest rates, inflation, and economic growth affect the availability of workers and should figure into organizational and HR plans and objectives. There is a considerable difference between finding qualified applicants in a 3% unemployment market and in a 7% unemployment market. In the 3% unemployment market, significantly fewer qualified applicants are likely to be available for any kind of position. Applicants who are available may be less employable because they are less educated, less skilled, or unwilling to work. As the unemployment rate rises, the number of qualified people looking for work increases, making it easier to fill jobs.

Geographic and Competitive Concerns

In making HR plans, employers must consider a number of geographic and competitive concerns. The *net migration* into a particular region is important. For example, in the past decade, the populations of U.S. cities in the South, Southwest, and West have grown rapidly and provided a ready source of labor. However, many areas in the Northeast and Midwest have had declining populations.

Within the last decade, many workers, especially those with working spouses, have expressed an increasing reluctance to accept *geographic relocation* as a precondition of moving up in organizations. This trend has forced organizations to change their employee development policies and practices as well as their HR plans.

Direct competitors are another important external force in HR planning. Failure to consider the competitive labor market and to offer pay scales and benefits competitive with those of organizations in the same general industry and geographic location may cost a company dearly in the long run. Underpaying or "undercompeting" may result in a much lower-quality workforce. Also, *other employers* in a geographic region can greatly expand or diminish the labor supply. For instance, if a new Wal-Mart or Target store opens in a suburban location, other retail employers in the area may see greater turnover and face greater difficulty in recruiting new employees.

Finally, the impact of *international competition* must be considered as part of environmental scanning. Global competition for labor intensifies as global competitors shift jobs and workers around the world, as illustrated by the outsourcing of jobs from the U.S. to countries with cheaper labor.

Workforce Composition

Changes in the composition of the workforce, combined with the use of different work patterns, have created workplaces and organizations that are notably different from those of a decade ago. Many organizations face major concerns about having sufficient workers with the necessary capabilities. When scanning the workforce, it is important to consider a number of variables, including these:

- ◆ Aging of the workforce
- ◆ Growing diversity of workers
- ◆ Women workers and work/life balancing concerns
- ◆ Availability of "contingent workers"
- ◆ Outsourcing possibilities

When considering these factors, it is important to analyze how they affect the current and future availability of workers with specific capabilities and experience. For instance, in the oil and gas industry, the median age of petroleum engineers is about 50 years, and the supply of engineering graduates is not sufficient to replace such employees as they retire.[23]

■ ASSESSING THE INTERNAL WORKFORCE

Analyzing the jobs that will need to be done and the skills of people who are currently available in the organization to do them is the next part of HR planning. The needs of the organization must be compared against the labor supply available inside the organization.

Jobs and Skills Audit

The starting point for evaluating internal strengths and weaknesses is an audit of the jobs being done in the organization. A comprehensive analysis of all current jobs provides a basis for forecasting what jobs will need to be done in the future. Much of the data to answer the questions in the audit should be available from existing staffing and organizational databases. The following questions are addressed during the internal assessment:

- What jobs exist now?
- How many individuals are performing each job?
- What are the reporting relationships of jobs?
- How essential is each job?
- What jobs will be needed to implement future organizational strategies?
- What are the characteristics of anticipated jobs?

Organizational Capabilities Inventory

As HR planners gain an understanding of the current and future jobs that will be necessary to carry out organizational plans, they can make a detailed audit of current employees and their capabilities. The basic source of data on employees is the HR records in the organization. Different HR information databases can be used to identify the knowledge, skills, and abilities (KSAs) of employees. Planners can use KSA inventories to determine future needs for recruiting, selection, and HR development. The information in those inventories can also provide a basis for determining what additional capabilities will be needed in the future workforce.

Using Organizational Inventory Data

An inventory of organizational capabilities may consider a number of elements, including the following:

- Individual employee demographics (age, length of service in the organization, time in present job)
- Individual career progression (jobs held, time in each job, promotions or other job changes, pay rates)
- Individual performance data (work accomplishment, growth in skills)

All the details on an individual employee's skills that go into a data bank may affect the employee's career. Therefore, the data and their use must meet the same standards of job-relatedness and non-discrimination as when the employee was initially hired. Furthermore, security measures must ensure that sensitive information is available only to those who have specific use for it.

Managers and HR staff members can gather data on individual employees and aggregate details into profile of the current organizational workforce. This profile may reveal many of the current strengths and deficiencies. If some specialized expertise, such as advanced computer skills, is absent, the organization may find it difficult to take advantage of new technological developments. Or if a large group of experienced employees are all in the same age bracket, their eventual retirements about the same time might lead to future "gaps" in the organization.

▌ FORECASTING HR SUPPLY AND DEMAND

Forecasting
Using information from the past and the present to identify expected future conditions.

The information gathered from scanning the external environmental and assessing internal strengths and weaknesses is used to predict HR supply and demand in light of organizational objectives and strategies. **Forecasting** uses information from the past and the present to identify expected future conditions. Figure 2-7 shows the role of HR forecasting in the HR planning process. Projec-

Figure 2-7 | *HR Forecasting*

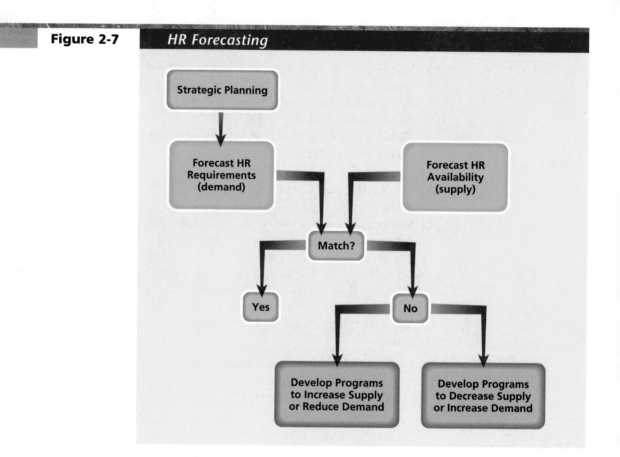

tions for the future are, of course, subject to error. Usually, though, experienced people are able to forecast with enough accuracy to benefit long-range organizational planning.

Forecasting Methods

Forecasting methods may be either judgmental or mathematical. Methods for forecasting human resources range from a manager's best guess to a rigorous and complex computer simulation. Despite the availability of sophisticated mathematical models and techniques, forecasting is still a combination of quantitative methods and subjective judgment. The facts must be evaluated and weighed by knowledgeable individuals, such as managers or HR planners, who use the mathematical models as tools and make judgments to arrive at decisions.

Forecasting Periods

HR forecasting should be done over three planning periods: short-range, intermediate-range, and long-range. The most commonly used planning period of six months to one year focuses on *short-range* forecasts for the immediate HR needs of an organization. Intermediate- and long-range forecasting are much more difficult processes. *Intermediate-range* plans usually project one to five years into the future, and *long-range* plans extend beyond five years.

Forecasting the Demand for Human Resources

The demand for employees can be calculated for an entire organization and/or for individual units in the organization. For example, a forecast might indicate that a firm needs 125 new employees next year, or that it needs 25 new people in sales and customer service, 45 in production, 20 in accounting and information systems, 2 in HR, and 33 in the warehouse. The unit breakdown obviously allows HR planners to better pinpoint the specific skills needed than the aggregate method does.

Demand for human resources can be forecast by considering specific openings that are likely to occur. The openings (or demands) are created when employees leave positions because of promotions, transfers, and terminations. The analysis always begins with the top positions in the organization, because from there, no promotions to a higher level are possible.

This analysis is used to develop decision rules (or "fill rates") for each job or level. For example, a decision rule for a financial institution might state that 50% of branch supervisor openings will be filled through promotions from customer service tellers, 25% through promotions from personal bankers, and 25% from new hires. Forecasters must be aware of chain effects throughout the organization, because as people are promoted, their previous positions become available. Continuing our example, forecasts for the need for customer service tellers and personal bankers would also have to be developed. The overall purpose of the forecast is to identify the needs for human resources by number and type for the forecasting period.

Forecasting the Supply of Human Resources

Once human resources needs have been forecast, then availability of human resources must be identified. Forecasting the availability considers both *external* and *internal* supplies. Although the internal supply may be easier to calculate, it is important to calculate the external supply as accurately as possible.

External Supply The external supply of potential employees available to the organization needs to be identified. Extensive use of government estimates of labor force populations, trends in the industry, and many more complex and inter-related factors must be considered. Such information is often available from state or regional economic development offices, including these:

- Net migration into and out of the area
- Individuals entering and leaving the workforce
- Individuals graduating from schools and colleges
- Changing workforce composition and patterns
- Economic forecasts for the next few years
- Technological developments and shifts
- Actions of competing employers
- Government regulations and pressures
- Circumstances affecting persons entering and leaving the workforce

Internal Supply Figure 2-8 shows in general terms how the internal supply can be calculated for a specific employer. Estimating internal supply considers that employees move from their current jobs into others through promotions, lateral moves, and terminations. It also considers that the internal supply is influenced by training and development programs, transfer and promotion policies, and retire-

FORECASTING
Identifies integrating information when doing forecasting.
Custom Search:
☑ ANALYSIS
Exact Phrase: Forecasting HR

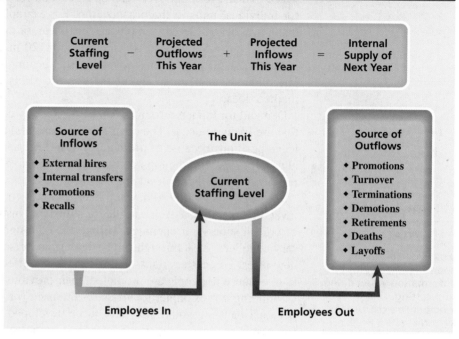

Figure 2-8 — *Estimating Internal Labor Supply for a Given Unit*

| Current Staffing Level | − | Projected Outflows This Year | + | Projected Inflows This Year | = | Internal Supply of Next Year |

Source of Inflows
- External hires
- Internal transfers
- Promotions
- Recalls

The Unit

Current Staffing Level

Source of Outflows
- Promotions
- Turnover
- Terminations
- Demotions
- Retirements
- Deaths
- Layoffs

Employees In   Employees Out

ment policies, among other factors. In forecasting the internal supply, data from the replacement charts and succession planning efforts are used to project potential personnel changes, identify possible backup candidates, and keep track of attrition (resignations, retirements, etc.) for each department in an organization.

DEVELOPING AND USING A STRATEGIC HR PLAN

With all the data collected and forecasts done, an organizational plan can be developed. Such a plan can be extremely sophisticated or rather rudimentary. Regardless of the degree of complexity, the ultimate purpose of the plan is to enable managers in the organization to match the available supply of labor with the demand that is expected given the strategies of the organization. If the necessary skill levels do not exist in the present workforce, the organization can train employees in the new skills or undertake outside recruiting. If the plan reveals that the firm employs too many people for its needs, a human resource surplus exists.

Succession Planning

Succession planning
Process of identifying a longer-term plan for the orderly replacement of key employees.

One important outcome of HR planning is **succession planning,** which is a process of identifying a longer-term plan for the orderly replacement of key employees. In larger organizations, such as the U.S. federal government, the aging of the workforce has significant implications for HR planning and succession planning. The HR Perspective highlights this concern.

One common flaw in succession planning is that too often it is limited to key executives. It may be just as critical to replace several experienced mechanical

U.S. Government Agencies Face Workforce Retirements

Many employers have experienced employees in their workforce who will be retiring in the next 10 years as the "baby-boomer" generation in the U.S. hits retirement age. When the employer has 1.5 million employees, and 20% are eligible to retire now, and 70% will be eligible to retire by 2012, that is a significant HR planning concern. When, as the following chart shows, the number of people who will be retiring annually is likely to increase from 5% in 2004 to nearly 35% in 2012, that is an even bigger concern.

U.S. government agencies as varied as the National Park Service, Army Corps of Engineers, Department of Veterans Affairs, and Department of Agriculture are just some of the ones facing significant possible losses of experienced workers. The situation has been labeled a "human capital crisis" by the U.S. Office of Personnel Management. Some analysts say that it may not be as big a crisis as forecast, because many people may not retire until several years after they are eligible to do so. Nevertheless, HR planning is needed. For example, Veterans Affairs is already facing competitive challenges in recruiting nurses due to the high demand in health care generally. Other agencies, such as NASA (National Aeronautics and Space Administration), are concerned about finding a significant number of specialized and experienced engineers, technical workers, and scientists.

This retirement situation among federal agencies illustrates two key points. First, general numbers projecting retirements may be interesting, but HR planning must focus on specific agencies and on occupational groups in those

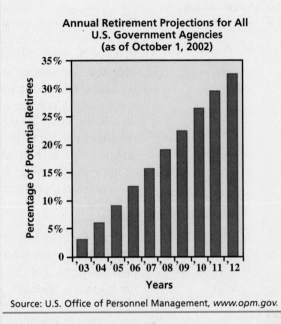

Source: U.S. Office of Personnel Management, *www.opm.gov.*

agencies. Second, identifying sources for potential replacements and developing "replacement charts" to ensure that the agencies continue to staff all their jobs, especially those requiring highly specialized education, experience, and qualifications, is a crucial part of strategic HR management.[24]

engineers or specialized nurses as to plan for replacing the CEO. Succession planning is discussed in detail in Chapter 10.

Managing a Human Resources Surplus

HR planning is of little value if no subsequent action is taken. The action taken depends on the likelihood of a human resources surplus or shortage. A surplus of workers can be managed within an HR plan in a variety of ways. Regardless of the means, the actions are difficult because workforce reductions are ultimately necessary.

Workforce Reductions and the WARN Act In this era of mergers, acquisitions, and downsizing, many workers have been laid off or had their jobs eliminated due to the closing of selected offices, plants, and operations. To provide employees with sufficient notice of such losses, a federal law passed, the Worker Adjustment and Retraining Notification (WARN) Act. This law requires employers to give a 60-day notice before implementing a layoff or facility closing that involves more than 50 people. However, part-time employees working fewer than 20 hours per week do not count toward the 50 employees. Also, seasonal employees do not have to receive WARN notification. The WARN Act imposes stiff fines on employers who do not follow the required process and give proper notice.[25]

Workforce Downsizing It has been given many names, including _downsizing, rightsizing,_ and _reduction in force (RIF),_ but it almost always means cutting employees. Focusing on trimming underperforming units or employees as part of a plan that is based on sound organizational strategies may make sense. After a decade of many examples and studies, it is clear that downsizing has worked for some firms. However, it does not generate additional revenue, and it only generates lower costs in the short term. When companies cannibalize the human resources needed to grow and innovate, disruption follows for some time. Also, downsizing can hurt productivity by leaving "surviving" employees overburdened and demoralized.

A common myth is that those who are still around after downsizing are so glad to have a job that they pose no problems to the organization. However, some observers draw an analogy between those who survive downsizing and those who survive wartime battles. They may experience guilt because they were spared while their friends were not. Bitterness, anger, disbelief, and shock all are common reactions. For those who survive workforce cuts, the culture and image of the firm as a "lifetime" employer often is gone forever.

Downsizing may adversely affect the performance of the survivors and communications throughout the organization. Survivors need information about why the actions had to be taken, and what the future holds for them personally. The more that employees are involved in the restructuring, the more likely the transition is to be smoother.[26] HR professionals and managers, too, find downsizing situations stressful and may react negatively to having to be the bearers of bad news.

The need for downsizing has inspired various innovative ways of removing people from the payroll, sometimes on a massive scale. Several different methods can be used when downsizing must occur: attrition, early retirement buyouts, and layoffs are the most common.

Attrition and Hiring Freezes _Attrition_ occurs when individuals quit, die, or retire and are not replaced. By use of attrition, no one is cut out of a job, but those who remain must handle the same workload with fewer people. Unless turnover is high, attrition will eliminate only a relatively small number of employees in the short run. Therefore, employers may combine attrition with a freeze on hiring. Employees usually understand this approach better than they do other downsizing methods.

Voluntary Separation Programs Organizations can downsize while also reducing legal liabilities if employees volunteer to leave. Often firms entice employees to volunteer by offering them additional severance and benefit payments.

Early retirement buyouts are widely used to encourage more senior workers to leave organizations early. As an incentive, employers make additional payments

LOGGING ON...

Challenger, Gray & Christmas
This firm provides commentary and research statistics on downsizing.
www.challengergray.com

to employees so that they will not be penalized too much economically until their pensions and Social Security benefits take effect. These buyouts are widely viewed as ways to accomplish workforce reduction without resorting to layoffs and individual firings.[27] In a FedEx buyout plan, of 14,000 eligible employees, 3,600 took the buyout. That plan offered eligible FedEx employees expanded health coverage and pension benefits after retirement.[28]

Volunteer separation programs appeal to employers because they can reduce payroll costs significantly over time. Although the organization faces some up-front costs, it does not incur as many continuing payroll costs. Using such programs is also viewed as a more humane way to reduce staff than terminating long-service, loyal employees. In addition, as long as buyouts are truly voluntary, the organization offering them is less exposed to age discrimination suits. One drawback is that some employees the company wishes would stay, as well as those it wishes would leave, can take advantage of a buyout. Also, employers must comply with WARN and other laws.

Layoffs Layoffs occur when employees are put on unpaid leaves of absence. If business improves for the employer, then employees can be called back to work. Layoffs may be an appropriate downsizing strategy during a temporary economic downturn in an industry. Nevertheless, careful planning of layoffs is essential. Care must be taken to ensure that age and other types of EEO discrimination do not occur.

Companies have no legal obligation to provide a financial cushion to laid-off employees; however, many do. When firms do provide severance pay, the most common formula is one week's pay for every year of employment. Larger companies tend to be more generous. Loss of medical benefits is a major problem for laid-off employees. However, under the federal Consolidated Omnibus Reconciliation Act (COBRA), displaced workers can retain their group medical coverage for up to 18 months for themselves, and for up to 36 months for their dependents, if they pay the premiums themselves.

Outplacement Services

Outplacement is a group of services provided to give displaced employees support and assistance. It is most often used with those involuntarily removed because of performance problems or job elimination. Outplacement services typically include personal career counseling, resume preparation and typing services, interviewing workshops, and referral assistance. Such services are generally provided by outside firms that specialize in outplacement assistance and whose fees usually are paid by the employer. It is important that outplacement be viewed as part of strategic HR planning.[29] Figure 2-9 shows that it is only one of five factors that should be considered to make downsizing more effective.

HR Planning in Mergers and Acquisitions

Another cause for downsizing has been the proliferation of mergers and acquisitions in many industries. One has only to look at the financial or telecommunications industry to see massive consolidation in the number of firms. A common result of most mergers and acquisitions (M&As) is an excess of employees once the firms have been combined, due to redundant departments, plants, and people. Because much of the rationale for combinations is financial, eliminating employees with overlapping responsibilities is a primary concern. However, studies

Figure 2-9 *Making Downsizing More Effective*

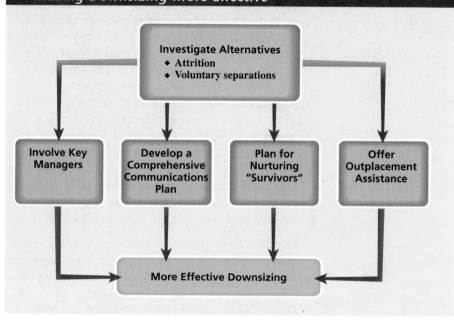

of numerous M&As reveal that a majority do not achieve their financial and strategic objectives.[30] Numerous studies have found that HR issues play a significant role in the success or failure of M&As, with the meshing of organizational cultures being crucial.[31]

HR management can contribute to the success of mergers and acquisitions. Experience with the failures shows clearly that for M&As to succeed, organizations have to ensure that different organizational cultures mesh. *Cultural compatibility* is the extent to which such factors as decision-making styles, levels of teamwork, information-sharing philosophies, and the formality of the two organizations are similar.

To address organizational culture concerns, HR professionals should be involved before, during, and after M&As.[32] Significant time must be spent identifying the cultural differences, how they are to be addressed, and ways to integrate managers and employees from both entities.[33]

Communicating Decisions The failures of M&As are often attributed to the incompatibility of the different organizational cultures involved. What changes will be made to the organization structure, how employee benefits will be meshed, what jobs and locations will get more or less staff, and many other issues must be decided and communicated. The longer such issues are left unanswered, the greater employee anxiety will be, and the more rumors will proliferate.[34]

Revising the Organization Structure A crucial part of HR is being sure that employee downsizing is handled legally and effectively. Also critical is the impact of job elimination on the remaining employees. Often, employee morale declines in the short term, and some firms see longer-term declines in employee morale after downsizing. Additionally, resignations and employee turnover may increase substantially in the year following downsizing if the HR issues are mismanaged.

Merging HR Activities Another key role played by HR in mergers and acquisitions is melding together the HR activities in each organization.[35] Compensation, benefits, performance appraisal systems, and employee relations policies all require significant attention by HR staff in both organizations. Who will head HR, and which employees will and will not have jobs in the new HR function, must be addressed. Compatibility of databases and information systems must be considered. Ultimately, how HR contributes to various aspects of mergers and acquisitions likely affects the overall effectiveness of the newly combined organizations.

MEASURING HR EFFECTIVENESS USING HR METRICS

A long-standing myth perpetuates the notion that one cannot really measure what the HR function does. That myth has hurt HR departments in some cases, because it suggests that any value added by HR efforts is somehow "mystical." That notion is, of course, untrue; HR—like marketing, operations, or finance—must be evaluated by considering the results of its actions and the value it adds to the organization.

Other departments, managers, and employees are the main "customers" for HR services. If those services are lacking, too expensive, or of poor quality, then HR loses some credibility in the organization. Unfortunately, the perceptions of managers and employees in many organizations is mixed because HR often has not measured and documented its contributions, or communicated those results to executives, managers, and employees.

During the past several years, the importance of measuring HR effectiveness has grown. A number of writers have stressed that HR cannot be a strategic business contributor without focusing on measuring its programs, its services, and its contributions to organizational success. It is through the development and use of metrics that HR can better demonstrate its value and track its performance.

Developing and Using HR Metrics

HR metrics are specific measures tied to HR performance indicators. A metric can be developed using costs, quantity, quality, timeliness, and other designated goals. One pioneer in developing HR measurements, Jac Fitz-Enz, has identified a wide range of HR metrics.[40] Some examples are shown in Figure 2-10.

HR metrics
Specific measures tied to HR performance indicators.

Figure 2-10	*Examples of Strategic and Operational HR Metrics*
Strategic	**Operational**
✦ Revenue generated per FTE	✦ Annual turnover rate
✦ Net income before taxes per FTE	✦ Benefits costs as percentage of payroll
✦ Ratio of managers to non-managers	✦ Training expenditures per FTE
✦ Labor costs as percentage of total operating costs	✦ Average time to fill openings
✦ ROI of human capital expenditures	✦ Workers' compensation costs per FTE
✦ HR department expenses as percentage of total expenses	✦ Number of applicants per opening
✦ Payroll/benefits costs as percentage of revenues	✦ Absenteeism by employee level/department

Technology Transforming HR

The Yellow Corporation and Boston Coach

Information technology is being used by small as well as large firms in ways that affect HR management. Two examples of how technology is affecting HR staffing and the payoffs from it are at Yellow Corporation and Boston Coach.

The Yellow Corporation, an Oklahoma-based trucking company, has invested millions of dollars on information technology, spending some of that money on identifying daily staffing needs at its 300 U.S. locations. To figure out how many of its 19,000 employees and 8,000 trucks are needed to handle over 60,000 orders daily, Yellow has developed computer software to manage its staffing.

The software allows both operating and HR managers at Yellow to identify how many drivers are needed for each shift at every location. If more or fewer drivers are needed, then adjustments and notifications are made. Employees whose schedules will be changed are notified by the company's intranet message system. Yellow has estimated that by calculating the number of employees needed and tracking staffing more effectively, this technology has led to over $100 million in savings.

Another transportation firm making effective use of technology is Boston Coach, which provides limousine service in a number of cities and at airports. The company has set up a wireless system to track locations of its vehicles and communicate customer data to its drivers. Instead of using two-way radios, Boston Coach drivers use wireless phones to contact dispatchers, who access a Web-based system and notify drivers where to pick up customers. Use of the system has led to 20% more rides for customers, better use of drivers, and fewer dispatchers. The large savings at Yellow and Boston Coach illustrate how technology can affect HR planning and staffing.[36]

LOGGING ON...

Saratoga Institute
This organization is well-known for its HR benchmarking data and studies.
www.saratogainstitute.com

Whether determining the cost of turnover, the average time needed to fill job openings, scores on employee satisfaction surveys, or the ratio of payroll expenditures to revenues, metrics provide specific data to track HR performance. Characteristics of good HR metrics include the following:

◆ Accurate data can be collected.
◆ Measures are linked to strategic and operational objectives.
◆ Calculations can be clearly understood.
◆ Measures provide information expected by executives.
◆ Results can be compared both externally and internally.
◆ Measurement data drives HR management efforts.

Metrics that meet all these characteristics give HR a better foundation for explaining and justifying its costs. Gathering and analyzing HR data and then using them for decision making is at the heart of measuring HR effectiveness. Data to evaluate performance can come from several sources. Some of those sources are already available in most organizations, but some data may have to be collected from existing HR records or HR research. For example, HR data can identify units with high turnover or an usual number of disciplinary problems. Or HR records on training can be compared with subsequent employee performance to determine if additional training expenditures are justified. Much of what has typically been measured by HR has focused on internal HR expenditures and effectiveness. A broader strategic perspective in measuring HR effectiveness is also needed.[37]

Fortunately in many organizations the growth in HR technology has made useful HR metric data much more available and its compilation much less time-consuming. The payoff for using technology to transform HR staffing at two transportation firm is highlighted in the HR Technology discussion.

Measures of Strategic HR Effectiveness

For HR to fulfill its role as a strategic business partner, HR metrics that reflect organizational strategies and goods must be used. Some of the more prevalent measures compare *full-time equivalents* (FTEs) with organizational measures. An FTE is a measure equal to one person working full-time for a year. For instance, two employees each working half-time would count as one FTE.

Return on Investment (ROI) A widely used financial measure that can be applied to measure the contribution and cost of HR activities is **return on investment (ROI),** which is a calculation showing the value of expenditures for HR activities. It can also be used to show how long it will take for the activities to pay for themselves. The following formula can be used to calculate the potential ROI for a new HR activity:

$$ROI = \frac{C}{A + B}$$

where:

A = Operating costs for a new or enhanced system for the time period
B = One-time cost of acquisition and implementation
C = Value of gains from productivity improvements for the time period

ROI is stressed because it is used in most other parts of organizations. It also is the "language" used by CFOs, CEOs, and Boards of Directors. To conduct ROI analyses, firms complete three stages:[38]

◆ Identify all potential/actual costs
◆ Determine the potential/actual benefits
◆ Calculate the ROI

Although it is recommended that ROI be calculated before programs are implemented, the reality is that such calculations often occur after the fact. This is counter to what would be typical in other parts of the organization, where the ROI of establishing a new plant or store would often be calculated before ever beginning the project. For instance, assume that a bank spent $100,000 on a customer service incentive program for employees to sell new services, and sales of the new services produced net revenues of $110,000. The ROI was $110,000/$100,000 or 10%, which was below the threshold ROI of 20% that the CFO used for other company expenditures. Although the incentive program was successful in adding revenues, looking at the ROI indicates that it could not be judged as successful using normal financial measures. Though data for this example could be easily tracked, trying to determine the ROI for overall employee benefits costs or for management development and training programs is much more difficult. Often, *utility analyses* or *cost/benefit analyses* are part of efforts to compute the ROI of HR efforts.

Economic Value Added (EVA) Another measure used is **economic value added (EVA),** which is the net operating profit of a firm after the cost of capital is deducted. Cost of capital is the minimum rate of return demanded by shareholders. When a company is making more than the cost of capital, it is creating wealth for shareholders. An EVA approach requires that all policies,

Return on investment (ROI)
Calculation showing the value of expenditures for HR activities.

Economic value added (EVA)
Net operating profit of a firm after the cost of capital is deducted.

procedures, measures, and methods use cost of capital as a benchmark against which their return is judged. Human resource decisions can be subjected to the same analyses.

HR and the Balanced Scorecard One effective approach to the measurement of the strategic performance of organizations, including their HR departments, is the *balanced scorecard.* Use of the balanced scorecard stresses measuring the strategic performance of organizations on four perspectives:[39]

- ◆ Financial
- ◆ Internal business processes
- ◆ Customer
- ◆ Learning and growth

Organizational measures in each of these areas are calculated to determine if the organization is progressing toward its strategic objectives. For example, some firms have noticed that when survey results show a decline in employee satisfaction, several months later there is a decline in customer loyalty and repeat customer sales. Or expenditures in employee leadership development training can be linked to lower employee turnover and reduced time to hire managers from outside the organization.

Using the balanced scorecard requires spending considerable time and effort to identify the appropriate HR measures in each of the four areas and how they tie to strategic organization success.[41] Both large companies, as diverse as Verizon, EDS (Electronic Data Systems Corporation), and Union Pacific, and smaller firms are using the balanced scorecard to ensure better alignment of HR measurement efforts and strategic goals.[42] However, regardless of the time and effort spent trying to develop and utilize objective measures in the balanced scorecard, subjectivity in what is selected and how the measures are interpreted can still occur.[43] In this book, HR metrics sections will be highlighted throughout the discussion of the various HR activities, using the special HR metrics icon that appears at the beginning of this section.

HR Measurement and Benchmarking

One approach to assessing HR effectiveness is **benchmarking,** which compares specific measures of performance against data on those measures in other organizations. HR professionals interested in benchmarking compare their measurement data with those from outside sources, including individual companies, industry sources, and professional associations.

Some diagnostic measures can be used to check the effectiveness of the HR function. For benchmarking overall HR costs, one useful source is data gathered each year by SHRM and the Bureau of National Affairs. This survey shows that HR expenditures by workforce size vary significantly, as Figure 2-11 depicts. As might be expected, the total number of staff needed to serve 1,000 employees is not significantly different from the number needed to serve 2,500 employees. But the cost per employee of having an HR department is greater in organizations with fewer than 250 employees.

Using benchmarking, HR effectiveness is best determined by comparing ratios and measures from year to year. But it is crucial that the benchmarking look at the strategic contributions HR makes to the organization, not just the operating efficiency measures.[44]

Benchmarking
Comparing specific measures of performance against data on those measures in other organizations.

Figure 2-11

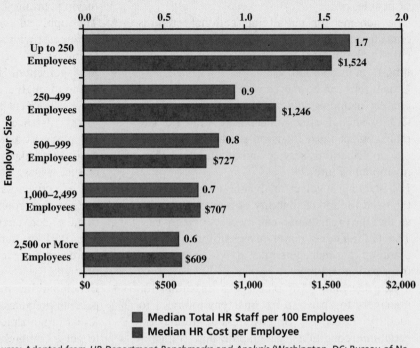

Costs per Employee of the HR Function

Median Total HR Staff per 100 Employees

Median HR Cost per Employee

Source: Adapted from *HR Department Benchmarks and Analysis* (Washington, DC: Bureau of National Affairs, 131, 140. 2004) To purchase this publication and find out more about other BNA HR solutions visit http://hrcenter.bna.com or call 800-372-1033. Used with permission.

HR Audit

HR audit

Formal research effort that evaluates the current state of HR management in an organization.

One general means for assessing HR is through an HR audit, which is similar to a financial audit. An **HR audit** is a formal research effort that evaluates the current state of HR management in an organization. This audit attempts to evaluate how well HR activities in each of the HR areas (staffing, compensation, health and safety, etc.) have been performed, so that management can identify areas for improvement. An HR audit often helps smaller organizations without a formal HR professional identify issues associated with legal compliance, administrative processes and recordkeeping, employee retention, etc.

Regardless of the time and effort placed on HR measurement and HR metrics, the most important consideration is that HR effectiveness and efficiency must be measured regularly for HR staff and other managers to know how HR is contributing to organizational success.

SUMMARY

- Organizations doing business internationally may evolve from organizations engaged in importing and exporting to multi-national enterprises, to global organizations.

- Legal, political, cultural, and economic factors influence global HR management.

- Culture consists of the societal forces affecting the values, beliefs, and actions of a distinct group of people.
- One scheme for classifying national cultures considers power distance, individualism, masculinity/femininity, uncertainty avoidance, and long-term orientation.
- Global jobs can be staffed with expatriates, host-country nationals, and third-country nationals.
- Organizational effectiveness and strategic HR management must focus on productivity, financial contributions, service and quality, and organizational culture.
- HR planning involves analyzing and identifying the need for and availability of human resources so that the organization can meet its objectives.
- The HR unit has major responsibilities in HR planning, but managers must provide supportive information and input.
- When developing HR plans, it is important for managers to scan the external environment to identify the effects of government influences, economic conditions, geographic and competitive concerns, and workforce composition changes.

- Assessing internal strengths and weaknesses as a part of HR planning requires auditing and inventorying current jobs and employee capabilities.
- The supply and demand for human resources can be forecast with a variety of methods and for differing periods of time.
- Management of HR surpluses may require downsizing through use of attrition and hiring freezes, early retirement buyouts, layoffs, and outplacement assistance.
- HR plays a crucial role in mergers and acquisitions, particularly in dealing with organizational culture issues.
- HR effectiveness must be measured using HR metrics that consider both strategic and operational effectiveness.
- The ROI of human capital and the balanced scorecard are two common means for HR measurement.
- Benchmarking allows an organization to compare its practices against "best practices" in different organizations, and HR audits can be used to get a comprehensive overview on HR activities.

REVIEW AND APPLICATION QUESTIONS

1. Discuss how cultural factors, both globally and inside organizations, must be addressed as part of strategic HR management.
2. What steps can HR professionals take to overcome the view that what HR accomplishes is not measurable?
3. As a newly hired HR manager for a medical clinic with 20 physicians and 100 employees, you want to identify and develop some HR metrics. Using the metrics discussed at *www.saratogainstitute.com* and other Web sources that you find, identify five specific metrics and discuss why those measures could be useful.

LEARNING REVIEW

To check your knowledge of the chapter, review the following. (Answers after the supplemental case.) For more questions, see the Study Guide.

1. A/An _____ has corporate units in a number of countries that are integrated to operate as one organization worldwide.
   a. multinational enterprise
   b. importing and exporting organization
   c. global organization
   d. traditional organization

2. _____ is the dimension of culture referring to the inequality among the people of a nation.
   a. Individualism
   b. Power distance
   c. Masculinity/femininity
   d. Long-term orientation

3. The HR planning process begins with _____.
   a. considering the objectives and strategies of the organization
   b. auditing the jobs currently being done in the organization
   c. analyzing the internal inventory of HR capabilities
   d. developing HR forecasts

4. One approach to assessing HR effectiveness is _____, which is comparing specific measures of performance against data on those measures in other organizations.
   a. benchmarking
   b. compa-valuation
   c. HR appraisal
   d. HR imitation

CASE
XEROX FOCUSES ON HR

Xerox is a widely known firm worldwide, but it has been through numerous crises in the past decade. In fact, at one point several years ago, there were questions about Xerox surviving as a firm. But no longer. Under the leadership of Anne Mulcahy as CEO, Xerox has rebounded. Numerous strategic business and financial decisions had to be made including reducing the workforce by 30,000. But Mulcahy also stressed that HR had to become a more strategic contributor.

One of the actions taken was to consolidate a number of HR functions from different business units into a corporate HR Service Center. This center performs many administrative transactions, and has added Internet-based systems to make HR services more accessible to managers and employees.

To track employees' views on the company and HR, employee surveys on the company intranet have been used for several years. Areas where lower scores were recorded have been addressed by HR staff and other managers. Using the survey results has led to another primary focus at Xerox, employee retention. With all of the reductions and organiza-tional restructurings, keeping the remaining employees, especially high-potential ones, has been a continuing emphasis. Xerox has invested significant time and resources into training and development of its employees, an important retention factor. Greater use of e-learning, technology, and leadership development have paid off in reducing turnover and convincing employees that career opportunities exist at Xerox.

Continuing competitive pressures are presenting new challenges for Xerox and its HR staff. The strategic importance of HR has been demonstrated in the past, and looks to be a part of the firm's future.[45]

Questions

1. Discuss the challenges faced by HR management when significant staff cutbacks occur and how they should be addressed.
2. Use of technology, employee retention, and HR development have been at the core of HR becoming more strategic at Xerox. Why have those areas been so key?

SUPPLEMENTAL CASE: Where Do You Find the Bodies?

This case identifies problems associated with HR planning and recruiting in a tight labor market. (For the case, go to http://mathis.swlearning.com.)

Learning Review Answers: 1. c 2. b 3. a 4. a

NOTES

1. Based on "Disconnect Persists Between Spending of HR Time and Money," *Connect, http://benefitnews.com,* November 18, 2003; and "EDS Study Reveals HR Departments Fail to Link Effectiveness to Overall Corporate Performance," *PRNewswire, www.harrisinteractive.com,* July 29, 2003, and Mark Lowrey, "A Balanced Approach," *Human Resource Executive,* June 16, 2003, 30–32.

2. Anil K. Gupta and Vijay Govindarajan, "Cultivating a Global Mindset," *Academy of Management Executive,* February 2002, 116–126.

3. Robert Gandossay and Elizabeth Varghese, "Global HR: The Next Frontier for Human Resources," *WorldatWork Journal,* Fourth Quarter 2003, 65–71.

4. Geert Hofstede, *Culture's Consequences: Comparing Values, Behaviors, Institutions, and Organizations Across Cultures,* 2nd ed. (Thousand Oaks, CA: Sage, 2001), and John W. Bing, "Hofstede's Consequences: The Impact of His Work on Consulting and Business Practices," *Academy of Management Executive,* February 2004, 80–87.

5. "Free Trade on Trial," *The Economist,* January 3, 2004, 13–16.

6. Sohel Ahmad and Roger G. Schroeder, "The Impact of Human Resource Management Practices on Operational Performance: Recognizing Country and Industry Differences," *Journal of Operations Management,* 21 (2003), 19–43.

7. For details on various approaches, see Richard H. Hall, *Organizations: Structures, Processes, and Outcomes* (Upper Saddle River, NJ: Prentice Hall, 2002), 236–278.

8. David E. Bowen and Cheri Ostroff, " Understanding HRM—Firm Performance Linkages: The Role of the "Strength of the HRM System," *Academy of Management Review,* 29 (2004), 203–221.

9. Fay Hansen, "The CFO Connection," *Workforce Management,* July 2003, 50–54.

10. Based on Patrick M. Wright, Timothy M. Gardner, and Lisa M. Moynihan, "The Impact of HR Practices on the Performance of Business Units," *Human Resource Management Journal,* 13 (2003), 21–36.

11. *Human Capital Management: The CFO's Perspective* (New York: Mercer Human Resource Consulting, 2003).

12. Vaughn C. Judd, "Achieving a Customer Orientation Using 'People Power,'" *European Journal of Marketing,* 37 (2003), 1301–1314.

13. Miles H. Overholt and Elena Granell, "Managing Strategic, Cultural, and HRM Alignment to Maximize Customer Satisfaction and Retention," *Human Resource Planning,* 25 (2002), 45–54.

14. Rosemary Batt, "Managing Customer Services: Human Resource Practices, Quit Rates, and Sales Growth," *Academy of Management Journal,* 45 (2003), 587–597.

15. Regular updates on customer satisfaction generally and by industry are available at *www.theacsi.org.*

16. Hale Kaynak, "The Relationship Between Total Quality Management Practices and Their Effects on Firm Performance," *Journal of Operations Management,* 21 (2003), 405–436.

17. Pamela Babcock, "Is Your Company Two-Faced?" *HR Magazine,* January 2004, 43–47.

18. Jeff Rosenthal and Mary Ann Masarech, "High-Performance Cultures: How Values Can Drive Business Results," *Journal of Organizational Excellence,* Spring 2003, 3–19.

19. Jeff Barbian, "Medicine for Managers," *Training,* February 2002, 22.

20. K. S. Lee, G. H. Lim, and W. S. Lim, "Family Business Succession: Appropriation Risk and Choice of Successor," *Academy of Management Review,* 28 (2003), 657–666.

21. Elini T. Stavrou, "Leadership Succession in Owner-Managed Firms Through the Lens of Extraversion," *International Small Business Journal,* 21 (2003), 331.

22. Pramodita Sharma, James J. Chrisman, and Jess H. Chua, "Predictions of Satisfaction with the Succession Process in Family Firms," *Journal of Business Venturing,* 18 (2003), 667.

23. "Facing a Generation Gap," *Omaha World-Herald,* November 24, 2002, 2CR.

24. Based on Brian Friel, "The Human Capital Crisis," *Government Executive,* May 2003, 20–27; and Virgil Larson, "Bye Bye 'Boomers,'" *Omaha World-Herald,* November 10, 2003, D1.

25. Joshua L. Ditelberg, "A Practical Guide to Workforce Reductions," *SHRM Legal Report,* March/April 2002.

26. Wayne F. Cascio, "Strategies for Responsible Restructuring," *Academy of Management Executive,* August 2002, 80–91.

27. Condon A. McGlothen, "Voluntary Separation Programs: A Safer Approach to Downsizing," *SHRM Legal Report,* March/April 2002, 1–5.

28. "More Workers Choosing to Retire Early," *Omaha World-Herald,* January 12, 2004, 2D.

29. Susan R. Silvano, "The HR Executive's Strategic Role in Outplacement," *Human Resource Executive,* January 26, 2004, *http://workindex.com.*

30. David Henry, "Mergers: Why Most Big Deals Don't Pay Off," *Business Week,* October 14, 2002, 60–70.

31. Jane Bryson, "Managing HRM Risk in a Merger," *Employee Relations,* 25 (2003), 14.

32. Teresa A. Daniel and Gary S. Metcalf, *The Management of People in Mergers and Acquisitions* (Westport, CT: Quorum, 2001).

33. Elissa D. Giffords and Richard P. Dina, "Changing Organizational Cultures," *Administration in Social Work,* 27 (2003), 69.

34. Steven H. Applebaum and Joy Gandell, "A Cross-Method Analyses of the Impact of Culture and Communications upon a Health-Care Merger," *Journal of Management,* 22 (2003), 370.

35. Christopher Cornell, "The Perfect Blend," *Human Resource Executive,* January 2004, 44–49.

36. Adapted from Michael Arndt, "Yellow," and Faith Arner "Boston Coach," *Web Smart 50, Business Week,* November 24, 2003, *www.businessweek.com.*

37. Jay Jamrog and Miles Overholt, "Building a Strategic HR Function: Continuing the Evaluation" (unpublished paper, Tampa, FL, 2004).

38. For details on these stages, see Brian E. Becher, Mark A. Huselid, and Dave Ulrich, *The HR Scorecard: Linking People, Strategy, and Performance* (Boston: Harvard Business School Press, 2001).

39. Robert S. Kaplan and David P. Norton, *The Strategy-Focused Organization: How Balanced Scorecard Companies Thrive in the New Business Environment* (Boston: Harvard Business School Press, 2001).

40. How to measure HR activities by areas is described in detail in Jac Fitz-Enz and Barbara Davidson, *How to Measure Human Resources* (New York: McGraw-Hill, 2002).

41. Steven Salterio and Allan Webb, "The Balanced Scorecard," *CA Magazine,* August 2003, 39–41.

42. Mark Lowery, "A Balanced Approach," *Human Resource Executive,* June 16, 2003, 30–32.

43. Christopher D. Itner, David F. Lancher, and Marshell W. Meyer, "Subjectivity and the Weighting of Performance Measures: Evidence from a Balanced Scorecard," *The Accounting Review,* 78 (2003), 725–758.

44. Brian E. Becker and Mark A. Huselid, "Measuring HR? Benchmarking is Not the Answer," *HR Magazine,* December 2003, 57–61.

45. Adapted from Ed Santalone, "Processing a Turnaround," *Human Resource Executive,* June 28, 2004, 1, 16–23.

CHAPTER 3

Organization/Individual Relations and Retention

After you have read this chapter, you should be able to:

- Identify the changing nature of the psychological contract.

- Describe different kinds of absenteeism and turnover.

- Explain two ways to measure absenteeism and turnover.

- Discuss how motivation is linked to individual performance.

- List the five major drivers of retention and activities related to them.

- Outline the steps in managing retention.

Myths About Retaining Employees

Keeping good employees is a challenge that all organizations share and that becomes even more difficult as labor markets tighten. Unfortunately, some myths have arisen about what it takes to retain employees. Consultants from Drake Beam Morin have identified some of the most prevalent of these myths:

1. *Money is the main reason people leave.* Money certainly is a powerful recruiting tool, and if people feel they are being paid inadequately, they are clearly more likely to leave. But if they are paid a competitive wage or salary, other parts of the job are more important.

2. *Hiring has nothing to do with retention.* This is not true. Recruiting and selecting the people who fit the jobs and who are less likely to leave in the first place, and then orienting them to the company, can greatly increase retention. Select for retention!

3. *If you train people, you are only training them for another employer.* Developing skills in employees may indeed make them more marketable, but it also tends to improve retention. When an employer provides employees with training and development assistance, job satisfaction may increase and employees are more likely to stay.

4. *Do not be concerned about retention during a merger.* That is exactly the time to worry about retention. While some people may have to be cut after a merger, the people the company would like to keep may have the most opportunity to leave voluntarily. During a merger, all employees are concerned about job security, and if they do not feel a part of the new organization early on, many will leave.

5. *If good people want to leave—the company cannot hold them.* Employees are best viewed as free agents. They can indeed leave when they want. The key to keeping good employees is to create an environment in which they *want* to stay and grow.[1]

"High performers are like frogs in a wheelbarrow—they can jump out at any time."

—McKinsey & Company study

Relationships between individuals and their employing organizations can vary widely. Both parties may view the employer/employee relationship as satisfactory. Or one may see it as satisfactory and one may not. Or both may be looking for a way to end the relationship. *Job satisfaction* and *commitment* often help determine whether an employee will want to stay. The *individual's performance* is a major part of whether the employer wants the employee to stay. However, understanding the relationship between individuals and organizations is more than just academically interesting. It is the basis for dealing successfully with absenteeism and turnover, a key to understanding individual performance, and vital to retaining employees.

▌▌ INDIVIDUAL/ORGANIZATIONAL RELATIONSHIPS

The long-term economic health of most organizations depends on the efforts of employees with both the appropriate capabilities and the motivation to do their jobs well. Organizations that are successful over time can usually demonstrate that relationships with their employees *do* matter.

Perhaps no organizational events have influenced employees and the way they view their relationships with their employers as much as has the recent wave of downsizing, mergers, and acquisitions.[2] A vice president of a just-merged company found that out when meeting with line managers. The VP repeatedly heard employees say, "I am just waiting for the economy to get better, and I am out of here" (in various forms). Yet the line managers thought their people were going to stay.[3] It has been estimated that one out of six employees may be ready to leave their current jobs.[4]

The Psychological Contract

One concept that has been useful in discussing employees' relationships with organizations is that of a **psychological contract,** which refers to the unwritten expectations employees and employers have about the nature of their work relationships. Because the psychological contract is individual and subjective, it focuses on expectations about "fairness" that may not be defined clearly by employees.

Both tangible items (such as wages, benefits, employee productivity, and attendance) and intangible items (such as loyalty, fair treatment, and job security) are encompassed by unwritten psychological contracts between employers and employees. Many employers attempt to detail their expectations through employee handbooks and policy manuals, but those materials are only part of the total "contractual" relationship.

The Changing Psychological Contract At one time, employees expected to exchange their efforts and capabilities for a secure job that offered rising pay, good benefits, and career progression within the organization. But as organizations have downsized and cut workers who have given long and loyal service, a growing number of employees question whether they should or should not be loyal to their employers. Closely related to the psychological contract is the concept of *psychological ownership.*[5] When individuals feel that they have some control and perceived rights in the organization, they are more likely to be committed to the organization.[6]

Rather than just paying employees to follow orders and put in time, increasingly, employers are expecting them to utilize their knowledge, skills, and abili-

Psychological contract
The unwritten expectations employees and employers have about the nature of their work relationships.

ties to accomplish organizational results. A psychological contract that can help achieve those ends recognizes the following components:

Employers Provide:	Employees Contribute:
◆ Competitive compensation and benefits	◆ Continuous skill improvement and increased productivity
◆ Flexibility to balance work and home life	◆ Reasonable time with the organization
◆ Career development opportunities	◆ Extra effort when needed

Recent research suggests that psychological contracts can be strengthened and employee commitment enhanced when the organization is involved in a cause the employee values highly. Conversely, psychological contracts can be violated not only in reaction to personal mistreatment, but from a perception that the organization has abandoned an important principle or cause.[7] The unethical and illegal behavior of upper management in Enron and WorldCom are good examples of contract violations. When a psychological contract is violated, employees may feel anger, distrust, reduced loyalty and commitment, and increased willingness to leave.[8]

Generational Differences Much has been written about the differing expectations of individuals in different generations. Many of these observations are anecdotal and give only generalizations about individuals in the various age-groups. Some common generational labels are:

- ◆ Matures (born before 1945)
- ◆ Baby boomers (born 1945–1965)
- ◆ Generation Xers (born 1966–1980)
- ◆ Generation Yers (born 1980–1990)

Rather than identifying the characteristics cited for each of these groups, it is most important here to emphasize that people's expectations about psychological contracts differ between generations, as well as within generations. For employers, the differing expectations present challenges. For instance, many baby boomers and matures are concerned about security and experience. However, younger generation Yers are often seen as the "why" generation, who expect to be rewarded quickly, are very adaptable, and tend to ask more questions about why managers and organizations make the decisions they do.[9] Consider the dynamics of a mature manager directing generation X and Y individuals, or generation X managers supervising older, more experienced baby boomers. Generational differences are likely to continue to create challenges and conflicts in organizations because of the different expectations inherent in different generations.

LOGGING ON...

AON Loyalty Institute
This Web site contains research and information on workplace loyalty.
www.aon.com

JOB SATISFACTION, LOYALTY, AND COMMITMENT

Employees *do* behave as if there is a psychological contract, and hope their employers will honor the "agreement." Many employees want security and stability, interesting work, a supervisor they respect, and competitive pay and benefits. If these elements are not provided, employees may feel a diminished need to contribute. When organizations merge, lay off large numbers of employees, outsource work, and use large numbers of temporary and part-time workers,

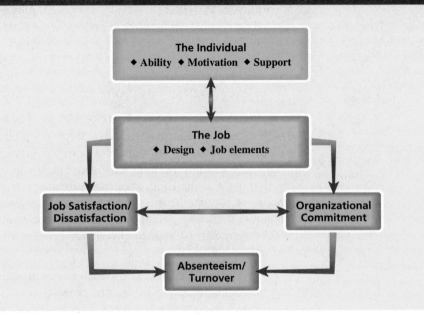

Job satisfaction
A positive emotional state resulting from evaluating one's job experiences.

employees experience job insecurity concerns and in turn see fewer reasons to give their loyalty to those employers.

In its most basic sense, **job satisfaction** is a positive emotional state resulting from evaluating one's job experiences. Job *dis*satisfaction occurs when one's expectations are not met. For example, if an employee expects clean and safe working conditions, then the employee is likely to be dissatisfied if the workplace is dirty and dangerous.

Dimensions of job satisfaction frequently mentioned include work, pay, promotion opportunities, supervision, and co-workers. Job satisfaction appears to have declined somewhat in recent years, and elements of the employee/employer relationship were cited among the major reasons in a 10-year study of 10,000 people.[10] More demanding work, fewer traditional hierarchical relationships with management, shorter relationships, and less confidence in long-term rewards were the reasons cited most frequently.

Loyalty and Organizational Commitment

Even though job satisfaction itself is important, perhaps the "bottom line" is how job satisfaction influences organizational commitment, which then affects employee turnover. As Figure 3-1 depicts, the interaction of the individual and the job determines levels of job satisfaction and organizational commitment.

"Loyal" employees are more than just satisfied with their jobs; they are pleased with the relationship with their employers. One study found that only about one-third of employees are committed to their employers at that level and plan to stay with the organization at least two years.[11] Additionally, employers find that in tight labor markets, turnover of key people occurs more frequently when employee loyalty is low, which in turn emphasizes the importance of a loyal and committed workforce.[12]

Organizational commitment
The degree to which employees believe in and accept organizational goals and desire to remain with the organization.

Organizational commitment is the degree to which employees believe in and accept organizational goals and desire to remain with the organization. A related idea is *employee engagement,* which is the extent to which an employee is willing and able to contribute. Various research studies have revealed that people who are relatively satisfied with their jobs will be somewhat more committed to the organization.

A logical extension of organizational commitment focuses more specifically on *continuance commitment* factors, which suggests that decisions to remain with or leave an organization ultimately are reflected in employee absenteeism and turnover statistics. Individuals who are not as satisfied with their jobs or who are not as committed to the organization are more likely to withdraw from the organization.

The relationships among satisfaction, commitment, and absenteeism and turnover have been affirmed across cultures, full- and part-time work, genders, and occupations.[13] Absenteeism and turnover are related, as both involve withdrawal from the organization. Absenteeism is temporary withdrawal, while turnover is permanent.

EMPLOYEE ABSENTEEISM

Absenteeism is any failure to report for work as scheduled or to stay at work when scheduled. The cause does not matter when counting someone absent. Absenteeism is expensive, costing an estimated $645 per employee each year.[14] Being absent from work may seem like a small matter to an employee. But if a manager needs 12 people in a unit to get the work done, and 4 of the 12 are absent most of the time, the work of the unit will decrease some, or additional workers will have to be hired to provide a margin.

Though some absences are justified, many are of the "three-day weekend" or "mental health days" variety. Many employees feel that such absences are acceptable. Such incidental absences account for as much as 80% of all absences and 33% of lost workdays.[15] For a company with 16,000 employees who cost the employer an average of $50,000 a year each (in compensation, benefits, etc.), incidental absences will incur about $16 million annually in direct costs. One study suggested that companies spend 15% of their payrolls on absenteeism each year.[16]

Types of Absenteeism

Employees can be absent from work for several reasons. Clearly, some absenteeism is inevitable because illness, death in the family, and other personal reasons for absences are unavoidable and understandable. Many employers have sick leave policies that allow employees a certain number of paid days each year for those types of *involuntary* absences. However, much absenteeism is avoidable, or *voluntary.* Often, a relatively small number of individuals are responsible for a disproportionate share of the total absenteeism in an organization.

Many people see no real concern about being absent or late to work. One nurse supervisor who managed a chronically understaffed unit confronted a nurse's aide who had been absent the previous day. The aide said, "My sister and I are having a party, and we had to audition a band." She clearly thought that was an adequate explanation and being absent was acceptable.[17]

Punctuality and tardiness are related to absenteeism. A recent study found that three factors distinguished between people who were late frequently and those

THOMSON
——————★——————
WEST ™

ABSENTEEISM AND TARDINESS POLICY
Contains a sample policy on absenteeism and tardiness control.
Custom Search:
☑ ANALYSIS
Exact Phrase: Employee absenteeism and tardiness

Figure 3-2

Reasons for Unscheduled Absences

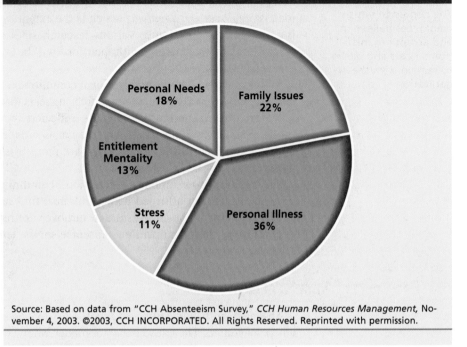

Source: Based on data from "CCH Absenteeism Survey," *CCH Human Resources Management,* November 4, 2003. ©2003, CCH INCORPORATED. All Rights Reserved. Reprinted with permission.

who were not: type A personality, organizational commitment, and age of the employee's youngest child (younger children were associated with more lateness).[18] Figure 3-2 shows the most common reasons for unscheduled absences.

Controlling Absenteeism

Voluntary absenteeism is easiest to control if managers understand its causes clearly. Once they do, they can use a variety of approaches to reduce it. Organizational policies on absenteeism should be stated clearly in an employee handbook and stressed by supervisors and managers. Approaches to control absenteeism fall into several categories:

- *Disciplinary approach:* Many employers use a disciplinary approach. People who are absent the first time receive an oral warning, and subsequent absences bring written warnings, suspension, and finally dismissal.
- *Positive reinforcement:* Positive reinforcement includes such methods as giving employees cash, recognition, time off, or other rewards for meeting attendance standards. Offering rewards for good attendance, giving bonuses for missing fewer than a certain number of days, and "buying back" unused sick leave are all positive methods of reducing absenteeism.
- *Combination approach:* A combination approach ideally rewards desired behaviors and punishes undesired behaviors. This "carrot and stick" approach uses policies and discipline to punish offenders, and various programs and rewards to recognize employees with outstanding attendance. One firm that has used attendance incentives effectively is Continental Airlines. As part of its "Go Forward" Program, employees with perfect attendance receive incentives of travel and other rewards.

- *"No fault" policy:* With a "no fault" policy, the reasons for absences do not matter, and the employees must manage their own attendance unless they abuse that freedom. Once absenteeism exceeds normal limits, then disciplinary action up to and including termination of employment can occur. The advantages of the "no fault" approach are that all employees can be covered by it, and supervisors and HR staff do not have to judge whether absences count as excused or unexcused.
- *Paid-time-off (PTO) programs:* Some employers have paid-time-off programs, in which vacation time, holidays, and sick leave for each employee are combined into a PTO account. Employees use days from their accounts at their discretion for illness, personal time, or vacation. If employees run out of days in their accounts, then they are not paid for any additional days missed. PTO programs generally have reduced absenteeism, particularly one-day absences, but they often increase overall time away from work because employees use all of "their" time off by taking unused days as vacation days.

The disciplinary approach is the most widely used means for controlling absenteeism, with most employers using policies and punitive practices. Figure 3-3 shows the various actions that employers use to control employee absenteeism.

EMPLOYEE TURNOVER

Turnover
The process in which employees leave an organization and have to be replaced.

Like absenteeism, turnover is related to job satisfaction and organizational commitment. **Turnover** occurs when employees leave an organization and have to be replaced.

Many organizations have found that turnover is a costly problem, as documented by a number of studies. In one study, 45% of surveyed employers estimated annual turnover costs to exceed $10,000 per person. In the hotel/hospitality industry, the average turnover cost per leaving employee is $4,100 and the total turnover costs for a typical hotel are $631,400 annually.[19] In many service industries, the turnover rates and costs are very high. In the retail industry, turnover

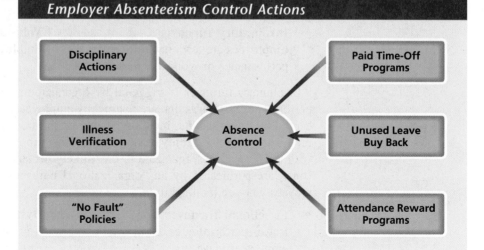

Figure 3-3   *Employer Absenteeism Control Actions*

- Disciplinary Actions
- Illness Verification
- "No Fault" Policies
- Paid Time-Off Programs
- Unused Leave Buy Back
- Attendance Reward Programs
- Absence Control

Turnover in India's Call Centers

In less than five years, India's call center industry has gone from nothing—to a $3 billion industry answering calls from the U.S. on a variety of products and services. But as the need for English-speaking employees in India has grown dramatically, turnover rates have risen too.

Many of the call center jobs are monotonous, and the turnover rates in some Indian firms have jumped to 35% to 45% annually. That is much lower than rates for similar jobs in the U.S., but it is "the single biggest issue" in the industry, according to the CEO of one of the Indian call center firms. Companies see their costs go up as they have to invest in ongoing training and recruiting. Also, productivity

dips until new people learn their jobs, and customer satisfaction has declined with some Indian call centers.

Companies are taking several actions to retain employees—agreeing not to poach workers from other firms, recruiting from rural areas in India, giving more attention to increasing workers' job satisfaction—much as American call centers have. But turnover is forcing the Indian companies to overstaff in anticipation of more turnover as they are tapping ever deeper into the pool of English speakers. Turnover, or attrition, as it is often referred to, has become an industry issue there just as it has in the U.S., the country that popularized call centers.[20]

averages 124% a year for part-time workers and 74% a year for full-time workers. In supermarkets, the typical stay for an employee is only 97 days. The nation's grocers and other retailers spend billions on turnover, with the costs for each full-time employee who leaves estimated to be between $6,900 and $10,500, depending on the type of retailer.[21] For higher-level executives and professionals, turnover costs can run as much as two times the departing employees' annual salaries.

Turnover costs are certainly not unique to the United States. HR Globally describes turnover in the growing call centers of another country—a problem similar to that faced by the industry in the United States.

Types of Turnover

Turnover is classified in a number of ways. Each of the following classifications can be used, and the two are not mutually exclusive:

+ **Involuntary Turnover**
  Employees are terminated for poor performance or work rule violations

+ **Voluntary Turnover**
  Employees leave by choice

Involuntary turnover is triggered by organizational policies, work rules, and performance standards that are not met by employees. Voluntary turnover can be caused by many factors, including career opportunities, pay, supervision, geography, and personal/family reasons. Voluntary turnover also appears to increase with the size of the organization, most likely because larger firms are less personal, are permeated by an "organizational bureaucracy," and have more employees who are inclined to move.

+ **Functional Turnover**
  Lower-performing or disruptive employees leave

+ **Dysfunctional Turnover**
  Key individuals and high performers leave at critical times

Not all turnover is negative for organizations; on the contrary, some workforce losses are desirable, especially if those who leave are lower-performing, less reliable individuals, or disrupt co-workers. Unfortunately for organizations, dysfunctional turnover does occur. That happens when key individuals leave, often at crucial work times. For example, a software project leader left in the middle of a system upgrade in order to take a promotion at another firm in the city. His departure caused the system upgrade timeline to slip by two months due to the difficulty of replacing that project leader.

♦ **Uncontrollable Turnover**
Employees leave for reasons outside the control of the employer

♦ **Controllable Turnover**
Employees leave for reasons that could be influenced by the employer

Employees quit for many reasons that cannot be controlled by the organization. These reasons include: (1) the employee moves out of the geographic area, (2) the employee decides to stay home with young children or elder relatives, (3) the employee's spouse is transferred, and (4) the employee is a student worker who graduates from college. Even though some turnover is inevitable, many employers today recognize that reducing turnover is crucial, and that they must address turnover that is controllable. Organizations are better able to retain employees if they deal with the concerns of employees that are leading to turnover.

It appears that the amount of money an organization invests in its employees is one of those concerns because it increases the costs of turnover. With respect to turnover and expense, firms that have invested significantly in employees have had lower turnover rates and their profits are affected positively. Tactics for adapting to ongoing turnover include simplifying jobs, outsourcing, and cross training.

HR METRICS: MEASURING ABSENTEEISM AND TURNOVER

A major step in reducing the expense of absenteeism and turnover is to decide how the organization is going to record those events and what calculations are necessary to maintain and benchmark their rates. A number of considerations are required.

Measuring Absenteeism

Controlling or reducing absenteeism must begin with continuous monitoring of the absenteeism statistics in work units. Such monitoring helps managers pinpoint employees who are frequently absent and departments that have excessive absenteeism. Various methods of measuring or computing absenteeism exist. One formula suggested by the U.S. Department of Labor is as follows:

$$\frac{\text{Number of person-days lost through job absence during period}}{(\text{Average number of employees}) \times (\text{Number of workdays})} \times 100$$

(This rate also can be based on number of hours instead of number of days.)

One source of extremely detailed information on absenteeism and turnover calculation has been prepared by Wayne Cascio. He suggests calculating the employee hours lost each month (or some other period) and the cost of those hours (including benefits), then calculating the cost of supervisory time lost to the management of absenteeism problems. The combination of the two costs is the cost of absenteeism for that period.[23] Sometimes it takes a six- or seven-figure cost number to get the attention of management to address absenteeism levels. Calculations of the costs of absenteeism should usually include these variables:

- Lost wages
- Benefits
- Overtime for replacements
- Fees for temporary employees, if incurred
- Supervisor's time
- Substandard production
- Overstaffing necessary to cover absences

Additional information can be gained by separating absenteeism data into long- and short-term categories. Different problems are caused by employees who are absent for 1 day 10 times during a year, and employees who are absent 1 time for 10 days. Other useful measures of absenteeism might include:

- *Incidence rate:* The number of absences per 100 employees each day
- *Inactivity rate:* The percentage of time lost to absenteeism
- *Severity rate:* The average time lost per absent employee during a specified period of time (a month or a year)

Measuring Turnover

The U.S. Department of Labor estimates that the cost of replacing a lower-level employee is one-third of the new hire's annual salary. Using only $7 an hour for an example, that equals $4,853 for each departing employee. Professional and managerial replacement rates are higher—perhaps as much as 2 or 2.5 times the new hire's annual salary.[24]

The turnover rate for an organization can be computed in different ways. The following formula from the U.S. Department of Labor is widely used; in it, *separations* means departures from the organization.

$$\frac{\text{Number of employee separations during the month}}{\text{Total number of employees at midmonth}} \times 100$$

Common turnover rates range from almost 0% to more than 100% a year and vary among industries. Often a part of HR management systems, turnover data can be gathered and analyzed in a number of different ways, including the following categories:

- Job and job level
- Department, unit, and location
- Reason for leaving
- Length of service
- Demographic characteristics
- Education and training
- Knowledge, skills, and abilities
- Performance ratings/levels

Two examples illustrate why detailed analyses of turnover are important. One manufacturing organization had a company-wide turnover rate that was not severe, but 80% of the turnover occurred within one department. That imbalance indicated that some action was needed to resolve problems in that unit. A health-care institution found that its greatest turnover in registered nurses occurred 24–36 months after hire, so the firm instituted a two-year employee recognition program and expanded the career development and training activities for em-

| **Figure 3-4** | **Simplified Turnover Costing Model** |

Job Title: _____

A. Typical annual pay for this job _____

B. Percentage of pay for benefits multiplied by annual pay _____

C. Total employee annual cost (add A + B) _____

D. Number of employees who voluntarily quit the job in the
   past 12 months _____

E. Number of months it takes for 1 employee to become fully
   productive _____

F. Per person turnover cost (multiply [E ÷ 12] × C × 50%*) _____

G. Annual turnover cost for this job (multiply F × D) _____

*Assumes 50% productivity throughout the learning period (E).

ployees with a least two years' service. For these example employers, the targeted turnover rates declined as a result of the actions taken in response to the turnover analyses that were done.

Determining Turnover Costs Determining turnover costs can be relatively simple or very complex, depending on the nature of the efforts and data used. Figure 3-4 shows a simplified costing model. In this model, if a job pays $20,000 (A) and benefits cost 40% (B), then the total annual cost for one employee is $28,000. Assuming that 20 employees quit in the previous year (D) and that it takes three months for 1 employee to be fully productive, the calculation in (F) results in a per person turnover cost of $3,500. Overall, the annual turnover costs would be $70,000 for the 20 individuals who left. In spite of its conservative and simple nature, this model makes the point that turnover is costly. For instance, if the job is that of a teller in a large bank where more than 150 people leave in a year, the conservative model produces turnover costs of more than $500,000 a year. More detailed and sophisticated turnover costing models consider a number of factors. Some of the most common areas considered include the following:

◆ *Separation costs:* Includes HR staff and supervisor time and salaries to prevent separations, exit interview time, unemployment expenses, legal fees for separations challenged, accrued vacation, continued benefits, etc.

◆ *Replacement costs:* Includes recruiting and advertising expenses, search fees, HR interviewer and staff time and salaries, employee referral fees, relocation and moving costs, supervisor and managerial time and salaries, employment testing costs, reference checking fees, pre-employment medical expenses, etc.

◆ *Training costs:* Includes paid orientation time, training staff time and salaries, costs of training materials, supervisors' and managers' time and salaries, co-worker "coaching" time and salaries, etc.

◆ *Hidden costs:* Includes costs not obvious but that affect lost productivity, decreased customer service, other employee turnover, missed deadlines, etc.

Competent employees who are satisfied with their employers, who know what is expected, and who have minimal absenteeism and reduced turnover potential are assets to the organization. But just as individuals in an organization can be a competitive advantage, they can also be a liability. When few employees know how to do their jobs, when people are constantly leaving, and when the employees who do remain work ineffectively, human resources are a problem that puts the organization at a competitive disadvantage. Individual performance, motivation, and employee retention are key for organizations to maximize the effectiveness of individual human resources.

INDIVIDUAL EMPLOYEE PERFORMANCE

The HR unit in an organization exists in part to analyze and address the performance of individual employees. Exactly how that should be done depends on what upper management expects. Like any management function, HR management activities should be developed, evaluated, and changed as necessary so that they can contribute to the competitive performance of the individuals at work and therefore of the organization.

Individual Performance Factors

The three major factors that affect how a given individual performs are illustrated in Figure 3-5. They are (1) individual ability to do the work, (2) effort expended, and (3) organizational support. The relationship of those factors is widely acknowledged in management literature as follows:

$$\text{Performance } (P) = \text{Ability } (A) \times \text{Effort } (E) \times \text{Support } (S)$$

Figure 3-5   *Components of Individual Performance*

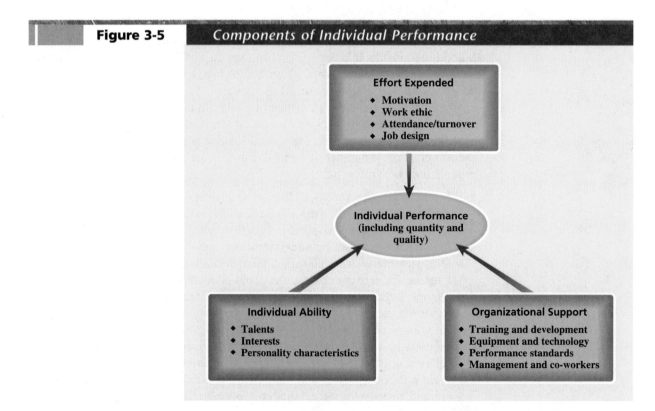

Individual performance is enhanced to the degree that all three components are present with an individual employee, and diminished if any of these factors is reduced or absent. For instance, assume that several production workers have the abilities to do their jobs and work hard, but the organization provides outmoded equipment or the management style of supervisors causes negative reactions by the workers. Or assume that a customer service representative in a call center has the necessary abilities and the employer provides excellent support, but the individual hates "being tied to a telephone cord" all day and is frequently absent because of that dislike, even though the job pays well. In both cases, individual performance is likely to be lower than it would be if all three components were present. Individual motivation, one of the variables that affects effort, is often missing from the performance equation.

Individual Motivation

Motivation
The desire within a person causing that person to act.

Motivation is the desire within a person causing that person to act. People usually act for one reason: to reach a goal. Thus, motivation is a goal-directed drive, and it seldom occurs in a void. The words *need, want, desire,* and *drive* are all similar to *motive,* from which the word *motivation* is derived. Understanding motivation is important because performance, reaction to compensation, turnover, and other HR concerns are affected by and influence motivation.

Approaches to understanding motivation vary because different theorists have developed their own views and models. Each approach has contributed to the understanding of human motivation, and details on different approaches can be found in various organizational behavior textbooks.

Management Implications for Motivating Individual Performance

Motivation is complex and individualized, and managerial strategies and tactics must be broadbased to address the motivation concerns of individuals. For instance, managers must determine whether inadequate individual behavior is due to employee deficiencies inconsistent reward policies, or low desire for the rewards offered. Additionally, managers may try training to improve employee performance or look at the methods by which they appraise and reward performance.

Finally, managers must investigate the desirability of the rewards given for performance. Even if skills and rewards for performance are both high, employees may not value the rewards. The rewards must be based on what the employees actually value, not what the managers think that employees want.

Many organizations spend considerable money to "motivate" their employees, using a wide range of tactics. For example, firms hire motivational speakers to inspire employees, with some of those "motivational coaches" commanding fees of as much as $50,000 a speech. Other employers give T-shirts, mugs, books, and videos to employees as motivators. Such efforts, not including sales motivation rewards, are estimated to cost in the billions of dollars a year. However, the effectiveness of those expenditures has been questioned, particularly given the short-term nature of many of the programs and rewards.

In summary, answering the question often asked by managers, "How do I motivate my employees?" requires managerial diagnoses of employees' efforts, abilities, and expectations. For that reason, the relationships between individuals and their organizations are an integral part of effective HR management, and affect employee retention—the focus of the remainder of the chapter.

▌▌ RETENTION OF HUMAN RESOURCES

Retention must be viewed as a strategic business issue. Until a few years ago, turnover was a routine HR matter requiring records and reports, but top management did not get involved. However, what was once a bothersome detail can become a substantial money issue for many employers. There are now fewer qualified and productive people in the workforce, and the good ones are even more in demand. Companies are being forced to study why employees leave and why they stay. While experts can (and do) make some observations, each organization must determine the causes for its own specific retention situation.

Some employers have placed such a high priority on employee retention that they have designated retention officers. Often an individual in the HR area is assigned a specific focus of retention to ensure that it receives high priority.

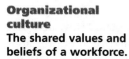

LOGGING ON...

Talent Keepers
This organization offers Web-based employee retention solutions.
www.talentkeepers.com

Why People Stay or Leave

Conventional wisdom says that employees leave if they are dissatisfied, and that money will make them stay. That greatly oversimplifies the issue.[25] People often leave jobs for reasons that have nothing to do with the jobs themselves. Mergers, unsolicited job offers, family responsibilities, a spouse's relocation, a poor performance appraisal, and administrative changes are all "shocks" that can bring on serious thoughts of leaving, even when people are not dissatisfied with their jobs. Further, people sometimes stay with jobs for non-work reasons. Some factors that limit individuals' willingness to leave the jobs are *links* between themselves and others; compatibility, or *"fit,"* with the job/organization/community; and potential *sacrifice,* or what they would have to give up if they left the job.

Those characteristics of the "stay or go" decision are personal and not entirely within the control of an employer. However, there are factors related to those individual decisions that an employer *can* control. Figure 3-6 shows those factors, and also indicates that they are "drivers" of retention, or forces that an employer can manage to improve retention.

▌▌ DRIVERS OF RETENTION

If employees choose to leave an organization for family reasons—because a spouse is transferring, to raise children, etc.—there are a limited number of actions the employer can take. However, there *are* significant actions that an employer *can* do to retain employees.

Characteristics of the Employer and Retention

A number of organizational characteristics influence individuals in their decisions to stay with or leave their employers. Organizations experience less turnover when they have positive, distinctive cultures; effective management; and recognizable job security.

Organizational culture
The shared values and beliefs of a workforce.

Culture and Values **Organizational culture** is a pattern of shared values and beliefs of a workforce. Those items provide organizational members with meaning and rules for behavior. In a recent study, employees gave employers a B+ on average, with 44% calling their employers' cultures "excellent" or "very good."[26]

One corporation well known for its culture and values is Southwest Airlines. The firm focuses considerable HR efforts on instilling its values of customer

Figure 3-6 *Drivers of Retention*

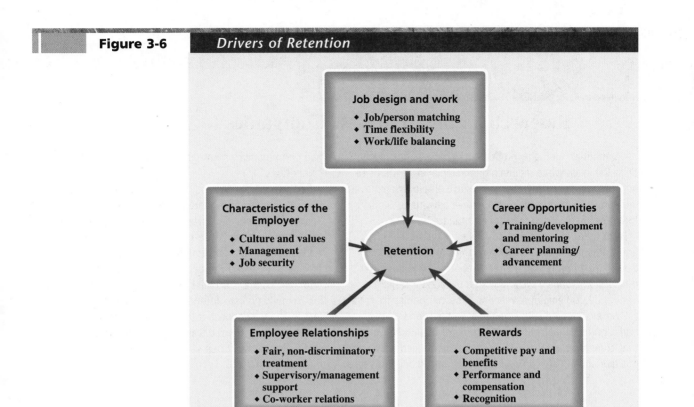

service and employee involvement. Those efforts have yielded greater performance, retention of employees, and a reputation as an "employer of choice" in the airline industry. Even after the terrorist attacks in September 2001, Southwest was the only airline that did not cut staff and significantly reduce its flights. The initiator of Southwest's culture, founding CEO Herb Kelleher, has repeatedly stated that showing respect for people is central to that culture.

Another firm that uses culture and values to retain employees is Starbucks, which has providing a "great work environment" as number one on its six-point mission statement. Also, the National Association of Insurance Commissioners, which is a small non-profit organization uses a high-quality workplace and values flexibility (in this case, allowing employees to bring babies to work) to compete with the higher salaries of competitors.[27]

The "100 Best Companies to Work For" have somewhat different cultures and values, yet their commitment to treating their employees well is a constant in good times and bad.[28] The HR Perspective on the next page looks at whether or not those firms are also performing better financially.

Management and Retention Other organizational components that affect employee retention are related to the management of the organization. Some organizations see external events as threatening, whereas others see changes as challenges requiring responses. The latter approach can be a source of competitive advantage, especially if an organization is in a growing, dynamic industry. The attitudes and approaches of management are the key.

Research on the "100 Best Companies to Work For"

Competition for highly productive employees has given firms the incentive to maintain good employee relations to assist in recruiting. However, do positive employer/employee relations give companies a competitive advantage, leading to better financial and market performance?

From the companies that have been listed at various times among the "100 Best Companies to Work For," 161 participated in a research project reported by Fulmer and others in *Personnel Psychology* that included a sample size of over 20,000 employee reactions. The companies from the list were compared with companies in the broad market and a group of matched firms. Results of the study found that companies on the "100 Best" list did indeed have very positive and stable employee attitudes, and those firms also had performance advantages over the broad market of competitors.

Financial performance data were analyzed for the three years before the firms were listed among the "100 Best" and for the three years after. Accounting ratios (return on assets) and the market-to-book value or equity of publicly traded companies were found to be generally better than those of a matched comparison group. Further, on long-term results, the "100 Best Companies" outperformed the broad market on stock returns. In summary, the study is the first to show a connection at the organizational level between the strategy of developing a positive workplace and performing better (often substantially better) financially than competitors.[29]

Another factor affecting how employees view their organizations is the visionary quality of organizational leadership. Often, leaders demonstrate their vision by having an identified strategic plan that guides how the firm responds to changes. If a firm is not effectively managed, then employees may be turned off by the ineffective responses and inefficiencies they deal with in their jobs. Organizations that have clearly established goals and hold managers and employees accountable for accomplishing results are viewed as better places to work, especially by individuals wishing to progress both financially and career-wise. Further, effective management provides the resources necessary for employees to perform their jobs well.

Job Security Many individuals have seen a decline in job security over the past decade. All the downsizings, layoffs, mergers and acquisitions, and organizational restructurings have affected employee loyalty and retention. Also, as co-workers experience layoffs and job reductions, the anxiety levels of the remaining employees rise. Consequently, employees start thinking about leaving before they too get cut. On the other hand, organizations in which job continuity and security are high tend to have higher retention rates. A survey by SHRM showed that about 75% of employees are at least somewhat satisfied with the job security provided by their employers, while 13% are at least somewhat dissatisfied. Younger employees experience more concern about job security than do older workers.[30]

But job security is not solely about one's personal security. A major issue in retention is the extent to which high-caliber top performers are retained by the company. Other employees view high turnover in this group and the company as a negative in the retention equation.[31]

Job Design/Work and Retention

Some jobs are considered "good" and others are thought to be "bad"—but not all people agree on which are which. People vary considerably in their preferences for particular job features. As a result, some people like some kinds of work and others like different kinds of work. That is fortunate, because it means there are people willing to do most jobs.

Job/Person Match Matching people with jobs they like and fit can be a challenge. Figure 3-7 shows some characteristics of people and jobs that might need to be matched.

If people do not fit their jobs well, they are more likely to look for other employment, so retention is affected by the *selection process.* A number of organizations have found that high turnover rates in the first few months of employment are often linked to inadequate selection screening efforts. An example illustrates the importance of a sound selection processes: A customer service call center experienced 89% annual turnover even though the firm paid above-market wages. Further analyses found that many people hired did not have the proper knowledge, skills, and abilities (KSAs) to perform the basic job requirements. The company reduced turnover by instituting new selection processes, including providing more realistic jobs previews to applicants and improving selection efforts by HR staff members.

Once individuals have been placed in jobs, several job/work factors affect retention. Because individuals spend significant time on the job, they expect to have modern equipment, technology, and *good working conditions,* given the nature of the work. Physical and environmental factors such as space, lighting, temperature, noise, and layout affect retention of employees.

Figure 3-7 *Some Characteristics of People and Jobs*

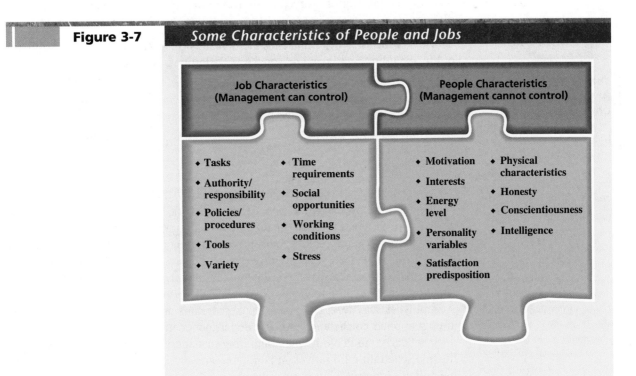

Additionally, workers want a *safe work environment,* where risks of accidents and injuries have been addressed. That is especially true for employees in such industries as manufacturing, agriculture, utilities, and transportation, which have higher safety risks than do many service industries and office environments.

Time Flexibility Flexibility in work schedules has grown in importance. Workload pressures have increased because of downsizing. On average, employees work 41.2 hours a week at their main jobs, but would prefer to work 34.5 hours a week. That discrepancy leads to 44% of employees working more than they want to and feeling overworked.[32] Further, with more Americans living longer, the need for elder care is increasing. Dual-income couples in the "sandwich generation," caring for children *and* aged parents, may find flexible scheduling options very desirable.

The Family and Work Institute surveyed 1,003 adults and found that over half felt overworked. Working more days or hours than they preferred contributed to that feeling. Technology also contributed to it, as over half of the respondents felt they were unnecessarily accessible to their employers through cell phones and e-mail. Finally, overworked employees felt they made more mistakes, were more angry with their employers, resented co-workers, and were more likely to look for other jobs.[33] Various work scheduling alternatives that are discussed in more detail in Chapter 6 can be used to improve time flexibility. Options include compressed scheduling, flexplace or telecommuting, flextime, part-time work, job sharing, and phased retirement.

Many approaches to time flexibility are informal. It is estimated that informal arrangements are more common than formal ones. However, informal schedule arrangements can cause communication problems among people who do not see each other, and hostility among some employees. Formal policies indicating who is eligible for schedule flexibility and how problems will be handled are needed.[34]

LOGGING ON...

You Can Work from Anywhere
One of the resources here is a tab on work/life balance that links to other useful sites.
www. youcanworkfromanywhere. com

Work/Life Balancing Balancing the demands of work with the responsibilities of life, including family and personal responsibilities, is a challenge; some may say it is an impossibility. Work/life balancing programs commonly used include:

- Different work arrangements
- Leave for childrens' school functions
- Compressed workweek
- Job sharing
- On-site child/adult care

- Telecommuting
- Employee assistance plans
- On-site health services
- Wellness programs
- Fitness facility

The purpose of all these offerings is to convey that employers recognize the challenges employees face when balancing work/life demands. The value of work/life programs has been documented by a number of employers. One large manufacturer worked to reduce absenteeism and increase employee commitment to the firm. A revised time-off program and more flexible work arrangements have reduced absenteeism and unscheduled time off, and increased employee satisfaction with the company.

Employees may tend to dismiss such programs as "window dressing" if they are not applied consistently. An HR department seminar on work/life balancing does not carry much clout when operating managers will not allow or encourage flexible scheduling initiatives. It is not uncommon to have effective work schedule policies identified but not practiced.[35]

Career Opportunities and Retention

Surveys of workers in all types of jobs consistently indicate that organizational efforts to aid career development can significantly affect employee retention. Such surveys have found that *opportunities for personal growth* lead the list of reasons why individuals took their current jobs and why they stay there. That component is even more essential for technical professionals and those under age 35, for whom opportunities to develop skills and obtain promotions rank above compensation as a retention concern.

Training/Development and Mentoring Organizations address training and development in a number of ways. Tuition aid programs, typically offered as a benefit by many employers, allow employees to pursue additional educational and training opportunities. These programs often contribute to higher employee retention rates. However, just offering such programs is not sufficient. Employers must also identify ways to use employees' new knowledge and capabilities inside the organization. Otherwise, employees are likely to feel that their increased "value" is not being recognized. Overall, training and development efforts are designed to meet many employees' expectations that their employers are committed to keeping their knowledge, skills, and abilities current.

Orientation is a type of training offered to new employees to help them adapt to their new jobs and employers. Increasing employee integration with the job through orientation during the first 90 days gets people proficient and makes them feel part of the company "team." Orientation that is well administered may increase employee retention rates by as much as 25%.[36]

Mentoring can increase retention, as it provides both career opportunities and development. Mentoring can be formal or informal. As the number of contacts grows through mentors or others, it turns into a career networking system, either inside the organization or outside, or perhaps both.

Career Planning/Advancement Organizations also increase employee retention through formal career planning efforts. Employees discuss with their managers career opportunities within the organization and career development activities that will help the employees grow. Career development and planning efforts may include formal mentoring programs. Also, companies can reduce attrition by showing employees that they are serious about promoting from within. In very large companies, it is not always easy to know who might be qualified for an open job. The Technology Transforming HR feature describes an effective solution.

Promotions reward individuals with status, security, and the opportunity for further development. They reward the organization by contributing to retention, therefore reducing the costs of training, recruiting, and turnover. Research suggests that when people have been promoted, they are less likely to leave the organization.[37] Individuals consider their own and others' promotion experiences in weighing opportunities, and eventually in deciding whether to stay or leave.

Rewards and Retention

The tangible rewards that people receive for working come in the form of pay, incentives, and benefits. Numerous surveys and experiences of HR professionals reveal that one key to retention is having *competitive compensation practices*. Many managers believe that money is the prime retention factor. Often, employees cite better pay or higher compensation as a reason for leaving one employer for another. However, the reality is a bit more complex.

Retention and Technology

Some companies are using Web-based solutions to help them identify internal talent for promotion. By taking an electronic look within the company, the firms not only save money, but also aid the prospects for retention of current employees because people see possible opportunities to move up.

Fireman's Fund Insurance is a California-based casualty and property insurer that has implemented an electronic system for internal recruiting. By logging on to the company intranet, an employee can create a personal profile including career objectives, education, skills, and salary expectations. When a job opens up, the program automatically looks in the company database for matches. Then appropriate candidates are notified by e-mail, and they can choose to go through the regular hiring process.

Using a "click and drag" technology, employees can register a profile easily and quickly. Previously, the task took employees 15–30 minutes to complete. It was so cumbersome that only 2,000 of the 7,000 employees submitted information to be considered for transfers or promotions. The advantage of the Web-based system is seen in statistics that show that in one year 38% of the positions at Fireman's Fund were filled internally, compared with 5% in the previous year.[38]

Competitive Pay and Benefits Pay and benefits *must be competitive,* which means they must be close to what other employers are providing and what individuals believe to be consistent with their capabilities, experience, and performance. If compensation is not close, often defined as within 10% of the "market" rate, then turnover is likely to be higher. This is especially true for individuals making less than $25,000 to $30,000 annually. Simply put, with the tight line they walk to meet their living costs and financial requirements, if those lower-paid workers can get $1 per hour more or add employer-paid family benefits elsewhere, they are more likely to move.

On the other hand, for more highly paid individuals, especially those earning $60,000 and more, retention is less affected by how close compensation is to the market rate. Other considerations are more likely to enter into their decisions to stay or leave. In fact, money may be why some people leave a job, but other factors may be why many stay. Offering health insurance, 401(k) retirement, tuition assistance, and other benefits commonly provided by competing employers often is vital to retention.

A number of employers have used a wide range of special benefits and perks to attract and retain employees. Some of the more exotic benefits offered are dry cleaning pickup and dropoff, car maintenance services in company parking lots, coffee and latte kiosks, and ATM machines in break rooms. By offering special benefits and perks, employers hope to be seen by employees more favorably, which may increase retention rates.[39]

Performance and Compensation Many individuals expect their rewards to be differentiated from those of others based on performance. That means, for instance, that if an employee receives about the same pay increase and overall pay as others who produce less, are absent more, and work fewer hours, then that person may feel that the situation is "unfair." This may prompt the individual to look for another job where compensation recognizes performance differences. Generally individuals are more satisfied with the actual levels of their pay than with the processes used to determine pay. That is why the performance management systems and performance appraisal processes in organizations must be designed so they are linked to compensation increases.

To strengthen links between organizational and individual performance, a growing number of private-sector firms are using variable pay and incentives programs. These programs offer cash bonuses or lump-sum payments to reward extra performance.

Recognition Employee recognition as a form of reward can be either tangible or intangible. Tangible recognition comes in many forms, such as "employee of the month" plaques and perfect-attendance certificates. Intangible and psychological recognition includes feedback from managers and supervisors that acknowledges extra effort and performance, even if monetary rewards are not given.

A franchise firm for the KFC food chain uses both tangible and intangible recognition as part of its employee retention efforts. Employees who receive recognition cards from customers or co-workers can exchange them for movie tickets and other rewards. Also, managers have been trained to make special efforts to recognize employee performance and service.[40] However, recognition programs *do not work* when used as substitutes for pay, or if they are viewed as "negative recognition" for those who are not recognized, or if the recognition is insincere.[41]

Employee Relationships and Retention

A final set of factors found to affect retention is based on the relationships that employees have in organizations. Such areas as the reasonableness of HR policies, the fairness of disciplinary actions, and the means used to decide work assignments and opportunities all affect employee retention. If individuals feel that policies are unreasonably restrictive or are applied inconsistently, then they may be more likely to look at jobs offered by other employers.[42]

The increasing demographic diversity of U.S. workplaces makes *fair* and *non-discriminatory treatment* of employees, regardless of gender, age, and other characteristics, particularly important. The organizational commitment and job satisfaction of ethnically diverse individuals are affected by perceived discriminatory treatment. A number of firms have recognized that proactive management of diversity issues results in greater retention of individuals of all backgrounds.

Other relationships that affect employee retention are *supervisory/management support* and *co-worker relations*. A supervisor or manager builds positive relationships and aids retention by being fair and non-discriminatory, allowing work flexibility and work/family balancing, giving feedback that recognizes employee efforts and performance, and supporting career planning and development.

Many individuals build close relationships with co-workers. Such friendships do not appear on employee records, but research suggests that they can be an important signal that a workplace is positive.[43]

MANAGING RETENTION

The foregoing section summarized the results of many studies and HR practices to identify factors that can cause retention difficulties. Now the focus turns to what a manager can do about retention issues. Figure 3-8 shows the keys to managing retention.

Figure 3-8   *Keys to Managing Retention*

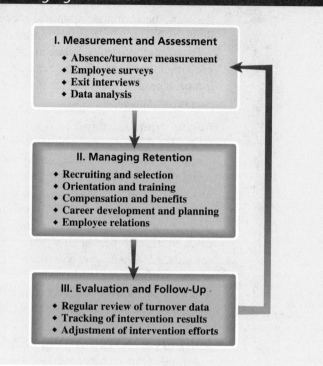

Retention Measurement and Assessment

To ensure that appropriate actions are taken to enhance retention, management decisions require data and analyses rather than subjective impressions, anecdotes of selected individual situations, or panic reactions to the loss of key people. Having several *absence and turnover measurements* to analyze is important. Two other sources of information might be useful before analysis is done: employee surveys and exit interviews.

Employee Surveys Employee surveys can be used to diagnose specific problem areas, identify employee needs or preferences, and reveal areas in which HR activities are well received or are viewed negatively. For example, questionnaires may be sent to employees to collect ideas for revising a performance appraisal system or to determine how satisfied employees are with their benefits programs. Regardless of the topic of a survey, obtaining employee input provides managers and HR professionals with data on the "retention climate" in an organization.

One specific type of survey used by many organizations is an **attitude survey** that focuses on employees' feelings and beliefs about their jobs and the organization. By obtaining data on how employees view their jobs, their supervisors, their co-workers, and organizational policies and practices, these surveys can be starting points for reducing turnover and increasing the length of time that employees are retained. Some employers conduct attitude surveys regularly (such as every year), while others do so intermittently. As the use of the Internet has spread, more organizations have begun conducting attitude surveys electronically.[44]

Attitude survey
A survey that focuses on employees' feelings and beliefs about their jobs and the organization.

HR *Practice*

Conducting Exit Interviews

One task commonly performed by HR staff members in organizations with significant turnover is conducting exit interviews. HR specialists, rather than department managers or supervisors, usually conduct these interviews. One reason for that is because a skilled HR interviewer may be able to gain useful information that departing employees may not wish to share with managers and supervisors, particularly if it pertains to problems and issues with those managers and supervisors. Departing employees may be reluctant to divulge their real reasons for leaving because they may wish to return to the company someday. Also, they may fear that candid responses will hinder their chances of receiving favorable references.

The following suggestions may be useful when conducting exit interviews:

◆ Decide who will conduct the exit interviews and when the discussions will occur. Usually, they are done on the last day of a departing individual's employment.

◆ Develop a checklist or a set of standard questions so that the information can be summarized. Typical areas

covered include reasons for leaving, supervision, pay, training, best- and least-liked aspects of the job, and organization to which the employee is moving.

◆ Emphasize that the information provided by departing employees will be treated confidentially, and will be summarized to use for making future improvements and changes in the organization.

◆ Regularly summarize the data by reasons for leaving, department, length of service, etc., to provide data for improving company retention efforts.

◆ If possible, contact departed employees a month or so after they leave. The "real reasons" for departure may be voiced at that time. One major reason employees commonly give for leaving their jobs is that they got an offer for more pay elsewhere; however, the pay increase may not be the only reason.

◆ Recognize that former employees may be more willing to provide information on questionnaires mailed to their homes or in telephone conversations conducted some time after they have left the organization.[45]

THOMSON
―――★―――™
WEST

EXIT INTERVIEW FORM
Contains a sample exit interview form.
Custom Search:
☑ ANALYSIS
Exact Phrase: Exit interview form

Exit interview
An interview in which individuals are asked to give their reasons for leaving the organization.

Attitude surveys are developed by consulting firms, academicians, and others. They can also be custom designed to address specific issues and concerns in an organization. Regardless of their type, only surveys that are valid and reliable can measure attitudes accurately. Often a "research" survey developed in-house is poorly structured, asks questions in a confusing manner, or leads employees to respond in ways that will give "favorable" results.[46]

By asking employees to respond candidly to an attitude survey, management is building up employees' expectations that action will be taken on the concerns identified. Therefore, a crucial part of conducting an attitude survey is providing feedback to those who participated in it. It is especially important that even negative survey results be communicated, to avoid fostering the appearance of hiding the results or placing blame.

Exit Interviews One widely used type of interview is the **exit interview,** in which individuals are asked to give their reasons for leaving the organization. In one survey of employers, 87% of them claimed to conduct exit interviews, and more than half used the information gathered to make changes to aid retention. A wide range of issues can be examined in exit interviews, as described in the HR Practice on conducting them.

LOGGING ON...

Insightlink
This organization offers design and analysis of employee surveys and exit interviews.
www.insightlink.com

Determining Retention Management Actions

The analysis of data mined from turnover and absenteeism records, surveys of employees, and exit interviews is an attempt to get at the cause of retention problems. Analysis should recognize that turnover and absenteeism are symptoms of other factors that may be causing problems. When the causes are treated, the symptoms will go away. Some of the first areas to consider when analyzing data for retention include the work, pay/benefits, supervision, and management systems.

There are numerous actions management might take to deal with retention issues. The choice of a particular action depends on the analysis of the turnover and retention problems in a particular organization and should be custom-tailored for that organization.

Retention Evaluation and Follow-Up

Once appropriate management actions have been implemented, it is important that they be evaluated and that appropriate follow-up be conducted and adjustments made. *Regular review of turnover data* can identify when turnover increases or decreases among different employee groups classified by length of service, education, department, and gender, etc.

Tracking of intervention results and *adjustment of intervention efforts* also should be part of evaluation efforts. Some firms may use pilot programs to see how changes affect turnover before extending them to the entire organization. For instance, to test the effect of flextime scheduling on employee turnover, a firm might try flexible scheduling in one department. If the turnover rate in that department drops in comparison with the turnover rates in other departments still working set schedules, then the experimental project may indicate that flexible scheduling can reduce turnover. Next, the firm might extend the use of flexible scheduling to other departments.

SUMMARY

- Psychological contracts are unwritten expectations that employees and employers have about the nature of their work relationships. Those contracts are changing along with employee loyalty to their employers.

- The interaction between individuals and their jobs affects both job satisfaction and organizational commitment.

- Absenteeism is expensive. It can be controlled by discipline, positive reinforcement, or use of a "no fault" policy and paid-time-off programs.

- Turnover is costly and can be classified in a number of ways, but it should be measured and its costs determined.

- Job satisfaction, commitment, and loyalty relate to turnover and absenteeism.

- The components of individual performance are individual ability, effort expended, and organizational support.

- Motivation deals with the needs and desires of human behavior. Various theories of motivation have been developed.

- Retention of employees is a major focus of HR efforts in organizations, as seen by the use of retention measures and the establishment of retention officers in some firms.

- The determinants of retention can be divided into five general categories, with the key organizational components being characteristics of the employer, job design and work, career opportunities, rewards, and employee relationships.

- The culture and values of the employer, management performance, and job security are employer characteristics that affect retention.
- The jobs and work done by employees affect retention, particularly if individuals are properly selected, work schedules are flexible, and work/life balancing programs are offered.
- Organizational career opportunities are frequently cited as crucial to employee retention.

- To enhance employee retention, rewards must be relatively competitive and tied to performance as well as employees having effective relationships with managers and co-workers.
- Retention management should be seen as a process involving measurement and assessment, interventions, and evaluation and follow-up.

REVIEW AND APPLICATION QUESTIONS

1. Describe your expectations for a job. How well is your employer meeting the expectations you bring to the psychological contract?
2. If you managed a restaurant with high absenteeism and high turnover, what actions would you take to get those issues under control?
3. As the HR manager, you have been asked to provide the senior management team with turnover costs for one high-turnover position. Using *www.talentkeepers.com* and *www.keepemployees.*

com, calculate turnover and analyze the variables involved. Also identify any other data that might be relevant.

The position is: **Machine Operator**
   Number of employees: 250
   Number of turnovers: 85
   Average wage: $11.50/hour
   Cost of benefits: 38% of payroll

LEARNING REVIEW

To check your knowledge of the chapter, review the following. (Answers after the supplemental case.) For more questions, see the Study Guide.

1. Research has confirmed that individuals whose psychological contract "obligations" are not being satisfied are _____.
   a. generally underpaid
   b. more likely to leave
   c. psychologically depressed
   d. more likely to commit acts of workplace violence
2. Which of the following circumstances has influenced employee loyalty and retention the most?
   a. a dynamic economy
   b. corporate downsizing
   c. affirmative action plans
   d. career development programs

3. Which of these items was *not* suggested as a reward issue affecting employee retention?
   a. recognition
   b. signing bonuses
   c. competitive benefits
   d. performance differentiation
4. By asking employees to respond candidly to an attitude survey, management is building up the employees' expectations that _____.
   a. their responses will be publicized
   b. an organizational restructuring is being considered
   c. the HR department is becoming more professional
   d. action will be taken on the concerns identified

CASE
ALEGENT HEALTH

Alegent Health is an Omaha-based non-profit health care system composed of seven hospitals with about 2,000 beds and more than 200 clinic and outpatient locations, 1,200 physicians, and over 7,500 other employees who work throughout the organization.

Several years ago, Alegent recognized that HR issues needed "acute care treatment." Turnover rates of 24%, coupled with over 500 unfilled positions, were costing the firm over $15 million annually.

Four years later, the turnover rates have declined to 12% and open positions have dropped to fewer than 100. Because of their improvements, Alegent's HR practices, and especially its retention successes, won several local and national awards. Alegent was named one of the "Best Places to Work in Omaha." The award was based on surveys of employees that asked about credibility, respect and fairness, pride, and camaraderie. Alegent also received a *Workforce Management's* Optimas Award in the financial impact category for its success at recruiting and retaining key staff. Alegent is clearly being effective with some HR activities to win all the awards.

Specifically regarding retention efforts, Alegent created an Employee Retention Task Force whose focus was to decrease turnover and increase employee satisfaction. The task force identified several strategies to be used.

One program illustrates how Alegent approached retention of nurses. The Nursing Residence Program has caught national attention. Each resident (or new nurse) is paired with an experienced nurse or "preceptor" based on interests, personality, and so on. Also, a mentor outside the nursing department adds support and encouragement to individuals. Nursing staff meet monthly for training. In addition, they can visit various other departments (pediatrics, cardiology, etc.) in which they may have career interests. Nurses interested in management can shadow the department director to see how the department is managed. Returning nurses who have been out of the field five or more years are enrolled, retrained, and paired with recently finished residents.

Alegent Health is the exception to the turnover levels in nursing. Compared to the U.S. health care industry rate of 20%, Alegent's turnover rate of 7.6% is exceptional. Another key to aiding nursing recruitment and retention is an extensive training and development program. Many different short courses and classes are provided to Alegent employees at no cost. As part of this program, Alegent pays up to $20,000 for employees selected for a career advancement program to obtain nursing degrees.[47]

Questions

1. Discuss how Alegent's practices match with the recommended retention practices covered in the chapter.
2. Why was a broadbased approach to nursing retention important?

SUPPLEMENTAL CASE: The Clothing Store

This case describes one firm's approach to improving employee retention. (For the case, go to http://mathis.swlearning.com.)

Learning Review Answers: 1. b   2. b   3. b   4. d

NOTES

1. Adapted from Ron Elsdon, "Dispelling the Myths About Employee Retention," *HR.Com,* October 31, 2003, 1–3, *www.hr.com.*

2. Jackie Ford and Nancy Harding, "Invoking Satan or the Ethics of the Employment Contract," *Journal of Management Studies,* 40 (2003), 1131–1150.

3. Matthew Levin, "End the Heartache and Disillusionment," *Workforce Management,* November 2003, 1–2, *www.workforce.com.*

4. Louis Lavelle, "Coming Next: A War for Talent," *Business Week Online,* September 29, 2003, 1, *www.businessweek.com.*

5. Denise Rousseau and Zipi Shperling, "Piece of the Action: Owners and the Changing Employment Relationship," *Academy of Management Review,* 28 (2003), 553–570.

6. Gregory Lee, "Towards a Contingent Model of Key Staff Retention: The New Psychological Contract Reconsidered," *South African Journal of Business Management,* 32 (2001), 1–9.

7. Jeffery Thompson and J. Stuart Bunderson, "Violations of Principle: Ideological Currency in the Psychological Contract," *Academy of Management Review,* 28 (2003), 571–586.

8. Lisa Scherer et al., "Breach and Fulfillment of the Psychological Contract: A Comparison of Traditional and Expanded Views," *Personnel Psychology,* 56 (2003), 895–934.

9. Virgil Larson, "Age Differences Key to Motivation," *Omaha World Herald,* March 17, 2003, D1.

10. "As Job Satisfaction Declines Further, Demands on Workers Rise, Surveys Say," *Bulletin to Management,* October 2, 2003, 314.

11. Richard F. Stolz, "Keeping the Crew," *Human Resource Executive,* December 2003, 1–26.

12. "Study Says 30 Percent of Workers Are Loyal," *Bulletin to Management,* September 11, 2003, 291.

13. S. Wasti, "Organizational Commitment, Turnover, Intentions and the Influence of Cultural Values," *Journal of Occupational and Organizational Psychology,* 76 (2003), 303–321; T. Thorsteinson, "Job Attitudes of Part-Time Vs. Full-Time Workers: A Meta-Analytic Review," *Journal of Occupational and Organizational Psychology,* 76 (2003), 151–177; M. E. G. van der Velde et al., "Gender Differences in the Influence of Professional Tenure on Work Attitudes," *Sex Roles,* 29 (2003), 153–162; and Lisa Kuokkanen et al., "Nurse Empowerment, Job Related Satisfaction and Organizational Commitment," *Journal of Nursing Care Quality,* 18 (2003), 184-192.

14. "2003 CCH Unscheduled Absence Survey," *CCH Incorporated,* November 4, 2003, 1.

15. Sharon Kaleta and Edward Anderson, "Here Today, Gone Tomorrow," *National Underwriter,* November 3, 2003, 28.

16. Sarah Fister Gale, "The Insider," *Workforce Management,* September 2003, 72.

17. L. Van Gelder, "On the Job," *New York Times,* May 27, 2001, 3.

18. M. Dishon-Berkovits and Meni Koslowsky, "Determinants of Employee Punctuality," *Journal of Social Psychology,* 142 (2002), 723–739.

19. Carla Joinson, "Capturing Turnover Costs," *HR Magazine,* July 2000, 107–109.

20. Adapted from Joanna Slater, "Attrition Besets India Call Centers," *Wall Street Journal,* December 31, 2003, A8.

21. "Employee Turnover," *Economist,* July 15, 2000, 64–65; and "Turnover Costs," *Wall Street Journal,* August 29, 2000, B12.

22. "Meet HR's New Best Friend: Turnover," *Workforce,* January 2003, 1.

23. Wayne Cascio, *Costing Human Resources,* 4th ed. (Cincinnati: South-Western College Publishing, 2003), 62–70.

24. Ibid., 24–25.

25. Terence Mitchell et al., "How to Keep Your Best Employees: Developing an Effective Retention Policy," *Academy of Management Executive,* 15, (2001), 96-107.

26. Robert Morgan, "Does Your Organization Make the Grade?" *Workspan,* February 2004, 19–20.

27. Maryann Hammers, "Starbucks Is Pleasing Employees and Pouring Profits," *Workforce Management,* October 2003, 58–59; and Maryann Hammers, "Babies Deliver a Loyal Workforce," *Workforce,* April 2003, 52.

28. Robert Levering and Milton Moskowitz, "100 Best Companies to Work For," *Fortune,* January 20, 2003, 127–150.

29. Ingrid Smithley Fulmer et al., "Are the 100 Best Better?" *Personnel Psychology,* 56 (2003), 965–993.

30. Eiren Esen, "Job Security Survey," *SHRM Research,* June 2003, 22.

31. Steve Bates, "Getting Engaged," *HR Magazine,* February 2004, 44–51.

32. Karen Lee, "Overworked Employees More Likely to Fall Ill and Leave," *Benefits News,* June 15, 2001, 1.

33. Ellen Galinsky et al., *Feeling Overworked: When Work Becomes Too Much,* (New York: Families and Work Institute, 2001), 6–14.

34. Sarah Fisker Gale, "Formalized Flextime: The Perk That Brings Productivity," *Workforce Management,* February 8, 2001, 39–42.

35. Patricia Chisholm et al., "Redesigning Work," *Maclean's,* May 3, 2001, 1–4.

36. "New Solution to Improving Employee Retention by as Much as 25%," *HR.Com,* March, 2003, 1, *www.hr.com.*

37. Ishak Saporta and Moshe Farjoun, "The Relationship Between Actual Promotions and Turnover Among Professional and Managerial-Administrative Occupational Groups," *Work and Occupations,* 30 (2003), 255–280.

38. Cindy Waxes, "Inside Jobs," *Human Resource Executive,* March 2, 2003, 36–37.

39. Mary Elizabeth Burke et al., "SHRM 2003 Benefits Survey," *SHRM Research,* June 2003, 1–56.

40. Lane Abrahamsen and Greg Boswell, "Employers Turn to Recognition to Motivate Employers," *Workspan,* December 2003, 24–26.

41. Jared Sandberg, "Cultural Culture," *The Wall Street Journal,* January 28, 2004, B1.

42. David Jones and Daniel Skarlicki, "The Relationship Between Perceptions of Fairness and Voluntary Turnover Among Retail Employees," *Journal of Applied Social Psychology,* 33 (2003), 1226–1243.

43. Sue Shellenbarger, "Work and Family," *The Wall Street Journal,* February 20, 2002, B1.

44. Marcie Levine and Peter Tobia, "Take Stock Then Take Action," *HR.Com,* January 2004, 1–5, *www.hr.com.*

45. Fay Hansen, "Weighing the Truth of Exit Interviews," *Workforce,* December 2002, 37; and Theresa Sweeney, "Exit Interviews," *Credit Union Management,* November 2002, 38–39.

46. Charlotte Garvey, "Getting Feedback You Can Depend On," *HR Magazine,* 48 (March 2003), 1–2.

47. Based on Christa Hines and Amy Protexter, *Alegent Health Press Releases* dated June 25, 2002, October 21, 2003, June 9, 2003, December 18, 2003, and February 26, 2004; and Eilene Zimmerman, "Strong Medicine," *Workforce Management,* March 2004, 40–42.

CHAPTER 4

Legal Framework of Equal Employment

After you have read this chapter, you should be able to:

- Define three basic EEO concepts and discuss the key provisions of Title VII of the Civil Rights Act of 1964.

- Give examples of three sex-based discrimination issues.

- Indicate the major requirements of the Americans with Disabilities Act of 1990.

- Discuss the two general approaches for complying with the 1978 Uniform Guidelines on Employee Selection Procedures.

- Identify typical EEO recordkeeping requirements and the records used in the EEO investigative process.

Mitsubishi Believes in EEO—NOW

Several years ago the Mitsubishi auto plant in Normal, Illinois, had a negative reputation. A lawsuit told the story: it alleged that sexual graffiti was written on fenders of cars being assembled before they passed female production workers, pornographic photos hung on the walls, male workers taunted women, and those women who complained were not promoted or perhaps were even fired.

Ultimately, Mitsubishi paid $34 million to settle a sexual harassment lawsuit brought on behalf of 500 workers at the plant. Further, Mitsubishi agreed to pay a multi-million-dollar settlement to African American and Hispanic employees who had claimed racial discrimination during the same time period as the sexual harassment claims. The plant's image was so bad that people were embarrassed to wear the company colors outside work.

Productivity was bad as well, and the company headquarters in Japan was considering closing the American plant. Rich Gilligan, a former Ford manager, was hired to run the plant and began to change the humiliating and illegal ways its women and racial minority employees were treated.

The plant today is moving toward being a model workplace of equal employment opportunity. Gilligan set up a department to investigate all employee complaints and to train employees in avoiding illegal discrimination issues. During monitoring for three years, there were 140 discrimination and harassment complaints. Fifty-two of those cases violated the zero-tolerance policy and resulted in 8 dismissals, 14 suspensions, and 30 additional disciplinary actions. "There is nothing better to change a culture than finding out there are consequences," said Nancy Kreiter, one of the monitors.[1]

The Mitsubishi case illustrates that there are consequences for violating EEO laws. Employers who choose not to deal with violations of EEO laws have paid hundreds of millions of dollars in fines to state and federal governments and in back wages and damages to employees. Since 1964, EEO has been the law of the land, and violations of that law can be expensive.

"All progress is precarious, and the solution of one problem brings us face-to-face with another problem."

—*Martin Luther King, Jr.*

King's words certainly apply to equal employment opportunity and its history in the United States. *Equal employment opportunity* is the concept that all individuals should have equal treatment in all employment-related actions. Initial concerns were especially with hiring, firing, pay, and promotion based on gender, religion, and race. But the idea spread to include age, pregnancy, and the disabled.

Amendments to the U.S. Constitution give all citizens rights to due process (Fifth Amendment), freedom from slavery (Thirteenth Amendment), and equal protection under the law (Fourteenth Amendment). Despite these protections, discrimination in employment has had a long history. Women and men working at exactly the same job have sometimes been paid differently; African Americans and Hispanics have simply not been considered for some jobs even if they are qualified.

The civil rights movement of the late 1950s and 1960s influenced public attitudes toward members of racial minorities and women. That change ultimately resulted in three decades of legislation designed to level the playing field in employment. Beginning in 1963 with the Equal Pay Act and continuing today with court interpretations of the EEO laws, employment opportunity is evolving. These laws, Executive Orders, and interpretations by courts and administrative agencies affect every part of HR management.

The fact that there are many examples of companies that have had to make significant payments for violating these laws makes the point that employers *must* be familiar with EEO laws and ensure that their practices are not illegally discriminatory. For employers operating worldwide, similar laws exist in other countries, as the HR Globally illustrates. This chapter focuses on EEO concepts and the major legal structures that support them. The next chapter will focus on managing for EEO compliance and diversity in the workforce.

EQUAL EMPLOYMENT OPPORTUNITY CONCEPTS

Equal employment
Employment that is not affected by illegal discrimination.

Blind to differences
Differences among people should be ignored and everyone should be treated equally.

Affirmative action
Employers are urged to hire groups of people based on their race, age, gender, or national origin, to make up for historical discrimination.

Not everyone agrees on the best way to achieve equal employment opportunity. There seems to be little disagreement that the goal is **equal employment,** or employment that is not affected by illegal discrimination. However, the way to achieve that goal is open to debate. One way is to use the **"blind to differences"** approach, which argues that differences among people should be ignored and everyone should be treated equally.[2] The second common approach is **affirmative action** through which employers are urged to hire groups of people based on their race, age, gender, or national origin. The idea is to make up for historical discrimination by giving groups who have been affected enhanced opportunities for employment. Affirmative action has been upheld by the courts, but only if it is used among equally qualified individuals. Affirmative action is covered in more detail in Chapter 5.

The word *discrimination* simply means "recognizing differences among items or people." For example, employers must discriminate (choose) among applicants for a job on the basis of job requirements and candidates' qualifications. However, discrimination is illegal in employment-related situations in which either: (1) different standards are used to judge different individuals, or (2) the same standard is used, but it is not related to the individuals' jobs. Charges of illegal discrimination continue to be filed, indicating that employers still do not deal with people fairly all the time.[3]

The Human Rights Act in the United Kingdom

In the United Kingdom, the Human Rights Act (HRA) of 2000 was enacted. This act allows workers in the United Kingdom (U.K.) to bring claims for employment discrimination and mistreatment in U.K. courts.

Increasingly, the act is affecting all employers even though it covers only public employees. Employment tribunals decide cases of unfair dismissal, discrimination, or detrimental treatment. The act is influencing the way cases are seen by the tribunals for private employees as well.

The human rights provided for by the act include:

- Prohibition of torture or inhumane or degrading treatment
- Right to a fair trial
- Right to respect for private and family life
- Right to freedom of expression

Most of the employment cases in the three years since enactment of the HRA have dealt with the right to a fair trial and respect for private and family life. Some of the more interesting findings of the courts in the U.K. include:

- Taking six years to conclude a hearing constitutes an unfair trial.
- Random drug testing is *not* infringement on respect for private life.
- Video surveillance is admissible in court.
- Dismissal for gross indecency outside working hours is fair.

Three years after the Human Rights Act passed, it is having an impact similar to that of U.S. EEO laws early on.[4]

Various laws have been passed to protect individuals who share certain characteristics, such as race, age, or gender. Those having the designated characteristics are referred to as a **protected class**, which is composed of individuals who fall within a group identified for protection under equal employment laws and regulations. The following bases for protection have been identified by various federal, state, and/or local laws:

Protected class
Individuals within a group identified for protection under equal employment laws and regulations.

- Race, ethnic origin, color (African Americans, Hispanic Americans, Native Americans, Asian Americans)
- Sex/gender (women, including those who are pregnant)
- Age (individuals over age 40)
- Individuals with disabilities (physical or mental)
- Military experience (Vietnam-era veterans)
- Religion (special beliefs and practices)
- Marital status (some states)
- Sexual orientation (some states and cities)

▮ MAJOR EQUAL EMPLOYMENT LAWS

Even if an organization has little regard for the principles of equal employment opportunity, it must follow federal, state, and local EEO laws and some affirmative action regulations to avoid costly penalties. Numerous federal, state, and local laws address equal employment opportunity concerns, as shown in Figure 4-1 on the next page. An overview of the major laws, regulations, and concepts follows.

Figure 4-1 — Major Federal Equal Employment Opportunity Laws and Regulations

Act	Year	Key Provisions
Broad-Based Discrimination		
Title VII, Civil Rights Act of 1964	1964	Prohibits discrimination in employment on basis of race, color, religion, sex, or national origin
Executive Orders 11246 and 11375	1965 1967	Require federal contractors and subcontractors to eliminate employment discrimination and prior discrimination through affirmative action
Executive Order 11478	1969	Prohibits discrimination in the U.S. Postal Service and in the various government agencies on the basis of race, color, religion, sex, national origin, handicap, or age
Vietnam Era Veterans' Readjustment Assistance Act	1974	Prohibits discriminations against Vietnam-era veterans by federal contractors and the U.S. government and requires affirmative action
Civil Rights Act of 1991	1991	Overturns several past Supreme Court decisions and changes damage claims provisions
Congressional Accountability Act	1995	Extends EEO and Civil Rights Act provisions to U.S. congressional staff
Race / National Origin Discrimination		
Immigration Reform and Control Act	1986 1990 1996	Establishes penalties for employers who knowingly hire illegal aliens; prohibits employment discrimination on the basis of national origin or citizenship
Gender / Sex Discrimination		
Equal Pay Act	1963	Requires equal pay for men and women performing substantially the same work
Pregnancy Discrimination Act	1978	Prohibits discrimination against women affected by pregnancy, childbirth, or related medical conditions; requires that they be treated as all other employees for employment-related purposes, including benefits
Age Discrimination		
Age Discrimination in Employment Act (as amended in 1978 and 1986)	1967	Prohibits discrimination against persons over age 40 and restricts mandatory retirement requirements, except where age is a bona fide occupational qualification
Older Workers Benefit Protection Act of 1990	1990	Prohibits age-based discrimination in early retirement and other benefits plans
Disability Discrimination		
Vocational Rehabilitation Act and Rehabilitation Act of 1974	1973 1974	Prohibit employers with federal contracts over $2,500 from discriminating against individuals with disabilities
Americans with Disabilities Act	1990	Requires employer accommodations for individuals with disabilities

Civil Rights Act of 1964, Title VII

Although the first civil rights act was passed in 1866, but it was not until passage of the Civil Rights Act of 1964 that the keystone of anti-discrimination employment legislation was put into place. The Equal Employment Opportunity Commission (EEOC) was established to enforce the provisions of Title VII, the portion of the act that deals with employment.

Title VII of the Civil Rights Act states that it is illegal for an employer to:

(1) fail or refuse to hire or discharge any individual, or otherwise discriminate against any individual with respect to his compensation, terms, conditions, or privileges of employment because of such individual's race, color, religion, sex, or national origin, or (2) to limit, segregate, or classify his employees or applicants for employment in any way that would deprive or tend to deprive any individual of employment opportunities or otherwise adversely affect his status as an employee because of such individual's race, color, religion, sex, or national origin.

Title VII Coverage Title VII, as amended by the Equal Employment Opportunity Act of 1972, covers most employers in the United States. Any organization meeting one of the criteria in the following list is subject to rules and regulations that specific government agencies have established to administer the act:

- All private employers of 15 or more persons who are employed 20 or more weeks a year
- All educational institutions, public and private
- State and local governments
- Public and private employment agencies
- Labor unions with 15 or more members
- Joint labor/management committees for apprenticeships and training

Title VII has been the basis for several extensions of EEO law. For example, in 1980, the EEOC interpreted the law to include sexual harassment. Further, a number of concepts identified in Title VII are the foundation for court decisions, regulations, and other laws discussed later in the chapter. Some of those concepts are depicted in Figure 4-2.

Business Necessity and Job Relatedness As has been emphasized by regulations and court decisions, employers are expected to use job-related employment practices. In a Michigan case, a federal court ruled that a staffing agency was discriminating illegally by filling job requests from employers with such limitations as "males only," "no applicants with accents," and "no Detroit residents." The court ruled that such criteria were not job-related and that little business necessity could be shown for these requests being made by employers using the staffing service.[5]

Business necessity
Practice necessary for safe and efficient organizational operations.

A **business necessity** is a practice necessary for safe and efficient organizational operations. Business necessity has been the subject of numerous court decisions. Educational requirements often are based on business necessity. However, an employer who requires a minimum level of education, such as a high school diploma, must be able to defend the requirement as essential to the performance of the job. For instance, equating a degree or diploma with the possession of math or reading abilities is considered questionable.

Figure 4-2

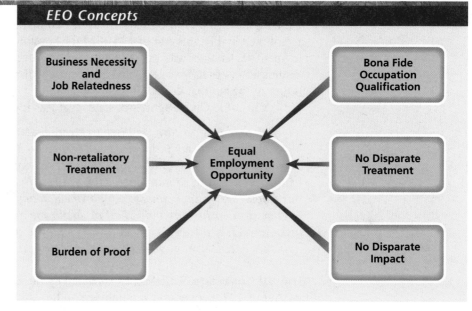

EEO Concepts

Bona Fide Occupational Qualification (BFOQ) Title VII of the 1964 Civil Rights Act goes on to state that employers may discriminate on the basis of sex, religion, or national origin if the characteristic can be justified as a "bona fide occupational qualification reasonably necessary to the normal operation of the particular business or enterprise." Thus, a **bona fide occupational qualification (BFOQ)** is a characteristic providing a legitimate reason why an employer can exclude persons on otherwise illegal bases of consideration. What constitutes a BFOQ has been subject to different interpretations in various courts across the U.S. Legal uses of BFOQs have been found for hiring Asians to wait on customers in a Chinese restaurant or Catholics to serve in certain religious-based positions in Catholic churches.

A recent case found that under certain circumstances, it is not illegal for a religious institution to discriminate against an employee for "objectionable religious speech." A clerk had been warned three times not to attempt "saving souls" on the premises of a Catholic non-profit clinic. He was fired and he filed a lawsuit. The court held that religious organizations have the right to "define themselves and their religious message" and may fire workers for violating that right.[6]

Disparate Treatment and Disparate Impact It would seem that the motives or intentions of the employer might enter into the determination of whether discrimination has occurred—but they do not. The outcome of the employer's actions, not the intent, is considered by the regulatory agencies or courts when deciding whether or not illegal discrimination has occurred. Two concepts used to activate this principle are disparate treatment and disparate impact.

Disparate treatment occurs when members of a protected class are treated differently from others. For example, if female applicants must take a special skills test not given to male applicants, then disparate treatment may be occur-

Bona fide occupational qualification (BFOQ) Characteristic providing a legitimate reason why an employer can exclude persons on otherwise illegal bases of consideration.

Disparate treatment Occurs when members of a protected class are treated differently from others.

ring. If disparate treatment has occurred, the courts generally have indicated that intentional discrimination exists.

Disparate impact occurs when members of a protected class are substantially under-represented as a result of employment decisions that work to their disadvantage. The landmark case that established the importance of disparate impact as a legal foundation of EEO law is *Griggs v. Duke Power* (1971).[7] The decision of the U.S. Supreme Court established two major points:

1. It is not enough to show a lack of discriminatory intent if the employment tool results in a disparate impact that discriminates against one group more than another or continues a past pattern of discrimination.
2. The employer has the burden of proving that an employment requirement is directly job related as a "business necessity." Consequently, the intelligence test and high school diploma requirements of Duke Power were ruled not to be related to the job.

This and a number of other decisions make it clear that employers covered by Title VII must be able to document through statistical analyses that disparate treatment and disparate impact have not occurred. How to make these calculations is discussed later in this chapter.

Burden of Proof Another legal issue that arises when discrimination is alleged is the determination of which party has the **burden of proof,** which is what individuals who file suit against employers must prove in order to establish that illegal discrimination has occurred. Building on an earlier case, *McDonnell Douglas v. Green,* the U.S. Supreme Court in *Reeves v. Sanderson Plumbing Products* ruled that circumstantial evidence can shift the burden of proof to the employer.[8]

Based on the evolution of court decisions, current laws and regulations state that the plaintiff charging discrimination: (1) must be a *protected-class member,* and (2) must prove that *disparate impact* or *disparate treatment* existed. Once a court rules that a *prima facie* (preliminary) case has been made, the burden of proof shifts to the employer. The employer then must show that the bases for making employment-related decisions were specifically job related and consistent with considerations of business necessity.

Retaliation Employers are prohibited by EEO laws from retaliating against individuals who file discrimination charges. **Retaliation** occurs when employers take punitive actions against individuals who exercise their legal rights. For example, a construction company was ruled to have engaged in retaliation when an employee who filed a discrimination complaint had work hours reduced, resulting in a loss of pay, and no other employees' work hours were reduced.[9]

Civil Rights Act of 1991

The Civil Rights Act of 1991 requires employers to show that an employment practice is *job related for the position* and is consistent with *business necessity.* The act clarifies that the plaintiffs bringing the discrimination charges must identify the particular employer practice being challenged and must show only that protected-class status played *some role.* For employers, this requirement means that an individual's race, color, religion, sex, or national origin *must play no role* in their employment practices.

Compensatory/Punitive Damages and Jury Trials One major impact of the 1991 act is that it allows people who have been targets of intentional dis-

Disparate impact
Occurs when members of a protected class are substantially under-represented as a result of employment decisions that work to their disadvantage.

Burden of proof
What individuals who file suit against employers must prove in order to establish that illegal discrimination has occurred.

Retaliation Punitive actions taken by employers against individuals who exercise their legal rights.

crimination based on sex, religion, or disability to receive both compensatory and punitive damages. Compensatory damages typically include payments for emotional pain and suffering, loss of enjoyment of life, mental anguish, or inconvenience. However, limits were set on the amount of compensatory and punitive damages. Additionally, the 1991 act allows jury trials to determine the liability for and the amount of compensatory and punitive damages, subject to the caps just mentioned, instead of requiring those issues to be decided by judges.

Other Provisions The Civil Rights Act of 1991 also addressed other issues. Briefly, some of the key issues and the provisions of the act are as follows:

- *Race norming:* The act prohibited adjusting employment test scores or using alternative scoring mechanisms, depending on the race or gender of test takers. The concern addressed by this provision is the use of different passing or cutoff scores for members of protected classes.
- *International employees:* The act extended coverage of U.S. EEO laws to U.S. citizens working abroad, except where local laws or customs conflict.
- *Government employee rights:* Congress extended EEO law coverage to employees of the Senate, presidential appointees, and previously excluded state government employees.

Executive Orders 11246, 11375, and 11478

The changing laws over the last 30 years have forced employers to address additional areas of potential discrimination. Several acts and regulations apply specifically to government contractors. These acts and regulations specify a minimum number of employees and size of government contracts. The requirements primarily come from federal Executive Orders 11246, 11375, and 11478. Many states have similar requirements for firms with state government contracts.

Numerous executive orders require that employers holding federal government contracts not discriminate on the basis of race, color, religion, national origin, or sex. An *Executive Order* is issued by the President of the United States to provide direction to government departments on a specific area. The Office of Federal Contract Compliance Programs (OFCCP) in the U.S. Department of Labor has responsibility for enforcing nondiscrimination in government contracts.

Laws on Sex/Gender Discrimination

A number of laws and regulations address discrimination on the bases of sex/gender. Historically, women experienced employment discrimination in a variety of ways. The inclusion of sex as a basis for protected-class status in Title VII of the 1964 Civil Rights Act has led to various areas of protection for women. It also has led to lawsuits, including the one against Wal-Mart discussed in the HR Perspective.

Pregnancy Discrimination The Pregnancy Discrimination Act (PDA) of 1978 requires that any employer with 15 or more employees treat maternity leave the same as other personal or medical leaves. Closely related to the PDA is the Family and Medical Leave Act (FMLA) of 1993, which requires that individuals be given up to 12 weeks of family leave without pay and also requires that those taking family leave be allowed to return to jobs (see Chapter 14 for details). The FMLA applies to both men and women.

Wal-Mart and Gender Discrimination Complaints

A class action lawsuit against retail giant Wal-Mart has alleged that women are paid less than men in similar jobs and that they are promoted less frequently than men. A class action lawsuit does not mean Wal-Mart is guilty of gender discrimination, but means that the claims filed are similar enough that they should be considered together. Class action lawsuits usually mean an extensive and time-consuming trial. As a result, class action suits seldom reach trial, but frequently are settled outside the courtroom.

The plaintiffs allege that Wal-Mart women get fewer promotions and they point out that 65% of hourly employees are women, but only 33% of managers are female. They further argue that women are paid less than men for similar jobs. This claim is based on a study by a labor economist hired by the plaintiffs, but Wal-Mart states that the study is flawed. Finally, the lawsuit charges that women are subject to sexist actions and gender stereotyping. Several examples of such situations are presented in the lawsuit to back this claim.

Wal-Mart is frequently praised as an innovative, growing company, but has in recent years struggled with complaints from employees that they are overworked and underpaid. The company recently has taken steps to change employment practices. It has restructured pay scales and added nationwide job posting systems. Further, executives will forego a bonus if they fail to meet specific employment diversity goals.

The plaintiffs and their lawyers must prove that the company knew about the problems and exhibited malice or reckless disregard in dealing with them. Plaintiff lawyers suggested that even if the company had no formal policy of gender discrimination, the corporate culture has cultivated differences in pay between men and women and restricted promotions for women. How these claims will be resolved will be determined through legal actions.[10]

Courts have generally ruled that the PDA requires employers to treat pregnant employees the same as non-pregnant employees with similar abilities or inabilities. Therefore, in one case, an employer was ruled to have acted properly when terminating a pregnant employee for excessive absenteeism due to pregnancy-related illnesses, because the employee was not treated differently from other employees with absenteeism problems.[11] However, in another case, a dental employee who was fired five days after she told her manager that she was pregnant was awarded $18,460 by a court decision that ruled that her employer violated the PDA.[12]

Two other areas somewhat related to pregnancy and motherhood have also been subjects of legal and regulatory action. The U.S. Equal Employment Opportunity Commission has ruled that denial of health insurance coverage for prescription contraceptives under employer-provided health plans violates the PDA. This ruling means that employers who have changed their health insurance plans to offer contraceptive coverage may face increases in benefit costs.

A number of states have passed laws that guarantee breast-feeding rights at work for new mothers. Attempts to enact such legislation at the federal level have not yet succeeded.

Pregnancy discrimination complaints nationwide rose about 10% in a recent year to 4,700. That is part of a long-term trend in which the number of complaints has risen 40% in the last decade.[13] In contrast, the number of job discrimination complaints in general edged downward during the same year. The

EEOC said over 80,000 complaints were filed, 35% for racial discrimination, 30% for gender discrimination, and 24% for age discrimination.[14]

Equal Pay and Pay Equity The Equal Pay Act of 1963 requires employers to pay similar wage rates for similar work without regard to gender. A *common core of tasks* must be similar, but tasks performed only intermittently or infrequently do not make jobs different enough to justify significantly different wages. Differences in pay may be allowed because of: (1) differences in seniority, (2) differences in performance, (3) differences in quality and/or quantity of production, and (4) factors other than sex, such as skill, effort, and working conditions. For example, a university was found to have violated the Equal Pay Act by paying a female professor a starting salary lower than salaries paid to male professors with similar responsibilities. In fact, the court found that the woman professor taught larger classes and had more total students than some of the male faculty members.[15]

Pay equity Idea that pay for jobs requiring comparable levels of knowledge, skill, and ability should be similar, even if actual duties differ significantly.

Pay equity is the idea that the pay for jobs requiring comparable levels of knowledge, skill, and ability should be similar, even if actual duties differ significantly. This theory has also been called *comparable worth* in earlier cases. But except where state laws have mandated pay equity for public-sector employees, U.S. federal courts generally have ruled that the existence of pay differences between jobs held by women and jobs held by men is not sufficient to prove that illegal discrimination has occurred.

A major reason for the development of the pay equity idea is the continuing gap between the earnings of women and men. For instance, in 1980, the average annual pay of full-time women workers was 60% of that of full-time men workers. By 2003, the reported rate of 76% showed some progress. More in-depth data and research studies have shown that when differences between the education, experience, and time at work of men and women are considered, women earn over 90% of what comparable male workers earn.[16]

Sexual Harassment The Equal Employment Opportunity Commission has issued guidelines designed to curtail sexual harassment. **Sexual harassment** refers to actions that are sexually directed, are unwanted, and subject the worker to adverse employment conditions or create a hostile work environment. Sexual harassment can occur between a boss and a subordinate, among co-workers, and when non-employees have business contacts with employees.

Sexual harassment Actions that are sexually directed, are unwanted, and subject the worker to adverse employment conditions or create a hostile work environment.

According to EEOC statistics, more than 90% of the sexual harassment charges filed involve harassment of women by men. However, some sexual harassment cases have been filed by men against women managers and supervisors, and for same-sex harassment. An in-depth discussion of prevention and investigation of sexual harassment complaints appears in Chapter 5.

Americans with Disabilities Act (ADA)

The passage of the Americans with Disabilities Act (ADA) in 1990 expanded the scope and impact of laws and regulations on discrimination against individuals with disabilities. The ADA affects more than just employment matters, as Figure 4-3 shows. All employers with 15 or more employees are covered by the provisions of the ADA, which are enforced by the EEOC, and the act applies to private employers, employment agencies, and labor unions. State government employees are not covered by the ADA, which means that they cannot sue in federal courts for redress and damages. However, they may still bring suits under state laws in state courts.

LOGGING ON...

Americans with Disabilities Act
This is the U.S. Department of Justice's home page on the Americans with Disabilities Act (ADA).
www.ada.gov

	Figure 4-3		*Major Sections of the Americans with Disabilities Act*		
Title I:	**Title II:**	**Title III:**	**Title IV:**	**Title V:**
Employment Provisions	**Public Participation and Service**	**Public Access**	**Telecommunications**	**Administration and Enforcement**
Prohibits employment-related discrimination against persons with disabilities	Prohibits discrimination related to participation of disabled persons in government programs and for public transportation	Ensures accessibility of public and commercial facilities	Requires provision of telecommunications capabilities and television closed captions for persons with hearing and speech disabilities	Describes administrative and enforcement provisions and lists who is not covered by ADA

Disabled person
Someone who has a physical or mental impairment that substantially limits life activities, who has a record of such an impairment, or who is regarded as having such an impairment.

Who Is Disabled? As defined by the ADA, a **disabled person** is someone who has a physical or mental impairment that substantially limits that person in some major life activities, who has a record of such an impairment, or who is regarded as having such an impairment. In spite of the EEOC guidelines, some confusion still remains as to who is disabled. Court decisions have found individuals who have high blood pressure, epilepsy, allergies, obesity, and color blindness to be disabled. For example, in another high-profile case, the U.S. Supreme Court decided that professional golfer Casey Martin, who suffers from a severe circulatory disorder in his legs, must be allowed to ride a golf cart while competing in PGA tournaments. The Supreme Court has said that the means used to mitigate an individual's physical or mental impairments, such as corrective eyeglasses or controlling medications, must be considered when determining if someone is disabled as defined by the ADA.

THOMSON

WEST

ADA COVERED DISABILITIES
Identifies disabilities covered by ADA and court decisions.
Custom Search:
☑ ANALYSIS
Exact Phrase: What is a disability

Mental Disabilities A growing area of concern under the ADA is individuals with mental disabilities. A mental illness is often more difficult to diagnose than a physical disability. Employers must be careful when considering "emotional" or "mental health" factors such as depression in employment-related decisions. They must not stereotype individuals with mental disabilities, but base their evaluations on sound medical information.[17]

Life-Threatening Illnesses In recent years, the types of disabilities covered by various local, state, and federal acts prohibiting discrimination have been expanded. One of the most feared contagious diseases is acquired immunodeficiency syndrome (AIDS). A U.S. Supreme Court decision ruled that individuals infected with human immunodeficiency virus (HIV), not just those with AIDS, have a disability covered by the ADA.[18]

Essential job functions Fundamental duties of a job.

ADA and Job Requirements The ADA contains a number of specific requirements that deal with employment of individuals with disabilities. Discrimination is prohibited against individuals with disabilities who can perform the **essential job functions**—the fundamental job duties—of the employment positions that those individuals hold or desire. These functions do not include marginal functions of the position. For a qualified person with a disability, an employer must make a **reasonable accommodation,** which is a modification or adjustment to a job or work environment that gives that individual an equal employment opportunity. EEOC guidelines encourage employers and individuals to work together to determine what are appropriate reasonable accommodations, rather than employers alone making those judgments.

Reasonable accommodation is restricted to actions that do not place an undue hardship on an employer. An **undue hardship** is a significant difficulty or expense imposed on an employer in making an accommodation for individuals with disabilities. The ADA offers only general guidelines in determining when an accommodation becomes unreasonable and places undue hardship on an employer. Most accommodation expenditures by employers have been relatively modest. A survey of British and American firms found that most employer changes were easy to make and inexpensive. The exception to that was making information available for people with visual, learning, or hearing impairments.[19]

For some businesses, overtime is a necessity. But for some employees with disabilities, overtime may be not only a nuisance but difficult. It is not entirely clear when the ADA requires employers to allow people with disabilities to avoid overtime. In general, the inability to work overtime is *not* a substantial limitation on the "major life activity" of working and is therefore not a disability.[20]

Further, a U.S. Supreme Court case found that an employee who had been fired for drug addiction was not entitled to be rehired, as his addiction was not a disability. The ADA does not protect current users of illegal drugs, but it does protect those who are recovering addicts.[21]

ADA Restrictions and Medical Information The ADA contains restrictions on obtaining and retaining medically related information on applicants and employees. Restrictions include prohibiting employers from rejecting an individual because of a disability and from asking job applicants any question about current or past medical history until a conditional job offer is made. The HR Practice discusses how employment applications and interview questions should be handled to comply with the ADA restrictions. Also, the ADA prohibits the use of pre-employment medical exams, except for drug tests, until a job has been conditionally offered. An additional requirement of the ADA is that all medical information be maintained in files separated from the general personnel files. The medical files must have identified security procedures, and limited access procedures must be identified.

Age Discrimination in Employment Act (ADEA)

The Age Discrimination in Employment Act (ADEA) of 1967, amended in 1978 and 1986, prohibits discrimination in terms, conditions, or privileges of employment against all individuals age 40 or older working for employers having 20 or more workers. However, the U.S. Supreme Court has ruled that state employees may not sue state government employers in federal courts because the ADEA is a federal law.

The act does not apply if age is a job-related occupational qualification. Age discrimination does not apply when an individual is disciplined or discharged for good cause, such as poor job performance. But targeting older workers for replacement is illegal. One case involving a supermarket found age discrimination

LOGGING ON...

Administration on Aging
This site provides information on aging and age discrimination from government agencies, associations, and organizations.
www.aoa.dhhs.gov

ADA and the Employment Process

The ADA prohibits asking job applicants any questions about past or current medical or health history until a conditional job offer is made, with the condition often being passing a physical exam or a medical background check. Any physical or medical requirements must be related to the specific job for which the applicant is being considered. Two specific HR areas that are affected are employment applications and interviews.

On employment applications, medical-related questions should be limited. Questions about past workers' compensation claims or injuries violate the ADA restrictions. Other medical history questions also should not be included on the initial application form. It is recommended that a question such as the following be used instead:

Can you perform the essential functions of the job for which you are applying with or without accommodation?

Court decisions have made it clear that employers are not expected to be clairvoyant and guess at a need for accommodation. By asking this question, employers can obtain useful information to determine whether or even what reasonable accommodations can be made. They are not required to make the specific accommodations requested by applicants, but must only make a reasonable effort to develop accommodations.

Several examples of questions concerning disabilities that should and should not be asked in employment interviews are shown in the chart below. As is evident, the questions that should be asked are specifically related to the job and address essential job functions. If an applicant reveals a medical condition or disability in answering interview questions, any use of that information must be related to the job and linked to identifying appropriate possible reasonable accommodations.

⊗ DO NOT ASK	✓ DO ASK
◆ Do you have any physical or mental disabilities? ◆ Why are you using crutches, and how did you become injured? ◆ How many times were you absent due to illness in the past two years? ◆ Have you been treated for any of the following medical conditions? ◆ Have you ever filed for or collected workers' compensation?	◆ How would you perform the essential tasks of the job for which you have applied? ◆ If hired, which tasks outlined in the job description that you reviewed would be more enjoyable and most difficult? ◆ Describe your attendance record on your last job. ◆ Describe any problems you would have reaching the top of a six-foot filing cabinet. ◆ What did your prior job duties consist of, and which ones were the most challenging?

when a district manager fired or demoted some older managers and replaced them with younger, less experienced individuals. Age-bias lawsuits tend to have larger-than-average settlements; however, plaintiffs in these suits are less likely to win than are plaintiffs in other EEO suits.

The Supreme Court ruled that while older workers can sue if they are not treated the same as younger workers, the reverse is *not* true. Two hundred General Dynamics employees had sued because they were too young to get benefits offered to colleagues age 50 and over. The workers (who were all in their 40s) argued reverse discrimination and lost.[22]

Older Workers Benefit Protection Act (OWBPA) This law is an amendment to the ADEA and is aimed at protecting employees when they sign liability waivers for age discrimination in exchange for severance packages. For example, an early retirement package that includes a waiver stating the employee will not sue for age discrimination if he or she takes the money for early retirement must:

♦ Include a written, clearly understood agreement
♦ Offer something of value beyond what the employee will receive without the package
♦ Advise the employee to consult an attorney
♦ Allow the employee at least 21 days to consider the offer
♦ Allow the employee 7 days to revoke the agreement after signing it[23]

Allstate Insurance was found guilty of age discrimination against 6,200 agents when the EEOC determined that its reorganization plan "Preparing for the Future" impacted agents age 40 and older. The plan was designed to convert agents, who were considered employees, to independent contractors, who were not. One agent said that the intent of the company was to avoid benefits costs associated with the older agents. Over 94% of the agents terminated in the Allstate plan were age 40 or older. The EEOC felt that the agents were employees even though Allstate called them independent contractors.[24]

Immigration Reform and Control Acts (IRCA)

Race is often a factor in discrimination based on national origin. The Immigration Reform and Control Acts (IRCA) and later revisions made it illegal for an employer to discriminate in recruiting, hiring, disciplining, or terminating employees based on an individual's national origin or citizenship. At the same time, the IRCA requires that employers who knowingly hire illegal aliens be penalized. Employers must ask for proof of identity, such as a driver's license with a picture, Social Security card, birth certificate, or immigration permit as part of completing the required I-9 form. This form must be completed by all new employees within 72 hours.

Revisions to the IRCA changed some of the restrictions on the entry of immigrants to work in U.S. organizations, particularly organizations with high-technology and other "scarce skill" areas. More immigrants were allowed legal entry, and categories for entry visas were revised.[25]

The number of Hispanic illegals who come across the southern border of the U.S. raises another immigration issue for employers. The U.S. has a population of 288 million. About 38 million are Hispanics, and an estimated 30% of those are thought to be immigrants—some legal and some illegal.[26] The law can present some real problems for an employer in deciding who is legal and who is not. For example, the government fined Wal-Mart $60,000 for requiring too much information (more verification than was required by law) to prove prospective hires were citizens. Later, in a series of raids, federal agents rounded up 250 illegal immigrants in 21 states from contractors who were cleaning stores for Wal-Mart. But anti-discrimination sections of the immigrant code had severely limited Wal-Mart's ability to investigate an individual's legal status.[27]

Other Discrimination Laws and Regulations

Several other types of discrimination have been identified as illegal. A number of issues in the area of religious discrimination require additional attention by employers.

Religious Discrimination Title VII of the Civil Rights Act identifies discrimination on the basis of religion as illegal. However, religious schools and institutions can use religion as a bona fide occupational qualification for employment practices on a limited scale. Also, the employers must make *reasonable accommodation* efforts regarding an employee's religious beliefs.

A major guide in this area was established by the U.S. Supreme Court in *TWA v. Hardison.* In this case, the Supreme Court ruled that an employer is required to make reasonable accommodation for an employee's religious beliefs. Because TWA had done so, the ruling denied the plaintiff's discrimination charges.[28] In a more recent case, a Muslim plumber was fired for leaving his job early on Fridays to attend Islamic prayer services. The individual was awarded more than $100,000 for being discriminated against for his religion, especially because his employer made no efforts to make reasonable accommodation.[29]

Genetic Bias Regulations Somewhat related to medical disabilities is the emerging area of workplace genetic bias. As medical research has revealed the human genome, medical tests have been developed that can identify an individual's genetic markers for various diseases. Whether these tests should be used and how they are used raise ethical issues.

Employers that use genetic screening tests do so for two primary reasons. Some employers use genetic testing to make workers aware of genetic problems that may exist, so that medical treatment can begin. Others use genetic testing to terminate employees who may make extensive use of health insurance benefits and thus raise the benefits costs and utilization rates of the employer. A major railroad company, Burlington Northern Santa Fe, had to publicly apologize to employees for secretly testing to determine if they were genetically predisposed to carpal tunnel syndrome. Several statutes potentially provide protection against genetic discrimination.[30]

Appearance and Weight Discrimination Several EEO cases have been filed concerning the physical appearance of employees. Court decisions consistently have allowed employers to set dress codes as long as they are applied uniformly. For example, establishing a dress code for women but not for men has been ruled discriminatory. Also, employers should be cautious when enforcing dress standards for women employees who are members of certain religions that prescribe appropriate and inappropriate dress and appearance standards. Some individuals have brought cases of employment discrimination based on height or weight. The crucial factor that employers must consider is that any weight or height requirements must be related to the job, such as when excess weight would hamper an individual's job performance.[31]

Cases also have addressed the issues of beards, mustaches, and hair length and style. African American men, who are more likely than white men to suffer from a skin disease that is worsened by shaving, have filed suits challenging policies prohibiting beards or long sideburns. Generally, courts have ruled for employers in such cases, except where certain religious standards expect men to have beards and facial hair.

Sexual Orientation Recent battles in a number of states and communities illustrate the depth of emotions that accompany discussions of "gay rights." Some states and cities have passed laws prohibiting discrimination based on sexual orientation or lifestyle. Even the issue of benefits coverage for "domestic partners," whether heterosexual or homosexual, has been the subject of state and city legislation. No federal laws of a similar nature have been passed. Whether gays and lesbians have rights under the equal protection amendment to the U.S. Constitution has not been decided by the U.S. Supreme Court.

Military Status The employment rights of military veterans and reservists have been addressed in several laws. The two most important laws are the Vietnam Era Veterans Readjustment Assistance Act of 1974 and the Uniformed Services Employment and Reemployment Rights Act (USERRA) of 1994. Under the latter, employees are required to notify their employers of military service obligations. Employers must give employees serving in the military leaves of absence, and those employees have re-employment rights for up to five years. Other provisions protect the right to benefits of employees called to military duty.[32]

With the increasing use of reserves and National Guard troops abroad, the provisions of USERRA have had more impact on employers. This act does not require employers to pay employees while they are on military leave, but many do provide some compensation, often a differential. Many requirements regarding benefits, disabilities, and re-employment are covered in the act as well.

Seniority and Discrimination Conflicts between EEO regulations and organizational practices giving preference to employees on the basis of seniority represent another area of regulation. Employers, especially those with union contracts, frequently make layoff, promotion, and internal transfer decisions by giving employees with longer service first consideration. However, the use of seniority often means disparate impact on protected-class members, who may be the workers most recently hired. The result of this system is that protected-class members who have obtained jobs through an affirmative action program are at a disadvantage because of their low levels of seniority. They may find themselves "last hired, first fired" or "last hired, last promoted." In most cases, the courts have held that a valid seniority system does not violate rights based on protected-class status. However, in a few cases, gender, racial, disability, or age considerations have been given precedence over seniority.

Conviction and Arrest Records Court decisions have consistently ruled that using records of arrests, rather than records of convictions, has a disparate impact on some racial and ethnic minority groups protected by Title VII. An arrest, unlike a conviction, does not show guilt. Statistics indicate that in some geographic areas, the arrest rates are higher for members of some minority groups than for others.

Generally, courts have held that conviction records may be used in determining employability if the offense is job related. For example, a bank could use an applicant's conviction for embezzlement as a valid basis for rejection. Some courts have held that only job-related convictions occurring within the most recent five to seven years may be considered. Consequently, employers inquiring about convictions often add a phrase such as "indication of a conviction will not be an absolute bar to employment."[33]

Subject of Inquiry	It May Not Be Discriminatory to Inquire About . . .	It May Be Discriminatory to Inquire About . . .
1. Name	a. Whether applicant has ever worked under a different name	a. The original name of applicant whose name has been legally changed b. The ethnic association of applicant's name
2. Age	a. If applicant is over the age of 18 b. If applicant is under the age of 18 or 21 if that information is job related (e.g., for selling liquor in a retail store)	a. Date of birth b. Date of high school graduation
3. Residence	a. Applicant's place of residence b. Alternative contact information	a. Previous addresses b. Birthplace of applicant or applicant's parents c. Length lived at current and previous addresses
4. Race or Color		a. Applicant's race or color of applicant's skin
5. National Origin and Ancestry		a. Applicant's lineage, ancestry, national origin, parentage, or nationality b. Nationality of applicant's parents or spouse
6. Sex and Family Composition		a. Sex of applicant b. Marital status of applicant c. Dependents of applicants or child-care arrangements d. Whom to contact in case of emergency
7. Creed or Religion		a. Applicant's religious affiliation b. Applicant's church, parish, mosque, or synagogue c. Holidays observed by applicant
8. Citizenship	a. Whether the applicant is a U.S. citizen or has a current permit/visa to work in U.S.	a. Whether applicant is a citizen of a country other than the U.S. b. Date of citizenship
9. Language	a. Language applicant speaks and/or writes fluently, if job related	a. Applicant's native tongue b. Language used at home

(Continued on next page.)

Pre-employment Inquiries

Figure 4-4 lists pre-employment inquiries and identifies whether they may or may not be discriminatory. The pre-employment inquiries labeled "may be discriminatory" have been so designated because of findings in a variety of court cases. Those labeled "may not be discriminatory" are legal, but only if they reflect a business necessity or are job related. Once an employer tells an applicant

Figure 4-4 Guidelines to Lawful and Unlawful Pre-employment Inquiries

Subject of Inquiry	It May Not Be Discriminatory to Inquire About . . .	It May Be Discriminatory to Inquire About . . .
10. References	a. Names of persons willing to provide professional and/or character references for applicant b. Previous work contacts	a. Name of applicant's religious leader b. Political affiliation and contacts
11. Relatives	a. Names of relatives already employed by the employer	a. Name and/or address of any relative of applicant b. Whom to contact in case of emergency
12. Organizations	a. Applicant's membership in any professional, service, or trade organization	a. All clubs or social organizations to which applicant belongs
13. Arrest Record and Convictions	a. Convictions, if related to job performance (disclaimer should accompany)	a. Number and kinds of arrests b. Convictions, unless related to job requirements and performance
14. Photographs		a. Photographs with application, with resume, or before hiring
15. Height and Weight		a. Any inquiry into height and weight of applicant, except where a BFOQ exists
16. Physical Limitations	a. Whether applicant has the ability to perform job-related functions with or without accommodation	a. The nature or severity of an illness or physical condition b. Whether applicant has ever filed a workers' compensation claim c. Any recent or past operations, treatments, or surgeries and dates
17. Education	a. Training applicant has received, if related to the job b. Highest level of education applicant has attained, if validated that having certain educational background (e.g., high school diploma or college degree) is needed to perform the specific job	a. Date of high school graduation
18. Military	a. Branch of the military applicant served in and ranks attained b. Type of education or training received in military	a. Military discharge details b. Military service records
19. Financial Status		a. Applicant's debts or assets b. Garnishments

he or she is hired (the "point of hire"), inquiries that were prohibited earlier may be made. After hiring, medical examination forms, group insurance cards, and other enrollment cards containing inquiries related directly or indirectly to sex, age, or other bases may be requested.

EEO Enforcement

Government agencies at several levels can investigate illegal discriminatory practices. At the federal level, the two most prominent agencies are the Equal Employment Opportunity Commission and the Office of Federal Contract Compliance Programs.

Equal Employment Opportunity Commission (EEOC)

The EEOC has enforcement authority for charges brought under a number of federal laws. Further, the EEOC issues policy guidances on many topics influencing EEO. Although the policy statements are not "law," they are "persuasive authority" in most cases.

Office of Federal Contract Compliance Programs (OFCCP)

While the EEOC is an independent agency, the OFCCP is part of the U.S. Department of Labor and ensures that federal contractors and subcontractors use non-discriminatory practices. A major thrust of OFCCP efforts is to require that covered employers take affirmative action to counter prior discriminatory practices.

State and Local Agencies

In addition to federal laws and orders, many states and municipalities have passed their own laws prohibiting discrimination on a variety of bases, and state and local enforcement bodies have been established. Compared with federal laws, state and local laws sometimes provide greater remedies, require different actions, or prohibit discrimination in more areas.

Evolving Nature of EEO Enforcement

Enforcement of EEO laws and regulations must be seen as a work in progress that is inconsistent and confusing at times. The court system is left to resolve the disputes and issue interpretations of the laws. The courts, especially the lower courts, have issued conflicting rulings and interpretations. The ultimate interpretation often has rested on decisions by the U.S. Supreme Court, although those rulings, too, have been interpreted differently.

Uniform Guidelines on Employee Selection Procedures

The 1978 Uniform Guidelines on Employee Selection Procedures are used by the U.S. EEOC, the U.S. Department of Labor's OFCCP, the U.S. Department of Justice, and the U.S. Office of Personnel Management. These guidelines attempt to explain how an employer should deal with hiring, retention, promotion, transfer, demotion, dismissal, and referral. Under the uniform guidelines, if sued, employers can choose one of two routes to prove they are not illegally discriminating against employees: no disparate impact, and job-related validity.

"No Disparate Impact" Approach

Generally, the most important issue regarding discrimination in organizations is the *effect* of employment policies and procedures, regardless of the *intent* of the employer. *Disparate impact* occurs when protected-class members are substantially under-represented in employment decisions. Under the guidelines, dis-

parate impact is determined with the **4/5ths rule.** If the selection rate for a protected group is less than 80% (4/5ths) of the selection rate for the majority group or less than 80% of the majority group's representation in the relevant labor market, discrimination exists. Thus, the guidelines have attempted to define discrimination in statistical terms. Disparate impact should be checked by employers both internally and externally.

Internal Metrics for Disparate Impact This compares the results of employer actions received by protected-class members with those received by non-protected-class members. HR activities that can be checked most frequently for internal disparate impact include the following:

♦ Selection of candidates for interviews from those recruited
♦ Pass rates for various selection tests
♦ Performance appraisal ratings as they affect pay increases
♦ Promotions, demotions, and terminations
♦ Identification of individuals for layoffs

Figure 4-5 calculates the internal disparate impact for men and women who were interviewed for jobs at a firm. In this case, the figure indicates that the selection process does have a disparate impact internally. The practical meaning of these calculations is that statistically, women have a lesser chance of being selected for jobs than men do, so much so that illegal discrimination exists unless the firm can demonstrate that its selection activities are specifically job related.

External Metrics for Disparate Impact Employers can check for disparate impact externally by comparing the percentage of protected-class members in their workforces with the percentage of protected-class members in the relevant labor markets. The relevant labor markets consist of the areas where the firm recruits workers, not just where those employed live. External comparisons can also consider the percentage of protected-class members who are recruited and who apply for jobs, to ensure that the employer has drawn a "representative sample" from the relevant labor markets. Although employers are not required to maintain exact proportionate equality, they must be "close." Courts have applied statistical analyses to determine if any disparities that exist are too high.

Figure 4-6 illustrates external disparate impact using impact analyses for a sample metropolitan area, Valleyville. Assume that a firm in that area, Acme

Figure 4-5	*Internal Disparate Impact Example*

Female applicants: 25% were selected for jobs
Male applicants: 45% were selected for jobs

Disparate Impact Determination

♦ Male selection rate of 45% × 4/5 (80%) = 36%
♦ Female selection rate = 25%
Disparate impact exists because the female selection rate is less than 4/5 of the male selection rate.

Figure 4-6

External Disparate Impact Example

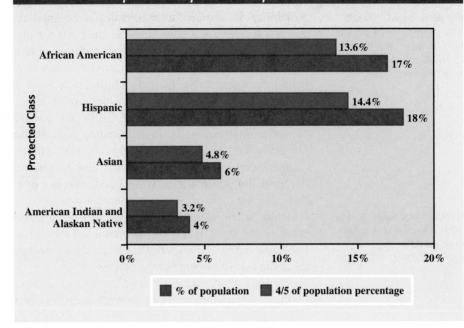

Company, has 500 employees, including 50 African Americans and 75 Hispanics. To determine if the company has external disparate impact, it is possible to make the following comparisons:

Protected Class	% of Total Employees at Acme Company	4/5 of Group in the Population (from Figure 4-6)	Disparate Impact?
African American	10% (50/500)	13.6%	Yes (10% <13.6%)
Hispanic	15% (75/500)	14.4%	No (15% >14.4%)

At Acme, external disparate impact exists for African Americans because the company employs fewer of them than the 4/5 threshold of 13.6%. However, because Acme has more Hispanic employees than the 4/5 threshold of 14.4%, there is no disparate impact for this group.

Statistical comparisons for determining disparate impact may use more complex methods.[34] HR professionals need to know how to do such calculations because external disparate impact must be computed and reported in affirmative action plans that government contractors submit to government agencies.

Job-Related Validation Approach

Under the job-related validation approach, virtually every factor used to make employment-related decisions—recruiting, selection, promotion, termination, discipline, and performance appraisal—must be shown to be job related. Hence, the concept of validity affects many of the common tools used to make HR decisions.

Validity is simply the extent to which a test actually measures what it says it measures. The concept relates to inferences made from tests. For instance, it may be valid to assume that performance on a mechanical knowledge test may predict

Validity Extent to which a test actually measures what it says it measures.

performance of a machinist in a manufacturing plant. However, it is probably invalid to assume that the same test scores indicate general intelligence or promotability for a manufacturing sales representative. An **employment "test"** is any employment procedure used as the basis for making an employment-related decision. For instance, for a general intelligence test to be valid, it must actually measure intelligence, not just a person's vocabulary. An employment test that is valid must measure the person's ability to perform the job for which she or he is being hired. For example, R. R. Donnelly & Sons of Lancaster, Pennsylvania, reached agreement with the OFCCP to pay $610,000 to protected-class applicants for unintentionally discriminating against them. The OFCCP found that Donnelly limited minority hires by requiring a high school diploma or its equivalent for certain jobs, without being able to show that a high school education made a valid difference between good and poor employee performance. Thus in this case, the diploma was considered a "test."[35]

Employment "test"
Any employment procedure used as the basis for making an employment-related decision.

Ideally, employment-related tests will be both valid and reliable. **Reliability** refers to the consistency with which a test measures an item. For a test to be reliable, an individual's score should be about the same every time the individual takes the test (allowing for the effects of practice). Unless a test measures a factor consistently (reliably), it is of little value in predicting job performance. Reliability can be measured by several statistical methodologies. The ones used most frequently are test-retest, alternate forms, and internal-consistency estimates. A more detailed methodological discussion is beyond the scope of this text.

Reliability Consistency with which a test measures an item.

VALIDITY AND EQUAL EMPLOYMENT

If a charge of discrimination is brought against an employer on the basis of disparate impact, a *prima facie* case must be established. The employer then must be able to demonstrate that its employment procedures are valid, which means demonstrating that they relate to the job and the requirements of the job. A key element in establishing job relatedness is conducting a *job analysis* to identify the *knowledge, skills, and abilities (KSAs)* and other characteristics needed to perform a job satisfactorily. A detailed analysis of the job provides the foundation for linking the KSAs to job requirements and job performance, as Chapter 6 discusses. Using an invalid instrument to select, place, or promote an employee has never been a good management practice, regardless of its legality.

In one sense, then, current requirements have done management a favor by forcing employers to use job-related employment procedures. There are two types of validation strategies: content validity and criterion-related validity (concurrent and predictive).

Content validity
Validity measured by a logical, non-statistical method to identify the KSAs and other characteristics necessary to perform a job.

Content validity is validity measured by a logical, non-statistical method to identify the KSAs and other characteristics necessary to perform a job. A test has content validity if it reflects an actual sample of the work done on the job in question. For example, an arithmetic test for a retail cashier might contain problems about determining amounts for refunds, purchases, and merchandise exchanges. Content validity is especially useful if the workforce is not large enough to allow other, more statistical approaches.

A content validity study begins with a comprehensive job analysis to identify what is done in the job and what KSAs are used. Then managers, supervisors, and HR specialists must identify the most important KSAs needed for the job.

Finally, a test is devised to determine if individuals have the necessary KSAs. The "test" may be an interview question about previous supervisory experience, or an ability test in which someone types a letter using a word-processing software program, or a knowledge test about consumer credit regulations.

Many practitioners and specialists see content validity as a commonsense standard for validating staffing requirements, and as more realistic than statistical standards. Consequently, content validity approaches are growing in use.

Criterion-Related Validity

Employment tests attempt to predict how well an individual will perform on the job. In measuring **criterion-related validity,** a test is the *predictor,* and the measures for job performance are the *criterion variables.* (See Figure 4-7.) Job analysis determines as exactly as possible what KSAs and behaviors are needed for each task in the job.

In the example in Figure 4-7, people who scored higher on the test also tended to do better on the job (a higher job performance score is better). The exact relationship between a test and performance is calculated by a correlation coefficient. A **correlation coefficient** is an index number giving the relationship between a predictor and a criterion variable. Correlation coefficients can range from -1.0 to $+1.0$. A correlation coefficient of $+.80$ (r^2) indicates that the test is a good predictor, whereas a correlation coefficient of $-.25$ indicates that the test is a poor predictor. Thus, a high correlation suggests that the test can differentiate between the better-performing employees and those with poor performance records.

There are two approaches to criterion-related validity. *Concurrent validity* is an "at-the-same-time" approach, and *predictive validity* is a "before-the-fact" approach. Figure 4-8 depicts both approaches.

Concurrent Validity *Concurrent* means "at the same time." As shown in Figure 4-8, **concurrent validity** is measured when an employer tests current employees and correlates the scores with their performance ratings on such

Criterion-related validity Validity measured by a procedure that uses a test as the predictor of how well an individual will perform on the job.

Correlation coefficient Index number giving the relationship between a predictor and a criterion variable.

Figure 4-7	Test Scores and Job Performance	
Applicant	**Predictor** (test score) (0–100, with 100 high)	**Criterion** (job performance, on a 5-point scale) (1–5 scale, 5 high)
Joe	60	2
Rashad	75	3
Anne	88	4
Sarah	52	1
Fred	80	4
Sally	95	5
Juan	85	4
Linda	58	2
Jeff	78	3
A. J.	65	3

Note: Correlation looks at the relationships between the test scores and job performance of the whole group.

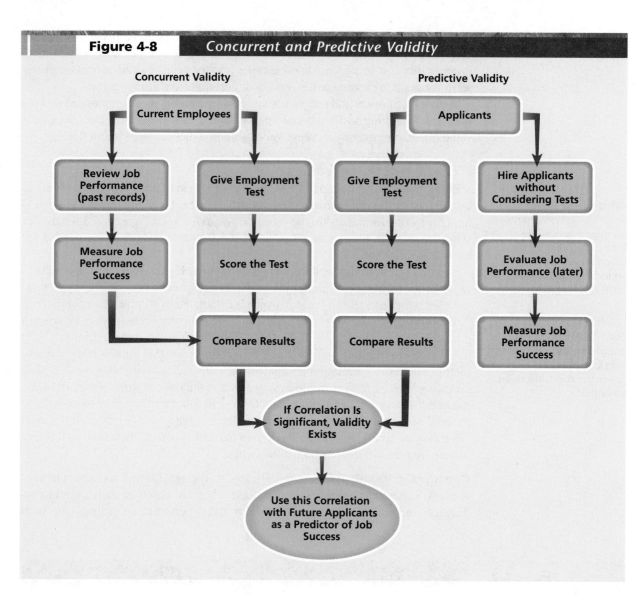

Figure 4-8   Concurrent and Predictive Validity

Concurrent Validity

Predictive Validity

Current Employees

Applicants

Review Job Performance (past records)

Give Employment Test

Give Employment Test

Hire Applicants without Considering Tests

Measure Job Performance Success

Score the Test

Score the Test

Evaluate Job Performance (later)

Compare Results

Compare Results

Measure Job Performance Success

If Correlation Is Significant, Validity Exists

Use this Correlation with Future Applicants as a Predictor of Job Success

Concurrent validity
Measured when an employer tests current employees and correlates the scores with their performance ratings.

Predictive validity
Measured when test results of applicants are compared with subsequent job performance.

measures as accident rates, absenteeism records, and supervisory performance appraisals. This type of validity is called *concurrent* because the job performance measures and the test scores are available at the same time (concurrently), rather than subject to a time lag as in the predictive validity approach.

A drawback of the concurrent validity approach is that employees who have not performed satisfactorily on the job are probably no longer with the firm and therefore cannot be tested, and extremely good employees may have been promoted or may have left the organization for better jobs. Also, any learning that has taken place on the job may influence test scores, presenting another problem.

Predictive Validity To measure **predictive validity,** test results of applicants are compared with their subsequent job performance. (See Figure 4-8.) Success on the job is measured by such factors as absenteeism, accidents, errors, and performance appraisals. If the employees who had one year of experience at the time of hire demonstrate better performance than those without such experience, as calculated by statistical comparisons, then the experience requirement is considered a valid predictor of performance and may be used in hiring future employees.

In the past, the EEOC has preferred predictive validity because it includes the full range of performance and test scores. However, predictive validity requires: (1) a fairly large number of people (usually at least 30), and (2) a time gap between the test and the performance (usually one year). As a result, predictive validity is not useful in many situations. Because of these and other problems, other types of validity are more popular.

■ EEO COMPLIANCE

Employers must comply with a variety of EEO regulations and guidelines. To do so, management should have an EEO policy statement and maintain all of the required EEO-related records.

EEO Policy Statement

It is crucial that all employers have a written EEO policy statement. They should widely communicate this policy by posting it on bulletin boards, printing it in employee handbooks, reproducing it in organizational newsletters, and reinforcing it in training programs. The contents of the policy should clearly state the organizational commitment to equal employment, and incorporate a listing of the appropriate protected classes.

EEO Records

All employers with 15 or more employees are required to keep certain records that can be requested by the Equal Employment Opportunity Commission, the Office of Federal Contract Compliance Programs, or numerous other state and local enforcement agencies. Under various laws, employers are also required to post an "officially approved notice" in a prominent place for employees. This notice states that the employer is an equal opportunity employer and does not discriminate.

Records Retention All employment records must be maintained as required by the EEOC. Such records include application forms and documents concerning hiring, promotion, demotion, transfer, layoff, termination, rates of pay or other terms of compensation, and selection for training and apprenticeship. Even application forms or test papers completed by unsuccessful applicants may be requested. The length of time documents must be kept varies, but generally *three years is recommended as a minimum.* Complete records are necessary to enable an employer to respond should a charge of discrimination be made.

Annual Reporting Form The basic report that must be filed with the EEOC is the annual report form EEO-1. The following employers must file this report:

- All employers with 100 or more employees, except state and local governments
- Subsidiaries of other companies if the total number of combined employees equals 100 or more
- Federal contractors with at least 50 employees and contracts of $50,000 or more
- Financial institutions with at least 50 employees, in which government funds are held or saving bonds are issued

THOMSON
―――★―――™
WEST

EEO-1 REQUIREMENTS
Provides explanation of the EEO-1 form requirements.
Custom Search:
☑ ANALYSIS
Exact Phrase: Employer Information Report Form

Applicant Flow Data Under EEO laws and regulations, employers may be required to show that they do not discriminate in the recruiting and selection of members of protected classes. Because employers are not allowed to collect such data on application blanks and other pre-employment records, the EEOC allows them to do so with a "visual" survey or a separate *applicant-flow form* that is not used in the selection process. The applicant-flow form is filled out voluntarily by the applicant, and the data must be maintained separately from other selection-related materials. Analyses of the data collected in applicant-flow forms may help show whether an employer has underutilized a protected class because of an inadequate flow of applicants from that class, in spite of special efforts to recruit them. Also, these data are reported as part of Affirmative Action Plans that are filed with the OFCCP.

EEOC Compliance Investigation Process

When a discrimination complaint is received by the EEOC or a similar agency, it must be processed. Figure 4-9 shows the employer's responses to an EEO complaint.

Figure 4-9 **Stages in the Employer's Response to an EEO Complaint**

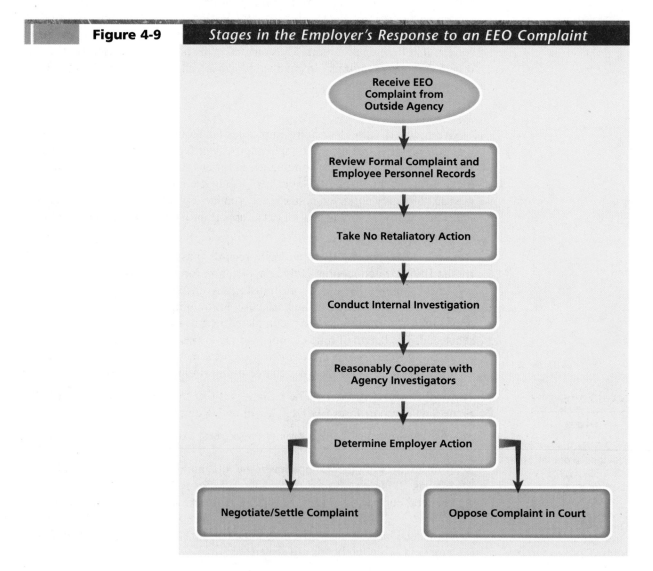

THOMSON
———✦———™
WEST

"Right to Sue"—EEO
Discusses when and how individuals can exercise "right to sue" in EEO cases.
Custom Search:
☑ ANALYSIS
Exact Phrase: Suits by individuals

Mediation Dispute resolution process by which a third party helps negotiators reach a settlement.

To handle a growing number of complaints, the EEOC has instituted a system that groups complaints into three categories: *priority, needing further investigation,* and *immediate dismissal.* If the EEOC decides to pursue a complaint, it uses the process outlined here.

In a typical situation, an EEO complaint goes through several stages before the compliance process is completed. First, the charges are filed by an individual, a group of individuals, or a representative. A charge must be filed within 180 days of when the alleged discriminatory action occurred. Then, the EEOC staff reviews the specifics of the charges to determine if it has *jurisdiction,* that is, to see if the agency is authorized to investigate that type of charge. If the EEOC has jurisdiction, it must serve a notice of the charge on the employer within 10 days after the filing; then the employer is asked to respond. Following the charge notification, the major effort of the EEOC turns to investigating the complaint.

During the investigation, the EEOC may interview the complaints, other employees, company managers, and supervisors. Also, it can request additional records and documents from the employer. If sufficient cause is found to support charges that the alleged discrimination occurred, the next stage involves mediation efforts by the agency and the employer. **Mediation** is a dispute resolution process by which a third party helps negotiators reach a settlement. The EEOC has found that use of mediation has reduced its backlog of EEO complaints and has resulted in faster resolution of complaints. Many employers using mediation said they would use it in future cases.[36]

If the employer agrees that discrimination has occurred and accepts the proposed settlement, then the employer posts a notice of relief within the company and takes the agreed-on actions. If the employer objects to the charge and rejects conciliation, the EEOC can file suit or issue a *right-to-sue letter* to the complainant. The letter notifies the complainant that he or she has 90 days to file a personal suit in federal court.

In the court litigation stage, a legal trial takes place in the appropriate state or federal court. At that point, both sides retain lawyers and rely on the court to render a decision. The Civil Rights Act of 1991 provides for jury trials in most EEO cases. If either party disagrees with the court ruling, either can file appeals with a higher court. The U.S. Supreme Court becomes the ultimate adjudication body.

SUMMARY

- Equal employment is an attempt to level the field of opportunity for all people at work.
- Title VII of the 1964 Civil Rights Act was the first significant equal employment law. The Civil Rights Act of 1991 both altered and expanded on the 1964 provisions.
- Employers may be able to defend their management practices using bona fide occupational qualifications (BFOQ), job relatedness, and business necessity.

- Disparate treatment occurs when members of a protected class are treated differently from others, regardless of discriminatory intent.
- Disparate impact occurs when employment decisions work to the disadvantage of members of protected classes, regardless of discriminatory intent.
- Employers have the burden of proof once a *prima facie* case of discrimination has been shown, and they should take care to avoid re-

taliation against individuals who exercise their rights.

- Several laws on sex/gender discrimination have addressed issues regarding pregnancy discrimination, unequal pay for similar jobs, and sexual harassment.

- The Americans with Disabilities Act (ADA) requires that most employers identify the essential functions of jobs, and that they make reasonable accommodation for individuals with disabilities unless doing so places undue hardship results.

- Age discrimination against persons over age 40 is illegal, according to the Age Discrimination in Employment Act.

- The Immigration Reform and Control Acts identify employment regulations affecting workers from other countries.

- A number of other concerns have been addressed by laws, including discrimination based on religion, genetic bias, appearance and weight, and sexual orientation.

- The Equal Employment Opportunity Commission (EEOC) and the Office of Federal Contract Compliance Programs (OFCCP) are the major federal enforcement agencies in the area of equal employment.

- The 1978 Uniform Guidelines on Employee Selection Procedures are used by enforcement agencies to examine recruiting, hiring, promotion, and many other employment practices. Two alternative compliance approaches are no disparate impact and job-related validation.

- Job-related validation requires that tests measure what they are supposed to measure (validity) in a consistent manner (reliability).

- Disparate impact can be determined through the use of the 4/5 rule.

- One type of validity is content validity, which uses a sample of the actual work to be performed. The two criterion-related validity strategies measure concurrent validity and predictive validity.

- Implementation of equal employment opportunity requires appropriate recordkeeping, such as completing the annual report (EEO-1) and keeping applicant flow data.

REVIEW AND APPLICATION QUESTIONS

1. If your employer asked you to review the decision *not to hire* an African American applicant for a job, what would you need to consider?

2. Explain why the use of content validity is growing. What practical problems do you see with predictive validity?

3. Use the text and the U.S. Department of Justice Web site (*www.usdoj.gov/crt/ada/*) to identify what is reasonable accommodation and how it is determined.

LEARNING REVIEW

To check your knowledge of the chapter, review the following. (Answers after the supplemental case.) For more questions, see the Study Guide.

1. The Civil Rights Act of 1991 emphasized the importance of _____ in establishing validity.
   a. test reliability
   b. affirmative action
   c. business necessity
   d. job descriptions

2. Which of the following rulings has generally been handed down in cases filed under the Pregnancy Discrimination Act?
   a. Employers are not required to accommodate the needs of pregnant employees.
   b. Pregnancy is a disability requiring special accommodation.
   c. Women must be assigned less strenuous tasks during pregnancy.
   d. Employers must treat pregnant employers the same as they treat non-pregnant employees with similar abilities or inabilities.

3. Which of the following groups would be considered disabled persons under the ADA?
   a. current users of illegal drugs
   b. compulsive gamblers
   c. individuals infected with HIV
   d. pregnant women

4. Which of the following statements is true?
   a. Using conviction records in employment decisions has been shown to be discriminatory.
   b. All convictions may be considered when making employment decisions.
   c. In general, only job-related convictions may be considered in employment decisions.
   d. Recent job-related arrests may be considered in employment decisions.

CASE
DIVERSITY IN THREE FORMS

Fortune magazine periodically puts together a list of the best companies for minority employment. The examples that the magazine found notable in several companies are interesting and illustrate different facets of workforce diversity.

Silicon Graphics, a computer workstation manufacturer, faced huge operating loses. Because of the loses, management identified that 1,000 employees, 10% of the workforce, probably would be terminated. The company was very concerned that the downsizing would affect their workforce diversity, so it monitored the layoffs to make certain that no one group of employees was disproportionately hit. This monitoring allowed the company to continue its diversity commitment through the downturn in its business.

SBC Communications of San Antonio, Texas, serves a customer group that is almost 35% minority group members. But, SBC has chosen not to use the representation of minority groups in the *workforce* as the basis for determining how many in each protected class should work in the company for affirmative action purposes. Instead, the firm attempts to mirror the population or customers they serve, a much larger proportion of protected-class people. When an economic slowdown required trimming the number of college graduates hired into the management development program, SBC held the percentage of minority participants steady in order to protect the diversity the firm had worked to build.

Advantica, the owner of Denny's Restaurants, was the target of a number of racial-based legal claims a decade ago. The company has responded with aggressive minority hiring and supplier-diversity efforts to show its commitment to diversity problems. Lawsuits pushed Advantica further on the road to diversity, but it now has apparently gotten the message and taken it to heart as it led the *Fortune* ranking of minority friendly companies for two years in a row.[37]

Questions
1. Discuss whether diversity efforts of these three companies are good business practices, not just being socially responsible.
2. If an employer is *forced* to deal with diversity as Denny's was, why is it proper to give an award?

SUPPLEMENTAL CASE: Keep on Trucking

This case illustrates the problems that can be associated with the use of employment tests that have not been validated. (For the case, go to **http://mathis.swlearning.com/**.)

Learning Review Answers: 1. c   2. d   3. c   4. c

NOTES

1. David Kiley, "Workplace Woes Almost Eclipse Mitsubishi Plant," *USA Today,* October 21, 2002, 1B.
2. William J. Collins, "The Labor Market Impact of State-Level Anti-discrimination Laws, 1940–1960," *Industrial and Labor Relations Review,* 56 (2003) 1–35.
3. U.S. Equal Employment Opportunity Commission, "EEOC Reports Discrimination Charge Filings Up," February 6, 2003, *www.eeoc.gov/press/2-6-03.html.*
4. "The Impact of the Human Rights Act on the Workplace," *Eversheds HR E-Briefing,* October 2003, *www.shrm.org/global.*
5. "Court Orders Michigan Employment Agency to End Wholesale Discrimination," *Wall Street Journal,* May 2, 2000, A1.
6. "Stage Court Backs Catholic Employer in Religious-Bias Case," *Omaha World-Herald,* May 17, 2002, 8A.
7. *Griggs v. Duke Power Co.,* 401 U.S. 424 (1971).
8. *Reeves v. Sanderson Plumbing Products, Inc.,* 530 U.S. 99-536 (June 12, 2000).
9. *O'Neal v. Ferguson Construction Co.,* 10th Cir. U.S. 99-2037 (January 24, 2001).
10. Ann Zimmerman, "Judge Certifies Wal-Mart Suit as Class Action," *Wall Street Journal,* June 23, 2004, A1 and A6; Stephanie Armour, "Plaintiffs Describe Their Lives at Wal-Mart," *USA Today,* June 24, 2004, 3B; and Stephanie Armour, "Women Say Wal-Mart Execs Knew of Sex Bias," *USA Today,* June 25, 2004, 1B.
11. *Arimindo v. Padlocker, Inc.,* 11th Cir., 99-4144 (April 20, 2000).
12. "Additional Pregnancy Bias Rulings," *Fair Employment Practices,* March 9, 2000, 78.
13. "Employee Pregnancy Disputes Are Rising," *Omaha World-Herald,* November 9, 2003, 8A.
14. Martin Crutsinger, "Job Discrimination Complaints Fell Slightly Last Year," *Laramie Boomerang,* March 9, 2004, 10.
15. *EEOC v. Eastern Michigan University,* E. D. Mich., 98-71806 (September 3, 1999).
16. Anne M. Alexander et al., "A Study of the Disparity in Wages and Benefits Between Men and Women in Wyoming," 2003, *www.wyomingbusiness.org/women.*
17. Andy Meisler, "The Mindfield of Depression," *Workforce Management,* September 2003, 57–60.
18. *Bragdon v. Abbott,* U.S. Supreme Court No. 97-156 (June 25, 1998).
19. "Implementation of the Employment Provisions of ADA/DDA," *www.shrm.org/global/.*
20. Joseph Mack III and Terrence M. Lewis, "The ADA vs. Overtime," *HR Magazine,* April 2002, 1–4.
21. Robert S. Greenberger, "High Court Issues Narrow Ruling on ADA's Scope," *Wall Street Journal,* December 3, 2003, A3.
22. Gina Holland, "Court: Bias Regarding Age Is a One-Way Street," *Denver Post,* February 25, 2004, C1.
23. "Provisions to Include in Any ADEA Waivers," *HR Focus,* June 2002, 1.
24. "Allstate Faces Age Bias Charge," *National Underwriters Property and Casualty,* September 15, 2003, 1.
25. Scott S. Moore, "H1-B Cap Countdown," *Baird Holm Labor and Employment Law Update,* May 2003, 1.
26. Milford Prewitt, "Many Borders to Cross," *Nation's Restaurant News,* July 7, 2003, 2.
27. Ann Zimmerman, "Labor Pains," *Wall Street Journal,* December 19, 2003, A1, A8.
28. *TransWorld Airlines v. Hardison,* 432 U.S. 63 (1977).
29. *Ansari v. Ray and Claude Goodwin, Inc.,* MD, Fla. 3:98-C-1052-J-20C (March 29, 2000).
30. "Genetic Information," *www.shrm.org/government/.*
31. Mark V. Roehling, "Weight Discrimination in the American Workplace," *Journal of Business Ethics,* 40 (2002), 177–189.
32. Ruth I. Major, "Military Leave: An Employer's Obligation," *Franchising World,* January 2002, 52–53.
33. Stephanie Armour, "Competitive Job Market Locks Out Former Offenders," *USA Today,* November 21, 2003, B1.
34. Kenneth M. York, "Disparate Results in Adverse Impact Tests: The 4/5th Rule and the Chi Square Test," *Public Personnel Management,* 31 (2002) 253–262.
35. Jennifer L. Gatewood, "Company Pays for Unintentional Bias," *Human Resource Executive,* October 20, 2002, 14.
36. "Albertsons Agrees to Mediation Program," *Laramie Boomerang,* October 7, 2003, 13.
37. Based on Jeremy Kahn, "Diversity Trumps the Downtown," *Fortune,* July 9, 2001, 114–116.

CHAPTER 5

Managing Equal Employment and Diversity

After you have read this chapter, you should be able to:

- Evaluate several arguments supporting and opposing affirmative action.

- Describe how women are affected by work/family and job assignment issues in organizations.

- Explain the two types of sexual harassment and how employers should respond to sexual harassment complaints.

- Identify two means that organizations are using to deal with the aging of their workforces.

- Discuss how reasonable accommodation is made when managing individuals with disabilities and differing religious beliefs.

- Define diversity management and discuss why it is important.

Diversity Backlash!

Equal employment opportunity, demographic changes among workers, and differences in the labor markets have combined to make for a much more diverse workforce. The concept of diversity recognizes that there are differences among people and that those differences provide both opportunities and challenges for employers. After many years of progress on the diversity front, HR departments are seeing backlash from employees in some areas. Consider these examples:

- A diversity class at a San Francisco airport became an issue when attendees complained that the presentation was anti-American and anti-Israeli. Attendees complained that topics covered in the class were harsh political attacks against the foreign policies of both the U.S. and Israel.
- In Minnesota, state workers went to court against diversity training, on religious grounds, after being reprimanded for reading their Bibles in protest during the training.
- In Connecticut, police officers objected to comments in a diversity training class that were thought to be anti-American shortly after the anniversary of 9/11.
- An employee of Eastman Kodak was fired for expressing disapproval of a diversity initiative when he chose to do so in a widely distributed e-mail.

Tension among individuals from different racial and ethnic backgrounds, religions, age groups, and genders is not new. But economic concerns and the threat of international terrorism seem to have put some of these issues at the forefront again. In addition, same sex and gay marriage issues seem to be generating more "pushback" from employees.

Effective diversity trainers suggest that problems stem from what employees see as attempts to change what they believe. Trainers emphasize that the key to avoiding backlash in diversity efforts is to stress that people can believe whatever they wish, but at work, their values are less important than their *behaviors.* Dealing with diversity is not about what people can and cannot *say,* it is about being *respectful* to others. The organization has the right to say, "We will respect all employees," and it also has the right to enforce that. Unfortunately, not all diversity integration efforts take that approach, which can create organizational and individual conflicts.[1]

"Can't we all just get along?"

—*Unknown*

The philosophy and legal requirements of equal employment opportunity (EEO) were discussed in Chapter 4. Understanding what the laws say is important, but knowing how to manage HR for EEO compliance requires significant HR efforts. This chapter considers the EEO areas covered in Chapter 4 with a different emphasis, focusing on the special issues and HR problems presented by each. The second part of this chapter examines diversity in the workforce and HR approaches and responses to that diversity.

RACE, NATIONAL ORIGIN, AND CITIZENSHIP ISSUES

The original purpose of the Civil Rights Act of 1964 was to address race and national origin discrimination. This concern continues to be important today, and employers must be aware of HR issues that are based on race, national origin, and citizenship in order to take appropriate actions.

Racial/Ethnic Demographics

Recent data from the U.S. Census Bureau reveal that the racial/ethnic mix of the U.S. population continues to shift. As Figure 5-1 shows, the white population has declined from 76% of the workforce in 1990 to about 69% in 2003. The greatest growth has been in the Hispanic population. In earlier census reports, there was confusion about how to count Hispanics. The latest census defined a Hispanic as someone who was born in or whose ancestors came from Cuba, Mexico, Puerto Rico, or South or Central America. According to the census data, the number of individuals identifying themselves as being of Hispanic origin grew by 58%, whereas the U.S. population as a whole grew by 13%. As a result,

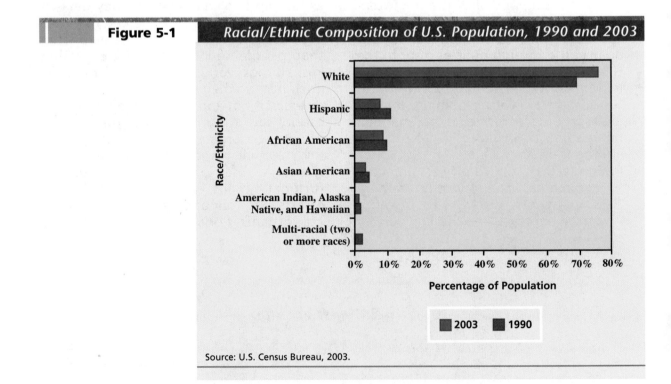

Figure 5-1 Racial/Ethnic Composition of U.S. Population, 1990 and 2003

Source: U.S. Census Bureau, 2003.

EEOC Sees Rise in Complaints of Color Bias

Under federal law, discriminating against people because of skin color is just as illegal as discriminating because of race. In the last decade, EEOC complaints on this issue have gone from about 300 a year to over 1,500 a year. Color discrimination is not necessarily racial bias. For example, one might be guilty of color discrimination but not racial discrimination if a Caucasian hired light-skinned African-Americans over dark-skinned people. Some examples illustrate how color bias has generated lawsuits.

In 2003, a Mexican restaurant in San Antonio was sued by the Equal Employment Opportunity Commission on behalf of a Caucasian supervisor. The Mexican-American owner had told him not to allow dark-skinned Hispanics to work in the dining room. The restaurant was ordered to pay $100,000 in fines. In another study, Dwight Burch, an African-American with very dark skin, was fired by his manager, an African-American with lighter skin. The EEOC sued for Burch, saying the firing was retaliatory because the two had verbally abused each other, each insulting the other's skin tone. The employer, Applebee's, settled for $40,000 and agreed to report all color harassment claims.

Many color bias situations go unreported because people simply do not understand that such a distinction is covered by law. People feel they have to put up with it because they are embarrassed to talk about it, an EEOC lawyer notes.[2]

the 35.3 million Hispanic Americans compose about the same percentage of the U.S. population as do African Americans.

The Society for Human Resource Management (SHRM) surveyed 450 HR managers about the impact of a more ethnically diverse workforce. The results showed there were few specific changes required at most employers (43%). However, 28% of those surveyed said there has been a greater need for bilingual communications, and 27% said there has been a need for more language training.[3]

Sociologically, the races most widely represented in the U.S. labor force are becoming somewhat more alike in terms of fertility, later marriage, and mortality.[4] However, more dissimilarities are found with employment and income among the various groups.[5] Employers have seen a number of other issues arising from racial and ethnic sources at work. One of these, color discrimination allegations, is discussed in the HR Perspective.

Affirmative Action

Affirmative action was mentioned previously as a requirement for federal government contractors to document the inclusion of women and racial minorities in the workforce. As part of those government regulations, covered employers must submit plans describing their attempts to narrow the gaps between the composition of their workforces and the composition of labor markets where they obtain employees. A practical concern with affirmative action efforts is how to "count" individuals with a multi-racial background, such as golfer Tiger Woods, whose father is African American and mother is Asian American. In fact, in the latest U.S. census, almost 7 million people classified themselves as multi-racial, and in California, almost 5% of the population classified themselves as being of two or more races.

LOGGING ON...

The Affirmative Action and Diversity Project
Discusses differing opinions about affirmative action and its economic and cultural aspects.
http://racerelations.about.com

Affirmative Action Is Still Needed

1. **Affirmative action is needed to overcome past injustices or eliminate the effects of those injustices.** Proponents of affirmative action believe that it is necessary because women and members of certain racial and ethnic groups historically have been subjected to unfair and illegal employment treatment by being relegated to lower positions (such as clerical and low-paying jobs), being discriminated against for promotions, and being disciplined more often. Without affirmative action, the inequities will continue to exist for individuals who are not white males.

2. **Affirmative action creates more equality for all persons, even if temporary injustice to some individuals may result.** White males, in particular, may be disadvantaged temporarily in order for affirmative action to create broader opportunities for all. Proponents argue for programs to enable women, minorities, and members of other protected groups to be competitive with males and whites. Otherwise, they will never "catch up" and have appropriate opportunities.

3. **Raising the employment level of protected-class members will benefit U.S. society in the long run.** Statistics consistently indicate that the greatest percentage of those in lower socioeconomic groups are in protected classes. As affirmative action assists people in these groups, it addresses socioeconomic disparities. Without affirmative action, proponents argue that many in the U.S. will be permanently economically disadvantaged. When economic levels are low, other social ills proliferate, such as crime, drug use, and disparities in educational opportunities.

4. **Properly used, affirmative action does not discriminate against males or whites.** An affirmative action plan should include a deadline for accomplishing long-term goals, but in the short term, case by case, individuals must meet the basic qualifications for jobs. Once all the criteria for jobs are established, *qualified* women or members of other protected groups should be chosen. Then, those not selected are discriminated against only in the sense that they did not get the jobs.

5. **Goals indicate progress needed, not quotas.** The proponents of affirmative action stress that affirmative action involves *goals,* not *quotas.* The difference is that quotas are specific, required numbers, whereas goals are targets for "good faith" efforts to ensure that members of protected classes truly are given consideration in employment-related decisions.

Debate on Affirmative Action Supporters offer many reasons why affirmative action is important, while opponents argue firmly against it. The reasons given most frequently by both sides are highlighted in the HR Perspective debate. Readers can examine the points of both sides in the debate and compare them with their personal views of affirmative action. The authors of this text believe that whether one supports or opposes affirmative action, it is important to understand why its supporters believe that it is needed and why its opponents believe it should be discontinued.

Employers use affirmative action *goals, targets,* and *timetables* to specify how many of which types of individuals they hope to have in their workforces in the future. By specifying these goals, employers say they are trying to "appropriately include protected group members" or "ensure a balanced and representative workforce." These claims and others like them are commonly used to describe affirmative action.

However, critics of affirmative action say that regardless of the language used, subsequent actions lead to the use of *preferential selection* for protected-class

Affirmative Action Is No Longer Needed

1. **Affirmative action penalizes individuals (males and whites) even though they have not been guilty of practicing discrimination.** Opponents argue that affirmative action is unfair to "innocent victims"—males and whites. These individuals had nothing to do with past discrimination or disparate impact, and were not even present at the time those occurred. Thus, opponents of affirmative action wonder why these individuals should have to pay for the remediation of past discriminatory actions.

2. **Creating preferences of certain groups results in reverse discrimination.** Those opposed to affirmative action believe that discriminating *for* someone means discriminating *against* someone else. If equality is the ultimate aim, then it is wrong to discriminate for or against anyone on any basis other than the knowledge, skills, and abilities needed to perform a job. Thus, discrimination in reverse is counter to creating a truly equal society.

3. **Affirmative action results in greater polarization and separatism along gender and racial lines.** The opponents of affirmative action believe that it establishes two groups: (1) women, racial minorities, and others in protected classes, and (2) everyone else. For any job, a person will clearly fall into one group or the other.

Thus, affirmative action affects males and whites negatively because of their gender or other inherent characteristics. Consequently, they become bitter against protected group individuals, and their bitterness leads to greater racism, prejudice, and societal conflicts.

4. **Affirmative action stigmatizes those it is designed to help.** Because affirmative action is viewed by some people as placing unqualified members of protected groups in jobs, it reinforces the belief held by some persons that women and members of minorities would not have succeeded on their own efforts. This belief leads to the conclusion that women or minority employees in responsible positions are there only because of who they are, not because of what they can do and have done. Additionally, when members of protected groups perform poorly in jobs because they do not have the knowledge, skills, and abilities needed, the result is to reinforce gender or racial/ethnic stereotypes.

5. **Goals become quotas by forcing employers to "play by the numbers."** Opponents of affirmative action state that regardless of the language used, when goals or targets are set, they become quotas to be met. If they are not met, employers are subjected to legal actions and condemnation.

Reverse discrimination When a person is denied an opportunity because of preferences given to protected-class individuals who may be less qualified.

members over equally qualified white males and others not covered by the EEO regulations. The result is **reverse discrimination,** which occurs when a person is denied an opportunity because of preferences given to protected-class individuals who may be less qualified.

Affirmative action focuses on hiring, training, and promoting protected-class members who are *under-represented* in an organization in relation to their availability in the labor markets from which recruiting occurs. Sometimes, employers have instituted affirmative action voluntarily, but many times, employers have been required to do so because they are government contractors with more than 50 employees and over $50,000 in government contracts annually.

Affirmative Action and the Courts Generally, the courts have upheld the legality of affirmative action, but recently they have limited it somewhat. One major case involved a University of Michigan policy of allotting every minority applicant 20 out of the 150 points necessary to guarantee admission. The U.S. Supreme Court held that the system violated the Fourteenth Amendment's "equal

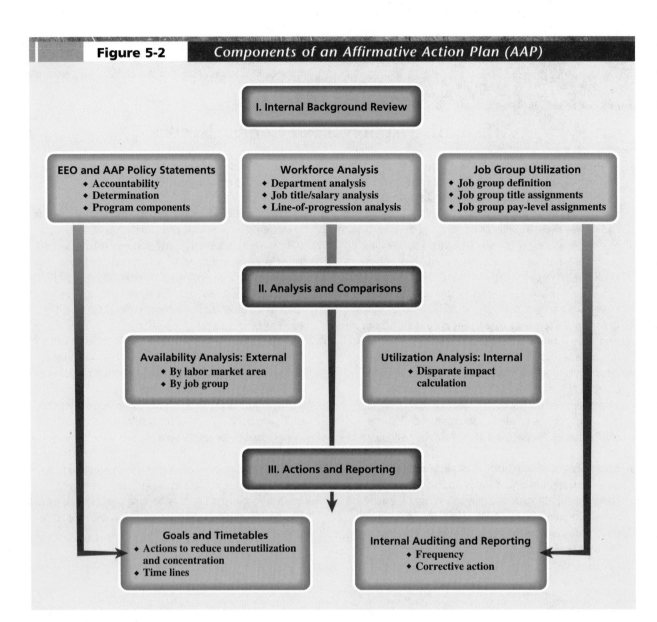

Figure 5-2   Components of an Affirmative Action Plan (AAP)

I. Internal Background Review

EEO and AAP Policy Statements
- Accountability
- Determination
- Program components

Workforce Analysis
- Department analysis
- Job title/salary analysis
- Line-of-progression analysis

Job Group Utilization
- Job group definition
- Job group title assignments
- Job group pay-level assignments

II. Analysis and Comparisons

Availability Analysis: External
- By labor market area
- By job group

Utilization Analysis: Internal
- Disparate impact calculation

III. Actions and Reporting

Goals and Timetables
- Actions to reduce underutilization and concentration
- Time lines

Internal Auditing and Reporting
- Frequency
- Corrective action

protection" clause. However, in another case, the court upheld affirmative action, ruling that the University of Michigan law school was justified in trying to ensure that a "critical mass" of minority students was admitted, even if that meant denying admission to white students with better grades or higher test scores.[6]

Surveys of Americans' beliefs on affirmative action show that 63% feel that affirmative action has been good for minorities. However, only 42% say affirmative action is still necessary to achieve diversity at work.[7] Other research on affirmative action suggests that increases in diversity recruiting efforts by employers, raises employer willingness to hire minority applicants, increases the numbers of minority applicants and employees, and increases tendencies to provide training and formally evaluate employees. Overall, the study found that affirmative action generally does not lead to lower credentials of workers.[8]

Affirmative action plan (AAP) Formal document that an employer compiles annually for submission to enforcement agencies.

Affirmative Action Plans (AAPs) Federal, state, and local regulations require many government contractors to compile affirmative action plans to report on the composition of their workforces. An **affirmative action plan (AAP)** is a formal document that an employer compiles annually for submission to enforcement agencies. Generally, contractors with at least 50 employees and $50,000 in government contracts annually must submit these plans. Courts have noted that any employer *may* have a *voluntary* AAP, although employers *must* have such a plan if they are government contractors. Some courts have ordered employers that are not government contractors to submit required AAPs because of past discriminatory practices and violations of laws.

The contents of an AAP and the policies flowing from it must be available for review by managers and supervisors within the organization. Plans vary in length; some are long and require extensive staff time to prepare. Figure 5-2 depicts the phases in the development of an AAP.

Availability analysis Identifies the number of protected-class members available to work in the appropriate labor markets for given jobs.

Utilization analysis Identifies the number of protected-class members employed in the organization and the types of jobs they hold.

AAP Measures The second phase is a crucial but time-consuming one in which two types of analyses and comparisons are done. The **availability analysis** identifies the number of protected-class members available to work in the appropriate labor markets for given jobs. This analysis can be developed with data from a state labor department, the U.S. Census Bureau, and other sources. The **utilization analysis** identifies the number of protected-class members employed in the organization and the types of jobs they hold.

One difficulty in conducting the analyses is how to report and count individuals who are multi-racial or multi-ethnic. Under long-standing regulations, a multi-racial person such as Tiger Woods would be reported in two or more categories. The enforcement agencies have recognized such concerns and are expected to develop new reporting categories and guidelines within the next few years.

Once all the data have been analyzed and compared, then the *underutilization* statistics must be calculated by comparing the workforce analyses with the utilization analysis. It is useful to think of this stage as a comparison of whether the internal workforce is a "representative sampling" of the available external labor force from which employees are hired.

Using the underutilization data, *goals and timetables* for reducing the underutilization of protected-class individuals must then be identified. Actions that will be taken to recruit, hire, promote, and train more protected-class individuals are described. The AAP must be updated and reviewed each year to reflect changes in the utilization and availability of protected-class members. If the AAP is audited by the Office of Federal Contract Compliance Programs (OFCCP), the employer must be prepared to provide additional details and documentation.

Requirements for Immigrants and Foreign-Born Workers

Although immigrants are a smaller percentage of the U.S. population now than they were a century ago, their overall numbers have increased dramatically. Much of the growth in various racial and ethnic groups is due to immigration from other countries. Immigrants come into the country as temporary workers, visitors, students, illegals, etc. Recent statistics indicate that for many types of jobs, particularly the lower-skilled jobs in such areas as hospitality and agricultural businesses, workers with limited educational skills are coming from Mexico, Sudan, the Balkan countries, and poorer Latin American and

Asian countries. The U.S. economy relies on immigrant workers for the following reasons:[9]

- Many U.S.-born citizens finish high school, leaving few dropouts for the low-end, less-skilled jobs.
- The migration from rural areas to the cities is declining, ending that source of entry-level employees for employers in metropolitan areas.
- More women are in careers in the labor force, and are thus less likely to accept low-paying, dead-end jobs.

Visas and Documentation Requirements The increasing number of foreign-born workers means that employers must comply with the provisions of the Immigration Reform and Control Acts. Employers are required to obtain and inspect I-9 forms, and verify documents such as birth certificates, passports, visas, and work permits. They can be fined if they knowingly hire illegal aliens.

Visas are granted by U.S. consular officers (there are more than 200 such officers throughout the world). Once a visa is granted, an alien will be accepted for transportation to the U.S. However, at the border (or airport), a Bureau of Citizenship and Immigration Services (BCIS) official decides whether the person will be admitted. Many different types of visas exist. Among those most commonly encountered by employers are the B1 for business visitors, B2 for pleasure visitors, H-1B for professional or specialized workers, and L-1 for intra-company transfers.

H-1B visas are designed to allow workers with scarce skills to come into the U.S. for a six-year period. An employer must sponsor the worker. Companies cannot hire H-1B employees to displace U.S. workers, and they must file documents with the Labor Department and pay prevailing U.S. wages to the visa holders.

An L-1 visa can be used to transfer international company employees to the U.S. and is not subject to the constraints on the H-1B employees. Some 330,000 foreigners work in the U.S. under the L-1 visa program despite some concerns that the program is used to circumvent the limits put on hiring foreign workers to displace U.S. workers.[10]

Identity "Mismatch" Besides visas, employers have other challenges deciding which individuals meet federal restrictions for verifying the legality of employment in the U.S. Employers may hear from the U.S. Social Security Administration (SSA) that a Social Security number they have on file for an employee does not match the number on file with the SSA. If an employee has provided a false Social Security number, that person may be an illegal alien and not qualified to work in the U.S. By employing an alien, the employer could be violating federal immigration law. Reasons for a mismatch could include an unreported name change, marital status change, stolen identity, or clerical error. Certainly these possibilities should be checked before concluding that the person is an illegal alien and dismissing the person.

Language Issues and EEO

As the diversity of the workforce increases, more employees have language skills beyond English. Interestingly, some employers have attempted to restrict the use of foreign languages, while other employers have recognized that bilingual employees have valuable skills.

English-Only Requirements A number of employers have policies requiring that employees speak only English at work. These employers contend that the policies are necessary for valid business purposes. For instance, a manufacturer requires that all employees working with dangerous chemicals use English in order to communicate hazardous situations to other workers and to read chemical labels.

The EEOC has issued guidelines clearly stating that employers may require workers to speak only English at certain times or in certain situations, but the business necessity of the requirements must be justified. Teaching, customer service, and telemarketing are examples of positions that may require English skills and voice clarity. However, because language characteristics are closely related to national origin, employers must make sure that the business reasons justify any impingement on workers' rights.[11]

Bilingual Employees A growing number of employers have found it beneficial to have bilingual employees so that foreign-language customers can contact someone speaking their languages. Some employers do not pay bilingual employees extra, believing that paying for the jobs being done is more appropriate than paying for language skills that are used infrequently on those jobs. Other employers pay "language premiums" if employees must speak to customers in another language. For instance, one employer pays workers in some locations a bonus if they are required to use a foreign language a majority of the time with customers. Bilingual employees are especially needed among police officers, airline flight personnel, hospital interpreters, international sales reps, and travel guides.

At Fazoli's restaurants in Lexington, Kentucky, and Atlanta, Georgia, various work-related training materials have been translated into Spanish and the managers take courses in Spanish. These actions have improved the managers' understanding of spoken Spanish to about 80%. The company uses its Spanish immersion program for managers to court Spanish-speaking employees and consumers.[12] Regardless of the HR policies and practices used, the reality is that language issues must be dealt with as part of managing a racially and ethnically diverse workforce.

Racial/Ethnic Harassment

The area of racial/ethnic harassment is such a concern that the EEOC has issued guidelines on it. It is recommended that employers adopt policies against harassment of any type, including ethnic jokes, vulgar epithets, racial slurs, and physical actions. The advantage of taking quick remedial action is shown in a case in which an employee filed suit against Delta Airlines because co-workers told racist jokes and hung nooses in his workplace. Delta was able to show that each time any employee, including the plaintiff, reported an incident, management quickly conducted an investigation and took corrective and disciplinary actions against the offending employees. Following the management actions, further incidents did not occur, so the court ruled for Delta Airlines in this case.[13]

▌ SEX/GENDER ISSUES

The influx of women into the workforce has major social, economic, and organizational consequences. As Figure 5-3 on the next page shows, the percentage of women in the total U.S. civilian workforce has increased dramatically since 1950, to almost 50% today.

Figure 5-3

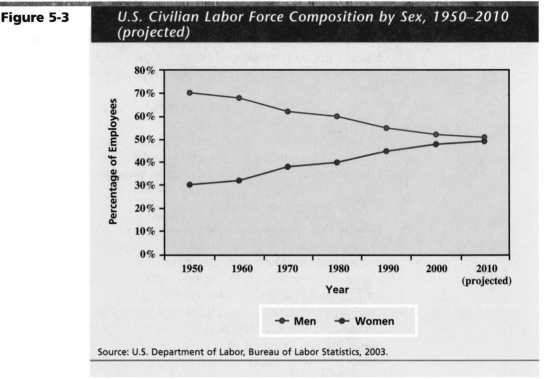

U.S. Civilian Labor Force Composition by Sex, 1950–2010 (projected)

Source: U.S. Department of Labor, Bureau of Labor Statistics, 2003.

A major result of the increasing share of women in the workforce is that more women with children are working. According to the U.S. Bureau of Labor Statistics, about three-fourths of women ages 25–54 are in the workforce. Further, about half of all women currently working are single, separated, divorced, widowed, or otherwise single heads of households. Consequently, they are "primary" income earners, not co-income providers, and must balance family and work responsibilities.

The increasing number of working mothers with children has led employers to take steps to establish policies compatible with workers who are pregnant or are new parents. Due to the Pregnancy Discrimination Act discussed in Chapter 4, employers must not discriminate against pregnant women when making selection, promotion, training, or other employment-related decisions. The Family and Medical Leave Act (FMLA) requirements also affect the management of pregnant workers and new parents. This act applies to both female and male employees who are new parents, through either adoption or natural birth. Many employers have policies allowing new mothers to leave their work sites during business hours in order to nurse or use breast pumps.

Sex Discrimination

The growth in the number of women in the workforce has led to more sex/gender issues related to jobs and careers. A significant issue is related to biology (women bear children) and to tradition (women have a primary role in raising children). In the 1960s, about 44% of women worked during pregnancy; currently, around 67% do. During the 1960s, about 63% of working women who were pregnant with their first children quit their jobs around the time of the birth.

Today, only about 17% quit after the birth, and 78% are back at work within 12 months of the birth.[14]

The signals on this trend are mixed because a growing number of women at the peak of their careers are dropping out to stay home with their families.[15] At the same time, a much publicized option—that of the father staying home and raising the children—is clearly not widely used, and a stigma still seems to be attached to men who choose that alternative.[16]

Pay Inequity In Chapter 4, it was shown that on average, women earn less than men. That discrepancy depends to a large extent on differences between jobs, industries, and time spent at work. However, there is probably a discrimination component to the problem as well.[17] To guard against pay inequities that are considered illegal under the Equal Pay Act, employers should follow these guidelines:[18]

- Include benefits and other items that are part of remuneration to calculate pay for the most accurate overall picture.
- Make sure people know how the pay practices work.
- Base pay on the value of jobs and performance.
- Benchmark against local and national markets so that pay structures are competitive.
- Conduct frequent audits to ensure there are no gender-based inequities and that pay is fair internally.

Nepotism Practice of allowing relatives to work for the same employer.

Nepotism and Nontraditional Jobs Many employers have policies that restrict or prohibit **nepotism,** the practice of allowing relatives to work for the same employer. Other firms require only that relatives not work directly for or with each other or not be placed in positions where collusion or conflict could occur. The policies most frequently cover spouses, brothers, sisters, mothers, fathers, sons, and daughters. Generally, employer anti-nepotism policies have been upheld by courts, in spite of the concern that they tend to discriminate against women more than men (because women tend to be denied employment or to leave employers more often as a result of marriage to other employees).

Figure 5-4 shows some of the typically male-dominated occupations in which women constitute relatively few of those employed. An additional result

Figure 5-4

Nontraditional Occupations for Women	
Occupation	Percentage Female
Welders and cutters	4.9
Truck drivers	4.7
Airplane pilots and navigators	3.9
Construction laborers	3.7
Firefighting and fire prevention occupations	3.6
Excavating and loading machine operators	3.1
Tool and die makers	2.7
Operating engineers	1.7
Crane and tower operators	1.4
Motion picture projectionists	<1.0

Source: U.S. Department of Labor, Women's Bureau, 2003, available at *www.dol.gov/dol/wb.*

of the increasing number of women in the workforce is the movement of women into jobs traditionally held by men. The U.S. Department of Labor defines nontraditional occupations for women as those in which women constitute 25% or less of the total number employed. Even though the nature of the work and working conditions may contribute some to this pattern, many of these jobs pay well, and as more women enter these occupations, women's earnings will rise.

The right to re-assign women from hazardous jobs to ones that may be lower paying because of health-related concerns is another gender-related issue encountered by employers. Fears about higher health insurance costs, and even possible lawsuits involving such problems as birth defects caused by damage sustained during pregnancy, have led some employers to institute reproductive and fetal protection policies. However, the U.S. Supreme Court has ruled that such policies are illegal. Also, having different job conditions for men and women is usually held to be discriminatory.

Glass Ceiling For years, women's groups have alleged that women in workplaces encounter a **glass ceiling,** which refers to discriminatory practices that have prevented women and other protected-class members from advancing to executive-level jobs. Women in the U.S. are making some progress: today, overall, 39% of women are in managerial or professional jobs, up from 24% in 1977.[19] Nevertheless, women held only 5.1% of the highest-ranking executive management jobs in Fortune 500 companies. By comparison, women held 2% of the same kinds of jobs in France, 3% in Germany and Brazil, and 3.6% in the United Kingdom.[20]

"Glass Walls" and "Glass Elevator" A related problem is that women have tended to advance to senior management in a limited number of support or staff areas, such as HR and corporate communications. Because executive jobs in these "supporting" areas tend to pay less than jobs in sales, marketing, operations, or finance, the overall impact is to reduce women's career progression and income. Limits that keep women from progressing only in certain fields have been referred to as "glass walls" or "glass elevators."

"Breaking the Glass" A number of employers have recognized that "breaking the glass," whether ceilings, walls, or elevators, is good business for both women and racial minorities. The HR Perspective shows the results of a study on both. Some of the most common means used to "break the glass" are as follows:

◆ Establishing formal mentoring programs for women and members of racial/ethnic minorities[21]

◆ Providing opportunities for career rotation into operations, marketing, and sales for individuals who have shown talent in accounting, human resources, and other areas

◆ Increasing the memberships of top management and boards of directors to include women and individuals of color[22]

◆ Establishing clear goals for retention and progression of protected-class individuals and holding managers accountable for achieving these goals

◆ Allowing for alternative work arrangements for employees, particularly those balancing work/family responsibilities

Glass ceiling Discriminatory practices that have prevented women and other protected-class members from advancing to executive-level jobs.

LOGGING ON...

Catalyst Organization
This nonprofit research and advisory organization is dedicated to advancing women in business.
www.catalystwomen.org

Research on the Glass Ceiling

Foley, Kidder, and Powell examined the relationship of a perceived glass ceiling to several employment outcomes. Their results were reported in the *Journal of Management.* The researchers focused on 204 Hispanic lawyers who worked full-time in private law firms. In the sample 39% were female, 65% of whom were married and had about one child each.

The study confirmed that for female Hispanic lawyers, the glass ceiling did indeed exist. Gender was related to the perception of a glass ceiling. More women than men perceived that the glass ceiling existed. Belief that a glass ceiling exists decreased the perception that promotions were fair and based on merit. When people felt promotions were fair, there was much less likelihood that they also felt there was a glass ceiling. When it was believed that promotions were fair, people had more positive views of their own chances

for promotion in the future. Further, the study found a relationship between the perception that a glass ceiling exists and the intentions of the Hispanic lawyers to leave their current employment.

The study concluded that Hispanic women are more concerned with social "treatment" factors than are Hispanic men. The greater awareness of such factors might be a part of the increased perception of a glass ceiling as might the fact that women may have seen discrimination based on both gender and ethnicity. Promotions tend to be an important part of employee aspirations. If the protected-class employees feel that promotions are less fair due to discrimination, they may change their work-related attitudes. The study suggested that management should provide all employees with the same explicit feedback about the reasons for promotion in the firm to minimize perceptions of unfairness.[23]

Individuals with Differing Sexual Orientations

As if demographic diversity did not place enough pressure on managers and organizations, individuals in the workforce today have widely varying lifestyles that can have work-related consequences. Legislative efforts have been made to protect individuals with differing lifestyles or sexual orientations from employment discrimination, though at present only a few cities and states have passed such laws.

One specific issue that some employers have had to address is that of individuals who have had or are undergoing sex-change surgery and therapy. Federal court cases and the EEOC have ruled that sex discrimination under Title VII applies to a person's gender at birth. Thus, it does not apply to the new gender of those who have had gender-altering operations. Sexual orientation or sex-change issues that arise at work include:

- *Clarification of HR policies:* Access to company benefits plans must be clarified. Also, the "restroom issue" is often the most sensitive. At some firms, the policy is that whatever restroom the individual wishes to use, that is the one that is acceptable.
- *Reactions of co-workers:* It is crucial to ensure that co-workers understand that the employer will not tolerate snide remarks or harassment of individuals over these issues.
- *Continuing acceptance:* If an employer believes that it is important to retain every worker who is performing satisfactorily, then keeping an employee who is in a same-sex relationship or is transgendered is just as important as retaining any other employee. Managers and supervisors must ensure that

such an individual is evaluated fairly and not discriminated against in work assignments, raises, training, or promotions.

SEXUAL HARASSMENT AND WORKPLACE RELATIONSHIPS

As more women have entered the workforce, more men and women work together in teams and on projects. Consequently, more employers are becoming concerned about the close personal relationships that develop at work.

Consensual Relationships and Romance at Work

When work-based friendships lead to romance and off-the-job sexual relationships, managers and employers face a dilemma: Should they "monitor" these relationships to protect the firm from potential legal complaints, thereby "meddling" in employees' private, off-the-job lives? Or do they simply ignore these relationships and the potential problems they present?

Different actions may be taken if a relationship is clearly consensual than if it involves a supervisor-subordinate relationship. The greatest concerns are romantic relationships between supervisors and subordinates, because the harassment of subordinates by supervisors is the most frequent type of sexual harassment. Some employers have addressed the issue of workplace romances by establishing policies dealing with them. However, only 12% of the firms responding to a survey by the American Management Association had such a policy.[24]

A survey by SHRM found that most executives and HR professionals (as well as employees) agree that workplace romances are risky because they have great potential for causing conflict. Seventy percent agreed that romance must not take place between a supervisor and a subordinate.[25] Two-thirds of the respondents in yet another survey believed that office romances are harmful, but most also felt that such relationships are personal and private and are none of the employer's business.[26] Of special concern is what will happen if or when the office romance turns into sexual harassment. As shown by Figure 5-5, individuals in many different roles can be sexual harassers.

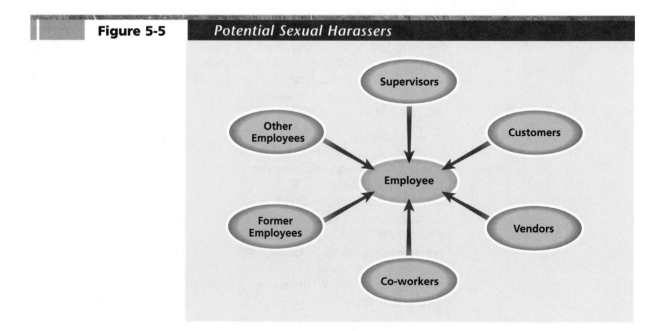

Figure 5-5   *Potential Sexual Harassers*

Technology Transforming HR

Electronic Sexual Harassment

Much has been made of the advantages of the Internet and its positive effects on HR management. However, electronic information technology is creating new problems for HR managers as well, because sexual harassment occurs in e-mails and Internet access systems.

Cyber sexual harassment is a growing concern because it occurs in a variety of forms. It may be an employee forwarding an e-mail joke with sexual content received from a friend outside the company. Or it may be an employee repeatedly sending e-mails asking another employee to meet for lunch or a date.

Another more troublesome form is employees accessing pornographic Web sites at work, and then sharing some content with other employees. Even something such as an employee having a screen saver of his wife in a revealing outfit or an actress dressed in a bikini has led to complaints by other employees.

Many employers have developed policies addressing the inappropriate use of e-mail and company computer systems. Most employers have policies on electronic technology usage, and many of those policies have "zero tolerance," whereby disciplinary action occurs regardless of the proclaimed innocence of the employee.

More serious situations have led to employee terminations, as evidenced by some examples. Blue Cross Blue Shield of Michigan fired seven employees for sending pornographic e-mails. Dow Chemical disciplined more than 200 employees and fired 50 of them for having e-mailed pornographic images and other inappropriate materials using the company information system. A well-publicized case occurred at the New York Times, where 20 employees were fired for sending offensive and inappropriate e-mails—many of the individuals repeatedly doing so.

HR managers are handling cyber sexual harassment in a number of ways. First, having a policy is important, but it is even more crucial to train all employees on sexual harassment and electronic usage policies. Additionally, many employers have equipped their e-mail systems and Web sites with scanners that screen for inappropriate words and images. Offending employees receive the warnings and disciplinary actions associated with "flagged" items. As with all sexual harassment situations, HR professionals should document the incidents, their investigative efforts, and the actions taken to prevent further cyber sexual harassment.[27]

Nature of Sexual Harassment

Sexual harassment is a significant concern in many organizations and can occur in a variety of workplace relationships. Third parties who are not employees also have been found to be harassers. Both customer service representatives and food servers have won sexual harassment complaints because their employers refused to protect them from regular sexual harassment by aggressive customers.

Most frequently, sexual harassment occurs when a male in a supervisory or managerial position harasses women within his "power structure." However, women managers have been found guilty of sexually harassing male employees. Also, same-sex harassment has occurred. Court decisions have held that a person's sexual orientation neither provides nor precludes a claim of sexual harassment under Title VII. It is enough that the harasser engaged in pervasive and unwelcome conduct of a sexual nature.[28] As computer and Internet technology has spread, the number of electronic sexual harassment cases has grown, as the Technology Transforming HR describes.

Types of Sexual Harassment Two basic types of sexual harassment have been defined by EEOC regulations and a large number of court cases. The two types are different in nature and defined as follows: 1. **Quid pro quo** is harassment in which employment outcomes are linked to the individual granting sexual favors. 2. **Hostile environment** harassment exists when an individual's work performance or psychological well-being is unreasonably affected by intimidating or offensive working conditions.

In quid pro quo harassment, an employee may be promised a promotion, a special raise, or a desirable work assignment, but only if the employee grants some sexual favors to the supervisor. Unfortunately, hostile environment harassment is much more prevalent, partially because the standards and consequences are more varied.

A number of court cases have emphasized that commenting on appearance or attire, telling jokes that are suggestive or sexual in nature, allowing revealing photos and posters to be on display, or making continual requests to get together after work can lead to the creation of a hostile work environment.

Regardless of the type of sexual harassment, it is apparent that sexual harassment has significant consequences on the organization, other employees, and especially those harassed. Follow-up interviews and research with victims of sexual harassment reveal that the harassment has both job-related and psychological effects. Also, harassment even has a ripple effect on others who fear being harassed or view their employer more negatively if prompt, remedial actions do not occur. Thus, how employers respond to sexual harassment complaints is crucial for both legal reasons and employee morale.

Legal Standards on Sexual Harassment

One survey found that 21% of American women and 7% of American men report being sexually harassed at work. If the workplace culture fosters harassment, and policies and practices do not inhibit harassment, an employer is wise to re-evaluate and solve the problem before lawsuits follow.[29]

Only if the employer can produce evidence of an affirmative defense in which the employer took reasonable care to prohibit sexual harassment does the employer have the possibility of avoiding liability. Critical components of ensuring reasonable care include the following:

◆ Establishing a sexual harassment policy
◆ Communicating the policy regularly
◆ Training employees and managers on avoiding sexual harassment
◆ Investigating and taking action when complaints are voiced

As Figure 5-6 indicates, if an employee suffered any tangible employment action (such as being denied raises, being terminated, or being refused access to training) because of sexual harassment, then the employer is liable. Even if the employee suffered no tangible employment action, if the employer has not produced an affirmative defense, then employer liability still exists.

▌▌ AGE ISSUES AND EEO

The populations of most developed countries—including Australia, Japan, most European countries, and the United States—are aging. The aging of a pop-

Figure 5-6

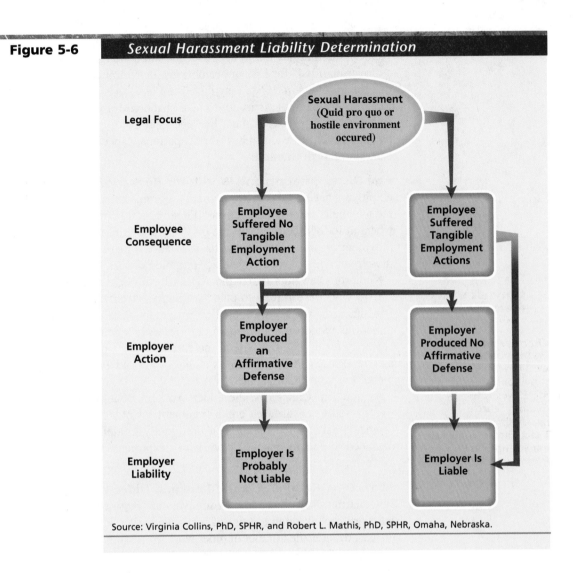

Sexual Harassment Liability Determination

Source: Virginia Collins, PhD, SPHR, and Robert L. Mathis, PhD, SPHR, Omaha, Nebraska.

ulation means many "mature workers" in organizations. As older workers with a lifetime of experience and skills retire, HR faces significant challenges in replacing them with workers having the capabilities and work ethic that characterize many mature workers. Many older people stay active in the workforce. For instance, more than half of both men and women workers over age 70 are employed part-time. Also, full-time workforce participation does not drop significantly until age 65, especially for women.[30]

Employment discrimination against individuals age 40 and older is prohibited by the Age Discrimination in Employment Act (ADEA), as mentioned in Chapter 4. The ADEA and other anti-bias laws do not preclude an employer from firing older workers if necessary. It does increase the necessity to be able to prove that employment actions do not have a disproportionate impact on older workers. Employers must be aware of a number of HR issues associated with managing older workers.

Job Opportunities and Older Employees

One issue that has led to age discrimination charges is labeling older workers as "overqualified" for jobs or promotions. In a number of cases, courts have ruled that the term *overqualified* may have been used as a code word for workers being too old, thus causing them not to be considered for employment. Also, selection and promotion practices must be "age neutral." Older workers face substantial barriers to entry in a number of occupations, especially those requiring significant amounts of training.

Age Discrimination and Workforce Reductions In the past decade, many employers have used early retirement programs and organizational downsizing to reduce their employment costs. Illegal age discrimination sometimes occurs when an individual over the age of 40 is forced into retirement or is denied employment or promotion on the basis of age. If disparate impact or treatment for those over age 40 exists, age discrimination occurs.

Numerous lawsuits under the ADEA have been filed involving workers over age 40 who were forced to take "voluntary retirement" when organizational restructuring or workforce reduction programs were implemented. However, terminations based on documented performance deficiencies not related to age are perfectly legal. Additionally, in the case of older employees, care must be taken that references to age (such as "That's just old Fred" or "We need younger blood") in conversations are not used.

As noted in Chapter 4, the Older Workers Benefit Protection Act (OWBPA) was passed to ensure that equal treatment for older workers occurs in early retirement or severance situations. Additionally, guidelines issued by the EEOC are designed to ensure that older workers are protected when early retirement and downsizing programs include severance agreements and employee waivers.

Attracting, Retaining, and Managing Older Workers To counter significant staffing difficulties, some employers are recruiting older people to return to the workforce through the use of part-time and other scheduling options. During the past decade, the number of older workers holding part-time jobs has increased. It is likely that the number of older workers interested in working part-time will continue to increase, and that they will work more hours than previously.

A strategy used by employers to retain the talents of older workers is **phased retirement,** whereby employees gradually reduce their workloads and pay. This option is growing in use as a way to allow older workers with significant knowledge and experience to have more personal flexibility, while the organization retains them for their valuable capabilities. Figure 5-7 shows what two studies identified as the advantages and disadvantages of retaining older workers. It also lists what those studies say are consequences that employers may face with those employees.[31] Some firms also re-hire their retirees as part-time workers, independent contractors, or consultants. One survey found that more than 60% of surveyed organizations are using such means.[32]

INDIVIDUALS WITH DISABILITIES IN THE WORKFORCE

Employers looking for workers with the knowledge, skills, and abilities to perform jobs often have neglected a significant source: individuals with physical or mental disabilities. At least 55 million Americans with disabilities are covered by the Americans with Disabilities Act (ADA), but only 25% of them are currently

OLDER WORKERS' BENEFIT PROTECTION ACT
Outlines OWBPA provisions on early incentives.
Custom Search:
☑ ANALYSIS
Exact Phrase: Voluntary early retirement incentive

Phased retirement
Approach in which employees gradually reduce their workloads and pay.

Figure 5-7	HR Managers' Views of Older Workers	
Advantages	**Disadvantages**	**Consequences**
◆ Are willing to work different schedules ◆ Serve as mentors ◆ Have invaluable experience ◆ Have strong work ethic ◆ Are more reliable	◆ Are weak on new technology ◆ Cause expenses to rise ◆ Are less flexible	◆ Health care usage ◆ Health care costs ◆ More training/retraining ◆ Employee stress

employed. Estimates are that as many as 10 million of these individuals could be added to the workforce if employers made appropriate accommodations.

Reasonable Accommodations

At the heart of employing individuals with disabilities is for employers to make reasonable accommodations in several areas. First, architectural barriers should not prohibit disabled individuals' access to work areas or restrooms. Second, appropriate work tasks must be assigned. Satisfying this requirement may mean modifying jobs, work area layouts, or work schedules, or providing special equipment.

Recruiting Individuals with Disabilities Some companies have specifically targeted individuals with disabilities as employees. Examples include the following:[33]

- Proctor & Gamble formed a special recruiting team to identify individuals with severe disabilities and how they can be employed.
- Microsoft hired summer interns with disabilities and made a video featuring Microsoft employees with disabilities. Also, to support diversity efforts, the video is shown as part of orientation training to all new employees in order to reinforce Microsoft's commitment to those with disabilities.

Key to making reasonable accommodations is identifying the essential job functions and then determining which accommodations are reasonable so that the individual can perform the core job duties. Fortunately for employers, most accommodations made are relatively inexpensive. Employers who show a positive interest in making accommodations are more likely to encourage individuals with disabilities to believe that they will receive appropriate considerations for employment opportunities.

Managing Employees Who Develop Disabilities For many employers, the impact of the ADA has been the greatest when handling employees who develop disabilities, not just when dealing with applicants who have disabilities. As the workforce ages, it is likely that more employees will develop disabilities in some of the following ways:

- An accounting manager suffers a heart attack and must limit how much she can travel to conduct audits at company locations throughout the United States.
- A utility repair worker suffers a back injury while on vacation skiing and is restricted from climbing ladders and poles or lifting items weighing more than 10 pounds.

LOGGING ON...

National Business and Disability Council
This Web site is a source for employers seeking to locate and integrate people with disabilities into the workplace.
www.business-disability.com

◆ An office employee is in a severe car accident, resulting in neck injuries that constrain how much time he can sit at computer terminals doing data input.

These and countless other examples illustrate that employers must develop responses for handling accommodation requests from individuals who have been satisfactory employees without disabilities, but now must be considered for accommodations if they are to be able to continue working. Handled inappropriately, these individuals are likely to file either ADA complaints with the EEOC or private lawsuits.

Employees sometimes can be shifted to other jobs where their disabilities do not affect them as much. For instance, the utility was able to move the injured repair worker to a dispatcher job inside, so that climbing and lifting were unnecessary. But the problem for employers is what to do with the next worker who develops problems if an alternative job is not available. Even if the accommodations are just for one employee, the reactions of co-workers must be considered.

Managing Individuals with Mental Disabilities More ADA complaints are being filed by individuals who have or claim to have mental disabilities. About 16% of all ADA claims are based on psychiatric or mental illness.[34] The cases that have been filed have ranged from individuals with a medical history of paranoid schizophrenia or clinical depression to individuals who claim that job stress has affected their marriage or sex life. Regardless of the type of employees' claims, it is important that employers respond properly, by obtaining medical verifications for claims of mental illnesses and considering accommodation requests for mental disabilities in the same manner as accommodation requests for physical disabilities.

Individuals with Life-Threatening Illnesses

The U.S. Supreme Court has determined that individuals with life-threatening illnesses are covered by the ADA. Individuals with leukemia, cancer, or AIDS are all considered as having disabilities, and employers must respond to them appropriately or face charges of discrimination. Additionally, the cost of supporting the health of disabled workers, such as AIDS patients in late stages, are huge. The HR Perspective examines this problem.

Unfortunately, employers and employees often react with fear about working with someone who has AIDS or a life-threatening illness. Educating other employees may be more appropriate than terminating the person who is ill. A medical leave of absence (without pay, if that is the general policy) can be used to assist the afflicted employee during medical treatments. Also, employees who indicate that they will not work with an afflicted employee should be told that their refusal to work is not protected by law, and that they could be subject to disciplinary action up to and including discharge.

RELIGION AND SPIRITUALITY IN WORKPLACES

Title VII of the Civil Rights Act of 1964 prohibits discrimination at work on the basis of religion; also, employers are prohibited from discriminating against employees for their religious beliefs and practices. Since the September 11, 2001, attacks, such considerations have become even more important in protecting Muslim individuals from discrimination and harassment.

Ethics, Disability, and Expensive Health Insurance

Polaroid was in bankruptcy and preparing to sell its assets to Bank One when it sent letters to 180 disabled employees telling them they had been fired. As a result, their health, life, and dental insurance were terminated too. For instance, one forklift operator who had been with the company for 21 years got the letter, while he was bedridden with kidney disease.

Disabled workers are becoming an increasingly common casualty of the need to cut health costs. Only a few years ago, companies would pay health insurance premiums for long-term, disabled employees until age 65 and were eligible for Medicare. But health insurance costs are climbing, and now more companies are firing disabled employees. One study found that 27% of surveyed firms dismiss employees when they go on long-term disability, and 24% dismiss workers after 6 or 12 months on long-term disability.

Because these employees are too sick to work, they typically get 60%–70% of their salaries through Social Security disability benefits and disability insurance policies purchased by the company. But the loss of the other benefits, especially health and life insurance, brings additional financial burden at a difficult time. The federal COBRA law allows them to keep health insurance for 18 months, but they must pay all the premiums, and coverage costs thousands of dollars a year for an individual.

Bankruptcies and takeovers often motivate companies to fire disabled workers. "It is arithmetic," one executive notes. "Profits are not being generated to cover health care programs of workers from the past."[35] But there definitely are ethical issues that can be raised when employees who become disabled are terminated.

Managing Religious Diversity in Workplaces

Employers increasingly are having to balance the rights of employees with differing religious beliefs. One way to do that is to make reasonable accommodation for employees' religious beliefs when assigning and scheduling work, because many religions have differing days of worship and holidays. For example, some firms have established "holiday swapping pools," whereby Christian employees can work during Passover or Ramadan or Chinese New Year, and employees from other religions work Christmas. Other firms allow employees a set number of days off for holidays, without specifying the holidays in company personnel policies.

Another potential area for conflict between employer policies and employee religious practices is dress and appearance. Some religions have standards about the appropriate attire for women. Also, some religions expect men to have beards and facial hair. For instance, a Muslim worker received $70,000 in back pay and damages because the company's policy of prohibiting beards violated the worker's religious standards.[36]

Another issue relates to religious expression. In the last several years, employees in several cases have sued employers for prohibiting them from expressing their religious beliefs at work. In one case, an individual won a court case because the employer would not let him pray during his work breaks and co-workers harassed him and wiped their shoes on his prayer rug. In other cases, employers have had to take action because of the complaints by workers that employees were aggressively "pushing" their religious views at work, thus creating a "hostile environment."[37] Other areas that may need to be considered when dealing with religion at work are food, on-site religion-based groups, office decoration, and religious practice at work.

MANAGING DIVERSITY

As the foregoing examples have shown, the U.S. workforce has become quite diverse, and EEO regulation has encouraged and protected that diversity. Figure 5-8 shows the tangible indicators of diversity that employers must consider.

Further, by the year 2050, current minority groups will likely be 49.9% of the population. The Census Bureau says non-Hispanic whites represent 69% of the population currently, and will be 50.1% in 2050. The Hispanic population will increase by 188%, to about one-quarter of the overall population. The Asian population will triple.[38] These increases in minority proportions suggest that in some cases, the company without a diversity plan may not have sufficient employees.[39] Many organizations have already begun to deal with the diversity challenge, but others have yet to begin.[40]

Different organizations approach the management of diversity from several perspectives. As Figure 5-9 shows, the continuum can run from resistance to creation of an inclusive diversity culture. The increasing diversity of the available workforce, combined with growing shortages of workers in many occupations and industries, has forced more employers to recognize that diversity must be managed.

Part of the process of solving the challenges of diversity may include diversity audits to see what the issues might be for a particular employer. Cummins, a global company based in Columbus, Indiana, sends diverse audit teams from site to site to conduct interviews with employees. The process is carried out with confidentiality. Cummins has seen several advantages in this approach.[41] A similar approach can be taken for global firms that face a more complicated diversity situation but similar problems. An audit of all their various national employment law and diversity issues might be necessary.[42]

Figure 5-8 *Indicators of Diversity*

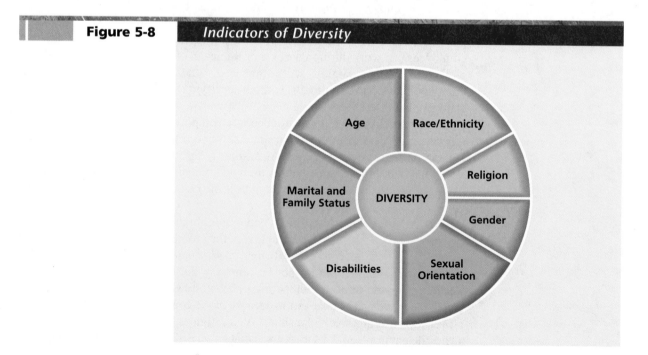

Figure 5-9

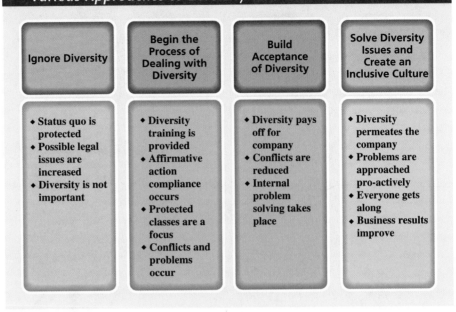

Various Approaches to Diversity and Their Results

Ignore Diversity	Begin the Process of Dealing with Diversity	Build Acceptance of Diversity	Solve Diversity Issues and Create an Inclusive Culture
◆ Status quo is protected ◆ Possible legal issues are increased ◆ Diversity is not important	◆ Diversity training is provided ◆ Affirmative action compliance occurs ◆ Protected classes are a focus ◆ Conflicts and problems occur	◆ Diversity pays off for company ◆ Conflicts are reduced ◆ Internal problem solving takes place	◆ Diversity permeates the company ◆ Problems are approached pro-actively ◆ Everyone gets along ◆ Business results improve

Diversity: The Business Case

Diversity can be justified on the basis of social justice, but does it make business sense? The answer is mixed. The "business case" for diversity can be argued based on the following points:

◆ Diversity allows new talent and new ideas from employees of different backgrounds.

◆ Diversity helps recruiting and retention, as people tend to prefer to work with others "like" themselves.

◆ Diversity allows for an increase of market share, as customers tend to prefer to buy from people of the same race or ethnic background.

◆ Diversity leads to lower costs because there may be fewer lawsuits.

Many "experts" have significant interests in diversity efforts.[43] It should be noted that an estimated $8 billion industry has developed around diversity: consultants, diversity officers, scorecards, benchmarks, best practices, training, conferences, and academies exist to deal with it.[44] Whether or not the money spent by employers is producing results has not been clearly documented.

A five-year study of several companies examined how diversity affects performance. It found that managing diversity leads to more effective performance on gender issues, but that racial and ethnic diversity may, in fact, have a negative impact on business performance unless specific controls are in place. If not managed properly, diversity can produce miscommunication, conflict, higher turnover, and lower performance.[45]

The study found that racial diversity was associated with poor performance under conditions of *competition* and *growth*. Diversity was found to have had a negative impact when groups did not treat it as a resource for innovation and learning, but it enhanced performance when diversity *was* treated as a source of

LOGGING ON...

Diversity, Inc.
This site provides news, resources, and other commentary on the role of diversity in corporations.
www.diversityinc.com

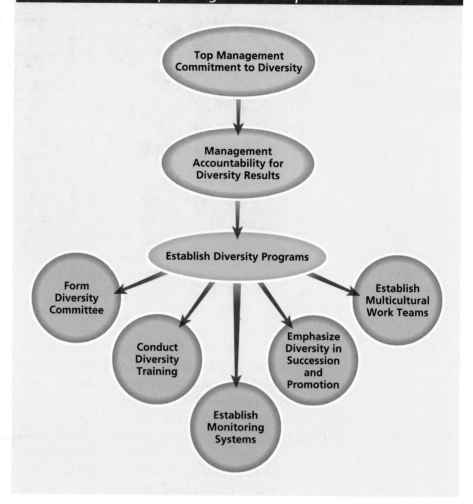

Figure 5-10 — *Common Diversity Management Components*

Top Management Commitment to Diversity

Management Accountability for Diversity Results

Establish Diversity Programs

Form Diversity Committee

Conduct Diversity Training

Establish Monitoring Systems

Emphasize Diversity in Succession and Promotion

Establish Multicultural Work Teams

innovation and learning. More diversity was a negative when diversity was defined as more women and the group was led by a woman, but not when teams were led by men. A final result showed that customers did not care whether they were served by people of the same gender or race.[46]

The study makes clear that we have more to learn on diversity and whether or not the business case is valid. Diversity can contribute to business success, *but* organizations need to learn how to maximize its benefits and minimize the problems. Good intentions alone do not guarantee good results in this area.

Diversity Management Programs and Activities

A wide variety of programs and activities have been used in organizations as part of diversity management efforts. Figure 5-10 shows common components of diversity management efforts. For diversity to succeed, the most crucial component is seeing it as a commitment throughout the organization, beginning with top management. Diversity results must be measured, and management accountability for achieving these results must be emphasized and rewarded. Once management accountability for diversity results has been established, then a number of different activities can be implemented as part of a diversity management program, including diversity training.

DIVERSITY TRAINING

There are a number of different goals for traditional diversity training. One prevalent goal is to minimize discrimination and harassment lawsuits. Other goals focus on improving acceptance and understanding of people with different backgrounds, experiences, capabilities, and lifestyles.

THOMSON

WEST

DIVERSITY TRAINING
Contains 10 diversity tips and links to diversity management and training information.
Custom Search:
☑ ANALYSIS
Exact Phrase: Consider diversity training

Components of Traditional Diversity Training

Approaches to diversity training vary, but often include at least three components. *Legal awareness* is the first and most common component. Here, the training focuses on the legal implications of discrimination. A limited approach to diversity training stops with these legal "do's and don'ts."

By introducing *cultural awareness,* employers hope to build greater understanding of the differences among people. Cultural awareness training helps all participants to see and accept the differences in people with widely varying cultural backgrounds.

The third component of diversity training—*sensitivity training*—is more difficult. The aim here is to "sensitize" people to the differences among them and how their words and behaviors are seen by others. Some diversity training includes exercises containing examples of harassment and other behaviors.

Effects of Diversity Training

The effects of diversity training are viewed as mixed by both organizations and participants. Relatively few studies have been done on the effectiveness of diversity training expenditures, other than asking participants how they felt about the training. There is some concern that the programs may be interesting or entertaining, but may not produce longer-term changes in people's attitudes and behaviors toward others with characteristics different from their own.

Mixed reviews about the effectiveness of diversity training suggest that either the programs or how they are implemented are suspect. Two common complaints are:

♦ Diversity training tends to draw attention to differences, building walls rather than breaking them down.
♦ Much of the content in diversity training is viewed as "politically correct," which means that it blames majority individuals, particularly white males, for past wrongs.

Some argue that traditional diversity training more often than not has failed, pointing out that it does not reduce discrimination and harassment complaints. Rather than reducing conflict, in a number of situations, diversity training has heightened hostility and conflicts.[47] In some firms, it has produced divisive effects, and has not taught the behaviors needed for employees to get along in a diverse workplace.

This last point, focusing on behaviors, seems to hold the most promise for making diversity training more effective. For instance, dealing with cultural diversity as part of training efforts for sales representatives and managers has produced positive results. Teaching appropriate behaviors and skills in relationships with others is more likely to produce satisfactory results than focusing just on attitudes and beliefs among diverse employees.

Backlash Against Diversity Efforts

The negative consequences of diversity training manifest themselves more broadly in a backlash against diversity efforts, as the chapter opener shows. This backlash takes two main forms. First, and somewhat surprisingly, the individuals in protected groups, such as women and members of racial minorities, sometimes see the diversity efforts as inadequate and nothing but "corporate public relations." Thus, it appears that by establishing diversity programs, employers are raising the expectation levels of protected-group individuals, but the programs are not meeting the expectations. This failure can result in further disillusionment and more negativity toward the organization by those who would initially appear to benefit the most from such programs.

On the other side, a number of individuals who are not in protected groups, primarily white males, believe that the emphasis on diversity sets them up as scapegoats for the societal problems created by increasing diversity. Surveys of white males frequently show hostility and anger at diversity efforts. Those programs are widely perceived as benefiting only women and minorities and taking away opportunities for men and non-minorities.[48] This resentment and hostility is usually directed at affirmative action programs that employers have instituted.

Managing diversity training, and indeed diversity itself, is more than assuming that "good intentions cannot hurt." Programs must be well thought out and implemented. Diversity is a reality for employers today, and effective diversity management is crucial to HR management.

SUMMARY

- Affirmative action has been intensely litigated, and the debate about it continues today.
- Discrimination on the basis of race and national origin is illegal, and employers must be prepared to deal with language issues and racial harassment as part of effectively managing racial/ethnic diversity.
- As more women have entered the workforce, sex/gender issues in equal employment have included discrimination in jobs and careers, as well as sexual harassment in its two forms, quid pro quo and hostile environment.
- Employers should develop policies on sexual harassment, have identifiable complaint procedures, train all employees on what constitutes sexual harassment, promptly investigate complaints, and take action when sexual harassment is found to have occurred.
- Aging of the U.S. workforce has led to more concerns about age discrimination, especially in the form of forced retirement and termination.

- Employers are recognizing the value of attracting and retaining older workers through greater use of part-time work and phased retirement programs.
- Individuals with disabilities represent a significant number of current and potential employees.
- Employers are making reasonable accommodations for individuals with disabilities, including those with mental or life-threatening illnesses.
- Reasonable accommodation also is a strategy that can be used to deal with the religious diversity of employees.
- Diversity management is concerned with organizational efforts to ensure that all people are valued regardless of their differences.
- The "business case" for diversity is built on its ability to allow new talent and ideas, aid in employee attraction and retention, allow for an increase in market share, and lead to lower costs. However, results are mixed.
- Diversity training has had limited success, possibly because it too often has focused on beliefs rather than behaviors.

REVIEW AND APPLICATION QUESTIONS

1. Explain why you agree or disagree with this statement: "Employers in the U.S. must learn to adjust to diversity if they are to be effective in the future."

2. From your own experience or that of someone you know, give examples of the two types of sexual harassment.

3. You need to convince upper management of the usefulness of a company-wide diversity program. How will you define diversity and what arguments can be made for doing so? Use the Web site *http://www.diversityworld.com* and the article "Workforce Diversity" on the site to gather the necessary information.

LEARNING REVIEW

To check your knowledge of the chapter, review the following. (Answers after the supplemental case.) For more questions, see the Study Guide.

1. Which of the following is a reason why organizations should be proactively addressing their diversity issues?
   a. There is a shortage of workers in many occupations and industries.
   b. It is "politically correct."
   c. Diversity creates conflict and problems.
   d. Doing so is the legal responsibility of organizations.

2. One result of the increasing number of women in the workforce is _____.
   a. conflict between men and women
   b. increased productivity
   c. the movement of women into jobs traditionally held by men
   d. an increase in the number of men staying home with children

3. By setting _____, _____, and _____ as part of affirmative action efforts, employers specify how many of which types of individuals they hope to employ in the future.
   a. quotas, goals, projections
   b. quotas, timetables, estimates
   c. goals, targets, timetables
   d. policies, procedures, goals

4. In a recent survey, employers listed the barriers to employment and advancement that individuals with disabilities face. Which barrier was mentioned by the largest percentage of employers?
   a. lack of experience
   b. cost of supervision
   c. lack of requisite skills and training
   d. attitudes or stereotypes

CASE

CONSTRUCTION INDUSTRY CONFRONTS DIVERSITY

The construction industry is a major employer in many states and communities throughout the United States. Unfortunately, another common characteristic of the construction industry is a high number of work-related accidents and injuries. Increasingly, the employees in the construction industry are individuals for whom English is not their primary language, and a number of construction site accidents have been attributed to the lack of English language skills

of some construction workers. For instance, it has been estimated that 40% of work-related accidents in the Houston, Texas, area involve Hispanic workers. Some specific examples illustrate the concerns:

- A worker demolishing a building in New York City was hit and killed by a demolition boom. He left the machine on and pushed the wrong boom control pedal. Even though a safety instruction manual was available in English, the worker spoke and understood only Polish.

♦ A Hispanic worker was killed when the window-washing lift he was on fell 30 feet because the lift platform had not been locked properly. None of the safety instructions and warnings were in Spanish.

Even if injuries or deaths do not result, the diversity of workers on many construction sites means different languages are being used by employees, with less English fluency than might be desirable. Assume that workers from Croatia, Mexico, Sudan, and Laos are all working on the same construction project. How would a supervisor who speaks only English communicate with them?

Fortunately, some progressive construction firms have recognized that the diversity of workers presents some opportunities for building better workplaces. By working with construction unions, some employers have developed English training programs for workers that are offered to non-English-speaking employees. Other employers have translated their safety training materials into Spanish or other languages. Also, greater use of pictures and diagrams rather than written instructions has helped with safer operation of equipment and machinery.

Some construction firms have conducted basic foreign language classes for English-speaking supervisors and managers. Still other employers have conducted diversity training in order to reduce conflicts among the different racial/ethnic groups and to promote better working relationships and greater understanding. This training also has helped reduce the number of racial harassment complaints and lawsuits.

The major benefit of these efforts is that the number of work-related accidents at some construction sites has declined. Another benefit is that whenever employees receive training in their own languages and/or their boss makes some effort to speak the native language of construction workers, employee morale appears to increase and turnover tends to decline. Thus it appears that addressing diversity issues pays off for construction employers.[49]

Questions

1. As the HR manager, how would you begin development of a diversity effort for a construction firm?
2. Discuss the difficulties in dealing with employees from a number of different racial/ethnic groups when developing and conducting safety training.

SUPPLEMENTAL CASE: Discrimination?

This case illustrates issues involved in a disciplinary action when a protected class individual is involved. (For the case, go to http://mathis.swlearning.com/)

Learning Review Answers: 1. a, b 2. c 3. c 4. b

NOTES

1. Christopher Cornell, "When 'Pushback' Comes to Shove," *Human Resource Executive,* May 16, 2003, 24–27.
2. Marjorie Valbrun, "EEOC Sees Rise in Inter-race Complaints of Color Bias," *Wall Street Journal,* August 7, 2003, B1.
3. Jessica Collison, "2002 Workplace Demographic Trends Survey," *SHRM Research,* 2002, 8.

4. Michael R. Haines, "Ethnic Differences in Demographic Behavior in the United States: Has There Been a Convergence?" *National Bureau of Economic Research Working Paper 9042,* July 2002, 1–45.
5. Roger O. Crockett and Peter Coy, "Progress Without Parity," *Business Week,* July 14, 2003, 101–102.

6. M. Lee Pelton, "After the Supreme Court Michigan Cases," *The Presidency,* Fall 2003, 18–27.
7. Stephen J. Hirschfeld, "Americans Believe Affirmative Action in Hiring Has Been Good," *Press Releases Polls/Surveys,* http://www.employmentlawalliance.com.
8. Harry Holzer and David Neumark, "What Does Affirmative Action Do?" *Industrial and Labor Relations*

Review, 53 (2000), 240–271; Markus Kemmelmeier, "Individualism and Attitudes Toward Affirmative Action," *Basic and Applied Social Psychology,* 25 (2003), 111–119; T. J. Elkins et al., "Promotion Decisions in an Affirmative Action Environment," *Journal of Applied Social Psychology,* 33 (2003), 1111–1139; and Daniel Sabbagh, "Judicial Uses of Subterfuge: Affirmative Action Reconsidered," *Political Science Quarterly,* 118 (2003), 411–436.

9. Steve Jordan, "Work Ethic Wins Over Employers," *Omaha World-Herald,* June 8, 2003, 5A.

10. Brian Grow and Manjeet Kripalani, "A Loophole as Big as a Mainframe," *Business Week,* March 10, 2003, 82–83.

11. Scott S. Moore, "EEOC Issues Guidance on National Origin Discrimination," *Baird Holm Labor and Employment Law Update,* January 2003, 1–2.

12. Donna H. Crecca, "Speaking in Tongues," *Chain Leader,* August 2002, 1–2.

13. *Hollins v. Delta Airlines,* 10th Cir. 99-4072 (January 29, 2001).

14. Margaret M. Clark, "Study Plots Trends in Maternity Leave, Women's Work Patterns," *HR Executive,* January 2002, 15.

15. Michelle Conlin and Diane Brady, "Goodbye, Boss Lady. Hello, Soccer Mom," *Business Week,* April 1, 2002, 79; Lisa Belkin, "The Opt-Out Option," *New York Times,* October 26, 2003, sec. 6, 42.

16. Kemba J. Dunham, "Stay-at-Home Dads Fight Stigma," *Wall Street Journal,* August 26, 2003, B1.

17. Anne M. Alexander et al., "A Study of the Disparity in Wages and Benefits Between Men and Women in Wyoming," 2003, *www.Wyomingbusiness.org/women.*

18. Diffusing the Equity Issue: How BC-BS Instituted a Gender Balanced Pay Plan," *Pay for Performance Report,* July 2003, 1–2.

19. Sue Shellenbarger, "Number of Woman Managers Rises," *Wall Street Journal,* September 30, 2003, D2.

20. "ILO Says U.S. Women Executives Outpace Foreign Counterparts," *Global Perspective,* Bureau of National Affairs, 2001, 1.

21. Linda Babcock et al., "Nice Girls Don't Ask," *Harvard Business Review,* October 2003, 14.

22. Kristi Arellano, "Undoing the Glass Ceiling," *The Denver Post,* December 22, 2003, 1E.

23. Sharon Foley, Deborah Kidder, and Gary Powell, "The Perceived Glass Ceiling and Justice Perceptions: An Investigation of Hispanic Law Associates," *Journal of Management,* 28 (2002), 471.

24. Sue Shellenbarger, "Getting Fired for Dating Co-worker: Office Romance Comes Under Attack," *Wall Street Journal,* February 14, 2004, D1.

25. "HR Managers/Executives Worry About Workplace Romance," *Human Resource Department Management Report,* April 2002, 1; "Workplace Romance," *SHRM Research,* April 2002, 3 and 6.

26. "Americans Overwhelmingly Disapprove of Romantic Relationships Between Supervisors and Employees," *Employment Law Alliance,* November 29, 2001, 1.

27. Karyn-Siobhan Robinson, "Cyber-Sex Permeates the Workplace," *HR News,* April 2001, 10.

28. "Sexual Orientation Irrelevant in Sex Harassment Claims," *HR News,* November 2002, 6.

29. Corrie Fishel et al., "Is There a 'Standard of Care' to Define Reasonable Harassment Investigation?" *SHRM White Paper,* August 2003, 1–12.

30. Patrick J. Pursell, "Older Workers: Employment and Retirement Trends," *Monthly Labor Review,* November 2003, 38–45.

31. "SHRM 2002 Workplace Demographic Trends Survey," *SHRM Research,* September 2002, 6.

32. Jessica Collison, "Older Workers Survey," *SHRM Research,* June 2003, 1–34.

33. Daniel B. Moskowitz, "Accessing the Disabled," *Human Resource Executive,* February 2001, 70–73.

34. "Coverage for Mental Disabilities Debated," *Bestwire,* November 27, 2001, 1.

35. Adapted from Joseph Pereira, "To Save on Health-Care Costs, Firms Fire Disabled Workers," *Wall Street Journal,* July 14, 2003, 1.

36. "Religion in the Workplace Survey," *SHRM Research,* 2001, 1–55.

37. Jill Elswick, "Firms Urged to Provide Benefits for Religious Diversity," *Benefits News Dot Com,* October 2003, 58–59.

38. Genaro C. Armas, "The U.S. in 2050: Minorities Will Be Half the Population," *Denver Post,* March 18, 2004, 23A.

39. "HR's Next Recruiting Challenge: No Diversity Plan; No Workers," *Human Resource Department Management Report,* January 2003, 1–2.

40. "Turn Diversity to Your Advantage," *Research Technology Management,* July 2003, 1–8.

41. Lin Grensing-Pophal, "A Balancing Act on Diversity Audits," *HR Magazine,* November 2001, 1–3.

42. Justine S. Juson et al., "A Global Approach: The Employment Law Audit for the Multi-Jurisdictional Employer," *SHRM Global Forum,* May 2003, 1–26.

43. "Hours of Diversity Training Has a Positive Bottom Line Impact," *SHRM/Fortune Survey of Diversity Initiatives on the Bottom Line,* in *Managing Training and Development,* July 2001, 1–6; Sheila Cschimpf, "Bottom Line Successes with Diversity Have Turned Employers into Advocates," *Bulletin to management BNA Inc.,* May 15, 2003, 153–160; and "Nextel Diversity Training Produces an ROI of 163%," *Manager's Training and Development,* February 2003, 1–3.

44. Fay Manson, "Diversity's Business Case: Doesn't Add Up," *Workforce,* April 2003, 28–33.

45. Thomas Kochan et al., "The Effects of Diversity on Business Performance: Report of the Diversity Research Network," *Human Resource Management,* 42 (2003), 3–21.

46. Mary Kwak, "The Paradoxical Effects of Diversity," *MIT Sloan Management Review,* 44 (2003), 7.

47. C. W. Von Bergen et al., "Unintended Negative Effects of Diversity Management," *Public Personnel Management,* 31 (2002), 1–12.

48. Martha Frase-Blunt, "Thwarting the Diversity Backlash," *HR Magazine,* June 2003, 137–144.

49. Based on Mike Florey, "Solving the Language Barrier," *Occupational Health and Safety,* January 2001, 37–38; and Tina Kelley "Foreign Languages Often Form Construction Barriers," *Omaha World-Herald,* February 27, 2000, 17G.

CHAPTER 6

Jobs and Job Analysis

After you have read this chapter, you should be able to:

- Discuss workflow analysis and business process re-engineering as approaches to organizational work.

- Define job design and identify five design characteristics for jobs.

- Explain how work schedules and telework are affecting jobs and work.

- Describe job analysis, and the stages in and methods used in the job analysis process.

- Indicate how job analysis has both behavioral and legal aspects.

- Identify the components of job descriptions.

Dramatic Changes Occurring in Work and Jobs

Work and jobs in organizations throughout the world are changing dramatically. Globalization and technology are primary drivers. Consider how some jobs have been shifted from the U.S. and Europe to China, India, Romania, Mexico, the Philippines, and other lower-wage countries.

Changes in work and jobs are being reported daily on television, on the Internet, and in other media. According to a recent study by RAND Corporation, key factors that will be affecting the jobs in many organizations are the following:[1]

* *Globalization of workers,* whereby much work can be done regardless of time zones and physical locations.
* *Organization of production,* in which firms are decentralizing work and using information technology (IT) to network with employees, contractors, co-workers in various other countries, and "e-lancers" (freelance contributors who use IT).

* *Changes in work and job skill requirements,* where jobs are increasingly falling into two tiers, requiring either highly skilled technical and professional workers or lower-skilled service employees.

The interplay of these factors, along with the demographic shifts occurring in many countries, will dramatically change how work is done, where work is done, and the number of jobs. The aging of the workforce and subsequent retirements of many experienced workers will provide employers opportunities to restructure or eliminate jobs. Information technology is being incorporated more extensively into jobs, which means more pressures on HR training efforts.

These are just two illustrations of how HR management is being affected by changes in jobs and work. How HR professionals deal with these pressures will significantly affect how HR is viewed by executives and managers.

"That is not in my job description."

—*A disgruntled employee*

One way to visualize an organization is as an entity that takes inputs from the surrounding environment and then, through some kind of "work," turns those inputs into goods or services. **Work** is effort directed toward accomplishing results. The work may be done by humans, machines, or both. But the entire amount of work to be done must be divided into jobs so that it can be coordinated in some logical way. A **job** is a grouping of tasks, duties, and responsibilities that constitutes the total work assignment for employees. These tasks, duties, and responsibilities may change over time, and therefore the job may change. Ideally, when all the jobs in an organization are added together, they should equal the amount of work that the organization needs to have done—no more, no less. The degree to which this ideal is met drives differences in organizational productivity.

Work Effort directed toward accomplishing results.

Job Grouping of tasks, duties, and responsibilities that constitutes the total work assignment for employees.

CHANGING NATURE OF WORK AND HR MANAGEMENT

During the past 10 years, domestic increases in organizational productivity in many industries have resulted in significant changes in work and jobs. A focus on productivity has led to replacing employees with technology, international outsourcing of work to lower-wage countries, and more flexibility in how and when work is done. These changes have led to political pressures, including efforts to stop "job exporting," and proposed restrictions on allowing foreign workers into the U.S. and some European countries.

Jobs that are "routinized," meaning jobs whose work can be divided into step-by-step tasks with little variation daily and weekly, are being affected the most. Routinization occurs in jobs ranging from assembling products on a manufacturing line, to doing repetitive computer programming, to handling simple customer service inquiries, to processing mortgage loan applications. Use of information and communications technologies has allowed the "knowledge" to perform these tasks to be built into computer programs and databases, so that individuals with less training and fewer skills can perform the work by just "following the programs." Jobs and work that cannot be routinized and that require significant communication or managerial capability are less likely to be affected by job losses.[2] Undoubtedly, the nature of jobs and work will continue to be affected as the drive for productivity and global competitiveness continue.

As Figure 6-1 indicates, organizational values and strategies linked to customer needs, affect the nature of work, which in turn influences the relationship of jobs, people, and HR management activities. For Southwest Airlines, organizational values and strategies are tied to having involved employees working in an enjoyable culture that delivers dependable service at low fares. Thus, Southwest has a high degree of flexibility in how its employees perform the work, even to the point that customer service agents may help clean planes or unload luggage if the workload demands it. Other airlines, such as American and United, have higher fares, more service amenities, but employees who have more narrowly defined jobs. The ways work is done and jobs are designed and performed vary significantly under the two approaches, and the differences impact the number of jobs and people needed.

In HR management, the most important activities associated with jobs are:

♦ *Workflow analysis:* Examining how work flows through the organization, in order to improve operating efficiency
♦ *Re-engineering:* Improving productivity by changing the jobs themselves
♦ *Job design:* Dividing up organizational work into jobs in order to utilize employee capabilities effectively

Figure 6-1   *Influences Affecting Jobs, People, and Related HR Policies*

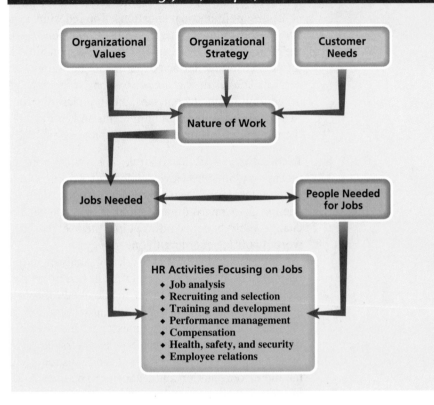

- *Job analysis:* Analyzing what people do in jobs currently
- *Job descriptions and job specifications:* Identifying the tasks, duties, and responsibilities in jobs, and the capabilities needed for people to perform jobs well

Workflow Analysis

Workflow analysis
Study of the way work (inputs, activities, and outputs) moves through an organization.

Workflow analysis is the study of the way work moves through an organization. Usually, it begins with an examination of the quantity and quality of the desired and actual *outputs* (goods and services). Then, the *activities* (tasks and jobs) that lead to the outputs are evaluated to see if they are achieving the desired outputs. Finally, the *inputs* (people, material, information, data, equipment, etc.) must be assessed to determine if they make the outputs and activities more efficient and better.

Several years ago, at an electric utility company, if a customer called with a service outage problem, a customer service representative typically took the information and entered it into a database. Then, in the operations department, a dispatcher accessed the database to schedule a line technician to repair the problem. Then, someone else called to tell the customer when the repair would be done. The line technician also received instructions from a supervisor, who got information on workload and locations from the dispatcher.

A workflow analysis showed that there were too many steps involving too many different jobs in this process. Therefore, the utility implemented a new customer information system and combined the dispatching function with customer service.

The redesign permitted the customer service representatives to access workload information and schedule the line technicians as part of the initial consumer phone calls, except in unusual situations. The redesign required redefining tasks, duties, and responsibilities of several jobs. Implementing the new jobs required training the customer service representatives in dispatching, as well as moving dispatchers into the customer service department and training them in all facets of customer service. The result was a more responsive workflow for customers, more efficient scheduling of line technicians, and broader jobs for customer service representatives. Ultimately, through retirements and employee attrition, the firm has reduced the number of customer service employees by 20%.

Technology and Workflow The utility company example illustrates how technology must be viewed as part of workflow analysis. With the rapid growth of the Internet and Web-based information systems, changes in the workflow are occurring in many organizations. For instance, having employees access and change their benefits information themselves has reduced HR administrative work by 60%, according to one survey.[3]

Another example of why workflow analysis may be helpful involves secretarial jobs. The number of secretaries has declined sharply over the last decade as technology has changed. Also, the demand for typists has dropped as more managers compose their own memos and reports on e-mail. Voice mail has reduced the need for someone taking messages, and copying and filing are done in many organizations through office service centers, not by individual secretaries. On the other hand, current office support functions require greater responsibility and entail more coordination and authority.[4] The job title today is more likely to be "administrative coordinator" or "administrative assistant" to reflect these changes, and organizations are doing workflow analysis to make adjustments.

Business Process Re-engineering

After workflow analysis provides an understanding of how work is being done, re-engineering generates the needed changes in the operations. The purpose of **business process re-engineering (BPR)** is to improve such activities as product development, customer service, and service delivery. BPR consists of three phases:

1. *Re-think:* Examine how the current organization of work and jobs affects customer satisfaction and service.
2. *Re-design:* Analyze how jobs are put together, the workflow, and how results are achieved; then redesign the process as necessary.
3. *Re-tool:* Look at new technologies (equipment, computers, software, etc.) as opportunities to improve productivity, service quality, and customer satisfaction.

In the past, HR has been excluded from BPR in many organizations because the focus of BPR has been operations areas. However, because of the desire to improve HR efficiency and effectiveness, BPR is increasingly being applied to HR management.[5] Global banks such as Barclays, Deutsche, and Standard Chartered have engaged in re-engineering and re-structuring their HR departments.[6] Key to successful BPR of HR or other organizational areas is providing effective and continuous communication, doing detailed planning, and training managers on the BPR processes. Without these efforts, the success rates of BPR are low, around 30%.[7]

Business process re-engineering (BPR) Measures for improving such activities as product development, customer service, and service delivery.

IMPORTANCE OF JOB DESIGN

Job design Organizing tasks, duties, and responsibilities into a productive unit of work.

Job design refers to organizing tasks, duties, and responsibilities into a productive unit of work. It addresses the content of jobs and the effect of jobs on employees. Identifying the components of a given job is an integral part of job design. Currently, job design is receiving greater attention for three major reasons:

- Job design can influence *performance* in certain jobs, especially those where employee motivation can make a substantial difference. Lower costs resulting from reduced turnover and absenteeism also are related to the effective design of jobs.
- Job design can affect *job satisfaction*. Because people are more satisfied with certain job configurations than with others, identifying what makes a "good" job becomes critical.
- Job design can affect both *physical* and *mental health*. Problems such as hearing loss, backache, and leg pain sometimes can be traced directly to job design, as can stress, high blood pressure, and heart disease.

Person/job fit Matching characteristics of people with characteristics of jobs.

Not everyone would enjoy being an HR manager, an engineer, a nurse, or a drill-press operator. But various people like and do well at each of these jobs. The **person/job fit** is a simple but important concept of matching characteristics of people with characteristics of jobs. Figure 6-2 depicts some of the personal factors and job functions that must mesh. If a person does not fit a job, either the person can be changed or replaced, or the job can be altered. In the past, it was much more common to try to make the "round" person fit the "square" job.

Figure 6-2 **Person/Job Fit**

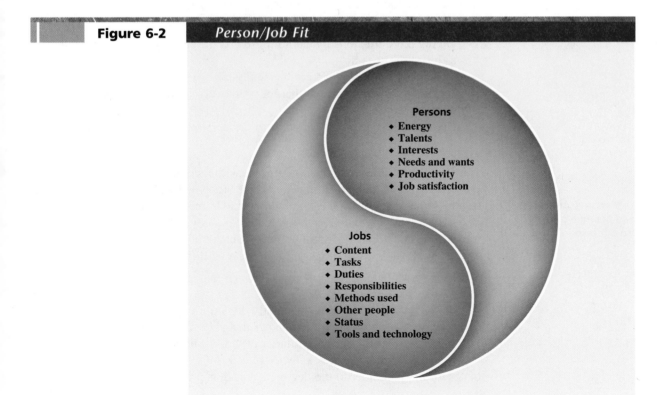

Persons
- Energy
- Talents
- Interests
- Needs and wants
- Productivity
- Job satisfaction

Jobs
- Content
- Tasks
- Duties
- Responsibilities
- Methods used
- Other people
- Status
- Tools and technology

But, it is hard to successfully reshape people. By re-designing jobs, the person/job fit may be improved more easily. Improving the person/job fit may affect individual responses to jobs because a job may be motivating to one person but not to someone else. Also, depending on how jobs are designed, they may provide more or less opportunity for employees to satisfy their job-related needs. For example, a sales job may furnish a good opportunity to satisfy social needs, whereas a training assignment may satisfy a need to expand expertise in a specific area. A job that gives little autonomy may not satisfy a need to be creative or innovative.

Nature of Job Design

One tactic for designing or re-designing jobs is to simplify the job tasks and responsibilities. Job simplification may be appropriate for jobs that are to be staffed with entry-level employees. However, making jobs too simple may result in boring jobs that appeal to few people, causing high turnover. Several different approaches are useful as part of job design.

Job Enlargement and Job Enrichment Attempts to alleviate some of the problems encountered in excessive job simplification fall under the general headings of job enlargement and job enrichment. **Job enlargement** involves broadening the scope of a job by expanding the number of different tasks to be performed. **Job enrichment** is increasing the depth of a job by adding responsibility for planning, organizing, controlling, or evaluating the job. A manager might enrich a job by promoting variety, requiring more skill and responsibility, providing more autonomy, and adding opportunities for personal growth. Giving an employee more responsibility for planning and controlling the tasks to be done also enriches a job. However, simply adding more similar tasks actually does not enrich a job. Some examples of job enrichment are:

◆ Giving the employee an entire job rather than just a piece of the work
◆ Giving more freedom and authority so that the employee can perform the job as he or she sees fit
◆ Increasing the employee's accountability for work by reducing external control
◆ Expanding assignments so that the employee can learn to do new tasks and develop new areas of expertise
◆ Giving feedback reports directly to the employee rather than only to management

Job Rotation One technique that can break the monotony of an otherwise simple, routine job is **job rotation,** which is the process of shifting a person from job to job. Some argue that job rotation does little in the long run—that although rotating a person from one boring job to another may help somewhat initially, the jobs are still perceived as boring. The advantage of job rotation is that it develops an employee's capabilities for doing several different jobs.

Characteristics of Jobs

A model developed by Hackman and Oldham identifies five important design characteristics of jobs. Figure 6-3 shows that *skill variety, task identity,* and *task significance* affect the meaningfulness of work; *autonomy* stimulates responsibility; and *feedback* provides knowledge of results. Each aspect can make a job better for the jobholder to the degree that each is present.

Job enlargement Broadening the scope of a job by expanding the number of different tasks to be performed.

Job enrichment Increasing the depth of a job by adding responsibility for planning, organizing, controlling, or evaluating the job.

Job rotation Process of shifting a person from job to job.

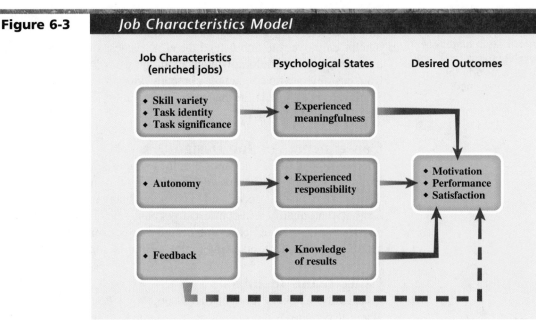

Figure 6-3   *Job Characteristics Model*

Skill Variety The extent to which the work requires several different activities for successful completion indicates its **skill variety.** For example, lower skill variety exists when an assembly-line worker performs the same two tasks repetitively. The more skills involved, the more meaningful the work becomes. Skill variety is not to be confused with *multi-tasking,* which is doing several tasks at the same time with computers, telephones, personal organizers, and other gadgets. The price of multi-tasking may be never getting away from the job—not a "better" outcome for everyone.

Skill variety Extent to which the work requires several different activities for successful completion.

Task Identity The extent to which the job includes a "whole" identifiable unit of work that is carried out from start to finish and that results in a visible outcome is its **task identity.** For example, in the utility company mentioned previously, now, when a customer calls with a problem, one employee, called a Customer Care Advocate, handles problems from maintenance to repair. As a result, more than 40% of customer problems are resolved by one person while the customer is still on the line. Previously, fewer than 1% of customer problems were resolved immediately because the customer service representative had to complete paperwork and forward it to operations, which then followed a number of separate steps using different people to resolve problems. In the current system, the Customer Care Advocate generally follows the problem from start to finish, solving the whole problem, not just a part of it, which makes the job more meaningful to the employees involved.

Task identity Extent to which the job includes a "whole" identifiable unit of work that is carried out from start to finish and that results in a visible outcome.

Task Significance The impact the job has on other people indicates its **task significance.** A job is more meaningful if it is important to other people for some reason. For instance, soldiers may experience more fulfillment when defending their country from a real threat than when merely training to stay ready in case a threat arises.

Task significance Impact the job has on other people.

Autonomy The extent of individual freedom and discretion in the work and its scheduling indicates **autonomy.** More autonomy leads to a greater feeling of personal responsibility for the work.

Autonomy Extent of individual freedom and discretion in the work and its scheduling.

Feedback The amount of information employees receive about how well or how poorly they have performed is **feedback.** The advantage of feedback is that it helps employees to understand the effectiveness of their performance and contributes to their overall knowledge about the work. At one firm, feedback reports from customers who contact the company with problems are given directly to the employees who handle the customers' complaints, instead of being given only to the department manager.

Consequences of Job Design

Jobs designed to take advantage of these important job characteristics are more likely to be positively received by employees. Job characteristics can help distinguish between "good" and "bad" jobs. Many approaches to enhancing productivity and quality reflect efforts to expand one or more of the job characteristics. Because of the effects of job design on performance, employee satisfaction, health, and other factors, changing the design of some jobs may be beneficial.

Using Teams in Jobs

Typically, a job is thought of as something done by one person. However, where it is appropriate jobs may be designed for teams. In an attempt to make jobs more meaningful and to take advantage of the increased productivity and commitment that can follow such a change, more organizations are assigning jobs to teams of employees instead of individuals. Some firms have gone as far as dropping such terms as *workers* and *employees,* replacing them with *teammates, crew members, associates,* and other titles that emphasize teamwork.

Special-Purpose Teams Organizations use several types of teams that function outside the scope of members' normal jobs and meet from time to time. One is the **special-purpose team,** which is formed to address specific problems, improve work processes, and enhance the overall quality of products and services. Often, special-purpose teams are a mixture of employees, supervisors, and managers.

Self-Directed Teams The **self-directed team** is composed of individuals who are assigned a cluster of tasks, duties, and responsibilities to be accomplished. Unlike special-purpose teams, self-directed work teams become the regular entities that use internal decision-making processes. Use of self-directed work teams must be planned well and fit the culture of the organization.[8]

The role of supervisors and managers changes with use of teams.[9] An interesting challenge for self-directed work teams involves the emergence or development of team leaders. The role of the team leader differs from the traditional role played by supervisors or managers. Rather than giving orders, the team leader becomes a facilitator to assist the team, mediate and resolve conflicts among team members, and interact with other teams and managers in other parts of the organization. Team members may need to share or rotate leadership for different phases of projects in which special expertise may be beneficial.

Global Virtual Teams With more firms operating globally, the use of global teams has increased significantly. Many times, members of global teams never or seldom meet in person. Instead, they "meet" electronically, using Web-based systems.[10]

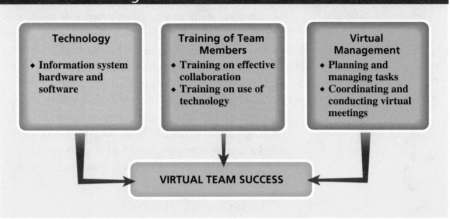

Figure 6-4

Factors Affecting Virtual Team Success

Technology
- Information system hardware and software

Training of Team Members
- Training on effective collaboration
- Training on use of technology

Virtual Management
- Planning and managing tasks
- Coordinating and conducting virtual meetings

VIRTUAL TEAM SUCCESS

Virtual team
Organizational team composed of individuals who are geographically separated but linked by communications technology.

The **virtual team** is composed of individuals who are separated geographically but linked by communications technology. Virtual teams are used by such firms as Hewlett-Packard, IBM, Ford, Toyota, and Johnson & Johnson.[11] Research by the Center for the Study of Work Teams indicates that the success of virtual work teams depends on a number of factors.[12] Some of the key factors are depicted in Figure 6-4.

Advantages and Disadvantages of Team Jobs

Doing work with teams has been a popular form of job redesign for the last decade. Improved productivity, increased employee involvement, more widespread employee learning, and greater employee ownership of problems are among the potential benefits. For example, the United Auto Workers (UAW) and Chrysler have used work teams effectively in a number of facilities, though this cooperative effort has not been successful in all locations.[13]

One study on the use of self-directed work teams in auto service garages found that productivity increased, especially when both individual and team compensation were used.[14] However, how to measure the performance of teams poses a problem. Compensating individual team members so that they see themselves as a team rather than just a group of individuals is a related issue not adequately addressed in many team situations.

Teams are more likely to be successful if they are allowed to function with sufficient authority to make decisions about their activities and operations. As a transition to work teams occurs, significant efforts are necessary to define the areas, scope of authority, and goals of the teams. Additionally, teams must recognize and address dissent and conflict. Contrary to what some might believe, suppressing dissent and conflict to preserve harmony ultimately becomes destructive to the effective operation of a team.

As seen in the example of the UAW and Chrysler, not every use of teams as a part of job design has been successful. In some cases, employers find that teams work better with "group-oriented" employees than with more individualistically focused workers. Further, much work does not really need a team, and many companies have used teamwork without much thought. Too often, *teamwork* can be a buzzword or "feel-good" device that may actually get in the way of effective decision making.

JOB DESIGN, WORK SCHEDULES, AND TELEWORK

A job consists of the tasks an employee does, the relationships required on the job, the tools the employee works with, and many other elements. Considerations that increasingly affect job design for both employers and employees are the time during which work is scheduled and the location of employees when working.

The pressures of employees' lives, coupled with the demands of their jobs, can lead to emotional imbalances that are collectively labeled *stress.* The main causes of job-related stress appear to be time pressures, fears of losing a job, deadlines, and fragmented work. The increasing use of technology means that many employees are "always on call" and can "burn out" on work. How employees view the demands of work have been identified in a study that found the following:[15]

◆ More than half of U.S. workers (52%) say they would be willing to trade a day off a week for a day's pay a week.

◆ Over 80% wish they had more time to spend with family, and this view is shared among adults with and without children.

◆ About 60% feel pressure to work too much.

To respond to stress and other concerns, employers are using different work schedule alternatives, flexible scheduling, and telework.

Work Schedules

The work schedules associated with different jobs vary. Some jobs must be performed during "normal" daily work hours and workdays, and some jobs require working nights, weekends, and extended hours.

Global Work Schedule Differences The number of work hours in a week varies from country to country. For instance, the European Union (EU) has issued the Working Time Directive, which states that employees in EU countries should work a maximum of 48 hours a week. However, EU workers can opt out of the maximum, and over one-third of British workers have such opt-outs.[16] France has a law limiting working hours to 35 hours a week, but because various exceptions are made, the weekly average is lower than 35. Workers in the U.S. average significantly more work hours than do workers in many other developed countries.[17]

Work Schedule Alternatives The traditional work schedule in the U.S., in which employees work 8 hours a day, 5 days a week at the employer's place of operation, is in transition. Throughout many organizations, many different work scheduling arrangements are being used, including the 4-day, 40-hour week; the 4-day, 32-hour week; the 3-day week; shift work and the compressed workweek; flexible scheduling; and job sharing.

Shift Work and the Compressed Workweek *Shift work* is a commonly used work schedule design. Many organizations need 24-hour coverage and therefore schedule three 8-hour shifts each day. Many employers provide some form of additional pay, called a *shift differential,* for working the evening or night shift. Shift work has been found to increase the number of workplace accidents, with employees who work the "graveyard" shift (11 P.M. to 7 A.M.) having 20% more accidents and five times as many work-related mistakes.[18] Also, shift work has long been known to cause difficulties for many employees with families.

On-line Bidding for Work Schedules

Many people today are familiar with on-line bidding for time-shares, merchandise, books, and other goods and services through Timeshares.com, eBay, Amazon.com, and other Web auction sites. But a growing number of employers, especially health-care organizations, have established on-line bidding for job assignments for nurses and other staff members who have skills that are scarce.

Hospitals in Florida, New York, Pennsylvania, and other states have established on-line bidding for additional work hours for nurses. For instance, at St. Peter's Hospital in Albany, New York, nurses wanting extra hours can go to St. Peter's Jobs Online to see shifts available. Individual nurses post their "wage bids," and the hospital receives their qualifications and bids to determine who fills which hours. The bidders are notified within 24 hours.

The benefit of "job auctions" is that hospitals fill their staffing schedules while avoiding the higher fees of temporary help firms and also allowing qualified nurses to pick up additional hours and income. St. Peter's management estimated that in one year, the "on-line jobs auction saved the hospital almost one million dollars."[19]

Employees like flexible scheduling because it helps them better balance their work and family life demands.[20] Employers benefit also. According to one study, flexible work practices increased profitability and employee retention in the surveyed firms.[21] Employers using flexible scheduling specifically have found it easier to attract and retain working mothers, many of whom wish to continue their careers while devoting time to family responsibilities.

Compressed workweek Schedule in which a full week's work is accomplished in fewer than 5 8-hour days.

Twelve-hour shifts, which some employees choose, often involve significant life changes. Nevertheless, many employers must have 24-hour, 7-day coverage, so shift work is likely to continue to be an HR concern.

One type of shift work is the **compressed workweek**, in which a full week's work is accomplished in fewer than 5 8-hour days. Compression simply alters the number of hours an employee works each day, usually resulting in more work hours each day and fewer workdays each week. The use of the compressed workweek illustrates how greater flexibility in work schedules is occurring.

Flextime Scheduling arrangement in which employees work a set number of hours a day but vary starting and ending times.

Flexible Scheduling Flexible work schedules allow organizations to make better use of workers by matching work demands to work hours. One type of flexible scheduling is **flextime,** in which employees work a set number of hours a day but vary starting and ending times. In another variation, employees work 30 minutes longer Monday through Thursday, take short lunch breaks, and leave work at 1 P.M. or 2 P.M. on Friday. Some firms allow employees to work reduced schedules and receive proportional wages/salaries. Certain levels of hours are worked weekly or monthly.

Flexible scheduling allows management to relax some of the traditional "time clock" control of employees, while still covering workloads. In the United States, over 30% of the full-time workforce vary their work hours from those in the traditional model, more than double the rate a decade ago. Also, over 60% of workers surveyed indicated that they had complete or some control over their work schedules.[22] One unique approach to work scheduling is described in the Technology Transforming HR.

Job Sharing Another alternative used to add flexibility and more work-life balancing is **job sharing,** in which two employees perform the work of one full-time job. For instance, a hospital allows two radiological technicians to fill one job, whereby each individual works every other week. Such arrangements are beneficial for employees who may not want to or be able to work full-time because of family, school, or other reasons. Job sharing also can be effective because each person can substitute for the other when illness, vacation, or other circumstances occur. The key to successful job sharing is that both "job sharers" work effectively together and each is competent in meeting the job requirements.[23]

Telework

The developments in information and communications technology mean that employees can work anywhere and anytime. As a result, a growing number of employers are allowing employees to work from widely varied locations. Some employees work partly at home and partly at an office, while others share office space with other "office nomads." According to the International Telework Association & Council, in a recent year, firms employed 23.5 million teleworkers. Additionally, about the same number of teleworkers are self-employed individuals who have their own businesses or work as independent contractors or contingent workers. These numbers represent a 40% increase in just two years.[23]

Some employees *telecommute,* which means they work via electronic computing and telecommunications equipment. Many U.S. employers have employees who telecommute one or more days a week, and who may work from home, a client's facility, an airport conference room, a work suite in a hotel resort, a business-class seat on an international airline flight, or even a vacation condominium. Telecommuting allows employees to work from home when bad weather or family illness prevents them from coming to office facilities.[24]

HR Management of Teleworkers A number of HR management issues and employee concerns must be addressed with teleworkers, as Figure 6-5 indicates. Because managers have less direct supervision of teleworkers, there is more self-

Figure 6-5	*Telework Concerns of Management and Employees*
Management Concerns	**Employee Concerns**
◆ Loss of control over staff	◆ Overworking and failing to create a distinction between work and home
◆ Employee perceptions of unequal treatment when only certain employees are permitted to telecommute	◆ Trouble with self-motivation and time management
◆ Security, especially with information systems	◆ Difficulty working among home distractions
◆ Diminished interaction with staff, and team-building problems	◆ Isolation and diminished interaction with colleagues
◆ Employees' spending time on non-work-related activities (e.g., child care)	◆ Negative impact on career development from less interaction with supervisors
◆ Telecommuters' straying from the culture and values of the organization	◆ Inadequate equipment or technology support

Source: "Telework Concerns of Management and Employees," *HR Executive Series: Focus on Telecommunicating Executive Summary,* Bureau of National Affairs, Winter 2002, 2. For more information about this publication and other HR solutions visit http://hrcenter.bna.com or call 800-372-1033. Used with permission.

scheduling by employees. Thus, employees have to be evaluated more on producing results and less on "putting in time."[25] HR must develop policies regarding teleworkers and must train supervisors and managers on how to "lead" employees who may not be physically present much of the time."[26]

Another concern comes from evidence that telecommuting employees may not advance as quickly as office-based executives, because of an "out-of-sight, out-of-mind" framework of some managers.[28] This is especially a concern for global employees, whose working hours may not be consistent with U.S. working times. For instance, the 15-hour time zone difference between the U.S. and some Asian countries may make it difficult for global employees to participate in conference calls. Despite these concerns, telework is likely to continue to increase, which may add to employee stress.

NATURE OF JOB ANALYSIS

Job design attempts to develop jobs that fit effectively into the flow of the organizational work that needs to be done. The more narrow focus of job analysis centers on using a formal system to gather data about what people do in their jobs. This data is used to generate job descriptions and job specifications. An overview of job analysis is depicted in Figure 6-6.

The most basic building block of HR management, **job analysis,** is a systematic way of gathering and analyzing information about the content, context, and human requirements of jobs. Using job analysis to document HR activities is im-

Job analysis Systematic way of gathering and analyzing information about the content, context, and human requirements of jobs.

Figure 6-6 *Job Analysis in Perspective*

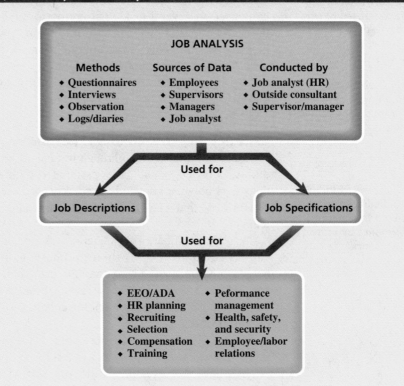

portant because the legal defensibility of an employer's recruiting and selection procedures, performance appraisal system, employee disciplinary actions, and pay practices rests in part on the foundation of job analysis.

Various methods and sources of data can be used to conduct job analyses. The real value of job analysis begins as the information is compiled into job descriptions and job specifications for use in virtually all HR activities. To justify HR actions as job related for EEO matters, accurate details on job requirements are needed. To be effective, HR planning, recruiting, and selection all must be based on job requirements and the capabilities of individuals.[29] Additionally, compensation, training, and employee performance appraisals all should be based on the specific needs of the job. Job analysis also is useful in identifying job factors and duties that may contribute to workplace health and safety issues. For instance, one study used job analysis to identify physical demands causing work-related injuries, and the steps to be taken to reduce those injuries.[30] Finally, job analysis plays a key role in employee/labor relations issues.

Job analysis involves collecting information on the characteristics of a job that differentiate it from other jobs. The information generated by job analysis may be useful in redesigning jobs, but its primary purpose is to capture a clear understanding of what is done on a job and what capabilities are needed to do it as designed. There are two approaches to job analysis, one focusing on tasks performed in the job, the other on competencies needed for job performance.

Task-Based Job Analysis

Task Distinct, identifiable work activity composed of motions.

Task-based job analysis is the most common form and focuses on the tasks, duties, and responsibilities performed in a job. A **task** is a distinct, identifiable work activity composed of motions, whereas a **duty** is a larger work segment composed of several tasks that are performed by an individual. Because both tasks and duties describe activities, it is not always easy or necessary to distinguish between the two. For example, if one of the employment supervisor's duties is to interview applicants, one task associated with that duty would be asking questions. **Responsibilities** are obligations to perform certain tasks and duties.

Duty Larger work segment composed of several tasks that are performed by an individual.

Responsibilities Obligations to perform certain tasks and duties.

Competency-Based Job Analysis

Unlike the traditional approach to analyzing jobs, which identifies the tasks, duties, knowledge, and skills associated with a job, the competency approach considers how the knowledge and skills are used. **Competencies** are individual capabilities that can be linked to enhanced performance by individuals or teams.

Competencies Individual capabilities that can be linked to enhanced performance by individuals or teams.

A growing number of organizations use some facets of competency analysis in various HR activities.[31] The three primary reasons that organizations use a competency approach are: (1) to communicate valued behaviors within the organization; (2) to raise competency levels throughout the organization; and (3) to emphasize people's capabilities for enhancing the competitive advantage of the organization.

The concept of competencies varies widely from organization to organization.[32] *Technical competencies* often refer to specific knowledge and skills employees have. For example, skills for using specialized software to design Web pages or for operating highly complex machinery and equipment may be cited as

Competencies Needed in Hotels

In the last several years, significant attention in HR has been focused on identifying competencies needed in jobs. Studies made in various industries on the types of competencies have been helpful. To extend the understanding of competencies needed by middle managers in hotels, Brophy and Kiely focused on identification of managerial competencies in two departments common in many hotels: rooms management and food/beverage operations. The results of their study were published in the *Journal of European Industrial Training* and contained several interesting insights.

The study was conducted on 42 three-star hotels in Ireland and used input from both general managers and lower-level managers in the hotels. Data were gathered using interviews, task analyses, and critical incident documentation. The results of the study identified the following managerial competency areas as important in the two hotel departments:

- Providing customer care
- Maintaining quality and standards
- Managing staff
- Achieving profitability
- Growing the business

Within each of these areas, specific competencies were identified. In customer care, some competencies were: having good relations with hotel customers, handling dissatisfied customers, resolving complaints, and tracking customer satisfaction. In the area of strategic business, competencies included financial awareness and strategic thinking, among others. Though the competencies identified in this study are specific to the hotel industry, similar competencies may be needed in a number of other industries.[33]

competencies.[34] Some of the following have been identified as *behavioral competencies:*

- Customer focus
- Team orientation
- Technical expertise
- Results orientation
- Communication effectiveness

- Leadership
- Conflict resolution
- Innovation
- Adaptability
- Decisiveness

The competency approach also attempts to identify the hidden factors that are often critical to superior performance. For instance, many supervisors talk about employees' attitudes, but they have difficulty identifying exactly what they mean by "attitude." The competency approach uses a variety of methodologies to help the supervisors articulate examples of what they mean by attitude and how those factors affect performance. In some industries, research has been done to identify critical competencies, as the HR Perspective indicates.

Choosing a Job Analysis Approach

Whether to use the task-based or competency-based approach to job analysis is affected by the nature of jobs and how work is changing. In some high-technology industries, employees work in cross-functional project teams and shift from project to project. Organizations in these industries focus less on performing specific tasks and duties, and more on competencies needed to attain results. For example, a project team of eight employees in different countries who are developing software that will allow various credit cards to be used with ATMs worldwide will work on many different tasks and use various competencies, some individually and some with other team members. When that project is finished, those employees will move to other projects, possibly with other employees. Such shifts may happen several times a year. Therefore, the basis for recruiting, selecting, and compensating these individuals is their competencies and capabilities, not just the tasks they perform.

However, in many industries, traditional jobs will continue to exist. Studying these jobs and their work consequences is relatively easy because of the repetitiveness of the work and the limited number of tasks each worker performs, so the task-based approach to job analysis is appropriate. Studying different types of jobs—lower-skilled ones or more varied, highly technical ones—requires different approaches to job analysis. Some important considerations include how job analysis is done, who provides data, and who conducts and uses the data so that job descriptions and job specifications can be prepared and reviewed. Focusing on the competencies that individuals need in order to perform complete jobs, rather than on the tasks, duties, and responsibilities that compose a job, emphasizes how significantly people's capabilities influence organizational performance.

Traditional task-based job analysis can provide a defensible basis for such activities as compensation, selection, and training, all of which may be the subject of legal action by employees if they believe they are being wronged in some way. The traditional job analysis approach has been used successfully to substantiate employment decisions. Currently, there is little legal precedent regarding competency analysis, which leaves it open to legal challenge as not being documented as well as the traditional approach. For that reason, task-based job analysis is more widely used, and it is the primary focus of the rest of this chapter.

Job Analysis Responsibilities

Job analysis requires a high degree of coordination and cooperation between the HR unit and operating managers. Figure 6-7 shows a typical division of responsibilities in organizations with an HR unit. The assignment of responsibility for job analysis depends on who can best perform various aspects of the process. In large companies, the HR unit supervises the process to maintain its integrity, and writes the job descriptions and specifications for uniformity. The managers

Figure 6-7 — *Typical Division of HR Responsibilities: Job Analysis*

HR Unit	Managers
• Coordinates job analysis • Writes job descriptions and specifications for review by managers • Periodically reviews job descriptions and specifications • Reviews managerial input to ensure accuracy • May seek assistance from outside experts for difficult or unusual analyses	• Complete or help complete job analysis information • Review job descriptions and specifications and maintain their accuracy • Request new analysis as jobs change • Use job analysis information to identify performance standards • Provide information to outside experts

Figure 6-8 Stages in the Job Analysis Process

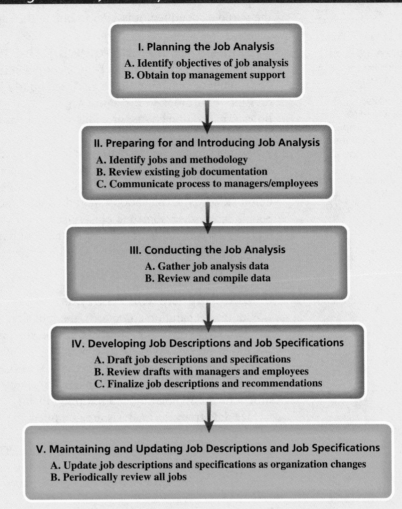

I. **Planning the Job Analysis**
A. Identify objectives of job analysis
B. Obtain top management support

II. **Preparing for and Introducing Job Analysis**
A. Identify jobs and methodology
B. Review existing job documentation
C. Communicate process to managers/employees

III. **Conducting the Job Analysis**
A. Gather job analysis data
B. Review and compile data

IV. **Developing Job Descriptions and Job Specifications**
A. Draft job descriptions and specifications
B. Review drafts with managers and employees
C. Finalize job descriptions and recommendations

V. **Maintaining and Updating Job Descriptions and Job Specifications**
A. Update job descriptions and specifications as organization changes
B. Periodically review all jobs

review the efforts of the HR unit to ensure accuracy and completeness. They also may request new job analyses when jobs change significantly. In small organizations, managers may perform all the job analysis responsibilities.

▌ STAGES IN THE JOB ANALYSIS PROCESS

The process of job analysis must be conducted in a logical manner, following appropriate management and professional psychometric practices. Therefore, analysts usually follow a multi-stage process, regardless of the specific job analysis methods used.[35] The stages for a typical job analysis, as outlined in Figure 6-8, may vary somewhat with the number of jobs included.

Planning the Job Analysis

A crucial aspect of the job analysis process is the planning done before gathering data from managers and employees. Probably the most important consideration is to identify the objectives of the job analysis, from just updating job descriptions to revising the compensation programs in the organization. Whatever the purpose identified, it is vital to obtain the support of top management.

Preparing for and Introducing the Job Analysis

Preparation for job analysis begins with identification of the jobs under review. For example, are the jobs to be analyzed hourly jobs, clerical jobs, all jobs in one division, or all jobs in the entire organization? Reviewing existing job descriptions, organization charts, previous job analysis information, and other industry-related resources is part of the planning.

This phase identifies those who will be involved in conducting the job analysis and the methods to be used. A crucial step is communicating and explaining the process to managers, affected employees, and other concerned people, such as union stewards. Explanations should address the natural concerns and anxieties people have when someone closely scrutinizes their jobs. When employees are represented by a union, it is essential that union representatives be included in reviewing the job descriptions and specifications, to lessen the possibility of future conflicts.

Conducting the Job Analysis

With the preparation completed, the job analysis can be conducted. The methods selected will determine the timeline for the project. If questionnaires are used, it is often helpful to have employees return them to supervisors or managers for review before giving them back to those conducting the job analysis. Questionnaires should be accompanied by a letter explaining the process and instructions for completing and returning them.

Once data from job analysis are compiled, the information should be sorted by job, organizational unit, and job family. This step allows for comparison of data from similar jobs throughout the organization. The data also should be reviewed for completeness, with follow-up as needed in the form of additional interviews or questions to be answered by managers and/or employees.

Developing Job Descriptions and Job Specifications

At the fourth stage, the job analysts draft job descriptions and job specifications. Generally, organizations find that having managers and employees write job descriptions is not recommended for several reasons. First, it reduces consistency in format and details, both of which are important given the legal consequences of job descriptions. Second, managers and employees vary in their writing skills. Also, they may write the job descriptions and job specifications to reflect what they do and what their personal qualifications are, not what the job requires.

Completed drafts should be reviewed with managers and supervisors. Whether employees review the drafts or wait to receive the final job descriptions is often determined by the managerial style of the supervisors/managers and the culture of the organization regarding employee participation and communication. When the job descriptions are finished, the HR department distributes them to managers, supervisors, and employees. Supervisors or managers should then review the completed descriptions with the appropriate employees to ensure understanding and agreement on the content that will be linked to the performance appraisals, as well as to all other HR activities.

Maintaining and Updating Job Descriptions and Job Specifications

Once job descriptions and specifications have been completed and reviewed by all appropriate individuals, a system must be developed for keeping them current. One effective way to ensure that appropriate reviews occur is to use job descriptions and job specifications in other HR activities. For example, each time a vacancy occurs, the job description and specifications should be reviewed and revised as necessary *before* recruiting and selection efforts begin. Similarly, in some organizations, managers and employees review their job descriptions during each performance appraisal interview.

▮▮▮ JOB ANALYSIS METHODS

LOGGING ON...

Job-Analysis.NETwork
This Web site has resources for conducting a job analysis, including different types of methods, legal issues, questionnaires, and job descriptions.
www.job-analysis.net

Job analysis information about what people are doing in their jobs can be gathered in a variety of ways. One consideration is who is to conduct the job analysis. Most frequently, a member of the HR staff coordinates this effort. Depending on which of the methods discussed next is used, others who often participate are managers, supervisors, and employees doing the jobs. For more complex analyses, industrial engineers may conduct time-and-motion studies.

Another consideration is the method to be used. Whatever method is chosen, it should be content based and should not reflect rater bias.[36] Common methods are observation, interviewing, questionnaires, and computerized systems. The use of a combination of these approaches depends on the situation and the organization.[37] Each of these methods is discussed next.

Observation

With the observation method, a manager, job analyst, or industrial engineer observes the individual performing the job and takes notes to describe the tasks and duties performed. Use of the observation method is limited because many jobs do not have complete and easily observed job duties or complete job cycles. Thus, observation may be more useful for repetitive jobs and in conjunction with other methods.

Work Sampling One type of observation, work sampling, does not require attention to each detailed action throughout an entire work cycle. This method allows a manager to determine the content and pace of a typical workday through statistical sampling of certain actions rather than through continuous observation and timing of all actions. Work sampling is particularly useful for routine and repetitive jobs.

Employee Diary/Log Another method requires employees to "observe" their own performances by keeping a diary/log of their job duties, noting how frequently those duties are performed and the time required for each one. Although this approach sometimes generates useful information, it may be burdensome for employees to compile an accurate log. Also, employees sometimes perceive this approach as creating needless documentation that detracts from the performance of their work.

Interviewing

The interview method of gathering information requires a manager or an HR specialist to visit each job site and talk with the employees performing each job.

| **Figure 6-9** | *Typical Areas Covered in a Job Analysis Questionnaire* |

Duties and Percentage of Time Spent on Each
- Regular duties
- Special duties performed less frequently

Supervision
- Supervision given to others
- Supervision received from others

Decisions Made
- Records and reports prepared
- Materials and equipment used
- Financial/budget responsibilities

Contact with Other People
- Internal contacts
- External contacts

Physical Dimensions
- Physical demands
- Working conditions

Jobholder Characteristics
- Knowledge
- Skills
- Abilities
- Training needed

A standardized interview form is used most often to record the information. Frequently, both the employee and the employee's supervisor must be interviewed to obtain a complete understanding of the job.

Sometimes, group or panel interviews are used. A team of "subject matter experts" (SMEs) who have varying insights about a group of jobs is assembled to provide job analysis information.[38] This option may be particularly useful for highly technical jobs and others for which a range of individuals can provide input.

The interview method can be quite time-consuming, especially if the interviewer talks with two or three employees doing each job. Professional and managerial jobs are often more complicated to analyze and usually require longer interviews. For these reasons, combining the interview method with one of the other methods is suggested.

Questionnaires

The questionnaire is a widely used method of gathering data on jobs. A survey instrument is developed and given to employees and managers to complete. The typical job questionnaire often covers the areas shown in Figure 6-9.

The questionnaire method offers a major advantage in that information on a large number of jobs can be collected inexpensively in a relatively short period of time. However, the questionnaire method assumes that employees can accurately analyze and communicate information about their jobs. Employees may vary in their perceptions of the jobs, and even in their literacy. Using interviewing and observation in combination with the questionnaire method allows analysts to clarify and verify the information gathered in questionnaires.

Position Analysis Questionnaire (PAQ) The Position Analysis Questionnaire is a specialized instrument incorporating checklists. Each job is analyzed on 27 dimensions composed of 187 "elements." The PAQ has a number of divisions, each containing numerous job elements. The divisions include:

- *Information input:* Where and how does the worker get information to do the job?
- *Mental process:* What levels of reasoning are necessary on the job?

- *Work output:* What physical activities are performed on the job?
- *Relationships with others:* What relationships are required while performing the job?
- *Job context:* What working conditions and social contexts are involved in the job?
- *Other:* What else is relevant to the job?

The PAQ focuses on "worker-oriented" elements that describe behaviors necessary to do the job, rather than on "job-oriented" elements that describe the technical aspects of the work. Although its complexity may deter many potential users, the PAQ is easily quantified and can be used to conduct validity studies on selection tests. It also may contribute to internal pay fairness because it considers the varying demands of different jobs.

Managerial Job Analysis Questionnaire Because managerial jobs differ in character from jobs with clearly observable routines and procedures, some specialized methods have evolved for their analysis. One well-known and widely used method is the Management Position Description Questionnaire (MPDQ). Composed of more than 200 statements, the MPDQ examines a variety of managerial dimensions, including decision making and supervising.

Computerized Systems

With the expansion of information technology, computerized job analysis systems have been developed. These systems all have several common characteristics, including the way they are administered. First, analysts compose task statements that relate to all jobs. Then, those statements are listed in questionnaires, which are distributed to employees. Next, employees respond on computer-scannable documents, which are fed into computer-based services capable of scoring, recording, analyzing, and reporting thousands of pieces of information about any job.

An important feature of computerized job analysis is the specificity of data that can be gathered. All this specific data is compiled into a job analysis database. As a result, a computerized job analysis system can often reduce the time and effort involved in writing job descriptions. These systems often store banks of job duty statements that relate to each of the task and scope statements of the questionnaires. Interestingly, a study found little variation in the results of job analysis data obtained by paper questionnaires and by computerized methods.[39] Thus, use of computerized methods will likely grow.

Job Analysis and the U.S. Department of Labor

A variety of resources related to job analysis are available from the U.S. Department of Labor (DOL). The resources have been developed and used over many years by various entities within the DOL, primarily the Employment and Training Administration.

Functional Job Analysis (FJA) This method is a comprehensive approach to job analysis. FJA considers: (1) goals of the organization, (2) what workers do to achieve those goals in their jobs, (3) level and orientation of what workers do, (4) performance standards, and (5) training content. A functional definition of what is done in a job can be generated by examining the three components of *data, people,* and *things.* The levels of these components are used to identify and compare important elements of jobs.

LOGGING ON...

PAQ Services, Inc.
This site provides information on position analysis questionnaires for management and administrative positions.
www.paq.com

O*Net On-line The DOL has made a major commitment to provide usable information on skills, abilities, knowledge, work activities, and interests associated with a wide range of jobs and occupations. O*Net is a database compiled by the U.S. Department of Labor to provide basic occupational data to anyone who is interested. Information in O*Net covers more than 950 occupations based on the Standard Occupational Classification (SOC) developed by the government.

O*Net also provides extensive linkages to additional resources on workplace issues. It is a valuable and time-saving resource for job analysis and for writing good descriptions and specifications.

Combination Methods

There are a number of different ways to obtain and analyze information about a job. Therefore, in dealing with issues that may end up in court, HR specialists and others doing job analysis must carefully document all the steps taken. Each method has strengths and weaknesses, and a combination of methods generally may be more appropriate than one method alone. Regardless of the methods used, in its most fundamental form job analysis provides the information necessary to develop job descriptions and job specifications.

BEHAVIORAL ASPECTS OF JOB ANALYSIS

Job analysis involves determining what the "core" job is. A detailed examination of jobs, although necessary, sometimes can be a demanding and disruptive experience for both managers and employees, in part because job analysis can identify the difference between what currently is being performed in a job and what *should* be done. Consequently, a number of behavioral factors can affect job analysis, some of which are discussed next.

"Inflation" of Jobs and Job Titles

Employees and managers have some tendency to inflate the importance and significance of their jobs. Because job analysis information is used for compensation purposes, both managers and employees hope that "puffing up" jobs will result in higher pay levels and greater "status" for resumes and more possible promotion opportunities.

Titles of jobs often get inflated too.[40] Some firms give fancy titles in place of pay raises, and others do it to keep well-paid employees from leaving for "status" reasons. Some industries, such as banking and entertainment, are well known for their title inflation. For instance, banking and financial institutions use officer designations to enhance status. In one small Midwestern bank, an employee who had three years' experience as a teller was "promoted" with no pay increase to Second Vice President and Senior Customer Service Coordinator. She basically became the lead teller when her supervisor was out of the bank, and now could sign a few customer account forms, but her duties remained basically the same. As the HR Globally identifies, the problem of job titles is not limited to U.S. firms.

Employee and Managerial Anxieties

Both managers and employees have concerns about job analysis. Through the information developed in a job analysis, the job description is ideally supposed

Japanese Job Titles and Global Competitiveness

The culture of Japan has long included extensive use of *keigo,* an honorific language that has traditionally been taught to children and continued throughout the society. Central to *keigo* is the formalization of how individuals are addressed. The formalization often includes language to honor older people, organizational managers, and others.

However, the global economic changes facing many Japanese companies has led a growing number of employers to issue policy directives to discontinue the use of job titles and such high formalization when addressing other employees and managers. For example, Elpida, a senior conductor manufacturer, issued a policy statement that employees should add *san* to their names, as in Tyuka-san, but

discontinue addressing each other by additional formal job titles, such as Department Chief Tyuka-san. Another factor contributing to the decline in formal language use by younger Japanese is that many of them have had education and travel experiences outside of Japan, and they use just first names or first and last names without any formalities.

Numerous older Japanese have resisted the changes, and Japanese schools have had to change educational curriculums to de-emphasize formalization. Thus HR professionals and managers from throughout the world who deal with Japanese companies, employees, and customers must be aware of the changes in job titling in Japan.[41]

to identify the nature of a job. However, it is difficult to capture all facets of a job, particularly for jobs in which employees perform a variety of duties and operate with a high degree of independence.

Managerial Straitjacket One primary concern of managers and supervisors is that the job analysis and job descriptions will unrealistically limit managerial flexibility. As workloads and demands change rapidly, managers and supervisors want to be able to move duties to other employees, cross-train employees, and have more dynamic, flexible ways to get work accomplished. If job descriptions are written restrictively, some employees may use an omission to limit managerial flexibility. The resulting attitude, "It's not in my job description," puts a straitjacket on a manager. In some organizations with unionized workforces, very restrictive job descriptions exist. Because of such difficulties, the final statement in many job descriptions is a *miscellaneous clause,* which consists of a phrase similar to "Performs other duties as needed upon request by immediate supervisor." This statement covers unusual situations that may occur in an employee's job. However, duties covered by this phrase cannot be considered essential functions under the Americans with Disabilities Act.

Employee Fears One fear that employees may have concerns the purpose of a detailed investigation of their job. Perhaps they feel that such a detailed look means someone thinks they have done something wrong. The attitude behind such a fear might be, "As long as no one knows precisely what I am supposed to be doing, I am safe."

Often the content of a job may reflect the desires and skills of the incumbent employee. For example, in one firm, an employee promoted to customer service supervisor continued to spend considerable time answering customer calls, rather than supervising employees taking the calls. As part of job analysis discussions, the customer service manager and the supervisor discussed the need for the supervisor to train his employees on handling special customer requests and to delegate more routine duties to the customer service representatives.

Also, some employees may fear that an analysis of their jobs will put a straitjacket on them, limiting their creativity and flexibility by formalizing their duties. However, analyzing a job does not necessarily limit job scope or depth. In fact, having a well-written, well-communicated job description can assist employees by clarifying their roles and the expectations within those roles.[42] One effective way to handle anxieties is to involve the employees in the revision process.

Current Incumbent Emphasis

As illustrated by the example of the customer service supervisor, a job analysis and the resulting job description and job specifications should not describe just what the person currently doing the job does and what his or her qualifications are. The incumbent may have unique capabilities and the ability to expand the scope of the job to assume more responsibilities. The company would have difficulty finding someone exactly like that individual if he or she left. Consequently, it is useful to focus on *core* duties and *necessary* knowledge, skills, and abilities (KSAs) by determining what the jobs would be if the incumbents quit or were no longer available to do the jobs.

▮▮ LEGAL ASPECTS OF JOB ANALYSIS

The previous chapters on equal employment laws, regulations, and court cases emphasized that legal compliance must focus on the jobs that individuals perform. The 1978 Uniform Guidelines on Employee Selection Procedures make it clear that HR requirements must be tied to specific job-related factors if the employers are to defend their actions as a business necessity.

Job Analysis and the Americans with Disabilities Act (ADA)

HR managers and their organizations must identify job activities and then document the steps taken to identify job responsibilities. One result of the ADA is increased emphasis by employers on conducting job analysis, as well as developing and maintaining current and accurate job descriptions and job specifications.

The ADA requires that organizations identify the *essential job functions,* which are the fundamental duties of a job. These do not include the marginal functions of the positions. **Marginal job functions** are duties that are part of a job but are incidental or ancillary to the purpose and nature of the job. Figure 6-10 shows three major considerations used in determining essential functions and marginal functions. Job analysts, HR staff members, and operating managers must evaluate and make decisions when information on the three considerations is not clear.

Marginal job functions Duties that are part of a job but are incidental or ancillary to the purpose and nature of the job.

Job analysis also can identify the physical demands of jobs.[43] An understanding of the skills and capabilities used on a job is critical. For example, a customer service representative must be able to hear well enough to take customer orders. However, hearing may be less essential for a heavy equipment operator in a quarry.

An important part of job analysis is obtaining information about what duties are being performed and what percentage of time is devoted to each duty. As the ADA suggests, the percentage of time spent on a duty generally indicates its rel-

Figure 6-10	Determining Essential and Marginal Job Functions	
Considerations	**Essential Functions**	**Marginal Functions**
Percentage of time spent on task	Significant percentage of time, often 20% or more, is spent on task.	Generally less than 10% of time is spent on task.
Frequency of task	Task is performed regularly: daily, weekly, or monthly.	Task is performed infrequently or when substituting in part of another job.
Importance of task	Task affects other parts of job and other jobs.	Task is unrelated to job, and there are few consequences if not performed.

ative importance. Also, if duties are regularly performed daily, weekly, and/or monthly, they are more likely to be seen as essential. In contrast, a task performed only infrequently or when helping another worker on a totally unrelated job more likely falls in the marginal category.[44]

Another consideration is the ease or difficulty of assigning a duty to be performed by someone else, or in a different job. For instance, assume an assembler of electronic components places the completed parts in a bin next to the work area. At the end of each day, the bin of completed parts must be carried to another room for use in the final assembly of a product. Carrying the bin to the other room probably would be defined as a marginal task, because assigning someone else to carry it would not likely create major workflow problems with other jobs and workers.

Job Analysis and Wage/Hour Regulations

Typically, job analysis identifies the percentage of time spent on each duty in a job. This information helps determine whether someone should be classified as exempt or non-exempt under the wage/hour laws.

As will be noted in Chapter 12, the federal Fair Labor Standards Act (FLSA) and most state wage/hour laws indicate that the percentage of time employees spend on manual, routine, or clerical duties affects whether they must be paid overtime for hours worked in excess of 40 a week. To be exempt from overtime, the employees must perform their *primary duties* as executive, administrative, professional, or outside sales employees. *Primary* has been interpreted to mean occurring at least 50% of the time.

Other legal-compliance efforts, such as those involving workplace safety and health, can also be aided through the data provided by job analysis. In summary, it is extremely difficult for an employer to have a legal staffing system without performing job analysis. Truly, job analysis is the most basic HR activity and the foundation for most other HR activities.

JOB DESCRIPTIONS AND JOB SPECIFICATIONS

The output from analysis of a job is used to develop a job description and its job specifications. Together, these summarize job analysis information in a readable format and provide the basis for defensible job-related actions. They also identify individual jobs for employees by providing documentation from management.

In most cases, the job description and job specifications are combined into one document that contains several sections. A **job description** identifies the tasks, duties, and responsibilities of a job. It describes what is done, why it is done, where it is done, and, briefly, how it is done. **Performance standards** flow directly from a job description, and indicate what the job accomplishes and how performance is measured in key areas of the job description.

Performance Standards

The reason for establishing performance standards linked to job descriptions and job responsibilities is clear. If employees know what is expected and how performance is to be measured, they have a much better chance of performing satisfactorily. Figure 6-11 shows job duty statements and some performance standards used for a customer response representative in a telecommunications firm.

Unfortunately, performance standards are often not developed as supplemental items from job descriptions. Even if performance standards have been identified and matched to job descriptions, they may not be communicated to employees if

Job description Identification of the tasks, duties, and responsibilities of a job.
Performance standards Indicators of what the job accomplishes and how performance is measured in key areas of the job description.

Figure 6-11	*Sample Job Duty Statements and Performance Standards*

Job Title: Customer Response Representative
Supervisor: Customer Response Supervisor

Duty	Performance Standards
Discusses non-payment of bills with customers and notifies them of non-payment disconnecting of service	◆ Flags accounts, within two days, that are not to be disconnected according to discussions with local manager ◆ Mails notices to cable television customers to be received at least five days before disconnection date ◆ Uses prior payment history to determine which accounts require credit deposit ◆ Calmly discusses with customers the non-payment status of accounts, along with options for reconnection ◆ Disconnects and reconnects long-distance calling cards for non-payment, with 100% accuracy
Receives and records trouble reports from customers and dispatches reports to appropriate personnel	◆ Completes all required trouble information on the trouble-reporting system accurately, with no more than five errors annually ◆ Dispatches trouble ticket information to voice mail with 100% accuracy ◆ Tests line if needed or as requested by technician for telephone troubles

HR *Practice*

Writing Job Descriptions

Although not the most exciting part of HR management, developing and maintaining current job descriptions is important. Some key suggestions for writing the essential functions and duties of a job follow:

- *Compose specific duty statements that contain most of the following elements:*
    - a precise action verb
    - an object of the verb
    - the expected outcome
    - the tools, equipment, aids, and processes to be used
    - the frequency of the duties
- *Be logical:* Make the job description easy for the reader to understand. If the job is repetitive, describe the tasks as they occur in the work cycle. For varied jobs, list the major tasks first, and follow those with the less frequent and/or less important tasks in order.
- *Use proper detail:* Make sure the description covers all the meaningful duties of the job. But recognize that excessive detail only makes the description difficult to read and use in other HR activities.
- *Use the active voice:* Start each statement with a functional verb in the present tense (third-person singular)—for instance, "Bends," "Approves," or "Analyzes." Avoid "Is responsible for" because each duty is already assumed to be a responsibility.

- *Eliminate unnecessary words:* Do not use personal pronouns, because they do not add to the description and the gender of the jobholder is irrelevant.
- *Quantify:* For example, instead of saying, "Lifts heavy packages," say, "Frequently lifts heavy packages weighing up to 50 pounds."
- *Describe, do not prescribe:* Say, "Operates electronic imaging machine," not, "Must know how to operate electronic image machine." (The latter is a job specification, not a job description.)
- *Be specific:* Specify what is done by the employee. Do not say, "Does clerical computations"; better, say, "Computes sales frequency percentages."
- *Avoid vague terms:* Avoid terms like *prepares, handles, maintains,* and *processes.* Substitute active, action verbs like *checks* and *reviews.*
- *Be consistent:* Define terms like *may, occasionally,* and *periodically.* For example, say, "*May* is used to describe tasks that only some of the employees in a job perform; *occasionally* can describe tasks performed once in a while and not by a particular employee on a job."
- *Prepare a miscellaneous clause:* This clause allows flexibility, and may be phrased such as "Performs other related duties as assigned by supervisory personnel."

---

the job descriptions are not provided to employees but are used only as tools. Such an approach limits the value of job descriptions.

Job Specifications

Job specifications
The knowledge, skills, and abilities (KSAs) an individual needs to perform a job satisfactorily.

While the job description describes activities to be done, the **job specifications** list the knowledge, skills, and abilities (KSAs) an individual needs to perform a job satisfactorily. KSAs include education, experience, work skill requirements, personal abilities, and mental and physical requirements. It is important to note that accurate job specifications identify what KSAs a person needs to do the job, not necessarily the current employee's qualifications.

Job Description Components

A typical job description contains several major parts. The HR Practice provides some suggestions for writing job descriptions. Overviews of the most common components are presented next.

Figure 6-12   *Sample Job Description*

Identification Section:

Position Title: Human Resource Manager

Department: Human Resources   **EEOC Class: O/M**

Reports to: President   **FLSA Status: Exempt**

General Summary: Directs HR activities of the firm to ensure compliance with laws and policies, and assists President with overall HR planning

Essential Job Functions:

1. Manages compensation and benefits programs for all employees, resolves compensation and benefits questions from employees, and negotiates with benefits carriers (20%)
2. Ensures compliance with both internal policies and applicable state and federal regulations and laws, including EEO, OSHA, and FLSA (20%)
3. Identifies HR planning issues and suggested approaches to President and other senior managers (15%)
4. Assists managers and supervisors create, plan, and conduct training and various development programs for new and existing employees (15%)
5. Recruits candidates for employment over telephone and in person. Interviews and selects internal and external candidates for open positions (10%)
6. Reviews and updates job descriptions, assisted by department supervisors, and coordinates performance appraisal process to ensure timely reviews are completed for all employees (10%)
7. Administers various HR policies and procedures and helps managers resolve employee performance and policy issues (10%)
8. Performs other duties as needed and directed by President

Knowledge, Skills, and Abilities:

- Knowledge of HR policies, HR practices, and HR-related laws and regulations
- Knowledge of company products and services and policies and procedures
- Knowledge of management principles and practices
- Skill in operating equipment, such as personal computer, software, and IT systems
- Skill in oral and written communication
- Ability to communicate with employees and various business contacts in a professional and courteous manner
- Ability to organize multiple work assignments and establish priorities
- Ability to negotiate with others and resolve conflicts, particularly in sensitive situations
- Ability to pay close attention to detail and to ensure accuracy of reports and data
- Ability to make sound decisions using available information while maintaining confidentiality
- Ability to create a team environment and sustain employee commitment

Education and Experience: Bachelor's degree in HR management or equivalent, plus 3–5 years' experience

Physical Requirements:	Percentage of Work Time Spent on Activity			
	0%–24%	25%–49%	50%–74%	75%–100%
Seeing: Must be able to read computer screen and various reports				X
Hearing: Must be able to hear well enough to communicate with employees and others				X
Standing/walking	X			
Climbing/stooping/kneeling	X			
Lifting/pulling/pushing	X			
Fingering/grasping/feeling: Must be able to write, type, and use phone system				X

Working Conditions: Good working conditions with the absence of disagreeable conditions

Note: The statements herein are intended to describe the general nature and level of work performed by employees, but are not a complete list of responsibilities, duties, and skills required of personnel so classified. Furthermore, they do not establish a contract for employment and are subject to change at the discretion of the employer.

Identification Figure 6-12 shows a sample job description and also contains job specifications. The first part of the job description is the identification section, in which the job title, department, reporting relationships, location, and date of analysis may be given. Usually, it is advisable to note other information that is useful in tracking jobs and employees through HR systems. Additional items commonly noted in the identification section are: job code, pay grade, exempt/non-exempt status under the Fair Labor Standards Act (FLSA) and the EEOC classification (from the EEO-1 form).

General Summary The second part, the general summary, is a concise statement of the general responsibilities and components that make the job different from others. One HR specialist has characterized the general summary statement as follows: "In thirty words or less, describe the essence of the job." It is generally recommended that the summary be written after all other sections are completed, so that a more complete overview is prepared.

Essential Functions and Duties The third part of the typical job description lists the essential functions and duties. It contains clear, precise statements on the major tasks, duties, and responsibilities performed. Writing this section is the most time-consuming aspect of preparing job descriptions.

Job Specifications The next portion of the job description gives the qualifications needed to perform the job satisfactorily. The job specifications typically are stated as: (1) knowledge, skills, and abilities, (2) education and experience, and (3) physical requirements and/or working conditions. The components of the job specifications provide information necessary to determine what accommodations might and might not be possible under the Americans with Disabilities Act.

Disclaimer and Approvals The final section on many job descriptions contains approval signatures by appropriate managers and a legal disclaimer. This disclaimer allows employers to change employees' job duties or to request employees to perform duties not listed, so that the job description is not viewed as a contract between the employer and the employee.

THOMSON

WEST

Job Specifications
Contains suggestions for preparing job qualification statements.
Custom Search:
☑ ANALYSIS
Exact Phrase: Needed job qualifications

SUMMARY

- Work is organized into jobs for people to do. Both workflow analysis and business process re-engineering are approaches used to check how well this has been done.
- Job design involves developing jobs that people like to do. It may include simplification, enlargement, enrichment, or rotation.
- Designing jobs so that they incorporate skill variety, task identity and significance, autonomy, and feedback is important for both employers and employees.
- There is a growing use of teams in jobs, especially with self-directed work and virtual teams.

- Greater flexibility in work schedules and the use of telework has affected the design of many jobs.
- Job analysis is a systematic investigation of the content, context, and human requirements of a job.
- Task-based job analysis focuses on the tasks, duties, and responsibilities associated with jobs. Competency-based job analysis focuses on basic characteristics that can be linked to enhanced performance, such as technical and behavioral competencies.
- The job analysis process has five stages, beginning with planning and ending with maintaining and updating job descriptions and job specifications.

- A number of methods of job analysis are used, with interviews and questionnaires being the most popular.
- Both the behavioral reactions of employees and managers and legal compliance issues must be considered as part of job analysis.

- The end products of job analysis are job descriptions, which identify the tasks, duties, and responsibilities of jobs, and job specifications, which list the knowledge, skills, and abilities needed to perform a job satisfactorily.

REVIEW AND APPLICATION QUESTIONS

1. For many individuals, the nature of work and jobs is changing. Describe some reasons for the changes and how they are affecting HR management and organizations.
2. Explain how you would conduct a job analysis in a company that had never had job descriptions.

3. As an HR specialist, you have been asked to develop job descriptions for a *computer support specialist* who assists with LAN/WAN networks. Using O*Net (*http://online.onetcenter.org*), job boards, and other Web-based resources, locate the details needed and prepare a job description using the format shown in Figure 6-11.

LEARNING REVIEW

To check your knowledge of the chapter, review the following. (Answers after the supplemental case.) For more questions, see the Study Guide.

1. A _____ is a grouping of tasks, duties, and responsibilities that constitutes the total work assignment for employees.
   a. job
   b. essential function
   c. job specification
   d. job design
2. A major limitation of the interview method of job analyses is that it is _____.
   a. less accurate than other methods
   b. very time-consuming
   c. too subjective
   d. a very complex process

3. The Americans with Disabilities Act calls the fundamental duties of the position that an individual with a disability holds or desires _____.
   a. essential job functions
   b. knowledge, skills, and abilities
   c. critical job elements
   d. job specifications
4. The essential functions and duties section of a job description should contain clear and precise statements on the _____.
   a. tasks, duties, and responsibilities performed
   b. qualifications needed to do the job satisfactorily
   c. conditions in which the work is performed
   d. mental and physical requirements of the job

CASE

JOBS AND WORK AT R.R. DONNELLEY

Changes in many industries are occurring, with a common thrust being efforts to increase productivity. Re-designing jobs, integrating information technology, and increasing HR training efforts are all critical. One example illustrates what happens when jobs and work are changed.

R. R. Donnelley is the leading commercial printing firm in the U.S. One of its primary facilities is in Roanoke, Virginia, where 3.5 million books a month are produced with about 300 employees. To improve productivity and profitability, Donnelley focused on lowering costs, improving workplace safety, and reducing errors. Because making numerous changes was likely to increase employees' concerns, significant time and effort were spent communicating with employees about the need for change, improvement in quality, and higher productivity. Training for all employees on quality and workflow changes were conducted that focused on specialized methods such as Six Sigma and other process improvement means. In addition, greater use was made of digital technology to receive and make printing film and plates, which changed numerous jobs at the plant and required employees to learn a number of new methods and technologies.

The payoff of these changes is seen in a number of ways. The production time for printing four-color books has been cut by 50% or more. Productivity is up 20% in the past three years. In fact, the increase in productivity has been great enough that Donnelley did not have to set up another production line, savings millions of dollars. For Donnelley employees, their fears that the Roanoke plant might close have been eliminated. They have been trained in new technology, have changed jobs, and work in a highly successful plant.[45]

Questions

1. Discuss why Donnelley had to coordinate HR activities with the changes in jobs and work.
2. Identify examples of how technology has changed jobs where you have worked and what HR activities were handled well and poorly.

SUPPLEMENTAL CASE: The Reluctant Receptionist

This case illustrates how incomplete job analysis and job descriptions create both managerial and employee problems. (For the case, go to **http://mathis.swlearning.com/.**)

Learning Review Answers: 1. a   2. b   3. a   4. a

NOTES

1. Lynn A Karoly and Constantin W. A. Panis, *The 21st Century at Work: Forces Shaping the Future Workforce and Workplace in the United States* (Santa Monica, CA: RAND Corporation, 2004).
2. "Special Report: Where Are the Jobs?" *Business Week,* March 22, 2004, 36–53.
3. "Study: Self-Service Is Finally Delivering," *Human Resource Executive,* January 2004, 52.
4. For details, see the International Association of Administrative Professionals, *www.iaap-hq.org,* and the International Association of Virtual Office Assistants, *www.iavoa.com.*
5. Figen Calzar, Umit S. Bitici, and Jillian McBryde, "A Business Process Approach to Human Resource Management," *Business Process Management,* 9 (2003), 190.
6. "Banks Invest in a New Look at HR," *Human Resource Management International Digest,* 11 (2003), 19–23.
7. Martin Smith, "Business Process Design: Correlates of Success and Failure," *Quality Management Journal,* 10 (2003), 38–50.
8. Robert J. Trent, "Planning to Use Work Teams Effectively," *Team Performance Management,* 9 (2003), 50.
9. Ceasar Douglas and William L. Gardner, "Transition to Self-Directed Work Teams," *Journal of Organizational Behavior,* 25 (2004), 47.
10. P. Christopher Earley and Cristina B. Gibson, *Multinational Work Teams* (Mahwah, NJ: Lawrence Erlbaum Associates, 2002).
11. Linda Arnison and Peter Miller, "Virtual Teams: A Virtue for the Conventional Team," *Journal of Workplace Learning,* 14 (2002), 166–174.
12. Carla Joinson, "Managing Virtual Teams," *HR Magazine,* June 2002, 69–73.
13. Larry W. Hunter, John P. Macduffie, and Lorna Doucet, "What Makes Teams Take? Employee Reactions to Work Teams," *Industrial and Labor Review* 55 (2002), 448.
14. Lawrence D. Fredenall and Charles Emery, "Productivity Increases Due to the Use of Teams in Service Garages," *Journal of Managerial Issues,* 15 (2002), 221–242.
15. "Poll Shows Americans Eager to Take Back Their Time," *Newsline,* October 6, 2003, www.timeday.com.
16. "Put Down That Tool," *The Economist,* January 10, 2004, 55–56.
17. Christopher Rhoods, "Short Work Hours Undercut Europe in Eco-

nomic Drive," *Wall Street Journal,* August 8, 2002, 1A.

18. Acacia Aguirre, *Health in Extended Hours Operations: Understanding the Challenges, Implementing Solutions,* 2003, *www.circadian.com.*

19. Adapted from Brian Gow, "How Much Do I Hear for This Nurse?" *Business Week,* December 8, 2003, 14.

20. "Employers Increase Work-Life Programs, According to Mellon Survey," January 15, 2004, *www.mellon.com.*

21. Edward Prewitt, "Flextime and Telecommuting," *CIO,* April 15, 2002, 30.

22. Families and Work Institute, 2002, *www.familiesandwork.org.*

23. "Sample Job-Sharing Policy and Request Form," *www.workforce.com.*

24. "In the House and on the Job," *Human Resource Executive,* November 2003, 10; and *American Interactive Consumer Survey,* International Telework Association and Council, *www.telecommute.org.*

25. "Telecommuting Advances Make Snow Days Less Unproductive," *Newsline,* January 28, 2004, *www.sunspot.com.*

26. Keri E. Pearlson and Coral S. Saunders, "There's No Place Like Home: Managing Telecommuting Paradoxes," *Academy of Management Executive,* 14 (2001), 117–128.

27. Jane W. Gibson et al., "Telecommuting in the 21st Century," *Journal of Leadership and Organizational Studies,* 8 (2002), 75–87.

28. Anne Freedman, "Remote Control," *Human Resource Executive,* October 6, 2002, 41–45.

29. Thiagarajan Srivinivasan and Brian Kleiner, "How to Hire Employees Effectively," *Management Research News,* 25 (2002), 65.

30. W. M. Keyserling et al., "Using Multiple Information Sources to Identify Opportunities for Ergonomic Interventions in Automotive Parts Distribution: A Case Study," *AIHA Journal,* 64 (2003), 690–702.

31. Donna Rodriguez et al., "Developing Competency Models to Promote Integrated Human Resource Practices," *Human Resource Management,* 41 (2002), 309.

32. Marcel R. Vander Klink and Jo Boon, "Competencies: The Triumph of a Fuzzy Concept," *International Journal of Human Resources Development and Management,* 3 (2003), 125.

33. Adapted from Monica Brophy and Tony Kiely, "Competencies: A New Sector," *Journal of European Industrial Training,* 26 (2002), 165–177.

34. For an illustration, see Francesa Sgobbi, "Web Design Skills and Competencies: An Empirical Analysis," *Human Systems Management,* 21 (2002), 115.

35. For a detailed discussion of the job analysis process and methods, see Michael T. Brannick and Edward Levine, *Job Analysis: Methods, Research, and Applications for Human Resource Management in the New Millennium* (Thousand Oaks, CA: Sage Publishing, 2002).

36. Kristen O. Prien, Erich P. Prien, and William Wooten, "Interrater Reliability in Job Analysis," *Public Personnel Management,* 32 (2003), 125–141.

37. I-Wei Chang and Brian H. Kleiner, "How to Conduct Job Analysis Effectively," *Management Research News,* 25 (2003), 73–82.

38. Dana C. Simmons, "Job Analysis, the Missing Ingredient in the Total Rewards Recipe," *Workspan,* September, 2002, 52–55.

39. Jeanne D. Mackiney et al., "Examining the Measurement Equivalence of Paper and Computerized Job Analysis Scales" (paper presented at the 18th annual conference of the Society for Industrial and Organizational Psychology, 2003).

40. Patrick Shannon and Bob Miller, "What's in a Title?" *WorldatWork Journal,* Fourth Quarter, 2003, 26–34.

41. Based on "Japanese Workplaces Drop Formalities to Enhance Output," *Omaha World-Herald,* November 16, 2003, 14A.

42. Merrie Spath, "Expanding Your Job Description," *Risk Management,* October 2002, 56.

43. Kenneth H. Pritchard, "Non-Prejudicial Language for ADA-Compliant Job Descriptions," *SHRM Forum,* November, 2002, *www.shrm.org.*

44. Chi Ming Chow and Brian H. Kleiner, "How to Differentiate Essential Job Duties from Marginal Duties," *Managerial Law,* 44 (2002), 121–128.

45. Adapted from Gene Bylinsky, "Elite Factories," *Fortune,* September 1, 2003, 154B–154J.

CHAPTER 7

Recruiting in Labor Markets

After you have read this chapter you should be able to:

- Identify different ways that labor markets can be identified and approached.

- Discuss the advantages and disadvantages of internal and external recruiting.

- Specify three internal sources for recruiting and issues associated with their use.

- List and briefly discuss five external recruiting sources.

- Explain why Internet recruiting has grown and how employers are conducting it.

- Discuss three factors to consider when evaluating recruiting efforts.

Employment "Branding" Can Help Recruiting

To become an "employer of choice" for excellent job candidates, companies find that it is advantageous to have a recognized "brand," or identity. Organizations seen as desirable employers are better able to attract more qualified applicants than are organizations with poor reputations. For example, one firm had good pay and benefits, but its work demands were seen as excessive, and frequent downsizings had resulted in some terminations and transfers. The result was high turnover and a low rate of individuals interested in applying for employment at the company.

Companies spend considerable effort and money establishing brand images for their products. Firms that regularly appear in the "100 Best Companies To Work For" as designated by *Fortune* magazine, like the Container Store, Southwest Airlines, Cisco Systems, and Edward Jones, have achieved success in establishing a brand image that helps their recruiting. An executive in one global firm noted that "the most compelling reason people join our company is pride in what the company stands for and where it is going."

Not only can the brand help generate more recruits, but it can also help with applicant self-selection. For example, McKinsey & Company is known for high pay, demanding jobs, and selectivity. Its mystique does not require mass marketing, because the press tells the McKinsey story for the firm, and only the brightest and best apply.

This marriage between marketing, public relations, and HR is not always easy, or may not be possible in some firms. But when it has occurred, indicators that branding has indeed worked include these:

- The employer experiences positive name recognition because both individuals inside and outside the company discuss it favorably.
- The employer is a top choice for high performers because they see the firm as a prestigious place that invests in their future.
- If individuals quit, they are more likely to return once they discover that another employer is not as desirable a place to work.
- The employer's sign-up lists at job fairs and colleges are longer than other employers', which aids both recruiting and enhances the employer's reputation with other potential candidates.[1]

"Ability will never catch up with the demand for it."

—*Malcolm Forbes*

The staffing process matches people with jobs through recruiting and selection. This chapter examines recruiting, and the next examines selection. **Recruiting** is the process of generating a pool of qualified applicants for organizational jobs. If the number of available candidates only equals the number of people to be hired, no real selection is required—the choice has already been made. The organization must either leave some openings unfilled or take all the candidates.

Recruiting is about finding qualified applicants, and doing that often requires much more than just running an ad in a newspaper. For example, simply acquiring the human capital necessary to replace normal attrition and provide for growth probably will require an employer to:[2]

♦ Know the business and industry to successfully recruit qualified employees
♦ Identify keys to success in the labor market, including ways to deal with competitors' recruiting efforts
♦ Cultivate networks and relationships with sources of prospective employees
♦ Promote the company brand so that the organization becomes known as a good place to work
♦ Create recruiting metrics in order to measure the effectiveness of recruiting efforts

Without significant HR attention recruiting can become just a set of administrative functions: coordinating internal openings, handling the flow of candidate data, dealing with regulatory reporting, and moving candidates through the system. These steps are important, but more important is tying the employer's business strategy to its recruiting strategy.[3]

STRATEGIC APPROACH TO RECRUITING

A strategic approach to recruiting becomes more important as labor markets shift and become more competitive. Strategic HR planning helps to align HR strategies with organizational goals and plans. Therefore, it is important that recruiting be a part of strategic HR planning. For example, at one time, Walgreens, the drugstore chain, had to cut back its plans to expand and open new stores, because of a shortage of trained pharmacists. Good recruiting and more lead time might have kept it from having to do that and allowed the strategic expansion to go forward.

Strategy is a general framework that provides guidance for actions. If a company is driven by technology, recruiting must determine how to bring in the best technologists. If the strategy of a company is based on marketing, the focus should be on where the company will look to find the best marketing candidates. Certainly, cost is an issue, and some employers are quite concerned about cost per hire. However, if an HR strategy focuses on *quality,* a company might choose to hire only from the top 15% of candidates for critical jobs, and from the top 30% of candidates for all other important positions.[4] This approach likely would improve workforce quality, but it would cost more per hire.

Strategic recruiting may sometimes need to go beyond just filling empty positions. It can focus on discovering talent *before* it is needed, capitalizing on windfall opportunities when there is an abundance of highly qualified people, or perhaps developing strong Internet recruiting abilities.[5] Generally, the recruiting decisions dictate not only the kinds and numbers of applicants, but also how difficult or successful recruiting efforts may be. Figure 7-1 shows an overview of the strategic recruiting stages.

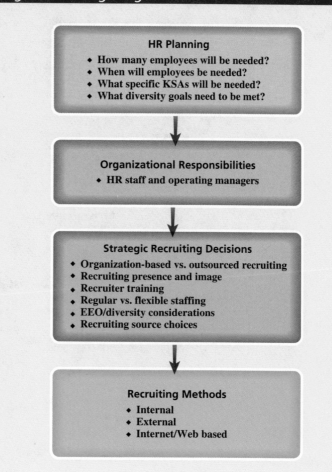

Figure 7-1 *Strategic Recruiting Stages*

HR Planning
- How many employees will be needed?
- When will employees be needed?
- What specific KSAs will be needed?
- What diversity goals need to be met?

Organizational Responsibilities
- HR staff and operating managers

Strategic Recruiting Decisions
- Organization-based vs. outsourced recruiting
- Recruiting presence and image
- Recruiter training
- Regular vs. flexible staffing
- EEO/diversity considerations
- Recruiting source choices

Recruiting Methods
- Internal
- External
- Internet/Web based

Even during periods of reduced hiring, implementing long-range plans means keeping in contact with outside recruiting sources to maintain visibility, while also maintaining employee recruiting channels inside the organization. These efforts allow management to match recruiting activity with organizational and human resource plans.

Employers have faced shortages of workers who have the appropriate knowledge, skills, and abilities. Further, as business cycles fluctuate demand for labor changes and the number of people looking for work changes.

LABOR MARKETS

Labor markets Exter-nal supply pool from which organizations at-tract employees.

Because staffing takes place in such variable labor markets, learning some basics about labor markets aids in understanding recruiting. **Labor markets** are the external supply pool from which employers attract employees. To understand where recruiting takes place, one can think of the sources of employees as a funnel, in which the broad scope of labor markets narrows progressively to the point of selection and job offers (see Figure 7-2). Of course, if the selected candidate rejects the offer, then HR staff members must move back up the funnel to the ap-

Figure 7-2

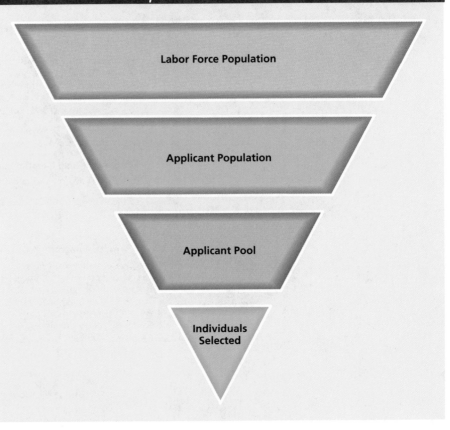

Labor Market Components

Labor Force Population

Applicant Population

Applicant Pool

Individuals Selected

plicant pool for other candidates, and in extreme cases to re-open the recruiting process. It is important for recruiting efforts to address a number of specific issues that affect employers in today's labor markets.

Labor Market Components

Labor force population All individuals who are available for selection if all possible recruitment strategies are used.

The broadest labor market component and measure is the **labor force population,** which is made up of all individuals who are available if all possible recruitment strategies are used. This large number of potential applicants may be reached using many different recruiting methods—for example, newspaper ads, Internet sites, college job fairs, and word of mouth. Each recruiting method will reach different segments of the labor force population.

Applicant population A subset of the labor force population that is available for selection using a particular recruiting approach.

The **applicant population** is a subset of the labor force population that is available for selection if a particular recruiting approach is used. For example, an organization might limit its recruiting for management trainees to MBA graduates from major universities. This recruiting method results in a different group of applicants from those who might apply if the employer advertises openings for management trainees on a local radio station or posts a listing on an Internet jobs board. At least four recruiting decisions affect reaching the applicant population:

◆ *Recruiting method:* Advertising medium chosen, including use of employment agencies

◆ *Recruiting message:* What is said about the job and how it is said

- *Applicant qualifications required:* Education level and amount of experience necessary, for example
- *Administrative procedures:* When recruiting is done, applicant follow-up, and use of previous applicant files

In tight labor markets, many employers try to expand the applicant population in a number of ways. One method that employers have used to expand the applicant population is to consider *ex-convicts.* Care is needed in evaluating the individuals and ensuring appropriate placements given their criminal backgrounds. But giving individuals a second chance has paid off in some situations and not in others, for both small and large employers.

The **applicant pool** consists of all persons who are actually evaluated for selection. Many factors can affect the size of the applicant pool, including the reputation of the organization and industry as a place to work, the screening efforts of the organization, the job specifications, and the information available. If a suitable candidate can be found, the organization then selects the individual and makes the job offer.

Applicant pool All persons who are actually evaluated for selection.

LOGGING ON...

Job Web
This Web site offers a job outlook section containing a special report about labor markets and jobs. Also, it contains information on career fairs, starting salaries, and researching potential employers.
www.jobweb.com

Labor Markets and Recruiting

The supply of workers in various labor markets substantially affects staffing. An organization can recruit in a number of labor markets, including geographic, industry and occupational, and educational and technical. The labor markets can be viewed in several ways to provide information that is useful for recruiting. Looking at projections for the labor force by age, participation rates, annual rates of labor force growth, and growth in employment in certain occupations will help alert recruiters to trends in the labor markets.

Geographic Labor Markets One common way to classify labor markets is based on geographic location. Some markets are local, some area or regional, some national, and others international. Local and area labor markets vary significantly in terms of workforce availability and quality. For instance, the state of Iowa found that even if it retained every high school graduate for 10 years, at the end of that time, it still would be short of workers for many jobs because of the aging populations in many Iowa counties. The shortage of workers had caused employers in some locations to close operations and relocate to areas with greater numbers of potential workers. Therefore, state agencies and Iowa employers developed an aggressive campaign to "import" workers. Efforts included recruiting native Iowans to return to the state, encouraging foreign immigrants to move to Iowa, and encouraging graduates of Iowa high schools and colleges to remain in the state.[6]

Changes in a geographic labor market may force changes in recruiting efforts. If a new major employer locates in a regional labor market, then other employers may see a decline in their numbers of applicants. For instance, following the opening of large automobile manufacturing plants in South Carolina, Tennessee, Kentucky, and Alabama, some nearby employers, particularly smaller manufacturing firms, had to raise their wages to prevent turnover of existing workers.

Attempting to recruit locally or in a limited geographic area for a job market that is really national will likely result in disappointing applicant rates. For example, a catalog retailer will likely not be able to recruit a senior merchandising manager from only the small town where the firm is located. Conversely, it may not need to recruit nationally for workers to fill administrative support jobs.

Global Labor Markets U.S. employers tap global labor markets when necessary and export work to overseas labor markets when doing so is advantageous. For example: U.S. hotels are likely to hire housekeeping staff from Croatia, Poland, Jamaica, Sudan, and the Philippines. Manufacturers, meatpackers, and roofing companies regularly use workers from Mexico, Haiti, Honduras, Sudan, Albania, and other countries. Public school systems in North Carolina, Georgia, California, and Texas have used teachers from Australia, Canada, Jamaica, Chile, England, and Ghana. Also, scores of Western firms have farmed out software development and back-office work to India and other countries with lower wages.

The migration of U.S. work overseas has been controversial. While many decry the loss of American jobs, some employers respond that they cannot be competitive in a global market if they fail to take advantage of labor savings. However, enormous advancements in American productivity means that it takes fewer employees in America to produce items instead of exporting more jobs to other countries.[7]

Recruiting employees for global assignments requires approaches and understanding different from those used for typical recruiting efforts in the home country. The recruiting processes must consider differences in culture, laws, and language. For instance, in Eastern Europe, potential recruits like to work for European and U.S. firms, so recruiters emphasize the "Western" image. In Hong Kong, recruiting ads often stress success factors by showing "typical employees" of a firm wearing expensive watches and stylish clothes.

Dealing with foreign labor markets can present challenges. In China, for example, recruiting is regulated and generally requires the approval of local personnel or labor authorities. Article 8 of the Labor Market Regulations sets out the specific channels that may be used for recruiting. Recruitment agencies, employment fairs, mass media, and the Internet are allowable. Unfortunately, two government bureaucracies, with different rules, have overlapping authority in recruiting, and the result is bureaucratic confusion as to what recruiting can be done.[8]

The growth of the Internet has made global recruiting much more accessible, particularly for individuals in search of professional management jobs. Those individuals and more technologically knowledgeable candidates can be reached using Internet advertising. Global search firms also can be used to locate specialized global managerial talent.

Industry and Occupational Labor Markets Labor markets also can be classified by industry and occupation. The demand for truck drivers, hotel workers, nurses, teachers, and others has been strong, creating tight labor markets in the industries served by those occupations.

Occupational labor markets are based on the KSAs required for the jobs. These markets include physical therapists, HR managers, engineers, accountants, welders, and bank tellers. One occupational area of extreme volatility in the past several years is the *information technology* (IT) labor market, which has fluctuated from being extremely tight several years ago, to rather soft after many dot.coms failed and employers began exporting software work. Forecasts for an increasingly limited supply of qualified IT workers in the U.S. in the future have lead to international outsourcing.

Educational and Technical Labor Markets Another way to look at labor markets is by considering educational and technical qualifications to define the people being recruited. Employers may need individuals with specific licenses, certifications, or educational backgrounds. For instance, a shortage of business professors with PhDs is forecasted to affect many colleges and universities in the next few years due to the retirement of many baby boomers from faculty positions. Other examples include shortages of certified auto mechanics, heating and air-conditioning technicians, and network-certified computer specialists.

Unemployment Rate and Labor Markets

When the unemployment rate is high in a given market, many applicants are looking for jobs. When the unemployment rate is low, there are few applicants. Of course, unemployment rates vary with the business cycle and present very different challenges for recruiting. For instance, several years ago when Associated Grocers in Seattle needed a generalist computer operator with basic skills, the company could barely find candidates—and when it did, those candidates wanted huge salaries and stock options. Later, in a period with a high unemployment rate that followed a recession and a big downturn in jobs for computer operators, a single employment ad for a computer operator placed by the same company generated over 700 applications. Such a candidate glut is a mixed blessing, as a down economy generates more unqualified candidates (who simply apply for anything) to sift through—but the big volume of applicants can mean more qualified people as well.[9]

▌ STRATEGIC RECRUITING DECISIONS

An employer must make a number of recruiting decisions based on the recruiting needs identified as part of HR planning. Important ones are discussed next.

Organization-Based vs. Outsourced Recruiting

An initial and basic decision is whether the recruiting will be done by the employer or outsourced. This decision need not be an "either-or" decision, with all recruiting done by organizational staff or else external resources used exclusively.

In most organizations, HR staff members handle the bulk of recruiting efforts. The distribution of recruiting responsibilities between the HR department and operating managers shown in Figure 7-3 is typical for all but the smallest organizations.

Because recruiting can be a time-consuming process, given all the other responsibilities of HR staff and other managers in organizations, outsourcing it is

| **Figure 7-3** | **Typical Division of HR Responsibilities: Recruiting** |

HR Unit	Managers
• Forecasts recruiting needs • Prepares copy for recruiting ads and campaigns • Plans and conducts recruiting efforts • Audits and evaluates all recruiting activities	• Anticipate needs for employees to fill vacancies • Determine KSAs needed from applicants • Assist in recruiting efforts with information about job requirements • Review success/failure of recruiting activities

a way to both decrease the number of HR staff needed and free up time for HR staff members. Recruiting can be outsourced in a number of ways. For example, some large employers outsource such functions as placement of advertisements, initial screening of resumes, and initial phone contacts with potential applicants. Once those activities are done, then the employer's HR staff take over the rest of the recruiting activities.

A common means of outsourcing is retaining search firms and employment agencies to recruit candidates. Currently, about 10% of all firms outsource large parts of recruiting operations, and about 58% plan to increase outsourcing at some point.[10] For example, Kellogg, with 14,000 employees worldwide, outsources the hiring of all but hourly employees. Outsourcing gives the firm more flexibility: when 200 salespeople were needed quickly, the vendor was able to fill those positions faster and cheaper ($3,800 per hire vs. $6,000 per hire) than in-house recruiters could have.[11]

Moen, a large manufacturer of plumbing fixtures with 3,500 employees, works with only one outsource recruiter. On any day, between 175 and 200 temporary workers are provided by the recruiting firm, which keeps two of its own full-time employees on-site to oversee HR issues with the temps, who are rated and receive points. All full-time employees are hired from those individuals with the highest scores in the temp pool.[12]

Professional Employer Organizations (PEOs) and Employee Leasing

A specific type of outsourcing uses professional employer organizations (PEOs) and employee leasing. This approach has grown rapidly in recent years. Some sources estimate that about 3 million individuals are employed by PEOs doing employee leasing.[13]

The employee leasing process is simple: An employer signs an agreement with the PEO, after which the existing staff is hired by the leasing firm and leased back to the company. For a fee, a small-business owner or operator turns the staff over to the leasing company, which then writes the paychecks, pays the taxes, prepares and implements HR policies, and keeps all the required records.

PEOs and employment agencies are different entities. An *employment agency* provides a "workfinding" service for job seekers and supplies employers with applicants they may then hire. A PEO has its own workforce, which it supplies by contract to employers with jobs. Small-business owners do not always know how to comply with EEOC, ADA, COBRA, OSHA, and other requirements. Using a PEO can be an advantage because the PEO handles the HR complexities.[14] There are, however, some legal and tax-related issues that must be considered when using a PEO, so employers should consult outside experts before shifting to PEOs for staffing.[15]

One advantage for employees of leasing companies is that they may receive better benefits than they otherwise would get in many small businesses. All this service comes at a cost. Leasing companies often charge employers between 4% and 6% of employees' monthly salaries. Thus, while leasing may save employers money on benefits and HR administration, it may also increase total costs of payroll.

Recruiting Presence and Image

Recruiting efforts may be viewed as either continuous or intensive. *Continuous* efforts to recruit offer the advantage of keeping the employer in the recruiting market. For example, with college recruiting, some organizations may find it ad-

LOGGING ON...

Professional Employer Organizations
This is an informational Web site about PEOs and contains a directory of PEOs.
www.peo.com/peo/

vantageous to have a recruiter on a given campus each year. Employers that visit a campus only occasionally are less likely to build a following in that school over time.

Intensive recruiting may take the form of a vigorous recruiting campaign aimed at hiring a given number of employees, usually within a short period of time. Such efforts may be the result of failure in the HR planning system to identify needs in advance or to recognize drastic changes in workforce needs due to unexpected workloads.

As noted in the chapter opener, a factor related to recruiting is portraying a positive image of the employer. The way the "employment brand" of the organization is viewed by both employees and outsiders is crucial to attracting applicants and retaining employees, who also may describe the organization in positive or negative terms to others.

Additionally, the recruiting image of an industry and an employer can significantly affect whether individuals ever consider a firm and submit applications. For example, in the fast-food industry, the product image and reputation of a firm affects the attractiveness of the firm as a potential employer of teenagers and retirees. Recruiting should be seen as part of organizational marketing efforts and linked to the overall image and reputation of the organization and its industry.

Training of Recruiters

Another important strategic issue is how much training will be given to recruiters. In addition to being trained on interviewing techniques, communications skills, and knowledge of the jobs being filled, it is crucial that recruiters learn the types of actions that violate EEO regulations and how to be sensitive to diversity issues with applicants. Training in those areas often includes interview do's and don'ts and appropriate language to use with applicants. Racist, sexist, and other inappropriate remarks hurt the image of the employer and may result in legal complaints. For instance, a male college recruiter regularly asked female candidates about their marital status, and if they were single and attractive, he later called applicants and asked them for dates. Only after two students complained to the university placement office did the employer learn of the recruiter's misconduct.

Incidents such as this one reinforce the importance of employers' monitoring recruiters' behaviors and actions. Some employers send interviewees follow-up surveys asking about the effectiveness of the recruiters and the image the candidates have of the employers as a result of their recruiting contacts.

Regular vs. Flexible Staffing

Another strategic decision affects how much recruiting will be done to fill staffing needs with regular full-time and part-time employees. Decisions as to who should be recruited hinge on whether to seek traditional employees or to use more flexible approaches, which might include temporaries or independent contractors. A number of employers feel that the cost of keeping a regular workforce has become excessive and grows worse due to increasing government-mandated costs. However, not just the money is at issue. The number of governmental regulations also constrains the employment relationship, making many employers reluctant to hire new employees.

Flexible staffing Use of workers who are not traditional employees.

Flexible staffing uses workers who are not traditional employees. Using flexible staffing arrangements allows an employer to avoid some of the cost of full-time benefits such as vacation pay and pension plans, as well as to recruit in a somewhat different market. These arrangements provide temporary workers, independent contractors, and employee leasing.

Temporary Workers Employers who use temporary employees can hire their own temporary staff members or contract with agencies supplying temporary workers on a rate-per-day or rate-per-week basis. Originally developed to provide clerical and office workers to employers, such agencies now provide workers in many other areas. The use of temporary workers may make sense for an organization if its work is subject to seasonal or other fluctuations. Hiring regular employees to meet peak employment needs would require that the employer find some tasks to keep employees busy during less active periods or resort to layoffs.[16]

Some employers hire temporary workers as a way for individuals to move into full-time, regular employment. Better-performing workers may move to regular positions when they become available. This "try before you buy" approach is potentially beneficial to both employers and employees. However, most temporary service firms bill client companies a placement charge if a temporary worker is hired full-time within a certain time period—usually 90 days.

Independent contractors Workers who perform specific services on a contract basis.

Independent Contractors Some firms employ **independent contractors**, who are workers that perform specific services on a contract basis. These workers must be independent as determined by a 20-item test used by the U.S. Internal Revenue Service and the U.S. Department of Labor, which is discussed in greater detail in Chapter 12. Independent contractors are used in a number of areas, including building maintenance, security, advertising, and others. One major reason for use of independent contractors is that some employers get significant savings by using independent contractors because benefits do not have to be provided to those individuals.

Recruiting and Diversity Considerations

As Figure 7-4 indicates, a number of factors go into ensuring that recruiting decisions meet diversity considerations. Recruiting as a key employment-related activity is subject to various legal considerations, especially equal employment laws and regulations. As part of legal compliance in the recruiting process, organizations must work to reduce external disparate impact, or under-representation of protected-class members compared with the labor markets utilized by the employer. If disparate impact exists, then the employer may need to make special efforts to persuade protected-class individuals to apply for jobs. For employers with affirmative action plans, special ways to reduce disparate impact may be identified as goals and listed in those plans. Some employers that emphasize internal recruiting should take actions to obtain protected-class applicants externally if disparate impact exists in the current workforce. When a particular protected class is under-represented in an organization, word-of-mouth referral by existing employees has been considered a violation of Title VII of the Civil Rights Act of 1964, because it continues a past pattern of discrimination.

Employment Advertising Employers covered by equal employment regulations must exercise care when preparing employment advertisements. The Equal Employment Opportunity Commission guidelines state that no direct or indirect

Figure 7-4 | *Recruiting and Diversity Considerations*

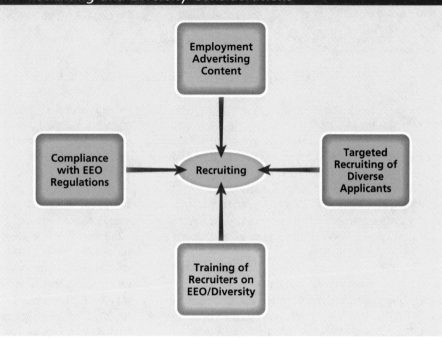

references implying gender or age are permitted. Some examples of impermissible terminology are: "young and enthusiastic," "recent college graduate," "Christian values," and "journeyman lineman."

Additionally, employment advertisements should indicate that the employer has a policy of complying with equal employment regulations. Typically, advertisements should contain a general phrase, such as Equal Opportunity Employer, or more specific designations, such as EEO/M-F/AA/ADA. Employers demonstrate inclusive recruiting by having diverse individuals represented in company materials, in advertisements, and as recruiters. Microsoft, Prudential Insurance, Bristol-Myers Squibb, and other firms have found that making diversity visible in recruiting efforts has helped them recruit more individuals with more varied backgrounds.[17]

Recruiting Diverse Workers The growing difficulty that many employers have had in attracting and retaining workers has led them to recruit workers from diverse backgrounds.[18] Three specific protected groups that have been attracted into the workforce effectively by some employers are individuals over 55 years of age, persons with disabilities, and members of racial/ethnic minorities.

When discussing the recruitment of older workers, the first task is to identify which individuals are included in this group. Senior and experienced individuals may include the following:

♦ *Mid-life career changers:* Those who are burned out in their jobs and career fields and leave voluntarily to try new fields
♦ *Displaced older workers:* Those who have worked but have been displaced, often involuntarily, through job reductions or plant closings
♦ *Retirees:* Those who took early retirement buyouts or formally retired from prior jobs

Research on Diversity in Recruiting Ads

Recruiting advertisements increasingly portray racial diversity in pictures associated with the ads. But a key question is how are such ads viewed by individuals of different races. To provide insights, Avery researched reactions to diversity in recruiting advertising and reported his findings in the *Journal of Applied Psychology*. The sample consisted of 144 African Americans and 129 whites selected from psychology classes at three southern universities. The average participant was 20 years old with 3 years of predominately part-time working experience.

Web site ads were constructed showing three types of organizations. The racial composition of the ads was manipulated through three pictures of employees at the job site. The first showed five white employees and three white managers. Those pictured were labeled as individuals with whom new hires would be working. The second type of ad showed some black co-workers and the same three white managers. The third type of ad was the same as the second except that one of the white managers had been replaced with a black manager.

The results of the study found that white viewers of the ad did not change their views based on any diversity shown in the Web site pictures. However, African American viewers were more positive because of the diversity shown in the ads.

The researcher concluded that seeing African Americans in managerial positions illustrates opportunities for advancement to other African Americans who might view the ad. Simply seeing another black face in the employee ranks did not have the same positive effect on their perceptions of an employer. But seeing African Americans in high-status positions likely conveys that promotions and other employment outcomes are made without discrimination.[19]

Individuals with disabilities provide a potential pool of recruits numbering more than 40 million. Jobs must be such that accommodation can be made for people with disabilities. Not every disability lends itself to every job for accommodations. However, in many cases, changes in job duties, work stations, and equipment might result in a job that a person with a disability can do—and do well. For example, a Marriott Worldwide reservations center has special monitors and software that is used by visually impaired individuals who take customer calls and make hotel reservations.

Employers that do business with federal and state governments must have affirmative action plans, as discussed in Chapter 5. Consequently, those employers may face pressures to increase proportionately the number of employees who are women or are members of racial/ethnic minorities. These pressures often are stronger for managerial, professional, and technical jobs than for unskilled, clerical, and blue-collar jobs. For an example of research on the effects of diversity recruiting ads, see the HR Perspective.

Recruiting Source Choices: Internal vs. External

Recruiting strategy and policy decisions entail identifying where to recruit, whom to recruit, and how to recruit. One of the first decisions determines the extent to which internal or external sources and methods will be used. Both promoting from within the organization (internal recruitment) and hiring from outside the organization (external recruitment) come with advantages and disadvantages. Figure 7-5 shows some of the major pluses and minuses of each.

Figure 7-5   *Advantages and Disadvantages of Internal and External Recruiting Sources*

Recruiting Source	Advantages	Disadvantages
Internal	• The morale of the promotee is usually high. • The firm can better assess a candidate's abilities. • Recruiting costs are lower for some jobs. • The process is a motivator for good performance. • The process causes a succession of promotions. • The firm has to hire only at entry level.	• "Inbreeding" results. • Those not promoted may experience morale problems. • Employees may engage in "political" infighting for promotions. • A management development program is needed.
External	• New "blood" brings new perspectives. • Training new hires is cheaper and faster because of prior external experience. • The new hire has no group of "political supporters" in the organization. • The new hire may bring new industry insights.	• The firm may not select someone who will fit the job or the organization. • The process may cause morale problems for internal candidates not selected. • The new employee may require a longer adjustment or orientation time.

Most employers combine the use of internal and external methods. Organizations that face rapidly changing competitive environments and conditions may need to place a heavier emphasis on external sources in addition to developing internal sources. However, for organizations existing in environments that change slowly, promotion from within may be more suitable. Once the various recruiting policy decisions have been addressed, then the actual recruiting methods can be identified and used. These include internal and external sources, as well as Internet/Web-based approaches.

INTERNAL RECRUITING

Pursuing internal recruiting with the advantages mentioned earlier means using various sources developed and managed inside the organization. The most common internal recruiting methods include: organizational databases, job postings, promotions and transfers, current-employee referrals, and re-recruiting of former employees and applicants.

Internal Recruiting Processes

Within the organization, tapping into databases, job postings, promotions, and transfers provides ways for current employees to move to other jobs. Filling openings internally may add motivation for employees to stay and grow in the organization rather than pursuing career opportunities elsewhere.

Organizational Databases The increased use of HR management systems allows HR staff members to maintain background and KSA information on existing employees. As openings arise, HR employment specialists can access databases by entering job requirements and then get a listing of current employees meeting those requirements. Various types of employment software sort employee data by occupational fields, education, areas of career interests, previous work histories, and other variables. For instance, if a firm has an opening for someone with an MBA and marketing experience, the key words *MBA* and *marketing* can be entered in a search field, and the program displays a list of all current employees with these two items identified in their employee profiles.

The advantage of such databases is that they can be linked to other HR activities. Opportunities for career development and advancement are major reasons why individuals stay or leave their employers. With databases, internal opportunities for individuals can be identified. Employee profiles are continually updated to include such items as additional training or education completed, special projects worked on, and career plans and desires noted during performance appraisal and career mentoring discussions.

Job Posting The major means for recruiting employees for other jobs within the organization is **job posting**, a system in which the employer provides notices of job openings and employees respond by applying for specific openings. Without some sort of job posting system, it is difficult for many employees to find out what jobs are open elsewhere in the organization. The organization can notify employees of job vacancies in a number of ways, including posting notices on the company intranet and Internet Web site, using employee newsletters, and sending out e-mails to managers and employees. In a unionized organization, job posting and bidding can be quite formal because the procedures are often spelled out in labor agreements. Seniority lists may be used by organizations that make promotions based strictly on seniority, so candidates are considered for promotions in the order of seniority.

Regardless of the means used, the purpose of the job posting system is to provide employees with more opportunities to move within the organization. When establishing and managing a job posting system, a number of answers to many potential questions must be addressed:

- What happens if no qualified candidates respond to postings?
- Must employees inform their supervisors that they are applying for another job?
- Are there restrictions on how long an employee must stay in a job before applying for another one?
- How much notice should an employee be required to give before transferring to a new department?
- What types of or levels of jobs will not be posted?

Job posting systems can be ineffective if handled improperly. Jobs generally are posted before any external recruiting is done. The organization must allow a reasonable period of time for present employees to check notices of available jobs before it considers external applicants. When employees' bids are turned down, they should discuss with their supervisors or someone in the HR area the knowledge, skills, and abilities they need in order to improve their opportunities in the future.

Some organizations use automated systems that combine elements of databases and job postings. The Technology Transforming HR presents examples of such systems.

Technology Transforming HR

Automated Job Posting

A number of vendors offer systems that allow large companies to match existing employees with new job openings. Taking a close look at their own employees saves firms money and helps loyalty. It has been noted that "if you are not recruiting your own employees, someone else will," and that if employees have no internal opportunities to advance, the best performers will look outside.

Most companies have had some kind of job posting systems for internal jobs; now more use pro-active efforts to get employees to apply through Web-based systems. For example, the job posting system at Fireman's Fund Insurance works like this: Employees log on to the company intranet and create personal profiles including career objectives, education, skill sets, and salary expectations. They may also attach a resume. When a job opens, the placement program automatically mines the database for matches. Candidates are notified by e-mail and go through the regular hiring cycle.

Thomson Legal and Regulatory, a legal publishing firm with 17,000 employees worldwide, uses a similar system.

After logging on to the intranet and creating profiles, applicants respond to a series of questions about their experiences, skills, and professional qualifications. These responses are scored and ranked automatically. If an applicant fits criteria set by a hiring manager, then a face-to-face interview can be scheduled.

At Whirlpool, 68,000 employees can use a somewhat similar system, making it simpler for employees to access job openings. They can go on-line to retrieve a list of jobs that match their backgrounds and to apply for jobs. Further, managers can enter job criteria and instantly receive names of internal and external candidates who fit them. More than half of the people Whirlpool hired in 2003 were internal candidates. The company estimates that it saved $1 million with the system that year.

These examples illustrate how automated job posting is paying off for employers. Use of such systems is expected to grow in the future.[20]

Promotions and Transfers Many organizations choose to fill vacancies through promotions or transfers from within whenever possible. Although most often successful, promotions and transfers from within have some drawbacks as well. A person's performance on one job may not be a good predictor of performance on another, because different skills may be required on the new job. For example, not every high-performing worker makes a successful supervisor. In most supervisory jobs, an ability to accomplish the work through others requires skills in influencing and dealing with people, and those skills may not have been a factor in non-supervisory jobs.

As employees transfer or are promoted to other jobs, individuals must be recruited to fill their vacated jobs. Planning on how to fill those openings should occur before the job transfers or promotions, not afterward. It is clear that people in organizations with fewer levels may have less frequent chances for promotion. Also, in most organizations, promotions may not be an effective way to speed the movement of protected-class individuals up through the organization if doing that is an organizational concern. Some promotions and transfers may require employee relocation as well.[21]

Employee-Focused Recruiting

One reliable source of potential recruits is suggestions from current or former employees. Because current and former employees are familiar with the employer, most employees usually do not refer individuals who are likely to be un-qualified or to make the employees look bad. Also, follow-up with former em-ployers is likely to be done only with persons who were solid employees previously.

Current-Employee Referrals A reliable source of people to fill vacancies is composed of acquaintances, friends, and family members of employees. The cur-rent employees can acquaint potential applicants with the advantages of a job with the company, furnish letters of introduction, and encourage candidates to apply. However, using only word-of-mouth or current employee referrals can vi-olate equal employment regulations if protected-class individuals are under-represented in the current organizational workforce. Therefore, some external recruiting might be necessary to avoid legal problems in this area.

Utilizing this source is usually one of the most effective methods of recruiting because many qualified people can be reached at a low cost. In an organization with numerous employees, this approach can develop quite a large pool of po-tential employees. Some studies have found that new workers recruited through current-employee referrals have longer tenure with organizations than do those recruited through other sources. According to a study, referral programs cost an average of $500 per salaried employee hired and $70 per hourly employee hired, whereas print advertising costs $2,884 per salaried employee hired and $726 per hourly employee hired.[22]

Tight labor markets in many geographic areas and certain occupational fields prompted many employers to establish employee referral incentive programs. Mid-sized and larger employers are much more likely to use employee referral bonuses. Some referral programs provide different amounts for hard-to-fill jobs compared with common openings.

Re-recruiting of Former Employees and Applicants Former employees and former applicants represent another source for recruitment. Both groups of-fer a time-saving advantage because something is already known about them. Seeking them out as candidates is known as *re-recruiting* because they were suc-cessfully recruited previously.

Former employees are considered an internal source in the sense that they have ties to the employer, and may be called "boomerangers" because they left and came back. Individuals who left for other jobs might be willing to return because the other jobs and employers turned out to be less attractive than initially thought. For example, Accenture, a consulting firm, attracted more than 100 people who had left in the prior two years by contacting them and offering them "loyalty grants." Firms such as Accenture, Microsoft, and others have established "alumni reunions" to keep in touch with individuals who have left, and also to allow them to re-recruit individuals as appropriate openings arise.[23] Key issues in the decision to re-recruit someone include the reasons why the individual left originally and whether or not the individual's performance and capabilities were good.

Another potential source of applicants is former applicants. Although these are not entirely an internal source, information about them can be found in the orga-nizational files or an applicant database. Re-contacting those who have previ-ously applied for jobs can be a quick and inexpensive way to fill unexpected openings. For instance, one firm that needed two cost accountants immediately contacted qualified previous applicants and was able to hire individuals who were disenchanted with their current jobs at other companies.

Re-recruiting has another meaning as well. The idea is to treat the best current employees as if they were top recruits. For example, if a company is giving signing bonuses to top recruits, perhaps it should give retention bonuses to top existing staff members. As one manager put it: "Think of your best staff member. What would you do or say if he or she was leaving? Do these things anyway."[24]

EXTERNAL RECRUITING SOURCES

Many external sources are available for recruiting. In some tight labor markets, multiple sources and methods may be used to attract candidates for the variety of jobs available in organizations. Some of the more prominent methods are highlighted next.

College and University Recruiting

College or university students are a significant source for entry-level professional and technical employees. Most universities maintain career placement offices in which employers and applicants can meet. A number of considerations affect an employer's selection of colleges and universities at which to conduct interviews. The major determinants are:

- Current and anticipated job openings
- Reputations of the colleges and universities
- Experiences with placement offices and previous graduates
- Organizational budget constraints
- Market competition for graduates
- Cost of available talent and typical salaries

College recruiting can be expensive; therefore, an organization should determine if the jobs it is trying to fill really require persons with college degrees. A great many jobs do not, yet many employers often insist on filling them with college graduates. The result may be employees who must be paid more and who are likely to leave if the jobs are not sufficiently challenging.

There is a great deal of competition for the top students in many college and university programs, and less competition for students with less impressive records. Attributes that recruiters seem to value most highly in college graduates—poise, oral and written communication skills, personality, and appearance—all are typically mentioned ahead of grade point average (GPA). However, for many employers, a high GPA is a major criterion for considering candidates for jobs during on-campus interviews. Research suggests that recruiters use GPA decision rules in a variety of ways to initially screen applicants in college recruiting. These include setting minimum GPA requirements to screen large applicant pools, not considering GPA at all, and screening out students with *high* GPA.[25]

A number of factors determine success in college recruiting. Some employers actively build continuing relationships with individual faculty members and career staff at designated colleges and universities. Maintaining presence on campus by providing guest speakers to classes and student groups increases the contacts for an employer.

The important point is that employers that show continuing presence and support on a campus are more likely to see better college recruiting results. For instance, Shell Oil has concentrated its college recruiting. Formerly, the company recruited at 84 colleges and universities. Today, it targets only 26 schools. As a

THOMSON

WEST

COLLEGE AND UNIVERSITY RECRUITING
Suggests ideas for effective college recruiting.
Custom Search:
☑ ANALYSIS
Exact Phrase: College recruiting efforts

Making Internships Work

An internship has the potential for being good situations for both the individual student intern and an employer. The student gets an opportunity to see if the employer and its culture fit, and the employer gets the equivalent of a 90-day interview instead of a 30-minute one. But not all internships actually are good situations for either party. Some basic guidelines for the employer can help improve the odds that internships will be rewarding:

♦ *Decide what the company needs.* A specific project is more challenging for the student and a better predictor of future employment capabilities for the company than just providing a job.

♦ *Require meaningful work.* Challenging assignments are best. Using interns as clerical replacements is usually not the best way to impress them.

♦ *Pay well.* Competitive wages help attract talent. In the past there were many unpaid internships, but most interns today are paid. Average pay of $3,000–$4,000 for a summer or $9–$10 per hour is typical.

♦ *Treat the intern like a new employee.* Interns need work space, appropriate tools for the job, Internet access, a telephone, training feedback, and someone to provide guidance when needed.

♦ *Look at several candidates.* Use a broad internship description to increase the chances of finding a talented person with appropriate capabilities.

result, recruiting costs have dropped, time-to-hire has dropped, and the acceptance rate for job offers has gone up.[26]

Another example is GE, which stresses internships in its college recruiting. About 65% of the 1,400 students it hires annually have had an internship or a type of cooperative experience. The company achieves better retention using internship and cooperative programs.[27] PricewaterhouseCoopers uses internships, focusing on early identification of potential candidates through contacts with professors and others. Ford uses an interactive assessment program posted on a Web site, and a weekend leadership conference that includes an interview. When the weekend is over, successful candidates know if they got a job, what the salary is, and when they start.[28]

As these examples illustrate, well-planned internships can be excellent sources for talented job candidates. For successful internship suggestions, see the HR Practice.

School Recruiting

High schools or vocational/technical schools may be good sources of new employees for some organizations. Many schools have a centralized guidance or placement office. Promotional brochures that acquaint students with starting jobs and career opportunities can be distributed to counselors, librarians, or others. Participating in career days and giving company tours to school groups are other ways of maintaining good contact with school sources. Cooperative programs in which students work part-time and receive some school credits also may be useful in generating qualified future applicants for full-time positions.

Until recently, students not going on to college received little guidance or training on finding jobs after high school. However, the number of "partnerships" with schools through "school to work" programs has grown. Companies are entering the classroom not only to recruit, but to tutor students in skills such as the reading and math needed for work. Internships during the summer and work/school programs also are widely used.[29]

Employers recognize that they may need to begin attracting students with capabilities while those students are in high school. For example, GE, IBM, and other corporations fund programs to encourage students with science and math skills to participate in engineering internships during summers. These and other employers specifically target talented members of racial minorities in high schools and provide them with career encouragement, summer internships, and mentoring programs. In addition to fulfilling some social responsibilities and aiding in workforce diversity, the organizations hope to generate employment interest from the students they assist, and that that interest may help fill future openings.

Labor Unions

Labor unions are a good source of certain types of workers. In such industries as electrical and construction ones, unions have traditionally supplied workers to employers. A labor pool is generally available through a union, and workers can be dispatched from it to particular jobs to meet the needs of the employers.

In some instances, the union can control or influence recruiting and staffing needs. An organization with a strong union may have less flexibility than a non-union company in deciding who will be hired and where that person will be placed. Unions can also benefit employers through apprenticeship and cooperative staffing programs, as they do in the building and printing industries.

Employment Agencies and Headhunters

Every state in the United States has its own state-sponsored employment agency. These agencies operate branch offices in many cities throughout the states and do not charge fees to applicants or employers.

Private employment agencies also operate in most cities. For a fee collected from either the employee or the employer, these agencies do some preliminary screening and put the organization in touch with applicants. Private employment agencies differ considerably in the levels of service, costs, policies, and types of applicants they provide. Employers can reduce the range of possible problems from these sources by giving complete descriptions and specifications for jobs to be filled.

Some employment agencies focus their efforts on executive, managerial, and professional positions. These executive search firms are split into two groups: (1) contingency firms that charge a fee only after a candidate has been hired by a client company, and (2) retainer firms that charge a client a set fee whether or not the contracted search is successful. Most of the larger firms work on a retainer basis. The fee charged by executive search firms may be 30% or more of the employee's first-year salary. In most cases, the employer pays the fee, but in some circumstances, the employee does. For placing someone in a high-level executive job, a search firm may receive $300,000 or more, counting travel expenses and the placement fee.[30] The size of the fees and the aggressiveness with which some firms pursue candidates for openings have led to such firms being called *headhunters.* However, search firms are ethically bound not to approach employees of client companies in their search for job candidates for another employer.[31]

Competitive Sources

Other sources for recruiting include professional and trade associations, trade publications, and competitors. Many professional societies and trade associations publish newsletters or magazines and have Web sites containing job ads. Such sources may be useful for recruiting specialized professionals needed in an industry.

Some employers have extended recruiting to customers. Retailers such as Target, Home Depot, and Best Buy have aggressive programs to recruit employees in stores. Customers at these firms can receive applications blanks, apply on-line using kiosks, or schedule interviews with managers or HR staff members, all while in the stores. Other firms have included employment announcements when sending out customer bills or newsletters.

Media Sources

Media sources such as newspapers, magazines, television, radio, and billboards are widely used. Some firms have used direct mail with purchased lists of individuals in certain fields or industries. Whatever medium is used, it should be tied to the relevant labor market and should provide sufficient information on the company and the job. Figure 7-6 shows information a good recruiting advertisement should include. Notice that details about the job and the application process, desired candidate qualifications, and an overview of the organization are all important.

Evaluating Ads HR recruiters should measure the responses they generate in order to evaluate the effectiveness of various media. The easiest way to track responses to ads is to use different contact names, e-mail addresses, or phone number codes in each ad. Then the employer can note which advertisement prompted each applicant response that is received.

Figure 7-6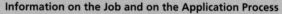

What to Include in an Effective Recruiting Ad

Information on the Job and on the Application Process
- Job title and responsibilities
- Location of job
- Starting pay range
- Closing date for application
- Whether or not to submit a resume and a cover letter
- Whether or not calls are invited
- Where to mail application or resume

Desired Candidate Qualifications
- Years of experience
- Three to five key characteristics of successful candidates

Information on the Organization
- That it is an EEO employer
- Its primary business

Although the total number of responses to each ad should be tracked, judging the success of an ad only by this number is a mistake. For example, it is better to have 10 responses with two qualified applicants than 30 responses with only one qualified applicant. Therefore, after the individuals are hired, follow-up should be done to see which sources produced employees who stayed longer and performed better.

Job Fairs and Special Events

Employers in tight labor markets or needing to fill a large number of jobs quickly have used job fairs and special recruiting events. Job fairs also have been held by economic development entities, employer associations, HR associations, and other community groups to help bring employers and potential job candidates together. For instance, to fill jobs in one metropolitan area, the local SHRM chapter annually sponsors a job fair at which 75–125 employers can meet applicants. Publicity in the city draws more than 1,000 potential recruits. One cautionary note: Some employers at this and other job fairs may see current employees "shopping" for jobs at other employers.

Another cautionary note: "General" job fairs are likely to attract many people including more unemployed (and unemployable) attendees. Industry- or skill-specific events offer more satisfactory candidates. For example, Prudential Insurance in Newark, New Jersey, found it was getting unemployable applicants at general job fairs. The firm started going to "targeted" job fairs for financial professionals or "diversity" events for specific protected-class individuals. Such job fairs can attract employed candidates who are looking casually but may not put their resumes out on the Internet.[32]

"Virtual" job fairs have been used by the federal government and others.[33] "Drive-through" job fairs at shopping malls have been used by employers in a number of communities. At one such event, interested persons can drive up to a tent outside the mall and pick up applications from a "menu board" of employers, then park and interview in the tent with recruiters if time allows. Some firms also use other methods as noted next.

Creative Recruiting Methods

In labor markets that are tight and in industries with significant shortages of qualified applicants, employers turn to more creative recruiting methods. Regardless of the methods used, the goal is to generate a pool of qualified applicants so that the jobs in organizations are filled in a timely manner. Some methods may be more effective at recruiting for certain jobs than others. To illustrate, here are some examples:

- Using a plane towing an advertising banner over beach areas
- Advertising jobs on local movie theater screens as pre-show entertainment
- Holding raffles for employees who refer candidates, with cars and trips being used as prizes
- Offering free rock concert tickets to the first 20 applicants hired
- Setting up recruiting tables at bowling alleys, minor-league baseball games, or stock car races
- Recruiting younger technical employees at video game parlors
- Arranging partnerships with downsizing firms to interview those being laid off

- Connecting with outplacement firms to find out about individuals who have lost their jobs
- Offering tuition assistance for those willing to work their way through college
- Sponsoring book fairs to recruit publishing company sales representatives
- Interviewing 2 hours a week even if the organization does not have any openings—and maintaining good files on those interviewed
- Taking candidates from among those who leave the armed forces (About 275,000 women and men, plus many of their spouses, leave the armed forces each year.)
- Partnering with U.S. military recruiters and guaranteeing enlistees jobs after they complete military service
- Parking motor homes—all set up for interviews, testing, and hiring—in parking lots at malls, with signs saying, "Want a job? Apply here."

▌ INTERNET RECRUITING

The Internet has become the primary means for many employers to search for job candidates and for applicants to look for jobs. The explosive growth in general Internet use is a key reason. Internet users tap the Internet to search for jobs almost as frequently as they read classified ads in newspapers. Many of them also post or submit resumes on the Internet.

🌐 Global Internet Recruiting

The percentage of Global 500 companies that use Web sites for recruiting has jumped to 88%. Use of the Internet has increased around the globe in part because it is cheaper. The Internet is used for recruiting most widely in the U.S.: 12.2% of Internet users in the U.S. visited a Web site for recruitment in 2003, while only 7.3% of Internet users in Europe did so.[34] The explosive growth of Internet recruiting can overwhelm HR professionals in breadth and scope.

E-Recruiting Methods

Several methods are used for Internet recruiting. The most common ones are Internet job boards, professional/career Web sites, and employer Web sites.

Internet Job Boards Numerous Internet job boards, such as Monster, Yahoo!, and HotJobs, provide places for employers to post jobs or search for candidates. Another prevalent one is America's Job Bank, operated in conjunction with the U.S. Department of Labor and state job services.

Job boards provide access to numerous candidates. However, many individuals accessing the sites are "job lookers" who are not serious about changing jobs, but are checking out compensation levels and job availability in their areas of interest. Various estimates are that about one-third of all visitors to job boards are just browsing, not seriously considering changing employment. Despite these concerns, HR recruiters find general job boards useful for generating applicant responses. Also, a recruiter for a firm can pretend to be an applicant in order to check out what other employers are looking for in similar job candidates and offering as compensation, in order to maintain recruiting competitiveness.

Professional/Career Web Sites Many professional associations have employment sections at their Web sites. As illustration, for HR jobs see the Society for Human Resource Management site, *www.shrm.org*, or the American Society for Training and Development site, *www.astd.org*. A number of private corporations

Effective Recruiting Through a Company Web Site

Using a company Web site for effective recruiting includes a number of suggestions. The primary ones are:

- Make the site easy to navigate. The "Careers" button should be on the home page and clearly labeled. Job information should be no more than three clicks away.
- Build a strong image for the company and the job. One company lists open positions and also describes the kind of work people would be doing in those positions, shows pictures of facilities and the people who work there, and describes the company climate and location.
- Make it easy to apply for a job. There should be a resume builder, or a place to paste an existing resume. On-line applications are important too.
- Use qualifying categories (location, job function, skills, keyword search, etc.) to help candidates find the jobs for

which they are eligible. Using such categories saves time, especially in a big company.

- Use self-assessment checklists to ask candidates about experience and interests and to direct them to the jobs that fit them the best.
- Include items people care about. Describe the company, its products and services, careers, and other unique advantages of working for the company.
- Link the site to a database. Doing this provides recruiters with a way to post jobs, search for resumes and applications, and screen applicants. Without this necessary step, it is impossible to manage a busy Web site.
- Collect metrics on the site. To determine how effective the site is, gather information such as the numbers of visitors, hits from ads, and actual hires.

---

maintain specialized career or industry Web sites to focus on IT, telecommunications, engineering, physician, or other areas. Using these more targeted Web sites limits somewhat the recruiters' search time and efforts. Also, posting jobs on such Web sites is likely to target applicants specifically interested in the job field and may reduce the number of less-qualified applicants who actually apply.

Employer Web Sites Despite the popularity of job boards and association job sites, many employers have found their own Web sites to be more effective and efficient when recruiting candidates. See the HR Practice for advice on designing an effective careers or employment section for a Web site.

Numerous employers have included employment and career information on their sites. Many company Web sites have a tab labeled "Careers" or "Employment." This is the place that recruiting (internal and external) is often conducted. On many of these sites, job seekers are encouraged to e-mail resumes or complete on-line applications. According to one survey, about 16% of hires come through a company Web site—a much higher proportion than come from on-line job boards.[35]

A good Web site can also help reach "passive" job seekers, who have a good job and are not really looking to change, but might consider a better opportunity if it were presented. These individuals often are not usually listed on job boards, but they might visit a company Web site for other reasons and check out the careers or employment section. A well-designed corporate Web site can help stimulate interest in some of passive job seekers, as well as other potential candidates.

It is important that the recruiting and employment portions of an employer Web site be seen as part of the marketing efforts of the firm. Therefore, the employment section of an organizational Web site must be shaped to market jobs and ca-

THOMSON

_____

WEST

EFFECTIVE RECRUITING WEB SITE
Describes results of Internet recruiting survey and tips for success.
Custom Search:
☑ ANALYSIS
Exact Phrase: Recruiting site needs

reers effectively. Also, a company Web site should market the employer by out-lining information on the organization, its products and services, organizational and industry growth potential, and organizational operations.

Advantages of Internet Recruiting

Employers have found a number of advantages in using Internet recruiting. A primary one is that many employers have saved money using Internet recruiting versus other recruiting methods such as newspaper advertising, employment agencies, and search firms.

Internet recruiting also can save considerable *time*. Applicants can respond quickly to job postings by sending e-mails, rather than using "snail mail." Recruiters can respond to qualified candidates more quickly, and establish times for interviews or request additional candidate information.

An expanded pool of applicants can be generated using Internet recruiting. In fact, a large number of candidates may see any given job listing, although exposure depends on which Internet sources are used. One side benefit of the Internet is that jobs literally are posted globally, so potential applicants in other geographic areas and countries can view job openings posted on the Internet. The Internet also improves the ability to target specific audiences through the use of categories, information, and other variables.[36]

Disadvantages of Internet Recruiting

The positives associated with Internet recruiting come with a number of disadvantages. In getting broader exposure, employers also may get more unqualified applicants. HR recruiters find that Internet recruiting creates additional work for HR staff members. More resumes must be reviewed, more e-mails need to be dealt with, and expensive specialized software may be needed to track the increased number of applicants resulting from many Internet recruiting efforts. A related concern is that many individuals who access job sites are just browsers who may submit resumes just to see what happens but are not seriously looking for new jobs.

Another issue with Internet recruiting is that some applicants may have limited Internet access, especially individuals from lower socio-economic groups and from certain racial/ethnic minority groups. A "digital divide" separates those who have Internet access from those who do not—and fewer Hispanic and African American job seekers than whites have Internet access at home or at all. Consequently, employers using Internet recruiting may not be reaching as diverse a recruitment pool as might be desired.

Privacy is another potential disadvantage with Internet recruiting. Sharing information gleaned from people who apply to job boards or even company Web sites has become common. But information sharing is being done in ways that might violate discrimination and credit reporting laws.[37]

Legal Issues in Internet Recruiting

With Internet recruiting comes new legal concerns. Several of the concerns have ethical and moral implications, as well as legal ones. For example:[38]

♦ When companies use screening software to avoid looking at each of the thousands of resumes they receive, are rejections really based on the qualifications needed for the job?

♦ Are protected classes being excluded from the process?

- As a company receives resumes from applicants, it is required to track those applicants and report to the federal government. How can a person's protected-class status and other information be collected and analyzed for those reports?
- Who are really applicants? Is someone who sent an e-mail asking if the employer has a job open really an applicant?
- General informality on-line can lead to discussions or information that might be improper if the person does not get the job.

▨▨▨▨ RECRUITING EVALUATION AND METRICS

To determine how effective various recruiting sources and methods have been, it is important to evaluate recruiting efforts. The primary way to find out whether recruiting efforts are cost-effective is to conduct formal analyses as part of recruiting evaluation. Several areas *can* be measured when trying to analyze recruiting effectiveness; five specific areas that *need* to be considered include: quantity of recruits, quality of recruits, time available for filling empty positions, cost per recruit, and satisfaction of parties involved. Metrics that look at the quality of the selection decisions made will be included here.

Evaluating Recruiting Quantity and Quality

As one means of evaluating recruiting, organizations can see how their recruiting efforts compare with past patterns and with the recruiting performance of other organizations. Certain measures of recruiting effectiveness are quite useful in indicating whether sufficient numbers of the targeted applicant population group are being attracted. Information on job performance, absenteeism, cost of training, and turnover by recruiting source also help adjust future recruiting. For example, some companies find that recruiting at certain colleges or universities furnishes stable, high performers, whereas recruiting at other schools provides employees who are more prone to leave the organization. General metrics for evaluating quantity and quality of recruiting include the following variables:

- *Quantity of applicants:* Because the goal of a good recruiting program is to generate a large pool of applicants from which to choose, quantity is a natural place to begin evaluation. The basic measure here considers whether the quantity of recruits is sufficient to fill job vacancies. A related question is: Does recruiting provide enough qualified applicants with an appropriate mix of protected-class individuals?
- *Quality of applicants:* In addition to quantity, a key issue is whether or not the qualifications of the applicant pool are sufficient to fill the job openings. Do the applicants meet job specifications, and do they perform the jobs well after hire? What is the failure rate for new hires for each recruiter? Measures that can be used include items such as performance appraisal scores, months until promotion, output, and sales volume for each hire.

Evaluating the Time Required to Fill Openings

Looking at the length of time it takes to fill openings is a common means of evaluating recruiting efforts. If openings are not filled quickly with qualified candidates, the work and productivity of the organization likely suffer. If it takes 75 days to fill empty positions, managers who need those employees will be unhappy.

Generally, it is useful to calculate the average amount of time it takes from contact to hire for each source of applicants, because some sources may produce recruits faster than others. For example, one firm calculated the following averages:

Source	Average Time from Contact to Hire
Agencies	25 days
Walk-ins	7 days
Internet	12 days

These data reveal that use of agencies takes significantly longer to fill openings than relying on other means. Therefore, it suggests matching the use of sources to the time available.

Evaluating the Cost of Recruiting

The major number for measuring cost is calculating recruiting expenses for the year divided by the number of hires for the year:

$$\frac{\text{Recruiting expenses}}{\text{Number of recruits hired}}$$

The problem with this approach is accurately identifying what should be included in the recruiting expenses. Should expenses for testing, background checks, relocations, or signing bonuses be included, or are they more properly excluded?

If those questions are answered, then the costs might be allocated to various sources to determine how much each hire from each source costs. The costs also can be sorted by type of job—costs for hiring managers, secretaries, bookkeepers, and sales personnel will all be different.

Evaluating Recruiting Satisfaction

The satisfaction of two groups is useful in evaluating recruiting. Certainly the views of managers with openings to fill are important, because they are "customers" in a very real sense. But also the applicants (those hired and those not hired) are an important part of the process and can provide useful input.

Managers can respond to questions about the quality of the applicant pool, the recruiter's service, the timeliness of the process, and any problems that they see. Applicants might provide input on how they were treated, their perceptions of the company, and the length of the recruiting process.

General Recruiting Process Metrics

Because recruiting activities are important, the costs and benefits associated with them should be analyzed. A cost-benefit analysis of recruiting efforts may include both direct costs (advertising, recruiters' salaries, travel, agency fees, etc.) and indirect costs (involvement of operating managers, public relations, image, etc.). Cost-benefit information on each recruiting source can be calculated. Comparing the length of time that applicants hired from each source stay in the organization with the cost of hiring from that source also offers a useful perspective.

Yield ratios Comparisons of the number of applicants at one stage of the recruiting process with the number at the next stage.

Yield Ratios One means for evaluating recruiting efforts is **yield ratios,** which compare the number of applicants at one stage of the recruiting process with the number at another stage. The result is a tool for approximating the necessary size of the initial applicant pool. It is useful to visualize yield ratios as a pyramid, in which the employer starts with a broad base of applicants that progressively

Figure 7-7 | *Sample Recruiting Evaluation Pyramid*

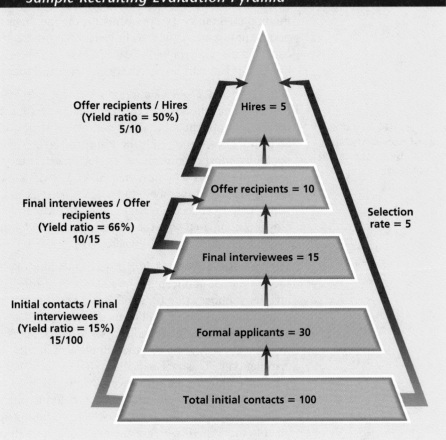

Offer recipients / Hires
(Yield ratio = 50%)
5/10

Hires = 5

Final interviewees / Offer
recipients
(Yield ratio = 66%)
10/15

Offer recipients = 10

Selection
rate = 5

Final interviewees = 15

Initial contacts / Final
interviewees
(Yield ratio = 15%)
15/100

Formal applicants = 30

Total initial contacts = 100

narrows. As Figure 7-7 depicts, to end up with five hires for the job in question, a sample company must begin with 100 applicants in the pool, as long as yield ratios remain as shown.

A different approach to using yield ratios suggests that over time, organizations can develop ranges for crucial ratios. When a given indicator ratio falls outside that range, it may indicate problems in the recruiting process. For example, in college recruiting, the following ratios might be useful:

$$\frac{\text{College seniors given second interview}}{\text{Total number of seniors interviewed}} = \text{Range of } 30\%\text{--}50\%$$

$$\frac{\text{Number who accept offer}}{\text{Number invited to the company to visit}} = \text{Range of } 50\%\text{--}70\%$$

$$\frac{\text{Number hired}}{\text{Number offered a job}} = \text{Range of } 70\%\text{--}80\%$$

$$\frac{\text{Number finally hired}}{\text{Total number interviewed on campus}} = \text{Range of } 10\%\text{--}20\%$$

Selection rate
Percentage hired from
a given group of
candidates.

Selection Rate Another useful calculation is the **selection rate,** which is the percentage hired from a given group of candidates. It equals the number hired divided by the number of applicants; for example, a rate of 30% indicates that

3 out of 10 applicants were hired. The selection rate is also affected by the validity of the selection process. A relatively unsophisticated selection program might pick 8 out of 10 applicants for the job. Four of those might turn out to be good employees. A more valid selection process might pick 5 out of 10 applicants but all perform well. Selection rate measures not just recruiting but selection issues as well. So do acceptance rate and success base rate.

Acceptance Rate Calculating the acceptance rate helps identify how successful the organization is at hiring candidates to employ. The **acceptance rate** is the percent of applicants hired divided by the total number of applicants. After the company goes through all the effort to screen, interview, and make job offers, hopefully, most candidates accept job offers. If they do not, then HR might want to look at reasons why managers and HR staff cannot "close the deal." It is common for HR staff members to track the reasons candidates turn down job offers, which help explain the rejection rate, in order to learn how competitive the employer is compared with other employers and what factors are causing candidates to choose employment elsewhere.

Acceptance rate Percent of applicants hired divided by total number of applicants.

Success Base Rate A longer-term measure of recruiting effectiveness is the success rate of applicants. The *success base rate* can be determined by comparing the number of past applicants who have become successful employees against the number of applicants they competed against for their jobs, using historical data within the organization. Also, the success base rate can be compared with the success rates of other employers in the area or industry, using benchmarking data. This rate indicates whether the quality of the employees hired results in employees who perform well and have low turnover. For example, assume that if 10 people were hired at random, one would expect 4 of them to be good employees. Thus, a successful recruiting program should be aimed at attracting the 4 in 10 who are capable of doing well on this particular job. Realistically, no recruiting program will attract only the 4 in 10 who will succeed. However, efforts to make the recruiting program attract the largest proportion of those in the base rate group can make recruiting efforts more effective.

Increasing Recruiting Effectiveness

The efforts to evaluate recruiting should be used to make recruiting activities more effective. Using the data to target different applicant pools, tap broader labor markets, use different recruiting methods, improve internal handling and interviewing of applicants, and train recruiters and managers all can increase recruiting effectiveness.

Another way to increase recruiting effectiveness rests on the recruiters themselves. Those involved in the recruiting process can turn off recruits or create excitement among them. Recruiters who are knowledgeable about the jobs and their employers and who treat applicants with respect and enthusiasm are viewed more positively. A positive image is more likely to result in more applicants pursuing employment opportunities with an employer.

SUMMARY

♦ Recruiting is the process of generating a pool of qualified applicants for organizational jobs through a series of activities.

♦ Recruiting must be viewed strategically, and discussions should be held about the relevant labor markets in which to recruit.

- A strategic approach to recruiting begins with human resource planning and decisions about organizational recruiting responsibilities.
- The components of labor markets are labor force population, applicant population, and applicant pool.
- Labor markets can be categorized by geographic area, industry, occupation, qualifications, and other characteristics.
- Employers must make decisions about organization-based versus outsourced recruiting, regular versus flexible staffing, and other strategic aspects of recruiting.
- Efforts should be made to recruit a diverse workforce, including older workers, individuals with disabilities, women, and members of racial/ethnic minorities.
- The decision to use internal or external sources should consider both the advantages and disadvantages of each source.
- The most common methods of internal recruiting include organizational databases, job postings, promotions and transfers, current-employee referrals, and re-recruiting of former employees and applicants.
- The most common external recruiting sources include colleges and universities, schools, labor unions, employment agencies and headhunters, competitive sources, media sources, job fairs and special events, and creative methods.
- Internet recruiting has grown in use through job boards and various Web sites.
- Internet recruiting can save costs and time, but they also can generate more unqualified applicants and frequently may not reach certain groups of potential applicants.
- Recruiting efforts should be evaluated to assess how effectively they are.
- Recruiting evaluation typically includes evaluating recruiting quantity and quality, tracking the time to fill openings, and examining the costs and benefits of various recruiting sources.

REVIEW AND APPLICATION QUESTIONS

1. What labor markets should be considered when recruiting to fill an opening for a sales representative for a pharmaceutical manufacturer?
2. Discuss ways a bank could effectively use the Internet to recruit management trainees.
3. Go to *www.recruitusa.com* and other sites to get ideas on evaluating recruiting efforts and then prepare a report for review.

LEARNING REVIEW

To check your knowledge of the chapter, review the following. (Answers after the supplemental case.) For more questions, see the Study Guide.

1. One of the advantages for the staffs of employee leasing companies is that _____.
   a. they usually receive many interesting assignments in a variety of start-up businesses
   b. they may receive better benefits than they would otherwise get in many small businesses
   c. they do not require Social Security taxes
   d. they can be regarded as self-employed for IRS purposes

2. Which of the following is given as an advantage of external recruiting?
   a. It allows for better assessment of abilities.
   b. It involves a shorter adjustment or orientation time.
   c. The new hire may bring new industry insights.
   d. The company has to hire only at entry level.

3. Which of the following statements regarding job posting and bidding is *false*?
   a. It gives each employee an opportunity to move to a better job within the organization.
   b. It makes it difficult for supervisors to develop employees over the long term.
   c. Jobs are generally posted before any external recruiting is done.
   d. In a unionized organization, job posting and bidding often is spelled out in the labor agreement.

4. Evaluating the success of recruiting efforts is important because it _____.
   a. provides input to the compensation system of the HR unit
   b. is one way to measure the reputation of the firm on the college campuses
   c. indicates how the employer measures up against competitors
   d. is the primary way to find out whether or not the efforts are cost effective

CASE
ENTERPRISE RECRUITING

Many customers use Enterprise Rent-A-Car each year, and it is bigger than its competitors Hertz, Avis, and National. In ten years Enterprise has doubled the number of cars in its fleet and increased its workforce over 30%, to 54,000 employees. What may not be widely known is that Enterprise recruits large numbers of college graduates each year for its management training program and other jobs. About 6,000 college graduates have been hired annually, so that Enterprise can staff its expanding number of offices.

Several innovative means are being used in addition to the typical recruiting approaches. On the company's Web site the on-line game called "Give Me the Business" gets many hits. The game is not directly related to renting cars, but it lets people experience the challenges of a customer-service business. The hidden message is its "virtual marketing" of Enterprise and its fun culture.

Another creative approach used was sponsoring a Personal Enterprise show on MTV, in which candidates for a job at Enterprise were viewed during two rounds of behavioral interviews. The candidates were asked questions, and they were "judged" on their answers. But unlike other TV reality shows where only one person wins, three of the four candidates were offered jobs.

The on-line games and the TV show were attention-getters, but the greatest source of Enterprise recruits comes from employee referrals. Enterprise employees who refer candidates who are hired and remain with the firm can receive incentives of $500 to $1,500 each. Often, referrals check out Enterprise or its Web site and mention the firm to others, which expands the pool of potential recruits.

Enterprise is somewhat unusual as an employer because it uses both traditional and creative recruiting means. The wide range of activities has helped Enterprise recruit more effectively, which aids its strategic goal of establishing its "employment brand." At the heart of its branding efforts is a program called *My Personal Enterprise*. This program is a theme of all of Enterprise's recruiting materials, advertisements, Web site, and other recruiting efforts. The main focus of *My Personal Enterprise* is to convince college graduates that there are career opportunities in the rental car firm, and that jobs in the company can be fun and fulfilling.[39]

Questions
1. How does having multiple recruiting means help Enterprise establish its brand?
2. Go to the Enterprise Web site (*www.enterprise.com*) and check out the game, career opportunities, and other components. Then evaluate how effective you feel the Web site is as an employment branding and recruiting resource.

SUPPLEMENTAL CASE: Northwest State College

This case shows how recruiting policies can work against successful recruiting when a tight labor market exists. (For the case, go to **http://mathis.swlearning.com/.**)

Learning Review Answers: 1. b   2. c   3. b   4. d

NOTES

1. John Sullivan, "How to Figure Out if You Are an Employer of Choice," *Workforce Online,* April 2003 *www.workforce.com;* Eilene Zimmerman, "Hospital President Sparks Groundbreaking Recruiting Campaign," *Workforce Online,* May 2003, *www.workforce.com;* Frank Jossi, "HR Is Turning into Brands," *Workforce Online,* July 2002, *www. workforce.com*; Jeff Dahlthorp, "Public Relations and Recruiting," IIRC Article, *www.iirc.com/;* "Five Great Recruiting Brands," *Workforce Online,* July 2003; "Global Execs Confirm Branding as Key Success Factor," *Right Communique,* Second Quarter 2002, 1; and Gene C. George et al., "Building the Brand through People," *Worldatwork Journal,* First Quarter 2004, 39–45.

2. Adapted from John Sumser, "Roses in the Thorn Bush," *Hire.com,* 2003, 4, *www.interbiznet.com.*

3. John Sumser, "What Is Recruiting?" *www.interbiznet.com*

4. Lou Adler, "Why Your Hiring Strategy Must Map Your Business Strategy," February 20, 2004, *www.erexchange.com.*

5. Jeff Garton, "Strategy Strong Enough to Beat the Competition," *Employment Management Today,* Spring 2002, 2.

6. "Iowa—the Future Is Foreign," *The Economist,* September 16, 2000, 36; and "Immigration Foes Take Aim at Vilsak," *Omaha World-Herald,* August 21, 2001, A14.

7. Jeff Thredgold, "Overseas Migration," *Rocky Mountain News,* September 27, 2003, 2C.

8. Dene Yeaman, "New Opportunities Old Shackles," *China Staff,* nd 7, 51–53, no. 02856020.

9. Martha Frase-Blunt, "Candidate Glut," *HR Magazine,* August 2003, 1.

10. Rachel King, "The Messy Challenge and Big Payoff of Outsourced Recruiting," *Workforce Management Online,* October 2003, 1.

11. Michelle Martinez, "Recruiting Here and There," *HR Magazine,* September 2002, 96–97.

12. Sara Fister Gold, "Permanent-Hire Program Reduces Turnover," *Workforce,* July 2002, 74–77.

13. "Leased Workers Ask: Who Is the Boss," *Omaha World-Herald,* May 13, 2002, 2D.

14. Harold F. Krieger Jr., "Is There a Professional Employer Organization in Your Future?" *National Public Accountant,* May 5, 2003.

15. John M. Polson, "The PEO Phenomenon," *Employment Law Journal,* Spring 2002, 7–25.

16. Debra Williams, "Temporary Benefits," *Area Development,* October 2002, 36–37.

17. William H. Burgess III, "Dibs on Diversity Recruiting," *Network Journal,* June 2003, 12–13.

18. Ruth E. Thaler-Carter, "Diversify Your Recruitment Advertising," *HR Magazine,* June 2001, 1–5.

19. Based on Derek R. Avery, "Reactions to Diversity in Recruitment Advertising," *Journal of Applied Psychology,* 88 (2003), 672–679.

20. Leslie Klaff, "New Internal Hiring Systems Reduce Cost and Boost Morale," *Workforce Management,* March 2004, 76-79; Cindy Waxer, "Inside Jobs," *Human Resource Executive,* June 10, 2003, 1; D. J. Chhabra, "Turbo Hiring," *Human Resource Executive,* March 2, 2004, 56–59; and Patrick J. Kiger, "CISCO's Homegrown Gamble," *Workforce,* March 2003, 28.

21. Lin Grensing-Pophal, "Transferring Employees Smoothly Takes Time," *HR Magazine,* September 2001, 1 and Lin Grensing-Pophal, "Rules for Hitting the Road," *HR Magazine,* May 2002, 1.

22. Carroll Lachnit, "Employee Referral Saves Times, Saves Money, Delivers Quantity," *Workforce,* June 2001, 67–72.

23. "Referral Programs that Result in Great Hiring and Retention," *SHRM Forum Employment Management Association,* 2002, *www.shrm.org/ema/library.*

24. Todd Raphael, "Think Twice: Why Stars Switch Galaxies," *Workforce,* April 2002, 89; and "Re-recruiting Employees," *Practical Accountant,* September 2003, 23–25.

25. Arlise P. McKinney et al., "Recruiters' Use of GPA in Initial Screening Decisions," *Personnel Psychology,* 56 (2003), 823–845.

26. Joe Mullich, "College Recruiting Goes for Niches," *Workforce Management,* February 2004, 1.

27. Carla Joinson, "Red Hot College Recruiting," *Employment Management Today,* Fall 2001, 1–5.

28. Ibid.

29. Phyllis G. Hartman, "Strategic Recruiting by Partnering with Suppliers," *SHRM Forum Employment Management Association,* June 2002, *www.shrm.org.*

30. Egon Zehnder, "A Simpler Way to Pay," *Harvard Business Review,* April 2001, 53–60.

31. "The Adoption of Quality Standards in Human-Asset-Intensive Service Organizations: The Case of Executive Search," *Global Competitiveness,* January 2002.

32. Martha Frase-Blunt, "Job Fair Challenges for HR," *HR Magazine,* April 2002, 1–5.

33. Ira Hobbs, "Virtual Job Fairs Are the Wave of the Future," *Government Computer News,* April 29, 2002, 1–2.

34. Anne Freedman, "The Web World-Wide," *Human Resource Executive,* March 6, 2002, 44–46.

35. Karen Frankola, "Better Recruiting on Corporate Web Sites," *Workforce Online,* May 2002, *www.workforce.com.*

36. P. Singh and D. Finn, "The Effects of Information Technology on Recruitment," *Journal of Labor Research,* 24 (2003), 395–408.

37. Ryan J. Foley, "Privacy Isn't Part of Online Job Hunt," *Wall Street Journal,* November 12, 2003, D2.

38. Gillian Flynn, "E-Recruiting Ushers in Legal Dangers," *Workforce,* April 2002, 70–72.

39. Based on Alison Stein Wellnar, "The Pickup Artists," July 2004, *Workforce Management Online, www.workforce.com.*

CHAPTER 8

Selecting Human Resources

After you have read this chapter, you should be able to:

- Diagram the sequence of a typical selection process.

- Identify three types of selection tests and legal concerns about their uses.

- Discuss several types of selection interviews and some key considerations in conducting these interviews.

- Explain how legal concerns affect background investigations of applicants and use of medical examinations in the selection process.

- Describe the major issues to be considered when selecting candidates for global assignments.

Pre-employment Testing Cuts Turnover

APAC Customer Services of Deerfield, Illinois, operates call centers for large organizations and employs 13,000 people to do so. In the past, each year, 28,000 employees quit or were fired for poor performance. The company hired virtually anyone who applied and then found that a high number of mismatches between people and jobs resulted in the need to continuously re-hire. A large amount of money was spent on staffing; recruiting costs alone were $1,200 a person.

Concerned about the high cost of turnover, APAC employed a consultant to design pre-employment tests to better place applicants. Now applicants for entry-level jobs complete four tests that usually take a total of about four hours. The first test is a work simulation in which candidates handle calls, making decisions from multiple-choice questions. If they pass that test, the next two tests are behavioral interviews conducted by HR. The fourth test is a Web-based personality assessment that classifies applicants as being at high or low risk for turnover.

"The only problem I cannot find a test for," comments one manager, is whether or not "applicants are going to be at work and come on time." Use of pre-employment testing has cut the attrition rate by 50% and is saving the company $14 million a year.[1]

"Selecting qualified employees is like putting money in the bank."

—*John Boudreau*

Selection decisions are an important part of successful HR management. Some even would argue that they are the *most* important part. Improvement in organizational performance may come from many sources—but unless the employer begins by having the necessary people with the appropriate capabilities in place, positive organization results are less likely to occur.

▋ SELECTION AND PLACEMENT

Selection Process of choosing individuals with qualifications needed to fill jobs in an organization.

Selection is the process of choosing individuals with qualifications needed to fill jobs in an organization. Without qualified employees, an organization is less likely to succeed. Perhaps the best perspective on selection and placement comes from two HR truisms that clearly identify the importance of an effective selection process:

♦ *"Hire hard, manage easy."* The amount of time and effort spent selecting the right people for jobs may make managing them as employees much less difficult because more problems will be eliminated.

♦ *"Good training will not make up for bad selection."* When the right people with the appropriate capabilities are not selected for jobs, employers have difficulty later adequately training those individuals who are selected.

Selection Responsibilities

Organizations vary in how they allocate selection responsibilities between HR specialists and operating managers. The need to meet EEO requirements has forced many organizations to better plan their selection efforts. Still, in some organizations, each department screens and hires its own employees. Many managers insist on selecting their own people because they are sure no one else can choose employees for them as well as they can themselves. This practice is particularly prevalent in smaller firms. But the validity and effectiveness of this approach may be questionable.

Other organizations have the HR unit do the initial screening of the candidates, and managers or supervisors make the final selection from a qualified group of individuals. As a rule, the higher the position being filled, the greater the likelihood that the ultimate hiring decisions will be made by operating managers rather than HR specialists. Typical selection responsibilities are shown in Figure 8-1.

Selection responsibilities are affected by the existence of a central employment office, which usually is part of an HR department. In smaller organizations, especially in those with fewer than 100 employees, a full-time employment specialist or unit may be impractical. But for larger employers, centralizing employment within one unit may be appropriate.

The employment function in any organization may be concerned with some or all of the following activities: (1) receiving applications, (2) interviewing applicants, (3) administering tests to applicants, (4) conducting background investigations, (5) arranging for physical examinations, (6) placing and assigning new employees, (7) coordinating follow-up of these employees, (8) conducting exit interviews with departing employees, and (9) maintaining appropriate records and reports.

Placement

Placement Fitting a person to the right job.

The ultimate purpose of selection is **placement,** or fitting a person to the right job. Placement of human resources should be seen as primarily a matching

Figure 8-1

Typical Division of HR Responsibilities: Selection	
HR Unit	**Managers**
◆ Provides initial reception for applicants ◆ Conducts initial screening interview ◆ Administers appropriate employment tests ◆ Obtains background and reference information and arranges for the employment physical examination, if used ◆ Refers top candidates to managers for final selection ◆ Evaluates success of selection process	◆ Requisition employees with specific qualifications to fill jobs ◆ Participate in selection process as appropriate ◆ Interview final candidates ◆ Make final selection decision, subject to advice of HR specialist ◆ Provide follow-up information on the suitability of selected individuals

process. How well an employee is matched to a job affects the amount and quality of the employee's work. This matching also directly affects training and operating costs. Individuals who are unable to produce the expected amount and quality of work can cost an organization a great deal of money and time.

Selection and placement activities typically focus on applicants' knowledge, skills, and abilities. The **person/job fit** is a simple but important concept that involves matching the KSAs of people with the characteristics of jobs. People already in jobs can help identify the most important KSAs for success, as part of job analysis.

In addition to matching individuals to jobs, employers also increasingly try to determine the congruence between individuals and organizational factors to achieve **person-organization fit.** Person-organization fit is important when general factors of job success are as important as specific KSAs.

Person/job fit
Matching the KSAs of people with the characteristics of jobs.

Person-organization fit The congruence between individuals and organizational factors.

Criteria, Predictors, and Job Performance

Whether an employer uses specific KSAs or a more general approach, effective selection of employees involves using criteria and predictors of job performance. At the heart of an effective selection system must be knowledge of what constitutes appropriate job performance and what employee characteristics are associated with that performance. First, an employer defines successful employee performance; then, using that definition as a basis, the employer determines the employee KSAs required to achieve that success. A **selection criterion** is a characteristic that a person must have to do that specific job successfully. Figure 8-2 shows that ability, motivation, intelligence, conscientiousness, appropriate risk, and permanence might be good selection criteria for many jobs.

Selection criterion
Characteristic that a person must have to do a job successfully.

Predictors
Measurable or visible indicators of a selection criterion.

To determine whether or not candidates might have a certain selection criterion (such as ability or motivation), employers try to identify **predictors** that are measurable or visible indicators—of that criterion. For example, in Figure 8-2 on the next page, three good predictors of permanence might be individual interests, salary requirements, and tenure on previous jobs.

The information gathered about an applicant through predictors should be focused on the likelihood that the applicant will be able to perform the job well.

Figure 8-2

Job Performance, Selection Criteria, and Predictors

Elements of Job Performance	Selection Criteria for Employee Characterisitics	Predictors of Selection Criteria
◆ Quantity of work ◆ Quality of work ◆ Compatibility with others ◆ Presence at work ◆ Length of service ◆ Flexibility	◆ Ability ◆ Motivation ◆ Intelligence ◆ Conscientiousness ◆ Appropriate risk for employer ◆ Appropriate permanence	◆ Experience ◆ Past performance ◆ Physical skills ◆ Education ◆ Interests ◆ Salary requirements ◆ Certificates/degrees ◆ Test scores ◆ Personality measures ◆ Work references ◆ Previous jobs and tenure ◆ Drug test ◆ Police record

Predictors can take many forms (for example, application form, test, interview, education requirements, or years of experience required), but they should be used only if they are valid predictors of job performance. Using invalid predictors can result in selecting the "wrong" candidate and rejecting the "right" one.

To illustrate how criteria and predictors can be beneficial, Bank of America wanted to reduce the number of bad hires and the time and cost of hiring for such jobs as deposit reporter, cash handler, and operations coordinator. The company created "competency profiles" consisting of the correct KSAs for the jobs. Current jobholders and managers were interviewed to confirm that the profiles were correct. Tests were developed and validated to act as predictors for some of the selection criteria chosen.

Applicants watched a job preview video, and then went to a computer terminal to key in application information about themselves and to complete three tests and inventories. A reaction survey was also built in, to gather candidate feedback for making changes to the process as needed.

Candidates who passed the tests were five times more likely to be satisfactory employees than those who did not, and the tests were able to distinguish between people who would later become high and low performers. Ninety-seven percent of the candidates expressed satisfaction with the process. Analyses broken out by race, gender, and age showed that the process treated all protected groups fairly, and the rate of return on investment for the selection system was very high.[2] This is a good example of how the needed job performance ultimately helps identify predictors, which are then used for hiring.

Validity In selection, validity is the correlation between a predictor and job performance. As mentioned in Chapter 4, validity occurs to the extent that a predictor actually predicts what it is supposed to predict. Validity depends on the situation in which the selection device is being used. For example, a psychological test designed to predict aptitude for child-care jobs might not be valid in predicting sales aptitude for marketing representative jobs. Clearly, if a test is not valid, it should not be used. A test must be validated for use in a specific company's application, not "in general" by the test vendor.[3]

Reliability Reliability of a predictor is the extent to which it repeatedly produces the same results, over time. For example, if a person took a test in December and scored 75, then took it again in March and scored significantly lower, the test may not be reliable. Thus, reliability has to do with the consistency of predictors used in selection.

Combining Predictors

If an employer chooses to use only one predictor (for example, a test) to select who will be hired, the decision is straightforward. If the test is valid and encompasses a major dimension of a job, and the applicant does well on the test, he or she can be hired. When an employer uses several predictors (for example, three years of experience, a college degree, and a certain score on an aptitude test), qualified candidates are those who possess sufficient amounts of each of those predictors. When more than one predictor is used, they must be combined in some way. Two approaches for combining predictors are:

- *Multiple hurdles:* A minimum cutoff is set on each predictor, and each minimum level must be "passed." For example, to be hired, a candidate for a sales representative job must achieve a minimum education level, a certain score on a sales aptitude test, and a minimum score on a structured interview.
- *Compensatory approach:* Scores from individual predictors are added together and combined into an overall score, thus allowing a higher score on one predictor to offset, or compensate for, a lower score on another. The combined index takes into consideration performance on all predictors. For example, admitting students into graduate business programs, a higher-score on the math portion of an admissions test may offset a lower score on the verbal part of the test.

■ THE SELECTION PROCESS

LOGGING ON...

"The Employment Strategist"
This Web site offers a free monthly newsletter focusing on the recruitment, selection, and retention of human resources in today's changing workforce.
www.cathyfyock.com

Most organizations take a series of consistent steps to process and select applicants for jobs. Variations on the basic process depend on organizational size, nature of the jobs to be filled, number of people to be selected, the use of electronic technology, and other factors. This process can take place in a day or over a much longer period of time. If the applicant is processed in one day, the employer usually checks references after selection. One or more phases of the process may be omitted or the order changed, depending on the employer. Figure 8-3 on the next page shows a selection process typical in many organizations.

Legal Concerns in the Selection Process

Selection is subject to a number of legal concerns, especially all the equal employment opportunity (EEO) regulations and laws introduced in previous chapters. Throughout the selection process, application forms, interviews, tests, background investigations, and any other selection activities must be conducted in a nondiscriminatory manner. Also, applicants who are not hired should be rejected only for job-related reasons; rejections based on protected-class status are illegal.

Figure 8-3 | *Selection Process Flowchart*

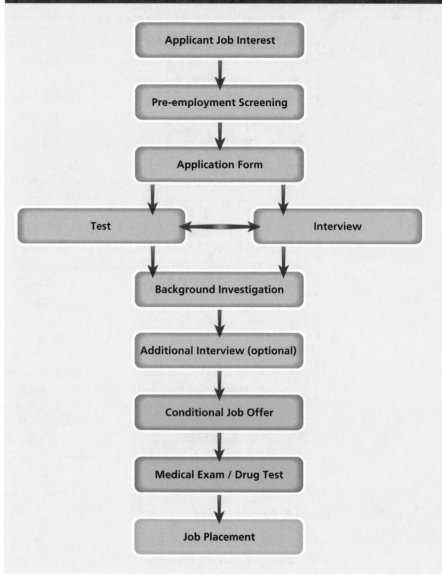

Defining Who Is an Applicant Employers are required to track applicants who apply for jobs at their companies. Gathering and logging data on applicants should be comprehensive and consistent.[4] It is increasingly important for employers to carefully define exactly who is an applicant and who is not, because many employers are required to track and report applicant information as part of equal employment and affirmative action plans. Also, it is important because employers may be targeted by scams involving individuals who claim to have applied for jobs but whose primary purpose is to file lawsuits. Without a clear definition of who is an applicant, employers might have to count as applicants all individuals who submit unsolicited resumes, respond electronically to Web site employment postings, or walk in to apply for jobs. The EEOC and OFCCP have agreed on this definition of *applicant* to be used when an application has been submitted via electronic means:[5]

- The employer must have taken steps to fill a particular job.
- The individual must have followed the employer's application procedure.
- The individual must have expressed interest in a particular position.

Applicant Flow Documentation Employers must collect data on the race, sex, and other demographics of applicants to fulfill EEO reporting requirements. Many employers ask applicants to provide EEOC reporting data in a flow form that may be attached to the application form. It is important that employers review this flow form separately and not use it in any other HR selection activities, or they may be accused of using applicant information inappropriately. Because completing the form is voluntary, employers can demonstrate that they tried to obtain the data.

Applicant Job Interest

Individuals desiring employment can indicate interest in a number of ways. Traditionally, individuals have submitted resumes by mail or fax, or applied in person at an employer's location. But with the growth in Internet recruiting, many individuals complete applications on-line or submit resumes electronically.

Regardless of how individuals express interest in employment, the selection process has an important public relations dimension. Discriminatory hiring practices, impolite interviewers, unnecessarily long waits, unreturned telephone inquiries, inappropriate testing procedures, and lack of follow-up responses can produce unfavorable impressions of an employer. Job applicants' perceptions of the organization, and even of the products or services it offers, will be influenced by how they are treated.

Realistic Job Previews Most job seekers appear to know little about organizations before applying to them for jobs. Consequently, when deciding whether or not to accept a job, they tend to give considerable weight to the information received from prospective employers in the recruiting/selection process. For applicants, information on pay, nature of the work, geographic location, and opportunity for promotion is useful. Unfortunately, some employers oversell their jobs in recruiting advertisements, making the jobs appear better than they really are.

Realistic job preview (RJP) Process through which a job applicant receives an accurate picture of a job.

Through the process of a **realistic job preview (RJP),** applicants are provided with an accurate picture of a job, including the "organizational realities" surrounding it, so that they can better evaluate their own job expectations. With an RJP, the organization hopes to prevent unrealistic expectations, which helps reduce employee disenchantment and ultimately employee dissatisfaction and turnover. A review of research on RJPs found that they tend to be effective in that regard.[6] The HR Perspective on the next page reports on a research study involving salespeople and RJPs.

Pre-employment Screening

Many employers conduct pre-employment screening to determine if applicants meet the minimum qualifications for open jobs. For example, a firm that hires security guards and armored-car drivers might use a pre-screening interview to ver-

Research on Salespeople and Realistic Job Previews

Insuring that prospective new employees are familiar with what their jobs would involve is important, but especially so with salespeople who receive more training than those in many other occupations. Salespeople who leave a firm before the cost of that training is recovered are a source of expense, and their departures can create serious problems for employers.

Barksdale, Bellenger, Boles, and Brashear studied 762 insurance salespeople in 54 companies to test the impact of realistic job previews (RJPs). The results were reported in the *Journal of Personal Selling and Sales Management*. Analysis of the data provided some interesting findings. One primary result suggests that management should focus RJPs on two separate but parallel tracks. One track involves productivity or performance, and the other involves commitment to the firm. In the area of performance, RJPs can directly improve a salesperson's understanding of her or his role in the job and can result in more positive perceptions of training. In other words, the need for training is clear when people understand what the job will entail and how training can help them do the job.

Commitment to or satisfaction with the firm can be enhanced with a realistic job preview as well. RJPs are related to the salespeople's satisfaction with the firm, commitment to continuing employment, and reduced turnover. Emphasizing why the firm is a good place to work, while making sure that an applicant understands the salesperson's job and role in the firm and industry, can increase commitment to stay if the individuals are hired.[7]

ify whether an applicant meets the minimum qualifications of having a valid driver's license, being free of any criminal convictions in the past seven years, and having been trained to use a pistol. Because these minimum standards are required, it would be a waste of time for any applicant who could not meet them to fill out an application form initially. Some areas typically covered by employers include types of available jobs, applicants' pay expectations, job location, and travel requirements.

Some employers have everyone who may be interested in a job fill out an application first. The completed application then becomes the basis for pre-screening information. But collecting, storing, and tracking all of these applications can create significant work for HR staff members. That is why pre-screening has grown to be more prevalent.

Electronic Screening Pre-employment screening done electronically has increased dramatically in the past few years. One type of screening uses computer software to scan for keywords in resumes or applications submitted electronically. Hundreds of large companies use types of text-searching or artificial intelligence (AI) software to scan, score, and track resumes of applicants. For example, a large financial firm streamlined its application process so that individuals can complete applications electronically. The applicants' qualifications are then electronically compared with job profiles to determine which candidates are likely to be successful, and those candidates are contacted for interviews.

Pre-screening sorts the serious job contenders from the often hundreds of electronic applicants, by looking for keywords, key skills, or experience. Assessment evaluates skill level, experience, or even attitudes through an on-line test of some sort taken by the candidate.[8]

These and other features are often parts of "applicant tracking systems" that are used for screening, tracking, testing, assessing, and reporting on the people who apply for jobs. Such software systems are used most often when:[9]

- The volume of applicants is large
- The quality of hires needs to be increased
- Hiring cycles need to be shortened
- The cost of hiring needs to be reduced
- The firm needs to reach geographic areas not visited by recruiters

Applicant reactions to these technological innovations have been mixed. Company Web sites as part of the electronic screening process have been well received. Computer-based testing (on-line or simply on a computer) has had mixed reviews, perhaps depending on the design, administration, and feedback associated with the test. Satisfaction rates of applicants for on-line interviewing are lower than those for face-to-face interviewing. Computerized job simulations or situational judgment tests have also had mixed reviews.[10] Regardless of the electronic pre-employment systems used, the analyses must be job-related, without using age, gender, or other data as screening criteria. Otherwise, potential illegal discrimination complaints could not be defended well.

Application Forms

Application forms are almost universally used and can take different formats. Properly prepared, the application form serves four purposes:

- It is a record of the applicant's desire to obtain a position.
- It provides the interviewer with a profile of the applicant that can be used in the interview.
- It is a basic employee record for applicants who are hired.
- It can be used for research on the effectiveness of the selection process.

Many employers use only one application form, but others need several. For example, a hospital might need one form for nurses and medical technicians, another form for clerical and office employees, another for managers and supervisors, and another for support workers in housekeeping and food-service areas.

Application Disclaimers and Notices Application forms need disclaimers and notices so that appropriate legal protections are stated by employers. The recommended disclosures and notices appearing on applications include:

- *Employment-at-will:* Indicates the right of the employer or the applicant to terminate the employment relationship at any time with or without notice or cause (where applicable by state law).
- *Reference contacts:* Requests permission to contact previous employers listed by applicants as references.
- *Employment testing:* Notifies applicants of required drug tests, pencil and paper tests, physical exams, or other tests.
- *Application time limit:* Indicates how long applications are active (typically six months) and that individuals must re-activate their applications after that period.
- *Information falsification:* Conveys to an applicant signing the form that falsification of application information is grounds for termination.

Immigration Forms The Immigration Reform and Control Act of 1986, as revised in 1990, requires that within 72 hours of hiring, an employer must determine whether a job applicant is a U.S. citizen, registered alien, or illegal alien. Applicants who are not eligible to work in this country must not be hired. Employers use the I-9 form to identify the status of potential employees. Employers are responsible for ensuring the legitimacy of documents submitted by new employees, such as U.S. passports, birth certificates, original Social Security cards, and driver's licenses. Also, employers who hire employees on special visas must maintain appropriate documentation and records.[11] Figure 8-4 shows documents that may be used to verify that new hires are eligible to work in the U.S.

EEO Considerations and Application Forms An organization should retain all applications and hiring-related documents and records for *three years.* Guidelines from the EEOC and court decisions require that the data requested on application forms must be job related. Employers of all types should review their application forms. Figure 8-5 shows a sample application form. Illegal questions frequently found on application forms ask for the following information:

- Marital status
- Height/weight
- Number and ages of dependents

- Information on spouse
- Date of high school graduation
- Contact in case of emergency

Concern about such questions stems from their potential disparate impact on some protected groups. For example, the question about dependents can be used

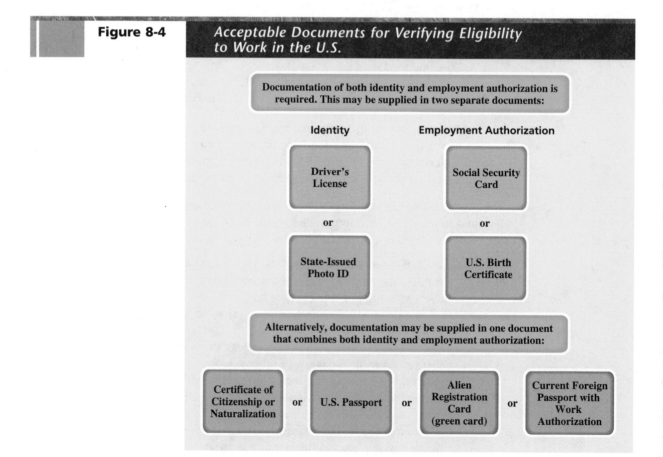

Figure 8-4   *Acceptable Documents for Verifying Eligibility to Work in the U.S.*

Documentation of both identity and employment authorization is required. This may be supplied in two separate documents:

Identity — Driver's License *or* State-Issued Photo ID

Employment Authorization — Social Security Card *or* U.S. Birth Certificate

Alternatively, documentation may be supplied in one document that combines both identity and employment authorization:

Certificate of Citizenship or Naturalization *or* U.S. Passport *or* Alien Registration Card (green card) *or* Current Foreign Passport with Work Authorization

Figure 8-5   *Sample Application Form*

Application for Employment
An Equal Opportunity Employer*

Today's Date _____

PERSONAL INFORMATION

Please Print or Type

Name (Last) (First) (Full middle name)	Social Security number
Current address City State Zip code	Phone number ( )
What position are you applying for?	Date available for employment?	E-mail address

Are you willing to relocate? ☐ Yes ☐ No	Are you willing to travel if required? ☐ Yes ☐ No	Any restrictions on hours, weekends, or overtime? If yes, explain.
Have you ever been employed by this Company or any of its subsidiaries before? ☐ Yes ☐ No		Indicate location and dates
Can you, after employment, submit verification of your legal right to work in the United States? ☐ Yes ☐ No		Have you ever been convicted of a felony? ☐ Yes ☐ No *Convictions will not automatically disqualify job candidates. The seriousness of the crime and the date of conviction will be considered.*

PERFORMANCE OF JOB FUNCTIONS

Are you able to perform all the functions of the job for which you are applying, with or without accommodation?

☐ Yes, without accommodation   ☐ Yes, with accommodation   ☐ No

If you indicated you can perform all the functions with an accommodation, please explain how you would perform the tasks and with what accommodation.

EDUCATION

School level	School name and address	No. of years attended	Did you graduate?	Course of study
High school				
Vo-tech, business, or trade school				
College				
Graduate school				

PERSONAL DRIVING RECORD

This section is to be completed ONLY if the operation of a motor vehicle will be required in the course of the applicant's employment.

How long have you been a licensed driver?	Driver's license number	Expiration date	Issuing State

List any other state(s) in which you have had a driver's license(s) in the past:

Within the past five years, have you had a vehicle accident? ☐ Yes ☐ No	Been convicted of reckless or drunken driving? ☐ Yes ☐ No If yes, give dates:	Been cited for moving violations? If yes, give dates: ☐ Yes ☐ No
Has your driver's license ever been revoked or suspended? ☐ Yes ☐ No If yes, explain:		Is your driver's license restricted? If yes, explain: ☐ Yes ☐ No

*We are an Equal Opportunity Employer. We do not discriminate on the basis of race, religion, color, gender, age, national origin, or disability.

to identify women with small children, who may not be hired because of a manager's perception that they will be absent more than women without small children. The high school graduation date more closely identifies a person's age, which can be used to discriminate against individuals over 40. The question about emergency contact might reveal marital status or other protected personal information.

Resumes as Applications Applicants commonly provide background information through resumes. Technically, a resume used in place of an application form must be treated by an employer as an application form for EEO purposes. Consequently, if an applicant's resume voluntarily furnishes some information that cannot be legally obtained, the employer should not use that information during the selection process. Some employers require that all who submit resumes complete an application form as well. Individuals who mail in resumes may be sent thank-you letters and application forms to be completed and returned.

Biodata and Weighted Application Forms Biographical data on an applicant can be gleaned from the application form, pencil-and-paper questionnaires, interviews, or communications with former employers. It is useful if there are large numbers of people doing the same job, or a large number of applicants for a small number of openings, as with on-line recruiting. In such cases, each data element will receive a score depending on the applicant's response. The scores for each applicant can be added, and the highest totals will indicate the applicants most likely to be satisfactory employees.

To develop biodata and weighted application forms, it is necessary to develop questions that can be asked legally and weights that differentiate between satisfactory and poor performance. An employer can then use numeric measurements to evaluate applicants' responses and compare them with a valid, job-related set of inquiries. This approach is at the heart of many electronic pre-employment screening systems.[12]

SELECTION TESTING

LOGGING ON...

Buros Institute
Affiliated with the University of Nebraska at Lincoln, the Institute provides publications and resources on the use and effectiveness of commercially available tests.
www.unl.edu/buros

Many kinds of tests may be used to help select good employees. Literacy tests, skills tests, psychological measurement tests, and honesty tests are the major categories. Carefully developed and properly administered employment tests allow employers to predict which applicants have the ability to do the job in question, who can learn in training, and who will stay. Tests are even available to screen out candidates who may create behavioral or other risks to the employer.[13]

A recent survey found that 41% of the employers polled use basic skills tests (essentially testing ability to read and do math) and 68% use some kind of job skills test (focusing on skills necessary to do a specific job). In addition, 29% use some kind of psychological measurement test (including cognitive ability, personality, and honesty).[14] A look at the most common types of tests follows.

Ability Tests

Tests that assess an individual's ability to perform in a specific manner are grouped as ability tests. These are sometimes further differentiated into *aptitude tests* and *achievement tests*.

Cognitive ability tests Tests that measure an individual's thinking, memory, reasoning, verbal, and mathematical abilities.

Cognitive ability tests measure an individual's thinking, memory, reasoning, verbal, and mathematical abilities. Tests such as these can be used to determine applicants' basic knowledge of terminology and concepts, word fluency, spatial orientation, comprehension and retention span, general and mental ability, and conceptual reasoning. The Wonderlic Personnel Test and the General Aptitude Test Battery (GATB) are two widely used tests of this type. One consideration when using cognitive ability tests is to ensure that the cognitive concepts tested are clearly job related.

General mental ability has been found to be a good predictor of job performance. The controversy in the use of general mental ability tests has to do with large differences in the scores of different racial groups.[15] Such tests cost less than personality tests and are highly reliable, and the verbal reasoning and numerical tests are valued for a wide range of jobs. However, certain racial minorities score one full standard deviation below non-minorities, and that discrepancy could result in adverse impact.[16]

Physical ability tests Tests that measure an individual's abilities such as strength, endurance, and muscular movement.

Physical ability tests measure an individual's abilities such as strength, endurance, and muscular movement. At an electric utility, line workers regularly must lift and carry equipment, climb ladders, and perform other physical tasks; testing of applicants' mobility, strength, and other physical attributes is job related. Some physical ability tests measure such areas as range of motion, strength and posture, and cardiovascular fitness. As noted later, care should be taken to limit physical ability testing until after a conditional job offer is made, in order to avoid violating the provisions of the Americans with Disabilities Act (ADA).

Psychomotor tests Tests that measure dexterity, hand-eye coordination, arm-hand steadiness, and other factors.

Different skill-based tests can be used, including **psychomotor tests,** which measure a person's dexterity, hand-eye coordination, arm-hand steadiness, and other factors. Such tests as the MacQuarie Test for Mechanical Ability can measure manual dexterity for assembly-line workers and others using psychomotor skills regularly.

Work sample tests Tests that require an applicant to perform a simulated job task.

Many organizations use situational tests, or **work sample tests,** which require an applicant to perform a simulated task that is part of the target job. Having an applicant for a financial analyst's job prepare a computer spreadsheet is one such test. Requiring a person applying for a truck driver's job to back a truck to a loading dock is another. An "in-basket" test is a work sample test in which a job candidate is asked to respond to memos in a hypothetical in-basket that are typical of the problems faced by people holding that job. The key for any work sample test is the behavioral consistency between the criteria in the job and the requirements for the test.

Situational judgment tests Tests that measure a person's judgment in work settings.

Situational judgment tests are designed to measure a person's judgment in work settings. The candidate is given a situation and a list of possible solutions to the problem. The candidate then has to make judgments about how to deal with the situation. Situational judgment tests are an additional form of job simulation.[17]

Assessment Centers An assessment center is not a place, but an assessment composed of a series of evaluative exercises and tests used for selection and development. Most often used in the selection process when filling managerial openings, assessment centers consist of multiple exercises and are evaluated by multiple raters. In one assessment center, candidates go through a comprehensive interview, a pencil-and-paper test, individual and group simulations, and work exercises. The candidates' performances are then evaluated by a panel of trained raters. It is crucial that the tests and exercises in an assessment center reflect the content of the job for which individuals are being screened, and the types of problems faced on that job.

Personality Tests

Personality is a unique blend of individual characteristics that affect interaction with a person's environment and help define a person. Many types of personality tests are available. One well-known version is the Minnesota Multiphasic Personality Inventory (MMPI), which was originally developed to diagnose major psychological disorders and has become widely used as a selection test. The Myers-Briggs test is another widely used instrument of the same type. From these and many other personality tests, an extensive number of personality characteristics can be identified and used.

The multitude of different personality traits has long frustrated psychologists, who have argued that there is a relatively small number of underlying *major* traits. The most widely accepted approach to studying these underlying personality traits (although not the only one) often refers to the "Big Five" personality traits. The Big Five that can be considered generally useful predictors of training success and job performance are shown in Figure 8-6.

Of the Big Five, conscientiousness has been found to be related to job success across most organizations and occupations. Extroversion has been found to predict success in jobs requiring social interaction, such as many sales jobs. The

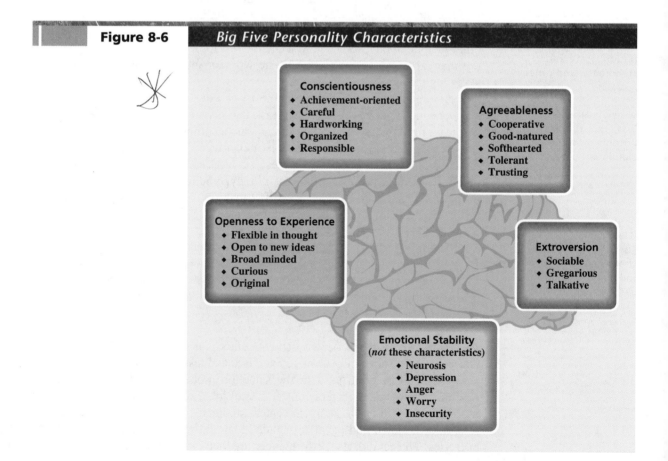

Figure 8-6 — *Big Five Personality Characteristics*

Conscientiousness
- Achievement-oriented
- Careful
- Hardworking
- Organized
- Responsible

Agreeableness
- Cooperative
- Good-natured
- Softhearted
- Tolerant
- Trusting

Openness to Experience
- Flexible in thought
- Open to new ideas
- Broad minded
- Curious
- Original

Extroversion
- Sociable
- Gregarious
- Talkative

Emotional Stability
(*not* these characteristics)
- Neurosis
- Depression
- Anger
- Worry
- Insecurity

usefulness of the other three traits varies depending on the kind of job and organization.

Personality testing can be useful in identifying interpersonal traits needed in jobs and can reveal more information about abilities and interests. However, intrusive questions, lack of face validity, and the need to use them with other selection methods can present problems.[18] Such tests have been used to predict many factors including success in training, ability to develop new business, and performance on managerial jobs.[19] When used in selection, psychological or personality testing must be solidly related to the job.[20]

"Fakability" and Personality Tests "Faking" is a major concern for employers using personality tests. Most test publishers do not dispute that test profiles can be falsified, and they try to reduce faking by including questions that together constitute a social desirability or "lie" scale.[21] Researchers generally favor the use of "corrections" based on components of the test to account for faking—a preference that also constitutes an argument for professional scoring of personality tests.[22]

Honesty/Integrity Tests

Different types of tests are being used by employers to assess the honesty and integrity of applicants and employees. They include standardized honesty/ integrity tests and polygraph tests. Both are controversial.

Employers use these tests for several reasons. Firms such as retailers use honesty tests to screen out potentially dishonest individuals and decrease the incidence of employee theft. These firms believe that giving honesty tests also sends a message to applicants and employees alike that dishonesty will not be tolerated.

Honesty/integrity tests may be valid as broad screening devices for organizations if used properly. However, it is important that the tests be chosen, used, and evaluated in ways that ensure that they are and remain valid and reliable. They should be used as one piece of the selection process, along with applications, interviews, and other data.[23] One documented concern about integrity tests, as about personality tests, is their "fakability." Research indicates that test takers are more able to fake honesty and pass integrity tests than to falsify profiles on personality tests.[24] Also, the use of honesty/integrity tests can have a negative impact on public relations with applicants. A final concern is that the types of questions asked may constitute invasion of individual privacy.

Polygraphs The polygraph, more generally and incorrectly referred to as the "lie detector," is a mechanical device that measures a person's galvanic skin response, heart rate, and breathing rate. The theory behind the polygraph is that if a person answers a question incorrectly, the body's physiological responses will "reveal" the falsification through the polygraph's recording mechanisms.[25] As a result of concerns, Congress passed the Employee Polygraph Protection Act, which prohibits the use of polygraphs for pre-employment screening purposes by most employers. Federal, state, and local government agencies are exempt from the act. Also exempted are certain private-sector employers such as security companies and pharmaceutical companies. The act does allow employers to continue to use polygraphs as part of internal investigations of thefts or losses. But in those situations, the polygraph test should be taken voluntarily, and the employee should be allowed to end the test at any time.

Controversial and Questionable Tests

Sometimes questionable tests are used in employee selection. Experts warn of the legal and ethical problems in using those techniques for employee selection. Graphology, psychics, and SAT scores are all questionable job selection tools that have been used by various employers.

Graphology "analyzes" an individual's handwriting. Such characteristics as how people dot an *i* or cross a *t*, whether they write with a left or right slant, and the size and boldness of the letters they form supposedly tell graphologists about the individuals' personalities and their suitability for employment. Graphology is popular in France, Israel, and several other countries, but is used on a limited basis in the United States. Formal scientific evaluations of graphology are not easily found. The value of this tool as a personality predictor is somewhat questionable, and use of this tool may not be easily validated as job related.

Some firms use *psychics* to help them select managerial talent. The psychics are supposedly able to determine if a person is suited for a job intellectually and emotionally. However, most businesses probably would not want anyone to know that they used psychic advisers.

Some employers have begun requiring that applicants have a minimum *SAT score* for consideration in a job. The Scholastic Aptitude Test that usually is taken by high school juniors and seniors (or the ACT test, which is similar) is designed as one measure for college admission. It predicts how well a person is likely to do in college. Some employers see using the scores from this test as one more way to choose among applicants. Of course, if the test has not been validated for specific jobs in a company, it *should* be if it is to be used for selection.[26]

Legal Concerns and Selection Testing

LOGGING ON...

Uniform Guidelines
This Web site is a free site on the use of selection procedures and tests to ensure compliance with federal laws.
www.uniformguidelines.com

Employers must make sure that the selection tests they use are valid, are job-related, and do not discriminate against protected-class members. Several court cases have ruled that some tests used by employers, particularly personality tests, are illegally discriminatory. For example, Rent-A-Center paid $2.1 million to settle a class action lawsuit that alleged that required psychological tests, the MMPI and the Bernreuter Personality Inventory, violated the Americans with Disabilities Act. In another case, a general knowledge test used by shipping firms and longshore unions was found to discriminate against minority applicants who applied for dock shipping jobs, because the failure rates for Hispanic, Asian, and African American applicants was significantly higher than for other applicants. In summary, the role of testing in the selection process must be kept in perspective because tests represent only one possible data source, and they must be used appropriately and legally.[27]

SELECTION INTERVIEWING

Selection interviewing of job applicants is done both to obtain additional information and to clarify information gathered throughout the selection process. Typically, interviews are conducted at two levels: first, as an initial screening interview simply to see if the person has minimum qualifications, and then later, as an in-depth interview perhaps involving HR staff members and operating managers in the departments where the individuals will work.

Before the in-depth interview, information from all available sources is pulled together so that interviewers can identify and ask questions about conflicting in-

Figure 8-7

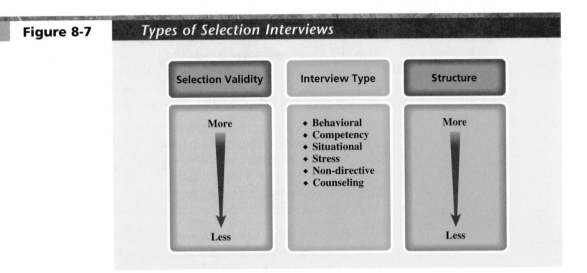

Types of Selection Interviews

formation that may have emerged from tests, application forms, and references. In addition, interviewers must obtain as much pertinent information about the applicants as possible during the limited time of the interview itself, and evaluate this information against job standards. As Figure 8-7 shows, there are a number of types of interviews. They range from structured to unstructured and vary in terms of appropriateness for selection.

Reliability and Validity of Interviews

To be useful, interviews must be reliable, allowing interviewers to pick the same capabilities again and again in applicants. Some interviewers may be better than others at selecting individuals who will perform well. A high *intra*-rater reliability (within the same interviewer) can be demonstrated, but only moderate-to-low *inter*-rater reliability (across different interviewers) is generally shown. Interrater reliability becomes important when each of several interviewers is selecting employees from a pool of applicants, or if the employer uses team or panel interviews with multiple interviewers.

The interview is popular with employers because it has high "face validity," that is, it seems valid to employers and they like it. It is often assumed that if someone interviews well and the information obtained in the interview is useful, then the individual will perform well on the job. However, research over several decades has consistently confirmed that an unstructured interview is not an especially valid predictor of job performance and success. That is why use of structured interviews has grown in popularity.

Structured Interviews

Structured interview
Interview that uses a set of standardized questions asked of all job applicants.

A **structured interview** uses a set of standardized questions asked of all applicants. The interviewer asks every applicant the same basic questions, so that comparisons among applicants can more easily be made. This type of interview allows an interviewer to prepare job-related questions in advance and then complete a standardized interviewee evaluation form that provides documentation indicating why one applicant was selected over another. The structured interview is especially useful in the initial screening phase because of the large number of applicants that may need to be considered in this step of the selection process. The structured interview does not have to be rigid. The pre-determined questions should be asked in a logical manner, but interviewers can avoid reading them word for word down the list. Also, the applicants should be allowed adequate opportunity to explain their answers, and each interviewer should probe with additional questions until she or he fully understands the responses. Sample questions that might be asked of all applicants for a retail sales clerk opening are as follows:

- "I noticed on your application that you were previously employed with _____. How did you get a job there?"
- "Tell me about your responsibilities and duties with _____."
- "Describe a time you were frustrated as a customer because of the way a store clerk treated you. What do you think should have been done?"
- "How did you handle an abusive and rude customer?"

Research on interviews consistently finds the structured interview to be more reliable and valid than other interview approaches. The structured format ensures that a given interviewer has similar information on each candidate. It also ensures that when several interviewers ask the same questions of applicants, there is greater consistency in the subsequent evaluation of those candidates.

These reasons are why structured interviews—in any of several forms, including biographical, behavioral, competency, and situational—are recommended for selection decisions. Their consistency raises the validity of the interview as a selection instrument. Less-structured or even unstructured interviews have their places as well but are usually not recommended for ordinary hiring situations.

Biographical Interview A biographical interview focuses on a chronological exploration of the candidate's past experiences. This type of interview is widely used and is often combined with situational, competency, and other forms of information. It contributes to the picture of a person by providing a sketch of past experiences.

Behavioral Interview Increasingly, interviewers are using an experience-based type of structured interview. In the **behavioral interview,** applicants are asked to give specific examples of how they have performed a certain task or handled a problem in the past. The notion that past behaviors are good predictors of future actions provides the logic behind behavioral interviews. Learning about how candidates describe their previous behaviors helps in determining which applicants may be best suited for current jobs. For example, applicants might be asked the following questions:

- "How did you handle a situation that had no rules or guidelines for employee discipline?"
- "Why did you choose that approach?"
- "How did your supervisor react?"
- "How was the situation finally resolved?"

Competency Interview The *competency interview* is similar to the behavioral interview except that the questions are designed specifically to provide the interviewer with something to measure the applicant's response against—that is, the "competency profile" for the position, which includes a list of competencies necessary to do that particular job.[28] Adler, a well-known selection expert, is credited with what he calls the one-question interview: "Describe your most significant accomplishment." The answers are expected to reveal the candidate's

Behavioral interview Interview in which applicants give specific examples of how they have performed a certain task or handled a problem in the past.

competencies in making that achievement.[29] A variation focuses on problems in the interviewing company and how the candidate would solve them.

Developing competency-based questions and behavioral-based questions is time-consuming. Further, competency and behavioral interviews may simply identify which candidate is the most articulate person or the best at creating a positive impression.

Situational Interview The **situational interview** is a structured interview composed of questions about how applicants might handle specific job situations. Interview questions are based on job analysis and checked by experts in the job so that they will be content valid. For some situational interviews, job experts also rate responses to the questions in order to facilitate the ranking of candidates. The interviewer can code the suitability of the answer, assign point values, and add up the total number of points an interviewee received. Some situational questions include:

Situational interview Structured interview composed of questions about how applicants might handle specific job situations.

♦   "You are a supervisor, and an employee consistently arrives late to work. What action do you take?"

♦   "One of your employees tells you in confidence that she has seen one of her co-workers steal. What do you do?"

♦   "You feel that your boss is discriminating against you because you are older than other employees. How do you handle this?"

Research on both behavioral and situational interviews shows that they can predict performance equally well.[30] However, when a descriptively anchored scale for rating answers was added, the behavioral or competency approach was found to have higher validity.[31]

NEW YORKER CARTOON
by Bernard Schoenbaum

"As an orange, how much experience have you had working with apples?"

Less-Structured Interviews

Some interviews are done unplanned and without any structure. Often, these interviews are conducted by operating managers or supervisors who have had little training on interviewing do's and don'ts. An *unstructured interview* occurs when the interviewer "wings it," asking questions that have no identified direct purpose, such as, "Tell me about yourself."

A *semistructured interview* is a guided conversation in which broad questions are asked and new questions arise as a result of the discussion. In the hands of a professional interviewer trained in the psychology of personality theory, semistructured interviews have been found to be better than structured interviews for accurately predicting personality.[32] However, personality can also be predicted with a pencil-and-paper or Web-based test if necessary.

A **non-directive interview** uses questions that are developed from the answers to previous questions. The interviewer asks general questions designed to prompt the applicant to discuss herself or himself. The interviewer then picks up on an idea in the applicant's response and uses it to shape the next question. For example, if the applicant says, "One reason that I enjoyed my last job was my supervisor," the interviewer might ask, "What type of supervisor do you most enjoy working with?"

With a non-directive interview, as with any less-structured interview, difficulties include keeping the conversation job related and obtaining comparable data on various applicants. Many non-directive interviews are only semiorganized; as a result, a combination of general and specific questions is asked in no set order, and different questions are asked of different applicants for the same job. Comparing and ranking candidates is more open to subjective judgments and legal challenges under this format. This is why it is best used only in very specific settings.

Stress Interview

A **stress interview** is a special type of interview designed to create anxiety and put pressure on applicants to see how they respond. In a stress interview, the interviewer assumes an extremely aggressive and insulting posture. Those who use this approach often justify doing so with individuals who will encounter high degrees of stress on the job, such as consumer-complaint clerks in a department store or air traffic controllers.

The stress interview is a high-risk approach for an employer. The typical applicant is already somewhat anxious in any interview, and the stress interview can easily generate a poor image of the interviewer and the employer. Consequently, an applicant that the organization wishes to hire might turn down the job offer. Even so, many interviewers deliberately put applicants under stress.

Who Does Interviews?

Interviews can be done individually, by several individuals in sequence, or by panels or teams of individuals. For some jobs, such as entry-level jobs requiring lesser skills, applicants often are interviewed by an HR representative alone. For other jobs, employers screen applicants by using multiple interviews, beginning with an HR representative and following up with interviews conducted by appropriate supervisors and managers. Then a selection decision is made based on discussions by those who have conducted the interviews. When an interviewee must see several people, often many of the interviews are redundant and therefore unnecessarily time-consuming.

In a **panel interview,** several interviewers meet with the candidate at the same time. All the interviewers hear the same responses. Panel interviews may be combined with individual interviews. For example, to select a new marketing manager in a distribution firm, three vice presidents interviewed the top two candidates after the Vice President of Sales had conducted individual interviews to identify the two finalists. On the negative side, without planning by the panel of interviewers, an unstructured interview can result. Also, applicants are frequently uncomfortable with the group interview format.

The prevalence of work teams has increased the use of the **team interview,** in which applicants are interviewed by the team members with whom they will work. Involving team members in the selection of their co-workers can improve the success of the team. However, training is required to make sure that team members understand the selection process, interviewing, and legal constraints. A selection procedure in which the team votes for the top choice may be inappropriate; usually, the decision should be made by consensus, which may take longer. A test has been developed to help select employees for team-based organizations; when an employer uses the test in combination with a team interview, its chances of picking a "team player" are increased.[33]

Video Interviewing A number of employers use video interviewing to augment or replace in-depth telephone interviews. Often, video interviews are used to narrow a pool of candidates down to two or three finalists, who are then interviewed in person. An applicant is asked to go to a video-conferencing facility scheduled by the employer. At the designated time, an applicant and those conducting the interview are video linked. Video technology using the Internet and digital cameras gives employers additional interviewing options.

Video interviewing is used most by large corporations; executive recruiting firms; and college and university placement offices, which offer the technology to aid both students and employers. Savings on time and travel costs are an advantage of video interviewing. A disadvantage is that applicants seem to be more skeptical of video interviews than face-to-face interviews.[34]

Effective Interviewing

Many people think that the ability to interview is an innate talent, but this contention is difficult to support. Just being personable and liking to talk is no guarantee that someone will be an effective interviewer. Interviewing skills are developed through training. A number of suggestions for making interviewing more effective have been developed. Three key ones commonly cited are as follows:

- *Plan the interview:* Interviewers should review pre-employment screening information, the application or resume, and the appropriate job description before beginning the interview, and then identify specific areas for questioning during the interview.
- *Control the interview:* This includes knowing in advance what information must be collected, systematically collecting it during the interview, and stopping when that information has been collected. Controlling the interview does not mean monopolizing the conversation; effective interviewers should talk no more than about 25% of the time in an in-depth interview.

Panel interview
Interview in which several interviewers meet with the candidate at the same time.

Team interview
Interview in which applicants are interviewed by the team members with whom they will work.

INTERVIEWING
Suggests effective employment interviewing tips.
Custom Search:
☑ ANALYSIS
Exact Phrase:
Interviewing tips

◆ *Use effective questioning techniques:* The questioning techniques used by an interviewer can and do significantly affect the type and quality of information obtained.[35] *Describe, who, what, when, why, tell me, how,* and *which* are all good words and phrases for beginning questions that will produce longer and more informative answers. Figure 8-8 lists questions commonly used in selection interviews.

Interview problems exist with both interviewers and applicants. The HR Perspective relates stories illustrating some negative situations.

Figure 8-8

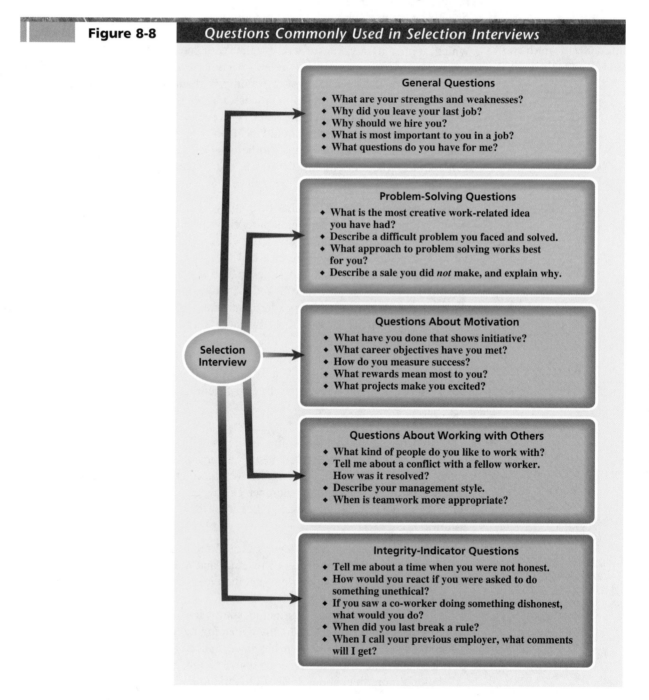

Questions Commonly Used in Selection Interviews

General Questions
- What are your strengths and weaknesses?
- Why did you leave your last job?
- Why should we hire you?
- What is most important to you in a job?
- What questions do you have for me?

Problem-Solving Questions
- What is the most creative work-related idea you have had?
- Describe a difficult problem you faced and solved.
- What approach to problem solving works best for you?
- Describe a sale you did *not* make, and explain why.

Questions About Motivation
- What have you done that shows initiative?
- What career objectives have you met?
- How do you measure success?
- What rewards mean most to you?
- What projects make you excited?

Questions About Working with Others
- What kind of people do you like to work with?
- Tell me about a conflict with a fellow worker. How was it resolved?
- Describe your management style.
- When is teamwork more appropriate?

Integrity-Indicator Questions
- Tell me about a time when you were not honest.
- How would you react if you were asked to do something unethical?
- If you saw a co-worker doing something dishonest, what would you do?
- When did you last break a rule?
- When I call your previous employer, what comments will I get?

Selection Interview

HR *Perspective*

Job Interview Tales

Some amusing, unbelievable, and even inappropriate actions are taken by both interviewers and applicants during job interviews. The following examples of poor interviewing behaviors and responses *are not* recommended for use!

Interviewers

College students have encountered some interviewers who act in strange or inappropriate ways:

- Interviewers asked the following questions:
  - ◊ "How many girlfriends do you have?"
  - ◊ "What method of birth control do you use?"
  - ◊ "Would you like to see my appendectomy scar?"
  - ◊ "What do your mother and father do for a living?"
  - ◊ "What will your boyfriend think of you working long hours?"
- An interviewer talked on the phone while the applicant answered questions.
- An interviewer asked the applicant to guess what his nationality was.
- An interviewer watched television over the applicant's shoulder during the interview.

Interviewees

Some applicants also apparently do not provide acceptable interview behaviors and responses:

- An applicant showed up in torn camouflage pants, a T-shirt, and hiking boots for a secretarial job interview.
- A graduate came to an interview wearing sunglasses and eating a hamburger and fries.
- An applicant put his head down on the interviewer's desk and complained of studying all night.
- A female applicant for an office job wore a shirt that left her midriff bare, exposing multiple tattoos on her stomach.
- An applicant vomited into the interviewer's trash can because, he said, he had been drinking for several hours before the interview.
- Interviewees made the following statements:
  - ◊ "Do I have to come to work before 9:00 A.M., because I work nights as a stripper?"
  - ◊ "My previous supervisor didn't like me—just like at my last three other companies."
  - ◊ "I haven't job hopped because I was fired from all of them [four jobs in the past year]."

Questions to Avoid Certain kinds of questions should be avoided in selection interviews:

- *Yes/no questions:* Unless verifying specific information, the interviewer should avoid questions that can be answered "Yes" or "No." For example, "Did you have good attendance on your last job?" will probably be answered simply, "Yes."
- *Obvious questions:* An obvious question is one for which the interviewer already has the answer and the applicant knows it.
- *Questions that rarely produce a true answer:* An example is, "How did you get along with your co-workers?" The likely answer is, "Just fine."
- *Leading questions:* A leading question is one to which the answer is obvious from the way that the question is asked. For example, "How do you like working with other people?" suggests the answer, "I like it."
- *Illegal questions:* Questions that involve information such as race, age, gender, national origin, marital status, and number of children are illegal. They are just as inappropriate in the interview as on the application form.
- *Questions that are not job related:* All questions should be directly related to the job for which the interviewee has applied.

Listening Responses to Avoid Effective interviewers avoid listening responses such as nodding, pausing, making casual remarks, echoing, and mirroring. A friendly but neutral demeanor is appropriate. Listening responses are an essential part of everyday, normal conversation, but they may unintentionally provide feedback to the applicant. Applicants may try to please interviewers and look to the interviewers' listening responses for cues. Even though the listening responses may be subtle, they do provide information to applicants. However, giving no response to applicants' answers may imply boredom or inattention. Therefore, interviewers should make a neutral comment, acknowledge the answers, or use a reply such as, "That is interesting information."

Problems in the Interview

Operating managers and supervisors are more likely to use poor interviewing techniques because they do not interview often or lack training. Several problems are commonly encountered in the interview.

Snap Judgments Unfortunately, many interviewers decide whether an applicant is suitable for the job within the first two to four minutes of the interview, and spend the balance of the interview looking for evidence to support their decision. This impression may be based on a review of the individual's application form or on more subjective factors such as dress or appearance. Ideally, the interviewer should collect all the information possible on an applicant before making a judgment.

Negative Emphasis As might be expected, unfavorable information about an applicant is the biggest factor considered in interviewers' decisions about overall suitability. Unfavorable information is usually given more weight than favorable information. Often, a single negative characteristic may bar an individual from being accepted, whereas no amount of positive characteristics will guarantee a candidate's acceptance.

Halo Effect Interviewers should try to avoid the *halo effect,* which occurs when an interviewer allows a prominent characteristic to overshadow other evidence. For instance, the halo effect is present if an interviewer lets a candidate's athletic accomplishments overshadow other characteristics, and then hires the applicant because "athletes make good salespeople." *Devil's horns* is the reverse of the halo effect. It occurs when an interviewer allows a negative characteristic, such as inappropriate dress or a low grade point average, to overshadow other evidence.

Biases and Stereotyping Personal biases and stereotyping of applicants should be avoided in interviews.[36] One type of bias, the "similarity" bias, occurs because interviewers tend to favor or select people they perceive to be similar to themselves. The similarity can be in age, race, sex, previous work experiences, personal background, or other factors. As workforce demographics shift, interviewers should be aware of any personal tendencies to stereotype individuals because of demographic characteristics and differences, and be careful to avoid doing so.

Cultural Noise Interviewers must learn to recognize and handle cultural noise, which comes from what the applicant believes is socially acceptable rather than what the applicant knows is factual.[37] An interviewer can handle cultural noise by not encouraging it. If the interviewer supports cultural noise, the applicant

Technology Transforming HR

Web-Based Background Checks

Recently, an employer learned a difficult lesson about hiring. The employer had hired a technical employee who was simply not performing well—he was often late and irresponsible—so he was fired. Then the employer got a call from a police officer who worked with the company. "You know that guy that was working with you? Well, he has a criminal record as long as my arm. Didn't you run a background check? Well, that's a security problem, isn't it?"

Some employers use outside firms to conduct background investigations. The growth of the Internet makes it even easier to contract with outside sources. Vendors that provide investigation services ask employers to have applicants complete a form. This form can be either faxed or e-mailed to the vendor. Most frequently, it is faxed because sending

to secure, dedicated fax machines provides a bit more security. The vendor taps databases containing criminal, credit, and other data on individuals. The vendor then e-mails the investigative report to a designated HR staff member at the employer. Financial institutions, government entities, public schools, retailers, and many other employers are using these services.

Some banks, child-care agencies, school systems, and other employers are using electronic fingerprint investigation services. Before these employers make a final job offer, fingerprints of candidates are screened through the Federal Bureau of Investigation's database. Technology also allows employers to obtain and transmit electronic fingerprint images, instead of using messy ink-based images.[38]

will take the cue and continue giving answers that reflect it. If the interviewer instead makes the applicant aware that he or she is not being taken in, the interviewer re-establishes control over the interview.

BACKGROUND INVESTIGATION

Background investigation may take place either before or after the in-depth interview. It costs the organization some time and money, but it generally proves beneficial when making selection decisions. Technology has played an increasing role in helping employers conduct background investigations, as the Technology Transforming HR illustrates.

A background screening has four goals: to show that the employer exercised due diligence in hiring; to provide factual information about a candidate; to discourage applicants with something to hide; to encourage applicants to be honest on applications and during interviews.[39]

A comprehensive background check costs $100–$200 per applicant.[40] A few states have passed laws enforcing limitations on background checking that have made the process more complex, and have encouraged employers to hire firms that specialize in checking backgrounds. International background checks present special challenges. A common but dangerous assumption is that if an applicant has a visa, she or he is a safe choice for employment.[41]

The value of background investigation is evident when the investigation reveals that applicants have misrepresented their qualifications and backgrounds. The most common pieces of false information given are length of prior employment, past salary, criminal record, and former job title. Additionally, many universities report that inquiries on former students often reveal that "graduates" never graduated, and sometimes reveal that "students" did not even attend the university. Another type of credential fraud uses the mail-order "degree mill." To enhance their chances of employment, individuals purchase unaccredited degrees from organizations posing as "universities." These entities provide their "students" degrees for fees and require "no exams, no studying, no classes."

The only way for employers to protect themselves from resume fraud and false credentials is to get verification on applicants either before or after hire. If hired, an employee can be terminated for falsifying employment information. It is unwise for employers to assume that "someone else has already checked." Too often, that assumption has been proved wrong. Two areas that have received special scrutiny since the 9/11 attacks are airline employees and truck drivers.[42]

Sources of Background Information

Background information can be obtained from a number of sources including the following:

- Previous-employment records
- Criminal records
- Drug tests
- Education/degree documentation
- Professional certifications/licenses
- Motor vehicle records
- Credit history
- Honesty tests
- Social Security number
- Sex offenders lists
- Worker's compensation records
- Military records

Personal references, such as those from relatives, clergy, or friends, are of little value, and should not even be used. No applicant seeks a recommendation from somebody who would give a negative response. Instead, work-related references from previous employers and supervisors should be relied on.

SHRM reports that the conducting of a criminal background check has increased by 29% in the last several years. Eighty percent of HR professionals say they conduct criminal checks, and 88% conduct some kind of background checks.[43] These checks reveal that 13% of those screened had failed to disclose a criminal background and 23% had misrepresented employment or education.[44]

Reference-Checking Methods

Several methods of obtaining information from references are available to an employer, with telephoning the reference the most commonly used method. Many experts recommend that employers conducting a telephone reference check use a form focusing on factual verification of information given by the applicant, such as employment dates, salary history, type of job responsibilities, and attendance record. Other items often include reasons for leaving the previous job, the individual's manner of working with supervisors and other employees, and other more subjective information. Many firms that are called for references will provide only factual information. But the use of the form can provide evidence that a diligent effort was made.

Written methods of reference checking are also used. Some organizations send pre-printed reference forms to individuals who are giving references for applicants. These forms often contain a release statement signed by the applicant, so that those providing references can see that they have been released from liability on the information they furnish. Specific or general letters of reference also are requested by some employers or provided by applicants. Employers can face conflicting thoughts when asked to give references for former employees, as the following discussion illustrates.

Giving References on Former Employees In a number of court cases, individuals have sued their former employers for slander, libel, or defamation of character as a result of what the employers said to other potential employers that prevented the individuals from obtaining jobs. Because of such problems, lawyers advise organizations that are asked about former employees to give out only name, employment date, and title; many organizations have adopted policies restricting the release of reference information.

However, employers are increasingly concerned that they could be found liable for *failing* to tell a prospective employer that the person about whom it is inquiring was fired for violent behavior, theft, criminal behavior, sexual harassment, etc.[45] For example, nurse Charles Cullen, accused of killing between 30 and 40 patients, was fired by five employers, and in at least three of those cases there was a suspicion that he was connected to patient deaths. However, when the last hospital he applied to called the previous employers for references on him, no one warned the prospective employer.[46]

Clearly, employers are in a difficult position. Because of threats of lawsuits, they must obtain information on potential employees but are unwilling to give out information in return. To address these concerns, 35 states have laws that protect employers from civil liability when giving, in good faith, reference information that is objective and factual in nature.[47] Still, if former employers will not cooperate, it is difficult. Changing the way that questions are asked may improve the chance for a response.[48]

Legal Constraints on Background Investigations

Various federal and state laws protect the rights of individuals whose backgrounds may be investigated during pre-employment screening. An employer's most important action when conducting a background investigation is to obtain from the applicant a signed release giving the employer permission to conduct the investigation.

Under the Federal Privacy Act of 1974, a government employer must have a signed release from a person before it can give information about that person to someone else. The recommendation is that during an exit interview, an employer obtains a signed release authorizing the employer to provide reference information on the former employee in the future.

Risks of Negligent Hiring and Negligent Retention The costs of failing to check references may be high. Some organizations have become targets of lawsuits that charge them with negligence in hiring workers who have committed violent acts on the job. Lawyers say that an employer's liability hinges on

Negligent hiring
Occurs when an employer fails to check an employee's background and the employee injures someone.

Negligent retention
Occurs when an employer becomes aware that an employee may be unfit for employment, continues to employ the person, and the person injures someone.

THOMSON
━━━━━★━━━━━™
WEST

FAIR CREDIT REPORTING ACT
Discusses provisions of the act and the use of consumer reports in employment decisions.
Custom Search:
☑ ANALYSIS
Exact Phrase: Using consumer reports

how well it investigates an applicant's background. Prior convictions and frequent moves or gaps in employment should be cues for further inquiry. Details provided on the application form by the applicant should be investigated to the greatest extent possible, so the employer can show that due diligence was exercised. Also, employers should document their efforts to check background information by noting who was contacted, when, and what information was or was not provided. This documentation can aid in countering negligent hiring claims.

Negligent hiring occurs when an employer fails to check an employee's background and the employee injures someone. There is a potential negligent hiring problem when: the employer hired an unfit employee who injures others, the employer did an inadequate background check, or the employer failed to find facts that would have led to rejection because of potential risk.[49] A related situation, **negligent retention,** occurs when an employer becomes aware that an employee may be unfit for employment, but continues to employ the person, and the person injures someone.

Fair Credit Reporting Act Many employers check applicants' credit histories. The logic is that poor credit histories may signal irresponsibility, an assumption which may or may not be correct. Firms that check applicants' credit records must comply with the federal Fair Credit Reporting Act. This act basically requires disclosing that a credit check is being made, obtaining written consent from the person being checked, and furnishing the applicant with a copy of the report. Some state laws also prohibit employers from getting certain credit information. Credit history should be checked on applicants for jobs in which use of, access to, or management of money is an essential job function. Commonly, financial institutions check credit histories on loan officers or tellers, and retailers conduct credit checks on cashiers and managerial staff.

Medical Examinations and Inquiries

Medical information on applicants may be used to determine their physical and mental capabilities for performing jobs. Physical standards for jobs should be realistic, justifiable, and geared to the job requirements. Workers with disabilities can perform satisfactorily in many jobs. However, in many places, they are rejected because of their disabilities, rather than being screened and placed in appropriate jobs.

ADA and Medical Inquiries The Americans with Disabilities Act (ADA) prohibits the use of pre-employment medical exams, except for drug tests, until a job has been conditionally offered. Also, the ADA prohibits a company from rejecting an individual because of a disability, and from asking job applicants any question related to current or past medical history until a conditional job offer is made. Once a conditional offer of employment is made, then some organizations ask the applicant to complete a pre-employment health checklist or the employer pays for a physical examination of the applicant. It should be made clear that the applicant who has been offered the job is not "hired" until successful completion of the physical inquiry.

Drug Testing Drug testing may be conducted as part of a medical exam, or it may be done separately. Use of drug testing as part of the selection process has increased in the past few years. If drug tests are used, employers should remember that their accuracy varies according to the type of test used, the item tested, and the quality of the laboratory where the test samples are sent. Because of the potential impact of prescription drugs on test results, applicants should complete a detailed questionnaire on this matter before the testing. If an individual tests positive for drug use, then a second, more detailed analysis should be administered by an independent medical laboratory. Whether urine, blood, saliva, or hair samples are used, the process of obtaining, labeling, and transferring the samples to the testing lab should be outlined clearly and definite policies and procedures should be established.

Genetic Testing Another controversial area of medical testing is genetic testing. Employers who use genetic screening tests do so for several reasons. First, the tests may be used to link workplace health hazards and individuals with certain genetic characteristics. Second, the tests may be used to make workers aware of genetic problems that could occur in certain work situations. Third, and most controversial, the tests may be used to exclude individuals from certain jobs if they have genetic conditions that increase their health risks. Because people cannot change their genetic makeup, the potential for discrimination based on a particular genetic characteristic, such as the probability of getting breast cancer, is real.

MAKING THE JOB OFFER

The final step of the selection process is offering someone employment. Job offers are often extended over the phone, and many are then formalized in letters and sent to applicants. It is important that the offer document be reviewed by legal counsel and that the terms and conditions of employment be clearly identified. Care should be taken to avoid vague, general statements and promises about bonuses, work schedules, or other matters that might change later. These documents also should provide for the individuals to sign an acceptance of the offer and return it to the employer, who should place it in the individual's personnel files.

STAFFING GLOBAL ASSIGNMENTS

Staffing global assignments involves selecting, placing, and locating employees in other countries. The need for individuals who can provide leadership in global organizations emphasizes the importance of global staffing.[50]

When staffing global assignments, cost is a major consideration. The cost of establishing a manager or professional in another country can run as high as $1 million for a three-year job assignment. The cost of placing a key manager outside the United States is often twice the manager's annual salary. If the manager is going to Japan, the cost may be even higher when housing expenses, schooling subsidies, and tax equalization payment are calculated. Further, if a manager, professional, or executive quits an international assignment prematurely or insists on a transfer home, associated costs can equal or exceed the annual salary. "Failure" rates for managers sent to other countries may run as high as 40%–50% in some firms or countries.[51]

Types of Global Employees

Global organizations can be staffed in a number of different ways, including with expatriates, host-country nationals, and third-country nationals. Each

LOGGING ON...

Etiquette International
This professional firm works with organizations to make their employees more effective and professional when working with other cultures.
www.etiquetteintl.com/

staffing option presents some unique HR management challenges. For instance, when staffing with citizens of different countries, different tax laws and other factors apply. HR professionals need to be knowledgeable about the laws and customs of each country represented in their workforce.

An **expatriate** is a citizen of one country who is working in a second country and employed by an organization headquartered in the first country. Experienced expatriates can provide a pool of talent that can be tapped as the organization expands its operations more broadly into even more countries.[52]

A **host-country national** is a citizen of one country who is working in that country and employed by an organization headquartered in a second country. Host-country nationals often know the culture, politics, laws, and business customs better than an outsider would.

A **third-country national** is a citizen of one country who is working in a second country and employed by an organization headquartered in a third country. For example, a U.S. citizen working for a British oil company as a manager in Norway is a third-country national. Staffing with third-country nationals shows a truly global approach.

Selection Process for Global Assignments

The selection process for an international assignment should provide a realistic picture of the life, work, and culture to which the employee may be sent. HR managers start by preparing a comprehensive description of the job to be done. This description notes responsibilities that would be unusual in the home nation, including negotiating with public officials; interpreting local work codes; and responding to ethical, moral, and personal issues such as religious prohibitions and personal freedoms.[53] Figure 8-9 shows the most frequently cited key competencies for successful global employees. The five areas are as follows:

- **Cultural Adjustment** Crucial to global success for individuals is how they adjust to the cultural differences in their foreign assignments.[54] Awareness of cultural issues and differences, and acceptance of diverse cultural demands and customs are important areas to examine.
- **Organizational Requirements** Many global employers find that knowledge of the organization and how it operates is important.
- **Personal Characteristics** The experiences of many global firms demonstrate that the best employees in the home country may not be the best employees in a global assignment, primarily because of personal characteristics of individuals.
- **Communication Skills** One of the most basic skills needed by expatriate employees is the ability to communicate orally and in writing in the host-country language. Inability to communicate adequately in the language may significantly inhibit the success of an expatriate.
- **Personal/Family Concerns** The preferences and attitudes of spouses and other family members are major staffing concerns. Two of the most common reasons for turning down international assignments are family considerations and spouses' careers.

Legal Issues in Selecting Global Employees

Some countries have varying government-controlled employment processes that require foreign employers to obtain government approval in order to hire lo-

Figure 8-9

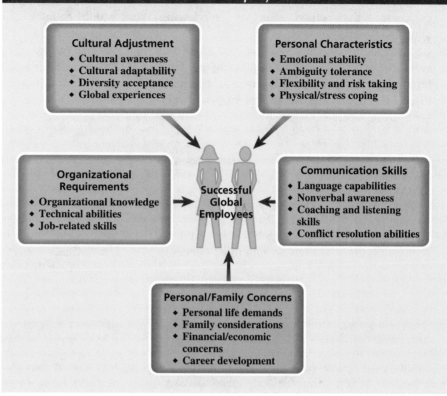

Selection Factors for Global Employees

cal employees. Many countries, including the U.S. and Australia, require foreign workers to apply for work permits or visas.

For U.S.-based firms, the assignment of women and members of racial/ethnic minorities to international posts involves complying with U.S. EEO regulations and laws. Also, most U.S. EEO regulations and laws do apply to foreign-owned firms operating in the U.S. Courts have treated the foreign-owned firms just as they would U.S.-owned employers.

SUMMARY

- Selection is the process that matches individuals and their qualifications to jobs in an organization.
- Placement of people should consider both person/job fit and person/organization fit.
- Predictors linked to criteria are used to identify the applicants who are most likely to perform jobs successfully.
- The selection process—from applicant interest through pre-employment screening, application, testing, interviewing, and background investigation—must be handled by trained, knowledgeable individuals.

- A growing number of employers use electronic pre-employment screening.
- Application forms must meet EEO guidelines and must ask only for job-related information.
- Selection tests include ability tests, assessment centers, personality tests, honesty/integrity tests, and other more controversial types of tests.
- Structured interviews, including behavioral and situational ones, are more effective and face fewer EEO compliance concerns than do unstructured interviews and non-directive interviews.

- Interviews can be conducted individually, by multiple individuals, or by video technology. Regardless of the method, effective interviewing questioning techniques should be used.
- Background investigation can be conducted in a variety of areas. When either requesting or giving reference information, employers must take care to avoid potential legal concerns such as negligent hiring, libel, and slander.
- Global organizations can be staffed by individuals who are expatriates, host-country nationals, or third-country nationals.
- Selection factors for global employees include cultural adjustment, personal characteristics, communication skills, personal/family concerns, and organizational requirements.

REVIEW AND APPLICATION QUESTIONS

1. Develop a structured interview for hiring assistant managers at a large retail store.
2. How would you do a complete background investigation on applicants to minimize concerns about negligent hiring?
3. Your Accounting Manager has decided that using a behavioral interview to select accountants will solve many hiring problems. What can you tell him? Check *www.job-interview.net* and other sources to gather information.

LEARNING REVIEW

To check your knowledge of the chapter, review the following. (Answers after the supplemental case.) For more questions, see the Study Guide.

1. More than anything else, placement of human resources should be seen as _____.
   a. a public relations activity
   b. an operating management responsibility
   c. a matching process
   d. an HR unit responsibility
2. What can employers do to comply with the EEO requirements of reporting the race and sex of applicants?
   a. Collect the data after the hiring decision has been made.
   b. Gather information on the application blank.
   c. Ask applicants to provide EEO reporting data on a separate form.
   d. Make visual assessments during the initial stages of the selection process.
3. Instruments that assess an individual's ability to perform in a specific manner are _____ tests.
   a. aptitude
   b. knowledge
   c. ability
   d. behavioral
4. The Employee Polygraph Protection Act _____.
   a. prohibits most employers from using polygraph tests for pre-employment screening
   b. prohibits employers from using polygraph tests to investigate theft
   c. prohibits government agencies from using polygraph tests
   d. permits the use of polygraph tests, but only when administered by trained experts

HIRING PUBLIC EMPLOYEES MORE QUICKLY

Individuals who have ever applied for a job with a governmental agency normally face a bureaucratic routine. Applicants go to the HR department of the city, county, state, or federal government agency and fill out applications. Then applicants are sent to a large room during business hours and take a test with numbers of other candidates. A month later applicants receive letters informing them of the test results and indicating that they may be called for an interview at some time in the future. The process is very slow and impersonal and the best candidates often have found other jobs before the appropriate government contacts them for an interview.

But Riverside County in California, which employs 16,000 people, has changed its selection process. Because the County has seen rapid growth, its managers decided that it was not competitive with the private sector in its selection process and was losing too many good applicants. County HR staff and others examined Internet-based testing as a way to screen candidates more quickly. Job seekers can log on to a Web site 24 hours per day and test for entry-level positions.

The screening test consists of two parts. The first part measures basic aptitudes in key areas and can be taken from any PC anywhere. The second part of the test is taken in a proctored environment to verify the identity of the person taking the test. The first test score is correlated with the second test score to see if the person likely had assistance from someone else (a family member, friend, neighbor, etc.) with the first part. If it is apparent there was outside help, the candidates are disqualified.

When Riverside County recently built a new juvenile detention facility, over 200 positions needed to be filled quickly. The new on-line testing allowed candidates to take the first part, and if they passed, a "pop up" announcement congratulated them immediately. Those who did not pass the test also were told they had not passed. The proctored portion was taken on computers at a central site and again scored instantly. Of the 436 applicants who took the initial test, 346 passed. Of the 133 who took the proctored second portion, 107 passed.

The response from candidates was very positive. Many indicated that they viewed the Riverside County process as an improvement from the typical government steps. Overall, the net effect has been a more efficient process and a more positive view of Riverside County by potential employees.[55]

Questions

1. Riverside County has taken some large steps to be more efficient in its recruiting practices. What other areas might be considered to improve the selection process?
2. How are the changes in the selection process likely to aid in attracting more and better qualified applicants?

SUPPLEMENTAL CASE: Selecting a Programmer

This case shows that using a test after a pool of candidates has already been interviewed can present some difficulties. (For the case, go to **http://mathis.swlearning.com/.**)

Learning Review Answers: 1. c 2. c 3. c 4. a

1. Carol Patton, "Test for the Best," *HR Executive,* June 16, 2003, 25–29.

2. "Merging Tests with Applicant Tracking Systems," *SHRM Forum,* January 2004, 1–2.

3. A. Wendell Williams, "'I'm in the Mood for Validity' or 'A Rose by any Other Name,'" *SHRM Forum,* June 2002, 1–2.

4. Mary-Jane Sinclair, "So Who Is an Applicant Anyway?" *SHRM Forum,* July 2003, 1–3.

5. Margaret M. Clark, "EEOC Proposes Definition of Internet Job 'Applicant,'" *www.shrm.org.* February 2004, 1-2.

6. Richard Buda and Bruce Charnov, "Message Processing in Realistic Recruitment Practices," *Journal of Management Issues,* 25 (2003), 302–316.

7. Hiram C. Barksdale Jr. et al., "The Impact of Realistic Job Previews and Perceptions of Training on Salesforce Performance and Continuance Commitment: A Longitudinal Test," *Journal of Personal Selling and Sales Management,* 23 (2003), 125–138.

8. Bob Calandra, "Boosting Better Hues," *HR Executive,* March 2, 2004, 47–50.

9. Derek Chapman and Jane Webster, "Technology Use in Screening and Selection," *SHRM Forum,* June 2003, 1–5.

10. Neil Anderson, "Applicant and Recruiter Reactions to New Technology in Selection," *International Journal of Selection and Assessment,* 2 (2003), 121–136.

11. W. J. Manning and Jorge R. Lopez, "New Concerns About Immigration Procedures Merit Review of I-9 Requirements," Jackson/Lewis, *www.Jacksonlewis.com/legalupdates/article.cfm?aid=77.*

12. Michelle Martinez, "Screening for Quality on the Web," *Employment Management Today,* Winter 2004, 1; and John Mooney, "Pre-employment Testing on the Internet," *Public Personnel Management,* 31 (2002), 41–52.

13. David Arnold and John Jones, "Who the Devil's Applying Now? Companies Can Use Tests to Screen Out Dangerous Job Candidates," *Security Management,* March 2002, 85.

14. "2001 AMA Survey on Workplace Testing," *AMA Research, www.amanet.org/research.*

15. James L. Outtz, "The Role of Cognitive Ability Tests in Employment Selection," *Human Performance,* 15 (2002), 161–171; Nathan R. Kuncel et al., "Academic Performance, Career Potential, Creativity and Job Performance: Can One Construct Predict All?" *Journal of Personality and Social Psychology,* 86 (2004), 148–161; Jesús F. Salgado et al., "International Validity Generalization of GMA and Cognitive Abilities," *Personnel Psychology,* 56 (2003), 573–605; Kevin R. Murphy, "Can Conflicting Perspectives on the Role of g in Personnel Selection Be Resolved?" *Human Performance,* 15 (2002), 173–186.

16. Leaetta M. Hough et al., "Determinants, Detection and Amelioration of Adverse Impact in Personnel Selection Procedures," *International Journal of Selection and Assessment,* 9 (2001), 152–193; Patrick McKay and Dennis Doverspike, "African-Americans' Test Taking Attitudes and Their Effect on Cognitive Ability Test Performance," *Public Personnel Management,* 20 (2001), 67-75; and Dening S. Ones and Neil Anderson, "Gender and Ethnic Group Differences on Personality Scales in Selection: Some British Data," *Journal of Occupational and Organizational Psychology,* 75 (2002), 255-276.

17. Michael A. McDaniel and Nhung T. Nguyen, "Situational Judgment Tests: A Review of Practice and Constraints Assessed," *International Journal of Selection and Assessment,* 9 (2001), 103–113.

18. David W. Oakes et al., "Cognitive Ability and Personality Predictors of Training Program Skill Acquisition and Job Performance," *Journal of Business and Psychology,* 15 (2001), 523–548; Jay E. Janovics and Neil D. Christiansen, "Profiling New Business Development: Personality Correlates of Successful Ideation and Implementation, *Social Behavior and Personality,* 31 (2003) 71–80; and C. Viswegvarn et al., "Do Impression Management Scales in Personality Inventories Predict Managerial Job Performance Ratings" *International Journal of Selection and Assessment,* 9 (2001), 277–289.

19. Joyce Hogan and Brent Holland, "Using Theory to Evaluate Personality and Job Performance Relations," *Journal of Applied Psychology,* 88 (2003), 100–112.

20. "Store Chain Settles Lawsuit over Testing," *Omaha World-Herald,* July 11, 2003, 7-M.

21. Lynn A. McFarland, "Warning Against Faking on a Personality Tests for Faking," *International Journal of Selection and Assessment,* 11 (2003), 265–276.

22. Richard D. Goffin and Neil D. Christiansen, "Correcting Personality Tests for Faking," *International Journal of Selection and Assessment,* 11 (2003), 340–344.

23. Gregory M. Hurtz and George M. Alliger, "Influence of Coaching on Integrity Test Performance and Unlikely Virtues Scale Scores," *Human Performance,* 15 (2002), 255–273; Dening S. Ones et al., "Personality and Absenteeism: A Meta Analysis of Integrity Tests," *European Journal of Personality,* 17 (2003), s19–s38.

24. Reagan D. Brown and Christopher M. Cothern, "Individual Differences in Faking Integrity Tests," *Psychological Reports,* 19 (2002), 691–702.

25. Ken Alder, "A Social History of Untruth: Lie Detection and Trust in Twentieth Century America," *Representations,* (Fall 2002), 11–33.

26. Kemba J. Dunham, "More Employers Ask Job Seekers for SAT Scores," *Wall Street Journal,* October 28, 2003, B1.

27. "Rent-A-Center to Pay $2.1 Million," *Bulletin to Management,* July 20, 2000, 89; and *Equal Employment Opportunity Commission v. Pacific Maritime Commission,* CD-CA, CV 00-01516 DT JWJ, February 22, 2000.

28. Michael A. Warech, "Competency Based Interviewing at the Buckhead Beef Company," *Cornell Hotel and Restaurant Administration Quarterly,* February 2002, 70–78.

29. Interviews That Cut to the Chase," *SHRM Forum,* May 2002, *www.shrm.org.*

30. Arla L. Day and Sarah A. Carroll, "Situational and Patterned Behavioral Description Interviews," *Human Performance,* 16 (2003), 25–47.
31. Paul J. Taylor and Bruce Small, "Asking Applicants What They Would Do Versus What They Did Do," *Journal of Occupational and Organizational Psychology,* 75 (2002), 277–294.
32. Melinda C. Blackman, "Personality Judgment and the Utility of the Unstructured Employment Interview," *Basic and Applied Social Psychology,* 24 (2002), 241–250; Melinda C. Blackman and David C. Funder, "Effective Interview Practices for Accurately Assessing Counter Productive Traits," *International Journal of Selection and Assessment,* 10 (2002), 109–116.
33. Anita C. McClough and Steven G. Rogelberg, "Selection in Teams: An Exploration of the Teamwork Knowledge, Skills, and Ability Test," *International Journal of Selection and Assessment,* 11 (2003), 56–65.
34. Susan G. Strauss et al., "The Effects of Video Conference, Telephone, and Face-to-Face Media on Interviewer and Applicant Judgments in Employment Interviews," *Journal of Management,* 27 (2001), 363–381.
35. Nora Cate Shaeffer and Stanley Presser, "The Science of Asking Questions," *Annual Review of Sociology,* 29, (2003), 65–88.
36. D. S. Chapman and P. M. Rowe, "The Impact of Videoconference Technology, Interview Structure, and Interviewer Gender on Interviewer Evaluations," *Journal of Occupational and Organizational Psychology,* 74 (2001), 279–298.
37. Lynn A. McFarland et al., "Field Study Investigation of Applicant Use of Influence Tactics in a Selection Interview," *Journal of Psychology,* 136 (2002), 383–398.
38. Jonathan Feldman, "Security's Hard Knocks," *Network Computing,* January 8, 2001, 1–2; and "Investigation Nation," *Incentive,* February 2002, 1.
39. Les Rosen, "Effective Pre-Employment Background Screening," *Protective Operations,* Spring 2002, 1–5.
40. Carroll Lachnit, "Protecting People and Profits with Background Checks," *Workforce,* February 2002, 50–54.
41. Ron Lasher, "Global Challenges of Background Checks," *Security Management,* March 2003, 105–108.
42. Rick Barrett, "Employers Run Background Check on Driver Applicants to Curb Liability Costs," *Knight-Ridder Tribune Business News,* March 10, 2004; and "U.S. to Start Airline Background Checks," *Information Management Journal,* March 2004, 1–2.
43. "SHRM Finds Employers Are Increasingly Conducting Background Checks to Ensure Workplace Safety," January 20, 2004, *www.shrm.org/press.*
44. Merry Mayer, "Background Checks in Focus," *HR Magazine,* January 2002, 1–4.
45. Rebecca Dean, "Are Employers Obligated to Reveal Information about a Former Employee's Misconduct to a Prospective Employer?" *www.elinfonet.com/fedarticles.*
46. Paul Salvatore, "The Risks of References: A Former Employer Is Accused," *Human Resource Executive,* March 10, 2004, 1–3.
47. "It Is Better to Give *and* Receive Employer References," *Bulletin to Management BNA Inc.,* March 21, 2002, 53.
48. Joe Mullich, "Cracking the Ex-Files," *Workforce Management,* September 2003, 51–54.
49. Pamela Babcock, "Spotting Lies," *HR Magazine,* October 2003, 1.
50. Andrea C. Poe, "Selection Savvy," *HR Magazine,* April 2002, 1–4.
51. "Employers Opt for Shorter-Term Expatriate Assignments," *Newsline,* November 17, 2003, *www.mercerhr.com.*
52. Yaping Gong, "Subsidiary Staffing in Multinational Enterprises: Agency Resources, and Performance," *Academy of Management Journal,* 46 (2003), 728–739.
53. Brett Clegg and Sidney J. Gray, "Australian Expatriates in Thailand: Some Insights for Expatriate Management Policies," *International Journal of Human Resource Management,* 13 (2002), 598–623.
54. Joel Millman, "Repats Help Payless Shoes Branch Out in Latin America," *Wall Street Journal,* December 24, 2003, B1.
55. Based on John Mooney, Pre Employment Testing on the Internet," *Public Personnel Management,* 31, (2002), 41–52.

Training and Developing Human Resources

Training Human Resources

After you have read this chapter, you should be able to:

- Define training and discuss why a strategic approach is important.

- Discuss the four phases of the training process.

- Identify three types of analyses used to determine training needs.

- Explain internal, external, and e-learning as training delivery approaches.

- Give an example for each of the four levels of training evaluation.

- Describe the importance of intercultural competence training for global employers.

Does Training Get the Respect It Deserves?

Company trainers often complain that training does not get the respect it deserves as a major means for accomplishing goals set by management. One indication of this concern is that drastic cuts in training budgets often are seen when the economy slows or a company's profitability declines. Those cuts call into question how essential training is when times get tough. Trainers argue that deferring training in organizations is like deferring maintenance on an automobile—it can come back to haunt the person who puts it off. An HR professor at Northwestern University suggests, "What happens is you start mortgaging your future. Employees cannot be as productive if they are not adequately trained."

During the last recession, Patricia Thorp, of Thorp & Company, demonstrated a better way to deal with training during difficult times. She moved her training in-house. No more did she offer "nice treat" seminars in New York and fee-for-service motivational speakers so that employees and managers could go to New York for recreation and entertainment as well. Instead, she re-evaluated the firm's training efforts and put her training dollars to work more effectively on the specific problems of individual employees. Also, she used internal trainers instead of outside training consultants.

Few companies measure the long-term effectiveness of training. Also, few firms develop maps for individual employee training and follow up after the training. Another problem is that employers seldom put constraints on the kind of training that is allowed. For instance, if someone wants to get a law degree through the company tuition reimbursement plan, even though the company does not need another lawyer, that degree is frequently paid for anyway.

In summary, training must be both desired by the employee and beneficial for the organization. It is crucial that employers follow up to see that what was learned as part of the training produces value for the company. As training becomes more efficient and effective, it likely will not be cut as much during tight budget times.[1]

"Knowledge management is the art of creating value by using the organization's intellectual capital."

—*John Lewison*

The competitive pressures facing organizations today require employees whose knowledge and ideas are current, and whose skills and abilities can deliver results. As organizations compete and change, training becomes even more critical than before. Employees who must adapt to the many changes facing organizations must be trained continually in order to maintain and update their capabilities. Also, managers must have training and development to enhance their leadership skills and abilities. In a number of situations, employers have documented that effective training produces productivity gains that more than offset the cost of the training.

NATURE OF TRAINING

Training Process whereby people acquire capabilities to perform jobs.

Training is the process whereby people acquire capabilities to perform jobs. Poorly trained employees may perform poorly and make costly mistakes. Training provides employees with specific, identifiable knowledge and skills for use in their present jobs. Sometimes a distinction is drawn between *training* and *development,* with development being broader in scope and focusing on individuals' gaining new capabilities useful for both present and future jobs. Development is discussed in Chapter 10; training is the focus of this chapter.

Training may include "hard" skills such as teaching a programmer how to use C++, an accountant how to make an income statement, or a machinist apprentice how to set up a drill press. "Soft" skills are critical in many instances and can be taught as well. They include communicating, mentoring, managing a meeting, and working as part of a team.[2]

New Context of Training

Contemporary training in organizations has evolved significantly over the past decade. Brought on by changes in the competitive environment and technology, this evolution is altering the way training is done. It has affected four areas in particular: organizational competitiveness, knowledge management, revenue, and performance.

Organizational Competitiveness and Training More employers are recognizing that training their human resources is vital. Currently, U.S. employers spend at least $60 billion annually on training. For the average employer, training expenditures average at least 1.5%–2% of payroll expenses, and run $677 per eligible employee, according to a study by the American Society for Training and Development (ASTD). Organizations that see training as especially crucial to business competitiveness average $1,665 in training expenditures per eligible employee.[3]

General Electric, Dell Computers, Motorola, Marriott, Cisco, FedEx, and Texas Instruments all emphasize the importance of training employees and managers. These companies and others recognize that training and HR development efforts are integral to competitive business success. In a sense, for these companies, training is similar to the "continuous improvement" practiced by some manufacturing firms. The nature of technological innovation and change is such that if employees are not trained all the time, they fall behind and the company becomes less competitive. For example, consider the telecommunications industry today compared with five years ago, with all the new technologies, wireless

LOGGING ON...

American Society for Training and Development
This Web site on training and development contains information on research, education seminars, and conferences.
www.astd.org

services, and competitive shifts. Without continual training, organizations may not have staff members with the KSAs needed to compete effectively.

Training also assists organizational competitiveness by aiding in the retention of employees. As emphasized in Chapter 3, a primary reason why many individuals stay or leave organizations is career training and development opportunities. Employers that invest in training and developing their employees enhance retention efforts.

Knowledge Management and Training For much of history, competitive advantage among organizations was measured in terms of physical capital. However, as the information age has evolved, "intelligence" became the raw material that many organizations make and sell through their "knowledge workers." **Knowledge management** is the way an organization identifies and leverages knowledge in order to be competitive. It is the art of creating value by using organizational intellectual capital, which is what the organization (or, more exactly, the people in the organization) knows, and it includes intellectual properties such as patents and copyrights.[4]

Multiple definitions of knowledge management exist, some referring to the technology used to transfer information. Technology can indeed help transmit knowledge, but having technology does not mean people will use it to manage knowledge to best effect. Knowledge management is a conscious effort to get the right knowledge to the right people at the right time so that it can be shared and put into action. It involves more than simply a technological infrastructure.[5]

Training as a Revenue Source Some organizations have identified that training can be a source of business revenue. For instance, Microsoft, Ceridian, Cisco, Hewlett-Packard, and other technology firms bundle training with products and services sold to customers. Also, manufacturers of industrial equipment offer customers training on machine upgrades and new features. Customers of many of these firms pay for additional training either by course, by participant, or as part of equipment or software purchases. Not only are the costs of the trainers' salary, travel, and other expenses covered, but the suppliers make a profit on the training through the fees paid by customers. As a side benefit, customer satisfaction and loyalty increase if customers know how to use the products and services purchased. Thus, customer training aids customer retention and enhances future sales revenues.

Integration of Performance and Training Job performance, training, and employee learning must be integrated to be effective. First, as training progressively moves "closer to the job" in order to produce "real-time" learning, the linkage between training and job performance is vital. Consider the following example: many U.S. Air Force flight-line personnel must undergo regular safety training. The days of sending them to a conference room where they watch a one-hour videotape on safety are gone. Today, they are taken out on the flight line and trained with the actual equipment (i.e., in a real situation, with real tools and equipment and people), not moved to an artificial learning environment. Trainees can watch the trainer put on the necessary gear in the proper manner, attempt to replicate the actions themselves, and receive real-time feedback in an actual work setting.

Second, organizations are seeking more authentic (and hence more effective) training experiences for their trainees, using real business problems to advance

Knowledge management The way an organization identifies and leverages knowledge in order to be competitive.

Figure 9-1   *Performance Consulting*

employee learning. Rather than separating the training experience from the context of actual job performance, trainers incorporate everyday business issues as learning examples, thus increasing the realism of training exercises and scenarios. As part of management training at GE, managers are given actual business problems to solve, and they must present their solutions to organizational business leaders. Using real situations for practice is yet another way of merging the lines between training, learning, and job performance.

Performance Consulting

Training should result in improved organizational performance. Ensuring that it does may require a "performance consulting" approach. **Performance consulting** is a process in which a trainer (either internal or external to the organization) and the organizational client work together to decide what needs to be done to improve results. That may or may not including training.

As Figure 9-1 depicts, performance consulting compares desired and actual organizational results with desired and actual employee performance. Once these comparisons are made, then performance consulting takes a broad approach to performance issues. It does so by:

♦ Focusing on identifying and addressing root causes of performance problems
♦ Recognizing that the interaction of individual and organizational factors influences employee performance
♦ Documenting the actions and accomplishments of high performers and comparing them with actions of more typical performers[6]

Regardless of whether the trainer is an internal employee or an outside consultant, a performance consulting approach recognizes that training alone cannot automatically solve every employee performance problem. Instead, training is

Performance consulting Process in which a trainer and the organizational client work together to determine what needs to be done to improve results.

one piece of a larger "bundled solution." For instance, some employee performance issues might be resolved by creating a training program for employees, and others might call for compensation or job design changes.

Managers are likely the best source of technical information used in employee skills training. They also are in a good position to decide when employees need training or re-training. Their close and continual interaction with employees puts managers in the most appropriate place to determine and discuss employee training possibilities and plans with individual employees. However, compared with individual operating managers, HR often operates with a more long-range view of employee training and development for the entire organization. This difference is especially true at lower levels in the organization. The performance consulting approach is most likely to come from HR or from a consultant that HR has hired. Therefore, a "training partnership" between the HR staff members and operating managers is important.

Chief Learning Officers (CLOs)

To emphasize the importance of training, some organizations have created a position entitled *Chief Learning Officer (CLO)* or *Chief Knowledge Officer (CKO)*. The CLO is not just a training director with an inflated new title. Instead, the CLO is a leader who designs knowledge through training for individual employees and the organization. CLOs must demonstrate a high level of comfort in working with boards of directors and the top management team, a track record of success in running some type of business unit, and an understanding of adult learning technologies and processes. If they possess these characteristics, then CLOs are more likely to take the lead in developing strategic training plans for their organizations.

TRAINING AND ORGANIZATIONAL STRATEGY

Training represents a significant expenditure in most organizations. But it is too often viewed tactically rather than strategically, as upper management is often not clear what it wants from training and therefore fails to connect training with the strategy and goals of the organization.[7] Figure 9-2 shows how training might be used to help accomplish various strategies in an organization. Ideally, the upper management group understands that the training function can provide valu-

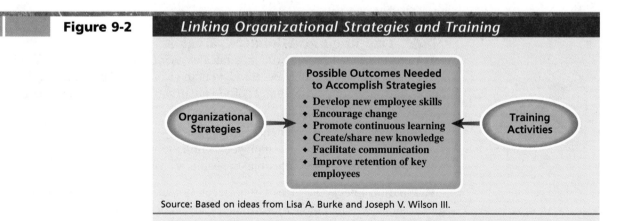

Figure 9-2 *Linking Organizational Strategies and Training*

Organizational Strategies → **Possible Outcomes Needed to Accomplish Strategies**
- Develop new employee skills
- Encourage change
- Promote continuous learning
- Create/share new knowledge
- Facilitate communication
- Improve retention of key employees

← Training Activities

Source: Based on ideas from Lisa A. Burke and Joseph V. Wilson III.

able intelligence about the necessary core skills. If the training unit understands the strategic direction of the organization, it can find creative ways to move people in the direction of the various strategies.

Training that is seen as being aligned with the direction that the organization is going gets higher usage; and providing support for people to get that training is viewed by employees as positive for the strategies of the organization.[8] If a company is trying to distinguish itself from its competition through the quality of its customer service, then significant customer service training is needed to support the strategic direction of the firm. If another firm differentiates itself from competitors with products or services that customers perceive as distinctive and unique, then training resources should be shifted to keeping employees abreast of the latest advertising and marketing ideas. For instance, an exclusive jewelry store selling Rolex watches and expensive jewelry must ensure that its employees are trained on all the models, features, and operations of such items.

Benefits of Strategic Training

The benefits of strategic training are numerous. First, strategic training enables HR and training professionals to get intimately involved with the business, partner with operating managers to help solve their problems, and make significant contributions to organizational results. Strategic training also may prevent HR professionals and trainers from chasing fads or the hottest or latest type of training gimmick.[9] Additionally, a strategic training mindset reduces the likelihood of thinking that training alone can solve most employee or organizational problems. It is not uncommon for operating managers and trainers to react to most important performance problems by saying, "I need a training program on X." With a strategic training focus, the organization is more likely to assess such requests to determine what training and/or non-training approaches might address the most important performance issues.

The value of strategic training can be seen at Walt Disney World where the company has established specific strategic training plans. Implementing those training plans results in a distinct and noted competitive advantage for the organization. For example, at the Disney Institute, employees (called "cast members") gain critical experience from the perspective of their guests. As a part of their training, individuals taking hotel reservations stay at a resort as guests in order to gain greater understanding of what they are selling and to experience the services themselves.

Training and Global Strategies

For global firms the most brilliant strategies ever devised will not work unless there are well-trained employees throughout the world to carry them out. For example, the successful development of *global strategies* is inhibited primarily by training deficits such as these:[10]

♦ Workforces with disparate competencies
♦ A declining pool of U.S. employees willing to go overseas
♦ Slow, expensive, and inflexible "on campus" training options

Halliburton Energy Services Group recently faced just such challenges to its global strategy. The company had historically relied on instructor-led training, which involved instructor travel, lodging, missed work time for students, limited capacity, little individualized training, and a cost of about $8 million a year. The training system that was developed to take the place of the old approach was directly tied to the skills needed to follow the direction identified in the company's strategic plan. The "blended" learning strategy used e-learning for building knowledge of certain basics, a Web-based virtual classroom for building skills, and about 50% traditional instructor-led training. The system now serves 35,000 employees at five Global Learning Centers successfully and at significantly less expense.[11]

DEVELOPING STRATEGIC TRAINING PLANS

Training plans allow organizations to identify what is needed for employee performance *before* training begins. It is at this stage that fit with strategic issues is ensured. A good training plan deals with the following questions:[12]

- Is there really a need for the training?
- Who needs to be trained?
- Who will do the training?
- What form will the training take?
- How will knowledge be transferred to the job?
- How will the training be evaluated?

Training Process

The way firms organize and structure the training affects the way employees experience the training, which in turn influences the effectiveness of the training.[13] Effective training requires the use of a systematic training process. Figure 9-3 shows the four phases of such a process: assessment, design, delivery, and evaluation. Using such a process reduces the likelihood that unplanned, uncoordinated, and haphazard training efforts will occur. A discussion of each phase of the training process follows.

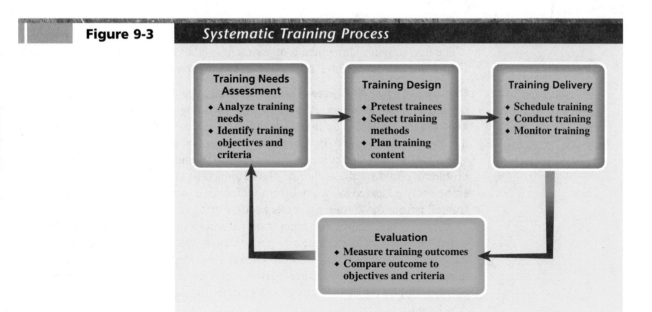

Figure 9-3   Systematic Training Process

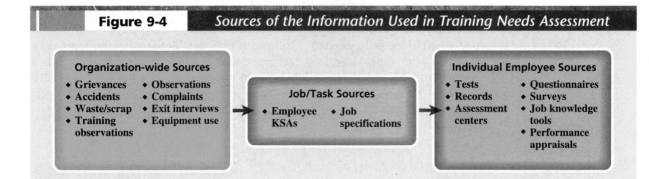

Figure 9-4 *Sources of the Information Used in Training Needs Assessment*

Organization-wide Sources
- Grievances
- Accidents
- Waste/scrap
- Training observations
- Observations
- Complaints
- Exit interviews
- Equipment use

Job/Task Sources
- Employee KSAs
- Job specifications

Individual Employee Sources
- Tests
- Records
- Assessment centers
- Questionnaires
- Surveys
- Job knowledge tools
- Performance appraisals

▊▊ TRAINING NEEDS ASSESSMENT

Assessing organizational training needs represents the diagnostic phase of a training plan. This assessment considers issues of employee and organizational performance to determine if training can help. Needs assessment measures the competencies of a company, a group, or an individual as they relate to what is required in the strategic plan. It is necessary to find out what is happening and what should be happening before deciding if training will help, and if it will help, what kind is needed.[14] For instance, suppose that in looking at the performance of clerks in a billing department, a manager identifies problems that employees have with their data-entry and keyboarding abilities, and she decides that they would benefit from instruction in these areas. As part of assessing the training needs, the manager has the clerks take a data-entry test to measure their current keyboarding skills. Then the manager establishes an objective of increasing the clerks' keyboarding speed to 60 words per minute without errors. The number of words per minute without errors is the criterion against which training success can be measured, and it represents the way in which the objective is made specific.

Analyzing Training Needs

The first step in training needs assessment is analyzing what training is needed. Figure 9-4 shows the three sources of analyzing training needs.

Organizational Analyses Training needs can be diagnosed through analyzing organizational outcomes. A part of HR planning is the identification of the knowledge, skills, and abilities that will be needed in the future as both jobs and the organization change. Both internal and external forces will influence training and must be considered when doing organizational analyses. For instance, the problems posed by the technical obsolescence of current employees and an insufficiently educated labor pool from which to draw new workers should be confronted before those training needs become critical.

One important source for organizational analyses comes from various operational measures of organizational performance. On a continuing basis, detailed analyses of HR data reveal training weaknesses. Departments or areas with high turnover, high absenteeism, low performance, or other deficiencies can be pinpointed. Following an analysis of such problems, training objectives then can be developed.

Job/Task Analyses The second way of diagnosing training needs is to analyze the jobs involved and the tasks performed in those jobs. By comparing the requirements of jobs with the knowledge, skills, and abilities of employees, training needs can be identified. Current job specifications can be a source for such an analysis. For example, at a manufacturing firm, analyses identified the tasks performed by engineers who served as technical instructors for other employees. By listing the tasks required of a technical instructor, management established a program to teach specific instructional skills; thus, the engineers were able to become more successful instructors.

Individual Analyses The third means of diagnosing training needs focuses on individuals and how they perform their jobs. The most common approach for making these individual analyses is to use performance appraisal data. In some instances, a good HR information system can be used to identify individuals who require training in specific areas in order to be eligible for promotion. To assess training needs through the performance appraisal process, the organization first determines an employee's performance inadequacies in a formal review. Then, it can design some type of training to help the employee overcome the weaknesses.

Another way of assessing individual training needs is to survey both managerial and non-managerial employees about what training is needed. Such surveys can also be useful in building support for training from those who will be trained, because the employees will have provided input for identifying their training needs. A training needs survey can take the form of questionnaires or interviews with supervisors and employees individually or in groups. The purpose is to gather information on problems perceived by the individuals involved. In addition to performance appraisals and training surveys, the following sources are useful for individual analyses:

- Skills tests
- Individual assessment tests
- Records of critical incidents
- Assessment centers

- Questionnaires
- Attitude surveys
- Job knowledge tools

Establishing Training Objectives and Priorities

Once training needs have been identified using appropriate analyses, then training objectives and priorities can be established by a "gap analysis," which indicates the distance between where an organization is with its employee capabilities and where it needs to be. Training objectives and priorities are set to close the gap. Three types of training objectives can be set:

- *Knowledge:* Impart cognitive information and details to trainees.
- *Skill:* Develop behavior changes in how jobs and various task requirements are performed.
- *Attitude:* Create interest in and awareness of the importance of training.

The success of training should be measured in terms of the objectives set. Useful objectives are measurable. For example, an objective for a new sales clerk might be to "demonstrate the ability to explain the function of each product in the department within two weeks." This objective checks on internalization, or whether the person really learned and is able to use the training.

Because training seldom is an unlimited budget item and because organizations have multiple training needs, prioritization is necessary. Ideally, management

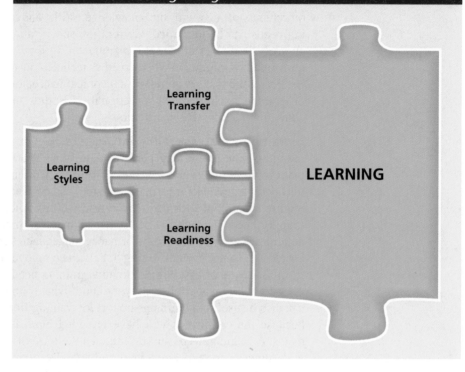

Figure 9-5 *Elements of Training Design*

Learning Transfer

Learning Styles

Learning Readiness

LEARNING

ranks training needs based on organizational objectives.[15] Conducting the training most needed to improve the performance of the organization will produce visible results more quickly.

TRAINING DESIGN

Once training objectives have been determined, training design can start. Whether job-specific or broader in nature, training must be designed to address the assessed specific needs. Effective training design considers learning concepts, different approaches to training, and legal issues.

Working in organizations should be a continual learning process, and learning is the focus of all training activities. Different approaches are possible, but learning is a complex psychological process.[16] As depicted in Figure 9-5, there are three primary considerations when designing training: (1) determining learner readiness, (2) understanding different learning styles, and (3) designing training for transfer. Each of these elements must be considered for the training design to mesh together.

Learner Readiness

For training to be successful, learners must be ready to learn.[17] Learner readiness means having the basic skills necessary for learning, the motivation to learn, and self-efficacy.

Ability to Learn Learners must possess basic skills, such as fundamental reading and math proficiency, and sufficient cognitive abilities. Companies may discover that some workers lack the requisite skills to comprehend their training effectively. Various firms have found that a significant number of job applicants and current employees lack the reading, writing, and math skills needed to do the jobs. Employers might deal with the lack of basic employee skills in several ways:

- Offer remedial training to people in their current workforce who need it.
- Hire workers they know are deficient and then implement specific workplace training.
- Work with local schools to help better educate potential hires for jobs.

Motivation to Learn A person's desire to learn training content is referred to as "motivation to learn" and is influenced by multiple factors. For example, the extent to which a student taking a college course is motivated to learn the course content might be influenced by personal career interests and values, degree plan requirements and area of study, the positive value the student places on getting an A in the course, or simply personal expectations of doing well in school. The student's motivation level may also be influenced by the instructor's motivation and ability, friends' encouragement to do well, classmates' motivation levels, the physical classroom environment, and the training methods used. Regardless of what the motivation is, without it, the student will not learn the material.

Self-efficacy Person's belief that he or she *can* successfully learn the training program content.

Self-Efficacy Learners must also possess **self-efficacy,** which refers to a person's belief that he or she *can* successfully learn the training program content. For learners to be ready for and receptive to the training content, they must feel that it is possible for them to learn it. As an example, some college students' levels of self-efficacy diminish in math or statistics courses when they do not feel adequately able to grasp the material. These perceptions may have nothing to do with their actual ability to learn, but rather reflect the way they see themselves and their abilities. Instructors and trainers must find appropriate ways to boost the confidence of trainees who are unsure of their learning abilities. For instance, people with a low level of belief that they can learn certain content may benefit from one-on-one training.

Learning Styles

In designing training interventions, trainers also should consider individual learning styles. For example, *auditory* learners learn best by listening to someone else tell them about the training content. *Tactile* learners must "get their hands on" the training resources and use them. *Visual* learners think in pictures and figures and need to see the purpose and process of the training. Trainers who address all these styles by using multiple training methods can design more effective training.

Training many different people from diverse backgrounds poses a significant challenge in today's work organizations. Research reveals that in addition to considering cultural, gender, and race/ethnicity diversity, training design sometimes must address some special issues presented by adult learning. For instance, assume a firm is training a group of 30 customer service representatives, 10 of whom are under age 25 and highly computer and Internet literate, and the remainder of whom are older and not as computer proficient. Certainly, the training design must consider that all the trainees are adults, but they come with widely varying learning styles, experiences, and anxieties.

Training older adults in technology may require greater attention to explaining the need for changes and to building the older trainees' confidence in their abilities to learn new technology. In contrast, younger adults are likely willing to try new technology because of their earlier exposure to computers and technology. As a consequence of differences such as these, a variety of training designs and delivery considerations must be assessed when developing training for adults of various ages.

Adult Learning Malcolm Knowles's classic work on adult learning suggests five principles for designing training for adults. That and subsequent work by others suggests that adults:

1. Have the need to know why they are learning something
2. Have a need to be self-directed
3. Bring more work-related experiences into the learning process
4. Enter into a learning experience with a problem-centered approach to learning
5. Are motivated to learn by both extrinsic and intrinsic factors

Adult learners in work organizations present different issues for training design based on Knowles's principles.[18] For instance, trainers cannot expect to do a "brain dump" of material without giving trainees the context or bigger picture of why participants need the training information. This concept is referred to as *whole learning* or *Gestalt learning*. As applied to job training, this means that instructions should be divided into small elements *after* employees have had the opportunity to see how all the elements fit together—that trainers should present the big picture first.

Adult learners should be encouraged to bring work-related problems to training as a way to make the material more relevant to them.[19] Effective training should involve participants in learning by actively engaging them in the learning and problem-solving process. **Active practice** occurs when trainees perform job-related tasks and duties during training. It is more effective than simply reading or passively listening. For instance, if a person is being trained as a customer service representative, after being given some basic selling instructions and product details, the trainee calls a customer and uses the knowledge received. Active practice can be structured in two ways. The first, **spaced practice,** occurs when several practice sessions are spaced over a period of hours or days. The second, **massed practice,** occurs when a person performs all the practice at once. Spaced practice works better for some types of skill or physical learning that require muscle memory, whereas for other kinds of learning, such as memorizing tasks, massed practice is usually more effective. Imagine the difficulty of trying to memorize the lists of options for 20 dishwasher models, one model a day for 20 days. By the time an appliance distribution salesperson learned the last option, the person likely would have forgotten the first one.

Behavior Modeling The most elementary way in which people learn—and one of the best—is **behavior modeling,** or copying someone else's behavior. The use of behavior modeling is particularly appropriate for skill training in which the trainees must use both knowledge and practice. For example, a new supervisor receives training and mentoring on how to handle disciplinary discussions with employees by observing as the HR director or department manager deals with such problems. Behavior modeling is used extensively as the primary means for training supervisors and managers in interpersonal skills. It can aid in the transfer and usage of those skills by the trained supervisors. Fortunately or unfortunately, many supervisors and managers end up modeling the behavior they

Active practice Performance of job-related tasks and duties by trainees during training.

Spaced practice Practice performed in several sessions spaced over a period of hours or days.

Massed practice Practice performed all at once.

Behavior modeling Copying someone else's behavior.

see their bosses use. For that reason, effective training should include good examples of how to handle interpersonal and other issues and problems.

Reinforcement and Immediate Confirmation The concept of **reinforcement** is based on the *law of effect,* which states that people tend to repeat responses that give them some type of positive reward and to avoid actions associated with negative consequences. Closely related is a learning concept called **immediate confirmation,** which is based on the idea that people learn best if reinforcement and feedback are given as soon as possible after training. Immediate confirmation corrects errors that, if made throughout the training, might establish an undesirable pattern that would need to be unlearned. It also aids with the transfer of training to the actual work done.

Transfer of Training

Finally, trainers should design training for the highest possible transfer from the class to the job. Transfer occurs when trainees actually use on the job what they learned in training. Estimates of how much training effectively gets transferred in corporate training are fairly dismal.[20]

Effective transfer of training meets two conditions. First, the trainees can take the material learned in training and apply it to the job context in which they work. Second, employees maintain their use of the learned material over time.

A number of approaches can increase the transfer of training.[21] Offering trainees an overview of the training content and process before the actual training seems to help with both short-term and longer-term training transfer. Another specific way to aid transfer of training to job situations is to ensure that the training mirrors the job context as much as possible. For example, training managers to be better selection interviewers should include role-playing with "applicants" who respond in the same way that real applicants would.

Training Categories

Training can be designed to meet a number of objectives and can be classified in various ways. Some common groupings include the following:

- *Required and regular training:* Complies with various mandated legal requirements (e.g., OSHA and EEO) and is given to all employees (new employee orientation)
- *Job/technical training:* Enables employees to perform their jobs, tasks, and responsibilities well (e.g., product knowledge, technical processes and procedures, and customer relations)
- *Interpersonal and problem-solving training:* Addresses both operational and interpersonal problems and seeks to improve organizational working relationships (e.g., interpersonal communication, managerial/supervisory skills, and conflict resolution)
- *Developmental and innovative training:* Provides long-term focus to enhance individual and organizational capabilities for the future (e.g., business practices, executive development, and organizational change)

Orientation: Training for New Employees The most important and widely conducted type of regular training is done for *new* employees. **Orientation** is the planned introduction of new employees to their jobs, co-workers, and the organization, and is offered by most employers. It requires cooperation between indi-

Effective New Employee Orientation

Effective new employee orientation requires planning and preparation. Unfortunately, orientation often is conducted rather haphazardly. To make orientation more effective, the following suggestions may be useful:

- *Prepare for new employees:* New employees must feel that they belong and are important to the organization. Both the supervisor and the HR unit should be prepared to give each new employee this perception. Further, co-workers should be prepared for a new employee's arrival. The manager or supervisor should discuss the purpose of hiring the new worker with all current employees before the arrival of the new worker.

- *Consider using mentors:* Some organizations assign co-workers or peers to serve as buddies or mentors as part of the new employees' orientation. It is particularly useful to involve more experienced and higher-performing individuals who can serve as role models for new employees.

- *Use an orientation checklist:* An orientation checklist can be used by HR department representatives, the new employee's supervisor, or both, to cover what the new employee needs to know now. Many employers have new employees sign the checklist to verify that they have been told of pertinent rules and procedures.

- *Cover needed information:* It is important to give employees information on the policies, work rules, and

benefits of the company. Policies about sick leave, tardiness, absenteeism, vacations, benefits, hospitalization, parking, and safety rules must be made known to every new employee. Also, the employee's supervisor or manager should describe the routine of a normal workday for the employee the first morning.

- *Present orientation information effectively:* Managers and HR representatives should determine the most appropriate ways to present orientation information. Employees will retain more of the orientation information if it is presented in a manner that encourages them to learn. In addition to videotapes, movies, slides, and charts, self-paced electronic orientation can be used.

- *Avoid information overload:* One common failing of many orientation programs is information overload. New workers presented with too many facts may ignore important details or inaccurately recall much of the information.

- *Evaluate and follow up:* An HR representative or manager can evaluate the effectiveness of the orientation by conducting follow-up interviews with new employees a few weeks or months after the orientation. Employee questionnaires also can be used for follow-up. Unfortunately, it appears that most employers do limited or no evaluation of the effectiveness of orientation.

viduals in the HR unit and operating managers and supervisors. In a small organization without an HR department, the new employee's supervisor or manager usually assumes most of the responsibility for orientation.[22] In large organizations, managers and supervisors, as well as the HR department, generally work as a team to orient new employees.

Effective orientation achieves several key purposes:

- Establishes a favorable employee impression of the organization and the job
- Provides organization and job information
- Enhances interpersonal acceptance by co-workers
- Accelerates socialization and integration of the new employee into the organization
- Ensures that employee performance and productivity begin more quickly

Effective orientation efforts contribute to both short-term and long-term success for employees. The HR Practice contains some suggestions on how to make employee orientation more effective.

Some research studies and employer surveys report that the socialization of new employees and their initial commitment to the organization are positively affected by orientation.[23] This socialization enhances the "person/organization fit," which reinforces the employee's positive view of the job, co-workers, and the organization. Additionally, employers have found that higher employee retention rates result when new employees receive effective orientation.

Orientation also contributes to overall organizational performance by helping employees to more quickly feel that they are a part of the organization and can begin contributing to organizational work efforts. For example, at First National Bank and Trust in Stuart, Florida, new hire orientation is three days. The two days right after hire deal with the mission, values, customer service and products of the bank, and a tour of the facility. A third day (after three months' service) deals with employees' being efficient in their personal lives.[24]

One way of expanding the efficiency of orientation is to use electronic resources. A number of employers place general employee orientation information on company intranets or corporate Web sites. New employees log on and go through much of the general material on organizational history, structure, products and services, mission, and other background, instead of sitting in a classroom where the information is delivered in person or by videotape.[25] Specific questions and concerns can be addressed by HR staff and others after employees review the Web-based information. Unfortunately, many new employee orientation sessions come across as boring, irrelevant, and a waste of time to both new employees and their department supervisors and managers.[26]

Cross training Training people to do more than one job.

Cross Training **Cross training** occurs when people are trained to do more than one job—theirs and someone else's. For the employer, the advantages of cross training are flexibility and development. If an employee gets sick or quits, there is someone already trained to do the job. However, while cross training is attractive to the employer, it is not always appreciated by employees, who often feel that it requires them to do more work for the same pay.

In some organizations, the culture may be such that people seek cross-training assignments to grow or prepare for a promotion, but that is not the case in all organizations. Unions typically are not in favor of cross training, as it threatens job jurisdiction and broadens jobs. Cross training may require scheduling work differently during training, and temporarily decreased productivity may result from it as people learn.

An effective cross-training program can overcome the concerns mentioned and has the potential to be good for both employer and employee. Learning "bonuses" can be awarded for successfully completing cross training, to make it more appealing to employees.

Legal Issues and Training

A number of legal issues must be considered when designing and delivering training. One concern centers on the criteria and practices used to select individuals for inclusion in training programs, making sure that those criteria are job related and do not unfairly restrict the participation of protected-class members.

Also, failure to accommodate the participation of individuals with disabilities in training exposes organizations to EEO lawsuits.

Another contemporary issue is employers' requiring trainees to sign contracts in order to protect the costs and time invested in specialized employee training. For instance, a telecommunications firm paid $77,000 to train four network technicians and certify them in specialized equipment. The firm required that the technicians sign training contracts whereby one-fourth of the cost would be forgiven each year the employee stayed with the organization following the training. A technician who left sooner would be liable to the firm for the unforgiven balance. Health-care organizations, IT firms, and some other employers use training contracts.

TRAINING DELIVERY

Once training has been designed, then the actual delivery of training can begin. It is generally recommended that the training be pilot-tested or conducted on a trial basis to ensure that the training meets the needs identified and that the design is appropriate. Regardless of the type of training done, a number of approaches and methods can be used to deliver it. The growth of training technology continues to expand the available choices.

Whatever the approach used, a variety of considerations must be balanced when selecting training delivery methods. The common variables considered are:

- Nature of training
- Subject matter
- Number of trainees
- Individual vs. team
- Self-paced vs. guided

- Training resources/costs
- E-learning vs. traditional learning
- Geographic locations
- Time allotted
- Completion timeline

To illustrate, a large firm with many new hires may be able to conduct employee orientation using the Internet, videotapes, and specific HR staff members. However, a small firm with few new hires may have an HR staff member meet individually with the new hires for several hours. Or a medium-sized company with three locations in a geographic area may bring supervisors together for a two-day training workshop once a quarter. However, a large, global firm may use Web-based courses to reach supervisors throughout the world, with content available in several languages. Frequently, training is conducted internally, but some types of training use external or technological training resources.

Internal Training

Internal training generally applies very specifically to a job. It is popular because it saves the cost of sending employees away for training and often avoids the cost of outside trainers. Frequently, skills-based, technical training is conducted inside organizations. Due to rapid changes in technology, the building and updating of technical skills have become crucial training needs. Basic technical skills training is also being mandated by federal regulations in areas where the Occupational Safety and Health Administration (OSHA), the Environmental Protection Agency (EPA), and other agencies have jurisdiction.

Informal training
Training that occurs through interactions and feedback among employees.

Informal Training One internal source of training is **informal training,** which occurs through interactions and feedback among employees. Much of what the

Figure 9-6

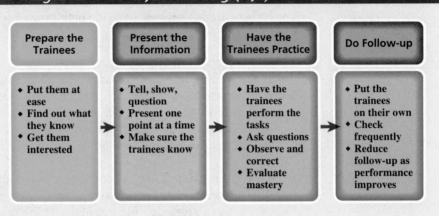

Stages for On-the-Job Training (OJT)

employees know about their jobs they learn informally from asking questions and getting advice from other employees and their supervisors, rather than from formal training programs.

On-the-Job Training (OJT) The most common type of training at all levels in an organization is *on-the-job training (OJT)*. In contrast with informal training, which often occurs spontaneously, OJT should be planned. The supervisor or manager conducting the training must be able to both teach and show the employees what to do. Based on a guided form of training known as *job instruction training (JIT)*, on-the-job training is most effective if a logical progression of stages is used, as shown in Figure 9-6.

On-the-job training is by far the most commonly used form of training because it is flexible and relevant to what employees do.[27] However, OJT has some problems. Often, those doing the training may have no experience in training, no time to do it, and no desire to participate in it. Under such conditions, learners essentially are on their own, and training likely will not be effective.[28] Another problem is that OJT can disrupt regular work. Unfortunately, OJT can amount to no training at all in some circumstances, especially if the trainers simply abandon the trainees to learn the job alone. Also, bad habits or incorrect information from the supervisor or manager can be transferred to the trainees. On the other hand, well-planned and well-executed OJT can be very effective.

External Training

External training, or training that takes place outside the employing organization, is used extensively by organizations of all sizes. Large organizations use external training if they lack the capability to train people internally or when many people need to be trained quickly. External training may be the best option for training in smaller firms due to limitations in the size of their HR staffs and in the number of employees who may need various types of specialized training. Whatever the size of the organization, external training occurs for several reasons:

♦ It may be less expensive for an employer to have an outside trainer conduct training in areas where internal training resources are limited.

♦ The organization may have insufficient time to develop internal training materials.

- The HR staff may not have the necessary level of expertise for the subject matter in which training is needed.
- There are advantages to having employees interact with managers and peers in other companies in training programs held externally.

Outsourcing of Training Many employers of all sizes outsource training to external training firms, consultants, and other entities. According to data from ASTD, approximately 28% of training expenditures go to outside training sources. Interestingly, over a recent three-year period, the outsourcing of training declined some.[29] The reasons for the decline may be cost concerns, a greater emphasis on internal linking of training to organizational strategies, and other issues.

A popular route for some employers is to use vendors and suppliers to train employees. Several computer software vendors offer employees technical certifications on their software. For example, being a Microsoft Certified Product Specialist gives employees credentials that show their level of technical expertise. Such certifications provide employees with items to put on their resumes should they decide to change jobs. These certifications also benefit employers, who can use them as job specifications for hiring and promotion.

Many suppliers, including software providers, host users' conferences, where employees from a number of firms receive detailed training on using the product and new features being added. Some vendors will conduct the training inside an organization as well if sufficient numbers of employees are to be trained.

Government-Supported Job Training Federal, state, and local governments provide a wide range of external training assistance. Government programs on both the state and federal levels provide training dollars to employers who hire new workers, particularly those who have been unemployed for a long time or have been receiving welfare benefits. The Workforce Investment Act (WIA) provides states with block grant programs that target adult education, disadvantaged youth, and family literacy. Employers hiring and training individuals who meet the WIA criteria receive tax credits and other assistance for six months or more, depending on the program regulations.

At state and local levels, employers who add to their workforces can take advantage of a number of programs that provide funding assistance to offset training costs. As examples, a number of states offer workforce training assistance for employers. Quick Start (Georgia), Smart Jobs (Texas), and Partnership (Alabama) are three well-known training support efforts. Often, such programs are linked to two-year and four-year colleges throughout the state.

Educational Assistance Programs Some employers pay for additional education for their employees. Typically, the employee pays for courses that apply to a college degree and is reimbursed upon successful completion of a course. The amounts paid by the employer are considered non-taxable income for the employee up to amounts set by federal laws.[30]

Traditional forms of employee educational programs pose risks for the employer, because upon completion of the degree, the employee may choose to take the new skills and go elsewhere. PricewaterhouseCoopers (PWC) deals with that situation. PWC will repay an employee's loan for an MBA within three years—but only if the employee stays for three years after getting the degree. The company does not agree to provide the opportunity for everyone; it offers the

Technology Transforming HR

Examples of E-learning Programs

Technology has enabled e-learning to take place, and employers are using it in many different ways and for many different kinds of training. For example: The National Insurance Crime Training Academy, operated by the National Insurance Crime Bureau, provides on-line courses aimed at teaching insurance personnel, prosecutors, and law enforcement officers how to prevent crime. Thousands have taken its courses. W. R. Grace uses e-learning in its Grace Global Learning Center, which is available 24/7 to its 6,000 employees worldwide. Sea Island Shrimp House has used e-learning in its seven restaurants to reduce the time managers have to spend on orientation in a high-turnover industry. The material is available in both English and Spanish.

In the transportation industry, e-learning has been used to ensure compliance with mandatory training regulations. American Airlines offers annual classes in flight-safety certification to its 24,000 flight attendants on-line, with completion monitored in a central database. Union Pacific Railroad uses e-learning to certify that 18,000 train service employees are trained on federal regulations. The railroad can automatically compensate employees for passing certain skill tests because its e-learning and payroll systems are integrated.

Other industries have also made effective use of e-learning. The Independent Grocers Association, through the IGA Institute, offers e-learning opportunities resulting in certification for three entry-level grocery store positions: stocker, courtesy clerk, and cashier. Banking, finance, and accounting professionals have access to a wide range of courses covering derivatives, credit, fixed-income securities, and much more. In all these cases, employers estimate significant cost savings with e-learning as opposed to conventional instructor-led training.[31]

arrangement only to those with several years of employment and potential to move up in the organization.[32]

E-learning: On-line Training

E-learning Use of the Internet or an organizational intranet to conduct training on-line.

E-learning is use of the Internet or an organizational intranet to conduct training on-line. An intranet is similar to the Internet, but it is a private organizational network behind "firewall" software that restricts access to authorized users, including employees participating in e-learning. Specific examples of how e-learning is being used in training are shown in the Technology Transforming HR.

E-learning caught on widely with employers because of its promise. The major advantages are cost savings and access to more employees. Over 15% of corporate training is conducted through learning technology today, almost double the percentage from two years ago. However, a recent survey of 375 corporate learners found the dropout rate *much* higher for e-learning than for conventional training: 26% versus 3%. Other studies have shown dropout rates as high as 70%.[33] An internal study for a large government agency found that only 67% of employees chose to begin compulsory on-line courses, and study after study has found that despite good intentions, e-learning, often has failed to capture and sustain the interest of employees.[34]

Even in information technology, where one would think that e-learning would be popular, it is not effective. Despite well-designed on-line courses with hands-on exercises, text-based peer interaction, and expert mentoring through e-mail discussions and telephone calls, e-learning is just not motivating voluntary, self-paced IT professionals to move beyond a few hours of training.[35] Research suggests that on-line courses are just as effective in delivering basic concepts such as basic economic ideas, but classroom instruction is more effective at delivering complex concepts such as advanced economic theories.[36] Further, if courses are optional or have little impact, low completion rates appear more likely. Also, in some situations, getting the necessary material might not require finishing the class. Finally, adults generally have positive attitudes about technology-based classes, but frustration and technology-related problems can change those attitudes.[37]

The solution seems to be "blended learning" programs that combine short, fast-paced, interactive computer-based lessons and teleconferencing with traditional classroom instruction and simulation. Deciding which training is best handled by which medium is important too.

Developing E-learning Rather than being adopted just for its efficiency, e-learning should meet strategic training needs. Certain criteria to consider before adopting e-learning include the following:

- Sufficient top management support and funding are committed to developing and implementing e-learning.
- Managers and HR professionals must be "re-trained" to accept the idea that training is being decentralized and individualized.
- Current training methods (compared with e-learning) are not adequately meeting organizational training needs.
- Potential learners are adequately computer literate and have ready access to computers and the Internet.
- Trainees attending pre-scheduled training programs are geographically separated, and travel time and costs are concerns.
- Sufficient numbers of trainees exist, and many trainees are self-motivated enough to direct their own learning.

Taking existing training materials, putting them on the Internet, and cutting the training budget is not the way to success in e-learning. An important question is: Can this material be learned just as well on-line as through conventional methods? To create a traditional eight-hour course for use in the classroom requires about 25% of the time required to create the same course for use on-line. Savings come from reducing learner costs (travel, time, hotel, etc.) and spreading the cost of developing the e-course over many trainees. Making e-learning pay often may require ensuring that many people participate as learners.[38]

Some people (especially those with reading problems) do not learn as well on-line. Companies have found that making some kind of on-line "lab" where employees can go to get away from their desks to study works best. Simulations, including those incorporating virtual classrooms, and marketing the training inside the company also increase the success of e-learning.[39]

Advantages and Disadvantages of E-learning The rapid growth of e-learning makes the Internet or an intranet a viable means for delivering training content. E-learning has both advantages and disadvantages that must be considered. In addition to being concerned about employee access to e-learning and desire to use it, some employers worry that trainees will use e-learning to complete courses quickly but will not retain and use much of their learning.

In sum, e-learning is the latest development in the evolution of training delivery. Some of the biggest obstacles to using it will continue to be keeping up with

Figure 9-7 — Advantages and Disadvantages of E-learning

Advantages	Disadvantages
• Is self-paced; trainees can proceed on their own time • Is interactive, tapping multiple trainee senses • Allows for consistency in the delivery of training • Enables scoring of exercises/assessments and the appropriate feedback • Incorporates built-in guidance and help for trainees to use when needed • Allows trainers to update content relatively easily • Can be used to enhance instructor-led training • Is good for presenting simple facts and concepts	• May cause trainee anxiety • Is something not all trainees may be ready for • Requires easy and uninterrupted access to computers, which not all trainees have • Is not appropriate for all training content (e.g., leadership and cultural change) • Requires significant up-front investment • Does not lead to significantly greater learning as evidenced in research studies • Requires significant support from top management to be successful

Source: Developed by Lisa A. Burke and Robert L. Mathis.

the rapid change in technological innovation, knowing when and how much to invest, and designing e-courses appropriately. Undoubtedly, e-learning will have a major impact on HR and training, but there are not "ten easy steps" to making e-learning successful. Figure 9-7 presents a listing of e-learning's most commonly cited advantages and disadvantages.

Training Approaches

Whether training is delivered internally, externally, or through e-learning, appropriate training approaches must be chosen. The following overview classifies common training approaches into several major groups. Some are used more for job-based training, while others are used more for development.

Cooperative Training Cooperative training approaches mix classroom training and on-the-job experiences. This training can take several forms. One form, generally referred to as *school-to-work transition,* helps individuals move into jobs while still in school or upon completion of formal schooling.[40] Such efforts may be arranged with high schools or with community colleges. For example, Union Pacific Railroad and Mid-Plains Community College, in North Platte, Nebraska, collaborate to provide training to students who want jobs as machinists and electricians, and training in safety and other areas to other railroad personnel. Over 8,000 employees have been trained in four years.[41]

A form of cooperative training called *internship* usually combines job training with classroom instruction from schools, colleges, and universities. Internships benefit both employers and interns. Interns get "real-world" exposure, a line on their resumes, and a chance to closely examine a possible employer. Employers get a cost-effective source of labor and a chance to see an intern at work before making a final hiring decision.

LOGGING ON...

Blackboard
Blackboard is a Web site
that offers a complete
set of software products
and services for
e-education
development.
www.blackboard.com

Another form of cooperative training used by employers, trade unions, and government agencies is *apprentice training.* An apprenticeship program provides an employee with on-the-job experience under the guidance of a skilled and certified worker. Certain requirements for training, equipment, time length, and proficiency levels may be monitored by a unit of the U.S. Department of Labor. Apprenticeships train people for jobs in skilled crafts, such as carpentry, plumbing, photoengraving, typesetting, and welding. Apprenticeships usually last two to five years, depending on the occupation. During this time, the apprentice usually receives lower wages than the certified individual.

Instructor-Led Classroom and Conference Training Instructor-led training is still the most prevalent approach to training. Employer-conducted short courses, lectures, and meetings usually consist of classroom training, whereas numerous employee development courses offered by professional organizations, trade associations, and educational institutions are examples of conference training. A particularly important aspect of classroom training is the need to recognize that adults in a classroom setting have different expectations and learning styles from those of younger students. A number of large firms have established their own "universities" to offer classroom and other training as part of curricula for employees. Because these corporate universities generally offer both training and development courses, they are discussed in Chapter 10.

Distance Training/Learning A growing number of college and university classes use some form of Internet-based course support. Blackboard and WebCT are two popular support packages that thousands of college professors use to make their lecture content available to students. These packages enable virtual chat and electronic file exchange among course participants, and also enhance instructor/student contact. Many large employers, as well as colleges and universities, use interactive two-way television to present classes. The medium allows an instructor in one place to see and respond to a "class" in any number of other locations. With a fully configured system, employees can take courses from anywhere in the world.

Simulations and Training The explosive growth in information technology in the past few years has revolutionized the way all individuals work, including how they are trained. Today, computer-based training involves a wide array of multimedia technologies—including sound, motion (video and animation), graphics, and hypertext—to tap multiple learner senses. Video streaming allows video clips of training materials to be stored on a firm's network server. Employees can then access the material using the firm's intranet.

Computer-supported simulations within organizational training can replicate the psychological and behavioral requirements of a task, often in addition to providing some amount of physical resemblance to the trainee's work environment. From highly complicated systems that replicate difficult landing scenarios for pilots, to programs that help medical trainees learn to sew sutures, simulations allow for safe training when the risks associated with failure are high. Virtual reality is also used to create an artificial environment for trainees so that they can participate in the training. For example, virtual reality is used in some military operations training and in the robotic manufacturing of electronic equipment.[42]

The new technologies incorporated into training delivery also affect the design, administration, and support of training. Some companies have invested in electronic registration and recordkeeping systems that allow trainers to register participants, record exam results, and monitor learning progress.

Generally, technology is moving from center stage to becoming embedded in the learning and training processes. As learning and work merge even closer in the future, technology is likely to integrate seamlessly into the work environment of more employees. This integration will allow employees to spend less time in the future learning how to use technology, and more time on learning the desired content.

TRAINING EVALUATION

Evaluation of training compares the post-training results to the pre-training objectives of managers, trainers, and trainees. Too often, training is conducted with little thought of measuring and evaluating it later to see how well it worked. Because training is both time-consuming and costly, it should be evaluated.[43]

Levels of Evaluation

It is best to consider how training is to be evaluated before it begins. Donald L. Kirkpatrick identified four levels at which training can be evaluated. As Figure 9-8 shows, the evaluation of training becomes successively more difficult as it moves from measuring reaction to measuring learning to measuring behavior and then to measuring results. But the training that affects behavior and results versus reaction and learning provides greater value.[44]

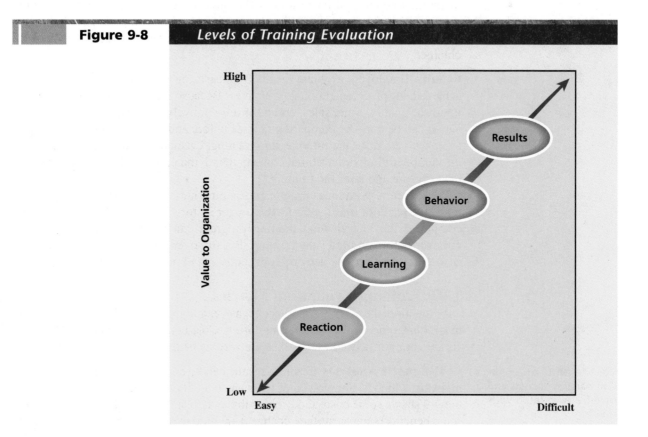

Figure 9-8 *Levels of Training Evaluation*

Reaction Organizations evaluate the reaction levels of trainees by conducting interviews with or administering questionnaires to the trainees. Assume that 30 managers attend a two-day workshop on effective interviewing skills. A reaction-level measure could be gathered by having the managers complete a survey that asked them to rate the value of the training, the style of the instructors, and the usefulness of the training to them. If the survey were administered immediately after the workshop, it might measure only how much the managers liked the training rather than how the training benefited them or how it affected the way they conduct interviews.

Learning Learning levels can be evaluated by measuring how well trainees have learned facts, ideas, concepts, theories, and attitudes. Tests on the training material are commonly used for evaluating learning, and they can be given both before and after training to provide scores that can be compared. If test scores indicate learning problems, then instructors get feedback and courses can be redesigned so that the content can be delivered more effectively. Of course, learning enough to pass a test does not guarantee that trainees will remember the training content months later or will change job behaviors.[45]

Behavior Evaluating training at the behavioral level means: (1) measuring the effect of training on job performance through interviews of trainees and their co-workers, and (2) observing job performance. For instance, the managers who participated in the interviewing workshop might be observed conducting actual interviews of applicants for jobs in their departments. If the managers asked questions as they had been trained and used appropriate follow-up questions, then behavioral indicators of the interviewing training exist. Behaviors are more difficult to measure than are reaction and learning. Even if behaviors do change after training, the results that management desires may not be obtained.

Results Employers evaluate results by measuring the effect of training on the achievement of organizational objectives. Because results such as productivity, turnover, quality, time, sales, and costs are relatively concrete, this type of evaluation can be done by comparing records before and after training. For the managers who attended the interviewing training, evaluators could gather records of the number of individuals hired compared with the number of employment offers made before and after the training.[46]

The difficulty with measuring results is pinpointing whether changes were actually the result of training or of other major factors. For example, managers who completed the interviewing training program can be measured on employee turnover before and after the training. But turnover also depends on the current economic situation, the demand for products, and many other variables.

||||||| Training Evaluation Metrics

As mentioned earlier, training is expensive, and therefore it is one HR function that requires measurement and monitoring. Cost-benefit analysis and ROI analysis are commonly used to do so, as are various benchmarking approaches.

Cost-benefit analysis
Comparison of costs and benefits associated with training.

Cost-Benefit Analysis Training results can be examined through **cost-benefit analysis,** which is comparison of costs and benefits associated with training. Figure 9-9 shows some costs and benefits that may result from training. Even though some benefits (such as attitude changes) are hard to quantify, comparison of costs

Figure 9-9

Some Typical Costs and Benefits of Training

Typical Costs
- Trainer's salary and time
- Trainee's salaries and time
- Materials for training
- Expenses for trainer and trainees
- Cost of facilities and equipment
- Lost productivity (opportunity cost)

Typical Benefits
- Increase in production
- Reduction in errors and accidents
- Reduction in turnover
- Less supervision necessary
- Ability to use new capabilities
- Attitude changes

and benefits associated with training remains a way to determine whether or not training is cost-effective. For example, one firm evaluated a traditional safety training program and found that the program did not lead to a reduction in accidents. Therefore, the safety training was re-designed, and better safety practices resulted. However, measurement of both the costs and the benefits listed in Figure 9-9 may be difficult.

Return on Investment (ROI) Analysis In organizations, training is often expected to produce a return on investment (ROI). Still, in too many circumstances, training is justified because someone liked it, rather than on the basis of resource accountability. Firms that measure ROI on training include LensCrafters, Sears, and Apple Computer.[47]

Benchmarking In addition to evaluating training internally, some organizations use benchmark measures to compare it with training done in other organizations. To do benchmarking, HR professionals gather data on training in their organization and compare them with data on training at other organizations in the same industry and of a similar size. Comparison data are available through the American Society for Training and Development and its Benchmarking Service. This service has training-related data from more than 1,000 participating employers who complete detailed questionnaires annually. Training also can be benchmarked against data from the American Productivity & Quality Center and the Saratoga Institute.

Training Evaluation Designs

With or without benchmarking data, internal evaluations of training programs can be designed in a number of ways. The rigor of the three designs discussed next increases with each level.

Post-Measure The most obvious way to evaluate training effectiveness is to determine after the training whether the individuals can perform the way management wants them to perform. Assume that a customer service manager has 20 representatives who need to improve their data-entry speeds. After a one-day training session, they take a test to measure their speeds. If the representatives can all type the required speed after training, was the training beneficial? It is difficult to say; perhaps most of them could have done as well before training. Tests after training do not always clearly indicate whether a performance is a result of the training or could have been achieved without the training.

LOGGING ON...

Scorecard for Skills
This Web site is dedicated to measuring the effectiveness of workplace programs. The site includes a tool to build your own balanced scorecard.
www.scorecardforskills.com

Pre-/Post-Measure By designing the evaluation differently, the issue of pretest skill levels can be considered. If the manager had measured the data-entry speed before and after training, she could have known whether the training made any difference. However, a question would have remained: Was any increase in speed a response to the training, or did these employees simply work faster because they knew they were being tested? People often perform better when they know their efforts are being evaluated.

Pre-/Post-Measure with a Control Group Another evaluation design can address this problem. In addition to testing the 20 representatives who will be trained, the manager can test another group of representatives who will not be trained, to see if they do as well as those who are to be trained. This second group is called a control group. After training, if the trained representatives work significantly faster than those who were not trained, the manager can be reasonably sure that the training was effective.

TRAINING FOR GLOBAL ASSIGNMENTS

The orientation and training that expatriates and their families receive before departure significantly affect the success of an overseas assignment. Unfortunately, various surveys have found that only 50%–60% of global employers provide formal training programs for expatriates and their families. When such programs are offered, most expatriates participate in them, and the programs usually produce a positive effect on cross-cultural adjustment.[48]

The most common topics covered in pre-departure training are: daily living conditions, cultural customs, business issues, country history, climate, and transportation and communication systems. Individuals selected to work outside their home countries need answers to many specific questions about their host countries.[49] Training in various areas helps expatriates and their families adjust to and deal with host-country counterparts. Training in customs and practices can be especially valuable to individuals who will not live outside the home country but will travel to other countries on business.

A related issue is the promotion and transfer of foreign citizens to positions in the United States. As more global organizations start or expand U.S. operations, more cross-cultural training will be necessary for international employees relocated to the United States. For example, many Japanese firms operating in the United States conduct training programs to prepare Japanese for the food, customs, labor and HR practices, and other facets of working and living in the U.S. Helping U.S. workers accept a foreign boss is another concern. These issues all underscore the importance of training and development for international adjustment.[50]

Intercultural Competence Training

Growing numbers of global employers are providing intercultural competence training for their global employees. Intercultural competence incorporates a wide range of human social skills and personality characteristics. As noted in Figure 9-10, three components of intercultural competence require attention when training expatriates for global assignments.

Figure 9-10

Intercultural Competence Training

Component	Possible Training
Cognitive	• Culture-specific training (traditions, history, cultural customs, etc.) • Language course
Emotional	• *Uneasiness:* Social skills training focusing on new/unclear and intercultural situations • *Prejudices:* Coaching may be clarifying • *Sensitivity:* Communication skills course (active listening, verbal/nonverbal cues, empathy)
Behavioral	• Culture Assimilator • International projects • Social skills training foucusing on intercultural situations

Source: Developed by Andrea Graf, PhD, Technical University of Braunschweig, Germany, and Robert L. Mathis, PhD, SPHR.

The key components are:

♦ *Cognitive:* What does the person know about other cultures?
♦ *Emotional:* How does the person view other cultures, and how sensitive is the person to cultural customs and issues?
♦ *Behavioral:* How does the person act in intercultural situations?

Increasingly, global employers are using training methods that allow individuals to behave in international situations and then receive feedback. One popular method is the Culture Assimilator. Used worldwide, especially by European-based firms, the Culture Assimilator is a programmed training and learning method consisting of short case studies and critical incidents. The case studies describe intercultural interactions and potential misunderstandings involving expatriates and host-country nationals.

SUMMARY

♦ Training is the process that provides people with the capabilities they need to do their jobs.
♦ Training affects factors such as organizational competitiveness, knowledge management, revenue, and performance.
♦ Performance consulting compares desired and actual results in order to identify needed training and non-training actions.
♦ A strategic approach to training links organizational strategies and HR planning to various training efforts.
♦ The training process consists of four phases: assessment, design, delivery, and evaluation.

♦ Training needs can be assessed using organizational, job/task, and individual analyses, and then training objectives can be set to help the organization meet those needs.
♦ Training design must consider learner readiness, learning styles, learning transfer, training categories, and legal issues.
♦ Orientation as a kind of training is designed to help new employees learn about their jobs.
♦ Training can be delivered internally through classes, informally, and on the job.
♦ External training may be delivered by outside sources such as government training programs.

- E-learning is training conducted using the Internet or an intranet, and its development must consider both its advantages and its disadvantages.
- Common training approaches include cooperative training, classroom and conference training, and distance training/learning.
- Various organizations are taking advantage of training that uses technology such as multimedia, video streaming, simulation, and virtual reality.
- Training can be evaluated at four levels: reaction, learning, behavior, and results.
- Training evaluation metrics may include cost-benefit analysis, return-on-investment analysis, and benchmarking.
- A pre-/post-measure with a control group is the most rigorous design for training evaluation; other, less rigorous designs can be used as well.
- Pre-departure orientation significantly affects the success of international assignments, but it is not universally offered.
- Intercultural competence training helps prepare employees to respond more appropriately to situations encountered during global assignments.

REVIEW AND APPLICATION QUESTIONS

1. What steps can HR professionals take to overcome the organizational tendency to cut training when money is tight?
2. Assume that you want to identify training needs for a group of sales employees in a luxury-oriented jewelry store. What would you do?
3. Develop a briefing for division managers that shows the advantages and disadvantages of e-learning. Use Web sources, including the following Web site: *www.e-learninghub.com.*

LEARNING REVIEW

To check your knowledge of the chapter, review the following. (Answers after the supplemental case.) For more questions, see the Study Guide.

1. Which is a way to determine whether or not training is cost-effective?
   a. Measure improvements in employee performance resulting from training.
   b. Compare costs and benefits associated with training.
   c. Identify attitude changes following training.
   d. Assess any reductions in voluntary turnover.
2. The performance consulting approach recognizes that it is important to consider _____.
   a. existing training methods
   b. the separation of training from development
   c. non-training factors such as compensation
   d. the cost of training programs
3. When they are ready to learn, people have the ability to learn, _____, and the belief that they can learn.
   a. the right attitude
   b. time
   c. a desire to learn
   d. organizational support
4. When a university asks students to complete an instructor-evaluation survey, it is evaluating training at the _____ level.
   a. results
   b. learning
   c. reaction
   d. behavior

CASE

HOTELS LINK TRAINING AND CUSTOMER SERVICE

Hotels, particularly upscale, luxury ones, focus on providing high-quality service to their guests. Hotel executives have learned that high-quality service is usually what determines if guests will return to resorts, even more so than price. Consequently, having a well-trained hotel staff is crucial to delivering the premium service guests expect.

The importance of training to deliver this service can be seen in several examples. At the Broadmoor Hotel in Colorado Springs with 1,600 employees, developing and conducting training for all employees is a priority. Beginning with extensive new employee orientation and training, employees learn how to greet guests, resolve problems, and respond to guests' requests. The value of this training is that when hotel guests fill out comments cards, many of them convey positive comments on the personalized service provided, a desire to return in the future, or other indications of the success of training at the Broadmoor.

Other upscale hotels and resorts see training as crucial as well. Rockresorts, which owns luxury properties in the United States and the Caribbean, averages $1,000 in training expenditures per staff member, or 400% greater than the industry average. One program is a three-day training session for all 1,400 Rockresorts employees. The objectives of this program include improving customer service, identifying ideas for improvements, and instilling customer service confidence in employees. Based on the results from employees who have completed the training, the objectives are being met. One indicator is an increase in the scores and comments on customer surveys and response cards. Another benefit of the training is that it has aided employee retention, particularly in the first year of employees' service.

The Starwood collection of hotels (St. Regis, Westin, Sheraton, Four Points, W Hotels) sees a specific focus on training as a contributor to competitive success. To increase the sales of beverages at the Starwood hotels and restaurants, a corporate initiative called "WineBuzz" was developed. With the specific goal of increasing wine sales through the Starwood hotel properties, Starwood executives recognized that guests purchasing wine expected to be served by knowledgeable, well-trained employees. Because serving beer is much different from serving wine, particularly given the different varieties and styles of wine, a training program on wine types and how to serve them was developed. A part of the training was Wine Camp, where food and beverage staff members from Starwood Hotels attended a multi-day session in Napa Valley, California. The 22 attendees from throughout the United States toured wineries, learned about viniculture and the different types of grapes used to produce different wines, and the wine production process. The trainees practiced opening bottles, discussing the merits of various grapes and wines, and other skills. Also, the Wine Camp contained "train-the-trainer" content, because the 22 attendees were then expected to conduct regional training sessions at Starwood hotels in their regional areas.

From these examples, it is evident that these hotels are investing in training. The payoffs of the training are likely to be seen in more satisfied guests, better-performing employees, and increased organizational revenues and profits.[51]

Questions

1. Discuss how these hotels are using a strategic and performance consulting approach to developing training efforts.
2. Identify how the effectiveness of Starwood's WineBuzz program might be measured several years later.

SUPPLEMENTAL CASE: The New Payroll Clerk

This case identifies the frustration that often accompanies the first day at work and why orientation often is important in aiding employee retention. (For the case, go to **http://mathis.swlearning.com/.**)

Learning Review Answers: 1. b   2. c   3. c   4. c

NOTES

1. "Training for Efficiency," *Omaha World-Herald,* October 14, 2002, D1–D2.
2. Kathryn A. Estrada, "In House Training for Soft Skills," *www.shrm.org/hrresources.*
3. ASTD, press release, March 26, 2001, *www.astd.org.*
4. John Lewison, "Knowledge Management," *SHRM White Paper,* October 2001, *www.shrm.org/hrresources.*
5. Chan Veng Seng et al., "The Contributions of Knowledge Management to Workplace Learning," *Journal of Workplace Learning,* 14 (2002), 138–147.
6. "Action Learning as a Strategy for Enhancing Market Competitiveness," *Global Competitiveness,* January 2002, 1–7.
7. Sharon Daniels, "Employee Training: A Strategic Approach to Better Return on Investment," *Journal of Business Strategy,* 24 (2003), 1–4.
8. Max Montesino, "Strategic Alignment of Training, Transfer-Enhancing Behaviors, and Training Usage," *Human Resource Development,* Spring 2002, 89–108.
9. Anastasios G. Karamono, "Complexity, Identity and the Value of Knowledge Intensive Exchanges," *Journal of Management Studies,* 40 (2003), 1871–1890; and Shari Caudron, "Just Say No to Training Fads," *T+D,* June 2002, 39–43.
10. Richard W. Oliver, "The Return on Human Capital," *Journal of Business Strategy,* 22 (2001), 7–10.
11. "The Business of Training: How Halliburton's 'I-Learn' Strategy Links to Its Business Mission," *Managing Training and Development,* February 2002, 1+.
12. Daniels, "Employee Training."
13. Amalia Santos and Mark Stuart, "Employee Perceptions and Their Influences on Training Effectiveness," *Human Resource Management Journal,* 13 (2003), 27–44; David N. Ashton, "The Impact of Organizational Structure and Practices on Learning in the Workplace," *International Journal of Training and Development,* 8 (2004), 43–53; and Paul M. Muchinsky, "When the Psychometrics of Test Development Meets Organizational Reality," *Personnel Psychology,* 57 (2004), 175–209.
14. Agnita D. Korsten, "Developing a Training Plan to Ensure Employees Keep Up with the Dynamics of Facility Management," *Journal of Facilities Management,* 1 (2003), 365–380.
15. Nicholas Clarke, "The Politics of Training Needs Assessment," *Journal of Workplace Learning,* 15 (2003), 141-153.
16. David C. Forman, "Eleven Common-Sense Learning Principles," *T+D,* September 2003, 39–46.
17. Ed Welsch, "Cautious Steps Ahead: A Slow Economy Means Readiness Assessments Are Back," *Online Learning,* January 2002, 20–24.
18. Paul Hager, "Lifelong Learning in the Workplace? Challenges and Issues," *Journal of Workplace Learning,* 16 (2004), 22–32.
19. Karen Evans et al., "Recognition of Tacit Skills: Sustained Learning Outcomes in Adult Learning," *International Journal of Training and Development,* 8 (2004), 54–72.
20. Jathan W. Janove, "Use It or Lose It," *HR Magazine,* April 2002, 1–3.
21. Chrysanthos Dellarocos: Learning Negotiation Skills: Four Models of Knowledge Creation and Transfer," *Management Science,* April 2003, 1–13.
22. "How 3 Companies Make New-Hire Training Mean Business," *Managing Training and Development,* September 2002, 1–3.
23. Charlotte Garvey, "The Whirlwind of a New Job," *HR Magazine,* (June 2001), 1–5.
24. "Training: New-Hire Orientation Can Build Support for Your Company's Mission," *Human Resource Department Management Report,* June 2002, 10–12.
25. Betty Sosnin, "Is a Video in Your Vision?" *HR Magazine,* February 2001, 1–5.
26. Tom Sarner, "Welcome E-Board," *Human Resource Executive,* March 6, 2002, 38–39.
27. Svernung Skule, "Learning Conditions at Work: A Framework to Understand and Assess Informal Learning in the Workplace," *International Journal of Training and Development,* 8 (2004), 8–20.
28. Jin Hyuk Kim and Chan Lee, "Implications of Near and Far Transfer of Training on Structured On-the-Job Training," *Advances in Developing Human Resources,* 3 (2001), 442–451.
29. Mark E. Van Buren, *ASTD State of the Industry Report, 2003* (Alexandria, VA: American Society of Training and Development, 2001), 11–12.
30. A. Pilzner, "Educational Assistance Programs," January 2002, *www.shrm.org.*
31. Michael Bradford, "Anti-Fraud Courses Available Online Helping Industry Meet Training Needs," *Business Insurance,* September 16, 2002, 1–2; K. Boxer and B. Johnson, "How to Build an Online Training Center," *T+D* August 2002, 1–6; "Chains Upgrade to Online Training," *Nation's Restaurant News,* March 10, 2003, 1–4; "All Aboard E-Learning at Air, Rail Companies," *Information Week,* November 8, 2002, 1; "Transfers of Knowledge," *Progressive Grocer,* February 15,

2004, 1–2; and "E-Learning Is a Better Chalkboard," *Financial Executive,* November 2003, 1–4.

32. Kevin Sweeney, "Education Benefits Adds ROI to MBA," *Employee Benefit News,* September 1, 2001, 1–3.

33. Joe Mullich, "A Second Act for E-Learning," *Workforce Management,* February 2004, 51–55.

34. Allison Rosset and Lisa Schafer, "What to Do About E-Dropouts," *T+D,* June 2003, 1–6; and Steve Alexander, "Do Not Pass Go: Why Do Learners Leave Online Courses Before Finishing Them?" *Online Learning,* March 2002, 1–3.

35. Leslie Laine, "Is E-Learning E-ffective for IT Training?" *T+D,* 57 (June 2003), 1–5.

36. "Online Lessons," *American City and County,* March 1, 2003, 1–4.

37. Elizabeth T. Welsh et al., "E-Learning: Emerging Uses, Empirical Results and Future Directions," *International Journal of Training and Development,* 7 (2003), 245–251.

38. Frank Diekmann, "Everything You Wanted to Know About E-Learning," *Credit Union Journal,* July 23, 2001, 1–3.

39. Holly Dolezalek, "Pretending to Learn," *Training,* July/August 2003, 20–26; and Wendy Webb, "Who Moved My Training?" *Training,* January 2003, 1–4.

40. "Survey: School-to-Work Lacks Sponsors," *HR News,* February 2002, 4.

41. Based on information provided by Jamie Herbert, SPHR. Union Pacific, Omaha, Nebraska.

42. Henry Simpson and Randall Oser, "Evaluating Large-Scale Training Simulations," *Military Psychology,* 15 (2003), 25–40.

43. Eduardo Salas et al., "Training Evaluations in the Military," *Military Psychology,* 15 (2003), 3–46.

44. Kathryn Tyler, "Evaluating Evaluations," *HR Magazine,* June 2002, 1–4.

45. Mark A. Davis, "Evaluating Cognitive Training Outcomes," *Journal of Business and Psychology,* 18 (2003), 191–206.

46. Linda Bjornberg, "Training and Development: Best Practices," *Public Personnel Management,* 31 (2002), 507–516.

47. How to Compute ROI for Online vs. Traditional Training," *HR Focus,* April 2002, 10–11.

48. Andy Meisler, "Companies Weigh the Cost of Prepping Expats," *Workforce Management,* February 2004, 60–63.

49. Kelley M. Blassingame, "Strangers in Strange Lands," *Employee Benefit News,* June 15, 2002, 1–2.

50. Jill Turbin, "Policy Borrowing: Lessons from European Transfer Training Practices," *International Journal of Training and Development,* 5 (2001), 96–111.

51. Based on Bill Kelley, "Refresher Course," *Human Resource Executive,* May 15, 2001, 59–64; and Jennifer J. Salopek, "Grape Expectations," *Training & Development,* August 2000, 52–57.

CHAPTER 10

Careers and HR Development

After you have read this chapter, you should be able to:

- Differentiate between organization-centered and individual-centered career planning.

- Discuss several career issues that organizations and employees face.

- List options for development needs analyses.

- Explain why succession planning has become more important.

- Identify several management development methods.

Developing Leaders Is a Challenge

Developing the talent in a workforce is challenging, but perhaps most demanding of all is developing future leadership talent for the organization. Development is different from training because it is not a one-time event, it is an ongoing process. One consultant suggests a rule of thumb: If an organization is going outside for leaders more than 20% of the time, its leadership development efforts are not effective.

Leader development programs are effective when addressing questions such as, What exactly do people need to be successful leaders? And what skill sets and behaviors do they require? Then the issues of succession planning, classroom training, coaching, work experiences, and appropriate pay must be dealt with in turn.

To emphasize the importance of leadership development, some firms base rewards for managers partly on how well the managers develop their employees, particularly those with leadership potential. In some cases, 10% to 20% of an executive's annual bonus may be based on how well talent under that executive is being developed. Another approach used is to consider the number of leaders an executive has developed and willingly given up to other parts of the organization—a "net talent exporter" approach. Contrast this approach to executives who "hoard" talent in their divisions so that they do not face turnover of their key staff.

Development, especially for leadership, has to be customized for each person so that individual strengths and areas for improvement are identified. The goal is to identify strengths that employees may not realize and also reveal areas where their abilities need to be enhanced. Every employee's development plan and activities will be different because each person has different capabilities. For the development of executives, it even may entail an external coach to assist individuals using a one-on-one process. Regardless of the means used, career development is important to both the organization and the individual, and doing it well is in the best interests of both.[1]

"Nothing is more important than growing your 'A' players and promptly dealing with your 'C' players."

—*Richard Brown*

Traditionally, career development efforts targeted managerial personnel to help them look beyond their current jobs and to prepare them for a variety of future jobs in the organization. But development for all employees, not just managers, is necessary for organizations to have the needed human resource capabilities for future growth and change.

Mergers, acquisitions, re-structurings, and layoffs all have influenced the way people and organizations look at careers and development. In the "new career," the individual—not the organization—manages her or his own development. Such self-development consists of personal educational experiences, training, organizational experiences, projects, and even changes in occupational fields.[2] Under this system, the individual defines career success, and the result may or may not coincide with the organizational view of success.

Organizations promote this "self-reliance" in career development by telling employees they should focus on creating employability for themselves in the uncertain future. However, employability must also be defined in such a way that it provides value for the employing organization. It is a dilemma of sorts that if employers give employees unrestricted access to development opportunities, employers may not be able to retain talent in the highly competitive labor markets of today.

▮▮ CAREERS AND CAREER PLANNING

Career Series of work-related positions a person occupies throughout life.

A **career** is the series of work-related positions a person occupies throughout life. People pursue careers to satisfy deeply individual needs. At one time, identifying with one employer seemed to fulfill many of those needs. Now, individuals and organizations view careers in distinctly different ways.

Indeed, in a few industries, changing jobs and companies every year or two is becoming more the norm than the exception. U.S. workers in high-demand fields often dictate their own circumstances to some extent. For instance, the average 30–35-year-old in the United States typically has already worked for up to seven different firms. However, workers in other fields change jobs infrequently. Physicians, teachers, economists, electricians and others do not change jobs as frequently. Valuable employees, deluged with job offers, switch jobs at a rate higher than in the past. Further, some individuals exhibit more loyalty to their careers than to an employer. Though organizations may use employment agreements containing non-compete clauses to put some restrictions on job hoppers, those clauses must be enforced in court, taking time and organizational resources. All these factors and more are changing how careers are defined and viewed.

Evolution of Careers

The old model of a career in which a person worked his or her way up the ladder in one organization is becoming rarer because smaller companies provide less room to move up. Also, various signs indicate that the patterns of individuals' work lives are changing in many areas: more freelancing, more working at home, more frequent job changes, more job opportunities but less security. Rather than letting jobs define their lives, more people set goals for the type of lives they want and then use jobs to meet those goals. However, for dual-career couples and working women, balancing work demands with personal and family responsibilities is a growing challenge.

For employers, career issues have changed too. The best people will not go to workplaces viewed as undesirable, because they do not have to do so. Employers must focus on retaining and developing talented workers by providing coaching, mentoring, and appropriate assignments.

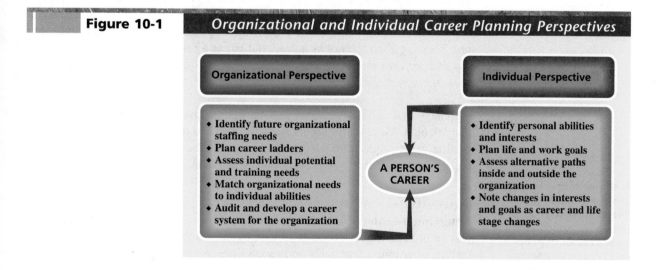 **Global Evolution of Careers** Insecurity caused by layoffs and downsizings marks a trend that stands in sharp contrast to the trend toward personal control over career goals. A greater number of older male American workers express fear of losing their jobs. This situation is not just a U.S. phenomenon. Many Japanese workers who have typically worked for one Japanese company their entire lives are experiencing similar job insecurity. In Europe, efforts to keep the traditional career system of job security are becoming more costly. Employers are pressuring European governments to dismantle outmoded labor rules that make eliminating employees difficult, while workers are pressuring the same governments to alleviate high unemployment rates. As a result, careers for many individuals contain both more flexibility and more insecurity.

Career Planning Perspectives

Careers are different and still evolving, and their evolution puts a premium on career development by both the employers and the employees. Employers that fail to help employees focus their careers in areas that benefit the organization may face shortages of employees who believe themselves to be ready to assume new jobs and responsibilities. Employees who fail to achieve psychological success, or a feeling of pride and accomplishment, in their careers may change careers, look outside work for "life success," or simply be unhappy. Effective career planning considers both organization-centered and individual-centered perspectives. Figure 10-1 summarizes the perspectives and interaction between the organizational and individual approaches to career planning. A look at each follows next.

Organization-centered career planning Career planning that focuses on identifying career paths that provide for the logical progression of people between jobs in an organization.

Organization-Centered Career Planning

Organization-centered career planning focuses on identifying career paths that provide for the logical progression of people between jobs in an organization. Individuals follow these paths as they advance in organizational units. For example, a person might enter the sales department as a sales representative, then be promoted to account director, to sales manager, and finally to vice president of sales.

Figure 10-1 *Organizational and Individual Career Planning Perspectives*

Organizational Perspective

- Identify future organizational staffing needs
- Plan career ladders
- Assess individual potential and training needs
- Match organizational needs to individual abilities
- Audit and develop a career system for the organization

A PERSON'S CAREER

Individual Perspective

- Identify personal abilities and interests
- Plan life and work goals
- Assess alternative paths inside and outside the organization
- Note changes in interests and goals as career and life stage changes

LOGGING ON...

Career Planner
This Web site can assist individuals with career planning.
www.careerplanner.com

Top management is responsible for developing career planning programs. A good program identifies career paths and includes performance appraisal, development, opportunities for transfer and promotion, and some planning for succession. To communicate with employees about opportunities and to help with planning, employers frequently use career workshops, a career "center" or newsletter, and career counseling. Individual managers must frequently play the role of coach and counselor in their direct contact with individual employees and within an HR-designed career management system.

For example, at one firm, major changes in the organization led to significant career dislocations. Previous career paths were closed, and management emphasized that employees had to take greater responsibility for their own careers. Into this potential chaos came managers who had been trained as "career coaches" for their employees. The entire process has changed from one in which employees "received" career planning to one in which they developed their own careers— roles for both managers and employees were changed.

The systems an employer uses to manage careers in the organization should be planned and managed in an integrated fashion to guide managers in developing employees' careers.[3] One such system is the career path, or "map," which is created and shared with the individual employee.

Career Paths Employees need to know their strengths and weakness, and they often discover those with some company-sponsored assessments. Then, career paths to develop the weak areas and fine-tune the strengths are developed. **Career paths** represent employees' movements through opportunities over time. While most career paths are thought of as leading upward, good opportunities also exist in cross-functional or horizontal directions.[4]

> **Career paths** Represent employees' movements through opportunities over time.

An innovative use of career paths called "skill supply chains" allows employees to move to other companies as they succeed where they are. For example, in Philadelphia, more than 200 employers (banks, fast-food restaurants, supermarkets, retailers, hotels, etc.) participate in a skill supply chain in the form of a "tiered employment" system aimed at underemployed entry-level workers. People enter the paths at tier 1 after receiving four weeks of customer service training, and find themselves flipping burgers or cleaning hotel rooms. They have to be successful for six months, with counselors checking attendance and performance. If they do well, they can apply for tier 2 positions either at their current employers or at another company in the system. After a year in tier 2, successful employees can apply for tier 3 jobs, which include entry-level store manager jobs. Viewing each job not as a dead end but as a rung on a ladder makes people stay and perform well. This kind of career path system is based on the same drivers as those that operate in a private employer's career path system.[5]

Organizational retrenchment and downsizing have changed career plans for many people. More and more individuals have had to face "career transitions"— in other words, they have had to find new jobs. These transitions have identified the importance of individual-centered career planning.

Individual-Centered Career Planning

Individual-centered career planning focuses on an individual's career rather than on organizational needs. It is done by the employees themselves when they analyze their individual goals and capabilities. Such efforts might consider situ-

> **Individual-centered career planning** Career planning focusing on an individual's career rather than on organizational needs.

ations both inside and outside the organization that could expand a person's career.[6] Although individuals are the only ones who can know for certain what they consider a successful career, even they are not always able to figure that out. For example, few college students enrolled in business programs know exactly what they want to do upon graduation; many can eliminate some types of jobs but might be interested in any of several others. For individuals to manage their own careers, three activities must happen:

- *Self-assessment:* Individuals need to think about what interests them, what they do not like, what they do well, and their strengths and weaknesses. Career advisors use a number of tools to help people understand themselves. Common professional tests include the Strong Interest Inventory to determine preferences among vocational occupations, and the Allport-Vernon-Lindzey Study of Values to identify a person's dominant values.
- *Feedback on reality:* Employees need feedback on how well they are doing, how their bosses see their capabilities, and where they fit in organizational plans for the future. One source of this information is through performance appraisal feedback.[7]
- *Setting of career goals:* Deciding on a desired path, setting some timetables, and writing down these items all set the stage for a person to pursue the career of choice. These career goals are supported by short-term plans for the individual to get the experience or training necessary to move forward toward the goals.

Because individual-centered career planning focuses on the individual, it may change depending on shifts in the individual's interests, abilities, circumstances, and family issues. A career based on such planning is referred to as "protean" because it is changeable. A successful "protean" career does not simply include *what* a person knows (although that knowledge keeps changing) but also includes *who* that person knows (through relationships and networking) and an understanding, based on experience, as to *why* activities are done the way they are done.[8] For individuals today, careers are rarely lived out in a single organizational setting. Instead, careers are "boundaryless" in that they might span several companies, industries, jobs, and projects.

How People Choose Careers

Four general individual characteristics affect how people make career choices. They are as follows:

- *Interests:* People tend to pursue careers that they believe match their interests. But over time, interests change for many people, and career decisions eventually are made based on special skills, abilities, and career paths that are realistic for them.
- *Self-image:* A career is an extension of a person's self-image, as well as a molder of it. People follow careers they can "see" themselves in and avoid those that do not fit with their perceptions of their talents, motives, and values.
- *Personality:* An employee's personality includes her or his personal orientation (for example, inclination to be realistic, enterprising, or artistic) and personal needs (including affiliation, power, and achievement needs). Individuals with certain personality types gravitate to different clusters of occupations.

- *Social backgrounds:* Socioeconomic status and the educational levels and occupations of a person's parents are included in that person's social background. Children of a physician or a welder know from a parent what that job is like and may either seek or reject it based on how they view the parent's job.

Less is known about how and why people choose specific organizations than about why they choose specific careers. One obvious factor is timing—the availability of a job when the person is looking for work. The amount of information available about alternatives is an important factor as well. Beyond these issues, people seem to pick an organization on the basis of a "fit" between the climate of the organization as they view it and their own personal characteristics, interests, and needs.

General Career Progression

The typical career of many individuals today probably includes different positions, transitions, and organizations—more so than in the past, when employees were less mobile and organizations were more stable as long-term employers. Therefore, it is useful to think about general patterns in people's lives and the effects on their careers.

Many theorists in adult development describe the first half of life as the young adult's quest for competence and for a way to make a mark in the world. According to this view, a person attains happiness during this time primarily through achievement and the acquisition of capabilities. The second half of life is different. Once the adult starts to measure time from the expected end of life rather than from the beginning, the need for competence and acquisition changes to the need for integrity, values, and well-being. For many people, internal values take precedence over external scorecards or accomplishments such as wealth and job title status. In addition, mature adults already possess certain skills, so their focus may shift to interests other than skills acquisition. Career-ending concerns, such as life after retirement, reflect additional shifts. Figure 10-2 shows a model identifying general career and life periods.

Contained within this life pattern is the idea that careers and lives are not predictably linear but cyclical. Individuals experience periods of high stability, fol-

| **Figure 10-2** | *General Career Periods* |

CAREER STAGE

Characteristics	Early Career	Mid-Career	Late Career	Career End
Age group	+/− 20 years	30–40 years	+/− 50 years	60–70 years
Needs	Identifying interests, exploring several jobs	Advancing in career; lifestyle may limit options, growth, opportunities	Updating skills; individual is settled in; individual is a leader whose opinions are valued	Planning for retirement, examining non-work interests
Concerns	External rewards, acquiring more capabilities	Values, contribution, integrity, well-being	Mentoring, disengaging, organizational continuance	Retirement, part-time employment

lowed by transition periods of less stability, and by inevitable discoveries, disappointments, and triumphs. These cycles of structure and transition occur throughout individuals' lives and careers. This cyclical view may be an especially useful perspective for individuals affected by downsizing or early career plateaus in large organizations. Such a perspective argues for the importance of flexibility in an individual's career. It also emphasizes the importance of individuals' continuing to acquire more and diverse knowledge, skills, and abilities.

Career Transitions and HR

Three career transitions are of special interests to HR: organizational entry and socialization, transfers and promotions, and job loss. Starting as a new employee can be overwhelming. "Entry shock" is especially difficult for younger new hires who find the work world very different from school. Entry shock includes the following concerns:

◆ *Supervisors:* The boss/employee relationship is different from the student/teacher relationship.
◆ *Feedback:* In school, feedback is frequent and measurable, although it is not that way in most jobs.
◆ *Time:* School has short (quarter/semester) time cycles, whereas time horizons are longer at work.
◆ *The work:* Problems are more tightly defined at school; at work, the logistical and political aspects of solving problems are less certain.

Job loss has been most associated with downsizing, mergers, and acquisitions. Losing a job is a stressful event in one's career, frequently causing depression, anxiety, and nervousness. The financial implications and the effects on family can be extreme as well. Yet the potential for job loss continues to increase and should be considered in career decision making.[9]

Transfers and promotions offer opportunities for employees to develop. However, unlike new hires, employees who have moved to new positions are often expected to perform well immediately, though that may not be realistic. International transfers cause even more difficulties than in-country transfers for many.

LOGGING ON...

Being Abroad
This Web site, which is geared toward expatriate workers, contains useful information about working abroad and repatriation.
www.beingabroad.com

Repatriation
Planning, training, and reassignment of global employees to their home countries.

🌐 Global Career Development

Many expatriates experience anxiety about their continued career progression. Therefore, the international experiences of expatriates must offer benefits both to the employer and to the expatriate's career as well.[10] Firms sometimes address this issue by bringing expatriates back to the home country for development programs and interaction with other company managers and professionals. Another useful approach is to establish a mentoring system that matches an expatriate with a corporate executive at the headquarters.[11]

Repatriation Another global development is **repatriation,** which involves planning, training, and reassignment of global employees to their home countries. For example, after expatriates are brought home, they no longer receive special compensation packages available to them during their assignments, which means that they experience a net decrease in income, even if they receive promotions and pay increases. In addition to dealing with concerns about personal finances, returning expatriates must often re-acclimate to U.S. lifestyles, transportation services, and other cultural circumstances, especially if they have been living in less-developed countries.

Back in the home organization, repatriated employees must re-adjust to closer working and reporting relationships with other corporate employees. Often, ex-patriates have had a greater degree of flexibility, autonomy, and independent decision making than their counterparts in the United States.

Another major concern focuses on the organizational status of expatriates upon return. Many expatriates wonder what jobs they will have, whether their international experiences will be valued, and how they will be accepted back into the organization. Unfortunately, many global employers do a poor job of repatriation.[12] To counter this problem, some companies provide career planning, the mentoring programs mentioned earlier, and even guarantees of employment upon completion of foreign assignments.

Development Issues Global managers are more expensive than home-country managers, and more problematic as well. Most global firms have learned that it is often a mistake to staff foreign operations with only personnel from headquarters, and they quickly hire nationals to work in a country. For this reason, global management development must focus on developing local managers as well as global executives. Development areas typically include: cultural issues, running a business, leading and managing, handling problematic people, personal qualities, self, and career.

Late-Career/Retirement Issues

Whether retirement comes at age 50 or age 70, it can require a major adjustment for many people. Some areas of emotional adjustment faced by many retirees include: self-direction, a need to belong, sources of achievement, personal space, and goals. To help address concerns over these issues, as well as anxieties about finances, some employers offer pre-retirement planning seminars for employees. Such seminars may make retirement less frightening for some and more possible for others.[13]

U.S. companies will face a severe shortage of badly needed skills in the coming decade unless they act now to convince top-performing older employees to delay or phase in their retirement.[14] Sixty-eight percent of full-time U.S. workers expect to work past age 65.[15] However, unless companies begin to make plans for using their older employees after retirement, those employees may be working for someone else.[16]

Career development for people toward the ends of their careers may be managed in a number of ways.[17] Phased-in retirement, consulting arrangements, and callback of some retirees as needed all act as means for gradual disengagement between the organization and the individual.

In an attempt to be mindful of the problems that retirement poses for some individuals, organizations are experimenting with phased retirement through gradually reduced workweeks and increased vacation time, accompanied by appropriate pay adjustments. These and other pre-retirement and post-retirement programs help individuals transition to a useful retirement and may keep experienced people available to the organization for a longer time.

However, phased retirement (which is widely seen as a good situation for all involved) faces a considerable obstacle in current pension law. Under many pension plans employees who are working may not receive pension benefits until they reach the normal retirement age. For example, a 54-year-old employee cannot cut back to 20 hours a week and collect a monthly retirement benefit. Benefits can be paid only when employment ceases. Future changes will require legislative and regulatory action.[18]

The phenomenon of "forced" early retirement often occurs as a result of downsizings and organizational restructurings. These events have required thousands of individuals, including many managers and professionals, to determine what is important to them while still active and healthy. As a result, some of the "younger retirees" begin second careers rather than focusing primarily on leisure activities or travel. To be successful with early retirement, management must avoid several legal issues such as forced early retirement and pressuring workers over age 55 to resign.[19]

Women and Careers

According to the U.S. Bureau of Labor Statistics, the percentage of women in the workforce has more than doubled since 1970, and will reach 48% by 2010. Women are found in all occupations and jobs, but their careers may have a different element than those of men. Women give birth to children, and in most societies are also primarily responsible for taking care of the children. The effect of this biology and sociology is that women's careers are often interrupted for child birth and child rearing.

The career approach for women frequently is to work hard before children arrive, step off the career track to be at home with the kids when they are young, and go back to work with a job that allows flexibility when they are older. This approach is referred to as "sequencing." But some women who sequence are concerned that the job market will not welcome them when they return, or that the time away will hurt their advancement chances. For example, Jennifer Lee was torn between two loves—her career as a hardware designer and her 10-month-old baby girl. She chose to stay home. Two years later, she still wrestles with her decision. She vacillates between feeling that she is doing what is right for her two daughters and wondering how she ended up at home. Her experience as a stay-at-home mom has been "halfway horrible," leaving her feeling isolated and frustrated. "My children are growing and will have a life. And I'll have a life again one day," she says.[20]

The interaction and conflicts among home, family, and a career affects the average woman differently than it does men.[21] By the time men and women have been out of school for six years, women have worked on average 30% less time than men. Sixteen years out of school, women average half as much work experience as men.[22] These and other career differences provide different circumstances for many females. Employers can tap into the female labor market to a greater extent with child care, flexible work policies, and a general willingness to be accommodative.

▉ SPECIAL CAREER ISSUES FOR ORGANIZATIONS AND INDIVIDUALS

The goals and perspectives in career planning may differ for organizations and individuals, but three issues can be problematic for both, although for different reasons. Those are career plateaus (or the lack of opportunity to move up), dealing with technical professionals who do not want to go into management, and dual-career couples.

Career Plateaus

Those who do not change jobs may face another problem: career plateaus. As the baby-boomer generation reaches mid-life and beyond, and as large employers cut back on their workforces, increasing numbers of employees find themselves "stuck" at a certain career level or "plateau." This plateauing may seem like a sign of failure to some people, and plateaued employees can cause problems for employers if their frustrations affect their job performance.

Many workers define career success in terms of upward mobility. As the opportunities to move up decrease, some employers try to convince employees they can find job satisfaction in lateral movement. Such moves can be reasonable if employees learn new skills that increase individual marketability in case of future layoffs, termination, or organizational re-structurings.[23]

One strategy for individuals to get off career plateaus is to take seminars and university courses. This approach may reveal new opportunities for plateaued employees. Rotating workers to other departments is another way to deal with career plateaus. A computer chip manufacturer instituted a formal "poaching" program that encouraged managers to recruit employees from other departments, thereby giving employees greater opportunities to experience new challenges without having to leave the employer. Some plateaued individuals change careers and go into other lines of work altogether.[24] Figure 10-3 shows a "portable" career path that can include major changes to deal with being plateaued. In summary, plateaued employees present a particular challenge for employers. They can affect morale if they become negative, but they may also represent valuable resources that are not being well used.

Technical and Professional Workers

Technical and professional workers, such as engineers, scientists, physical therapists, and IT systems experts, present a special challenge for organizations.[25] Many of these individuals want to stay in their technical areas rather than enter management; yet advancement in many organizations frequently requires a move into management. Most of these people like the idea of the responsibility and opportunity associated with advancement, but they do not want to leave the professional and technical puzzles and problems at which they excel.

The dual-career ladder is an attempt to solve this problem. As shown in Figure 10-4, a **dual-career ladder** is a system that allows a person to advance up either a management ladder or a corresponding ladder on the technical/professional side of a career. Dual-career ladders are now used at IBM and many other firms.

Dual-career ladder
System that allows a person to advance up either a management ladder or a corresponding ladder on the technical/professional side of a career.

Figure 10-3		"Portable" Career Path		
Beginning	**Expanding**	**Changing**	**Sustaining**	**Concluding**
Spend several years at large company to learn skills and build network	Use networking to develop broader skills and make contacts; establish good reputation	Change industries, or go to work for smaller companies; start a company	Refresh skills; take a sabbatical; go back to school; gain experience in non-profit organizations	Move to appealing projects as a temporary employee or subcontractor

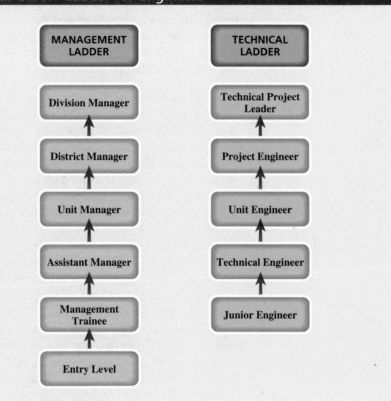

Figure 10-4 *Dual-Career Ladder for Engineers*

They are most common in technology-driven industries such as pharmaceuticals, chemicals, computers, and electronics. For instance, a telecommunications firm created a dual-career ladder in its data processing department to reward talented technical people who do not want to move into management. Different tracks, each with attractive job titles and pay opportunities, are provided.

Unfortunately, the technical/professional ladder is sometimes viewed as "second-class citizenship" within the organization. For a second or third career track to be taken seriously, the standards applied to technical/professional promotions must be just as rigorous as those applied to management promotions.

Dual-Career Couples

As the number of women in the workforce, particularly in professional careers, continues to increase, so does the number of dual-career couples. The U.S. Bureau of Labor Statistics estimates that 81% of all couples are dual-career couples. Marriages in which both mates are managers, professionals, or technicians doubled over the past two decades. Problem areas for dual-career couples include family issues and job transfers causing relocations.[26]

For dual-career couples with children, family issues may conflict with career progression. Thus, in job transfer situations, one partner's flexibility may depend on what is "best" for the family. Companies may consider part-time work, flex-time, and work-at-home arrangements as possible options, especially for parents with younger children.

It is important that the career development problems of dual-career couples be recognized as early as possible, especially if they involve transfer of locations. Early planning by employees and their supervisors can prevent crises from occurring. Whenever possible, having both partners involved in planning, even when one is not employed by the company, has been found to enhance the success of such efforts.[27]

Relocation of Dual-Career Couples Traditionally, employees accepted transfers as part of upward mobility in organizations. However, for some dual-career couples, the mobility required because of one partner's transfer often interferes with the other's career. In addition to having two careers, dual-career couples often have established support networks of co-workers, friends, and business contacts to cope with both their careers and their personal lives. Relocating one partner in a dual-career couple may mean upsetting this carefully constructed network for the other person or creating a "commuting" relationship.

Recruiting a member of a dual-career couple may mean having an equally attractive job available for the candidate's partner at the new location. Dual-career couples may lose some income when relocating; thus, they often have higher expectations, request more help, and expect higher salaries when asked to do so. In a company without a partner-assistance program, an employee may be hesitant to ask for services for a partner or may turn down a relocation request. Because the dual-career family has not been the norm for very long, traditional role expectations remain. In some cases, male employees may fear they will appear "unmanly" should their partners refuse to defer in support of career changes. On the other hand, some female employees may feel guilty about violating the traditional concept of male career dominance when they move and males must quit their jobs to follow.

Global Transfers Special difficulties exist when the transfer is overseas.[28] For example, a spouse who wants to work may not be able to get a work permit, may find that local residents have priority in the job market, or may find incompatible certification/licensing.

When setting HR policies on employee relocation assistance, organizations must consider the concerns of dual-career couples. The following approaches can help them do so:

- Paying employment agency fees for the relocating partner
- Paying for a designated number of trips for the partner to look for a job in the proposed new location
- Helping the partner find a job in the same company or in another division or subsidiary of the company
- Developing computerized job banks to share with other companies in the area that list partners available for job openings

DEVELOPING HUMAN RESOURCES

Development represents efforts to improve employees' abilities to handle a variety of assignments and to cultivate employees' capabilities beyond those required by the current job. Development benefits both organizations and individuals. Employees and managers with appropriate experiences and abilities

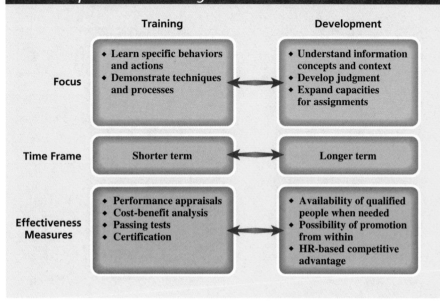

Figure 10-5 | *Development vs. Training*

	Training	Development
Focus	• Learn specific behaviors and actions • Demonstrate techniques and processes	• Understand information concepts and context • Develop judgment • Expand capacities for assignments
Time Frame	Shorter term	Longer term
Effectiveness Measures	• Performance appraisals • Cost-benefit analysis • Passing tests • Certification	• Availability of qualified people when needed • Possibility of promotion from within • HR-based competitive advantage

Development
Efforts to improve employees' abilities to handle a variety of assignments and to cultivate employees' capabilities beyond those required by the current job.

LOGGING ON...

Training and Development Community Center
This Web site provides over 300 Web site links for training and development.
www.tcm.com/trdev/

may enhance organizational competitiveness and the ability to adapt to a changing environment. In the development process, individuals' careers also may evolve and gain new or different focuses.

Development differs from training. It is possible to train most people to run a copy machine, answer customer service questions, drive a truck, operate a computer, or assemble a radio. However, development in areas such as judgment, responsibility, decision making, and communication presents a bigger challenge. These areas may or may not develop through life experiences of individuals. A planned system of development experiences for all employees, not just managers, can help expand the overall level of capabilities in an organization. Figure 10-5 profiles development and compares it with training.

At the organizational level of analysis, executives craft the broader organizational strategies and should establish a system for developing the people to manage and achieve those identified strategies. Development must be tied to this strategic planning because the firm needs to develop appropriate talents to carry out the plans. Successful HR development focuses on employee and managerial succession on several levels and in several different pathways as part of that development.

Currently, more jobs take on the characteristics of *knowledge work.* Workers in these jobs combine mastery of technical expertise with the ability to work in teams, form relationships with customers, and analyze their own practices. Managing such jobs involves guiding and integrating increasingly autonomous, highly skilled people.

HR planning anticipates the movement of people in the organization due to retirements, promotions, and transfers. Also, it helps identify the capabilities that will be needed by the organization in the future and the development necessary for people to be available to meet those needs. Figure 10-6 on the next page illustrates the HR development process.

Figure 10-6   *HR Development Process in an Organization*

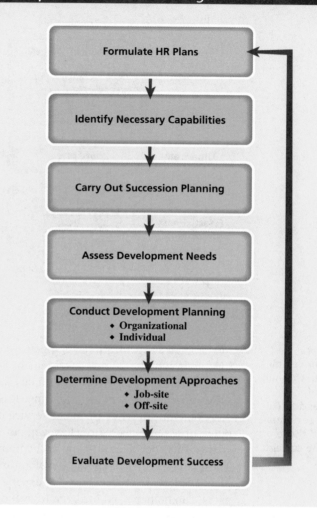

"Make or Buy"?

To some extent, employers face a "make-or-buy" choice: develop ("make") competitive human resources, or hire ("buy") them already developed from somewhere else. Current trends indicate that technical and professional people usually are hired because of the amount of skill development already achieved, rather than because of their ability to learn or their behavioral traits. Many organizations show an apparent preference for buying rather than making scarce employees in today's labor market. However, hiring rather than developing human resource capabilities may not contribute to a strategy of sustained competitive advantage through human resources. Like any financial decision, the make-or-buy decision can be quantified and calculated when some assumptions are made about time and costs.

Developing Specific Capabilities/Competencies

Exactly what kind of development individuals might require to expand their capabilities depends on both the individuals and the capabilities needed. Some important and common management capabilities often include an action orientation, quality decision-making skills, ethical values, and technical skills. Ability to build teams, develop subordinates, direct others, and deal with uncertainty are equally important but much less commonly developed capabilities for successful managers. For some tech specialties (tech support, database administration, network design, etc.), certain non-technical abilities must be developed as well: ability to work under pressure, work independently, solve problems quickly, and use past knowledge in a new situation.

Development frequently includes a focus on enhancing judgment and responsibility. How exactly to develop an "action orientation" or the "ability to work under pressure" must be addressed by organizations. These capabilities cannot successfully be taught in a course, and not everyone will develop them. As a result, development is more difficult in certain areas than in others.[29]

One point about development is clear: in studies that asked employees what they want out of their jobs, training and development ranked at or near the top. Because the assets individuals have to sell are their knowledge, skills, and abilities, many people view the development of their KSAs as an important part of their organizational package. This type of development works for many but not all.

Lifelong Learning

Learning and development are closely linked. For most people, lifelong learning and development are much more likely and desirable. For many professionals, lifelong learning may mean meeting continuing education requirements to keep certified. For example, lawyers, CPAs, teachers, dentists, and others must complete continuing education requirements in most states to keep their licenses to practice. For other employees, learning and development may involve training to expand existing skills and to prepare for different jobs, for promotions, or even for new jobs after retirement.[30]

Assistance from employers for needed lifelong development typically comes through programs at work, including tuition reimbursement programs. However, much of lifelong learning is voluntary, takes place outside work hours, and is not always formal.[31] Although it may have no immediate relevance to a person's current job, learning often can enhance the individual's confidence, ideas, or enthusiasm.[32]

Re-development

Whether due to a desire for career change or because the employer needs different capabilities, people may shift jobs in mid-life or mid-career. Re-developing or re-training people in the capabilities they need is logical and important. In the last decade, the number of college enrollees over the age of 35 has increased dramatically. But helping employees go back to college is only one way of re-developing them. Some companies offer re-development programs to recruit experienced workers from other fields. For example, different firms needing truck drivers, reporters, and IT workers have sponsored second-career programs. Public-sector employers have been using re-development opportunities as one recruiting tool as well.

Company Web Sites and Career Development

Many employers have Web sites, and on some of those Web sites is a section labeled "careers." The careers section can be used for many purposes, including listing open jobs for current employees looking to change jobs. The Web site is a link to the external world, but it can also be a link to existing employee development.

Sites also can be used for career assessment, information, and instruction.[33] Among the largest organizations in the U.S., it is estimated that 90% have a career section on the company Web site and 80% display open positions.[34] When designing Web sites, firms should consider the usefulness of the careers section for development.

▌▌ DEVELOPMENT NEEDS ANALYSES

Like employee training, employee development begins with analyses of the needs of both the organization and the individuals. Either the company or the individual can analyze what a given person needs to develop. The goal, of course, is to identify strengths and weaknesses. Methods that organizations use to assess development needs include assessment centers, psychological testing, and performance appraisals.

Assessment Centers

Assessment centers are collections of instruments and exercises designed to diagnose individuals' development needs.[35] Organizational leadership uses assessment centers for both developing and selecting managers. Many types of employers use assessment centers.

Assessment centers
Collections of instruments and exercises designed to diagnose individuals' development needs.

In a typical assessment-center experience, an individual spends two or three days away from the job performing many assessment activities. These activities might include role-playing, pencil-and-paper tests, cases, leaderless-group discussions, computer-based simulations, management games, and peer evaluations. Frequently, they also include in-basket exercises, in which the individual handles typical problems coming across a manager's desk. For the most part, the exercises represent situations that require the use of managerial skills and behaviors. During the exercises, several specially trained judges observe the participants.

Assessment centers provide an excellent means for determining management potential. Management and participants often praise them because they are likely to overcome many of the biases inherent in interview situations, supervisor ratings, and written tests. Experience shows that key variables such as leadership, initiative, and supervisory skills cannot be measured with paper-and-pencil tests alone. Assessment centers also offer the advantage of helping identify employees with potential in large organizations. Supervisors may nominate people for the assessment center, or employees may volunteer. For talented people, the opportunity to volunteer is invaluable because supervisors may not recognize their potential interests and capabilities.

Assessment centers can also raise concerns.[36] Some managers may use the assessment center to avoid making difficult promotion decisions. Suppose a plant supervisor has personally decided that an employee is not qualified for promotion. Rather than be straightforward and inform the employee, the supervisor sends the employee to the assessment center, hoping the report will show that the employee is unqualified for promotion. Problems between the employee and the supervisor may worsen if the employee earns a positive report. Using the assessment center for this purpose does not aid the development of the employee and is not recommended.

Psychological Testing

Psychological pencil-and-paper tests have been used for several years to determine employees' development potential and needs. Intelligence tests, verbal and mathematical reasoning tests, and personality tests are often given. Even a test that supposedly assesses common sense is available. Psychological testing can furnish useful information on individuals about such factors as motivation, reasoning abilities, leadership style, interpersonal response traits, and job preferences.

The biggest problem with psychological testing lies in interpretation, because untrained managers, supervisors, and workers usually cannot accurately interpret test results. After a professional scores the tests and reports the scores to someone in the organization, untrained managers may attach their own meanings to the results. Also, some psychological tests are of limited validity, and test takers can easily fake desirable responses. Thus, psychological testing is appropriate only when the testing and feedback process is closely supervised by a qualified professional.

Performance Appraisals

Well-done performance appraisals can be a source of development information. Performance data on productivity, employee relations, job knowledge, and other relevant dimensions can be gathered in such assessments. As noted in Chapter 11, appraisals designed for development purposes may be more useful in aiding individual employee development than appraisals designed strictly for administrative purposes.

■ SUCCESSION PLANNING

Succession planning
Process of identifying a longer-term plan for the orderly replacement of key employees.

Planning for the succession of key executives, managers, and other employees is an important part of HR development. **Succession planning** is the process of identifying a longer-term plan for the orderly replacement of key employees. The need to replace key employees results from promotions, transfers, retirements, deaths, disabilities, departures, and other events. Succession planning often focuses on top management, such as ensuring a CEO successor.[37] However, limiting succession planning just to top executive jobs is a mistake. For instance, in a health-care institution, identifying successors for accounting manager, marketing director, admissions supervisor, IT technician, physical therapist, and other key jobs is just as crucial as succession planning for the top executive jobs.

Succession in Small and Closely Held Organizations

Succession planning can be especially important in small and medium-sized firms, but studies show that few of these firms formalize succession plans. In fact, more than half of the respondents in one study named lack of succession planning as the biggest threat facing small businesses.[38] In closely held family firms (those that are not publicly traded on stock exchanges), many CEOs plan to pass the business on to a family member. Most of these firms would benefit from planning for orderly succession. Addressing development needs of the successor also helps to avoid a host of potential problems for both the organization and family member relationships.[39]

Succession Planning Process

Whether in small or large firms, succession planning is linked to strategic HR planning through the process shown in Figure 10-7. In that process, both the quantity and the capabilities of potential successors must be linked to organizational strategies and plans. For example, at Dole Food, with 61,000 workers in 90 countries, there is talent all over the world, but the company did not have comprehensive knowledge of who the managers were or what they could do. Dole is a highly decentralized company and feels the need for a succession planning process to bring forward the best for advancement. Part of its solution includes Web-based software to support the process.[40]

Two coordinated activities begin the actual process of succession planning. First, the development of preliminary replacement charts ensures that the right individuals with sufficient capabilities and experience to perform the targeted jobs are available at the right time. Replacement charts (similar to depth charts used by football teams) both show the backup "players" at each position and identify positions without a current qualified backup player. The charts identify who could take over key jobs if someone leaves, retires, dies unexpectedly, or otherwise creates a vacancy. Second, assessment of the capabilities and interests of current employees provides information that can be placed into the preliminary replacement charts. The HR Perspective discusses the importance of successful planning.

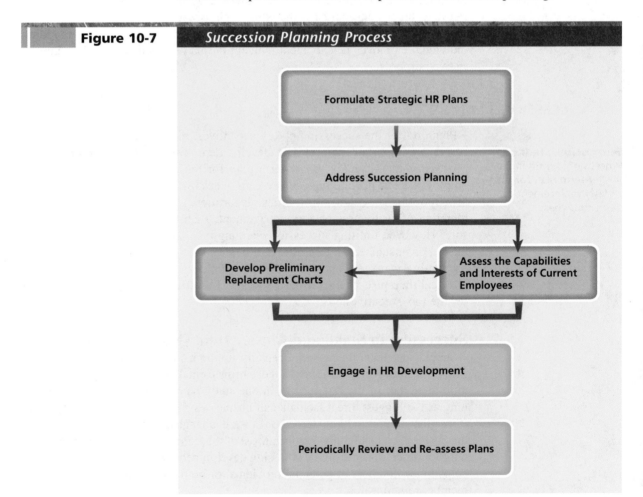

Figure 10-7 *Succession Planning Process*

Succession Planning Is Booming

Succession planning has become a greater concern in many U.S. firms as the supply of executives and managers is becoming more scarce. A huge shortage is ahead as the baby-boomer generation begins to retire. The boomers will be ages 46–64 by the year 2010, and their share of the labor market will drop from 49% in 2000 to 38% in 2010. About 24 million of them will leave their employers in the next decade. The critical concern in many firms is that these departing managers and executives represent some of the most experienced leaders.

Often the employees in the firms tapped to take their places are currently in their 30s and 40s and have 10–15 years' work experience. But these employees often have work/family issues that impact their careers. In particular,

some women in this group may have small children and may want to work part-time or shorter weeks. However, their jobs may not be compatible with such flexibility, which may affect succession planning and leadership development opportunities for them.

Succession planning is also important for the survival of a company; failing to plan for future leaders can leave a real gap. One firm that addressed this issue is Deloitte & Touche, a large accounting firm, where 17% of current partners and directors are women, up from 6.5% in 1993. "Succession planning is important for us because we feel strongly we need diversity in leadership," one director notes. That is why so many organizations want to plan rather than leave succession to chance.[41]

This traditional approach to succession planning does not always work in each employer. For example, at PepsiCo, a study showed that the succession planning process was taking too much time, so the company developed "acceleration pools." These pools focus on developing candidates for the executive level, rather than targeting one or two people for specific jobs. An executive resource board is responsible for placing pool members into situations where they can develop.[42] Other companies do succession planning as well. Eli Lilly, Dow Chemical, Bank of America, and Sonoco Products all use a system that identifies critical positions for development as part of the succession planning process.[43]

CHOOSING A DEVELOPMENT APPROACH

The most common development approaches can be categorized under two major headings: job-site development and off-site development. Both are appropriate in developing managers and other employees. Investing in human intellectual capital, whether on or off the job, becomes imperative for organizations as "knowledge work" aspects increase for almost all employers. Yet, identifying the right mix and approaches for development needs remains an art rather than a science.

Job-Site Development Approaches

All too often, unplanned and perhaps useless activities pass as development on the job. To ensure that the desired development actually occurs, managers must plan and coordinate development efforts. A number of job-site development methods can be used.

THOMSON
★
WEST ™

Coaching The oldest on-the-job development technique is **coaching,** which is the training and feedback given to employees by immediate supervisors. Coaching involves a continual process of learning by doing. For coaching to be effective, employees and their supervisors or managers must have a healthy and open relationship. Many firms conduct formal training courses to improve the coaching skills of their managers and supervisors.

Unfortunately, organizations may be tempted to implement coaching without any planning at all. Even someone who is good at a job or a particular part of a job will not necessarily be able to coach someone else to do it well. "Coaches" can easily fall short in guiding learners systematically, even if they know which experiences are best. Often the coach's job responsibilities take priority over learning and coaching of subordinates. Also, the intellectual component of many capabilities might be better learned from a book or a course before coaching occurs.

Sometimes, "executive" coaches, hired by either individual executives or employers, work with individual managers and executives. These outside coaches critique and advise the individuals. They are discussed along with management development, later in this chapter.

Committee Assignments Assigning promising employees to important committees may broaden their experiences and can help them understand the personalities, issues, and processes governing the organization. For instance, employees on a safety committee can gain a greater understanding of safety management, which would help them to become supervisors. They may also experience the problems involved in maintaining employee safety awareness. However, managers need to guard against committee assignments that turn into time-wasting activities.

Job Rotation The process of shifting a person from job to job is called **job rotation.** In some firms, job rotation is unplanned. In other organizations, managers follow elaborate charts and schedules, precisely planning a rotation program for each employee. Regardless of the approach, job rotation is widely used as a development technique. For example, a promising young manager may spend three months in the plant, three months in corporate planning, and three months in purchasing. When properly handled, such job rotation fosters a greater understanding of the organization.[44]

A disadvantage of job rotation is that it can be expensive because a substantial amount of time is taken when trainees change positions, because they must become acquainted with different people and techniques in each new unit.

When opportunities for promotion are scarce, job rotation through lateral transfers may help rekindle enthusiasm and develop employees' talents. The best lateral moves do one or more of the following: move the person into the core business, provide closer contact with customers, or teach new skills or perspectives.

"Assistant-to" Positions Some firms create "assistant-to" positions, which are staff positions immediately under a manager. Through such jobs, trainees can work with outstanding managers they might not otherwise have met. Some organizations set up "junior boards of directors" or "management cabinets" to which trainees may be appointed. These assignments provide useful experiences if they present challenging or interesting assignments to trainees.

On-line Development Technology can provide an appropriate tool for development. On-line development can take many forms, such as video conferencing, live chat rooms, document sharing, video and audio streaming, and Web-based courses. HR staff members can facilitate on-line development by providing a "learning portal," which is a centralized Web site for news, information, course listings, and materials.

On-line development allows participation in courses previously out of reach due to geographic or cost considerations. It allows costs to be spread over a larger number of people, and it can be combined with virtual reality and other technological tools to make presentations more interesting. It can eliminate travel as well. However, because of the time needed to develop on-line materials or perhaps because those materials are not seen as clearly appropriate for development efforts, on-line development is not widely used.

Corporate Universities and Career Development Centers Large organizations may use "corporate universities" to develop managers or other employees. Corporate universities take various forms. Sometimes regarded as little more than fancy packaging for company training, they often do not provide a degree, accreditation, or graduation in the traditional sense. A related alternative, partnerships between companies and traditional universities, continues where the universities design and teach specific courses for employers.

Career development centers are often set up to coordinate in-house programs and programs provided by suppliers. They may include assessment data for individuals, career goals and strategies, coaching, seminars, and on-line approaches.

Learning Organization Knowledge-based organizations, which deal primarily with ideas and information, must have employees who are experts at one or more conceptual tasks. These employees continuously learn and solve problems in their areas of expertise. Developing such employees requires an "organizational learning capacity" based on a culture of solving problems and learning new ways not previously used.[45] Figure 10-8 depicts some possible means for developing employees in a learning organization.

It is difficult to describe a "learning organization," except to say that it is an employer in which development occurs through shared information, culture, and leadership that values learning. It focuses on employees who want to learn to develop new capabilities. A learning mindset is probably difficult to introduce into

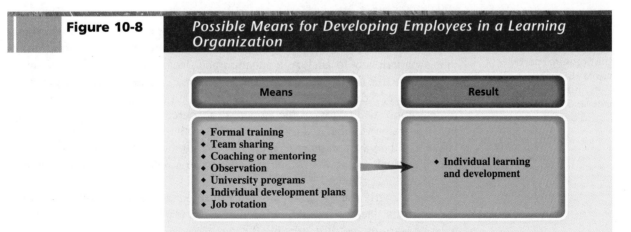

Figure 10-8 *Possible Means for Developing Employees in a Learning Organization*

Means

Result

- Formal training
- Team sharing
- Coaching or mentoring
- Observation
- University programs
- Individual development plans
- Job rotation

- Individual learning and development

an organization where it does not exist. But where it does exist, it represents the ultimate potential for development. It remains a theoretical and somewhat idealistic model in HR development.

Off-Site Development Approaches

Off-the-job development techniques give individuals opportunities to get away from the job and concentrate solely on what is to be learned. Moreover, contact with others who are concerned with somewhat different problems and come from different organizations may provide employees with new and different perspectives. Various off-site methods are used.

Classroom Courses and Degrees Most off-the-job development programs include some classroom instruction. Most people are familiar with classroom training, which gives it the advantage of being widely accepted. But the lecture system sometimes used in classroom instruction encourages passive listening and reduced learner participation, which is a distinct disadvantage. Sometimes trainees have little opportunity to question, clarify, and discuss the lecture material. The effectiveness of classroom instruction depends on multiple factors: group size, trainees' abilities, instructors' capabilities and styles, and subject matter.

Organizations often send employees to externally sponsored seminars or professional courses, such as those offered by the American Management Association. Many organizations also encourage continuing education by reimbursing employees for the costs of college courses. Tuition reimbursement programs provide incentive for employees to study for advanced degrees, such as MBAs, through evening and weekend classes, outside their regular workdays.

Human Relations Training This type of training attempts to prepare supervisors to deal with "people problems" brought to them by their employees. The training focuses on the development of the human relations skills a person needs to work well with others. Most human relations programs typically are aimed at new or relatively inexperienced first-line supervisors and middle managers. They cover motivation, leadership, employee communication, and other behavioral topics.

The most common reason employees fail after being promoted to management is poor teamwork with subordinates and peers. Other common reasons for management failure include not understanding expectations, failure to meet goals, difficulty adjusting to management responsibilities, and inability to balance work and home lives.

Simulation Technique that requires participants to analyze a situation and decide the best course of action according to data given.

Simulations (Business Games) Another development approach uses business games, or simulations, which are available commercially. A **simulation** requires participants to analyze a situation and decide the best course of action according to the data given. Often simulations are computer-interactive in nature. For example, individuals or teams draw up marketing plans for an organization to determine such factors as the amount of resources to allocate for advertising, product design, selling, and sales effort. The participants make a variety of decisions, and then the computer tells them how well they did in relation to competing individuals or teams. Managers have also used simulations to diagnose organizational problems.

When properly used, a simulation is a valuable management development tool. However, the lack of realism can diminish the learning experience. The focus must be learning, not just "playing the game."

Sabbaticals and Leaves of Absence A **sabbatical** is paid time off the job to develop and rejuvenate oneself. Popular for many years in the academic world, sabbaticals have been adopted in the business community as well. About 19% of U.S. corporations offer sabbaticals.[46] Some firms give employees three to six months off with pay to work on "socially desirable" projects. Such projects have included leading training programs in urban ghettos, providing technical assistance in foreign countries, and participating in corporate volunteer programs to aid non-profit organizations.

Companies that offer sabbaticals speak well of the results. Positive reasons for sabbaticals are to help prevent employee burnout, offer advantages in recruiting and retention, and boost individual employee morale. One obvious disadvantage of paid sabbaticals is the cost. Also, the nature of the learning experience generally falls outside the control of the organization, leaving it somewhat to chance.

Outdoor Training Many organizations send executives and managers off to ordeals in the wilderness, called outdoor training. As development tools, the rationale for using these wilderness excursions, which can last seven days or longer, is that such experiences can increase self-confidence and help individuals re-evaluate personal goals and efforts.[47] For individuals in work groups or teams, shared risks and challenges outside the office environment can create a sense of teamwork. The challenges may include rock climbing in the California desert, white-water rafting on a river, backpacking in the Rocky Mountains, or handling a longboat off the coast of Maine.

Survival-type management development courses may have more impact than many other management seminars. But companies must consider the inherent perils. Some participants have been unable to handle the physical and emotional challenges associated with rappelling down a cliff or climbing a 40-foot tower. The decision to sponsor such programs should depend on the personalities of the employees involved.[48]

To be effective, a development approach must mesh with HR strategies. Figure 10-9 on the next page summarizes the major advantages and disadvantages of the various on-site and off-site approaches to development.

MANAGEMENT DEVELOPMENT

Although development is important for all employees, it is essential for managers. Effective management development imparts the knowledge and judgment needed by managers. Without appropriate development, managers may lack the capabilities to best deploy and manage resources (including employees) throughout the organization.

Experience plays a central role in management development. Indeed, experience often contributes more to the development of senior managers than does classroom training, because much of it occurs in varying circumstances on the job over time. Yet, in many organizations it is difficult to find managers for middle-level jobs. Some individuals refuse to take middle-management jobs. As a middle manager, "you're a backstop, caught in the middle between upper management and the workforce," a cost accounting manager (who quit management) noted. "I was told 50 hours a week was not enough and that I had to work my people harder. . . . The few dollars more were not worth the pain." Similarly, not all companies seem to take the time to develop their own executive-level managers. In-

Figure 10-9 | *Advantages and Disadvantages of Major Development Approaches*

JOB-SITE METHODS	ADVANTAGES	DISADVANTAGES
• Coaching	• Is natural and job related	• Can lack good coaches because they are difficult to find
• Committee assignments	• Involve participants in critical processes	• Can be time wasters
• Job rotation	• Gives excellent overview of the organization	• Has a long start-up time
• "Assistant-to" positions	• Provide exposure to an excellent manager	• May be difficult to set up because of possible shortage of good assignments
• On-line development	• Is flexible	• Occupies a niche that is not yet well defined
• Corporate universities / career development centers	• Can combine academic and real world at work	• May be "universities" in name only
• Learning organizations	• Has perhaps the ideal mindset for development	• Has a mindset that is essentially a theoretical, idealistic notion for most organizations

OFF-SITE METHODS	ADVANTAGES	DISADVANTAGES
• Classroom courses and degrees	• Is familiar and accepted; has status	• Does not always improve performance
• Human relations training	• Deals with important management skills	• Is difficult to measure for effectiveness
• Simulations (business games)	• Offers realism and integration	• May involve inappropriate "game playing"
• Sabbaticals and leaves of absence	• Are rejuvenating as well as developmental	• Is expensive; employees may lose contact with job
• Outdoor training	• Increases self-confidence and teamwork through physical challenges	• Is not appropriate for all because of physical nature; may be dangerous

stead, executives often are hired from the outside. Figure 10-10 shows experience-based sources of managers' learning and lists some lessons important in effectively developing middle-managers and upper-level managers.

Management Development Methods

A number of approaches are used to mold and enhance the experience that managers need to be effective. The most widely used methods are leadership development, management modeling, management coaching, management mentoring, supervisory development, and executive education.

Leadership Development An effective leader creates positive change and is important for an organization. But like all developmental capacities, leadership cannot be taught to everyone.

Many companies have leadership development programs—but a recent survey found that only about 25% of those programs were rated high for quality.[49] In addition, the failure rate of new executives is around 50% in the first 18 months and two-thirds in five years.[50] Clearly, there is a need for better leadership development. However, what many people think of as leadership is really supervision

Figure 10-10 | *Management Lessons Learned from Job Experience*

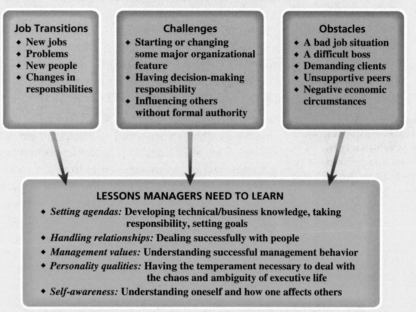

SOURCES OF MANAGERS' LEARNING

Job Transitions
- New jobs
- Problems
- New people
- Changes in responsibilities

Challenges
- Starting or changing some major organizational feature
- Having decision-making responsibility
- Influencing others without formal authority

Obstacles
- A bad job situation
- A difficult boss
- Demanding clients
- Unsupportive peers
- Negative economic circumstances

LESSONS MANAGERS NEED TO LEARN
- *Setting agendas:* Developing technical/business knowledge, taking responsibility, setting goals
- *Handling relationships:* Dealing successfully with people
- *Management values:* Understanding successful management behavior
- *Personality qualities:* Having the temperament necessary to deal with the chaos and ambiguity of executive life
- *Self-awareness:* Understanding oneself and how one affects others

and management—defining the job to be done and getting it done. Leadership is not only defining the job but also explaining why it must be done.

Management Modeling A common adage in management development says that managers tend to manage as they were managed. In other words, managers learn by behavior modeling, or copying someone else's behavior. This tendency is not surprising, because a great deal of human behavior is learned by modeling. Children learn by modeling the behaviors of parents and older children. Management development efforts can take advantage of natural human behavior by matching young or developing managers with appropriate models and then reinforcing the desirable behaviors exhibited by the learners. The modeling process involves more than straightforward imitation, or copying; it is considerably more complex. For example, one can learn what not to do by observing a model who does something wrong. Thus, exposure to both positive and negative models can benefit a new manager.

Management Coaching Coaching combines observation with suggestions. Like modeling, it complements the natural way humans learn. A brief outline of good coaching pointers often includes the following:

- Explaining appropriate behavior
- Making clear why actions were taken
- Accurately stating observations
- Providing possible alternatives/suggestions
- Following up and reinforcing behaviors used

In the context of management development, coaching involves a relationship between two managers for a period of time as they perform their jobs. Effective coaching requires patience and good communication skills.

A specific application of coaching is use of "executive coaching." Companies use executive coaches to help rising stars improve interpersonal skills or decision-making skills. In some cases they are used to help deal with problematic management styles. Executive coaches are predominately female and come from a psychology or counseling background. Some come to the office, but about half do their coaching by phone. Some coaches work for individual executives, but about three-quarters are paid by the executive's firm.[51] Coaches can serve many roles for a client by providing key questions and general directions.[52] Research on the effectiveness of coaching is scarce. The research that is available suggests that sometimes coaching can be beneficial.[53]

Management mentoring Relationship in which experienced managers aid individuals in the earlier stages of their careers.

Management Mentoring A method called **management mentoring** is a relationship in which experienced managers aid individuals in the earlier stages of their careers. Such a relationship provides an environment for conveying technical, interpersonal, and organizational skills from the more-experienced person to a designated less-experienced person. Not only does the inexperienced employee benefit, but the mentor may enjoy the challenge of sharing his or her wisdom.[54]

However, mentoring is not without its problems. Young minority managers frequently report difficulty finding mentors. Also, men generally show less willingness than women to be mentors. Further, mentors who are dissatisfied with their jobs and those who teach a narrow or distorted view of events may not help a young manager's development. Fortunately, many managers have a series of advisors or mentors during their careers and may find advantages in learning from the different mentors.[55] For example, the unique qualities of individual mentors may help less-experienced managers identify key behaviors in management success and failure. Further, those being mentored may find previous mentors to be useful sources for networking.[56] Figure 10-11 describes the four stages in most successful mentoring relationships.

Figure 10-11

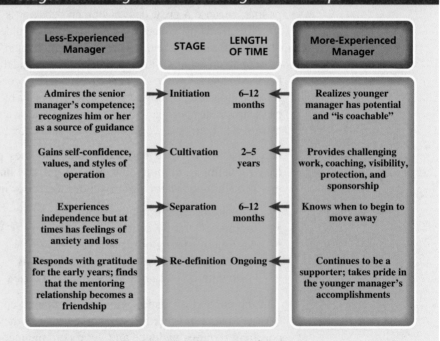

Stages in Management Mentoring Relationships

Less-Experienced Manager	STAGE	LENGTH OF TIME	More-Experienced Manager
Admires the senior manager's competence; recognizes him or her as a source of guidance	Initiation	6–12 months	Realizes younger manager has potential and "is coachable"
Gains self-confidence, values, and styles of operation	Cultivation	2–5 years	Provides challenging work, coaching, visibility, protection, and sponsorship
Experiences independence but at times has feelings of anxiety and loss	Separation	6–12 months	Knows when to begin to move away
Responds with gratitude for the early years; finds that the mentoring relationship becomes a friendship	Re-definition	Ongoing	Continues to be a supporter; takes pride in the younger manager's accomplishments

Management Mentoring and the Glass Ceiling In virtually all countries in the world, the proportion of women holding management jobs is lower than the proportion of men holding such jobs. The term *glass ceiling* has been used to describe the situation in which women fail to progress into top management positions. In the U.S. women are making slow but steady strides into management and the executive suite. Nationally, women hold 49% of managerial/professional positions and 12% of corporate officer positions, and those figures are higher in certain geographic regions.[57]

One approach to breaking through the glass ceiling is mentoring. For example, in some firms, women with mentors move up more often than those without mentors. Most of the literature on women and mentoring, based on various narratives of successful women executives, suggests that breaking the glass ceiling requires developing political sophistication, building credibility, refining a management style, and shouldering responsibilities. Women generally rate high in the skills needed for success where teamwork and partnering are important.

Supervisor Development At the beginning level for managerial development is the first-line supervisory job. It is often difficult to go from being one of the work group to being the boss. Further, the NYMs (new young managers), who are used to functioning as individual contributors, require new skills and mindsets to be successful supervisors.[58]

Development for supervisors may vary but usually contains common elements. The usual materials for supervisor training and development include several topics: basic management, performance evaluation, time management, conflict management, team building, and communication.

Executive Education Executives in an organization often face difficult jobs due to changing and unknown circumstances. "Churning" at the top of organizations and the stresses of executive jobs contribute to increased turnover in these positions. In an effort to decrease turnover, some organizations are experimenting with a relatively recent phenomenon: special education for executives. This type of training includes executive education traditionally offered by university business schools and adds strategy formulation, financial models, logistics, alliances, and global issues.

A female executive with Coca-Cola attended the four-day Harvard Business School program Women Leading Business. "My business is in a man's world—to have a group of peers, in one place, was very nice. And a good learning situation as well," she noted.[59] According to one survey, Harvard is in the number one place for executive education because of the nature and flexibility of its various programs.[60]

Problems with Management Development Efforts

Development efforts are subject to certain common mistakes and problems. Most of the management development problems in the United States have resulted from inadequate HR planning and a lack of coordination of HR development efforts.[61] Common problems include the following: failing to conduct adequate needs analysis, trying out fad programs or training methods, and substituting training for selecting qualified individuals.

Another common management development problem is **encapsulated development,** which occurs when an individual learns new methods and ideas in a development course and returns to a work unit that is still bound by old attitudes and methods. Therefore, the trainee cannot apply new ways to handle certain situations because of resistance from those having an investment in the status quo. The development was "encapsulated" in the classroom and is essentially not used on the job.

SUMMARY

- Career planning may focus on organizational needs, individual needs, or both.
- A person chooses a career according to interests, self-image, personality, social background, and other factors.
- A person's life is cyclical, as is his or her career. Looking at the two together offers a useful perspective for the future.
- Global career development has special challenges, including repatriation.
- Organizations increasingly are having to deal with individuals who have hit career plateaus, late career issues, and special issues with women employees.
- Technical employees sometimes may be able to follow dual-career ladders.
- Dual-career couples increasingly require relocation assistance for the partners of transferring employees.
- Development differs from training because it focuses on less tangible aspects of performance, such as attitudes and values.

- Successful development requires the support of top management and an understanding of how development relates to other HR activities.
- Assessment centers provide valid methods of assessing needs for management talent and development.
- Succession planning is the process that identifies how key employees are to be replaced.
- On-the job development methods include coaching, committee assignments, job rotation, assistant-to positions, on-line development, corporate universities/career development centers, and a learning mindset.
- Off-the-job development methods include classroom courses and degrees, human relations training, simulations, sabbaticals and leaves of absence, and outdoor training.
- Through mentoring and modeling, younger managers can acquire the skills and know-how necessary to be successful. Mentoring follows a four-stage progression in most cases.
- Supervisory development requires employees to develop new capabilities and mindsets to be successful.

REVIEW AND APPLICATION QUESTIONS

1. Identify problems that dual-career couples pose for employers and employees.
2. Why is succession planning important in businesses of all sizes today?
3. What two roles can be played by a company Web site with a careers section? Go to Hewlett-Packard's Web site, *www.jobshp.com*, as well as those of other firms, for examples.

LEARNING REVIEW

To check your knowledge of the chapter, review the following. (Answers after the supplemental case.) For more questions, see the Study Guide.

1. In recent years, the way people look at careers has changed. Now, the individual, not the organization, manages her or his own development. This switch has been caused by _____.
   a. an increase in moonlighting
   b. challenges to traditional ethical values
   c. corporate growth and international expansion
   d. mergers, acquisitions, re-structurings, and layoffs

2. Theorists in adult development believe that _____.
   a. lives and careers are predictably linear
   b. from early childhood, people have pre-ordained careers
   c. a person's career is the manifestation of the inner values affecting that person's life
   d. lives and careers must be viewed as cycles of structure and transition
3. A career plateau occurs when _____.
   a. a technical worker has no prospects for advancement
   b. a dual-career couple mutually agree to put their marriage ahead of their careers
   c. baby boomers reach mid-life and mid-career
   d. employees find themselves "stuck" at a career level

4. As a development technique, the best lateral transfers _____.
   a. provide a continual process of learning
   b. move the person into the core business
   c. ensure that trainees have an opportunity to deal with interesting assignments
   d. provide a monetary incentive for taking on new work

CASE

HENRICO COUNTY, VIRGINIA, AND SUCCESSION ISSUES

Henrico County, Virginia had a problem. The workforce was aging and there were fewer young employees ready to take their places. The County employs around 3,800 employees plus close to 1,000 temporary workers. Among upper management personnel, 29% were eligible for full retirement by 2005, and almost another 50% could retire then too, but with reduced benefits. To deal with the problem, the County designed a succession planning program. The goal was to provide opportunities for all employees, but especially for managers, to learn what development need they had to address in order to be ready to advance in the organization. The program had two parts to its design.

In the first part the County focused on *employee* needs. A variety of tools were available to help employees with their development efforts: ways to identify their interests, a "gap analysis" indicating how other people saw them, identification of their goals, and relevant organizational standards for different jobs.

The second part dealt with what the *organization* needed. The HR department at the County hosted sessions explaining the demographic shifts that were occurring and how the succession process would work. HR then identified holders of key positions and had them identify the key competencies necessary to do their jobs well. With this background as information, other employees who were interested in specific jobs then could use the listing of competencies as a guideline for their own development efforts.

The completion of the second part allowed HR managers and employees to match the key competencies with the individual development from part one. The development needed then became the responsibility of the employee.

The role of HR in the entire process was critical. Estimates by HR staff members is that they spent 400 hours or more on the program and expected to spend another 200 during the following year to maintain the program. One major result of the succession efforts is that there has been a surge in enrollments in the leadership development program the County offers. Also, of the six openings that have occurred since the program began, all have been filled from within the organization. This success is compared to the fact that only two of a previous six openings had been filled internally.[62]

Questions
1. What potential advantages and disadvantages might exist with the County's approach to succession planning?
2. Discuss factors that could be used to judge the readiness of a person to move up, and who should be making the analyses and decisions.

SUPPLEMENTAL CASE: Developed Today, Gone Tomorrow

This case illustrates a serious concern that some employers have about developing employees, only to have them leave. (For the case, go to **http://mathis.swlearning.com/.)**

Learning Review Answers: 1. d   2. d   3. d   4. b

NOTES

1. Christopher Cornell, "Follow the Leader," *Human Resource Executive,* February 2003, 28–32.
2. "The Top 25 Managers," *Business Week,* January 14, 2002, 65–68.
3. Yehuda Baruch, "Career Systems in Transition," *Personnel Review,* 32 (2003), 231–251.
4. Angela Karr, "Four Questions About Career Pathing," *Customer Interface,* June 2002, 38–43.
5. Eric Raimy, "Ladders of Success," *Human Resource Executive,* January 2002, 36–41.
6. "New and Emerging Occupations," *Occupational Outlook Quarterly,* September 2002, 1–13.
7. Steve H. Applebaum et al., "Career Management in Information Technology: A Case Study," *Career Development International,* 7 (2002), 142–159.
8. Roger D. Wessel et al., "Enhancing Career Development Through the Career Success Club," *Journal of Career Development,* 29 (2003), 265–276.
9. Julie Demers, "Keys to a Successful Career Transition," *CMA Management,* June 2002, 11–12.
10. Aldan Kelly et al., "Linking Organizational Training and Development Practices with New Forms of Career Structures," *Journal of European Industrial Training,* 27 (2003), 160.
11. Stephenie Overman, "Mentors Without Borders," *HR Magazine,* March 2004, 83–86; and George P. Hollenbeck and Morgan W. McCall Jr., "What Makes a Successful Global Executive?" *Business Society Review,* 12 (2001), 49–56.
12. Leslie Gross Klaff, "The Right Way to Bring Expats Home," *Workforce,* July 2002, 40–44.
13. Wilma G. Anderson, "Pre-retirees Offer Planning Opportunities," *National Underwriter Life and Health,* October 27, 2003, 40.
14. Bonnie Serino, "Cancel the Retirement Party," *Workspan,* July 2003, 35–41.
15. "Retirement Is the Next Stage of a Working Life," *Research Alert,* October 17, 2003, 1–6.
16. Stephen Dahlberg, "The New Elderhood," *Training,* February 2004, 46–49.
17. Martin M. Greller and Linda K. Stroh, "Extending Work Lives: Are Current Approaches Tools or Talismans?" in G. Adams and T. Beehr, eds., *Retirement: Reasons, Processes and Results* (New York: Springer Publishing, 2003), 115–135.
18. Jerry Geisel, "Rethinking Phased Retirement," *Business Insurance,* June 24, 2002, 3–5.
19. Todd J. Maurer and Nancy E. Rafuse, "Learning Not Litigating: Managing Employee Development and Avoiding Claims of Age Discrimination," *Academy of Management Executive,* November 2001, 110–121.
20. Michelle Quinn, "A New Generation of Women Is 'Sequencing,'" *Denver Post,* May 10, 2004, 6C.
21. L. B. Hammer et al., "Work-Family Conflict and Work-Related Withdrawal Behaviors," *Journal of Business and Psychology,* 17 (2003), 419–436; Linda M. Hite and Kimberly S. McDonald, "Career Aspirations of Non-Managerial Women: Adjustment and Adaptation," *Journal of Career Development,* 29 (2003), 221–235; M. Ferber and G. Green, "Career or Family: What Choices Do College Women Have?" *Journal of Labor Research,* 24 (2003), 145–161; and Toni Schindler et al., "Intimate Partnership: Foundation to the Successful Balance of Family and Work," *American Journal of Family Therapy,* 31 (2003), 107–124.
22. Anne M. Alexander et al., "A Study of the Disparity in Wages and Benefits Between Men and Women in Wyoming" Research Paper, (University of Wyoming, College of Business, 2003), 10.
23. Patrick Chang Boon Lee, "Going Beyond Career Plateaus," *Journal of Management Development,* 22 (2003), 538–551.
24. William D. Young, "Career Ladders," *SHRM White Paper,* November 2003, 1–5.
25. Keith Orndoff, "Developing Strategic Competencies," *Information Management Journal,* 36 (2002), 57–62.
26. Cenita Kupperbusch et al., "Predicting Husbands' and Wives' Retirement Satisfaction," *Journal of Social and Personal Relationships,* 20 (2003), 335–354; and Phyllis Moen, "Couples Work/Retirement Transitions," *Social Psychology Quarterly,* 64 (2001), 55–71.
27. Jeff D. Opdyke, "The Cost of a Mobile marriage," *Wall Street Journal,* January 7, 2004, D1.
28. Julie Cook, "The Dual-Income Dilemma," *Human Resource Executive,* June 6, 2002, 22–26; and Julie Cook, "Gender Gap," *Human Resource Executive,* August 2002, 24–29.
29. "Competitive Intelligence Education: Competencies, Sources, and Trends," *Information Management Journal,* 38 (2004), 56–64.
30. Kelly A. Chillaregen et al., "Learning from Our Mistakes: Error Management Training for Mature Learners," *Journal of Business and Psychology,* 17 (2003), 369–385.

31. Richard Dealtry, "The Savvy Learner," *Journal of Workplace Learning,* 16 (2004), 101–109.

32. Neal E. Thornberry, "Corporate Entrepreneurship: Teaching Managers to Be Entrepreneurs," *Journal of Management Development,* 22 (2003), 329–344.

33. JoAnn Harris-Bowlsby and James P. Sampson Jr., "Computer-Based Career Planning Systems: Dreams and Reality," *Career Development Quarterly,* 49 (2001), 250–260.

34. Vince Ryan, "Building a Company Career Web Site," *SHRM White Paper,* May 2001, 1–3, *www.shrm.org.*

35. Joel Schettler, "Building Bench Strength: Assessment Centers Methodology for Developing Talent," *Training,* June 2002, 55–60.

36. Cam Caldwell et al., "Ten Classic Assessment Center Errors," *Public Personnel Management,* 32 (2003), 73–88.

37. Errol L. Biggs, "CEO Succession Planning: An Emerging Challenge for Boards of Directors," *Academy of Management Executive,* February 2004, 105–107.

38. Khai Sheang Lee et al., "Family Business Succession: Appropriate Risk and Choice of Successor," *Academy of Management Review,* 28 (2003), 657–666.

39. James Hutchison, "Succession Planning: Can a Family Member Cut It?" *Practical Accountant,* May 2003, 38–42.

40. Bill Roberts, "Matching Talents with Tasks," *HR Magazine,* November 2002, 1–4.

41. Stephanie Armour, "Playing the Succession Game," *USA Today,* November 24, 2003, 3B.

42. William C. Byham, "A New Look at Succession Management," *Ivey Business Journal,* May 2002, 10–13.

43. Jay A. Conger and Robert M. Fulmer, "Developing Your Leadership Pipeline," *Harvard Business Review,* December 2003, 76.

44. Martha Frase-Blunt, "Ready, Set, Rotate!" *HR Magazine,* October 2001, 1–5.

45. David Boud and Heather Middleton, "Learning from Others at Work: Communities of Practice and Informal Learning," *Journal of Workplace Learning,* 15 (2003), 194–202; and Jan Betts and Rick Holden, "Organizational Learning in a Public Sector Organization: A Case Study of Muddled Thinking," *Journal of Workplace Learning,* 15 (2003), 280–287.

46. Toddi Garner, "The Pause That Refreshes," *Business Week,* November 19, 2001, 138.

47. Douglas P. Shuit, "Sound the Retreat," *Workforce Management,* September 2003, 39–48.

48. John P. Meyer, "Four Territories of Experience," *Academy of Management Learning and Education,* 2 (2003), 352–263.

49. Christopher Cornell, "Confidence Rating," *Human Resource Executive,* November 2003, 78–83.

50. Christopher Cornell, "Fail Safe," *www.workindex.com,*

51. "Corporate Therapy," *The Economist,* November 15, 2003, 61.

52. Juan J. Colombo and W. B. Weither Jr., "Strategic Career Coaching for an Uncertain World," *Business Horizons,* July/August 2003, 33–38.

53. Joy McGovern et al., "Maximizing the Impact of Executive Coaching," *Manchester Review,* 6 (2001), 1–9; and Suzy Wales, "Why Coaching?" *Journal of Change Management,* 3 (2002), 275–282.

54. Kathryn Tyler, "Find Your Mentor," *HR Magazine,* March 2004, 89–93.

55. Stephen Billett, "Workplace Mentors: Demands and Benefits," *Journal of Workplace Learning,* 15 (2003), 105–113.

56. Suzanne C. de Janasz et al., "Mentor Networks and Career Success," *Academy of Management Executive,* November 2003, 78–89.

57. Nancy Lockwood, "The Glass Ceiling," *HR Magazine 2004 Research Quarterly,* June 2004, 1–11.

58. Lynda McDermott, "Developing the New Young Managers," *T & D,* October 2001, 42–48.

59. Tom Starner, "Woman's Day," *HR Executive,* December 2003, 33–38.

60. Jennifer Merritt, "The Education Edge," *Business Week,* October 20, 2003, 86; and Paul Farris et al., "Executive Education Programs Go Back to School," *Journal of Management Development,* 22 (2003), 784–795.

61. E. Joy Mighty and William Ashton, "Management Development: Hoax or Hero," *Journal of Management Development,* 22 (2003), 14–31.

62. Based on "Creating 'Learning Culture' Helps County Achieve Excellence in Succession Planning," *Bulletin to Management,* BNA Inc. March 6, 2003, 73–74.

Performance Management and Appraisal

After you have read this chapter, you should be able to:

- Identify the components of performance management systems.

- Distinguish between performance management and performance appraisal, and between job criteria and performance standards.

- Explain the administrative and developmental uses of performance appraisal.

- Describe the advantages and disadvantages of multisource (360°) appraisals.

- Discuss the importance of training managers and employees about performance appraisal, and give examples of several rater errors.

- Identify several concerns about appraisal feedback and ways to make it more effective.

Performance Appraisals—Necessary but Not Popular

Many employees receive performance reviews from their managers and supervisors. Some of those reviews are very favorable, some are positive, and a few are negative. For managers and employees alike, the performance appraisal process, often done once a year, is not popular.

Various surveys have identified that a majority of employees view performance appraisals as "a joke," "an administrative game," "wasted time," "based on favoritism," and "not linked to pay." The most frequent criticisms include:

* With today's emphasis on teamwork, appraisals focus too much on the individual and do too little to develop employees to perform better.
* Many employees who receive reviews and supervisors who give reviews generally say that the appraisal process does not help improve workers' performance.
* Many appraisals are seen as inconsistent, focused on the short term, subjective, and valuable only for identifying employees who are performing extremely well or poorly.

However, employers must have some system for justifying the pay increases they give and the promotion or termination decisions they make. Also, most employees and managers want to communicate about how the employees are performing their jobs, and about additional training and development that would be beneficial. So, improvements in performance appraisals are needed to address the negative views held by many employees and managers.[1]

"Performance appraisal systems are like seat belts—most people believe they are necessary, but don't like to use them."

—*Dick Grote*

At the heart of organizational success is performance, which is driven by organizational and individual efforts leading to achieving goals and objectives. Performance management systems are a key means for HR management to contribute to organizational performance.

NATURE OF PERFORMANCE MANAGEMENT

Performance management Composed of the processes used to identify, measure, communicate, develop, and reward employee performance.

Performance management is composed of the processes used to identify, measure, communicate, develop, and reward employee performance. As shown in Figure 11-1, performance management links organizational strategies to results.

All performance management efforts should be driven by business strategies. Firms such as Payless ShoeSource and PPG Industries have developed performance management systems by breaking their business plans into sub-plans for

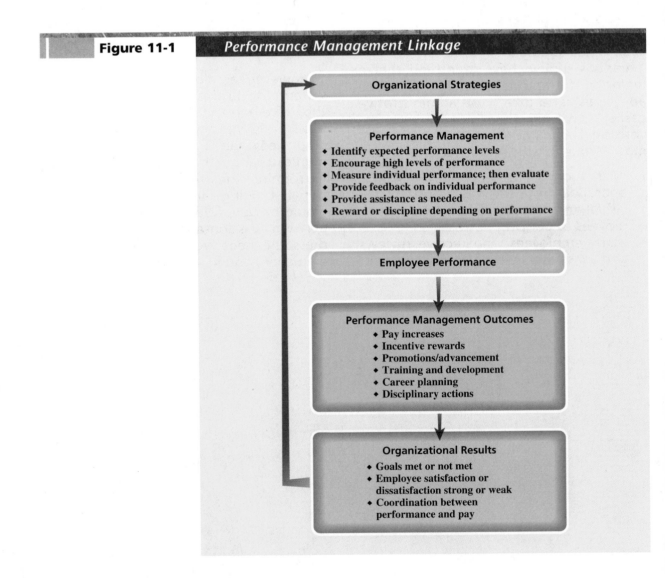

Figure 11-1   *Performance Management Linkage*

Organizational Strategies

Performance Management
- Identify expected performance levels
- Encourage high levels of performance
- Measure individual performance; then evaluate
- Provide feedback on individual performance
- Provide assistance as needed
- Reward or discipline depending on performance

Employee Performance

Performance Management Outcomes
- Pay increases
- Incentive rewards
- Promotions/advancement
- Training and development
- Career planning
- Disciplinary actions

Organizational Results
- Goals met or not met
- Employee satisfaction or dissatisfaction strong or weak
- Coordination between performance and pay

units and departments.[2] Those plans have then served as the foundation for accomplishing the following functions:

- Provide information to employees about their performance.
- Clarify the organizational performance expectations.
- Identify the development steps that are needed to enhance employee performance.
- Document performance for personnel actions.
- Provide rewards for achieving performance objectives.

Difference Between Performance Management and Performance Appraisals

In many organizations, managers and employees mistakenly equate performance appraisals with performance management. **Performance appraisal** is the process of evaluating how well employees perform their jobs and then communicating that information to the employees. Performance appraisal is also called *employee rating, employee evaluation, performance review,* and *performance evaluation.*

Sometimes, performance appraisal is incorrectly called *job evaluation.* Job evaluation is a compensation activity identifying the importance of jobs, whereas performance appraisal focuses on the actual performance of individuals and managers. It is easiest to think of performance appraisal as the way that performance management is implemented, as follows:

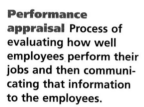

LOGGING ON...

Performance Management Technical Assistance Center
This Web site offers information on managing performance, and includes a Performance Management Handbook.
www.opm.gov/perform

| Performance Management | ⟹ | Performance Appraisals | ⟹ | Performance Feedback | ⟹ | Performance Rewards and Development |

Performance management systems in organizations can be effective in countering the narrow and negative views of performance appraisals. For instance, at Franciscan Health System, a non-profit health-care organization, the CEO and other executives support performance management as part of the corporate culture. Involvement and training of managers and employees are part of performance management efforts. Also, all performance reviews are linked to key performance "drivers," such as client satisfaction.[3]

▌ PERFORMANCE-FOCUSED ORGANIZATIONAL CULTURE

Organizational cultures vary dramatically on many dimensions, one of which is the emphasis on performance management. Both research and organizational experiences have identified a number of components of an effective performance management system.[4] The components are depicted in Figure 11-2 on the following page. Some corporate cultures are based on *entitlement,* meaning that adequate performance and stability dominate the organization. Employee rewards systems vary little from person to person and are not based on individual performance differences. As a result, the performance appraisal activities are seen as having little tie to performance and as being primarily a "bureaucratic exercise."

At the other end of the spectrum is a *performance-driven* organizational culture focused on corporate values, results, information sharing, and performance appraisal systems that link results to employee compensation and development. The importance of a performance-focused culture is seen in the results of several studies. One longitudinal study of 207 companies in 22 industries found

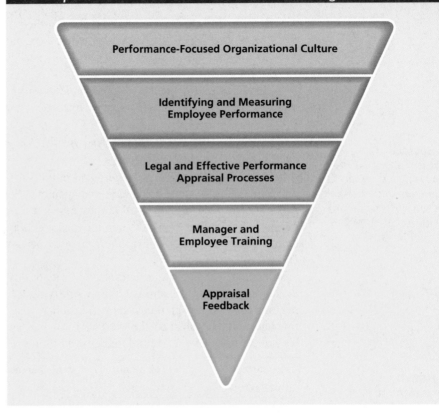

Figure 11-2   *Components of Effective Performance Management*

Performance-Focused Organizational Culture

Identifying and Measuring
Employee Performance

Legal and Effective Performance
Appraisal Processes

Manager and
Employee Training

Appraisal
Feedback

that firms with performance-focused cultures had significantly higher growth in company revenue, employment, net income, and stock prices than did companies with different cultures. Another study, by Becker, Huselid, and Ulrich, found that firms with strong performance cultures had dramatically better results as well.[5]

As the HR Globally indicates, wider cultural values affect performance management and organizational cultures. Those wider cultural values must be considered in a global workforce.

Executive Commitment to Performance Management

One crucial aspect of a performance-focused culture is executive involvement in continually reinforcing the performance message.[6] If top executives do performance reviews on employees who report directly to them, then they are supporting the performance culture. In many organizations, performance appraisals are supposed to be done by all managers, but senior executives never do them, nor are they held accountable for conducting feedback with their employees. Another indicator of a performance-focused culture is executive compensation plans that are clearly linked to company performance measures, rather than compensation systems that allow huge payouts for executives when results are mediocre and give employees small or no pay increases.

LOGGING ON...

International Society for Performance Improvement
This association is dedicated to improving human performance in the workplace. The Web site includes links to many valuable articles.
www.ispi.org

Cultural Differences in Performance Management

Performance management systems and performance appraisal processes are very common in the U.S. and in some other countries. When they are transported for use in other countries where multi-national organizations have operations, or when they are used with employees having non-American cultural backgrounds, problems can arise.

In some countries and cultures, it is uncommon for managers to rate employees or to give direct feedback, particularly if some points are negative. For instance, in several countries, including China and Japan, there is a high respect for authority and age. Consequently, expecting younger subordinates to engage in joint discussions with their managers through a performance appraisal process is uncommon. Use of such programs as multisource/360° feedback (discussed later in this chapter) would be culturally inappropriate.

In various other cultures, employees may view criticism from superiors as personally devastating rather than as useful feedback indicating training and development needs. Therefore, many managers do not provide feedback, nor do employees expect it.

Even in the physical settings for the appraisal discussions, "cultural customs" associated with formal meetings may need to be observed. In some Eastern European countries, it is common to have coffee and pastries or an alcoholic drink before beginning any formal discussion. These examples illustrate that the performance management processes may need to be adapted, or even not used in certain global settings.[7]

IDENTIFYING AND MEASURING EMPLOYEE PERFORMANCE

The second phase of an effective performance management system is that important performance measures are identified and used. Employee performance measures common to most jobs include the following elements:

◆ Quantity of output
◆ Quality of output
◆ Timeliness of output
◆ Presence at work

Job criteria Important elements in a given job.

Other dimensions of performance beyond these general ones apply to various jobs. Specific **job criteria,** or dimensions of job performance, identify the most important elements in a given job. For example, a college professor's job often includes the job criteria of teaching, research, and service. Job criteria are identified from well-written job descriptions that contain the most important factors of individual jobs. They define what the organization pays employees to do; therefore, the performance of individuals on job criteria should be measured and compared against standards, and then the results communicated to the employee.

Multiple job criteria are the rule rather than the exception in many jobs. Often, a given individual might demonstrate better performance on some job criteria than others. Also, some criteria might be more important than others to the organization. Weights can be used to show the relative importance of several job criteria in one job. For example, in a management job at a company that values revenue, cost control, and employee development, weights might be assigned as follows:

Management Job Criteria at Sample Firm	Weight
Revenue increase	40%
Cost control	30%
Employee development	30%
Total Management Performance	100%

Types of Performance Information

Managers can use three types of information about how employees are performing their jobs, as Figure 11-3 shows. *Trait-based information* identifies a character trait of the employee—such as attitude, initiative, or creativity—and may or may not be job related. Because traits tend to be ambiguous, and favoritism of raters can affect how traits are viewed, court decisions have generally held that trait-based performance appraisals are too vague to use when making performance-based HR decisions such as promotions or terminations.

Behavior-based information focuses on specific behaviors that lead to job success. For a salesperson, the behavior "verbal persuasion" can be observed and used as information on performance. Although more difficult to identify, behavioral information clearly specifies the behaviors management wants to see. A potential problem arises when any of several behaviors can lead to successful performance in a given situation. For example, identifying successful use of verbal persuasion for a salesperson might be difficult because an approach that is successful when used by one salesperson may not be successful when used by another.

Results-based information considers employee accomplishments. For jobs in which measurement is easy and obvious, a results-based approach works well. However, that which is measured tends to be emphasized, and that emphasis may leave out equally important but unmeasurable parts of the job. For example, a car sales representative who gets paid *only* for sales may be unwilling to do paperwork or other work not directly related to selling cars. Further, ethical or even legal issues may arise when only results are emphasized and how the results were achieved is not considered.

Performance measures can also be viewed as objective or subjective. *Objective* measures can be observed directly—for example, the number of cars sold or the number of invoices processed can be counted. *Subjective* measures require judgment on the part of the evaluator and are more difficult to determine. One exam-

Figure 11-3 *Types of Performance Information*

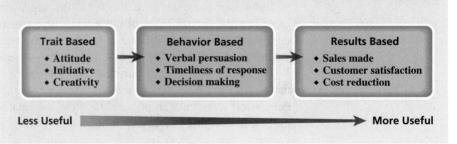

Trait Based	Behavior Based	Results Based
• Attitude	• Verbal persuasion	• Sales made
• Initiative	• Timeliness of response	• Customer satisfaction
• Creativity	• Decision making	• Cost reduction

Less Useful ➞ More Useful

ple of a subjective measure is a supervisor's ratings of an employee's "attitude," which cannot be seen directly. Consequently, both objective and subjective measures should be used carefully.

Relevance of Performance Criteria

Measuring performance requires the use of relevant criteria that focus on the most important aspects of employees' jobs. For example, measuring the initiative of customer service representatives in an insurance claims center may be less relevant than measuring the number of calls they handle properly. This example stresses that the most important job criteria should be identified in the employees' job descriptions.

Performance measures that leave out some important job duties are considered *deficient*. For example, measurement of an employment interviewer's performance is likely to be deficient if it evaluates only the number of applicants hired and not the quality of those hired or how long those hired stay at the company. On the other hand, including some irrelevant criteria *contaminates* the measure. For example, appearance might be a contaminating criterion in measuring the performance of a telemarketing sales representative whom customers never see. Managers need to guard against using deficient or contaminated performance measures.

Additionally, *overemphasis* on one or two criteria can lead to problems. For example, overstressing the number of traffic tickets written by a police officer, or the revenue generated by a sales representative, may lead to ignoring other performance areas. Ethical issues can arise because employees may falsify results in order to meet the one or two criteria that are overemphasized.[8] The corporate scandals involving Enron, WorldCom, Tyco, and others illustrate this concern.

Performance Standards

Performance standards define the expected levels of performance, and are "benchmarks" or "goals" or "targets"—depending on the approach taken. Realistic, measurable, clearly understood performance standards benefit both organizations and employees. In a sense, performance standards define what satisfactory job performance is. It is recommended that they be established *before* the work is performed. Well-defined standards ensure that everyone involved knows the levels of accomplishment expected.

Both numerical and non-numerical standards can be established. Sales quotas and production output standards are familiar numerical performance standards. A standard of performance can also be based on non-numerical criteria. The following performance standards illustrate both types:

Job Criterion: **Keep current on supplier technology.**
Performance Standards: **1. Every four months, invite suppliers to make presentation of newest technology. 2. Visit supplier plants twice a year. 3. Attend trade shows quarterly.**
Job Criterion: **Do price or cost analysis as appropriate.**
Performance Standard: **Performance is acceptable when employee follows all requirements of the procedure "Price and Cost Analysis."**

Performance standards can be set by managers, employees, or others such as quality control inspectors or financial analysts. Generally, it is recommended that

THOMSON

WEST ™

PERFORMANCE STANDARDS
Identifies what to consider when setting performance standards.
Custom Search:
☑ ANALYSIS
Exact Phrase: Developing standards

managers and supervisors review and discuss the standards with employees and get their input. The joint involvement of employees and their supervisors is critical to how the performance standards are perceived and used. Standards can be identified effectively by employees and their supervisors because both usually know what constitutes satisfactory performance of the dimensions of the employees' jobs.

LEGAL AND EFFECTIVE PERFORMANCE APPRAISAL PROCESSES

To be an effective part of performance management, performance appraisals must accomplish three major purposes: legal compliance and documentation, administrative uses, and developmental uses. Because these three purposes may have conflicting effects, achieving them all is challenging in many organizations. The decisions made in designing the appraisal process can influence the degree to which appraisals serve those purposes.

Legal Concerns and Performance Appraisals

Because appraisals are supposed to measure how well employees are doing their jobs, it may seem unnecessary to emphasize that performance appraisals must be job related. Yet courts have ruled in numerous cases that performance appraisals were discriminatory and not job related.[9] For instance, in a case involving an African American computer engineer at Hewlett-Packard, performance appraisals commended his technical skills and work efforts, but criticized his taking too much time analyzing problems. A few months after those appraisals were issued, the employee helped start a diversity group at the company. Shortly after that, his performance appraisal ratings declined, and his supervisor "encouraged" him to leave the company. The court ruled that there appeared to be enough irregularities in the performance appraisal documentation to raise questions about the fairness of the appraisal system. One concern was that the ratings were viewed as being overly subjective. A jury trial was ordered.[10]

Legal concerns have also arisen with the use of forced distribution rating systems, in which, for instance, managers are forced to rate a certain percentage of employees as "outstanding," another percentage as "satisfactory," and still another percentage as "needing improvement." For example, Ford, Goodyear Tire & Rubber, and Capital One have been sued and/or have settled lawsuits related to forced distribution ranking in performance appraisals. Ford paid $10.5 million to settle a lawsuit based on an employee's claim that the Ford appraisal system disproportionally and negatively affected the pay raises of older workers. Goodyear dropped its forced ranking appraisal system because of legal complaints that it discriminated on the bases of race and gender.[11]

A number of court decisions over 30 years have focused attention on performance appraisals, particularly on equal employment opportunity (EEO) concerns.[12] The uniform guidelines issued by the Equal Employment Opportunity Commission (EEOC) and various court decisions make it clear that performance appraisals must be job related, non-discriminatory, and documented.[13]

Clearly, employers should have fair and non-discriminatory performance appraisals. They should design their appraisal systems to satisfy the courts as well as performance management needs.

LOGGING ON...

AHI's Employment Law Resource
This Web site offers valuable legal management information on performance appraisals and other HR topics under the problem solver heading.
www.ahipubs.com

The elements of a performance appraisal system that can survive court tests can be determined from existing case law. Various cases have identified the elements of a legally defensible performance appraisal to include the following:

◆ Performance appraisal criteria based on job analysis
◆ Absence of disparate impact and evidence of validity
◆ Formal evaluation criteria that limit managerial discretion
◆ A rating instrument linked to job duties and responsibilities
◆ Documentation of the appraisal activities
◆ Personal knowledge of and contact with the appraised individual
◆ Training of supervisors in conducting appraisals
◆ A review process that prevents one manager, acting alone, from controlling an employee's career
◆ Counseling to help poor performers improve

Uses of Performance Appraisals

Organizations generally use performance appraisals in two potentially conflicting ways. One use is to provide a measure of performance for consideration in making pay or other administrative decisions about employees. This administrative role often creates stress for managers doing the appraisals. The other use focuses on the development of individuals. In this role, the manager acts more as counselor and coach than as judge, which may change the tone of the appraisal. The developmental performance appraisal emphasizes identifying current training and development needs, as well as planning employees' future opportunities and career directions. Figure 11-4 shows both uses for performance appraisal.

Administrative Uses of Appraisals Three administrative uses of appraisal impact managers and employees the most. They are: (1) determining pay adjustments; (2) making job placement decisions on promotions, transfers, and demotions; and (3) choosing employee disciplinary actions up to and including termination of employment.

A performance appraisal system is often the link between additional pay and other rewards that employees receive, and their job performance. Performance-based compensation affirms the idea that pay raises are given for performance ac-

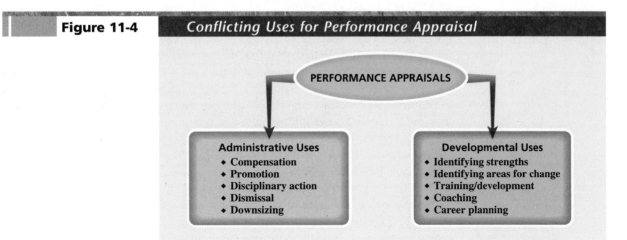

Figure 11-4 — *Conflicting Uses for Performance Appraisal*

PERFORMANCE APPRAISALS

Administrative Uses
◆ Compensation
◆ Promotion
◆ Disciplinary action
◆ Dismissal
◆ Downsizing

Developmental Uses
◆ Identifying strengths
◆ Identifying areas for change
◆ Training/development
◆ Coaching
◆ Career planning

complishments rather than based on length of service (seniority) or granted automatically to all employees at the same percentage levels. In pay-for-performance compensation systems, historically supervisors and managers have evaluated the performance of individual employees and also made compensation recommendations for the same employees. If any part of the appraisal process fails, better-performing employees may not receive larger pay increases, and the result is perceived inequity in compensation.

Many U.S. workers say that they see little connection between their performance and the size of their pay increases, due to flaws in the performance appraisal processes. However, the use of performance appraisals to determine pay is common. Consequently, many people argue that performance appraisals and pay discussions should be separated. Two major realities support this view. One is that employees often focus more on the pay amount received than on the appraisal feedback that identifies what they have done well or need to improve. The other is that managers sometimes manipulate performance appraisal ratings to justify the pay treatment they wish to give specific individuals. As a result of the second circumstance, many employees view the appraisal process as a "game," because compensation increases have already been determined before the appraisal decision.

To address these issues, numerous organizations have managers first conduct performance appraisals and discuss the results with employees, then several weeks later hold a shorter meeting in which pay is discussed. With this approach, the results of the performance appraisal can be considered before the amount of the pay adjustment is determined. Also, the performance appraisal discussions between managers/supervisors and employees can focus on the developmental uses of appraisals.

Employees are interested in the other administrative uses of performance appraisal as well, such as decisions about promotions, terminations, layoffs, and transfer assignments. Promotions and demotions based on performance must be documented through performance appraisals; otherwise, legal problems can result.

To improve the administrative processes of performance appraisals, many employers have implemented software so that managers can prepare appraisals electronically.[14] As the Technology Transforming HR indicates, even smaller firms are using such HR technology.

Developmental Uses of Appraisals For employees, performance appraisal can be a primary source of information and feedback, which are often key to their future development. In the process of identifying employee strengths, weaknesses, potentials, and training needs through performance appraisal feedback, supervisors can inform employees about their progress, discuss areas where additional training may be beneficial, and outline future development plans. The manager's role in such a situation parallels that of a coach, discussing good performance, explaining what improvement is necessary, and showing employees how to improve. After all, many employees do not always know where and how to improve, and managers should not expect improvement if they are unwilling to provide developmental feedback.

The purpose of such feedback is both to reinforce satisfactory employee performance and to address performance deficiencies. Positive reinforcement for desired behaviors contributes to both individual and organizational development. The development function of performance appraisal also can identify areas in which the employee might wish to grow. For example, in a performance appraisal interview targeted exclusively to development, an employee found out that the only factor keeping her from being considered for a management job in her firm

Implementing an E-System for Appraising Performance

Organizations of all sizes have found advantages in using technology to transform how performance appraisals are conducted. With 300 employees, Emprise Bank, based in Wichita, Kansas, had used a traditional paper-and-pencil form as part of its process. Under the guidance of Linda Erb, HR Director at Emprise, the bank implemented performance review software. There are many pre-written job competencies to choose from, or the HR staff and managers can modify them or write their own. Managers also can choose the weighting of each competency, so that accuracy may be weighted 10%, compliance 20%, etc., and the software calculates the overall rating.

When managers click on a rating for a particular competency, the sample wording appears. Managers can alter the wording because it is in a Microsoft Word document. They may access previous review forms and cut and paste relevant information from those forms to the new one. They may also review and cut and paste "log events," that is, is-

sues that have arisen over the past performance review period that might be noteworthy on the review form. The system also supplies coaching ideas that might help provide talking points for the performance feedback session.

Any salary or job title changes that need to be made following the performance appraisal may be electronically routed to the division manager for approval and then to payroll and HR for implementation. This system thus reduces the need for paper payroll change notices. The software offers many other features, such as reminders when reviews are due, that can be connected with e-mail.

Overall, this system has improved both the efficiency and effectiveness of the performance appraisal process at Emprise. The managers like the enhanced process, and it appears that the performance review sessions with employees are much more productive since the implementation of the appraisal software.[15]

was the lack of a working knowledge of cost accounting. Her supervisor suggested that she consider taking some night courses at the local college.

The use of teams provides a different set of circumstances for developmental appraisal. The manager may not see all of an employee's work, but the employee's team members do. Teams can provide developmental feedback. However, it is still an open question whether teams can handle administrative appraisals. When teams are allowed to design appraisal systems, they tend to "get rid of judgment" and avoid differential rewards. Thus, group appraisal may be best suited to developmental purposes, not administrative uses.

Decisions About Performance Appraisal Process

A number of decisions must be made when designing performance appraisal systems. Some important ones are identifying the appraisal responsibilities of the HR unit and of the operating managers, the type of appraisal system to use, the timing of appraisals, and who conducts appraisals.

Appraisal Responsibilities The appraisal process can benefit both the organization and the employees, if done properly. As Figure 11-5 on the next page shows, the HR unit typically designs a performance appraisal system. The operating managers then appraise employees using the appraisal system. During development of the formal appraisal system, managers usually offer input as to how the final system will work.

Figure 11-5 | *Typical Division of HR Responsibilities: Performance Appraisal*

HR Unit	Managers
• Designs and maintains appraisal system • Trains raters • Tracks timely receipt of appraisals • Reviews completed appraisals for consistency	• Typically rate performance of employees • Prepare formal appraisal documents • Review appraisals with employees • Identify development areas

It is important for managers to understand appraisals as *their* responsibility. Through the appraisal process, good employee performance can be developed to be even better, and poor employee performance can be improved or poor performers may be removed from the organization. Performance appraisal is not simply an HR requirement; it must also be a management process, because guiding employees' performance is among the most important responsibilities of managers.

Informal vs. Systematic Appraisal Processes Performance appraisals can occur in two ways: informally and/or systematically. A supervisor conducts an *informal appraisal* whenever necessary. The day-to-day working relationship between a manager and an employee offers an opportunity for the employee's performance to be evaluated. A manager communicates this evaluation through conversation on the job, over coffee, or by on-the-spot discussion of a specific occurrence.

Frequent informal feedback to employees can prevent "surprises" during a formal performance review. However, informal appraisal can become *too* informal. For example, a senior executive at a large firm so dreaded face-to-face evaluations that he recently delivered one manager's review while both sat in adjoining stalls in the men's room.

A *systematic appraisal* is used when the contact between manager and employee is formal, and a system is in place to report managerial impressions and observations on employee performance. One survey found that almost 90% of employers have a formal performance management system or process.[16] Although informal appraisal is useful and necessary, it should not take the place of formal appraisal.

Systematic appraisals feature a regular time interval, which distinguishes them from informal appraisals. Both employees and managers know that performance will be reviewed on a regular basis, and they can plan for performance discussions.

Timing of Appraisals Most companies require managers to conduct appraisals once or twice a year, most often annually. Employees commonly receive an appraisal 60–90 days after hiring, again at six months, and annually thereafter. "Probationary" or "introductory" employees, who are new and in a trial period, should be informally evaluated often—perhaps weekly for the first month, and monthly thereafter until the end of the introductory period. After that, annual reviews are typical. For high-demand employees, some employers use accelerated appraisals—every six months instead of every year. This is done to retain turnover-prone employees because more feedback has been given and pay raises have occurred more often.

To separate the administrative and developmental uses of appraisals, some employers implement the following appraisal schedule: First there is a performance review and discussion. Some time after that there is a separate training, development, and objective-setting session. Within two weeks of that there is a compensation adjustment discussion. Having three separate discussions provides both the employee and the employee's manager with opportunities to focus on the administrative, developmental, and compensation issues. Using this framework is generally better than addressing all three areas in one discussion of an hour or less, once a year.

■ Who Conducts Appraisals?

Performance appraisals can be conducted by anyone familiar with the performance of individual employees. Possible combinations include the following:

- Supervisors rating their employees
- Employees rating their superiors
- Team members rating each other
- Employees rating themselves
- Outside sources rating employees
- A variety of parties providing multisource, or 360°, feedback

The rating of employees by their immediate supervisors or managers to whom supervisors report is the most common method. The immediate superior has the main responsibility for appraisals in most organizations, although often the supervisor's boss may review and approve the appraisals. The growing use of teams and a concern with customer input contribute to two fast-growing sources of appraisal information: team members and parties outside the organization. Multisource (or 360°) feedback combines numerous methods and has recently grown in usage.

Supervisory Rating of Subordinates

The most widely used means of rating employees is based on the assumption that the immediate supervisor is the person most qualified to evaluate an employee's performance realistically and fairly. To help themselves provide accurate evaluations, some supervisors keep performance logs noting their employees' accomplishments. These logs provide specific examples to use when rating performance. Figure 11-6 on the next page shows the traditional review process by which supervisors conduct performance appraisals on employees.

Employee Rating of Managers

A number of organizations today ask employees or group members to rate the performance of supervisors and managers. A prime example of this type of rating takes place in colleges and universities, where students evaluate the performance of professors in the classroom. Performance appraisal ratings also are used for management development purposes.

Having employees rate managers provides three primary advantages. First, in critical manager/employee relationships, employee ratings can be quite useful for

Figure 11-6

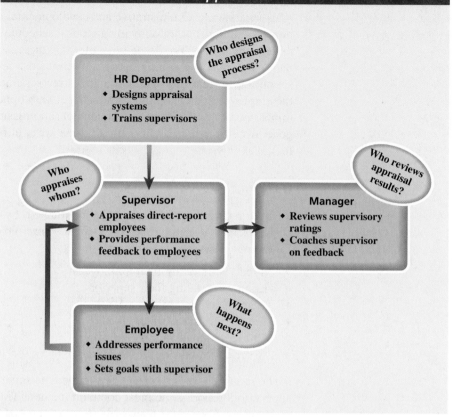

identifying competent managers. The rating of leaders by combat soldiers is one example of such a use. Second, this type of rating program can help make a manager more responsive to employees. This advantage can quickly become a disadvantage if the manager focuses on being "nice" rather than on managing; people who are nice but have no other qualifications may not be good managers in many situations. Finally, employee appraisals can contribute to career development efforts for managers by identifying areas for growth.

A major disadvantage of having employees rate managers is the negative reaction many superiors have to being evaluated by employees. Also, the fear of reprisals may be too great for employees to give realistic ratings. This fear may prompt workers to rate their managers only on the way the managers treat them, not on critical job requirements. The problems associated with this appraisal approach limit its usefulness to certain situations, including managerial development and improvement efforts.

Team/Peer Rating

Having employees and team members rate each other is another type of appraisal with potential both to help and to hurt. Peer and team ratings are especially useful when supervisors do not have the opportunity to observe each employee's performance, but other work group members do. One challenge of this approach is how to obtain ratings with virtual or global teams, in which the individuals work primarily through technology, not in person. Another challenge is how to obtain ratings from and for individuals who are on different special project teams throughout the year.

Some contend that any performance appraisal, including team/peer ratings, can negatively affect teamwork and participative management efforts. Although team members have good information on one another's performance, they may not choose to share it. They may unfairly attack, or "go easy" to spare feelings. Some organizations attempt to overcome such problems by using anonymous appraisals and/or having a consultant or HR manager interpret team/peer ratings. Despite the problems, team/peer performance ratings are probably inevitable, especially where work teams are used extensively.[17]

Self-Rating

Self-appraisal works in certain situations. As a self-development tool, it forces employees to think about their strengths and weaknesses and set goals for improvement. Employees working in isolation or possessing unique skills may be the only ones qualified to rate themselves. However, employees may not rate themselves as supervisors would rate them; they may use quite different standards. Evidence showing whether people tend to be more lenient or more demanding when rating themselves is mixed, with self-rating frequently higher than supervisory ratings. Still, employee self-ratings can be a useful source of performance information for development.

Outsider Rating

People outside the immediate work group may be called in to conduct performance reviews. This field review approach can include someone from the HR department as a reviewer, or completely independent reviewers from outside the organization. Examples include a review team evaluating a college president, and a panel of division managers evaluating a supervisor's potential for advancement in the organization. A disadvantage of this approach is that outsiders may not know the important demands within the work group or organization.

The customers or clients of an organization are obvious sources for outside appraisals. For sales and service jobs, customers may provide very useful input on the performance behaviors of employees. One firm measures customer service satisfaction to determine bonuses for top marketing executives. Use of such input has led to multisource ratings.

DILBERT reprinted by permission of United Feature Syndicate, Inc.

Figure 11-7

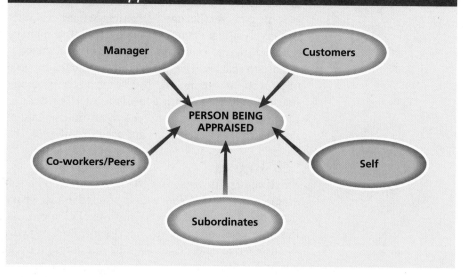

Multisource Appraisal

Multisource/360° Feedback

Multisource rating, or 360° feedback, has grown in popularity. Multisource feedback recognizes that for a growing number of jobs, employee performance is multi-dimensional and crosses departmental, organizational, and even global boundaries. The major purpose of 360° feedback is *not* to increase uniformity by soliciting like-minded views. Instead, it is to capture evaluations of the individual employee's different roles. Figure 11-7 shows graphically some of the parties who may be involved in 360° feedback. For example, an HR manager for an insurance firm deals with seven regional sales managers, HR administrators in five claims centers, and various corporate executives in finance, legal, and information technology. The Vice President of HR uses 360° feedback to gather data on all facets of the HR manager's job before completing a performance appraisal on the manager. Similar examples can be cited in numerous managerial, professional, technical, operational, and administrative jobs.

Significant administrative time and paperwork are required to request, obtain, and summarize feedback from multiple raters. Use of Web-based systems can significantly reduce the administrative demands of multisource ratings.

Developmental Use of Multisource Feedback As originally designed and used, multisource feedback focuses on the use of appraisals for future development of individuals. Conflict resolution skills, decision-making abilities, team effectiveness, communication skills, managerial styles, and technical capabilities are just some of the developmental areas that can be examined. Even in a multisource system, the manager remains a focal point, both to receive the feedback initially and to follow up with the employee appropriately.

Administrative Use of Multisource Feedback The popularity of 360° feedback systems has led to the results being used for making compensation, promotion, termination, and other administrative decisions. When using 360° feedback for administrative purposes, managers must anticipate potential problems.[18] Differences among raters can present a challenge, especially in the use of 360° ratings for discipline or pay decisions. Bias can just as easily be rooted in customers, subordinates, and peers as in a boss, and the lack of accountability of those sources can affect the ratings. "Inflation" of ratings is common when the sources know that their input will affect someone's pay or career. Also, issues of the confidentiality of the input and whether it is truly kept anonymous have led to lawsuits. Even though multisource approaches to performance appraisal offer possible solutions to the well-documented dissatisfaction with performance appraisal, a number of questions arise as multisource appraisals become more common.

Evaluating Multisource Feedback Research on multisource/360° feedback has revealed both positives and negatives. Studies have found that there can be more variability than expected in the ratings given by the different sources. Thus, supervisor ratings must carry more weight than peer or subordinate input to resolve the differences.[19] Other studies have found differences between employee self-ratings and multisource ratings. One concern is that those peers who rate poor-performing co-workers tend to inflate the ratings of those people so that the peers themselves can get higher overall evaluation results.[20]

One concern is whether 360° appraisals improve the process or simply multiply the number of problems by the total number of raters. Also, some wonder whether multisource appraisals really create better decisions that offset the additional time and investment required. These issues appear to be less threatening when the 360° feedback is used *only for development*. But they may effectively reduce the use of multisource appraisals as an administrative tool in many situations.

■ METHODS FOR APPRAISING PERFORMANCE

Performance can be appraised by a number of methods. Some employers use one method for all jobs and employees, some use different methods for different groups of employees, and others use a combination of methods. The following discussion highlights different methods and some of the pluses and minuses of each.

Category Scaling Methods

The simplest methods for appraising performance are category scaling methods, which require a manager to mark an employee's level of performance on a specific form divided into categories of performance. A *checklist* uses a list of statements or words from which raters check statements most representative of the characteristics and performance of employees. Often, a scale indicating perceived level of accomplishment on each statement is included, which becomes a type of graphic rating scale.

Graphic rating scale
Scale that allows the
rater to mark an em-
ployee's performance
on a continuum.

Graphic Rating Scales The **graphic rating scale** allows the rater to mark an employee's performance on a continuum. Because of its simplicity, this method is used frequently. Figure 11-8 on next page shows a sample appraisal form combining graphic rating scales with essays. Three aspects of performance are appraised using graphic rating scales: *descriptive categories* (such as quantity of work, attendance, and dependability), *job duties* (taken from the job description), and *behavioral dimensions* (such as decision making, employee development, and communication effectiveness).

Each of these types can be used for different jobs. How well employees meet established standards is often expressed either numerically (e.g., 5, 4, 3, 2, 1) or verbally (e.g., "outstanding," "meets standards," "below standards"). If two or more

| Figure 11-8 | Sample Performance Appraisal Form |

Date sent: 4/19/05

Name: Joe Hernandez

Department: Receiving

Employment status (check one): Full-time __x__ Part-time _____

Rating period: From: 5/12/04 **To:** 5/12/05

Reason for appraisal (check one): Regular interval __x__ Introductory ____ Counseling only ____ Discharge ____

Return by: 5/01/05

Job title: Receiving Clerk

Supervisor: Marian Williams

Date of hire: 5/12/00

Using the following definitions, rate the performance as I, M, or E.

I—Performance is below job requirements and improvement is needed.

M—Performance meets job requirements and standards.

E—Performance exceeds job requirements and standards most of the time.

SPECIFIC JOB RESPONSIBILITIES: List the prinicipal activities from the job summary, rate the performance on each job duty by placing an X on the rating scale at the appropriate location, and make appropriate comments to explain the rating.

I ———————————————— M ———————————————— E

Job Duty #1: Inventory receiving and checking
Explanation: _____

_____

_____

I ———————————————— M ———————————————— E

Job Duty #2: Accurate recordkeeping
Explanation: _____

_____

_____

I ———————————————— M ———————————————— E

Attendance (including absences and tardies):   **Number of absences** ____   **Number of tardies** ____
Explanation: _____

_____

Overall rating: In the box provided, place the letter—I, M, or E—that best describes the employee's overall performance.

Explanation: _____

_____

_____

Figure 11-9

Terms Defining Standards at One Company

5 — Outstanding: The person is so successful at this job criterion that special note should be made, and performance ranks in the top 10%.

4 — Exceeds Expectations: Performance is better than average for the unit, given the common standards and unit results.

3 — Meets Expectations: Performance is at or above the minimum standards. This level is what one would expect from most experienced, competent employees.

2 — Below Expectations: Performance is somewhat below the minimum standards. However, potential to improve within a resonable time frame is evident.

1 — Unsatisfactory: Performance is well below standard. Whether the person can improve to meet the minimum standards is questionable.

people are involved in the rating, they may find it difficult to agree on the exact level of performance achieved relative to the standard. Figure 11-9 defines the terms one company uses in evaluating employee performance. Notice that each level specifies performance standards or expectations in order to reduce variation in interpretations of the standards by different supervisors and employees.

Concerns with Graphic Rating Scales Graphic rating scales in many forms are widely used because they are easy to develop; however, they encourage errors on the part of the raters, who may depend too heavily on the form to define performance. Also, graphic rating scales tend to emphasize the rating instrument itself and its limitations. If they fit the person and the job, the scales work well. However, if they fit poorly, managers and employees who must use them frequently complain about "the rating form."

A key point must be emphasized. Regardless of the scales used, the focus should be on the job duties and responsibilities identified in job descriptions. The closer the link between the scales and what people actually do, as identified in current and complete job descriptions, the stronger the relationship between the ratings and the job, as viewed by employees and managers. Also, should the performance appraisal results be challenged by legal actions, the more performance appraisals are tied to what people actually do, the more likely employers are to prevail in those legal situations.

An additional drawback to graphic rating scales is that often, separate traits or factors are grouped together, and the rater is given only one box to check. For example, "dependability" could refer to meeting deadlines for reports, or it could refer to attendance and tardiness. If a supervisor gives an employee a rating of 3, which aspect of "dependability" is being rated? One supervisor might rate her employees on meeting deadlines, while another supervisor rates his employees on attendance.

Another drawback is that the descriptive words sometimes used in scales may have different meanings to different raters. Terms such as *initiative* and *cooper-*

I'm Rated a 4; Why Not a 5?

One of the biggest areas of contention with appraisals is how many points to use on a graphic rating scale. Scales of 1–10, 1–7, 1–5, 1–4, and 1–3 are all used. In some firms, 1 is low; in others, 1 is high. Confusion is compounded if the meanings of the numbers are not identified.

Odd-numbered scales are used more frequently than even-numbered ones because they allow a mid-point to be identified. Probably the most widely used scale has 5 points, ranging from 1 ("low") to 5 ("high"), with 3 being labeled "satisfactory" or "meeting standards." However, in reality, many supervisors do not rate employees at either the highest or lowest levels. A comment often heard is, "If an employee is rated a 1, he or she will be terminated, and no one deserves a 5 because no one is a superstar." Couple this distorted thinking with the reaction of employees who receive a 4, which is a solid rating: often their first question is, "What do I have to do to be rated a 5?" The rating manager may reply "A 4 is a really good rating; no one gets a 5." Logically, the employee thinks, "If no one can get a 5, why is it on the form?"

Use of 10-point scales poses similar problems, with it well understood that "no one gets a 10" and "if someone gets lower than a 6, that person has a limited employment future." Similar problems exist with 7-point and 4-point scales.

The "numbers game" would not be a big concern, except that the ratings are often tied to pay increase amounts. For instance, a 3 rating may mean a 2%–3% raise, a 4 rating a 4%–5% raise, and a 5 rating a 6%–7% raise.

What is the solution? Research and the experiences of many organizations suggest that there has to be a good definition of what each level means, and then a clear description of the performance standards associated with each level for each job duty and responsibility. Without close links between the rating levels, the job duties and responsibilities, and the performance accomplishments, the appraisal number and "the form," not the performance, become the focus. Training supervisors and managers is the most significant way to improve the performance appraisal process.

ation are subject to many interpretations, especially if used in conjunction with words such as *outstanding, average,* and *poor.* Also, the number of scale points and how they are used can create problems, as the HR Perspective indicates.

Behavioral Rating Scales In an attempt to overcome some of the concerns with graphic rating scales, employers may use behavioral rating scales, which are designed to assess an employee's *behaviors* instead of other characteristics. There are different approaches, but all describe specific examples of employee job behaviors. In a behaviorally anchored rating scale (BARS), these examples are "anchored" or measured against a scale of performance levels.

Identifying important *job dimensions,* which are the most important performance factors in a job description, begins the construction of a behavioral scale. Short statements describe both desirable and undesirable behaviors (anchors). These are then "translated," or assigned, to one of the job dimensions. Anchor statements are usually developed by a group of people familiar with the job. Assignment to a dimension usually requires the agreement of 60%–70% of the group. The group then assigns each anchor a number that represents how good or bad the behavior is, and the anchors are fitted to a scale. Figure 11-10 contains an example that rates customer service skills for individuals taking orders for a national catalog retailer. Spelling out the behaviors associated with each level of

The Customer Service Representative

Outstanding	5	Used positive phrases to explain product
	4	Offered additional pertinent information when asked questions by customer
Satisfactory	3	Referred customer to another product when requested item was not available
	2	Discouraged customer from waiting for an out-of-stock item
Unsatisfactory	1	Argued with customer about suitability of requested product

performance helps minimize some of the problems noted for the graphic rating scale.

Several problems are associated with the behavioral approaches. First, developing and maintaining behaviorally anchored rating scales require extensive time and effort. In addition, various appraisal forms are needed to accommodate different types of jobs in an organization. For instance, because nurses, dietitians, and admissions clerks in a hospital all have distinct job descriptions, a separate BARS form needs to be developed for each.

Comparative Methods

Comparative methods require that managers directly compare the performance levels of their employees against one another. For example, the Information Systems Supervisor would compare the performance of a programmer with that of other programmers. Comparative techniques include ranking and forced distribution.

Ranking The **ranking** method lists all employees from highest to lowest in performance. The primary drawback of the ranking method is that the sizes of the differences between individuals are not well defined. For example, the performances of individuals ranked second and third may differ little, while the performances of those ranked third and fourth differ a great deal. This drawback can be overcome to some extent by assigning points to indicate the sizes of the gaps. Ranking also means someone must be last, which ignores the possibility that the last-ranked individual in one group might be equal to the top-ranked employee in a different group. Further, the ranking task becomes unwieldy if the group to be ranked is large.

Ranking Performance appraisal method in which all employees are listed from highest to lowest in performance.

Forced Distribution Forced distribution is a technique for distributing ratings that are generated with any of the other appraisal methods, and comparing the

Forced distribution
Performance appraisal method in which ratings of employees' performance are distributed along a bell-shaped curve.

ratings of people in a work group. With the **forced distribution** method, the ratings of employees' performance are distributed along a bell-shaped curve. For example, a medical clinic administrator ranking employees on a five-point scale would have to rate 10% as a 1 ("unsatisfactory"), 20% as a 2 ("below expectations"), 40% as a 3 ("meets expectations"), 20% as a 4 ("above expectations"), and 10% as a 5 ("outstanding").

Forced distribution is used in some form by an estimated 30% of all firms with performance appraisal systems. At General Electric, in the "20-70-10" program, managers identify the top 20% and reward them richly so that few will leave. The bottom 10% are given a chance to improve or leave. The forced distribution system is controversial because of both its advantages and its disadvantages, which are discussed next.[21]

Advantages and Disadvantages of Forced Distribution One reason why firms have mandated the use of forced distributions for appraisal ratings is to deal with "rater inflation." If employers do not require a forced distribution, performance appraisal ratings often do not approximate the normal distribution of the bell-shaped curve (see Figure 11-11).

The use of a forced distribution system makes managers identify high, average, and low performers. Thus, high performers can be rewarded and developed, while low performers can be "encouraged" to improve or leave. Advocates of forced ranking also state that forced distribution ensures that compensation increases truly are differentiated by performance rather than being spread somewhat equally among all employees.[22]

But the forced distribution method suffers from several drawbacks.[23] One problem is that a supervisor may resist placing any individual in the lowest (or the

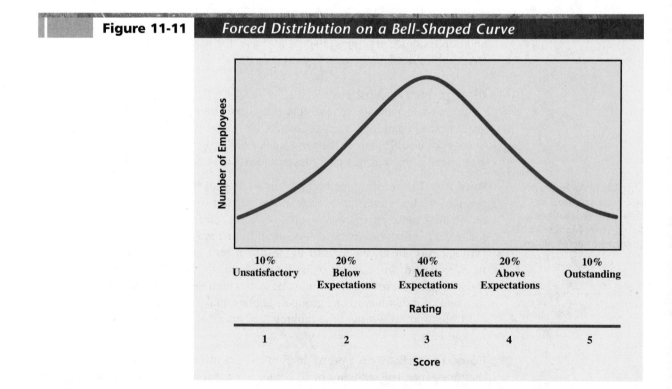

Figure 11-11 | Forced Distribution on a Bell-Shaped Curve

highest) group. Difficulties also arise when the rater must explain to an employee why she or he was placed in one group and others were placed in higher groups. Further, with small groups, the assumption that a bell-shaped or other distribution of performance occurs may be faulty. Finally, in some cases, the manager may make false distinctions between employees. By comparing people against each other, rather than against a standard of job performance, supervisors trying to fill the percentages may end up giving employees subjective ratings.

As a result of such drawbacks, forced distribution systems have been challenged legally. For instance, Capital One has been sued by over 60 former employees and the American Association of Retired Persons (AARP) for age discrimination. The lawsuit states that compared with previous performance rating systems, a forced ranking system introduced several years ago resulted in a greater proportion of workers over age 40 being fired. Several individuals over age 50 with years of experience had received satisfactory or better ratings until the forced ranking system was implemented. Capital One has defended its actions as justified because poor performers have been terminated. Court decisions will ultimately determine the outcome of the lawsuit.[24] Ford and Goodyear Tire & Rubber have already settled similar lawsuits and agreed to modify their performance appraisal processes.

A number of actions are recommended to address these problems if a forced distribution system is to be used. They include many that are similar to those for making other methods of appraisals more legal and effective.[25]

- Use specific, objective criteria and standards.
- Involve employees in planning and designing the programs.
- Ensure that sufficient numbers of people are rated, so that statistical rankings are relevant.
- Train managers, and review their ratings to ensure that they are job related, not based on favoritism.

Narrative Methods

Managers and HR specialists are required to provide written appraisal information. However, some appraisal methods are entirely written. Documentation and description are the essence of the critical incident method and the essay method.

Critical Incident In the critical incident method, the manager keeps a written record of both highly favorable and unfavorable actions performed by an employee during the entire rating period. When a "critical incident" involving an employee occurs, the manager writes it down. The critical incident method can be used with other methods to document the reasons why an employee was given a certain rating.

Essay The essay method requires a manager to write a short essay describing each employee's performance during the rating period. Some "free-form" essays are without guidelines; others are more structured, using prepared questions that must be answered. The rater usually categorizes comments under a few general headings. The essay method allows the rater more flexibility than other methods do. As a result, appraisers often combine the essay with other methods.

The effectiveness of the essay approach often depends on a supervisor's writing skills. Some supervisors do not express themselves well in writing and as a result produce poor descriptions of employee performance, whereas others have excellent writing skills and can create highly positive impressions.

Management by Objectives (MBO)

Management by objectives (MBO) specifies the performance goals that an individual and manager mutually identify. Each manager sets objectives derived from the overall goals and objectives of the organization; however, MBO should not be a disguised means for a superior to dictate the objectives of individual managers or employees. Other names for MBO include *appraisal by results, target coaching, work planning and review, performance objective setting,* and *mutual goal setting.*

MBO Process Implementing a guided self-appraisal system using MBO is a four-stage process. The stages are as follows:

1. *Job review and agreement:* The employee and the superior review the job description and the key activities that constitute the employee's job. The idea is to agree on the exact makeup of the job.
2. *Development of performance standards:* Together, the employee and his or her superior develop specific standards of performance and determine a satisfactory level of performance that is specific and measurable. For example, a quota of selling five cars a month may be an appropriate performance standard for a salesperson.
3. *Setting of objectives:* Together, the employee and the superior establish objectives that are realistically attainable.
4. *Continuing performance discussions:* The employee and the superior use the objectives as bases for continuing discussions about the employee's performance. Although a formal review session may be scheduled, the employee and the supervisor do not necessarily wait until the appointed time to discuss performance. Objectives can be mutually modified as warranted.

The MBO process seems to be most useful with managerial personnel and employees who have a fairly wide range of flexibility and control over their jobs. When imposed on a rigid and autocratic management system, MBO often has failed. Emphasizing penalties for not meeting objectives defeats the development and participative nature of MBO.

LOGGING ON...

Combinations of Methods

No single appraisal method is best for all situations. Therefore, a performance measurement system that uses a combination of methods may be sensible in certain circumstances. Using combinations may offset some of the advantages and disadvantages of individual methods. Category scaling methods sometimes are easy to develop, but they usually do little to measure strategic accomplishments. Further, they may make interrater reliability problems worse. Comparative approaches help reduce leniency and other errors, which makes them useful for administrative decisions such as determining pay raises. But comparative approaches do a poor job of linking performance to organizational goals, and they do not provide feedback for improvement as well as other methods do.

Research on Performance Raters and Performance Appraisals

How managers and supervisors complete performance appraisals on employees is affected by how the raters view the appraisal process. The impact of raters' attitudes and beliefs was examined by Tziner, Murphy, and Cleveland in a study published in the *International Journal of Selection and Assessment*.

The study was based on surveys of about 250 managers from different organizations, and all those managers had responsibilities for doing performance appraisals on employees. One area studied was the extent to which raters felt they had the information and skills needed to accurately rate their subordinates. Additionally, the researchers addressed rater attitudes and beliefs about the appraisal system, rater conscientiousness, and rating behaviors.

Results of the study found that raters who viewed the appraisal system more favorably tended to make greater distinctions when rating employees. Those raters also reported being more comfortable making performance rating distinctions among subordinates in comparison with managers with a more negative view of appraisal systems. The analyses also found that raters who were less confident and conscientious let their more negative views of the appraisal process affect their ratings.

From an HR perspective, this study emphasizes the importance of training in order to create a more positive view of performance appraisal systems. That training can help generate more realistic and objective appraisals.[26]

Narrative methods work well for development because they potentially generate more feedback information. However, without good definitions of criteria or standards, they can be so unstructured as to be of little value. Also, these methods work poorly for administrative uses. The management-by-objectives approach works well to link performance to organizational goals, but it can require much effort and time for defining expectations and explaining the process to employees. Narrative and MBO approaches may not work as well for lower-level jobs as for jobs with more varied duties and responsibilities.

When managers can articulate what they want a performance appraisal system to accomplish, they can choose and mix methods to realize those advantages. For example, one combination might include a graphic rating scale of performance on major job criteria, a narrative of developmental needs, and an overall ranking of employees in a department. Different categories of employees (e.g., salaried exempt, salaried non-exempt, and maintenance) might require different combinations of methods.

TRAINING OF MANAGERS AND EMPLOYEES

Court decisions on the legality of performance appraisals and research on appraisal effectiveness both stress the importance of training managers and employees on performance management and conducting performance appraisals. As the HR Perspective describes, managers with positive views of the performance appraisal system are more likely to use the system effectively. Unfortunately, such training occurs only sporadically or not at all in many organizations. One survey found that over half of all employers provide employees with little or no performance management training, and a third provide managers with little or no such training.[27]

For employees, performance appraisal training focuses on the purposes of appraisal, the appraisal process and timing, and how performance criteria and standards are linked to job duties and responsibilities. Some training also discusses how employees should rate their own performance and use that information in discussions with their supervisors and managers.

Most systems can be improved by training supervisors in doing performance appraisals.[28] Because conducting the appraisals is critical, training should center around minimizing rater errors and providing raters with details on documenting performance information.

Training is especially essential for those who have recently been promoted to jobs in which conducting performance appraisals is a new experience for them. Without training, managers and supervisors often "repeat the past." This means they appraise others much as they have been appraised in the past, which often will have been done poorly. The list below is not comprehensive, but it does identify some topics frequently covered in appraisal training.

- Appraisal process and timing
- Performance criteria and job standards that should be considered
- How to communicate positive and negative feedback
- When and how to discuss training and development goals
- Conducting and discussing the compensation review
- How to avoid common rating errors

Rater Errors

There are many possible sources of error in the performance appraisal process. One of the major sources is mistakes made by raters. Although completely eliminating these errors is impossible, making raters aware of them through training is helpful. Figure 11-12 lists some common rater errors.

Recency effect Occurs when a rater gives greater weight to recent events when appraising an individual's performance.

Varying Standards When appraising employees, a manager should avoid applying different standards and expectations for employees performing similar jobs. Such problems often result from the use of ambiguous criteria and subjective weightings by supervisors.

Primacy effect Occurs when a rater gives greater weight to information received first when appraising an individual's performance.

Recency and Primacy Effects The **recency effect** occurs when a rater gives greater weight to recent events when appraising an individual's performance. Giving a student a course grade based only on his performance in the last week of class, and giving a drill press operator a high rating even though she made the quota only in the last two weeks of the rating period are examples. The opposite is the **primacy effect,** which occurs when a rater gives greater weight to information received first.

Central tendency error Occurs when a rater gives all employees a score within a narrow range in the middle of the scale.

Central Tendency, Leniency, and Strictness Errors Ask students, and they will tell you which professors tend to grade easier or harder. A manager may develop a similar *rating pattern*. Appraisers who rate all employees within a narrow range in the middle of the scale (i.e., rate everyone as "average") commit a **central tendency error,** giving even outstanding and poor performers an "average" rating.

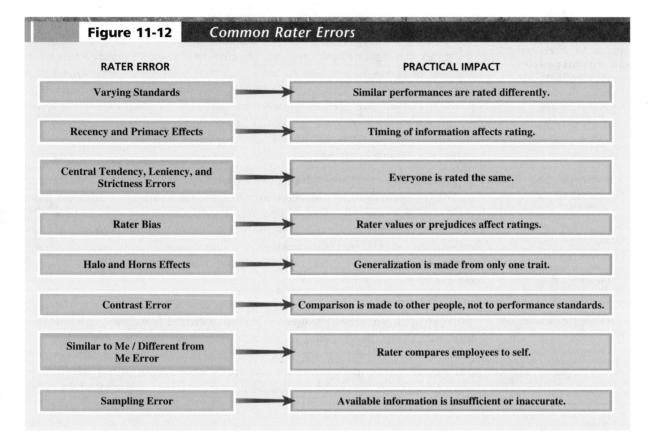

Figure 11-12   Common Rater Errors

RATER ERROR	PRACTICAL IMPACT
Varying Standards	Similar performances are rated differently.
Recency and Primacy Effects	Timing of information affects rating.
Central Tendency, Leniency, and Strictness Errors	Everyone is rated the same.
Rater Bias	Rater values or prejudices affect ratings.
Halo and Horns Effects	Generalization is made from only one trait.
Contrast Error	Comparison is made to other people, not to performance standards.
Similar to Me / Different from Me Error	Rater compares employees to self.
Sampling Error	Available information is insufficient or inaccurate.

Leniency error
Occurs when ratings of all employees fall at the high end of the scale.

Strictness error
Occurs when ratings of all employees fall at the low end of the scale.

Rater bias Occurs when a rater's values or prejudices distort the rating.

Halo effect Occurs when a rater scores an employee high on all job criteria because of performance in one area.

Rating patterns also may exhibit leniency or strictness. The **leniency error** occurs when ratings of all employees fall at the high end of the scale. The **strictness error** occurs when a manager uses only the lower part of the scale to rate employees. To avoid conflict, managers often rate employees higher than they should. This "ratings boost" is especially likely when no manager or HR representative reviews the completed appraisals.

Rater Bias **Rater bias** occurs when a rater's values or prejudices distort the rating. Such bias may be unconscious or quite intentional. For example, a manager's dislike of certain ethnic groups may cause distortion in appraisal information for some people. Use of age, religion, seniority, sex, appearance, or other "classifications" also may skew appraisal ratings if the appraisal process is not properly designed. A review of appraisal ratings by higher-level managers may help correct this problem.

Halo and Horns Effects The **halo effect** occurs when a rater scores an employee high on all job criteria because of performance in one area. For example, if a worker has few absences, her supervisor might give her a high rating in all other areas of work, including quantity and quality of output, without really thinking about the employee's other characteristics separately. The opposite is the *"horns" effect,* occurring when a low rating on one characteristic leads to an overall low rating.

Contrast Error Rating should be done using established standards. One problem is the **contrast error,** which is the tendency to rate people relative to others rather than against performance standards. For example, if everyone else in a group performs at a mediocre level, a person performing somewhat better may be rated as "excellent" because of the contrast effect. But in a group where many employees are performing well, the same person might receive a lower rating. Although it may be appropriate to compare people at times, the performance rating usually should reflect comparison against performance standards, not against other people.

Similar to Me / Different from Me Error Sometimes, raters are influenced by whether people show characteristics that are the same as or different from their own. For example, if a manager has an MBA degree, he might give subordinates with MBAs higher appraisals than those with only bachelor's degrees. The error comes in measuring an individual against another person rather than measuring how well the individual fulfills the expectations of the job.

Sampling Error If the rater has seen only a small sample of the person's work, an appraisal may be subject to sampling error. For example, assume that 95% of the reports prepared by an employee have been satisfactory, but a manager sees only the 5% that has had errors. If the supervisor rates the person's performance as "poor," then a sampling error has occurred. Ideally, the work being rated should be a broad and representative sample of all the work done by the employee.

APPRAISAL FEEDBACK

After completing appraisals, managers need to communicate the results in order to give employees a clear understanding of how they stand in the eyes of their immediate superiors and the organization. Organizations commonly require managers to discuss appraisals with employees. The appraisal feedback interview provides an opportunity to clear up any misunderstandings on both sides. In this interview, the manager should focus on coaching and development, and not just tell the employee, "Here is how you rate and why." Emphasizing development gives both parties an opportunity to consider the employee's performance as part of appraisal feedback.[29]

Appraisal Interview

The appraisal interview presents both an opportunity and a danger. It can be an emotional experience for the manager and the employee because the manager must communicate both praise and constructive criticism. A major concern for managers is how to emphasize the positive aspects of the employee's performance while still discussing ways to make needed improvements. If the interview is handled poorly, the employee may feel resentment, which could lead to conflict in future working relationships.

Employees usually approach an appraisal interview with some concern. They may feel that discussions about performance are both personal and important to their continued job success. At the same time, they want to know how their managers feel about their performance. Figure 11-13 summarizes hints for an effective appraisal interview for supervisors and managers.

Figure 11-13 | *Appraisal Interview Hints*

DO	DO NOT
◆ Prepare in advance ◆ Focus on performance and development ◆ Be specific about reasons for ratings ◆ Decide on specific steps to be taken for improvement ◆ Consider the supervisor's role in the subordinate's performance ◆ Reinforce desired behaviors ◆ Focus on future performance	◆ Do all the talking ◆ Lecture the employee ◆ Mix performance appraisal and salary or promotion issues ◆ Concentrate only on the negative ◆ Be overly critical or "harp on" a failing ◆ Feel it is necessary that both parties agree in all areas ◆ Compare the employee with others

Feedback as a System

The three commonly recognized components of a feedback system are data, evaluation of that data, and some action based on the evaluation. *Data* are factual pieces of information regarding observed actions or consequences. Most often, data are facts that report what happened, such as "Charlie solved an engineering problem" or "Mary spoke harshly to an engineer." Data alone rarely tells the whole story. For instance, Mary's speaking harshly may have been an instance of poor communication and reflective of a lack of sensitivity, or it may have been a proper and necessary action. Someone must evaluate the meaning or value of the data.

Evaluation is the way the feedback system reacts to the facts, and it requires performance standards. Managers might evaluate the same factual information differently than would customers (for example, regarding merchandise exchange or credit decisions) or co-workers. Evaluation can be done by the person supplying the data, by a supervisor, or by a group.

For feedback to cause change, some decisions must be made regarding subsequent *action*. In traditional appraisal systems, the manager makes specific suggestions regarding future actions the employee might take. Employee input often is encouraged as well. In 360° feedback, people from whom information was solicited might also suggest actions that the individual may consider. It may be necessary to involve those providing information if the subsequent actions are highly interdependent and require coordination with the information providers. Regardless of the process used, the feedback components (data, evaluation, and action) are necessary parts of a successful performance appraisal feedback system.

Reactions of Managers

Managers and supervisors who must complete appraisals of their employees often resist the appraisal process. Many managers feel that their role calls on them to assist, encourage, coach, and counsel employees to improve their performance. However, being a judge on the one hand and a coach and a counselor on the other hand may cause internal conflict and confusion for many managers.[30]

Knowing that appraisals may affect employees' future careers also may cause altered or biased ratings. This problem is even more likely when managers know that they will have to communicate and defend their ratings to the employees,

HR *Practice*

Lessons from Two Different Performances: A Supervisor's Story

My employees who do the best work are usually easy to get along with, but not always. I worked with one employee who alienated me and all his colleagues with his fierce competitiveness. He was quick to point out our mistakes, never spoke positively, and usually whined when someone else had a good project that he thought should have been his instead. I tried praising him and sought out his counsel to ease his obvious insecurities, but he was no fun to be around. However, he *was* productive. He got to work early and left late, was always eager to do more, and frequently worked overtime. He always did good work, could be counted on, and never missed a deadline. When he finally left, I realized I had come to rely on him, even though I did not miss his sour jealousy. He would not change.

Another employee and I shared common interests: some hobbies, the same work values and goals, and other inter-

ests. He was generous and willing to help, and his colleagues liked and appreciated him. Early on, he was a good producer, but later, he began procrastinating and often turned in incomplete work. I discussed it with him, and he promised to do better. But he did not. Project after project either flopped or was not done properly. Finally, I told him he would have to improve or find another job. The fact that I considered him a friend made that conversation painful, and I put it off longer than I should have. He told me he felt betrayed, and quit. Yet, when he got a new job, he called to say he had been unhappy but had been unable to move until I had pushed.[32]

What conclusions about performance management and performance appraisal can you draw from these two real-world examples?

their bosses, or HR specialists.[31] Managers can easily avoid providing negative feedback to an employee in an appraisal interview, and thus avoid unpleasantness in an interpersonal situation, by making the employee's ratings positive. But avoidance helps no one. A manager owes an employee a well-done appraisal, as the HR Practice indicates.

Reactions of Appraised Employees

Employees may well see the appraisal process as a threat and feel that the only way for them to get a higher rating is for someone else to receive a low rating. This win/lose perception is encouraged by comparative methods of rating. Emphasis on the self-improvement and developmental aspects of appraisal appears to be the most effective means to reduce these reactions from those participating in the appraisal process.[33]

Another common employee reaction resembles students' reactions to tests. A professor may prepare a test he or she feels is fair, but it does not necessarily follow that students will feel the test is fair; they simply may see it differently. Likewise, employees being appraised may not necessarily agree with the manager doing the appraising. However, in most cases, employees will view appraisals done well as what they are meant to be—constructive feedback.[34]

Effective Performance Management

Regardless of the approach used, managers must understand the intended outcome of performance management. When performance management is used to develop employees as resources, it usually works. When one key part of performance management, a performance appraisal, is used to punish employees, performance management is less effective. In its simplest form as part of performance management, performance appraisal is a manager's observation: "Here are your strengths and weaknesses, and here is a way to develop for the future." Done well, performance management can lead to higher employee motivation and satisfaction. To be effective, a performance management system, including the performance appraisal processes, should be:

- Consistent with the strategic mission of the organization
- Beneficial as a development tool
- Useful as an administrative tool
- Legal and job related
- Viewed as generally fair by employees
- Effective in documenting employee performance

SUMMARY

- Performance management systems attempt to identify, measure, communicate, develop, and reward employee performance.
- Performance management has a broad organizational focus, whereas performance appraisals are the processes used to evaluate how employees perform their jobs and then communicate that information to employees.
- Effective performance management has a number of components, beginning with a performance-focused organizational culture.
- Job criteria identify important elements of a job, and the relevance of job criteria affects the establishment of performance standards.
- Federal employment guidelines and numerous court decisions affect the design and use of the performance appraisal process.
- Appraising employee performance serves both administrative and developmental purposes.
- Performance appraisals can be done either informally or systematically.
- Appraisals can be conducted by superiors, employees (rating superiors or themselves), teams, outsiders, or a variety of sources.

- Appraisal methods include: category scaling, comparative, narrative, and management by objectives.
- Category scaling methods, especially graphic rating scales and behavioral rating scales, are widely used.
- Comparative methods include ranking and forced distribution, which both raise methodological and legal concerns.
- Narrative methods include the critical incident technique and the essay approach.
- Training managers and employees on conducting performance appraisals can contribute to the effectiveness of a performance management system.
- Many performance appraisal problems are caused by a number of different rater errors.
- The appraisal feedback interview is a vital part of any appraisal system, and the reactions of both managers and employees must be considered.

REVIEW AND APPLICATION QUESTIONS

1. Describe how an organizational culture and the use of performance criteria and standards affect the remaining components of a performance management system.

2. Suppose you are a supervisor. What errors might you make when preparing a performance appraisal on a clerical employee? How might you avoid those errors?

3. Review the performance appraisal process and appraisal form used by a current or former employer, and compare them with those provided by other students. Also review other appraisal forms by going to *www.shrm.org/HRtools* and looking under *sample HR forms—employee relations.* Then, develop a report suggesting changes to make the performance appraisal form and process you reviewed more effective.

LEARNING REVIEW

To check your knowledge of the chapter, review the following. (Answers after the supplemental case.) For more questions, see the Study Guide.

1. Specific _____, or dimensions, of job performance identify the most important elements in a given job.
   a. job criteria
   b. essential functions
   c. tasks
   d. performance criteria
2. A legally defensible performance appraisal system should include _____.
   a. appraisal criteria based on job analysis
   b. opportunity for self-appraisals
   c. informal evaluation criteria to permit managerial discretion
   d. input from outsiders who can provide objective feedback

3. A method frequently used by supervisors to rate the performance of subordinates on a continuum is _____.
   a. critical incidents
   b. graphic rating scales
   c. essay
   d. ranking
4. The _____ is the tendency to rate people relative to others rather than against performance standards.
   a. contrast error
   b. halo effect
   c. rater bias
   d. central tendency error

CASE

PERFORMANCE MANAGEMENT IMPROVEMENTS FOR BRISTOL-MYERS SQUIBB

Bristol-Myers Squibb (BMS) is one of the world's largest pharmaceutical firms and is widely known for its innovative research. But the firm has not limited its innovations to products. Several years ago BMS leaders decided that the company's performance management system needed to be reinvented. Specifically, they determined that the existing performance appraisal process was not working. Managers were "form focused," meaning that they were so concentrated on filling out the performance review forms, that the content of the forms was not being used for employee coaching and development. Also, most of the attention of managers and employees was historical and what employees had done in the past. Little attention was being given

to how employees could develop and improve in the future.

The most radical steps taken were to totally eliminate the appraisal forms and their rating scales and to request that managers not discuss pay increases during performance review sessions. Instead, a new "performance partnership" became the focus. At all levels of BMS, managers were trained to hold regular meetings with their employees. At these meetings managers and employees review performance goals expectations. Together they set expectations and timelines for accomplishing the goals. Rather than meeting just once a year, the performance partnership update occurs throughout the year.

The changes in the performance management system have led to several positive results. First, employees are more active participants, rather than just getting their ratings on forms and then passively listening to the managers. Also, a greater amount of time is spent on coaching because managers were trained on use of a guided feedback approach. This approach has led to more discussions in which employees and managers emphasize joint problem-solving and goal achievements. Although the system takes more managerial and employee time, the coaching and employee involvement have created a more positive relationship and improved individual and managerial performance.[35]

Questions

1. Discuss how this case illustrates the conflict between the administrative use and developmental use of appraisals.
2. What would be some of the advantages and disadvantages of eliminating the use of appraisal forms and ratings?

SUPPLEMENTAL CASE: Unequal/Equal Supervisors

This case identifies the consequences of giving appraisal ratings that may not be accurate. (For the case, go to http://mathis.swlearning.com/.)

Learning Activity Answers: 1. a   2. a   3. b   4. a

NOTES

1. "U.S. Workers Give Performance Management Programs a Failing Grade," *Newsline,* April 19, 2004, *www.worldatwork.org*; and Susan R. Hobbs, "If Everyone Hates Performance Evaluations, Why Do Them?" *Bulletin to Management,* February 7, 2002, 47.
2. Kathy Goagne, "One Day at a Time: Using Performance Management to Translate Strategy into Results," *Workspan,* February 2002, 20–25.
3. Andrea Ozias, "Exploring the Role of Performance Management," *Workspan,* June 2003, 50–55.
4. Leslie A. Weatherly, "Performance Management: Getting It Right from the Start," *SHRM Research Quarterly,* January 2004, 1–11.
5. Brian E. Becker, Mark A. Huselid, and Dave Ulrich, *The HR Scorecard: Linking People, Strategy, and Performance* (Boston, MA: Harvard Business School Press, 2001).
6. Edward E. Lawler III and Michael McDermatt, "Current Performance Management Practices," *Worldat-*

Work Journal, Second Quarter 2003, 49–60.
7. Stefan Groeschl, "Cultural Implications for the Appraisal Process," *Cross-Cultural Management* 10 (2003), 67–80; and Kelly Woodford and Jeanne D. Maes, "Employee Performance Evaluations: Administering and Writing Them Correctly in the Multinational Setting," *Equal Opportunities International,* July 2002, 1–9.
8. Inge C. Kerssens–von Dronghen and Olaf Fisscher, "Ethical Dilemmas in Performance Management," *Journal of Business Ethics,* June 2003, 51.
9. Stuart Buttrick, "How to Do Appraisals," *Indiana Employment Law Letter,* December 2003.
10. *Garrett v. Hewlett-Packard Company,* 305 F.3d 1210 (10th Cir. 2002).
11. Andy Meisler, "Dead Man's Curve," *Workforce Management,* July 2003, 44–49.
12. *Britov v. Zia Co.,* 478 F.2d 1200 (10th Cir. 1973).

13. John Goemaat, "Documentation Makes the Difference," *Security Management,* September 2003, 94–102.
14. France Lampron and Linda Koski, "Implementing Web-Enabled Performance Management," *Workspan,* January 2004, 35–38.
15. Based on information provided by Linda Erb, Emprise Bank, Wichita, KS, 2004.
16. "Performance Management Practices," *www.ddi.com.*
17. Susanne G. Scott and Walter O. Einstein, "Strategic Performance Appraisal in Team-Based Organizations: One Size Does Not Fit All," *Academy of Management Executive,* May 2001, 107–116.
18. Ginka Toegel and Jay A. Conger, "360-Degree Assessment: Time for Reinvention," *Academy of Management Learning and Education,* 2 (2003), 297–311.
19. Gary J. Greguras, John M. Ford, and Stepane Brutus, "Manager Attention to Multisource Feedback," *Journal*

of *Management Development,* 22 (2003), 345.

20. Paul Atkins and Robert E. Wood, "Self- Versus Others' Ratings as Predictors of Assessment Center Ratings: Validation Evidence for 360-Degree Feedback Programs," *Personnel Psychology,* 55 (2002), 871–904.

21. Mark Lowrey, "Forcing the Issue," *Human Resource Executive,* October 16, 2003, 26–29.

22. Camille A. Olson and Gregory M. Davis, "Pro's and Con's of Forced Ranking and Other Relative Performance Ranking Systems," *SHRM Legal Report,* March 2003, 1–7.

23. Michael O'Malley, "Forced Ranking," *WorldatWork Journal,* First Quarter 2003, 31–39.

24. Kristen B. Frasch, "Lawsuit Ties Performance Rankings to Age Discrimination," *Human Resource Executive,* July 2003, 13.

25. Orna Guralnik and Lori Anne Wordi, "Forced Distribution: A Controversy," *SHRM White Paper,* August 2003.

26. Based on Alron Tziner, Kevin R. Murphy, and Jeanette N. Cleveland, "Does Conscientiousness Moderate the Relationship Between Attitudes and Beliefs Regarding Performance Appraisal and Rating Behavior?" *International Journal of Selection and Assessment,* 10 (2002), 218–224.

27. Colleen O'Neill and Lori Holsinger, "Effective Performance Management Systems," *WorldatWork Journal,* Second Quarter 2003, 61–67.

28. Eileen Piggot-Irvine, "Appraisal Training Focused on What Really Matters," *International Journal of Education Management,* 17 (2003), 254.

29. Gary E. Roberts, "Employee Performance Appraisal System Participation," *Public Personnel Management,* 31 (2002), 333–334.

30. Jonathan R. Anderson, "Measuring Human Capital: Performance Appraisal Effectiveness," (presentation, Indianapolis, IN Midwest Academy of Management, October 2002).

31. Bob Losyk, "How to Conduct a Performance Appraisal," *Public Management,* April 2002, 8–11.

32. Adapted from Carol Hymowitz, "What to Do When Your Favorite Workers Don't Make the Grade," *Wall Street Journal,* April 11, 2000, B1.

33. Annette Simmons, "When Performance Reviews Fail," *T+D*, September 2003, 47–52.

34. Jay M. Jackman and Myra H. Strober, "Fear of Feedback," *Harvard Business Review,* April 2003, 101–107.

35. Based on "Adding New Life to Performance Reviews Keeps Employees, Managers Rejuvenated," *Bulletin to Management,* February 7, 2002, 41–42.

Compensating Human Resources

CHAPTER 12

Compensation Strategies and Practices

After you have read this chapter, you should be able to:

- Identify the two general types of compensation and the components of each.

- Discuss four issues of strategic compensation design.

- List the basic provisions of the Fair Labor Standards Act (FLSA).

- Describe the two means of valuing jobs.

- Outline the process of building a base pay system.

- Explain two ways individual pay increases are determined.

Compensation Strategies Differ at Costco and Wal-Mart

Different firms follow different compensation strategies due to varying business strategies. Those differences are evident in Costco Wholesale and Wal-Mart in the discount retail industry. Costco's business strategy stresses customer service and selling higher margin products to more affluent customers. This means that it needs to have lower employee turnover, higher productivity, and employees providing quality customer service. To retain and motivate its employees, Costco has adopted a compensation strategy that provides an average hourly wage of $15.97, and broad-based health and retirement benefits. Over 80% of all Costco employees participate in the Costco benefits plans. One payoff for Costco is that employee turnover rates average about 6% annually.

Wal-Mart, which has Sam's Club and Wal-Mart stores, uses a different compensation strategy that is consistent with its business strategy of keeping prices low and constantly reducing costs. This strategy has been successful in reducing prices of goods sold to Wal-Mart customers. The average wage for Wal-Mart employees is $9.47 an hour and for Sam's Club employees is $11.52 an hour (excluding 25% of the workers, who are part-timers and are paid lower rates). Wal-Mart also has required employees to pay more of their benefits costs in the past few years, and as a result has seen significantly less employee participation in the benefits plans. The turnover rate for first-year employees at Sam's Club averages over 20%, and the turnover rate for all employees at Wal-Mart has been about 50% a year. This overall rate means that Wal-Mart must hire 600,000 individuals a year just to keep the same size workforce. When staffing of new stores is included, over 1 million people must be hired annually.[1]

The differences between the compensation strategies of Costco and Wal-Mart do not mean that one strategy is better than the other. Instead, they illustrate how compensation strategies are aligned with business strategies, and the operational consequences of those strategies. It will be interesting to observe to what extent the compensation strategies shift in each firm as competitive pressures continue to grow.

"Money is power, freedom, a cushion,
the root of all evil, the sum of blessings."

—*Carl Sandburg*

Compensation costs represent significant expenditures in most organizations. For instance, at one large health-care organization, employee payroll and benefits expenditures constitute almost 60% of all costs. Although actual compensation costs can be easily calculated, the value derived by employers and employees proves more difficult to identify. Compensation systems in organizations must be linked to organizational objectives and strategies. As the opening discussion illustrates, different firms have different strategies for compensation. Additionally, compensation systems must balance the interests and costs of the employers with the needs and expectations of employees.

NATURE OF COMPENSATION

Compensation is an important factor affecting how and why people choose to work at one organization versus others. To attract and retain competent employees, employers must be reasonably competitive with several types of compensation.

Types of Compensation

Rewards can be both intrinsic and extrinsic. *Intrinsic rewards* may include praise for completing a project or meeting performance objectives. Other psychological and social forms of compensation also reflect the intrinsic type of rewards. *Extrinsic rewards* are tangible and take both monetary and non-monetary forms. Tangible components of a compensation program are of two general types (see Figure 12-1). With *direct compensation,* the employer exchanges monetary rewards for work done. Employers provide *indirect compensation*—like health insurance—to everyone simply for being members of the organization. *Base pay* and *variable pay* are the most common forms of direct compensation. Indirect compensation commonly consists of employee *benefits.*

Base pay Basic compensation that an employee receives, usually as a wage or a salary.

Base Pay The basic compensation that an employee receives, usually as a wage or a salary, is called **base pay.** Many organizations use two base pay categories,

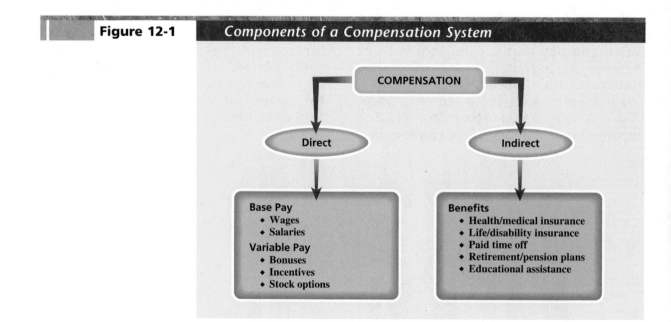

Figure 12-1 — Components of a Compensation System

COMPENSATION

Direct

Indirect

Base Pay
- Wages
- Salaries

Variable Pay
- Bonuses
- Incentives
- Stock options

Benefits
- Health/medical insurance
- Life/disability insurance
- Paid time off
- Retirement/pension plans
- Educational assistance

Wages Payments directly calculated on the amount of time worked.

Salaries Consistent payments made each period regardless of the number of hours worked.

Variable pay Compensation linked directly to individual, team, or organizational performance.

Benefit Indirect reward given to an employee or a group of employees for organizational membership.

hourly and *salaried,* which are identified according to the way pay is distributed and the nature of the jobs. Hourly pay is the most common means and is based on time. Employees paid hourly receive **wages,** which are payments directly calculated on the amount of time worked. In contrast, people paid **salaries** receive consistent payments each period regardless of the number of hours worked. Being paid a salary has typically carried higher status for employees than has being paid a wage. Some organizations maintain an all-salaried approach with their manufacturing and clerical employees in order to create a greater sense of loyalty and organizational commitment. However, they still must pay overtime to certain employees as defined by federal and state laws.

Variable Pay Another type of direct pay is **variable pay,** which is compensation linked directly to individual, team, or organizational performance. The most common types of variable pay for most employees are bonuses and incentive program payments. Executives often receive longer-term rewards such as stock options. Variable pay, including executive compensation, is discussed in Chapter 13.

Benefits Many organizations provide numerous extrinsic rewards in an indirect manner. With indirect compensation, employees receive the tangible value of the rewards without receiving actual cash. A **benefit** is an indirect reward—for instance, health insurance, vacation pay, or a retirement pension—given to an employee or a group of employees for organizational membership, regardless of performance, but they do not directly pay for all of that benefit.

Compensation Responsibilities

To administer compensation expenditures wisely, HR specialists and operating managers must work together. A typical division of compensation responsibilities is illustrated in Figure 12-2. HR specialists guide the development and administration of an organizational compensation system and conduct job evaluations and wage surveys. Also, because of the technical complexity involved, HR specialists typically assume responsibility for developing base pay programs and salary structures and policies. HR specialists may or may not do actual payroll processing. This labor-intensive responsibility is typically among the first to be outsourced. Also, as the HR technology discussion on the next page indicates, some employers have changed how "paychecks" are given to employees. Operating managers evaluate the performance of employees and consider their performance when deciding compensation increases within the policies and guidelines established by the HR unit and upper management.

Figure 12-2

Typical Division of HR Responsibilities: Compensation

HR Unit	Managers
◆ Develops and administers the compensation system ◆ Evaluate jobs and analyzes pay surveys ◆ Develops wage/salary structures and policies	◆ Identify job descriptions and compensation concerns ◆ Recommend pay rates and increases according to HR guidelines ◆ Evaluate employee performance for compensation purposes

Technology Transforming HR

Plastic Paychecks

The use of technology by HR staff is changing how employees receive compensation. For years, employers have encouraged employees to use electronic or automatic deposits of paychecks. Still, large numbers of employees, especially in smaller organizations, receive paper paychecks.

The costs of issuing paper paychecks and security concerns about them have led more employers to use plastic debit cards as "paychecks." Employers as varied as Burger King, Office Depot, Pilgrim's Pride, Cutting Edge Pizza, and the City of Dallas use payroll debit cards. The cards are issued by Visa or MasterCard, and can be used in ATMs (automatic teller machines) or accepted by merchants just as any other payment card.

For employers, the major advantage of plastic paychecks is seen in cost savings. For example, the City of Dallas estimates that it saves $150,000 annually by not having paper paychecks. Employees still get paycheck reports, either in person, through the mail, or electronically. The immediate availability of cash value is a plus for employees, especially many of those who receive lower wages and may have used expensive check-cashing services.

The biggest disadvantage for employees is that if their "paycheck" is stolen or lost, they lose any amount on the card that is spent before the theft or loss is reported. Despite this concern, estimates are that over 6 million employees will be receiving plastic paychecks annually.[2]

STRATEGIC COMPENSATION

An effective compensation system in an organization should be linked to the organizational strategies and objectives. Because so many organizational funds are spent on compensation-related activities, it is critical for top management and HR executives to match compensation systems and practices with what the organization is trying to accomplish.

According to the strategic view of compensation, organizations must make a number of important decisions about the nature of a compensation system to achieve the following compensation objectives:

LOGGING ON...

World at Work
Formerly the American Compensation Association, this Web site lists products, services, and research on compensation and benefits.
www.worldatwork.org

♦ Legal compliance with all appropriate laws and regulations
♦ Cost effectiveness for the organization
♦ Internal, external, and individual equity for employees
♦ Performance enhancement for the organization

Employers must balance compensation costs at a level that both ensures organizational competitiveness and rewards employees sufficiently for their knowledge, skills, abilities, and performance accomplishments. Decisions about compensation systems should be guided by the compensation philosophy of the organization.

Compensation Philosophies

Two basic compensation philosophies lie on opposite ends of a continuum, as shown in Figure 12-3. At one end of the continuum is the *entitlement* philosophy; at the other end is the *performance* philosophy. Most compensation systems fall somewhere in between.

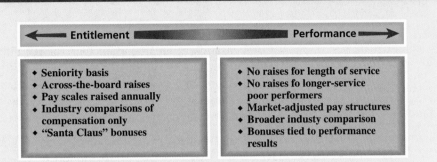

Figure 12-3 Continuum of Compensation Philosophies

← Entitlement ▬▬▬▬▬▬▬▬ Performance ▬▶

- ◆ Seniority basis
- ◆ Across-the-board raises
- ◆ Pay scales raised annually
- ◆ Industry comparisons of compensation only
- ◆ "Santa Claus" bonuses

- ◆ No raises for length of service
- ◆ No raises fo longer-service poor performers
- ◆ Market-adjusted pay structures
- ◆ Broader industy comparison
- ◆ Bonuses tied to performance results

Entitlement philosophy Assumes that individuals who have worked another year are entitled to pay increases, with little regard for performance differences.

Entitlement Philosophy The **entitlement philosophy** assumes that individuals who have worked another year are entitled to pay increases, with little regard for performance differences. Many traditional organizations that give automatic increases to their employees every year practice the entitlement philosophy. Further, most of those employees receive the same or nearly the same percentage increase each year.

Commonly, in organizations with an entitlement philosophy, base pay increases are referred to as *cost-of-living* raises, even if they are not tied specifically to economic indicators. Following an entitlement philosophy some employers guarantee that pay scales will be raised each year, which ultimately means that employer costs increase, regardless of employee performance or organizational competitive pressures. Market comparisons of compensation tend to be made within an industry, rather than more broadly among firms of all types. Bonuses in many entitlement-oriented organizations are determined in a paternalistic manner that often fails to reflect operating results. Therefore, employees "expect" the bonuses, and the bonuses become another form of entitlement.

Pay-for-performance philosophy Requires that compensation changes reflect individual performance differences.

Performance Philosophy The **pay-for-performance philosophy** requires that compensation changes reflect individual performance differences. Organizations operating under this philosophy do not guarantee additional or increased compensation simply for completing another year of organizational service. Instead, they structure pay and incentives to reflect performance differences among employees. Employees who perform well receive larger increases in compensation; those who do not perform satisfactorily see little or no increase in compensation.[3] Thus, employees who perform satisfactorily or better maintain or advance their positions in relation to market compensation levels, whereas poor or marginal performers may fall behind. Also, bonuses and incentives are based on individual, group, and/or organizational performance.

Few organizations totally follow performance-oriented compensation practices, but there is an overall trend to greater use of pay-for-performance systems. A survey of Fortune 1000 firms found that over 80% of the firms use some types of performance-based compensation plans. The study found that growth in the past decade had been greater in individual incentive plans and team/group reward systems than organization-wide gainsharing, profit sharing, and stock option plans.[4] Such plans may help reduce employee turnover and increase employee commitment and retention.[5] An outgrowth of different compensation philosophies is the use of varying approaches to implementing compensation systems.

Compensation Approaches

Compensation is an important tool for recruiting, motivating, and retaining good people. Indeed, those purposes change little over time, but the ways in which some companies approach them have altered dramatically. Figure 12-4 presents some of the choices organizations must make between the traditional compensation approach and a total rewards approach.

Traditional Compensation Approach Traditional compensation systems have evolved over a period of time to reflect a logical, rational approach to compensating employees. Job descriptions identify tasks and responsibilities, and are then used to decide which jobs are more valuable. These systems use a job evaluation to calculate the value that each job contributes to the organization. That value is then used to establish a pay range that reflects a person's progression as he or she grows and presumably gets better at the job.

For some organizations that are in relatively stable industries, a traditional compensation approach makes sense and offers certain advantages in specific competitive situations. This approach may be more legally defensible, less complex, and viewed as more "fair" by average and below-average employees. However, the total rewards approach helps retain top performers, can be more flexible when the economy goes up or down, and is favored by top-performing companies.

Total Rewards Approach The total rewards approach tries to place a value on individuals rather than just on jobs. When determining compensation, managers factor in elements such as how much an employee knows or how competent an employee is. Currently, some organizations have variable pay programs as part of a total rewards approach for all levels of employees. Widespread use of various incentive plans, team bonuses, organizational gainsharing programs, and other designs links growth in compensation to results.[6] The positive effects of a total rewards approach have been identified by Harrah's Entertainment, owner of

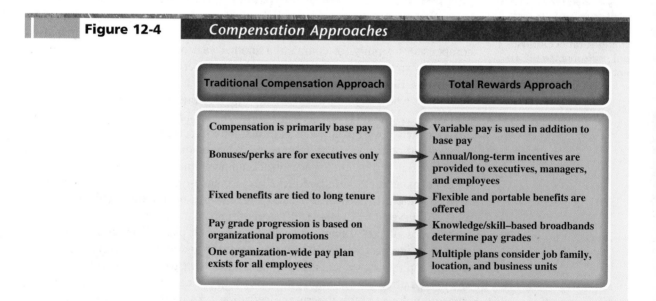

Figure 12-4   *Compensation Approaches*

Traditional Compensation Approach	Total Rewards Approach
Compensation is primarily base pay	Variable pay is used in addition to base pay
Bonuses/perks are for executives only	Annual/long-term incentives are provided to executives, managers, and employees
Fixed benefits are tied to long tenure	Flexible and portable benefits are offered
Pay grade progression is based on organizational promotions	Knowledge/skill–based broadbands determine pay grades
One organization-wide pay plan exists for all employees	Multiple plans consider job family, location, and business units

Figure 12-5

HR Metrics for Compensation

HR Performance Area	Method of Calculation
1. Pay and benefits as percentage of operating expense	Total pay and benefits expenditures
2. Human value added	Revenue − Operating expense − Pay and benefits = Adjusted profit ÷ Full-time-equivalent employees (FTEs)
3. Return on human capital invested	Revenue − Operating expense − Pay and benefits = Adjusted profit ÷ Pay and benefits
4. Employee cost factor	Total compensation and benefits ÷ Full-time-equivalent employees (FTEs)

numerous casinos. Using data from its total incentive program, Harrah's has determined that the program has contributed to increasing customer satisfaction and ultimately its financial results.[7]

HR Metrics and Compensation

Employers spend huge amounts of money for employee compensation. Just like any other area of expenditures, compensation expenditures should be evaluated to determine their effectiveness. Many measures can be used for this evaluation. One survey of 1,200 companies found that employee turnover/retention is widely used.[8] This usage assumes that how well compensation systems operate affects employees' decisions about staying or leaving the organization. Other more specific measures are used as well, such as the ones in Figure 12-5.[9]

The numbers for calculating these measures are readily available to most HR professionals and Chief Financial Officers, but in a large number of firms, such calculations are not made. To be even more useful, these compensation metrics should be computed each year, and then compared with metrics from past years to show how the rate of compensation changes compares with the rate of changes in the organization overall (revenues, expenses, etc.).

COMPENSATION SYSTEM DESIGN ISSUES

Depending on the compensation philosophies, strategies, and approaches identified for an organization, a number of decisions are made that affect the design of the compensation system. Some important ones are highlighted next beginning with global issues.

Global Compensation Issues

Organizations with employees in different countries face some special compensation issues. Variations in laws, living costs, tax policies, and other factors all must be considered in establishing the compensation for local employees and managers, as well as managers and professionals brought in from other countries. Even fluctuations in the values of various monetary currencies must be tracked and adjustments made as the currencies rise or fall in relation to currency rates in other countries. With these and numerous other concerns, developing and managing a global compensation system becomes extremely complex.

One significant global issue in compensation design is how to compensate the employees from different countries. As mentioned in Chapter 8, there are three types of global employees:

- *Host-country nationals:* Citizens of one country who are working in that country and employed by an organization headquartered in a second country.
- *Third-country nationals:* Citizens of one country who are working in a second country and employed by a global firm headquartered in a third country.
- *Expatriates:* Citizens of one country who are working in a second country and employed by an organization headquartered in the first country.

Compensating Host-Country Nationals In many countries, the local wage scales vary significantly. For instance, in some less-developed countries, pay levels for degreed professionals may range from $15,000 to $30,000 a year, whereas in Europe and the U.S., individuals with the same qualifications are paid $50,000 to $80,000 a year. Lower-skilled local workers may make as little as $300 a month in less-developed countries, whereas comparable employees make $1,500 to $2,000 a month in the United States and Europe. These large compensation differences have led to significant "international outsourcing" of jobs to lower-wage countries. The movement of call-center and information technology jobs to India and manufacturing jobs to China, the Philippines, and Mexico are examples.

In designing a compensation system, an organization must decide whether local wages are to be paid to host-country nationals, or more global wage levels are to be considered. Many global employers pay local wages to most employees, except those in senior management and technical positions. Those employers get accused of paying "slave wages," even though the host-country employees have jobs in countries with high unemployment rates and are often paid significantly more than if they worked for local employers.

Compensating Third-Country Nationals Decisions about the compensation levels for third-country nationals are often a function of the originating country of the employees. For example, Indonesians who are working in Turkey may be paid wages that are similar to or lower than those of locals. However, a German engineering manager working in Thailand is likely to be paid about the same as or more than in Germany, much like an expatriate.

Compensating Expatriates The typical components of an international compensation package for expatriates are shown in Figure 12-6. Notice that a number of items are often included.

The two primary approaches to international compensation for expatriates are the balance-sheet approach and the global market approach. The **balance-sheet approach** is a compensation plan that equalizes cost differences between the international assignment and the same assignment in the home country of the individual or the corporation. It has been estimated that the aggregate employer costs for an expatriate, including all allowances, is three to four times the expatriate's salary.[10] Thus, if an expatriate's salary is $120,000, the actual cost of employing that person is likely $360,000–$480,000.

Unlike the balance-sheet approach, the global market approach views international assignments as continual, not just temporary, if they may take employees

Balance-sheet approach Compensation plan that equalizes cost differences between identical international and home-country assignments.

Figure 12-6

Typical Components of Expatriate Compensation

Global market approach Compensation plan that attempts to be more comprehensive in providing base pay, incentives, benefits, and relocation expenses regardless of the country to which the employee is assigned.

Tax equalization plan Compensation plan used to protect expatriates from negative tax consequences.

to different countries for differing lengths of time. The **global market approach** attempts to be more comprehensive in providing base pay, incentives, benefits, and relocation expenses regardless of the country to which the employee is assigned. Further, the reactions of host-country nationals to the pay practices for expatriates must be considered.[11] Therefore, the global market approach to compensation requires greater flexibility, more detailed analyses, and significant administrative effort.

Many international compensation systems attempt to protect expatriates from negative tax consequences by using a **tax equalization plan.** Under such a plan, the company adjusts an employee's base income downward by the amount of estimated home-country tax to be paid for the year. Thus, the employee pays only the foreign-country tax. For instance, a tax equalization plan helps ensure that U.S. expatriates will not pay any more or less in taxes than if they were working in the United States. Because of the variation in tax laws and rates from country to country, tax equalization is very complex to determine.

Market Competitiveness and Compensation

Providing competitive compensation to employees, whether globally, domestically, or locally, is a concern for all employers. Some organizations establish specific policies about where they wish to be positioned in the labor market. These policies use a *quartile strategy,* as illustrated in Figure 12-7 on the next page. Data in pay surveys reveal that the dollar differential between quartiles is generally 15%–20%.

Figure 12-7 | *Compensation Quartile Strategies*

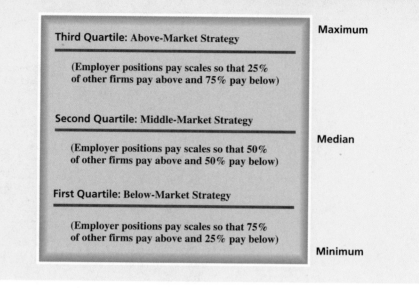

"Meet the Market" Strategy Most employers choose to position themselves in the *second quartile* (median), in the middle of the market, as identified by pay data from surveys of other employers' compensation plans. Choosing this level attempts to balance employer cost pressures and the need to attract and retain employees, by providing mid-level compensation scales that "meet the market" for the employer's jobs.

"Lag the Market" Strategy An employer using a *first-quartile* strategy may choose to "lag the market" by paying below market levels, for several reasons. If the employer is experiencing a shortage of funds, it may be unable to pay more. Also, when an abundance of workers is available, particularly those with lower skills, a below-market approach can be used to attract sufficient workers at a lesser cost. The downside of this strategy is that it increases the likelihood of higher worker turnover. If the labor market supply tightens, then attracting and retaining workers becomes more difficult.

"Lead the Market" Strategy A *third-quartile* strategy uses an aggressive approach to "lead the market." This strategy generally enables a company to attract and retain sufficient workers with the required capabilities and to be more selective when hiring. Because it is a higher-cost approach, organizations often look for ways to increase the productivity of employees receiving above-market wages.

Selecting a Quartile Deciding which quartile to position pay structures in is a function of a number of considerations. The financial resources available, competitiveness pressures, and the market availability of employees with different capabilities are external factors. Some employers with extensive benefits programs or broad-based incentive programs may choose a first-quartile strategy, so that their overall compensation costs and levels are competitive. Other firms may have union contracts and many long-term employees that together have resulted

Research on Pay Levels, Pay Structures, and Organizational Performance

The extent to which organizational compensation systems can affect organizational performance has been widely discussed. To gather specific insights, Brown, Sturman, and Simmering conducted a study on how organizational pay structures and pay levels were tied to organizational performance in over 300 hospitals in California. The results were discussed in the *Academy of Management Journal*.

The researchers examined how the market pay level strategies used in the hospitals were linked to organizational performance measures. Specifically, this study found that pay level and pay structure decisions were significantly related to financial return on assets, patient outcomes, and resource usage efficiencies. For example, having higher pay

levels was related to greater efficiency in the use of resources and in patient outcome measures such as average length of stay.

The general message of this study reinforces the proposition that compensation decisions about pay structures and pay levels do influence organizational performance. For instance, compensation decisions may influence employee turnover or retention, which can contribute to higher or lower employee performance and productivity. Also, compensation decisions play a role in whether or not individuals accept employment, which may ultimately affect organizational performance.[12]

---

in a third-quartile strategy. A firm in a highly competitive industry or in a remote rural location may choose to use a third-quartile strategy in order to attract and retain specialized talent. As the HR Perspective discusses, the pay levels and pay structures used can affect organizational performance.

One point of clarification is important to make: Choosing a quartile strategy means identifying at what broad level the firm will set its compensation levels. Individual employee pay levels will vary around the quartile level, depending on experience, performance, and other individual factors.

Competency-Based Pay

The design of most compensation programs rewards employees for carrying out their tasks, duties, and responsibilities. The job requirements determine which employees have higher base rates. Employees receive more for doing jobs that require a greater variety of tasks, more knowledge and skills, greater physical effort, or more demanding working conditions. However, the design of some compensation programs emphasizes competencies rather than tasks performed.

Competency-based Rewards individuals for the capabilities they demonstrate and acquire.

Competency-based pay rewards individuals for the capabilities they demonstrate and acquire. Because competencies are basic capabilities that can be linked to enhanced performance, paying for competencies rewards employees who exhibit more versatility and continue to develop their competencies. In knowledge-based pay (KBP) or skill-based pay (SBP) systems, employees start at a base level of pay and receive increases as they learn to do other jobs or gain additional skills and knowledge and thus become more valuable to the employer.[13] For example, a printing firm operates two-color, four-color, and six-color presses. The more colors, the more skills required of the press operators. Under a KBP or SBP system, press operators increase their pay as they learn how to operate the more complex presses, even though sometimes they may be running only two-color jobs.

The success of competency plans requires managerial commitment to a philosophy different from the traditional one in organizations. Both the organization and employees can benefit from a properly designed and implemented competency-based system.

When an organization moves to a competency-based system, considerable time must be spent identifying the required competencies for various jobs. Reliance on items such as relevant college diplomas and degrees may provide more emphasis on demonstrated knowledge and competencies.[14] *Progression* of employees must be possible, and employees must be paid appropriately for all their competencies. Any *limitations* on the numbers of people who can acquire more competencies should be clearly identified. *Training* in the appropriate competencies is particularly critical. Also, a competency-based system needs to acknowledge or certify employees as they acquire certain competencies, and then to verify the maintenance of those *competencies*. In summary, use of a competency-based system requires significant investment of management time and commitment.[15]

Individual vs. Team Rewards

As some organizations have shifted to using work teams, they face the logical concern of how to develop compensation programs that build on the team concept. At issue is how to compensate the individual whose performance may also be evaluated on the basis of team achievement. Paying everyone on a team the same amount, even though they demonstrate differing competencies and levels of performance, obviously creates concerns for many employees.

Many organizations use team rewards as variable pay above base pay. For base pay, they compensate individuals on the basis of competencies. Variable pay rewards for teams are most frequently distributed annually as specified dollar amounts, not as percentages of base pay. But team-based rewards may not succeed. At Lantech, a machinery manufacturer in Kentucky, team-based pay resulted in a number of dysfunctional consequences. Employees tried to get friends onto their teams, and others off their teams. Also, some employees exerted influence to get team members to favor them when pay decisions were made. Competition and acrimony between teams created internal conflicts. Consequently, the firm dropped the team-based plan and shifted to a company-wide incentive program, which has been successful.[16]

The most successful uses of team-based compensation have been as variable pay on top of base pay. Rather than substituting for base pay, team-based rewards appear to be useful when compensating a team for performance beyond the satisfactory level. Discussion of team-based incentives is contained in Chapter 13.

Compensation Fairness

Most people in organizations work in order to gain rewards for their efforts. Except in volunteer organizations, people expect to receive fair value, in the form of tangible compensation, for their efforts. Whether employees are considering base pay, variable pay, or benefits, the extent to which they perceive that compensation to be fair often affects their performance and how they view their jobs and employers.

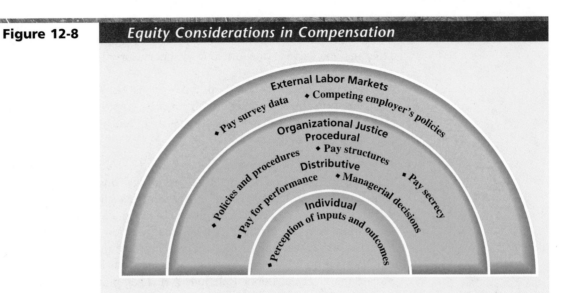

Figure 12-8 Equity Considerations in Compensation

Equity Perceived fairness between what a person does and what the person receives.

Equity is the perceived fairness between what a person does (inputs) and what the person receives (outcomes). Individuals judge equity in compensation by comparing their input (effort and performance) against the effort and performance of others and against the outcomes (the rewards received). These comparisons are personal and are based on individual perceptions, not just facts. A sense of inequity occurs when the comparison suggests an imbalance between input and outcomes. Figure 12-8 indicates the individual, organizational, and external dimensions of equity related to compensation.

External Equity If an employer does not provide compensation that employees view as equitable in relation to the compensation provided to employees performing similar jobs in other organizations, that employer is likely to experience higher turnover. Other drawbacks include greater difficulty in recruiting qualified and high-demand individuals. Also, by not being competitive, the employer is more likely to attract and retain individuals with less knowledge and fewer skills and abilities, resulting in lower overall organizational performance. Organizations track external equity by using pay surveys, which are discussed later in this chapter, and by looking at the compensation policies of competing employers.

Internal Equity in Compensation Equity internally means that employees receive compensation in relation to the knowledge, skills, and abilities they use in their jobs as well as their responsibilities and accomplishments. Two key issues—procedural justice and distributive justice—relate to internal equity.

Procedural justice Perceived fairness of the process and procedures used to make decisions about employees.

Procedural justice is the perceived fairness of the process and procedures used to make decisions about employees, including their pay. As it applies to compensation, the entire process of determining base pay for jobs, allocating pay increases, and measuring performance must be perceived as fair.

Distributive justice Perceived fairness in the distribution of outcomes.

A related issue that must be considered is **distributive justice,** which is the perceived fairness in the distribution of outcomes. As one example, if a hardworking employee whose performance is outstanding receives the same across-the-board raise as an employee with attendance problems and mediocre performance, then inequity may be perceived. Likewise, if two employees have similar performance records but one receives a significantly greater pay raise, the other may perceive an inequity due to supervisory favoritism or other factors not related to the job.

To address concerns about both types of justice, some organizations establish compensation appeals procedures. Typically, employees are encouraged to contact the HR department after discussing their concerns with their immediate supervisors and managers.

Pay Secrecy vs. Openness Another equity issue concerns the degree of secrecy or openness that organizations have regarding their pay systems. Pay information kept secret in "closed" systems includes how much others make, what raises others have received, and even what pay grades and ranges exist in the organization. Some firms have policies that prohibit employees from discussing their pay with other employees, and violations of these policies can lead to disciplinary action.[17] However, several court decisions have ruled that these policies violate the National Labor Relations Act. If employees who violate these "secrecy" policies are disciplined, the employers can be liable for back pay, damages, and other consequences.[18]

A number of organizations are opening up their pay systems to some degree by providing employees with more information on compensation policies, distributing a general description of the compensation system, and indicating where an individual's pay is within a pay grade. Such information allows employees to make more accurate equity comparisons. For instance, Ace Hardware formerly had a pay secrecy policy, but it has discarded it and found that pay openness allows managers to manage their employees more effectively.[19] Having a more open pay system has been found to have positive effects on employee retention and organizational effectiveness.[20]

LEGAL CONSTRAINTS ON PAY SYSTEMS

Compensation systems must comply with many government constraints. The important areas addressed by the laws include minimum-wage standards and hours of work. The following discussion examines the laws and regulations affecting base compensation; laws and regulations affecting incentives and benefits are examined in later chapters.

Fair Labor Standards Act (FLSA)

The major federal law affecting compensation is the Fair Labor Standards Act (FLSA), which was passed in 1938. Amended several times to raise minimum wage rates and expand the range of employers covered, the FLSA affects both private- and public-sector employers. Very small, family-owned and family-operated entities, and family farms generally remain excluded from coverage. Most federal, state, and local government employers also are subject to the provisions of the act, but military personnel, volunteer workers, and a few other limited groups are excluded.

Compliance with FLSA provisions is enforced by the Wage and Hour Division of the U.S. Department of Labor. To meet FLSA requirements, employers must keep accurate time records and maintain those records for three years. Penalties for wage and hour violations often include awards of up to two years of back pay for affected current and former employees. Well-known firms such as Wal-Mart, Royal Caribbean International, Waffle House, Bank of America, SBC Communications, and Farmers Insurance Group have all had to pay large sums to settle lawsuits for failure to pay overtime to employees in various jobs.

Changes in FLSA Regulations Many experts, lawyers, and HR professionals have argued that the nearly 70-year-old law has created great difficulties for employers trying to follow all the requirements of the law. For instance, it has been difficult to use the older regulations when examining jobs, such as software developer, insurance claims adjuster, and telecommunications engineer, that did not exist in 1938 or that have changed significantly since then.

To update and modernize the provisions of the FLSA, the U.S. Department of Labor in 2004 proposed some changes. However objections by labor unions and a number of politicians delayed the adoption of the changes. The details of what finally was approved can be found at *www.dol.gov/esa/whd/*. The provisions of both the original act and subsequent revisions focus on the following major areas:

- ◆ Establish a minimum wage.
- ◆ Discourage oppressive use of child labor.
- ◆ Encourage limits on the number of hours employees work per week, through overtime provisions (exempt and non-exempt statuses).

Minimum Wage The FLSA sets a minimum wage to be paid to the broad spectrum of covered employees. The actual minimum wage can be changed only by congressional action. A lower minimum wage is set for "tipped" employees, such as restaurant workers, but their compensation must equal or exceed the minimum wage when average tips are included. Minimum wage levels continue to spark significant political discussions and legislative maneuvering.

There also is a debate about the use of a living wage versus the minimum wage. A **living wage** is one that is supposed to meet the basic needs of a worker's family. In the United States, the living wage typically aligns with the amount needed for a family of four to be supported by one worker so that family income is above the officially identified "poverty" level. Currently in the United States, at about $8.20 an hour, the living-wage level is significantly higher than the minimum wage.

Without waiting for U.S. federal laws to change, over 80 cities have passed local living-wage laws. Those favoring living-wage laws stress that even the lowest-skilled workers need to earn wages above the poverty level.[21] Those opposed to living-wage laws point out that many of the lowest-paid workers are single, which makes the "family of four" test inappropriate. Obviously, there are ethical, economic, and employment implications on both sides of this issue.[22]

Child Labor Provisions The child labor provisions of the FLSA set the minimum age for employment with unlimited hours at 16 years. For hazardous occupations (see Chapter 15), the minimum is 18 years of age. Individuals 14–15 years old may work outside school hours with certain limitations. Many employers require age certificates for employees because the FLSA makes the employer responsible for determining an individual's age. A representative of a state labor department, a state education department, or a local school district generally issues such certificates.

Exempt and Non-exempt Statuses Under the FLSA, employees are classified as exempt or non-exempt. **Exempt employees** hold positions classified as

---

Living wage One that is supposed to meet the basic needs of a worker's family.

THOMSON

WEST

CHILD LABOR RESTRICTIONS
Describes occupational restrictions under child labor regulations.
Custom Search:
☑ ANALYSIS
Exact Phrase: Occupational restrictions

Exempt employees Employees to whom employers are not required to pay overtime under the Fair Labor Standards Act.

Non-exempt employees Employees who must be paid overtime under the Fair Labor Standards Act.

LOGGING ON...

Wage and Hour Division

This government Web site from the Wage and Hour Division of the U.S. Department of Labor provides an overview of the exemptions under the Fair Labor Standards Act.

www.dol.gov/esa/regs

Compensatory time off Hours given to an employee in lieu of payment for extra time worked.

executive, administrative, professional, or *outside sales,* for which employers are not required to pay overtime. **Non-exempt employees** must be paid overtime under the Fair Labor Standards Act.

In 2004, the FLSA regulations changed the terminology used to identify whether or not a job qualifies for exempt status. The categories of exempt jobs are:

♦ Executive
♦ Administrative
♦ Professional (Learned or Creative)
♦ Computer Employees
♦ Outside Sales

The regulations identify factors related to salaried pay levels per week, discretionary authority, and other criteria that must exist for jobs to be categorized as exempt. To review the details for each exemption, go to the Web site at the Wage and Hour Division noted in the Logging On.

In base pay programs, employers often categorize jobs into groupings that tie the FLSA status and the method of payment together. Employers are required to pay overtime for *hourly* jobs in order to comply with the FLSA. Employees in positions classified as *salaried non-exempt* are covered by the overtime provisions of the FLSA and therefore must be paid overtime. Salaried non-exempt positions sometimes include secretarial, clerical, and salaried blue-collar positions. The FLSA does not require employers to pay overtime for *salaried exempt* jobs, although some organizations have implemented policies to pay a straight rate for extensive hours of overtime. For instance, some electric utilities pay first-line supervisors extra using a special rate for hours worked over 50 a week during storm emergencies. A number of salaried exempt professionals in various information technology jobs also receive additional compensation for working extensive hours.

Overtime The FLSA establishes overtime pay requirements. Its provisions set overtime pay at one and one-half times the regular pay rate for all hours over 40 a week, except for employees who are not covered by the FLSA. Overtime provisions do not apply to farmworkers, who also have a lower minimum-wage schedule.

The workweek is defined as a consecutive period of 168 hours (24 hours × 7 days) and does not have to be a calendar week. If they wish to do so, hospitals and nursing homes are allowed to use a 14-day period instead of a 7-day week, as long as overtime is paid for hours worked beyond 8 in a day or 80 in a 14-day period. No daily number of hours requiring overtime is set, except for special provisions relating to hospitals and other specially designated organizations. Thus, if a manufacturing firm operates on a 4-day/10-hour schedule, no overtime pay is required by the act.

The most difficult part of the act is distinguishing who is and is not exempt. Some recent costly settlements have prompted more white-collar workers to sue for overtime pay. Retail managers, reporters, sales reps, personal bankers, engineers, computer programmers, and claims adjusters have won in some cases.

Compensatory Time Off Often called *comp-time,* **compensatory time off** is hours given to an employee in lieu of payment for extra time worked. Unless it is given to non-exempt employees at the rate of one and one-half times the number of hours over 40 that are worked in a week, comp-time is illegal in the private sector. Also, comp-time cannot be carried over from one pay period to another.

The only major exception to these provisions is for public-sector employees, such as fire and police employees, and a limited number of other workers. Because they often work 24-hour shifts, these individuals may receive compensatory time off. Police and fire officers can accumulate up to 480 hours; all other covered public-sector employees can accumulate up to 240 hours. When those hours are used, the employees must be paid at their normal rates of pay and the comp-time hours used do not count as hours worked in the paid week.

Independent Contractor Regulations

The growing use of contingent workers by many organizations has focused attention on another group of legal regulations—those identifying the criteria that independent contractors must meet. Figure 12-9 illustrates some of the key differences between an employee and an independent contractor. The IRS considers 20 factors in making such a determination.

For the employer classifying someone as an independent contractor rather than an employee offers a major advantage. The employer does not have to pay Social Security, unemployment, or workers' compensation costs. These additional payroll levies may add 10% or more to the costs of hiring the individual as an employee. Most other federal and state entities rely on the criteria for independent contractor status identified by the Internal Revenue Service (IRS). Firms such as Wal-Mart, Allstate, and Microsoft have faced lawsuits for mis-classifying individuals as independent contractors.[23]

Acts Affecting Government Contractors

Several compensation-related acts apply to firms having contracts with the U.S. government. The *Davis-Bacon Act of 1931* affects compensation paid by firms engaged in federal construction projects valued at over $2,000. It deals only with

Figure 12-9	**IRS Test for Employees and Independent Contractors**

An Employee	An Independent Contractor
• Must comply with instructions about when, where, and how to work • Renders services personally • Has a continuing relationship with the employer • Usually works on the premises of the employer • Normally is furnished tools, materials, and other equipment by the employer • Can be fired by the employer • Can quit at any time without incurring liability	• Can hire, supervise, and pay assistants • Generally can set own hours • Usually is paid by the job or on straight commission • Has made a significant investment in facilities or equipment • Can make a profit or suffer a loss • May provide services to two or more unrelated persons or firms at the same time • Makes services available to the public

Source: U.S. Internal Revenue Service, *www.irs.gov.*

federal construction projects and requires that the "prevailing" wage be paid on all federal construction projects. The *prevailing wage* is determined by a formula that considers the rate paid for a job by a majority of the employers in the appropriate geographic area.

Two other acts require firms with federal supply or service contracts exceeding $10,000 to pay a prevailing wage. Both the *Walsh-Healy Public Contracts Act* and the *McNamara-O'Hara Service Contract Act* apply only to those who are working directly on a federal government contract or who substantially affect its performance.

Legislation on Equal Pay and Pay Equity

Various legislative efforts have addressed the issue of wage discrimination on the basis of gender. The Equal Pay Act of 1963 applies to both men and women and prohibits using different wage scales for men and women performing substantially the same jobs. Pay differences can be justified on the basis of merit (better performance), seniority (longer service), quantity or quality of work, or factors other than gender. Similar pay must be given for jobs requiring equal skills, equal effort, or equal responsibility or jobs done under similar working conditions.

Pay equity Similarity in pay for all jobs requiring comparable knowledge, skills, and abilities, even if actual duties and market rates differ significantly.

Pay equity is not the same as equal pay for equal work; instead, it is similar to comparable worth. **Pay equity** is the concept that the pay for all jobs requiring comparable knowledge, skills, and abilities should pay the same even if job duties and market rates differ significantly. A number of states and the Canadian province of Ontario have laws requiring pay equity for public-sector jobs. However, simply showing the existence of pay disparities for jobs that are significantly different has not been sufficient to prove discrimination in court in many cases.

State and Local Laws

Many states and municipalities have enacted modified versions of federal compensation laws. If a state has a higher minimum wage than that set under the Fair Labor Standards Act, the higher figure becomes the required minimum wage in that state. On the other end of the spectrum, many states once limited the number of hours women could work. However, these laws have generally been held to be discriminatory in a variety of court cases, and states have dropped such laws.

Garnishment Laws

Garnishment A court action in which a portion of an employee's wages is set aside to pay a debt owed a creditor.

Garnishment occurs when a creditor obtains a court order that directs an employer to set aside a portion of an employee's wages to pay a debt owed a creditor. Regulations passed as a part of the Consumer Credit Protection Act established limitations on the amount of wages that can be garnished and restricted the right of employers to discharge employees whose pay is subject to a single garnishment order. All 50 states have laws applying to wage garnishments.

▮ DEVELOPMENT OF A BASE PAY SYSTEM

As Figure 12-10 shows, a base compensation system is developed using current job descriptions and job specifications. These information sources are used when *valuing jobs* and analyzing *pay surveys*. These activities are designed to en-

Figure 12-10   *Compensation Administration Process*

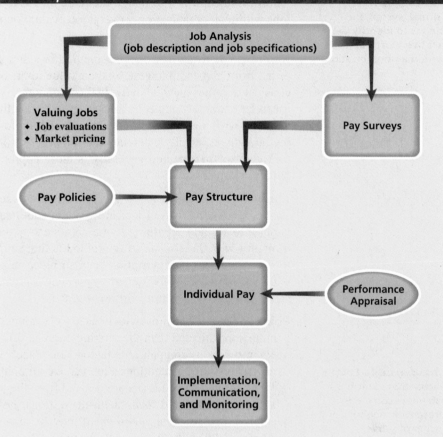

sure that the pay system is both internally equitable and externally competitive. The data compiled in these two activities are used to design *pay structures,* including *pay grades* and minimum-to-maximum *pay ranges.* After pay structures are established, individual jobs must be placed in the appropriate pay grades and employees' pay must be adjusted according to length of service and performance. Finally, the pay system must be monitored and updated.

Employers want their employees to perceive their pay as appropriate in relation to pay for jobs performed by others inside the organization. Frequently, employees and managers make comments such as, "This job is more important than that job in another department, so why are the two jobs paid about the same?" To provide a systematic basis for determining the relative value of jobs within an organization, the employer evaluates every job in the organization on the following features:

- ◆ Knowledge, skills, and abilities needed to perform the job satisfactorily
- ◆ Nature of job tasks, duties, responsibilities, and competencies
- ◆ Difficulty of the job, including the physical and mental demands

Two general approaches for valuing jobs are available: job evaluation and market pricing. Both approaches are used to determine initial values of jobs in relation to other jobs in an organization.

Valuing Jobs with Job Evaluation Methods

Job evaluation
Formal, systematic means to identify the relative worth of jobs within an organization.

Job evaluation is a formal, systematic means to identify the relative worth of jobs within an organization. Several job evaluation methods are available for use by employers of different sizes.

Ranking Method The ranking method is a simple system that places jobs in order, from highest to lowest, by their value to the organization. The entire job is considered rather than the individual components. A problem with ranking is that it can be extremely subjective, leaving managers the difficult task of explaining why one job is ranked higher than another to employees whose pay is affected by the ranking, especially when the ranking involves a large number of jobs. Therefore, the ranking method generally is more appropriate in a small organization having relatively few jobs.

Classification Method In the classification method of job evaluation, descriptions of each class of jobs are written, and then each job in the organization is put into a grade according to the class description it best matches. The major difficulty with the classification method is that subjective judgments are needed to develop the class descriptions and to place jobs accurately in them. With a wide variety of jobs and generally written class descriptions, some jobs could easily fall into two or three different grades.

Point Method The most widely used job evaluation method, the point method, is more sophisticated than the ranking and classification methods. It breaks jobs down into various compensable factors and places weights, or *points,* on them. A **compensable factor** identifies a job value commonly present throughout a group of jobs. Compensable factors are derived from the job analysis. For example, for jobs in warehouse and manufacturing settings, *physical demands, hazards encountered,* and *working environment* may be identified as compensable factors and weighted heavily. In contrast, for most office and clerical jobs, those factors are of little importance and other factors are more important. Figure 12-11 shows examples of compensable factors for different types of jobs.

Compensable factor
Factor that identifies a job value commonly present throughout a group of jobs.

A special type of point method used by a consulting firm, the Hay Group, has received widespread application, although it is most often used with exempt employees. The *Hay system* uses three factors and numerically measures the degree to which each of these factors is required in a job.[24] The three factors and their sub-factors are as follows:

Know-How	Problem-Solving Ability	Accountability
• **Functional expertise**	• **Environment**	• **Freedom to act**
• **Managerial skills**	• **Challenge**	• **Impact of end results**
• **Human relations**		• **Magnitude**

The point method has been widely used because it is relatively simple to use and it considers the components of a job rather than the total job. However, point systems have been criticized for reinforcing traditional organizational structures and job rigidity. Although not perfect, the point method of job evaluation is generally better than the classification and ranking methods because it quantifies job elements.

Factor-Comparison Method The factor-comparison method is a quantitative and quite complex combination of the ranking and point methods. A major advantage of the factor-comparison method is that it is tailored specifically to one organization. Each organization must develop its own key jobs and its own fac-

THOMSON
WEST

JOB EVALUATION
Describes factors affecting the choice of a job evaluation process.
Custom Search:
☑ ANALYSIS
Exact Phrase: Picking a job evaluation process

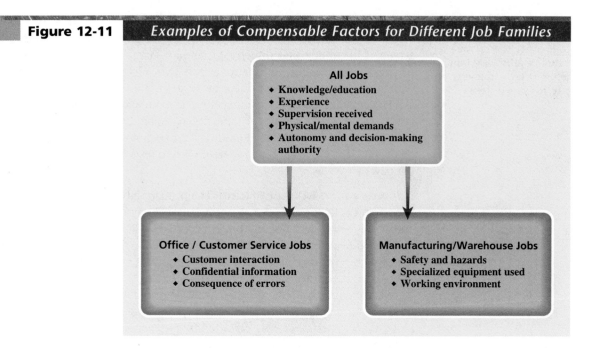

tors. The major disadvantages of the factor-comparison method are that it is complex, difficult to use, and time-consuming to establish and develop.

Integrated and Computerized Systems Some organizations are linking the components of wage and salary programs through computerized and statistical techniques. From a bank of compensable factors, employers can select those most relevant for the different job families in the organization, rate the jobs, and then analyze job evaluation and pay survey relationships. These systems are less separate methods than they are applications of information technology and advanced statistics to the process of developing a wage and salary program.

Legal Issues and Job Evaluation Employers usually view the task of evaluating jobs to determine rates of pay as separate from the tasks of selecting individuals for those jobs and taking disciplinary action against employees. However, because job evaluation affects the employment relationship, specifically the pay of individuals, it involves several legal issues that may cross over into broader employment concerns and that must be addressed.

Critics have charged that traditional job evaluation programs place less weight on knowledge, skills, and working conditions for many female-dominated jobs in office and clerical areas than on the same factors for male-dominated jobs in craft and manufacturing areas. These critics have attacked typical job evaluations as being gender biased. Employers counter that because they base their pay rates heavily on external equity comparisons in the labor market, they are simply reflecting rates the "market economy" sets for jobs and workers, rather than discriminating.

Valuing Jobs Using Market Pricing

A growing number of employers have scaled back their use of "internal valuation" through traditional job evaluation methods and switched to using market pricing more.[25] **Market pricing** uses market pay data to identify the relative value of jobs based on what other employers pay for similar jobs. Jobs are arranged in groups tied directly to similar survey data amounts. Well-known firms such as Marriott International and Dow Chemical are among employers who are relying on market pricing more and more.[26]

Key to market pricing is identifying relevant market pay for jobs that are good "matches" with the employer's jobs, geographic considerations, and company strategies and philosophies about desired market competitiveness levels.[27] Obviously, much of the accuracy of market pricing rests on the sources and quality of the pay surveys used.

Advantages of Market Pricing The primary advantage cited for use of market pricing is that it closely ties organizational pay levels to what is actually occurring in the market, without being distorted by "internal" job evaluation.[28] For years, criticisms of job evaluation have focused on the subjectivity of traditional job evaluations caused by organizational "politics," or the biases of those doing the ranking, classifications, or pointing.

An additional advantage of market pricing is that it allows an employer to communicate to employees that the compensation system is truly "market linked," rather than sometimes being distorted by internal issues. Employees often see a compensation system that was developed using market pricing as having "face validity" and as being more objective than a compensation system that was developed using the traditional job evaluation methods.

Disadvantages of Market Pricing The foremost disadvantage of market pricing is that it relies on accurate and appropriate market survey data, yet, for numerous jobs, pay survey data is limited or may not be gathered in methodologically sound ways. A closely related problem is that the responsibilities of a specific job in a company may be somewhat different from those of the "matching" job identified in the survey.

The scope of market data is another concern. Some employers who are labor market "competitors" may not participate in surveys, and the absence of their data can distort the market values used. A practical concern is that market pricing requires a firm to obtain a wide range of sources, particularly if it is geographically and globally dispersed.

Finally, tying pay levels to market data can lead to wide fluctuations based on market conditions. One has only to look back at the extremes of the information technology job market from 1999 to today, when pay levels increased dramatically then fell back because of the "dot.com" boom and bust. For these and other types of jobs, the debate over the use of job evaluation versus market pricing is likely to continue because both approaches have pluses and minuses associated with them.[29]

Pay Surveys

A **pay survey** is a collection of data on compensation rates for workers performing similar jobs in other organizations. Both job evaluation and market pricing are tied to surveys of the pay that other organizations provide for similar jobs.

Because jobs may vary widely in an organization, it is particularly important to identify **benchmark jobs**—jobs that are found in many other organizations. Often these jobs are performed by individuals who have similar duties that require similar KSAs. For example, benchmark jobs commonly used in clerical/office

LOGGING ON...

**The Institute of
Management and
Administration**
This Web site contains
information on salary
survey sources that are
reviewed by IOMA.
www.ioma.com

situations are accounts payable processor, word-processing operator, and receptionist. Benchmark jobs are used because they provide "anchors" against which individual jobs can be compared.

An employer may obtain surveys conducted by other organizations, access Internet data, or conduct its own survey. Many different surveys are available from a variety of sources. National surveys on many jobs and industries come from the U.S. Department of Labor, Bureau of Labor Statistics; professional and national trade associations; and various management consulting companies. In many communities, employers participate in wage surveys sponsored by the local chamber of commerce or local HR associations, to provide information relevant to jobs in the community.

Internet-Based Pay Surveys HR professionals can access a wide range of pay survey data on-line. In many cases, pay survey questionnaires are distributed electronically rather than as printed copies, and HR staff members complete the questionnaires electronically. Entities that have moved partially or totally to Web-based questionnaires report increased member participation and satisfaction. For example, the Credit Union Executives Society (CUES), an association for financial credit unions, has seen member participation rates increase 25% as it has transitioned to on-line surveys.[30]

The move to electronic surveys has had several advantages.[31] First, HR or account specialists can complete the electronic surveys by linking company payroll databases to the survey data requested. Doing this requires significantly less time than would be spent filling out printed survey forms. Also, submitting the survey data electronically reduces the time needed to enter the data and prepare the final report to send back to participating firms.

It is anticipated that over the next five years, most pay surveys will be conducted using electronic, Web-based technology. Also, the Internet provides a large number of pay survey sources and data. However, use of these sources requires caution because their accuracy and completeness may not be verifiable or may not be applicable to individual firms and employees. The HR Practice on the next page discusses how to address employee questions regarding pay survey data that is accessible from the Internet.

Using Pay Surveys The proper use of pay surveys requires evaluating a number of factors to determine if the data is relevant and valid. Areas that should be examined for each survey include the following questions:

◆ *Participants:* Does the survey cover a realistic sample of the employers with whom the organization competes for employees?
◆ *Broad-based:* Does the survey include data from employers of different sizes, industries, and locales?
◆ *Timeliness:* How current are the data (determined by the date the survey was conducted)?
◆ *Methodology:* How established is the survey, and how qualified are those who conducted it?
◆ *Job matches:* Does the survey contain job summaries so that appropriate matches to job descriptions can be made?

Pay Surveys and Legal Issues One reason for employers to use outside sources for pay surveys is to avoid charges that the employers are attempting "price-fixing" on wages. The federal government has filed suit against Exxon

Questions About Internet Pay Survey Data

One challenge facing HR professionals and managers is how to respond to employees who find salary information on Internet sources, such as *www.Salary.com*. Other pay data are available to individuals through e-newsletters from various professional and trade associations and through member-access Web pages. It is becoming common for employees who are dissatisfied with their pay to bring Internet data to HR professionals or their managers and ask why their current pay is different from the pay in that Internet data.

Responding to such questions from employees requires addressing a number of areas. Even *Salary.com* includes explanations on its Web site, under the links *my salary is lower* and *my salary is higher*. Points to be made in discussing employee concerns include the following:[32]

♦ *Job titles and responsibilities:* Comparison should be made against the employee's full job description, not just job titles and the brief job summaries on the Web sites.

♦ *Experience, KSAs, and performance:* Individuals in different organizations may have jobs with similar descriptions but vary significantly in their experience levels,

KSAs, and performance. Most pay survey data on the Internet is an average of multiple companies and of multiple employees in those companies.

♦ *Geographic differences:* Many pay survey sites on the Internet use geographic index numbers, not actual data from employers in a particular area. For certain jobs, surveys of actual employers and jobs from a specific local area may reflect different numbers than those index numbers.

♦ *Company size and industry:* Pay levels may vary significantly by company size, with smaller firms often having lower pay. Also, pay levels for comparable jobs are often lower in certain industries, such as retail and banking, than they are in utilities or highly unionized manufacturing firms.

♦ *Base pay vs. total compensation:* Employers vary in the use of benefits and incentive compensation programs. An employee may work in a firm with a benefits or incentive program that is significantly better or worse than the programs offered by firms whose data appear in Internet surveys. However, Internet data usually reflect only base pay amounts.

Mobil and 13 other oil companies, alleging that by sharing wage data, the employers attempted to hold wages down artificially in violation of the Sherman Antitrust Act. The final outcome of that case is still in litigation.[33]

Another case involved the Utah Society for Healthcare Human Resources Administration and nine hospitals in the Salt Lake City area. The consent decree that resulted prohibits all health-care facilities in Utah from designing, developing, or conducting a wage survey. The hospitals can participate in surveys conducted by independent third-party firms only if privacy safeguards are met.[34]

▮ PAY STRUCTURES

Job family Group of jobs having common organizational characteristics.

Once job valuations and pay survey data are gathered, pay structures can be developed using the process identified in Figure 12-12. Data from the valuation of jobs and the pay surveys may lead to the establishment of several different pay structures for different job families, rather than just one structure for all jobs. A **job family** is a group of jobs having common organizational characteristics. In organizations, there can be a number of different job families. Examples of some common pay structures based on different job families include: (1) hourly and

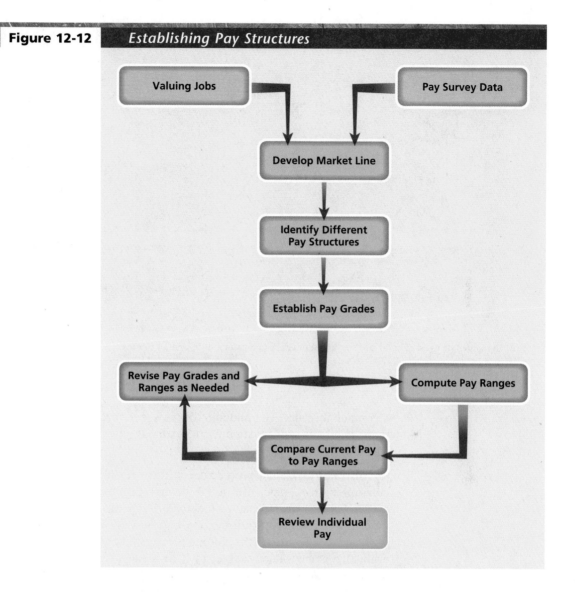

Figure 12-12   *Establishing Pay Structures*

salaried; (2) office, plant, technical, professional, and managerial; and (3) clerical, information technology, professional, supervisory, management, and executive. The nature, culture, and structure of the organization are considerations for determining how many and which pay structures to have.

Pay Grades

In the process of establishing a pay structure, organizations use **pay grades** to group individual jobs having approximately the same job worth. Although no set rules govern establishing pay grades, some overall suggestions can be useful. Generally, 11–17 grades are used in small and medium-sized companies, that is, companies with fewer than 500 employees. Two methods are commonly used to establish pay grades: market banding and use of job evaluation data.

Setting Pay Grades Using Market Banding Closely linked to the use of market pricing to value jobs, **market banding** groups jobs into pay grades based on similar market survey amounts. Figure 12-13 shows two "bands" for jobs in

Pay grades
Groupings of individual jobs having approximately the same job worth.

Market banding
Grouping jobs into pay grades based on similar market survey amounts.

Figure 12-13   *Market-Banded Pay Grades for Community Bank*

Grade	Job	Pay Survey Summary	Pay Grade		
			Minimum	Midpoint*	Maximum
1	Bookkeeper	$22,913			
	Loan Clerk	$22,705			
	Customer Service Representative	$22,337	$17,966	$22,458	$26,950
	Data Entry / Computer Operator	$22,309			
	Head Teller	$22,305			
	Special Teller	$22,179			
2	Mail Clerk / Messenger	$19,167			
	Proof Machine Operator	$18,970	$14,962	$18,703	$22,444
	General Office Clerk	$18,594			
	Receptionist	$18,184			

*Computed by averaging the pay survey summary data for the jobs in each pay grade.

a community bank. The midpoint of the survey average is used to develop pay range minimums and maximums, the methods of which are discussed later in this chapter.

Setting Pay Grades Using Job Evaluation Points The second approach to determining pay grades uses job evaluation points or other data generated from the traditional job evaluation methods discussed earlier in the chapter. This process ties pay survey information to job evaluation data by plotting a *wage curve* and *scattergram*. This plotting involves first making a graph that charts job evaluation points and pay survey rates for all surveyed jobs. The graph shows the distribution of pay for the surveyed jobs, allowing a linear trend line to be developed by the *least-squares regression method*. Also, a curvilinear line can be developed by multiple regression and other statistical techniques. The end result is the development of a **market line** that shows the relationship between job value as determined by job evaluation points and pay survey rates. The statistical analysis done when determining market lines particularly focuses on the r^2 levels from the regression when the data is analyzed by different job families and groups. Generally, an r^2 of $+.85$ or higher is desired. (Details on the methods and statistical analyses can be found in compensation texts.)[35]

Figure 12-14 shows a market line and how jobs having similar point values have been grouped into pay grades. Pay ranges have been computed for each pay grade. Each dot represents an individual employee's current pay in relation to the pay ranges that have been developed.

Market line Graph line that shows the relationship between job value as determined by job evaluation points and job value as determined by pay survey rates.

Pay Ranges

The pay range for each pay grade also must be established. Using the market line as a starting point, the employer can determine minimum and maximum pay

Figure 12-14

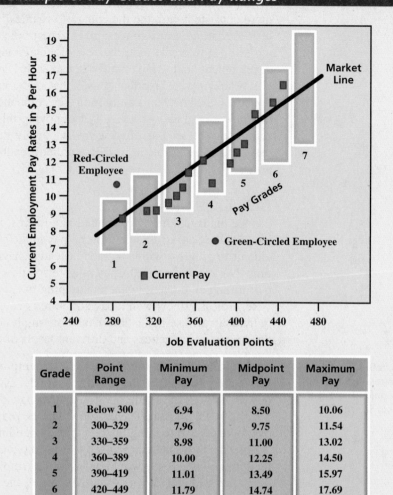

Grade	Point Range	Minimum Pay	Midpoint Pay	Maximum Pay
1	Below 300	6.94	8.50	10.06
2	300–329	7.96	9.75	11.54
3	330–359	8.98	11.00	13.02
4	360–389	10.00	12.25	14.50
5	390–419	11.01	13.49	15.97
6	420–449	11.79	14.74	17.69
7	Over 450	12.79	15.99	19.18

levels for each pay grade by making the market line the midpoint line of the new pay structure (see Figure 12-14). For example, in a particular pay grade, the maximum value may be 20% above the midpoint located on the market line, and the minimum value may be 20% below it.

Once pay grades and ranges have been computed, then the current pay of employees must be compared with the draft ranges. If the pay of a significant number of employees falls outside the ranges, then a revision of the pay grades and ranges may be needed. Also, once costing and budgeting scenarios are run to assess the financial impact of the new pay structures, then pay policy decisions about market positioning may have to be revised, by either lowering or raising the ranges. A growing number of employers are reducing the number of pay grades and expanding pay ranges by broadbanding.

Broadbanding Broadbanding is the practice of using fewer pay grades with much broader ranges than in traditional compensation systems. Combining many

Broadbanding
Practice of using fewer pay grades with much broader ranges than in traditional compensation systems.

grades into these broadbands is designed to encourage horizontal movement and therefore more skill acquisition. The main advantage of broadbanding is that it is more consistent with the flattening of organizational levels and the growing use of jobs that are multi-dimensional.[36] The primary reasons for using broadbanding are: (1) to create more flexible organizations, (2) to encourage competency development, and (3) to emphasize career development.

A problem with broadbanding is that many employees have become "conditioned" to the idea that a promotion is accompanied by a pay raise and movement to a new pay grade. As a result of removing this grade progression, the organization may be seen as offering fewer upward promotion opportunities. Despite these and other problems, it is likely that broadbanding will continue to grow in usage.

Individual Pay

Once managers have determined pay ranges, they can set the pay for specific individuals. Setting a range for each pay grade gives flexibility by allowing individuals to progress within a grade instead of having to move to a new grade each time they receive a raise. A pay range also allows managers to reward the better-performing employees while maintaining the integrity of the pay system.

Regardless of how well a pay structure is constructed, there usually are a few individuals whose pay is lower than the minimum or higher than the maximum due to past pay practices and different levels of experience and performance.

Red-Circled Employees A **red-circled employee** is an incumbent who is paid above the range set for the job. For example, assume that an employee's current pay is $10.92 an hour, but the pay range for that person's pay grade is $6.94–$10.06 an hour. The person would be red circled. Management would try over a year or so to bring the employee's rate into grade.

Several approaches can be used to bring a red-circled person's pay into line. Although the fastest way would be to cut the employee's pay, that approach is not recommended and is seldom used. Instead, the employee's pay may be frozen until the pay range can be adjusted upward to get the employee's pay rate back into the grade. Another approach is to give the employee a small lump-sum payment but not adjust the pay rate when others are given raises.

Green-Circled Employees An individual whose pay is below the range is a **green-circled employee.** Promotion is a major contributor to this situation. Generally, it is recommended that the green-circled individual receive fairly rapid pay increases to reach the pay grade minimum. More frequent increases can be used if the minimum is a large amount above the incumbent's current pay.

Pay Compression One major problem many employers face is **pay compression,** which occurs when the pay differences among individuals with different levels of experience and performance become small. Pay compression occurs for a number of reasons, but the major one involves situations in which labor market pay levels increase more rapidly than current employees' pay adjustments.

In response to shortages of particular job skills in a highly competitive labor market, managers may occasionally have to pay higher amounts to hire people with those scarce skills. For example, suppose the job of specialized information systems analyst is identified as a $48,000–$68,000 salary range in one company, but qualified individuals are in short supply and other employers are paying

Red-circled employee Incumbent who is paid above the range set for the job.

Green-circled employee Incumbent who is paid below the range set for the job.

Pay compression Occurs when the pay differences among individuals with different levels of experience and performance become small.

$70,000. To fill the job the firm likely will have to pay the higher rate. Suppose also that several analysts who have been with the firm for several years started at $55,000 and have received 4% increases each year. These current employees may still be making less than the $70,000 paid to attract and retain new analysts from outside with less experience. One partial solution to pay compression is to have employees follow a step progression based on length of service, assuming performance is satisfactory or better.[37]

DETERMINING PAY INCREASES

Decisions about pay increases are often critical ones in the relationships between employees, their managers, and the organization. Individuals express expectations about their pay and about how much of an increase is "fair," especially in comparison with the increases received by other employees. There are several ways to determine pay increases, including: performance, seniority, cost-of-living adjustments, and lump-sum increases. These methods can be used separately or in combination.

Pay Adjustment Matrix

Some system for integrating appraisals and pay changes must be developed and applied equally. Often, this integration is done through the development of a *pay adjustment matrix,* or *salary guide chart.* Use of pay adjustment matrices bases adjustments in part on a person's **compa-ratio,** which is the pay level divided by the midpoint of the pay range. To illustrate, the compa-ratio for two employees would be:

Compa-ratio Pay level divided by the midpoint of the pay range.

$$\text{Employee } R = \frac{\$16.50 \text{ (current pay)}}{\$15.00 \text{ (midpoint)}} \times 100 = 110 \text{ (Compa-ratio)}$$

$$\text{Employee } J = \frac{\$13.05 \text{ (current pay)}}{\$15.00 \text{ (midpoint)}} \times 100 = 87 \text{ (Compa-ratio)}$$

Salary guide charts reflect a person's upward movement in an organization. That movement often depends on the person's performance, as rated in an appraisal, and on the person's position in the pay range, which has some relation to experience as well. A person's placement on the chart determines what pay raise the person should receive. For example, if employee *J* is rated as exceeding expectations (2) with a compa-ratio of 87, that person is eligible for a raise of 7%–9%, according to the chart in Figure 12-15 on the next page.

Two interesting facets of the sample matrix illustrate the emphasis on paying for performance. First, individuals whose performance is below expectations receive small to no raises, not even a so-called cost-of-living raise. This approach sends a strong signal that poor performers will not continue to receive increases just by completing another year of service.

Second, as employees move up the pay range, they must exhibit higher performance to obtain the same percentage raise as those lower in the range performing at the "meets performance expectations" (2) level. This approach is taken because the firm is paying above the market midpoint but receiving only satisfactory performance rather than above-market performance. Charts can be constructed to reflect the specific pay-for-performance policy and philosophy in an organization.

Figure 12-15

Pay Adjustment Matrix

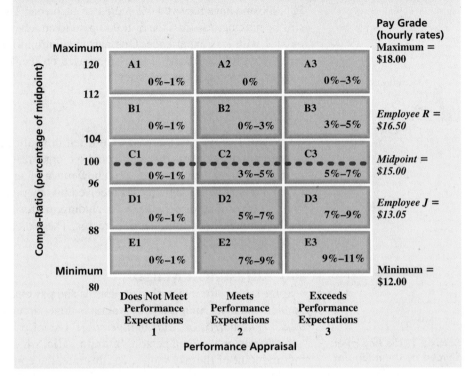

Seniority

Seniority Time spent in the organization or on a particular job.

Seniority, or time spent in the organization or on a particular job, can be used as the basis for pay increases. Many employers have policies that require a person to be employed for a certain length of time before being eligible for pay increases. Pay adjustments based on seniority often are set as automatic steps once a person has been employed the required length of time, although performance must be at least satisfactory in many non-union systems.

Cost-of-Living Adjustments (COLAs)

A common pay-raise practice is the use of a *cost-of-living adjustment (COLA).* Often, these adjustments are tied to changes in the Consumer Price Index (CPI) or some other general economic measure. However, numerous studies have revealed that the CPI overstates the actual cost of living.

Unfortunately, some employers give across-the-board raises and call them *merit raises,* which they are not. If all employees get a pay increase, it is legitimately viewed as a cost-of-living adjustment that has little to do with merit or good performance. For this reason, employers should reserve the term *merit* for any amount above the standard raise, and they should state clearly which amount is for performance and which is the "automatic" COLA.

Lump-Sum Increases (LSIs)

Most employees who receive pay increases, either for merit or for seniority, first receive an increase in the amount of their regular monthly or weekly paycheck. For example, an employee who makes $12.00 an hour and then receives a 3% increase will move to $12.36 an hour.

Lump-sum increase (LSI) One-time payment of all or part of a yearly pay increase.

In contrast, a **lump-sum increase (LSI)** is a one-time payment of all or part of a yearly pay increase. The pure LSI approach does not increase the base pay. Therefore, in the example of a person making $12.00 an hour, if an LSI of 3% is granted, then the person receives a lump sum of $748.80 ($0.36 an hour × 2,080 working hours in the year). However, the base rate remains at $12.00 an hour, which slows down the progression of the base wages. The firm can vary the amount of the "lump" from one year to the next, without having to continually raise the base rate. Some organizations place a limit on how much of a merit increase can be taken as a lump-sum payment. Other organizations split the lump sum into two checks, each representing one-half of a year's pay raise.

An LSI plan offers advantages and disadvantages. The major advantage of an LSI plan is that it heightens employees' awareness of what their performance "merited." Another advantage is that the firm can use LSIs to slow down the increase of base pay, and thus reduce or avoid the compounding effect on succeeding raises. One disadvantage of LSI plans is that workers who take a lump-sum payment may become discouraged because their base pay has not changed. Unions generally resist LSI programs for this reason; unions also resist LSI programs because of their impact on pensions and benefits, unless the total amount paid including the LSI is used in pension computations.

SUMMARY

- Compensation provided by an organization can come directly through base pay and variable pay and indirectly through benefits.
- For compensation expenditures to be administered effectively, compensation responsibilities of both HR specialists and managers must be performed well.
- Compensation practices are closely related to the strategies, objectives, culture, and philosophies of organizations.
- A continuum of compensation philosophies exists, ranging from an entitlement philosophy to a performance philosophy.
- A number of companies are using a total rewards approach to compensation.
- HR metrics can and should be used to measure the effectiveness of compensation.
- Compensation practices for international employees are much more complex than those for domestic employees, because they are affected by many more factors.
- Decisions about compensation must always consider market competitiveness and positioning, use of competency-based pay, team rewards, and fairness.

- When designing and administering compensation programs, internal and external equity, organizational justice, and pay openness all must be considered.
- The Fair Labor Standards Act (FLSA), as amended, is the major federal law that affects pay systems. It requires most organizations to pay a minimum wage and to comply with overtime provisions, including appropriately classifying employees as exempt or non-exempt and as independent contractors or employees.
- A base pay system is developed using information from valuations of jobs and pay surveys, both of which are designed to ensure that the pay system is internally equitable and externally competitive.
- The values of jobs can be determined using either job evaluation or market pricing.
- Once a firm has collected pay survey data, it can develop a pay structure, which is composed of pay grades and pay ranges.
- Broadbanding, which uses fewer pay grades with wider ranges, provides greater career movement possibilities for employees and has grown in popularity.

- Individual pay must take into account the placement of employees within pay grades. Problems involving "red-circled" jobs, whose rates are above pay range, and "green-circled" jobs, whose rates are below pay range, may be addressed in a number of ways.

- Individual pay increases can be based on performance, seniority, cost-of-living adjustments, lump-sum increases, or a different combination of approaches.

REVIEW AND APPLICATION QUESTIONS

1. Discuss the compensation philosophies and approaches that have been used at organizations where you have worked. What have been the consequences of those philosophies and approaches?

2. You have been named Human Resources Manager for a company that has 180 employees and no formal base pay system. What steps will you take to develop such a coordinated system?

3. You are the HR Director for an insurance company with regional offices in several states. For each office, you want to be sure that the administrative assistants reporting to the Regional Manager are paid appropriately. Go to *www.Salary.com* to find geographic pay survey data for this job in Hartford, Connecticut; Atlanta, Georgia; Omaha, Nebraska; and Phoenix, Arizona. Then, recommend pay ranges; identify the low, median, and high of each pay range. To present the data, list the offices in order from lowest median pay to highest median pay.

LEARNING REVIEW

To check your knowledge of the chapter, review the following. (Answers after the supplemental case.) For more questions, see the Study Guide.

1. The entitlement philosophy of compensation is characterized by _____.
   a. pay structures adjusted to market pressures
   b. broad pay comparisons beyond specific industry practices
   c. bonuses tied to performance
   d. across-the-board raises

2. Most employers position their pay programs in the _____ quartile of their market as identified by data from surveys of other employers' compensation plans.
   a. first
   b. second
   c. third
   d. fourth

3. _____ are paid a salary for the standard workweek but are subject to the overtime provisions of the FLSA.
   a. Salaried exempt employees
   b. Independent contractors
   c. Hourly employees
   d. Salaried non-exempt employees

4. Pay compression occurs primarily because _____.
   a. employers fail to conduct performance appraisals
   b. organizations fail to conduct pay surveys
   c. labor market pay levels increase more than employers' pay adjustments
   d. employers pay below the minimum of their pay ranges

CASE

COMPENSATION CHANGES AT JC PENNEY

Having been in business for over 100 years, JC Penney has experienced highs and lows in organizational performance. In the past decade the firm has faced a dramatically changing retail environment from competitors such as Target, Wal-Mart, the Gap, and others. As a result, JC Penney increasingly became seen by customers and analysts of the retail industry as lagging in its merchandising strategies.

Even the compensation system at JC Penney was viewed as traditional and paternalistic in nature, because it emphasized rewarding employees primarily for their length of service. Also, most promotions were made internally, which created a more static organizational culture. The traditional pay structure at the firm contained many pay grades and was based on job evaluations to establish those grades. Its performance review system emphasized employee tenure and effort to a greater degree than performance results.

To respond to the competitive environment, the firm's executives decided that JC Penney had to become more dynamic and able to change more quickly. One of the changes identified was that a new compensation system was needed. The restructured compensation system that was developed and implemented focused heavily on market value, using pay survey data that specifically matched job responsibilities. The greatest change was the development of "career bands." These career bands grouped jobs together based on survey data and job responsibilities, which resulted in there being fewer grades with wider ranges. The career bands represented a broadbanding approach that was based on benchmark jobs for which market pricing data were available. Jobs for which market data could not be found were analyzed using a job evaluation system.

Use of the career bands was designed to identify career paths for employees throughout the company, as well as better link compensation to all of the jobs. By having career bands, greater flexibility was provided for employees to be rewarded for both current performance and continuing career growth. To support this new compenation system, a revised performance management system was developed. This system used performance goals and measures more closely tied to business strategies and objectives. Important to implementing the new performance management system was managerial training. This training was needed so that the managers could use the new system effectively and to describe to employees the importance of performance and its link to compensation.

Implementation of the new compensation system required extensive communications efforts. Newsletters were prepared for all managers explaining the new compensation system. Then departmental and store meetings were held with managers and employees to describe the new system. A number of printed materials and videos discussing the importance of the new compensation plan were prepared and utilized. A final part of communications was to prepare letters for individual employees that informed them about their job band and market pay range.[38]

Questions

1. Discuss why JC Penney's shift to a more performance-oriented compensation system had to be linked to market pricing.
2. Why does having fewer pay bands aid the career development for employees?

SUPPLEMENTAL CASE: Scientific Turmoil

This case discusses the concerns associated with having a formal base pay system, and communication issues that occur. (For the case, go to **http://mathis.swlearning.com/.**)

Learning Review Answers: 1. d 2. b 3. d 4. c

NOTES

1. Based on Stanley Holmes and Wendy Zeller, "The Costco Way," *Business Week,* April 12, 2004, 76–77; "How Big Can IT Grow?" *The Economist,* April 17, 2004, 67–69; and "People Problems on Every Aisle," *Workforce Management,* February 2004, 26–34.

2. Based on Elayne Robertson Demby, "Plastic Paychecks," *HR Magazine,* April 2003, 89–94; and "The Paycheck Is in the Card," *Business Week,* December 22, 2003, 16.

3. Steve Bates, "Top Pay for Best Performance," *HR Magazine,* January 2003, 31–38.

4. Edward E. Lawler III, "Pay Practices in *Fortune 1000* Corporations," *WorldatWork Journal,* Fourth Quarter 2003, 45–54.

5. Michael C. Sturman et al., "Is It Worth It to Win the Talent War? Evaluating the Utility of Performance-Based Pay," *Personnel Psychology,* 56 (2003), 997–1035.

6. Frank H. Lyons and Dan Ben-Ora, "Total Rewards Strategy," *Compensation & Benefits Review,* March/April 2002, 34–40.

7. Gary Loveman, "Diamonds in the Data Mine," *Harvard Business Review,* May 2003, 109.

8. DowScott et al., "Linking Compensation Policies and Programs to Organizational Effectiveness, *WorldatWork Journal,* Fourth Quarter 2003, 35–44.

9. Jac Fitz-Enz and Barbara Davison, *How to Measure Human Resources Management,* 3rd ed. (New York: McGraw-Hill, 2002); and *www.shrm.org/hrtools.*

10. Julie Cook, "Local Living," *Human Resource Executive,* November 11, 2003, *www.workindex.com.*

11. Soo Min Toh and Angelo S. Denisi, "Host Country National Reactions to Expatriate Pay Policies," *Academy of Management Review,* 28 (2003), 606–621.

12. Based on Mark P. Brown, Michael C. Sturman, and Marcia J. Simmering, "Compensation Policy and Organizational Performance: The Efficiency, Operational, and Financial Implications of Pay Levels and Pay Structures," *Academy of Management Journal,* 46 (2003), 752–762.

13. Sofiane Sahraoui, "How to Pay for Knowledge," *Human Systems Management,* 21 (2002), 159.

14. R. Eugene Hughes, "Skill or Diploma? The Potential Influence of Skill-Based Pay Programs on Sources of Skills Acquisition and Degree Programs," *WorkStudy,* 45 (2003), 179.

15. Patricia K. Zingheim and Jay R. Schuster, "Reassessing the Value of Skill-Based Pay," *WorldatWork Journal,* Third Quarter 2002, 72–77.

16. Charlotte Garvey, "Steer Teams with the Right Pay," *HR Magazine,* May 2002, 71–78.

17. Jonathan A. Segal, "Labor Pains for Union-Free Employers," *HR Magazine,* March 2004, 113–118.

18. Rafael Gely and Leonard Bierman, "Pay Secrecy/Confidentiality Rules and the National Labor Relations Act," *Journal of Labor and Employment Law,* Fall 2003.

19. Lin Grensing-Pophal, "Communication Pays Off," *HR Magazine,* May 2003, 77-82.

20. Paul W. Mulvey et al., "Study Finds that Knowledge of Pay Processes Can Beat Out Amount of Pay in Employee Retention, Organizational Effectiveness," *Journal of Organizational Excellence,* Autumn 2002, 29; and Robert L. Heneman, Paul W. Mulvey, and Peter V. LeBlanc, "Improve Base Pay ROI by Increasing Employee Knowledge," *WorldatWork Journal,* Fourth Quarter 2002, 21–27.

21. David Neumark, "Detecting Effects of Living Wage Laws," *Industrial Relations,* 42 (2003), 531–565.

22. Julie Liedman, "Making a Living," *Human Resource Executive,* November 2002, 70–73.

23. Carolyn Hirschman, "Are Your Contractors Legal?" *Insurance Networking,* February 2002, 1.

24. Craig Skenes and Brian H. Kleiner, "The HAY System of Compensation," *Management Research News,* 26 (2003), 109–116.

25. Brian Hinchcliffe, "The Juggling Act: Internal Equity and Market Pricing," *Workspan,* February 2003, 46–48.

26. Fay Hansen, "Power to the Line People," *Workforce,* June 2003, 71–75.

27. For details on how to conduct market pricing, see *Market Pricing: Unraveling the Mystery* (Scottsdale, AZ: WorldatWork, 2002).

28. Howard Risher, "Planning a 'Next Generation' Salary System," *Compensation & Benefits Review,* November/December 2002, 13–24.

29. Robert L. Heneman, "Job and Work Evaluation: A Literature Review," *Public Personnel Management,* 32 (2003), 47–72.

30. Karen Bankston, "Make Way for Web Surveys," *Association Management,* April 2003, 51–55.

31. Nona Tobin, "Can Technology Ease the Pain of Salary Surveys?" *Public Personnel Management,* 31 (2002), 65–78.

32. For further details and discussion, see *www.Salary.com.*

33. *Todd v. Exxon Corporation,* 275 F.3d 191 (2nd Cir. 2001).

34. *District of Utah, U.S. District Court v. Utah Society for Healthcare Human Resources Administration, et al. Federal Register,* March 1994, No. 14203.

35. For example, see Richard I. Henderson, *Compensation Management in a Knowledge-Based World,* 9th ed. (Upper Saddle River, NJ: Prentice Hall, 2003).

36. Andrew S. Rosen and David Turetsky, "Broadbanding: The Construction of a Career Management Framework," *WorldatWork Journal,* Fourth Quarter 2002, 45–55.

37. Andrew L. Klein, Kimberly M. Keating, and Lisa M. Ruggerio, "The Perils of Pay Inequity: Addressing the Problems of Compression," *WorldatWork Journal,* Fourth Quarter 2002, 56–62.

38. Based on Donna R. Graebner and Kevin A. Seward, "Bringing It All Inside," *Workspan,* August 2004, 30–35.

Variable Pay and Executive Compensation

After you have read this chapter, you should be able to:

- Define variable pay and identify three elements of successful pay-for-performance plans.

- Discuss three types of individual incentives.

- Explain three ways that sales employees are typically compensated.

- Identify key concerns that must be addressed when designing group/team variable pay plans.

- Discuss why profit sharing and employee stock ownership are common organizational incentive plans.

- Identify the components of executive compensation and discuss criticisms of executive compensation levels.

Pay-for-Performance Plans

Pay-for-performance incentive plans are growing in popularity. Over 80% of all firms report that they have some type of plan whereby employees receive additional compensation tied to performance. Sales, customer service, productivity, attendance, safety, and executive incentive plans are the common ones. The performance rewarded can be individual, group, or organizational, or a combination of these.

One firm that has successfully made use of pay-for-performance plans is Intuit. Best known for its Quicken, TurboTax, and QuickBooks software, Intuit has used incentive plans to increase employee retention and customer response service at its call centers, which handle thousands of calls a day. Concerned by a past 30% annual turnover rate and too many errors and missed sales opportunities, Intuit developed a pay-for-performance program that focuses on sales productivity, accuracy, and customer feedback analyses. Specific performance goals were set that trigger the payment of incentives. Under the new program, employees who perform better on those criteria receive greater rewards. Since the firm introduced the plan, turnover has dropped to 12%, and accuracy, sales, and customer service ratings all have improved. Follow-up evaluation of the program revealed that Intuit has received a significant return on its investment (ROI) in the incentive program.

It appears that other firms that use pay-for-performance plans need to learn from Intuit. Even though companies overall spend an average of 9% of payroll costs on such pay plans, almost half of them report that they use no formal means to assess the effectiveness of those plans. Just as disturbing is that over 20% of companies using incentive plans do not communicate the performance goals to employees. Fortunately, over three-fourths of the firms that do communicate their plans and goals report that those efforts have contributed to better business results, which is the purpose of having such plans.[1]

"Some people make more money, others make less. More is better."

—*Anonymous employee*

Pay-for-performance is being utilized by a growing number of employers. In today's competitive global economy, many employers believe that people become more productive if compensation varies directly according to performance. A significant number of employers are adding to their traditional base pay programs by offering employees additional compensation. The amount of payment varies based on the degree to which individual, group/team, and organizational performance goals are attained.

VARIABLE PAY: INCENTIVES FOR PERFORMANCE

Variable pay Compensation linked to individual, group/team, and/or organizational performance.

Variable pay is compensation linked to individual, group/team, and/or organizational performance. Traditionally also known as *incentives,* variable pay plans attempt to provide tangible rewards to employees for performance beyond normal expectations. The philosophical foundation of variable pay rests on several basic assumptions:

◆ Some jobs contribute more to organizational success than others.
◆ Some people perform better and are more productive than others.
◆ Employees who perform better should receive more compensation.
◆ Some of employees' total compensation should be tied directly to performance.

Pay-for-performance has a different philosophical base than does the traditional compensation system based on seniority or length of service. In the traditional organization, length of service is a primary differentiating factor between people. Differences in job responsibilities are recognized through different amounts of base pay. However, giving additional rewards to some people and not others is seen as potentially divisive and as hampering employees' working together. These thoughts are why many labor unions oppose pay-for-performance programs. However, many individual workers expect to be rewarded for performance differences that increase organizational results.

Developing Successful Pay-for-Performance Plans

Employers adopt variable pay or incentive plans for a number of reasons. The main ones include desires to do the following:

◆ Link more directly strategic business goals and employee performance.
◆ Enhance organizational results and reward employees financially for their contributions.
◆ Reward employees to recognize different levels of employee performance.
◆ Achieve HR objectives, such as increasing retention, reducing turnover, recognizing training, or rewarding safety and attendance.

Variable pay plans can be considered successful if they meet the objectives the organization had for them when they were initiated. Figure 13-1 shows three elements that can affect the success of a variable pay plan. These elements are discussed next.

Does the Plan Fit the Organization? In the case of pay-for-performance plans, one size does not fit all. A plan that has worked well for one company will not necessarily work well for another. Obviously, the plan must be linked to the objectives of the organization. For example, a distribution company based in New Jersey, NYF, uses a teamsharing compensation plan as part of efforts to cre-

Figure 13-1 | *Effective Incentive Plans*

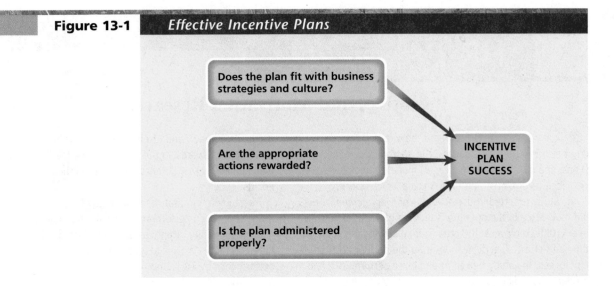

ate an organizational culture that permits the firm to respond to competitive changes more easily. One indication of success is a sales increase of 700% in target markets since implementation of the teamsharing program. In this program, all employees, whether sales, warehouse, office, or managerial, are rewarded if the company's sales goals are met.[2]

The success of any variable pay program relies on its consistency with the culture of the organization. For example, if an organization is autocratic and adheres to traditional rules and procedures, an incentive system that rewards flexibility and teamwork is likely to fail. The incentive plan is "planted" in the wrong growing environment.

Does the Plan Reward the Appropriate Actions? Variable pay systems should be tied as much as possible to desired performance. Employees must see a direct relationship between their efforts and their financial rewards.

Because people tend to produce what is measured and rewarded, organizations must make sure that what is being rewarded ties to meeting organizational objectives. Use of multiple measures helps ensure that various performance dimensions are not omitted. For example, assume a hotel reservation center wants to set incentives for employees to increase productivity by lowering the time they spend on each call. If that reduction is the only measure, the quality of customer service and the number of reservations made might drop as employees rush callers in order to reduce talk time. Therefore, the center should consider basing rewards on multiple measures, such as talk time, reservations booked, and the results of customer satisfaction surveys.

Linking pay to performance may not always be appropriate. For instance, if the output cannot be measured objectively, management may not be able to correctly reward the higher performers with more pay. Managers may not even be able to accurately identify the higher performers. Under those circumstances, individual variable pay is inappropriate.

Is the Plan Administered Properly? A variable pay plan may be complex or simple, but it will be successful only if employees understand what they have to do to be rewarded. The more complicated a plan is, the more difficult it will be

THOMSON

WEST

USE OF INCENTIVES
Identifies advantages and disadvantages of using incentives.
Custom Search
☑ ANALYSIS
Exact Phrase: Pros and cons of rewards

Incentives and Motivation Research

Stajkovic and Luthans compared the effects on productivity of four incentive approaches. The approaches were: (1) routine pay-for-performance, (2) monetary incentives, (3) social recognition, and (4) performance feedback.

The study reported in the *Academy of Management Journal* took place in the operations division of a company with over 7,000 employees. The organization spent significant time and effort objectively measuring the performance of employees. The study looked at employee performance and productivity in light of each of the four different types of incentives.

The "routine pay-for-performance" group simply got extra pay for increased performance. The "monetary incentives" group also received pay-for-performance, but supervisors were trained to use the pay as a consequence when critical performance was exhibited. In the "social recognition"

group, recognition and attention were used by trained supervisors as rewards. In the "performance feedback" group, individuals received detailed feedback on their performance results.

The study found that the routine pay-for-performance approach increased performance over the baseline by 11%, and the monetary incentives approach increased performance by 32%. The social recognition approach increased performance by 24%, and the performance feedback approach by 20%.

Overall, the results of the study indicate that pay can indeed improve performance. However, it apparently works best when it is presented contingently (that is, based on productivity and performance) and accompanied by social recognition and performance feedback.[3]

to communicate it meaningfully to employees. Experts generally recommend that a variable pay plan include several performance criteria. However, having two or three areas of focus should not overly complicate the calculations necessary for employees to determine their own incentive amounts. Managers also need to be able to explain clearly what future performance targets need to be met and what the rewards will be.

Successful plans clearly identify how much is provided to employees separate from their base pay amounts. That separation makes a distinct connection between performance and pay. It also reinforces the notion that part of the employees' pay must be "re-earned" in the next performance period. The HR Perspective describes a study on incentives and motivation.

Measuring the Success of Variable Pay Plans

The results of variable pay plans, like those in other areas of HR, should be measured to determine the success of the programs. Different measures of success can be used, depending on the nature of the plan and the goals set for it.[4] Figure 13-2 shows some examples of different measures that may be used to evaluate variable pay plans.

Regardless of the plan, the critical decision is to gather and evaluate data to determine if the expenditures on it are justified by increased performance and results. If the measures show positive analyses, then the plan is truly pay-for-performance in nature.

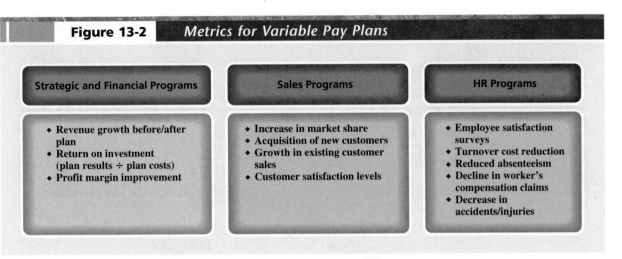

Figure 13-2 *Metrics for Variable Pay Plans*

Strategic and Financial Programs	Sales Programs	HR Programs
◆ Revenue growth before/after plan ◆ Return on investment (plan results ÷ plan costs) ◆ Profit margin improvement	◆ Increase in market share ◆ Acquisition of new customers ◆ Growth in existing customer sales ◆ Customer satisfaction levels	◆ Employee satisfaction surveys ◆ Turnover cost reduction ◆ Reduced absenteeism ◆ Decline in worker's compensation claims ◆ Decrease in accidents/injuries

Successes and Failures of Variable Pay Plans

Even though variable pay has grown in popularity, some attempts to implement it have succeeded and others have not. Incentives *do* work, but they are not a panacea because their success depends on the circumstances.

The positive view that many employers have for variable pay is not shared universally by all employees. If individuals see incentives as desirable, they are more likely to put forth the extra effort to attain the performance objectives that trigger the incentive payouts. As one indicator, a survey of employees found that only 29% believe that they are rewarded when doing a good job. Discouragingly for firms with incentive plans, approximately the same low percentage of employees indicated that they were motivated by their employers' incentive plans.[5] One problem is that many employees prefer that performance rewards increase their base pay, rather than be given as a one-time, lump-sum payment. Further, many employees prefer individual rewards to group/team or organizational incentives.

Providing variable pay plans that are successful can be complex and requires significant, continuing efforts. Some suggestions that appear to contribute to successful incentive plans are as follows:

◆ Develop clear, understandable plans that are continually communicated.
◆ Use realistic performance measures.
◆ Keep the plans current and linked to organizational objectives.
◆ Clearly link performance results to payouts that truly recognize performance differences.
◆ Identify variable pay incentives separately from base pay.

Types of Variable Pay

Individual incentives are given to reward the effort and performance of individuals. Some common means of providing variable pay to individuals are piece-rate systems, sales commissions, and bonuses. Others include special recognition rewards such as trips or merchandise. With individual incentives, employees may focus on what is best for them personally and may block or inhibit the performance of other individuals with whom they are competing. That is why group/team incentives have been developed.

When an organization rewards an entire group/team for its performance, cooperation among the members may increase as well. The most common *group/team*

LOGGING ON...

Synygy Inc.
At this Web site, the largest provider of software and services for managing variable pay plans provides free case studies and publications.
www.synygy.com

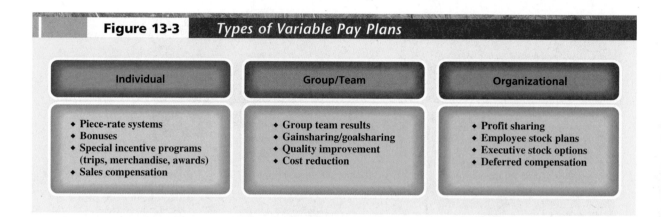

Figure 13-3 *Types of Variable Pay Plans*

Individual	Group/Team	Organizational
• Piece-rate systems • Bonuses • Special incentive programs (trips, merchandise, awards) • Sales compensation	• Group team results • Gainsharing/goalsharing • Quality improvement • Cost reduction	• Profit sharing • Employee stock plans • Executive stock options • Deferred compensation

incentives are gainsharing or goalsharing plans, in which employee teams that meet certain goals share in the gains measured against performance targets. Often, those programs focus on quality improvement, cost reduction, and other measurable results.

Organizational incentives reward people according to the performance results of the entire organization. This approach assumes that all employees working together can generate greater organizational results that lead to better financial performance. These programs often share some of the financial gains made by the firm with employees through payments calculated as a percentage of the employees' base pay. The most prevalent forms of organization-wide incentives are profit-sharing plans and employee stock plans. Figure 13-3 shows some of the programs under each type of incentive or variable pay plan.

INDIVIDUAL INCENTIVES

Individual incentive systems try to tie individual effort to additional rewards. Conditions necessary for the use of individual incentive plans are as follows:

- *Individual performance must be identified:* The performance of each individual must be measured and identified because each employee has job responsibilities and tasks that can be separated from those of other employees.
- *Independent work must be performed:* Individual contributions result from independent work and effort given by individual employers.
- *Individual competitiveness must be desired:* Because individuals generally pursue the incentives for themselves, competition among employees often occurs. Therefore, independent competition in which some individuals "win" and others do not must be desired.
- *Individualism must be stressed in the organizational culture:* The culture of the organization must be one that emphasizes individual growth, achievements, and rewards. If an organization emphasizes teamwork and cooperation, then individual incentives may be counterproductive.

Straight piece-rate system Pay system in which wages are determined by multiplying the number of units produced by the piece rate for one unit.

Piece-Rate Systems

The most basic individual incentive systems are piece-rate systems, whether straight or differential. Under the **straight piece-rate system,** wages are determined by multiplying the number of units produced (such as garments sewn or service calls handled) by the piece rate for one unit. Because the cost is the same for each unit, the wage for each employee is easy to figure, and labor costs can be accurately predicted. A *differential piece-rate system* pays employees one piece-rate wage for units produced up to a standard output and a higher piece-rate wage for units produced over the standard. Many possible combinations of straight and differential piece-rate systems can be used, depending on situational factors.

Despite their incentive value, piece-rate systems are difficult to apply because determining standards is a complex and costly process for many types of jobs. In some instances, the cost of determining and maintaining the standards may be greater than the benefits derived. Also, jobs in which individuals have limited control over output or in which high standards of quality are necessary may be unsuited to piecework.

Bonuses

Bonus One-time payment that does not become part of the employee's base pay.

Individual employees may receive additional compensation in the form of a **bonus,** which is a one-time payment that does not become part of the employee's base pay. Growing in popularity, individual bonuses are used at all levels in some firms.

A bonus can recognize performance by an employee, a team, or the organization as a whole. When performance results are good, bonuses go up. When performance results are not met, bonuses go down. Most employers base part of an employee's bonus on individual performance and part on company results, as appropriate.

Bonuses can also be used to reward employees for contributing new ideas, developing skills, or obtaining professional certifications. When the skills or certifications are acquired by an employee, a pay increase or a one-time bonus may follow. For example, a financial services firm provides the equivalent of two weeks' pay to employees who master job-relevant computer skills. Another firm gives one week's pay to members of the HR staff who obtain professional certifications such as Professional in Human Resources (PHR), Senior Professional in Human Resources (SPHR), or Certified Compensation Professional (CCP).

"Spot" Bonuses A special type of bonus used is a "spot" bonus, so called because it can be awarded at any time. Spot bonuses are given for a number of reasons. For instance, a spot bonus reward may be given to an information technology employee who installed a computer software upgrade, which required extensive time and effort. Other examples are to compensate a nurse who dealt successfully with a difficult patient and to pay a customer service employee who resolved the problems of a major client.

Often, spot bonuses are given in cash, although some firms provide managers with gift cards, travel vouchers, or other rewards. The keys to successful use of spot bonuses are to keep the amounts reasonable and to provide them for exceptional performance accomplishments.[6] The downside to their use is that it can create jealousy and resentment from other employees, who may feel that they were deserving but did not get a spot bonus.

Special Incentive Programs

Numerous special incentive programs have been used to reward individuals, ranging from one-time contests for meeting performance targets to awards for performance over time. For instance, safe-driving awards are given to truck drivers with no accidents or violations on their records during a year. Although special programs can be developed for groups and for entire organizations, they often focus on rewarding only high-performing individuals. Figure 13-4 shows purposes for special incentives.

Performance Awards Cash, merchandise, gift certificates, and travel are the most frequently used incentive rewards for significant performance. Cash is still highly valued by many employees because they can decide how to spend it. However, travel awards, particularly to popular destinations such as Disney World, Las Vegas, Hawaii, and international locations, appeal to many employees.

According to a study by *Incentive* magazine, the most effective incentives for sales employees are travel, cash, merchandise, or a combination of these means.[7] Generally, employees appreciate the "trophy" value of such awards as much as the actual monetary value.[8]

Recognition Awards Another type of program recognizes individual employees for their performance or service. For instance, many organizations in industries, such as hotels, restaurants, and retailers, have established "employee of the month" and "employee of the year" awards. Hotels often use favorable guest comment cards as the basis for providing recognition awards to front desk representatives, housekeepers, and other hourly employees. Shell uses recognition awards at its gasoline stations, and it has seen an increase in the favorable ratings of customers at stations where those awards have been given.[9]

Recognition awards often work best when given to acknowledge specific efforts and activities that the organization has targeted as important. The criteria for selecting award winners may be determined subjectively in some situations; however, formally identified criteria provide greater objectivity and are more likely to be seen as rewarding performance rather than as favoritism. When giving recognition awards, organizations should use specific examples to describe clearly how those receiving the awards were selected.

Service Awards Another type of reward given to individual employees is the *service award.* Although service awards may often be portrayed as rewarding performance over a number of years, in reality, they recognize length of service and have little linkage to employees' actual performance.

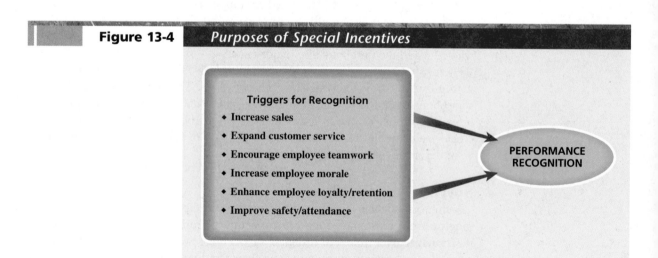

Figure 13-4   *Purposes of Special Incentives*

Triggers for Recognition
- Increase sales
- Expand customer service
- Encourage employee teamwork
- Increase employee morale
- Enhance employee loyalty/retention
- Improve safety/attendance

PERFORMANCE RECOGNITION

Ethical Concerns and Sales Compensation

Commission programs can effectively drive the behavior of sales representatives, especially if the performance measures are based wholly or mostly on sales volume and revenues. However, certain employees may act unethically to obtain incentives.

A number of legal experts and academics express concerns that some sales incentives programs encourage unethical behavior, particularly if compensation is based solely on commissions. For instance, there have been reports that individuals in other countries buying major industrial equipment have received bribes or kickbacks from sales representatives. The bribes are paid from the incentives received by the sales representatives. This criticism applies especially with major transactions such as large industrial machines, aircraft contracts, and even large insurance policies.

One way of addressing these ethical issues uses a mixture of guaranteed base salary and lowered commission rates. Other approaches use other sales-related dimensions, such as customer service, repeat business, and customer satisfaction. For instance, sales commissions for investment brokers might be linked to increasing a client's net portfolio value, rather than only to generating trades. How realistic such methods are in a variety of sales situations may be debated. But clearly, ethical issues must be considered when developing and managing sales incentive plans.[10]

SALES COMPENSATION

The compensation paid to employees involved with sales and marketing is partly or entirely tied to individual sales performance. Salespeople who sell more receive more total compensation than those who sell less. Sales incentives are perhaps the most widely used individual incentives. With some sales compensation plans, ethical issues and conflicts can arise, as the HR Perspective describes.[11]

Types of Sales Compensation Plans

Sales compensation plans can be of several general types, depending on the degree to which total compensation includes some variable pay tied to sales performance. A look at three general types of sales compensation and some challenges to sales compensation follows.

Salary-Only Some companies pay salespeople only a salary. The *salary-only approach* is useful when an organization emphasizes serving and retaining existing accounts, over generating new sales and accounts. This approach is frequently used to protect the income of new sales representatives for a period of time while they are building up their sales clientele. Generally, the employer extends the salary-only approach for new sales representatives to no more than six months, at which point it implements a salary-plus-commission or salary-plus-bonuses system (discussed later in this section). Salespeople who want extrinsic rewards function less effectively in salary-only plans because they are less motivated to sell without additional performance-related compensation.

Commission Compensation computed as a percentage of sales in units or dollars.

Straight Commission An individual incentive system that is widely used in sales jobs is the **commission,** which is compensation computed as a percentage of sales in units or dollars. Commissions are integrated into the pay given to sales

Technology Transforming HR

Enterprise Incentive Management Systems

To improve the administration of incentive plans, employers are turning to HR technology. Use of enterprise incentive management (EIM) software has become widespread. These systems are advantageous because they can track the performance of numerous employees worldwide who may be covered by different incentive plans. Consider a company that has different product lines, geographic locations, and company subsidiaries, and imagine tracking the performance of hundreds or thousands of sales representatives for a sales incentive program. Or imagine manually tracking attendance, safety, and training incentives for firms with many employees worldwide.

Such was the challenge facing Carl Zeiss, a manufacturer of optical and optoelectronic products that is headquartered

in Germany and operates in over 30 countries. Carl Zeiss decided to cut administrative time and costs, as well as increase the accuracy and timeliness of incentive information, by switching to an EIM software system. After several years, the new system allows different business groups to administer their own sales incentive plans. The system also allows managers to identify the most productive sales representatives. With this information, managers can arrange for those high producers to provide "success stories" to other salespeople, who then can adapt their sales approaches. Overall, it is evident that the data provided by the EIM system are helping executives and managers worldwide at Carl Zeiss to support and manage their sales forces more effectively.[12]

---

workers in three common ways: straight commission, salary plus commission, and bonuses.

In the *straight commission system,* a sales representative receives a percentage of the value of the sales made. Consider a sales representative working for a consumer products company. She receives no compensation if no sales are made, but she receives a percentage of the total amount of all sales revenue made in her territory. The advantage of this system is that it requires sales representatives to sell in order to earn. The disadvantage is that it offers no security for the sales staff.[13]

Draw Amount advanced from and repaid to future commissions earned by the employee.

To offset this insecurity, some employers use a **draw** system, in which sales representatives can draw advance payments against future commissions. The amounts drawn are then deducted from future commission checks. Arrangements must be made for repayment of drawn amounts if individuals leave the organization before earning their draws in commissions.

Salary-Plus-Commission or Bonuses The form of sales compensation used most frequently is the *salary-plus-commission,* which combines the stability of a salary with the performance aspect of a commission. A common split is 70% salary to 30% commission, although the split varies by industry and by numerous other factors. Many organizations also pay salespeople salaries and then offer bonuses that are a percentage of the base pay, tied to how well the employee meets various sales targets or other criteria.

Sales Compensation Challenges

Sales incentives work well, especially when they are tied to strategic initiatives of the organization.[14] However, they do present many challenges—from calculating total pay correctly, to dealing with sales in e-business, to causing competition among salespeople. Often, sales compensation plans become quite complex, and tracking individual incentives can be demanding. As the HR Technology identifies, Internet-based software has helped because companies can use it to post results daily, weekly, or monthly and salespeople can use it to track their results.

The last few years have seen the growth of sales compensation plans with different design features. Many of them are multi-tiered and can be rather complex. Selling over the Internet brings challenges to incentive compensation as well. Some sales organizations combine individual and group sales bonus programs. In these programs, a portion of the sales incentive is linked to the attainment of group sales goals.[15] This approach is supposed to encourage cooperation and teamwork among the salespeople, but that may not always occur.

Sales Performance Metrics Successfully using variable sales compensation requires establishing clear performance criteria and measures. Generally, no more than three sales performance measures should be used in a sales compensation plan. Consultants criticize many sales commission plans as being too complex to motivate sales representatives. Other plans may be too simple, focusing only on the salesperson's pay, not on organizational objectives. Many companies measure performance primarily by comparing an individual's sales revenue against established quotas. The plans would be better if the organizations used a variety of criteria, including obtaining new accounts and selling high-value versus low-value items that reflect marketing plans. Figure 13-5 shows the criteria commonly used to determine incentive payments for salespeople and how they are part of determining sales effectiveness.

Effectiveness of Sales Incentive Plans There are so many organizations with sales incentive plans that it would be logical to think those plans are effective. However, many sales compensation plans are not seen as effective by either salespeople or managers and executives. One study found that sales productivity was not above targets in over half of all the surveyed firms and that the respondents were dissatisfied with their sales incentive plans. Consequently, almost 80% of the firms had made at least six changes in those plans in a two-year period.[16] Such frequent changes reduce the effectiveness of plans and create concerns and frustrations with the sales representatives and managers. HR

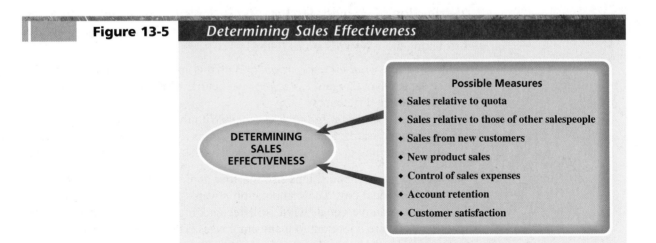

Figure 13-5   *Determining Sales Effectiveness*

DETERMINING SALES EFFECTIVENESS

Possible Measures
- Sales relative to quota
- Sales relative to those of other salespeople
- Sales from new customers
- New product sales
- Control of sales expenses
- Account retention
- Customer satisfaction

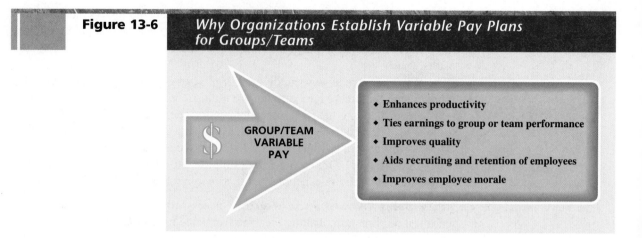

Figure 13-6 *Why Organizations Establish Variable Pay Plans for Groups/Teams*

GROUP/TEAM VARIABLE PAY

♦ Enhances productivity

♦ Ties earnings to group or team performance

♦ Improves quality

♦ Aids recruiting and retention of employees

♦ Improves employee morale

professionals may be involved in designing, revising, and communicating sales incentive plans, as well as in responding to the complaints and concerns of sales representatives.

GROUP/TEAM INCENTIVES

The use of groups/teams in organizations has implications for compensation. Although the use of groups/teams has increased substantially in the past few years, the question of how to compensate their members equitably remains a significant challenge. As Figure 13-6 notes, a number of reasons prompt organizations to establish variable pay plans for groups/teams. According to several studies, about 80% of large firms provide rewards for work groups or teams in some way.[17]

Design of Group/Team Incentive Plans

In designing group/team incentive plans, organizations must consider a number of issues. The main concerns are how and when to distribute the incentives, and who will make decisions about the incentive amounts.

Distribution of Group/Team Incentives Several decisions about how to distribute and allocate group/team rewards must be made. The two primary ways for distributing those rewards are as follows:

1. *Same-size reward for each member:* With this approach, all members receive the same payout, regardless of job level, current pay, seniority, or individual performance differences.
2. *Different-size reward for each member:* With this approach, employers vary individual rewards depending on such factors as contribution to group/team results, current pay, years of experience, and skill levels of jobs performed.

Generally, more organizations use the first approach in addition to different levels of individual pay. The combination rewards performance by making the group/team incentive equal, while still recognizing that individual pay differences exist and are important to many employees. The size of the group/team incentive can be determined either by using a percentage of base pay for the individuals or the group/team as a whole, or by offering a specific dollar amount.

For example, one firm pays members individual base rates that reflect years of experience and any additional training that they have. Additionally, the group/team reward is distributed to all as a flat dollar amount.

Timing of Group/Team Incentives How often group/team incentives are paid out is another important consideration. Some of the choices seen in firms with group/team incentives are monthly, quarterly, semiannually, and annually. The most common period used is annually. However, the shorter the time period, the greater the likelihood that employees will see a closer link between their efforts and the performance results that trigger the award payouts. Employers may limit the group/team rewards to $1,000 or less, allowing them to pay out rewards more frequently. The nature of the teamwork, measurement criteria, and organizational results must all be considered when determining the appropriate time period.

Decision Making About Group/Team Incentive Amounts To reinforce the effectiveness of working together, some group/team incentive programs allow members to make decisions about how to allocate the rewards to individuals. In some situations, members vote; in some, a group/team leader decides. In other situations, the incentive "pot" is divided equally, thus avoiding conflict and recognizing that all members contributed to the team results. However, many companies have found group/team members unwilling to handle incentive decisions for co-workers.

Problems with Group/Team Incentives

The difference between rewarding team members *equally* and rewarding them *equitably* triggers many of the problems associated with group/team incentives. Rewards distributed in equal amounts to all members may be perceived as "unfair" by employees who work harder, have more capabilities, or perform more difficult jobs. This problem is compounded when an individual who is performing poorly prevents the group/team from meeting the goals needed to trigger the incentive payment. Also, employees working in groups/teams have shown a relatively low level of satisfaction with rewards that are the same for all, versus rewards based on performance, which often may be viewed as more equitable.

Generally, managers view the concept of people working in groups/teams as beneficial. But many employees still expect to be paid according to individual performance, to a large extent. Until this individualism is recognized and compensation programs that are viewed as more equitable by more "team members" are developed, caution should be used in creating and implementing group/team incentives.

Successes and Failures of Group/Team Incentives

The unique nature of each group/team and its members figures prominently in the success of establishing incentive rewards.[18] The employer must consider the history of the group and its past performance. The success of team incentives was demonstrated at a garment manufacturing plant where worker productivity increased 14% after a shift was made to a group compensation system from an individual piece-rate compensation system.[19] However, simultaneously introducing the teamwork concept and changing to group/team incentives has not been as successful in other organizations.[20]

LOGGING ON...

HR Guide—Compensation
This Web site discusses incentives in detail.
www.hr-guide.com

Another consideration for the success of these incentives is the number of employees in the group/team. If it becomes too large, employees may feel that their individual efforts will have little or no effect on the total performance of the group and the resulting rewards. But group/team incentive plans may encourage cooperation in small groups where interdependence is high. Therefore, in those groups, the use of group/team performance measures is recommended. Such plans have been used in many industries. Conditions for successful team incentives are shown in Figure 13-7. If these conditions cannot be met, then either individual or organizational incentives may be more appropriate.

Types of Group/Team Incentives

Group/team reward systems use various ways of compensating individuals. The components include individual wages and salaries in addition to the additional rewards. Most organizations using group/team incentives continue to pay individuals based either on the jobs performed or the individuals' competencies and capabilities. The two most frequently used types of group/team incentives situations are work team results and gainsharing.

Group/Team Results Pay plans for groups/teams may reward all members equally on the basis of group output, cost savings, or quality improvement. The design of most group/team incentives is based on a "self-funding" principle, which means that the money to be used as incentive rewards is obtained through improvement of organizational results. A good example is gainsharing, which can be extended within a group or plantwide.

Gainsharing
System of sharing with employees greater-than-expected gains in profits and/or productivity.

Gainsharing The system of sharing with employees greater-than-expected gains in profits and/or productivity is **gainsharing.** Also called *teamsharing* or

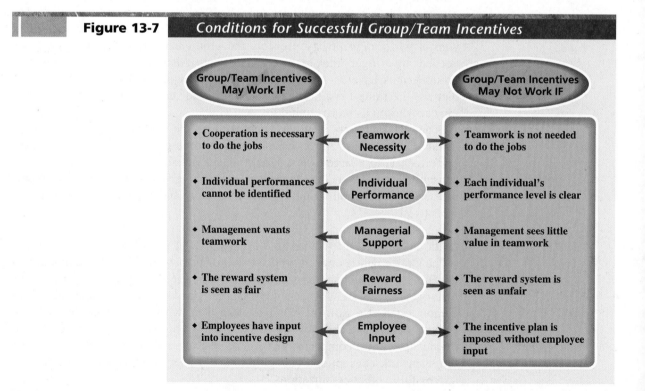

Figure 13-7 **Conditions for Successful Group/Team Incentives**

Group/Team Incentives May Work IF

Group/Team Incentives May Not Work IF

	Teamwork Necessity	
Cooperation is necessary to do the jobs		Teamwork is not needed to do the jobs
Individual performances cannot be identified	Individual Performance	Each individual's performance level is clear
Management wants teamwork	Managerial Support	Management sees little value in teamwork
The reward system is seen as fair	Reward Fairness	The reward system is seen as unfair
Employees have input into incentive design	Employee Input	The incentive plan is imposed without employee input

Successful Goalsharing Plans

Employers in different industries have had success with goalsharing plans. One well-known program exists at Corning, the large fiber and technology equipment firm. The Corning goalsharing system can provide employees with up to an additional 10% of their base pay if all goals are met. One-fourth of the plan is based on corporate earnings per share; the rest is tied to attainment of individual and business unit goals. Employees are extensively involved in the establishment and communication of goals.

Rothschild Berry Farms, based in Ohio, manufactures and sells gourmet jellies, preserves, and sauces. As a small company with 50 employees, Rothschild has a close-knit workforce. Several years ago, the company decided to implement

a goalsharing plan so that employees could better see how their performance linked to company strategies. A committee of 10 employees developed a goalsharing plan that has a variety of measures, including quality, cost control, sales growth, and return on assets. Payments based on results are made to employees quarterly, and have varied from year to year.

Both Corning and Rothschild have seen highly positive business results, and the goalsharing plans receive significant credit for enhancing those results. These goalsharing plans appear to be effective for the employees and the companies alike.[21]

goal-sharing, the focus is to increase "discretionary efforts," that is, the difference between the maximum amount of effort a person can exert and the minimum amount of effort that person needs to exert to keep from being fired. Workers in many organizations are not paid for discretionary efforts, but are paid to meet the minimum acceptable level of effort required. When workers do demonstrate discretionary efforts, the organization can afford to pay them more than the going rate, because the extra efforts produce financial gains over and above the returns of minimal efforts. Some organizations have labeled their programs *goalsharing* to emphasize the attainment of results based on business strategy objectives. Two successful goalsharing programs are described in the HR Perspective.

To develop and implement a gainsharing or goalsharing plan, management must identify the ways in which increased productivity, quality, and financial performance can occur and decide that some of the gains should be shared with employees. Often, measures such as labor costs, overtime hours, and quality benchmarks are used. Both organizational measures and departmental measures may be used, with the weights for gainsharing split between the two categories. Plans frequently require that an individual must exhibit satisfactory performance to receive the gainsharing payments.

Two older approaches similar to gainsharing exist. One, called Improshare, sets group piece-rate standards and pays weekly bonuses when the standard is exceeded. The other, the Scanlon plan, uses employee committees and passes on savings to the employees.

ORGANIZATIONAL INCENTIVES

An organizational incentive system compensates all employees in the organization according to how well the organization as a whole performs during the year. The basic concept behind organizational incentive plans is that overall results may depend on organization-wide or plantwide cooperation. The purpose of these plans is to produce better results by rewarding cooperation throughout the organization. For example, conflict between marketing and production can be overcome if management uses an incentive system that emphasizes organization-wide profit and productivity. To be effective, an organizational incentive program should include everyone from non-exempt employees to managers and executives. Two common organizational incentive systems are profit sharing and employee stock plans.

Profit Sharing

Profit sharing System to distribute a portion of the profits of the organization to employees.

As the name implies, **profit sharing** distributes some portion of organizational profits to employees. The primary objectives of profit-sharing plans include the following:

♦ Increase productivity and organizational performance.
♦ Attract or retain employees.
♦ Improve product/service quality.
♦ Enhance employee morale.

Typically, the percentage of the profits distributed to employees is set by the end of the year before distribution. In some profit-sharing plans, employees receive portions of the profits at the end of the year; in others, the profits are deferred, placed in a fund, and made available to employees on retirement or on their departure from the organization. Figure 13-8 shows how profit-sharing plans can be funded and allocated.

Unions sometimes are skeptical of profit-sharing plans. Often, the level of profits is influenced by factors not under the employees' control, such as accounting decisions, marketing efforts, competition, and elements of executive compensation. However, in recent years, some unions have supported profit-sharing plans that tie employees' pay increases to improvements against organizational performance measures, not just the "bottom-line" numbers.

Drawbacks of Profit-Sharing Plans When used throughout an organization, including with lower-echelon workers, profit-sharing plans can have some drawbacks. First, employees must trust that management will disclose accurate financial and profit information. As many people know, both the definition and level of profit can depend on the accounting system used and on decisions

THOMSON
WEST

PROFIT-SHARING PLANS
Describes advantages and disadvantages of profit-sharing plans.
Custom Search:
☑ ANALYSIS
Exact Phrase: Advantages of profit-sharing plans

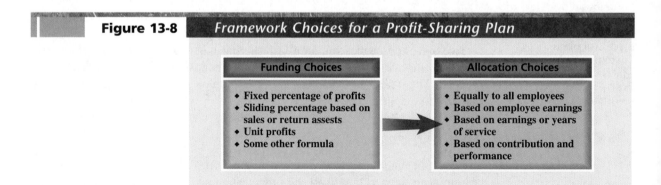

Figure 13-8   *Framework Choices for a Profit-Sharing Plan*

Funding Choices	Allocation Choices
♦ Fixed percentage of profits ♦ Sliding percentage based on sales or return assets ♦ Unit profits ♦ Some other formula	♦ Equally to all employees ♦ Based on employee earnings ♦ Based on earnings or years of service ♦ Based on contribution and performance

Stock option plan
Plan that gives employ-
ees the right to pur-
chase a fixed number of
shares of company stock
at a specified price for a
limited period of time.

**Employee stock
ownership plan
(ESOP)** Plan whereby
employees have signifi-
cant stock ownership in
their employers.

LOGGING ON...

**My Stock
Options.com**
This Web site provides
tools for communicat-
ing, educating, and
training employees
about stock options.
www.mystockoptions.com

made. To be credible, management must be willing to disclose sufficient financial and profit information to alleviate the skepticism of employees, particularly if profit-sharing levels fall from those of previous years. Second, profits
may vary a great deal from year to year, resulting in windfalls or losses beyond
the employees' control. Third, payoffs are generally far removed from employees' efforts, and therefore, higher rewards may not be strongly linked to
better performance.

Employee Stock Plans

Two types of organizational incentive plans use employer stock ownership to
reward employees. The goal of these plans is to get employees to think and act
like "owners."[22]

A **stock option plan** gives employees the right to purchase a fixed number of
shares of company stock at a specified exercise price for a limited period of time.
If the market price of the stock exceeds the exercise price, employees can then
exercise the option and buy the stock. The number of firms giving stock options
to non-executives has declined some in recent years, primarily due to changing
laws and accounting regulations.

Employee Stock Ownership Plans (ESOPs) An **employee stock ownership
plan (ESOP)** is designed to give employees significant stock ownership in their
employers. According to the National Center for Employee Ownership, an estimated 15,000 firms in the United States offer broad employee-ownership programs. Within these firms, approximately 11,000 have established ESOPs
covering about 9 million workers. Well-known supermarket firms that offer
ESOPs include Publix, Hy-Vee, Price Chopper, and Houtchens. Firms in many
other industries have ESOPs as well.[23]

Establishing an ESOP creates several advantages. The major one is that the
firm can receive favorable tax treatment on the earnings earmarked for use in the
ESOP. Another is that an ESOP gives employees a "piece of the action" so that
they can share in the growth and profitability of their firm. Employee ownership
may motivate employees to be more productive and focused on organizational
performance.[24]

Many people approve of the concept of employee ownership as a kind of "people's capitalism." However, the sharing can also be a disadvantage for employees
because it makes both their wages/salaries and their retirement benefits dependent on the performance of their employers. This concentration poses even greater
risk for retirees because the value of pension fund assets is also dependent on
how well the company does. The financial bankruptcy and travails of several airlines illustrates that an ESOP does not necessarily guarantee success for the employees who become investors.[25]

▌ EXECUTIVE COMPENSATION

Many organizations, especially large ones, administer compensation for executives differently from compensation for lower-level employees. At the heart of
most executive compensation plans is the idea that executives should be rewarded if the organization grows in profitability and value over a period of years.
Therefore, variable pay distributed through different types of incentives is a significant part of executive compensation.

Figure 13-9 | *Components of Executive Compensation Packages*

Global Executive Compensation

Executive compensation packages vary significantly from country to country. In multi-national firms, the differences may be less pronounced because executives are often part of global corporate compensation plans. In comparable-size firms in Europe and the U.S., total cash compensation for Chief Executive Officers (CEOs) is similar, about $2.5 million a year. But long-term incentives are used more in French and German companies than in the United Kingdom. Scandinavian firms pay their CEOs about 30% less than do other European firms.[26] Also, Japanese CEOs are paid about one-third of what U.S. CEOs in comparable-size firms are paid.[27] Critics of executive pay levels point out that in the U.S., many corporate CEOs make almost 200 times more than do average workers in their firms, up from 35 times more in the 1970s. In Japan, the ratio is 15:1, and in Europe, 20:1. Worldwide, the various elements of compensation shown in Figure 13-9 are used to different degrees.

Elements of Executive Compensation

Because high-salaried executives are in higher tax brackets, many executive compensation packages are designed to offer significant tax savings. These savings occur through use of deferred compensation methods whereby taxes are not due until after the executives leave the firm. According to a review of the compensation packages of CEOs of 350 large companies, long-term incentives constitute 68% of the total CEO compensation.[28]

Executive Salaries Salaries of executives vary by the type of job, size of organization, industry, and other factors. In some organizations, particularly non-profits, salaries often make up 90% or more of total compensation. In contrast, in large corporations, salaries may constitute 30% or less of the total package. Survey data on executive salaries are often reviewed by Boards of Directors to ensure that their organizations are competitive.

Executive Benefits Many executives are covered by *regular benefits plans* that are also available to non-executive employees, including traditional retirement, health insurance, and vacations plans. In addition, executives may receive *supplemental benefits* that other employees do not receive. For example, executive health plans with no co-payments and with no limitations on deductibles or physician choice are popular among small and middle-size businesses. Corporate-owned insurance on the life of the executive is also popular; this insurance pays both the executive's estate and the company in the event of death. One supplemental benefit that has grown in popularity is company-paid financial planning for executives. Trusts of various kinds may be designed by the company to help the executives deal with estate-planning and tax issues. Deferred compensation is another possible means of helping executives with tax liabilities caused by incentive compensation plans.

Perquisites (perks)
Special benefits—usually non-cash items—for executives.

Executive Perquisites (Perks) In addition to the regular benefits received by all employees, executives often receive benefits called perquisites. **Perquisites (perks)** are special benefits—usually non-cash items—for executives. Many executives value the status enhancement of these visible symbols, which allow them to be seen as "very important people" both inside and outside their organizations. Perks can also offer substantial tax savings because some of them are not taxed as income. Some commonly used executive perks are company cars, health club and country club memberships, first-class air travel, use of private jets, stress counseling, and chauffer services.[29]

Annual Executive Incentives and Bonuses Annual incentives and bonuses for executives can be determined in several ways. One way is to use a discretionary system whereby the CEO and the board of directors decide bonuses; the absence of formal, measurable targets detracts significantly from this approach. Another way is to tie bonuses to specific measures, such as return on investment, earnings per share, and net profits before taxes. More complex systems create bonus pools and thresholds above which bonuses are computed. Whatever method is used, it is important to describe it so that executives attempting to earn additional compensation understand the plan; otherwise, the incentive effect will be diminished.

Performance Incentives: Long-Term vs. Short-Term Use of executive performance-based incentives try to tie executive compensation to long-term growth and success of the organization. However, whether these incentives really emphasize the long term or merely represent a series of short-term rewards is controversial. Short-term rewards based on quarterly or annual performance may not result in the kind of long-run-oriented decisions necessary for the company to perform well over multiple years.

As would be expected, the total amount of pay-for-performance incentives varies by management level, with CEOs receiving significantly more than subsidiary or other senior managers. One study found that the typical CEO gets about half of all the total incentives paid to all senior managers and executives.[30]

The most widely used long-term incentives are stock option plans. A stock option gives individuals the right to buy stock in a company, usually at an advantageous price. Despite the prevalence of such plans, research has found little relationship between providing CEOs with stock options and subsequent firm performance.[31] Because of the numerous corporate scandals involving executives at Enron, WorldCom, Tyco, and others who received outrageously high compensation due to stock options, the use of stock options has declined.[32] Instead, more firms with publicly traded stock are using means such as *restricted stock, phantom stock, performance shares,* and other specialized technical forms, which are beyond the scope of this discussion.

LOGGING ON...

eComp
This Web site contains compensation data on thousands of Senior Executives, discusses Board of Directors' Pay practices, and includes other search tools and reports.
www.ecomponline.com

Is Any Executive Worth Over $50 Million a Year?

The staggeringly large amounts of some annual compensation packages for executives have raised ethical questions. A primary question is if any single CEO is really deserving of compensation totaling over $50 million when stock option profits, retirement bonuses, and other payments are included.

To illustrate, in a recent year, the following corporate executives received huge sums: Ruben Mark (Colgate-Palmolive), $141.1 million; Steve Jobs (Apple Computer), $74.8 million; and George David (United Technologies), $70.5 million. Numerous other CEOs received yearly compensation of over $20 million, including long-term stock option gains and other payments.

On top of these large annual amounts, executives have negotiated "departure agreements." Richard Grasso, former CEO of the New York Stock Exchange, was to receive over $180 million in the year he was asked to quit, as well as a "retirement agreement." Controversy over the package caused him to relinquish some of this amount.

"Departure-and-consulting agreements" for executives are another area of concern. These arrangements were provided for retiring CEOs such as Jack Welsh (GE), who received up to $3.4 million, and John Bryan (Sara Lee), who received $5 million. Major controversies arose at American Airlines and Delta Airlines when it was publicized that the departing CEOs at those companies were to receive $3 million or more a year after resigning. That disclosure occurred at the same time that unionized airline employees were being asked to negotiate wage and benefits reductions.[34]

Of course, these figures, large as they are, provide little meaning unless put into context. If the company is doing well and performing above competitors and expectations, the huge packages might be justifiable to stockholders. Certainly, the opposite can be true as well. The question that still must be addressed by Boards of Directors, stockholders, and executives is: How realistic and ethical is it to provide such huge amounts to one person, when many other executives have contributed to organizational performance and do not receive such lavish payouts? What do you think?

Another outcome of the recent corporate abuses by executives was the passage of the Sarbanes-Oxley Act of 2002. This act has numerous provisions that have affected the accounting and financial reporting requirements of different types of executive compensation.[33] Also, the Financial Accounting Standards Board (FASB) has adopted rules regarding the expensing of stock options.[35] Microsoft and IBM have been leaders in restructuring stock plans.

"Reasonableness" of Executive Compensation

The notion that monetary incentives tied to performance result in improved performance makes sense to most people. However, there is an ongoing debate about whether executive compensation in the United States is truly linked to performance. This is particularly of concern given the astronomical amounts of some executive compensation packages, as highlighted in the HR Perspective.

The reasonableness of executive compensation is often justified by comparison to compensation market surveys, but these surveys usually provide a range of compensation data that requires interpretation. Various questions have been suggested for determining if executive pay is "reasonable," including the following useful ones:

◆ Would another company hire this person as an executive?
◆ How does the executive's compensation compare with that for executives in similar companies in the industry?

- Is the executive's pay consistent with pay for other employees within the company?
- What would an investor pay for the level of performance of the executive?

Linkage Between Executive Compensation and Corporate Performance Of all the executive compensation issues that are debated, the one discussed most frequently is whether or not executive compensation levels are sufficiently linked to organizational performance.[36] One key aspect of evaluating all the studies on this topic is the performance measures used. Numerous studies have examined different facets of this topic.[37] In many settings, financial measures such as return on equity, return to shareholders, earnings per share, and net income before taxes are used to measure performance. However, a number of firms also incorporate non-financial organizational measures of performance when determining executive bonuses and incentives. Customer satisfaction, employee satisfaction, market share, productivity, and quality are other areas measured for executive performance rewards.

Measurement of executive performance varies from firm to firm. Some executive compensation packages use a short-term focus of one year, which may lead to large rewards for executive performance in a given year even though corporate performance over a multi-year period is mediocre. This difference is especially pronounced if the yearly measures are carefully chosen. Executives can even manipulate earnings per share by selling assets, liquidating inventories, or reducing research and development expenditures. All these actions may make organizational performance look better, but they may impair the long-term growth of the organization.

A number of other executive compensation issues and concerns are discussed. Figure 13-10 highlights the criticisms and counterarguments of some common points of contention.

Figure 13-10 *Common Executive Compensation Issues*

Criticisms	Counterarguments
Executive compensation often does not reflect company performance.	A competitive market for executives drives compensation package increases.
Boards give sizable rewards to both high- and low-performing executives.	The CEO is in charge and responsible for results.
Executives should not get rewards and bonuses for laying off much of the workforce.	Sports and entertainment stars earn as much as executives, or more, for playing games and acting.
Total compensation packages are excessive.	CEOs earn their money with endless hours, great pressures, major decisions.
Many people, not just the CEO, contribute to the success of a company.	Measuring company performance by short-term earnings and stock prices is insufficient.

One of the more controversial issues is that some executives seem to get large awards for negative actions. It seems contradictory from an employee's perspective to reward executives who often improve corporate results by cutting staff, laying off employees, changing pension plans, or increasing the deductible on the health insurance. But sometimes cost-cutting measures are necessary to keep a company afloat. However, a sense of reasonableness may be appropriate too; if rank and file employees suffer, giving bonuses and large payouts to executives appears counterproductive, and even hypocritical.

Executive Compensation and Boards of Directors In most organizations, the Board of Directors is the major policy-setting entity and must approve executive compensation packages. The **compensation committee** usually is a subgroup of the Board, composed of directors who are not officers of the firm. Compensation committees generally make recommendations to the Board of Directors on overall pay policies, salaries for top officers, supplemental compensation such as stock options and bonuses, and additional perquisites for executives.

> **Compensation committee** Subgroup of the board of directors, composed of directors who are not officers of the firm.

Increasingly, the independence of these committees has been criticized.[38] One major concern voiced by many critics is that the base pay and bonuses of CEOs are often set by the members of Board compensation committees, many of whom are CEOs of other companies with similar compensation packages. Also, the compensation advisors and consultants to the CEOs often collect large fees, and critics charge that those fees distort the objectivity of the advice given.

To counter criticism, some corporations have changed the composition of the compensation committees by taking actions such as prohibiting "insider" company officers from serving on them.[39] Also, some firms have empowered the compensation committees to hire and pay compensation consultants without involving executive management.

SUMMARY

- Variable pay, also called incentives, is compensation that can be linked to individual, group/team, and/or organizational performance.
- Effective variable pay plans should fit both business strategies and organizational cultures, appropriately award actions, and be administered properly.
- Piece-rate and bonus plans are the most commonly used individual incentives.
- Sales employees may have their compensation tied to performance on a number of sales-related criteria. Sales compensation can be provided as salary only, commission only, or salary plus commission or bonuses.
- The design of group/team variable pay plans must consider how the incentives are to be distributed, the timing of the incentive payments, and who will make decisions about the variable payout.
- Organization-wide rewards include profit sharing and stock ownership plans.
- Executive compensation must be viewed as a total package composed of salaries, bonuses, long-term performance-based incentives, benefits, and perquisites (perks).
- Performance-based incentives often represent a significant portion of an executive's compensation package.
- A compensation committee, which is a subgroup of the Board of Directors, generally has authority over executive compensation plans.

REVIEW AND APPLICATION QUESTIONS

1. Discuss why pay-for-performance plans have become more popular and what elements are needed to make them successful.

2. Give examples of individual incentives used by an organization in which you were employed. Then describe why those plans were successful and/or unsuccessful.

3. Suppose you have been asked to lead a task force to evaluate the sales incentive plans at your firm. The task force is to develop a list of strategies and issues to be evaluated. Using information from *www.alexandergroupinc.com/selfassessments/ selfassessment.htm* and various other Web sites, identify and develop preliminary material for the task force.

LEARNING REVIEW

To check your knowledge of the chapter, review the following. (Answers after the supplemental case.) For more questions, see the Study Guide.

1. Which of the following is a philosophical foundation of variable pay?
   a. Some people perform better than others.
   b. Time spent each day is the primary measure of contributions.
   c. Length of service within the organization is the primary differentiating factor between people.
   d. Contributions to the organization are recognized through different amounts of base pay.

2. The most frequently used form of sales compensation is the _____.
   a. straight commission
   b. draw against commission
   c. salary plus commission
   d. piece-rate system

3. The most prevalent form of organization-wide incentives is _____.
   a. individual incentives
   b. gainsharing
   c. bonuses
   d. profit-sharing plans

4. Which of the following executive incentive is used to emphasize the long-term growth and success of the organization?
   a. executive perquisites
   b. executive bonus plans
   c. golden parachutes
   d. stock options

CASE

INCENTIVE PLANS FOR FUN AND TRAVEL

For incentive plans to payoff for companies, the plans must stimulate employee interest and motivate them to perform well. Firms in several different industries have been creative in developing incentive plans, which have resulted in the companies receiving *Top Motivator Awards* from *Incentive* magazine. A look at two of the recent winners illustrates the variety of plans being used.

Houston-based Pappas Restaurants has over 10,000 employees working in restaurants such as

Pappadeux Seafood Kitchen, Pappas Pizza, and others. As a key part of creating and maintaining a "fun culture," Pappas has created an unusual job as part of its management structure, a Director of Fun Stuff. This individual's role is to develop and conduct activities that reinforce the performance-oriented, fun culture that Pappas wants. By stressing this culture, the firm hopes to ensure that both customers and employees enjoy Pappas restaurants. One successful incentive program is called "Rising Stars." Employees working as bartenders, food servers, and other customer contact jobs receive $20 gift certificates weekly for such actions as favorable customer comments, attendance, and working extra shifts as needed. But employees without primary customer roles are not forgotten, because Pappas has a "Kitchen Superstars" program for its dishwashers, cooks, and clean-up workers, who can receive gift certificates also. Purchased from well-known retailers such as Target, Blockbuster, and other retailers located near Pappas restaurants, the gift certificates provide immediate reinforcement for positive actions, as well as providing an easily used reward.

In a very different work setting, Washington Mutual, an insurance and financial services firm based in Seattle, has used sales incentive programs effectively. One successful program was called "Fresh Perspectives." To motivate sales employees to generate a greater number and volume of home loans, the company developed several different incentive plans. In the primary plan, the firm's sales representatives accumulated points for loan product sales. Sales results for employees were tracked and posted monthly so that everyone knew where they were in comparison to other sales representatives. The 400

top-producing sales people became members of the President's Club. To provide special recognition of their accomplishments, the President's Club members were rewarded with a five-day trip to Cancun. Unique entertainment events, jungle safaris, and other activities were participated in by the club members and key executives. The Cancun trip was both an incentive to encourage performance and a reward for the top sales performers.

Numerous other firms spend considerable time and money on various incentive programs. The key focus of those programs, as well as the ones used at Pappas Restaurants and Washington Mutual, are to motivate and reward performance.[40]

Questions
1. Why might use of incentives providing small amounts as gift certificates be better than just providing cash to employees?
2. What are some advantages and disadvantages of a sales incentive program where the top performers receive a trip or other large reward, while other sales individuals receive lesser or different types of rewards?

SUPPLEMENTAL CASE: "Cash Is Good, Card Is Bad"

Both the positive and negative issues associated with the use of an incentive plan are discussed in this case. (For the case, go to **http://mathis.swlearning.com/.**)

Learning Review Answers: 1. a   2. c   3. d   4. d

NOTES

1. Adapted from Julie Cook, "Getting Intuit," *Human Resource Executive,* June 20, 2002, 28–34; and Kathleen H. Van Neck and Jessica Smilko, "Variable Pay Plans: Creating a Financial Partnership with the Workforce," *WorldatWork Journal,* Fourth Quarter 2002, 74–79.
2. Dorren Remmen, "Performance Pays Off," *Strategic Finance,* March 2003, 27–32.
3. Alexander D. Stajkovic and Fred Luthans, "Differential Effects of Incentive Motivators on Work Performance," *Academy of Management Journal,* 43 (2001), 580–590.
4. For details, see Leo Jakobson, "ROI: Show Me the Money," *Incentive,* March 2004, 26–29; Donna Oldenburg, "ROI Incentives: Tools for Measuring Excellence," *HR Magazine,* October 2002, 71–79; and Ravin Jesuthasan, "Business Performance Management: Improving Return on Rewards Investments,"
WorldatWork Journal, Fourth Quarter 2003, 55–64.
5. Tom Wilson and Harold N. Altmansberger, "Taking Variable Pay to a New Level," *Workspan,* December 2003, 44–47.
6. Chris Taylor, "On-the-Spot Incentives," *HR Magazine,* May 2004, 80–84.
7. "2004 Sales Facts Reports," *Incentive,* February 2004, 34–37.

8. Carol Patton, "Creative Motivation," *Human Resource Executive,* March 16, 2004, 23–25.

9. Leo Jakobson, "Shell Goes Further," *Incentive,* May 2004, 20.

10. Charles H. Schwepker Jr., "An Exploratory Investigation of the Relationship Between Ethical Conflict and Salesperson Performance," *Journal of Business & Industrial Marketing,* 18 (2003), 45.

11. Jill Harrington, "Look Who's Creeping," *Incentive,* March 2004, 16.

12. Peter Kurlander and Scott Barton, "Improving Your Odds: Successful Incentive Compensation Automation," *Workspan,* January 2004, 30–33; and "Offers They Can't Refuse," February 17, 2003, *www.fortune.com/sections.*

13. Jeff Bailey, "Market Spurs More Commission-Only Sales," *Wall Street Journal,* July 22, 2003, B4.

14. David H. Johnston, "Strategic Initiatives in Sales Compensation," *WorldatWork Journal,* Second Quarter 2003, 75–83.

15. John M. Bremen and Jan Blackburn, "Where Is Sales Compensation Heading?" *Workspan,* January 2003, 47–60.

16. "Pay-for-Performance Sales Comp Not Living Up to Expectations," *Newsline,* September 24, 2003, available at *www.deloite.com.*

17. Edward E. Lawler III, "Pay Practices in *Fortune* 1000 Corporations," *WorldatWork Journal,* Fourth Quarter 2003, 45–54.

18. Bianca Beersma et al., "Cooperation, Competition, and Team Rewards: Toward a Contingency Approach," *Academy of Management Journal,* 46 (2003), 572–590.

19. Barton H. Hamilton, Jack A. Nickerson, and Hideo Owen, "Team Incentives and Worker Heterogeneity," *Journal of Political Economy,* 111 (2003), 465.

20. Jerry McAdams and Elizabeth J. Hawk, "Making Group Incentive Plans Work," *WorldatWork Journal,* Third Quarter 2000, 28–34.

21. Based on Steve Bates, "Goalsharing at Corning," *HR Magazine,* January 2003, 33; and Robert L. Heneman et al., "Taking a Middle Stance," *WorldatWork Journal,* Second Quarter 2002, 65–70.

22. Stephen H. Wagner, Christopher P. Parker, and Neil D. Christiansen, "Employees that Think and Act Like Owners," *Personnel Psychology,* 56 (2003), 847–871.

23. For current data, see the National Center for Employee Ownership, *www.nceo.org.*

24. Corey Rosen, "To Grant or Not to Grant," *Workspan,* March 2004, 40–44.

25. "A Capital Idea," *Economist,* March 29, 2003, 70.

26. "Pay Packages of European Execs Reach U.S. Levels," January 21, 2004, *www.haygroup.com.*

27. Louis Aguilar, "Exec-Worker Pay Gap Widens to Gulf," *The Denver Post,* July 8, 2001, 16A.

28. "The WSJ/Mercer 2003 CEO Compensation Survey," *Wall Street Journal,* April 12, 2004, R6; and *The Mercer Report,* May 2004.

29. Anne Freedman, "Executive Bounty," *Human Resource Executive,* May 2, 2004, 44–47; and Alex Frangos, "Perks, Minus the Pizzazz," *Wall Street Journal,* April 14, 2003, R4.

30. R. K. Aggarwal and A. A. Samwick, "Performance Incentives Within Firms: The Effect of Managerial Responsibility," *Journal of Finance,* 58 (2003), 1613–1650.

31. Jean McGuire and Elie Matta, "CEO Stock Options: The Silent Dimension of Ownership," *Academy of Management Journal,* 46 (2003), 255–265.

32. Seymour Burchman and Blair Jones, "The Future of Stock Options," *WorldatWork Journal,* First Quarter 2004, 29–38.

33. Rodney K. Platt, "Sarbanes-Oxley Bane or Boon?" *Workspan,* March 2004, 22–27.

34. "Executive Compensation," *Business Week,* April 19, 2004, 106–120; and Gary Strauss, "CEOs Cash in After Tenure," *USA Today,* April 5, 2002, 1B–2B.

35. For details on FASB quality-based compensation accounting, see the Financial Accounting Standards Board Web site, *www.fasb.org.*

36. Charles Elson, "What's Wrong with Executive Compensation?" *Harvard Business Review,* January 2003, 68.

37. For example, see James J. Corderio and Rajaram Viliyath, "Beyond Pay for Performance: A Panel Study of the Determinants of CEO Compensation," *American Business Review,* 21 (2003), 57–67; and Dan Dalton et al., "Meta-Analyses of Financial Performance and Equity: Fusion or Confusion?" *Academy of Management Journal,* 46 (2003), 13–26.

38. Jane T. Romweber, "The Effects of Good Compensation Committee Governance," *Workspan,* May 2003, 40–43; and Amy Hillman and Thomas Dalziel, "Boards of Directors and Firm Performance," *Academy of Management Review,* 28 (2003), 383–396.

39. Sydney Finkelstein and Ann C. Mooney, "Not the Usual Suspects: How to Use Board Process to Make Boards Better," *Academy of Management Executive,* May 2003, 101–113.

40. Based on Kenneth Hein, "Motivators of the Year," *Incentive,* October 2003, 40–44.

CHAPTER 14

Managing Employee Benefits

After you have read this chapter, you should be able to:

◆ Define a benefit and identify four strategic benefit considerations.

◆ Distinguish between mandated and voluntary benefits and list three examples of each.

◆ Discuss the shift of retirement plans from defined-benefit to defined-contribution plans.

◆ Explain the importance of managing the costs of health benefits and identify some methods of doing so.

◆ Describe the growth of financial, family-oriented, and time-off benefits and their importance to many employees.

◆ Summarize benefits communication and flexible benefits as considerations in benefits administration.

Employers and Employees Face Escalating Benefits Costs

A permeating concern in the U.S. workforce is anxiety about benefits. With good reasons, employees become anxious as employers try to reduce benefits in order to control costs. Employers have seen benefits costs grow to about 42% of employee payroll, which represents about $18,000 per employee annually, according to an annual benefits study conducted by the U.S. Chamber of Commerce. The biggest cost increases have been in health benefits, which have been rising at an average of 12% per year for the past several years.

To counter the cost increases, employers are taking steps to reduce or even eliminate benefits. Actions that companies are taking include increasing the amount that employees and retirees have to pay for health insurance, reducing employer contributions to 401(k) and other pension programs, and implementing prescription drug management programs.

These actions have reduced employee satisfaction with their benefits, especially in smaller companies. According to an SHRM survey, only 47% of employees in firms with fewer than 100 workers are satisfied with their benefits, whereas 74% of employees in larger firms are pleased with their benefits. Many employees voice concerns that their annual pay increases only cover the extra benefits charges they must pay. But, the pressures on benefits costs is likely to continue, and the employer/employee conflicts and anxieties over benefits costs will grow.[1]

"Despite rising costs, employers continue to offer a broad array of benefits to workers."

—Bruce Josten

Benefit Indirect reward given to an employee or a group of employees for organizational membership.

Employers provide benefits to their workers for being part of the organization. A **benefit** is an indirect reward given to an employee or a group of employees for organizational membership. Benefits often include retirement plans, vacations with pay, health insurance, educational assistance, and many more programs.

In the United States, employers often fill the role of major provider of benefits for citizens. In many other nations, citizens and employers are taxed to pay for government-provided benefits, such as health-care and retirement programs. Although federal regulations require U.S. employers to provide certain benefits, U.S. employers voluntarily provide many others.

Benefits are costly for the typical U.S. employer. They average over 40% of payroll expenses for employers, and in highly unionized manufacturing and utility industries, they may be as high as 80% of payroll. Figure 14-1 shows how the typical benefits dollar is spent on different types of benefits.

STRATEGIC PERSPECTIVES ON BENEFITS

Benefits should be looked at as a vital part of the overall compensation strategies of the organization.[2] For instance, an organization can choose to compete for employees by providing base compensation, variable pay, or benefits, or

Figure 14-1 — How the Typical Benefits Dollar Is Spent

Insurance Payments (medical premiums, vision care, dental care, life insurance, etc.) *About 25%*

Payment for Time Not Worked (leaves, vacations, holidays, etc.) *About 25%*

Legally Required Contributions (Social Security, unemployment, and workers' compensation) *About 20%*

Paid Rest Periods (coffee breaks, lunch period, travel time) *About 10%*

Miscellaneous Benefits (educational assistance, severance pay, child care, etc.) *About 5%*

Retirement Plans (pensions, 401(k) plans, etc.) *About 15%*

Source: Based on information from the U.S. Department of Labor, Bureau of Labor Statistics, *National Compensation Survey: Employee Benefits in Private Industry in the United States,* 2003; and *Employee Benefits Study,* 2003 ed. (Washington, DC: U.S. Chamber of Commerce, 2004).

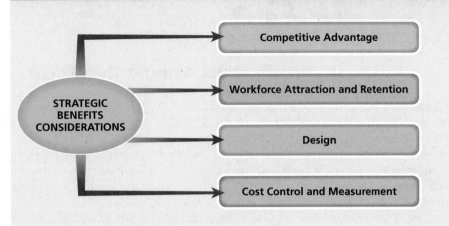

Figure 14-2   *Strategic Benefits Considerations*

- STRATEGIC BENEFITS CONSIDERATIONS
  - Competitive Advantage
  - Workforce Attraction and Retention
  - Design
  - Cost Control and Measurement

LOGGING ON...

Employee Benefit News
This Web site consists of surveys, archived articles, and the latest trends and information regarding employee benefits.
www.benefitnews.com

perhaps all three. Which approach is chosen depends on many factors, such as competition, organizational life cycle, and corporate strategy. For example, a new firm may choose to have lower base pay and use high variable incentives to attract new employees, but keep the cost of benefits as low as possible for a while. Or an organization that hires predominately younger female employees might choose a family-friendly set of benefits such as child-care assistance to attract and retain employees, but offer little variable pay and market-level base pay.

The reasons why employers offer benefits are multi-faceted and tie into strategic considerations. As Figure 14-2 indicates, there are four aspects to looking at benefits strategically.

Benefits as Competitive Advantage

Employers offer some benefits to aid recruiting and retention, some because they are required to do so, and some simply because doing so reinforces the company philosophy of social and corporate citizenship. Employers with good benefits are viewed positively within a community and the industry by customers, civic leaders, current employees, and workers in other firms. Conversely, the employers who are seen as skimping on benefits, cutting benefits, or taking advantage of workers may be viewed negatively.

The benefits offered can aid in reducing employee absenteeism and turnover, which may boost organizational performance. Employee wellness benefits at both large and small employers have been shown to reduce absenteeism due to illness problems and employee turnover because of health concerns. Time-off leave programs aid in reducing absenteeism and turnover as well. An additional strategic challenge that can affect the competitive advantage of a firm is the differences in benefits worldwide, as the HR Globally discussion illustrates.

Benefits and Workforce Attraction/Retention

The composition of the U.S. workforce is changing, and expectations about benefits of different generations of employees are affecting benefit decisions. For instance, in some employers many "baby boomers" who are approaching retire-

Benefits Around the World

Benefits vary from country to country. In many countries, retirement, health, and other benefits are provided as part of government services. Employers are taxed heavily to pay into government funds that cover the benefits. This model is very different from the one in the U.S., where most benefits are provided by employers directly.

Health-care benefits differ significantly worldwide. Many countries, including Great Britain and Canada, have national health services. Some global firms require employees to use the medical services available from host countries, whereas other global employers provide special coverage that allows expatriates to receive health care from private providers. Arranging quality private coverage becomes an especially important issue for global employees located in various underdeveloped countries where the availability and quality of medical facilities and treatment varies widely.

Retirement and pension systems are provided by the government in many countries as well. National pension programs in Germany, France, and Japan, among other countries, are facing significant financial pressures due to their aging workforces and populations. Such challenges also face the Social Security and Medicare systems in the U.S.

The amount of leave and vacation time also varies significantly around the globe. Of 130 countries, only the United States, Australia, and Ethiopia do not provide paid leave for new parents. The annual leave/vacation in European countries averages 36 days per year, whereas the United States and Canada average the lowest amounts of annual vacation leave of many developed countries. These examples illustrate the challenges facing firms with employees located in different countries.[3]

ment age are more concerned about retirement benefits and health care. Many younger generations, workers are more interested in portable flexible benefits. However, all generations, expect medical and dental insurance. Having benefits plans that appeal to the different groups is vital to attracting and retaining all employees.

It is well established that benefits influence employees' decisions about which particular employer to work for, whether to stay with or leave an employer, and when to retire. A major advantage of benefits is that they generally are not taxed as income to employees. For this reason, they represent a somewhat more valuable reward to employees than an equivalent cash payment. For example, assume that employee Clara Smith is in a 25% tax bracket. If Clara earns an extra $400, she must pay $100 in taxes on this amount (disregarding exemptions). But if her employer provides prescription drug coverage in a benefits plan, and she receives the $400 as payments for prescription drugs, she is not taxed on the amount, and she receives the value of the entire $400 not just $300. This feature makes benefits a desirable form of compensation to employees.

Benefits Design

Benefits plans can provide flexibility and choices for employees, or can be standardized for all employees. Increasingly, employers are finding that providing employees with some choices and flexibility allows individuals to tailor their benefits to their own situations. However, the more choices available, the more administrative demands placed on organizations.

A number of decisions are part of benefits design. Some key ones are the following:

◆ How much total compensation, including benefits, should be provided?
◆ What part of the total compensation of individuals should benefits constitute?
◆ What expense levels are acceptable for each benefit offered?
◆ Why is each type of benefit offered?
◆ Which employees should be given or offered which benefits?
◆ What is being received by the organization in return for each benefit?
◆ How does having a comprehensive benefits package help minimize turnover or maximize recruiting and retention of employees?
◆ How flexible should the package of benefits be?

Total benefits costs can be funded by contributions from both the employer and the employee. If the employer fully subsidizes a benefit, the cost to the employee is zero. But if an employer chooses to pay $400 a month toward an employee's health insurance premium and the premium costs $550 a month, the cost to the employee is $150 a month.

Part-Time Employee Benefits Another key design issue is whether or not to provide benefits coverage to employees who are not regular full-time employees. Many employers do not provide part-time employee benefits, except some time-off leave benefits. According to a study by the U.S. Bureau of Labor Statistics, only 24% of part-time workers are in company retirement plans, and only 17% are eligible for health care benefits.[4] Part-time employees who do receive benefits usually do so in proportion to the percentage of full-time work time they provide.

UPS, the package delivery firm, provides health benefits to most part-time employees. Wegmans Food Markets and Starbucks also provide benefits to part-timers. All these firms indicate that providing benefits positively affects their ability to attract and retain part-time workers in tight labor markets.[5]

Benefits Cost Control and Measurement

Many employees tend to take benefits for granted. So many organizations offer health insurance that employees expect it. Because benefits expenditures have risen significantly in the past few years, particularly for health care, employers are focusing more attention on measuring and controlling benefits costs, even reducing or dropping benefits offered to employees. Employers are using metrics shown in Figure 14-3.[6]

Figure 14-3	*Common Measurements of Benefits Effectiveness*

◆ **Benefits as a percentage of payroll (pattern over a multi-year period)**
◆ **Benefits expenditures per full-time equivalent (FTE) employee**
◆ **Benefits costs by employee group (full-time vs. part-time, union vs. non-union, office, management, professional, technical, etc.)**
◆ **Benefits administration costs (including staff time multiplied by the staff pay and benefits costs per hour)**
◆ **Health-care benefits costs per participating employee**

Benefits Effectiveness Metrics The significant costs associated with benefits require that analyses be conducted to determine the payoffs for the benefits. With the wide range of benefits that are offered, numerous HR metrics can be used.

Other metrics are used to measure the return on the expenditures for various benefits programs provided by employers. Some common benefits that employers track using HR metrics are workers' compensation, wellness programs, prescription drug costs, leave time, tuition aid, and disability insurance. The overriding point is that both benefits expenditures generally and costs for individual benefits specifically need to be measured and evaluated as part of strategic benefits management.

TYPES OF BENEFITS

A wide range of benefits are offered by employers. Some are mandated by laws and government regulations, while others are offered voluntarily by employers as part of their HR strategies.

Government-Mandated Benefits

There are many mandated benefits that employers in the United States must provide to employees by law. Social Security and unemployment insurance are funded through a tax paid by the employer based on the employee's compensation. Workers' compensation laws exist in all states. In addition, under the Family and Medical Leave Act (FMLA), employers must offer unpaid leaves to employees with certain medical or family difficulties. Other mandated benefits are funded in part by tax, through Social Security. The Consolidated Omnibus Budget Reconciliation Act (COBRA) mandates that an employer continue health-care coverage paid for by the employees after they leave the organization. The Health Insurance Portability and Accountability Act (HIPAA) requires that most employees be able to obtain coverage if they were previously covered in a health plan and provides privacy rights for medical records.

Additional mandated benefits have been *proposed* for many other areas, but as yet none of the proposals have been adopted. Areas in which coverage has been proposed are as follows:

* Universal health-care benefits for all workers
* Child-care assistance
* Pension plan coverage that can be transferred by workers who change jobs
* Core benefits for part-time employees working at least 500 hours a year
* Paid time off for family leave

A major reason for these proposals is that federal and state governments would like to shift many of the social costs for health care and other expenditures to employers. This shift would relieve some of the budgetary pressures facing government entities that otherwise might have to raise taxes and/or cut spending.

Voluntary Benefits

Employers voluntarily offer other types of benefits to compete for and retain employees. By offering additional benefits, organizations are recognizing the need to provide greater security and benefits support to workers with widely var-

LOGGING ON...

Employee Benefit Research Institute
This Web site provides the latest legislative and research information affecting benefits.
www.ebri.com

Figure 14-4 | *Types of Benefits*

☐ **Government mandated** ☐ **Employer voluntary**

Security	Health Care	Family Oriented
• Workers' compensation • Unemployment compensation	• COBRA and HIPAA provisions	• FMLA provisions
• Supplemental unemployment benefits (SUBs) • Severance pay	• Medical and dental • Prescription drugs • Vision • PPO, HMO, and CDH plans • Wellness programs • Flexible spending accounts	• Adoption benefits and dependent-care assistance • Domestic partner benefits
Retirement		**Time Off**
• Social Security • ADEA and OWBPA provisions	**Financial**	• Military reserve time off • Election and jury leaves
• Early retirement options • Health care for retirees • Pension plans • Individual retirement accounts (IRAs) • Keogh plans • 401 (k), 403 (b), and 457 plans	• Financial services (e.g., credit unions and counseling) • Relocation assistance • Life insurance • Disability insurance • Long-term care insurance • Legal insurance • Educational assistance	• Lunch and rest breaks • Holidays and vacations • Family leave • Medical and sick leave • Paid time off • Funeral and bereavement leaves
		Miscellaneous
		• Social and recreational programs and events • Unique programs

ied personal circumstances. In addition, as jobs become more flexible and varied, both workers and employers recognize that choices among benefits are necessary, as evidenced by the growth in flexible benefits and cafeteria benefit plans. Figure 14-4 lists seven types of mandated and voluntary benefits. The following sections describe them by type.

SECURITY BENEFITS

A number of benefits provide employee security. These benefits include some mandated by laws and others offered by employers voluntarily. The primary benefits found in most organizations include workers' compensation, unemployment compensation, and severance pay.

Workers' Compensation

Workers' compensation provides benefits to persons injured on the job. State laws require most employers to supply workers' compensation coverage by purchasing insurance from a private carrier or state insurance fund or by providing self-insurance. U.S. government employees are covered under the Federal Employees Compensation Act, administered by the U.S. Department of Labor.

The workers' compensation system requires employers to give cash benefits, medical care, and rehabilitation services to employees for injuries or illnesses occurring within the scope of their employment. In exchange, employees give up

Workers' compensation
Security benefits provided to persons injured on the job.

the right of legal actions and awards. The costs to employers for workers' compensation average about 2.2% of total payroll, and cost about $1.68 per $100 in wages per worker.[7]

Unemployment Compensation

Another benefit required by law is unemployment compensation, established as part of the Social Security Act of 1935. Because each U.S. state operates its own unemployment compensation system, provisions differ significantly from state to state. Employers finance this benefit by paying a tax on the first $7,000 (or more, in 37 states) of annual earnings for each employee. The tax is paid to state and federal unemployment compensation funds. The percentage paid by individual employers is based on "experience rates," which reflect the number of claims filed by workers who leave.

An employee who is out of work and is actively looking for employment normally receives up to 26 weeks of pay, at the rate of 50%–80% of normal pay. Most employees are eligible. However, workers fired for misconduct or those not actively seeking employment generally are ineligible. Only about 40% of eligible people use the unemployment compensation system. This underutilization may be due both to the stigma of receiving unemployment and the complexity of the system, which some feel is simply not worth the effort.

Supplemental unemployment benefits (SUBs) are closely related to unemployment compensation, but they are not required by law. A provision in some union contracts requires organizations to contribute to a fund that supplements the unemployment compensation available to employees from federal and/or state sources.

Criticisms of Unemployment Insurance Two problems explain changes in unemployment insurance laws proposed at state and federal levels: (1) abuses are estimated to cost billions each year, and (2) many state unemployment funds are exhausted during economic slowdowns. Some states allow striking union workers to collect unemployment benefits despite strike fund payments from the union, a provision bitterly opposed by many employers.

Severance Pay

Severance pay Security benefit voluntarily offered by employers to employees who lose their jobs.

Severance pay is a security benefit voluntarily offered by employers to the employees who lose their jobs. Severed employees may receive lump-sum severance payments if their employment is terminated by the employer. For example, if a facility closes because it is outmoded and no longer economically profitable to operate, the employees who lose their jobs may receive lump-sum payments based on their years of service. Severance pay provisions often provide higher severance payments corresponding to an employee's level within the organization and the person's years of employment. Severance pay is frequently offered for individuals whose jobs are eliminated or who leave by mutual agreement with their employers. The Worker Adjustment and Retraining Notification Act (WARN) of 1988 requires that many employers give 60 days' notice if a mass layoff or facility closing is to occur. The act does not require employers to give severance pay.

Some employers have offered reduced amounts of cash severance and replaced some of the severance value with continued health insurance and outplacement assistance. Through *outplacement assistance,* ex-employees receive resume writing instruction, interviewing skills workshops, and career counseling.

■ RETIREMENT BENEFITS

The aging of the workforce in many countries is affecting retirement planning for individuals and retirement plan costs for employers and governments. In the U.S., the number of citizens at least 55 years or older will increase 46% between 2004 and 2010, and older citizens will constitute 38% of the population in 2010. Simultaneously, the age of retirement will decline, as it has been for decades (see Figure 14-5). With more people retiring earlier and living longer, retirement benefits are becoming a greater concern for employers, employees, and retired employees.

Retirement Benefits and Age Discrimination

According to a 1986 amendment to the Age Discrimination in Employment Act (ADEA), most employees cannot be forced to retire at a specific age. As a result, employers have had to develop policies to comply with these regulations. In many employer pension plans, "normal retirement" is the age at which employees can retire and collect full pension benefits. Employers must decide whether individuals who continue to work past normal retirement age (perhaps 65) should receive the full benefits package, especially pension credits. As possible future changes in Social Security may increase the age for full benefits past 65, modifications in policies are likely. Despite the removal of mandatory retirement provisions, the age at which individuals retire has continued to decline in the United States. About 75% of all workers retire before age 65.

Early Retirement Many pension plans include provisions for early retirement to give workers voluntary opportunities to leave their jobs. After spending 25–30 years working for the same employer, individuals may wish to use their talents in other areas. Phased-in and part-time retirements offer alternatives that individuals and firms are using.

Some employers use early retirement buyout programs to cut back their workforces and reduce costs. Employers must take care to make these early retirement

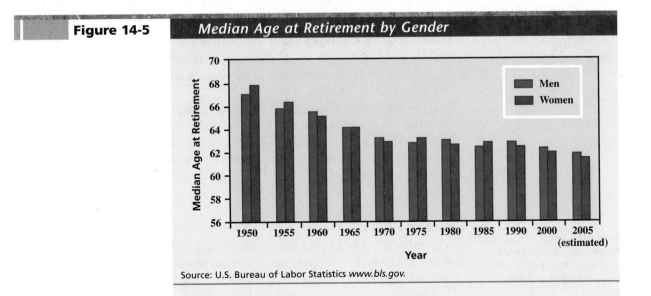

Figure 14-5

Median Age at Retirement by Gender

Source: U.S. Bureau of Labor Statistics *www.bls.gov.*

programs truly voluntary. Forcing workers to take advantage of an early retirement buyout program led to the passage of a federal law discussed next.

Older Workers Benefit Protection Act (OWBPA) Passed in 1990, the Older Workers Benefit Protection Act (OWBPA) amended the ADEA and overturned a decision by the U.S. Supreme Court in *Public Employees Retirement System of Ohio v. Betts*.[9] This act requires equal treatment for older workers in early retirement or severance situations. It also sets forth some specific criteria that must be met when older workers sign waivers promising not to sue for age discrimination.

Retiree Benefits Some employers choose to offer their retirees benefits, which may be paid for by the retirees, the company, or both. These benefits are usually available until the retiree is eligible for Medicare. The costs of such coverage have risen dramatically. To ensure that firms adequately reflect the liabilities for retiree health benefits, the Financial Accounting Standards Board (FASB) issued Rule 106, which requires employers to establish accounting reserves for funding retiree health-care benefits.

One problem with retiree pension benefits that some firms are facing is unfunded pension liabilities. General Motors has a liability of $9 billion. Other firms with large unfunded liabilities include ChevronTexaco ($2.6 billion), Hewlett-Packard ($2.6 billion), and Bank of America ($109 million).[10]

Unfortunately, most U.S. citizens have inadequate savings and retirement benefits for funding their retirements. According to a study by the Employee Benefit Research Institute, almost 70% of individuals over age 55 have less than $250,000 in savings and investments.[11] Therefore, they are heavily dependent on employer-provided retirement benefits. But many employers with fewer than 100 workers do not offer retirement benefits.

Social Security

The Social Security Act of 1935, with its later amendments, established a system providing *old-age, survivor's, disability,* and *retirement* benefits. Administered by the federal government through the Social Security Administration, this program provides benefits to previously employed individuals. Employees and employers share in the cost of Social Security through a tax on employees' wages or salaries.

Social Security Changes Since the system's inception, the Social Security payroll taxes have risen to 15.3% currently, with employees and employers each paying 7.65% up to an established maximum. In addition, Medicare taxes have more than doubled, to 2.9%.

Because the Social Security system affects a large number of individuals and is government operated, it is a politically sensitive program. Congress has responded to public pressure by raising payments and introducing cost-of-living adjustments. Now, Congress must respond to widespread criticisms that the system is not financially sound and must consider alternatives to ensure the future viability of the Social Security system.

Pension Plans

Pension plan
Retirement program established and funded by the employer and employees.

A **pension plan** is a retirement program established and funded by the employer and employees. Organizations are not required to offer pension plans to employees, and fewer than half of U.S. workers are covered by them. Small firms offer pension plans less often than do large ones.

Defined-Benefit Pension Plans A "traditional" pension plan, in which the employer makes the contributions and the employee will get a defined amount each month upon retirement, is no longer the norm in the private sector. Through a **defined-benefit plan,** employees are promised a pension amount based on age and service. The employees' contributions are based on actuarial calculations on the *benefits* to be received by the employees after retirement and the *methods* used to determine such benefits. A defined-benefit plan gives employees greater assurance of benefits and greater predictability in the amount of benefits that will be available for retirement. Defined-benefit plans are often preferred by workers with longer service, as well as by small-business owners.[12]

Defined-benefit plan
Retirement program in which an employee is promised a pension amount based on age and service.

If the funding in a defined-benefit plan is insufficient, the employer may have to make up the shortfall. Therefore, many employers have dropped defined-benefit plans in favor of defined-contribution plans so that their contribution liabilities are known.[13] Notice in Figure 14-6 that only unionized employees participate to a greater extent in defined-benefit plans.

Defined-contribution plan Retirement program in which the employer makes an annual payment to an employee's pension account.

Defined-Contribution Pension Plans In a **defined-contribution plan,** the employer makes an annual payment to an employee's pension account. The key to this plan is the *contribution rate;* employee retirement benefits depend on fixed contributions and employee earnings levels. Profit-sharing plans, employee stock ownership plans (ESOPs), and 401(k) plans are common defined-contribution plans. Because these plans hinge on the investment returns on the previous contributions, which can vary according to profitability or other factors, employees' retirement benefits are somewhat less secure and predictable. But because of their structure, these plans are sometimes preferred by younger, shorter-service employees.

Cash Balance Pension Plans Some employers have changed traditional pension plans to cash balance plans, which are hybrids based on ideas from both defined-benefit and defined-contribution plans. One type of plan is a

---

Figure 14-6   **Worker Participation in Pension Plan**

Category of Workers	Type of Pension Plan	
	Defined Benefit	Defined Contribution
All	20%	40%
White-collar	22%	51%
Blue-collar	24%	38%
Service	7%	16%
Full-time	24%	48%
Part-time	8%	14%
Union	72%	39%
Non-union	14%	40%
In firms with 1–99 workers	8%	51%
In firms with 100 or more workers	33%	51%

Source: U.S. Bureau of Labor Statistics, 2004, *www.bls.gov*.

Cash balance plan
Retirement program in which benefits are based on an accumulation of annual company contributions, expressed as a percentage of pay, plus interest credited each year.

cash balance plan, where retirement benefits are based on an accumulation of annual company contributions, expressed as a percentage of pay, plus interest credited each year. With these plans retirement benefits accumulate at the same annual rate until an employee retires. Because cash balance plans spread funding across a worker's entire career, these plans work better for mobile younger workers.

However, conversions to cash balance plans have caused discontent and even lawsuits among older employees at AT&T, EDS, and most notably IBM. At IBM, workers in the age 40 group would have lost a significant amount of retirement under the new plan. Their vocal protests and agitation caused IBM to change its initial plans for the new pension system, but a lawsuit is still in litigation.[14]

Many smaller employers do not offer pension plans for a number of reasons. The primary reason, in addition to their cost, is the administrative burdens imposed by government legislation, such as the law discussed next.

Employee Retirement Income Security Act (ERISA) The widespread criticism of many pension plans led to passage of the Employee Retirement Income Security Act (ERISA) in 1974. The purpose of this law is to regulate private pension plans so that employees who put money into them or depend on a pension for retirement funds actually receive the money when they retire.

ERISA essentially requires many companies to offer retirement plans to all employees if they offer retirement plans to any employees. Accrued benefits must be given to employees when they retire or leave. The act also sets minimum funding requirements, and plans not meeting those requirements are subject to financial penalties imposed by the IRS. Additional regulations require that employers pay plan termination insurance to ensure payment of employee pensions should the employers go out of business. To spread out the costs of administration and overhead, some employers use plans funded by multiple employers.

Retirement Equity in Pension Plans In the *Arizona Governing Committee v. Norris* ruling, a U.S. Supreme Court decision forced pension plan administrators to use "unisex" mortality tables, which do not reflect the gender differential in mortality.[15] To bring legislation in line with this decision, in 1984, Congress passed the Retirement Equity Act as an amendment to ERISA and the Internal Revenue Code. It liberalized pension regulations that affect women, guaranteed access to benefits, prohibited pension-related penalties due to absences from work such as maternity leave, and lowered the vesting age.

Qualified Domestic Relations Order (QDRO) Created by provisions of ERISA, a *qualified domestic relations order (QDRO)* is an agreement between a divorcing couple that identifies who gets assets in a retirement plan. Use of a QDRO provides protection for both individuals and their children in a divorce. Also, use of a QDRO provides some beneficial tax provisions.[16]

Contributory plan
Pension plan in which the money for pension benefits is paid in by both employees and employers.

Non-contributory plan Pension plan in which all the funds for pension benefits are provided by the employer.

Vesting Right of employees to receive certain benefits from their pension plans.

Pension Terms and Concepts Pension plans can be either contributory or non-contributory. In a **contributory plan,** money for pension benefits is paid in by both employees and the employer. In a **non-contributory plan,** the employer provides all the funds for pension benefits. As expected, the non-contributory plans are generally preferred by employees and labor unions.

Certain rights are attached to employee pension plans. Various laws and provisions have been passed to address the right of employees to receive benefits from their pension plans. Called **vesting,** this right assures employees of a certain pen-

sion, provided they work a minimum number of years. If employees resign or are terminated before they have been employed for the required time, no pension rights accrue to them except the funds they have contributed. If employees stay the allotted time, they retain their pension rights and receive the funds contributed by both the employer and themselves.

Another feature of some employee pensions is **portability.** In a portable plan, employees can move their pension benefits from one employer to another. A number of firms offer portable pension plans. Instead of requiring workers to wait until they retire to move their traditional pension plan benefits, the portable plan takes a different approach. Once workers have vested in a plan for a period of time, such as five years, they can transfer their fund balances to other retirement plans if they change jobs.

Individual Retirement Options

The availability of several retirement benefit options makes the pension area more complex. The most prominent options are individual retirement accounts (IRAs) and 401(k), 403(b), 457, and Keogh plans. These plans may be available in addition to company-provided pension plans and usually are contributory plans.

The **401(k) plan** gets its name from section 401(k) of the federal tax code. This plan is an agreement in which a percentage of an employee's pay is withheld and invested in a tax-deferred account. As Figure 14-7 indicates, many employers match employee 401(k) contributions, up to a percent of the employees pay. As a result, a significant number of employees contribute to 401(k) plans, and employers frequently have programs to encourage employees to contribute to 401(k) plans.[17] The use of 401(k) plans and of the assets in them has grown significantly in the past few years. The advantage to most employees, except for highly-compensated individuals, is that they can save pre-tax income toward their retirement.[18]

Figure 14-7

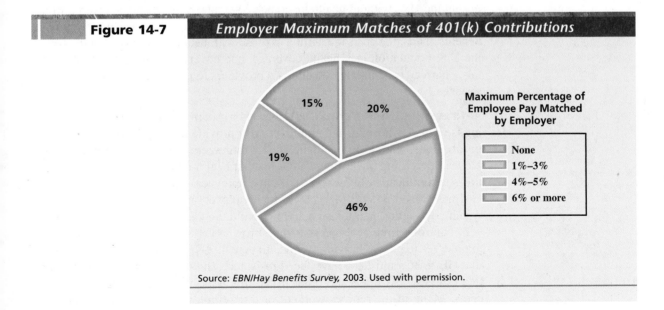

Employer Maximum Matches of 401(k) Contributions

Maximum Percentage of Employee Pay Matched by Employer
- None
- 1%–3%
- 4%–5%
- 6% or more

Source: *EBN/Hay Benefits Survey,* 2003. Used with permission.

Employers provide a variety of health-care and medical benefits, usually through insurance coverage. The most common plans cover medical, dental, prescription drug, and vision care expenses for employees and their dependents. Basic health-care insurance to cover both normal and major medical expenses is desired by most employees. Dental insurance is also important to many employees. Some dental plans include orthodontic coverage, which is a major expense for some families. If employers provide health insurance benefits, almost 70% of them offer vision insurance. But a larger percentage of the vision care plans require employees to pay all or part of the coverage costs.[19] Most firms do not cover the costs for Lasik and other elective surgeries to correct vision.

Increases in Health Benefits Costs

For several decades, the costs of health care have escalated at a rate well above the rates of inflation and changes in workers' earnings. Since the mid-1990s, employer health-care benefits costs have been increasing significantly faster than inflation or workers' earnings. Estimates are that average health-care benefits costs per employee are over $6,300 a year.[20]

As a result of these large increases, many employers find that dealing with health-care benefits is time-consuming and expensive. This is especially frustrating for employers who have found that many employees seem to take their health benefits for granted. Consequently, a growing number of firms, particularly smaller ones, have asked, "Why are we offering these benefits anyway?" and have answered the question by discontinuing or dramatically cutting health benefits. Only 60% of firms with under 200 workers offer health benefit coverage, down about 8% in the past few years. But 99% of all large firms offer health benefits.[21] Two major groups of workers that have contributed to the increasing costs are uninsured workers and retirees.

Uninsured Workers Some of the health benefits cost pressures are due to health-care providers having to cover the costs for the rising number of individuals in the U.S. without health insurance coverage. Some of the uninsured workers are illegal immigrants; others work for employers that do not provide benefits. Thus, the costs are shifted to those with health insurance. About 16% of the U.S. population lack health coverage, and covering their costs forces hospitals, pharmacies, and other health-care providers to raise their rates on all patient services.

Retirees Health Benefits Costs Another group whose benefits costs are rising is retirees whose former employers still provide health benefit coverage. For instance, at General Motors, there are 2.4 retired employees for every active employee. Increasing the problem at GM is that health-care usage rates for older retirees is significantly higher than current employees. The shocking statistic is that GM has to add $1,400 per vehicle for employee and retiree health-care costs, which costs more than the steel used to build the cars.[22]

To control retiree health costs, some firms are cutting their benefits or requiring retirees to pay higher rates for health benefits. Naturally, such efforts by firms like GE, SBC, and IBM have faced resistance and even lawsuits from disgruntled retirees.[23] At these and other firms, this issue raises troubling ethical concerns. Many of the retirees worked for their employers for 20, 30, 40, or more

years. Yet the reward for their long and loyal service increasingly is a reduction in health-care benefits.

Controlling Health-Care Benefits Costs

Employers offering health-care benefits are taking a number of approaches to controlling their costs. The most prominent ones are changing co-payments and employee contributions, using managed care, and switching to consumer-driven health plans.

Changing Co-Payments and Employee Contributions As health insurance costs rise, employers have tried to shift some of those costs to employees. The **co-payment** strategy requires employees to pay a portion of the cost of insurance premiums, medical care, and prescription drugs.

Co-payment Strategy requiring employees to pay a portion of the cost of insurance premiums, medical care, and prescription drugs.

Notice in Figure 14-8 that requiring new or higher employee contributions and co-payments is the most prevalent cost-control strategy identified by 400 employers surveyed. Employers who have raised the per-person deductible from $50 to $250 have realized significant savings in health-care expenses due to decreased employee usage of health-care services and prescription drugs. The "gatekeeper" role mentioned in the figure is important because many employers have found that some of the health care provided by doctors and hospitals is unnecessary, incorrectly billed, or deliberately overcharged. Consequently, both employers and insurance firms often require that medical work and charges be audited through a **utilization review.** This process may require a second opinion, a review of the procedures done, and a review of the charges for the procedures done.

Utilization review Audit of the services and costs billed by health-care providers.

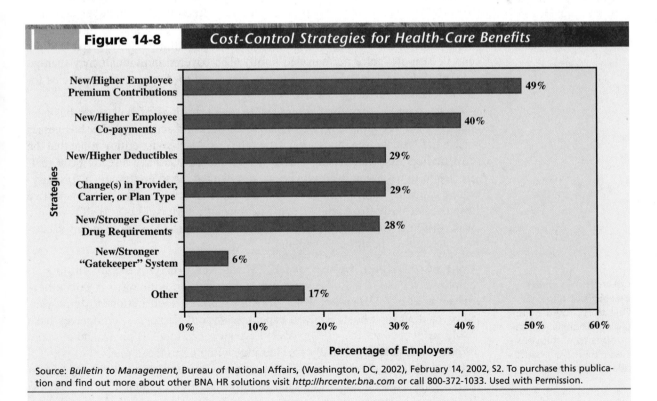

Figure 14-8 *Cost-Control Strategies for Health-Care Benefits*

Strategies / Percentage of Employers

- New/Higher Employee Premium Contributions — 49%
- New/Higher Employee Co-payments — 40%
- New/Higher Deductibles — 29%
- Change(s) in Provider, Carrier, or Plan Type — 29%
- New/Stronger Generic Drug Requirements — 28%
- New/Stronger "Gatekeeper" System — 6%
- Other — 17%

Source: *Bulletin to Management,* Bureau of National Affairs, (Washington, DC, 2002), February 14, 2002, S2. To purchase this publication and find out more about other BNA HR solutions visit *http://hrcenter.bna.com* or call 800-372-1033. Used with Permission.

These changes are facing significant resistance by employees, especially those who have had *first-dollar coverage.* With this type of coverage, all expenses, from the first dollar of health-care costs, are paid by the employee's insurance. Experts claim that when first-dollar coverage is included in a basic health plan, many employees see a doctor for every slight illness, which results in an escalation of the benefits costs.

Many union contracts have first-dollar coverage, and attempts by employers to negotiate co-payments or increases in co-payments have led to numerous strikes. One of the longest strikes over such benefits as a central issue involved 70,000 grocery store workers in Southern California and lasted for several months.[24]

Using Managed Care Several other types of programs attempt to reduce health-care costs paid by employers. **Managed care** consists of approaches that monitor and reduce medical costs through restrictions and market system alternatives. Managed care plans emphasize primary and preventive care, the use of specific providers who will charge lower prices, restrictions on certain kinds of treatment, and prices negotiated with hospitals and physicians.

One managed care approach is the **preferred provider organization (PPO),** a health-care provider that contracts with an employer or an employer group to supply health-care services to employees at a competitive rate. Employees have the freedom to go to other providers if they want to pay the differences in costs. *Point-of-service plans* are somewhat similar, offering financial incentives to encourage employees to use designated medical providers.

Another prominent managed care approach is a **health maintenance organization (HMO),** which provides services for a fixed period on a pre-paid basis. The HMO emphasizes both prevention and correction. An employer contracts with an HMO and its staff of physicians and medical personnel to furnish complete medical care, except for hospitalization. The employer pays a flat rate per enrolled employee or per enrolled family. The covered individuals may then go to the HMO for health care as often as they need to. Supplemental policies for hospitalization are also provided.

Critics contend that competing HMOs spend millions of dollars on business matters such as conducting destructive price wars and acquiring other businesses instead of focusing on innovation in health care. Also, some critics argue that the cost savings associated with managed care and HMOs have already been realized. Additionally, many employees do not like having to go through a "primary-care physician" before being able to see medical specialists. The HR Perspective discusses a study on employee satisfaction with HMOs. While HMOs remain widely used, a growing number of employers are focusing on other means to control the costs of health-care benefits.

Consumer-Driven Health (CDH) Plans Many employers are turning to employee-focused health benefits plans. The most prominent is a **consumer-driven health (CDH) plan,** which provides financial contributions to employees to cover their own health-related expenses. Various surveys of companies have identified that over 10% of employers have switched to CDH plans, and as many as one-third more are actively considering switching to these plans.[25]

In these plans, which are also called *defined-contribution health plans,* an employer places a set amount into each employee's "account" and identifies a number of health-care alternatives that are available. Then, individual employees

Managed care
Approaches that monitor and reduce medical costs through restrictions and market system alternatives.

Preferred provider organization (PPO)
A health-care provider that contracts with an employer group to supply health-care services to employees at a competitive rate.

Health maintenance organization (HMO)
Plan that provides services for a fixed period on a pre-paid basis.

Consumer-driven health (CDH) plan
One that provides employer financial contributions to employees to cover their own health-related expenses.

HR *Perspective*

Research on Satisfaction with Health Benefits

As employers have expanded the used of managed care in health benefits plans, there has been concern about how employees view those plans. Akinci and Sinay addressed this issue in a study published in *Health Services Management Research*.

The study was conducted in Pennsylvania using telephone interviews of almost 400 individuals, most of whom had health insurance coverage. Of those with coverage, 43% had HMOs, 30% had traditional health benefits plans, and the others had Medicare and Medicaid. The study found that satisfaction with access to medical care was related to the type of health plan, insurance costs, co-payments, and other factors. Results of the study revealed several areas of inter-

est. Over 20% of the respondents had complaints about the time spent in the doctors' offices or waiting rooms.

Of particular note, individuals covered under HMOs were much less satisfied with access to care than were individuals with traditional fee-for-service health plans. One important factor that contributed to the findings about HMOs was the respondents' negative views of HMOs because they thought co-payment levels were too high.

This study illustrates that different types of health benefits plans affect individuals' satisfaction. It also indicates that managed care, particularly through HMOs, is viewed negatively by a number of individuals.[26]

---

select from those health-care alternatives and pay for them from their accounts. For instance, assume an employer sets aside $250 a month for each employee. One employee may choose an HMO costing $230 a month, and use her remaining $20 for purchasing additional life insurance. Another employee may choose a family plan costing $480 a month, and have the additional $230 deducted from his paycheck.

CDH plans can be coupled with *health flexible spending accounts* (discussed later), *health reimbursement arrangements, medical savings accounts,* and *health savings accounts.* Although slightly different in terms of tax regulations, these programs all allow individuals to make regular tax-free deposits into accounts.[27] Then, the money can be withdrawn to pay for qualified medical expenses, health insurance premiums, catastrophic health expenses, and other approved health-related costs not covered by employer contributions.[28]

There are two advantages to such plans for employers. One is that more of the increases in health-care benefits are shifted to employees, because the employer contributions need not increase as fast as health-care costs. Second, the focus of controlling health-care usage falls on employees, who may have to choose when to use and not use health-care benefits.

Many employers offer programs to educate employees about health-care costs and how to reduce them. Newsletters, formal classes, and many other approaches are all designed to help employees understand why health-care costs are increasing and what they can do to control them. Some employers even have *wellness programs* offering financial incentives to improve health habits. These programs, discussed more in Chapter 15, reward employees who stop smoking, lose weight, and participate in exercise programs, among other activities.

Employee Reactions to Cost-Control Efforts

As would be expected, many employees are skeptical about or even hostile to employer efforts to control health benefits costs. Surveys of employees have found that they are more dissatisfied with changes to their health benefits than with the moderation of base pay increases. In fact, over half of the employees in one survey said that they would forgo any pay increase to keep their health benefits unchanged.[29]

For cost-control efforts to work for employers, the gap between employees' and employers' views on benefits must be bridged, which requires significant communication and education of employees to counter their negative reactions.[30] Yet, one survey found that over 60% of employees spend less than one hour selecting benefits plans, and half spend less than 30 minutes.[31] Key in communicating about controlling health benefits cost is sharing information and having a continuing communication plan. At First Tennessee Bank, communication methods include a newsletter, wellness programs, employee workshops, and intranet Q&As.[32]

Health-Care Legislation

The importance of health-care benefits to employers and employees has led to a variety of federal and state laws. Some laws have been enacted to provide protection for employees who leave their employers, either voluntarily or involuntarily. To date, the two most important ones are COBRA and HIPAA.

THOMSON
*
WEST

COBRA
Displays a sample COBRA election letter.
Custom Search:
☑ ANALYSIS
Exact Phrase: COBRA election letter

COBRA Provisions The Consolidated Omnibus Budget Reconciliation Act (COBRA) requires that most employers (except churches and the federal government) with 20 or more employees offer extended health-care coverage to certain groups, as follows:

- Employees who voluntarily quit
- Widowed or divorced spouses and dependent children of former or current employees
- Retirees and their spouses whose health-care coverage ends

Employers must notify eligible employees and/or their spouses and qualified dependents within 60 days after the employees quit, die, get divorced, or otherwise change their status. The chart in Figure 14-9 shows the coverage that must be offered depending on the qualifying circumstances. The individual no longer employed by the organization must pay the premiums, but the employer may charge this individual no more than 102% of the premium costs to insure a similarly covered employee.

Figure 14-9	Overview of COBRA Provisions	
Qualifying Event	**Qualified Beneficiaries**	**Coverage Period**
Employee termination / reduction in hours (except for misconduct)	Employee, spouse, and dependent children	18–29 months
Divorce or death of employee	Spouse and dependent children	36 months

For most employers, the COBRA requirements mean additional paperwork and related costs. For example, firms must not only track the former employees but also notify their qualified dependents. The 2% premium addition generally does not cover all relevant costs, because those costs often run several percentage points more.

HIPAA Provisions The Health Insurance Portability and Accountability Act (HIPAA) of 1996 allows employees to switch their health insurance plans when they change employers, and to get new health coverage with the new company regardless of pre-existing health conditions. The legislation also prohibits group insurance plans from dropping coverage for a sick employee, and requires them to make individual coverage available to people who leave group plans.

One of the greatest impacts of HIPAA comes from its provisions on the privacy of employee medical records. These provisions require employers to provide privacy notices to employees. They also regulate the disclosure of protected health information without authorization.[33]

Flexible Spending Accounts

Under current tax law (specifically, Section 125 of the Internal Revenue Code), employees can divert some pre-tax income into **flexible spending accounts** to fund certain additional benefits. Under tax law at the time of this writing, the funds in the account can be used to purchase only the following: (1) additional health care (including off-setting deductibles), (2) life insurance, (3) disability insurance, and (4) dependent-care benefits. An example illustrates the advantage of these accounts to employees. Assume an employee earns $3,000 a month and has $100 a month deducted to put into a flexible spending account. That $100 does not count as gross income for tax purposes, so the employee's taxable income is reduced. The employee uses the money in the account to purchase additional benefits.

Flexible spending accounts have grown in popularity as more varied health-care plans have been adopted by more employers. Of course, such plans and their tax advantages can be changed as Congress passes future health-care and new tax-related legislation.[34]

FINANCIAL BENEFITS

Employers may offer workers a wide range of special benefits that provide financial support to employees: financial services, relocation assistance, insurance benefits (in addition to health insurance), educational assistance, and others. Employers find that such benefits can be useful in attracting and retaining employees. Workers like receiving these benefits, which often are not taxed as income.

Financial Services

Financial benefits include a wide variety of items. A *credit union* sponsored by the employer provides saving and lending services for employees. *Purchase discounts* allow employees to buy goods or services from their employers at reduced rates. For example, a furniture manufacturer may allow employees to buy furniture at wholesale cost plus 10%, or a bank may offer employees use of a safe deposit box and free checking.

Employee *thrift plans, savings plans,* or *stock investment plans* of different types may be available. To illustrate, in a **stock purchase plan,** the employer

Flexible spending accounts Benefits plans that allow employees to contribute pre-tax dollars to buy certain additional benefits.

provides matching funds equal to the amount invested by the employee for the purchase of stock in the company. Often, employees may buy the stock at a discount. This type of plan allows employees to benefit from the future growth of the corporation. Also, the intent of such a plan is to develop greater employee loyalty and interest in the organization and its success.[35]

Financial planning and counseling are especially valuable services for executives, many of whom may need information on investments and tax shelters, as well as comprehensive financial counseling, because of their higher levels of compensation. The importance of these financial planning benefits likely will grow as a greater percentage of workers approach retirement age and need to plan financially for retirement.

Relocation Assistance

Relocation benefits of various types are offered by many firms. Some employers offer temporary relocation benefits, while others provide assistance in finding a job for the spouse of a transferred employee. Numerous other financial-related benefits may be offered as well, including the use of a company car, company expense accounts, and assistance in buying or selling a house.

Insurance Benefits

In addition to health-related insurance, some employers provide other types of insurance. These benefits offer major advantages for employees because many employers pay some or all of the costs. Even when employers do not pay any of the costs, employees still benefit because of the lower rates available through group programs. The most common types of insurance benefits are the following:

- *Life insurance:* Bought as a group policy, the employer pays all or some of the premiums. A typical level of coverage is one-and-a-half or two times an employee's annual salary.
- *Disability insurance: Short-term* and *long-term disability insurance* provides continuing income protection for employees who become disabled and unable to work. Long-term disability insurance is much more common because many employers cover short-term disability situations through sick leave programs.
- *Long-term care insurance:* Usually voluntary, these plans allow employees to purchase insurance to cover costs for long-term health care in a nursing home, an assisted-living facility, or at home. Though employees pay for the premiums, they get cheaper rates through employer sponsored group plans.
- *Legal insurance:* In these plans employees (or employers) pay a flat fee for a set amount of legal assistance time each month. In return, they have the right to use the service of a network of lawyers to handle their legal problems.

Educational Assistance

Another benefit that saves financial resources of employees comes in the form of *educational assistance* and tuition aid, which pays some or all of the costs associated with formal education courses and degree programs, including the costs of books and laboratory materials. Some employers pay for schooling on a proportional schedule, depending on the grades received; others simply require a passing grade of C or above. Unless the education paid for by the employer meets certain conditions, the cost of educational aid must be counted as taxable income by employees.

▐▐▐▐▐ **ROI of Tuition Aid** Providing educational benefits through tuition aid programs is a very popular benefit with employees. It has been estimated that in one year, U.S. employers spend over $10 billion for tuition aid, but only 2% of those firms conduct HR analyses to determine the return on their investment in tuition aid for those involved in these programs.[36] To make educational benefits programs more effective, the following factors could be measured: employee retention, internal promotions, increased employee satisfaction, and others.

▐▐▐ FAMILY-ORIENTED BENEFITS

The composition of families in the United States has changed significantly in the past few decades. The number of traditional families, in which the man went to work and the woman stayed home to raise children, has declined significantly, while the percentage of two-worker families has more than doubled. The growth in dual-career couples, single-parent households, and work demands on many workers have increased the emphasis some employers are placing on family-oriented benefits. As mentioned in earlier chapters, balancing family and work demands presents a major challenge to many workers at all levels of organizations. Therefore, employers have established a variety of family-oriented benefits. Since 1993, employers have also been required to provide certain benefits to comply with the Family and Medical Leave Act.

Family and Medical Leave Act (FMLA)

The Family and Medical Leave Act (FMLA) covers all federal, state, and private employers with 50 or more employees who live within 75 miles of the workplace. Only employees who have worked at least 12 months and 1,250 hours in the previous year are eligible for leaves under the FMLA.[37]

FMLA Leave Provisions The law requires that employers allow eligible employees to take a total of 12 weeks' leave during any 12-month period for one or more of three situations. Those situations are:

- Birth, adoption, or foster care placement of a child
- Caring for a spouse, a child, or a parent with a serious health condition
- Serious health condition of the employee

A **serious health condition** is one requiring in-patient, hospital, hospice, or residential medical care or continuing physician care. An employer may require an employee to provide a certificate from a doctor verifying such an illness.

The FMLA provides a number of guidelines regarding employee leaves. The guidelines are as follows:

- Employees taking family and medical leave must be able to return to the same job or a job of equivalent status or pay.
- Health benefits must be continued during the leave at the same level and conditions. If, for a reason other than serious health problems, the employee does not return to work, the employer may collect the employer-paid portion of the premiums from the non-returning employee.
- The leave may be taken intermittently rather than in one block, subject to employee and employer agreements, when birth, adoption, or foster child

THOMSON
✳
™
WEST

FMLA Policy
Contains sample FMLA policy statements.
Custom Search:
☑ ANALYSIS
Exact Phrase: Model family and medical leaves

Serious health condition One requiring in-patient, hospital, hospice, or residential medical care or continuing physician care.

care is the cause. For serious health conditions, employer approval is not necessary.

♦ Employees can be required to use all paid-up vacation and personal leave before taking unpaid leave.

♦ Employees are required to give 30-day notice, where practical.

Results of the FMLA Since the passage of the act, several factors have become apparent. First, a significant percentage of employees have been taking family and medical leave. As Figure 14-10 indicates, women and employees in the 25–34 age-group take more family and medical leave, primarily due to childbirth reasons.

Second, many employers have not paid enough attention to the law. Some employers are denying leaves or failing to reinstate workers after leaves are completed. Consequently, numerous lawsuits have resulted, many of which are lost by employers. Many employers' problems with the FMLA occur because of the variety of circumstances in which employees may request and use family leave. Often, employers have difficulty interpreting when and how the provisions are to be applied.[38] It took a U.S. Supreme Court decision in *Ragsdale v. Wolverine Worldwide* to clarify the notice obligations that employers have regarding FMLA leave granted to employees.[39]

Third, employers are not required to pay employees for leave taken under the FMLA, other than for sick leave or accumulated unused vacation time. However, some states have passed or are considering laws requiring employers to provide *paid family leave.* California law provides workers as much as 55% of their pay up to a weekly maximum, for leaves as long as six weeks. This controversial and complex law covers about 13 million workers in California.[40]

Finally, one challenge for employers has been covering the workload for employees on family leave. This difficulty is compounded because the law requires

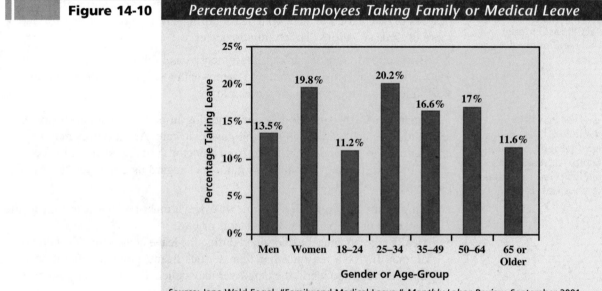

Figure 14-10   *Percentages of Employees Taking Family or Medical Leave*

Source: Jane Wald Fogel, "Family and Medical Leave," *Monthly Labor Review,* September 2001, 17–23; and U.S. Bureau of Labor Statistics, *www.bls.gov.*

that workers on these leaves be offered similar jobs at similar levels of pay when they return to work. Balancing work demands for many different employees and their family and medical situations has placed significant demands on HR professionals to ensure compliance with FMLA provisions.

Family-Care Benefits

Family issues are growing in importance for many organizations and for many workers. One repercussion of this emphasis is that employees without families may feel some resentment against those who seem to get special privileges because they have families. Many employees do not have children under the age of 18 and are offered fewer opportunities to use personal days off, flexible scheduling, telecommuting, etc. Further, they are more frequently asked to travel or put in overtime because they "don't have a family."[41] Nevertheless, a variety of family benefits are available in many organizations.

Adoption Benefits Many employers provide maternity and paternity benefits to employees who give birth to children. A comparatively small number of employees adopt children, and in the interest of fairness, some organizations provide benefits for them. For example, Microsoft gives a cash benefit and four weeks of paid leave to employees who adopt children. Wendy's provides cash payments to cover adoption expenses and up to six weeks of paid leave for employee adoptions. Overall, about 36% of surveyed firms provide some type of adoption benefits.[42]

Child-Care Assistance Balancing work and family responsibilities is a major challenge for many workers. Whether single parents or dual-career couples, these employees often experience difficulty obtaining high-quality, affordable child care. Employers are addressing the child-care issue in the following ways:

- Providing referral services to help parents locate child-care providers
- Establishing discounts at day-care centers, which may be subsidized by the employer
- Arranging with hospitals to offer sick-child programs partially paid for by the employer
- Developing after-school programs for older school-age children, often in conjunction with local public and private school systems
- Offering on-site child-care centers

Elder-Care Assistance Another family issue of importance is caring for elderly relatives.[43] Various organizations have surveyed their employees and found that as many as 25%–30% of them have had to miss work to care for aging relatives. The responsibilities associated with caring for elderly family members have resulted in reduced work performance, increased absenteeism, and more personal stress for the affected employees.[44] Lost productivity and absenteeism caused by workers caring for elders cost employers billions of dollars a year. Some responses by employers have included conducting needs surveys, providing resources, and giving referrals to elder-care providers.

Measuring the Effectiveness of Family Benefits

Employers that have provided child-care and other family-friendly assistance have found the programs beneficial for several reasons. The greatest advantage is in aiding employee retention.[45] Employees are more likely to stay with employers who aid them with work/life balancing. One study of child-care benefits identified savings of $5.50 for every $1.00 spent.[46] The savings are primarily due to decreased employee absenteeism and turnover. Analyses of elder-care costs/benefits show similar results. To determine such metrics, costs for recruiting, training, turnover, and lost productivity are included.[47]

Benefits for Domestic Partners

As lifestyles change in the United States, employers are being confronted with requests for benefits by employees who are not married but have close personal relationships with others. The terms often used to refer to individuals with such arrangements are *domestic partners* or *spousal equivalents.* The employees who are submitting these requests are: (1) unmarried employees who are living with individuals of the opposite sex and (2) gay and lesbian employees who have partners.

The argument made by these employees is that if an employer provides benefits for the spouses of married employees, then benefits should be provided for employees without spouses but with alternative lifestyles and relationships. This view is reinforced by data showing that a significant percentage of heterosexual couples live together before or instead of formally marrying. Also, there is increasing openness of more gay employees about their lifestyles. The debate about *same-sex marriages* has amplified the issue for HR professionals and their employers. In 13 states and 150 cities, laws have been enacted to require employers to grant domestic partners the same benefits rights that they give to traditional married couples.[48]

Estimates are that about 30% of employers provide domestic partner benefits, but some limit the benefits to heterosexual couples only. Organizations with those benefits usually have policies that define what the qualifying relationship is and what documentation is required to verify eligibility.[49] At some firms, both the employee and the "eligible partner" must sign an Affidavit of Spousal Equivalence. With this affidavit, the employee and the partner are asked to affirm the following:

- Each is the other's only spousal equivalent.
- They are not blood relatives.
- They are living together and jointly share responsibility for their common welfare and financial obligations.

Decisions to extend benefits to domestic partners have come under attacks from certain religious leaders opposed to homosexual lifestyles. However, it must be noted that most employees using the domestic partner benefits are of the opposite sex and are in heterosexual relationships.

▌▌ TIME-OFF BENEFITS

Time-off benefits represent an estimated 5%–13% of total compensation. Employers give employees paid time off in a variety of circumstances. Paid lunch breaks and rest periods, holidays, and vacations are common. But time off is given for a number of other purposes as well. As Figure 14-11 indicates, time-off benefits also include various leaves of absence.

Holiday Pay

Most employers provide pay for a variety of holidays. U.S. employers commonly offer 10–12 holidays annually. Employers in many other countries are re-

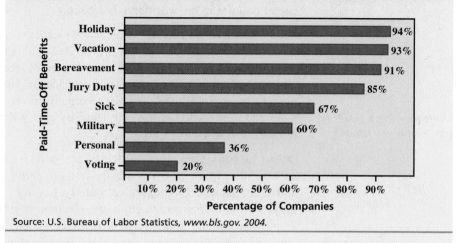

Figure 14-11 *Percentage of Companies with Various Paid-Time-Off Plans*

Source: U.S. Bureau of Labor Statistics, *www.bls.gov. 2004.*

quired to provide a significantly higher number of holidays, approaching 20–30 days in some cases. In both the U.S. and other countries, the number of holidays offered can vary depending on state/provincial laws and union contracts.

As an abuse-control measure, employers commonly require employees to work the last scheduled day before a holiday and the first scheduled workday after a holiday to be eligible for holiday pay. Some employers pay time-and-a-half to hourly employees who must work holidays. Also, some employers provide some company holiday parties and holiday bonus programs such as food gifts (turkeys at Thanksgiving) or holiday gift cards.

Vacation Pay

Paid vacations are a common benefit. Employers often use graduated vacation-time scales based on employees' lengths of service. Some organizations have a "use it or lose it" policy whereby vacation time cannot be carried over from year to year. Such policies are outlawed in California and a few other places.[50]

Some employers have policies to "buy back" unused vacation time. Other employers, such as banks, may have policies requiring employees to take a minimum number of vacation days off in a row. Regardless of the vacation policies used, employees are often required to work the day before and the day after vacation time off.

Leaves of Absence

Employers grant *leaves of absence,* taken as time off with or without pay, for a variety of reasons. All the leaves discussed here add to employer costs even if unpaid, because the missing employee's work must be covered, either by other employees working additionally or by temporary employees working under contract.

Family Leave As mentioned earlier in the chapter, the passage of the Family and Medical Leave Act clarified the rights of employees and the responsibilities of most employers. Even though *paternity leave* for male workers is available under FMLA, a relatively low percentage of men take it. The primary reason for the low usage is a perception that it is not as socially acceptable for men to stay home for child-related reasons. That view has begun changing as the number of dual-career couples in the workforce has risen.

Medical and Sick Leave Medical and sick leave are closely related. Many employers allow employees to miss a limited number of days because of illness without losing pay. Some employers allow employees to accumulate unused sick leave, which may be used in case of catastrophic illnesses. Others pay their employees for unused sick leave. Some organizations have shifted emphasis to reward people who do not use sick leave by giving them **well-pay**—extra pay for not taking sick leave.

Other Leaves Other types of leaves are given for a variety of purposes. Some, such as *military leave, election leave,* and *jury leave,* are required by various state and federal laws. Employers commonly pay the difference between the employee's regular pay and the military, election, or jury pay. Some firms grant the employees military time off and provide regular pay while the employees also receive military pay. Federal law prohibits taking discriminatory action against military reservists by requiring them to take vacation time when deployed or in training. However, the leave request must be reasonable and truly required by the military.

Funeral leave or *bereavement leave* is another common type of leave offered. Absence of up to three days for the death of immediate family members is usually granted. Some policies also give unpaid time off for the death of more distant relatives or of friends.

Paid-Time-Off (PTO) Plans

Other employers have made use of a **paid-time-off plan,** which combines sick leave, vacations, and holidays into a total number of hours or days that employees can take off with pay. Various studies have found that about two-thirds of all employers have PTO plans, up from one-third in the past several years. More importantly, about 60% of those employers have found PTO plans more effective than other means of reducing absenteeism and in having time off scheduled more efficiently.[51] Additionally, employee understanding and acceptance of leave policies may improve.[52]

▌▌ MISCELLANEOUS BENEFITS

Employers offer a wide variety of miscellaneous benefits. Some of the benefits are voluntary, meaning that employees can participate in them and pay for the costs themselves, often at group discount rates. Others are unique to employers and are provided at little or no cost to employees.

Social and Recreational Benefits

Some benefits and services are social and recreational in nature, such as tennis courts, bowling leagues, picnics, parties, employer-sponsored athletic teams, organizationally owned recreational lodges, and other sponsored activities and interest groups. As interest in employee wellness has increased, more firms are providing recreational facilities and activities. The idea behind social and recreational programs is to promote employee happiness and team spirit. Employees may appreciate this type of benefit, but managers should not necessarily expect

Well-pay Extra pay for not taking sick leave.

Paid-time-off (PTO) plans Plans that combine all sick leave, vacation time, and holidays into a total number of hours or days that employees can take off with pay.

increased job productivity or job satisfaction as a result. Further, employers should retain control of all events associated with their organizations because of possible legal responsibility.

Unique Benefits Offered

Employers provide a wide variety of unique benefits, ranging from transportation subsidies to self-defense training to company food services to health-club memberships. More unusual ones include pet insurance, which is offered by a number of employers, including the Weather Channel. In this program, employees get group rates on pet insurance that provides discounts when they pay for veterinarian services, pet food and supplies, and boarding/kennel services.[53]

Another unique benefit is provided through the Professional Association of Diving Instructors (PADI). In its corporate program, employees get discounts when getting scuba diving certifications. The PADI program is available at 4,700 dive centers worldwide.[54] There are other unusual benefits, too many to mention, all designed to differentiate employers from others and to provide unique benefits to employees.

BENEFITS ADMINISTRATION

With the myriad of benefits and regulations, it is easy to see why many organizations must make coordinated efforts to administer benefits programs. Figure 14-12 shows how benefits administration responsibilities can be split between HR specialists and operating managers. HR specialists play the more significant role, but managers must assume responsibility for some of the communication aspects of benefits administration.

Benefits Communication

Employees generally do not know much about the values and costs associated with the benefits they receive from employers, so benefits communication and benefits satisfaction are linked. Consequently, many employers have instituted special benefits communication systems to inform employees about the value of the benefits they provide. For instance, the retailer Pier 1 Imports uses various means, including videos, CDs, electronic alerts, newsletters, and employee meetings, to ensure that employees are knowledgeable about their benefits.[55]

Benefits Statements Some employers also give each employee a "personal statement of benefits" that translates benefits into dollar amounts. Federal regu-

Figure 14-12 **Typical Division of HR Responsibilities: Benefits Administration**

HR Unit	Managers
◆ Develops and administers benefits systems ◆ Answers employees' technical questions on benefits ◆ Monitors benefits usage ◆ Suggests benefits cost-control approaches	◆ Answer simple questions on benefits ◆ Maintain liaison with HR specialist on benefits ◆ Maintain good communications with employees near retirement ◆ Coordinate use of time-off benefits

On-line Benefits

Use of the Internet for a variety of benefits-related purposes is widespread. Many firms provide health-plan and wellness information to employees on-line. Communicating such information is especially important as firms try to hold down health benefits costs through consumer-driven health plans.

Cigna, a large health and retirement insurance firm, provides a Web site for 16 million members whose employers use Cigna as a vendor. On that Web portal, individuals can review health plan options, track the status of their medical claims, and locate medical providers.

Other firms use Web sources for accessing health and wellness information. Xerox and Johnson & Johnson each make wellness information available to employees on-line. Employees can complete confidential personal health profiles and in return get health and wellness analyses. These analyses suggest various wellness activities and direct employees to on-line resources they can review. Xerox employees who participate enter a drawing for gift certificates. Participation of the 40,000 Johnson & Johnson employees has grown to 90% in two years, and provides the company with both healthier employees and savings of over $8.5 million a year. These examples illustrate that both employers and employees gain from on-line resources for employee benefits.[57]

lations under ERISA require that employees receive an annual pension-reporting statement, which also can be included in the personal statement. Employers hope that by educating employees about their benefits and the costs, they can better manage expenditures and can give employees a better appreciation of the value of employers' payments.

HR Technology and Benefits

The spread of HR technology, particularly Internet-based systems, has significantly changed the benefits administration time and activities for HR staff members. Internet-based systems are being used to communicate benefits information, conduct employee benefits surveys, and facilitate other benefits communications. The Technology Transforming HR describes ways that companies are using technology to communicate health benefits information to employees.

Use of information technology also allows employees to change their benefits choices, track their benefits balances, and submit questions to HR staff members and external benefits providers. Use of the Internet for benefits enrollment has tripled in three years.[56] The greatest use has been to allow employees to sign up for, change, or update their benefits choices through Web-based systems. Previously, HR departments had to send out paper forms, hold numerous benefits meetings, and answer many phone calls from employees. The switch to on-line enrollment and communications has led to reductions in HR staff and benefits administration costs.

Flexible Benefits

As part of both benefits design and administration many employers have flexible benefits plans that offer employees choices.

Flexible benefits plan Program that allows employees to select the benefits they prefer from groups of benefits established by the employer.

A **flexible benefits plan,** sometimes called a *flex plan* or *cafeteria plan,* allows employees to select the benefits they prefer from groups of benefits established by the employer. By having a variety of "dishes," or benefits, available, each employee can select an individual combination of benefits within some overall limits.

As a result of the changing composition of the workforce, flexible benefits plans have grown in popularity. Flexible benefits systems recognize that individual employee situations differ because of age, family status, and lifestyle. For instance, dual-career couples may not want the same benefits from two different employers. Under a flex plan, one of them can forgo some benefits that are available in the partner's plan and take other benefits instead.[58]

Problems with Flexible Plans A problem with flexibility in benefits choice is that an *inappropriate benefits package* may be chosen by an employee. A young construction worker may not choose a disability benefit; however, if he or she is injured, the family may suffer financial hardship. Part of this problem can be overcome by requiring employees to select a core set of benefits (life, health, and disability insurance) and then offering options on other benefits.

Adverse selection Situation in which only higher-risk employees select and use certain benefits.

Another problem can be **adverse selection,** whereby only higher-risk employees select and use certain benefits. Because many insurance plans are based on a group rate, the employer may face higher rates if insufficient numbers of employees select an insurance option.

Finally, because many flexible plans have become so complex, they require more administrative time and information systems to track the different choices made by employees. Despite all these disadvantages, flex plans will likely continue to grow in popularity.

The ability to match all the various benefits available to differing employee needs, while also controlling some costs, will be a continuing challenge for employers of all sizes. But doing so is critical to effective HR management and may ultimately affect organizational success.

SUMMARY

- Benefits provide additional compensation to some employees as a reward for organizational membership.

- Because benefits generally are not taxed, they are highly desired by employees. The average employee now receives an amount equal to about 40% of pay in benefit compensation.

- Strategic considerations for benefits include their value in creating a competitive advantage and aiding in attracting and retaining employees.

- Benefits design and cost-control actions are crucial to strategic benefits efforts.

- Benefits can be viewed as mandatory or voluntary. The general types of benefits include security, retirement, health care, financial, family oriented, and time off.

- Three prominent security benefits are workers' compensation, unemployment compensation, and severance pay.

- Organizations provide retirement benefits through defined-benefit, defined-contribution, or cash balance plans.

- The pension area is a complex one that is governed by the Employee Retirement Income Security Act (ERISA) and other laws.

- Use of defined-contribution plans and individual retirement accounts is growing.

- Because health-care benefits costs have increased significantly, employers are managing their health benefits costs more aggressively.

- Efforts to control the costs of health benefits have included changing employee co-payments and employee contributions, using managed care, and switching to consumer-driven health (CDH) plans.

- ◆ Various types of financial services, relocation assistance, insurance benefits, educational assistance, and other benefits enhance the appeal of an organization to employees.
- ◆ Family-oriented benefits include complying with the Family and Medical Leave Act (FMLA) of 1993 and offering adoption benefits, child-care assistance, and elder-care assistance.

- ◆ Holiday pay, vacation pay, and various leaves of absence are means of providing time-off benefits to employees.
- ◆ Because of the variety of benefit options available and the costs involved, employers must develop effective systems to communicate those options and costs to their employees.
- ◆ Flexible benefits plans, which can be tailored to individual needs and situations, are increasing in popularity.

REVIEW AND APPLICATION QUESTIONS

1. Why are benefits strategically important to employers, and what are some key strategic considerations?
2. Discuss the following statement: "Health-care costs are out of control in the United States, and increasing conflicts between employers and employees are likely as employers try to reduce their health-benefits costs."

3. Assume that as an HR staff member, you have been asked to research consumer-driven health plans because your employer is considering implementing one. Go to a leading benefits information resource, *Employee Benefit News,* at *www.benefitnews.com,* and identify the elements of a successful CDH and some examples of firms with them.

LEARNING REVIEW

To check your knowledge of the chapter, review the following. (Answers after the supplemental case.) For more questions, see the Study Guide.

1. Employee benefits cost employers about _____ of payroll costs.
   a. 30%
   b. 40%
   c. 50%
   d. 60%
2. An employee's right to receive benefits from a pension plan is called _____.
   a. funding
   b. contributory
   c. portable
   d. vesting

3. A _____ is an employee's portion of the cost of both insurance premiums and medical care.
   a. pre-payment
   b. co-payment
   c. contribution
   d. annual payment
4. The Family and Medical Leave Act (FMLA) requires employers to allow eligible employees to take a total of _____ weeks' leave in a _____-month period.
   a. 6; 12
   b. 12; 12
   c. 12; 18
   d. 12; 24

CASE

DELIVERING BENEFITS

Employers of all sizes and in a variety of industries have made changes in their benefits programs to deal with rising costs. How FedEx Corporation, the worldwide transportation and shipping firm, responded to the cost pressures resulted in the firm receiving the Optimas award from *Workforce Man-*

agement magazine. The decisions made by FedEx provide some insights on approaches that other employers may wish to consider.

For years FedEx offered health-care benefits only through managed care programs such as HMOs and PPOs. But beginning in 2004, FedEx established a program that allows employees to use health-care providers inside or outside of the designated network of providers. Employees who want "freedom of choice" have a higher co-payment and payroll deduction. Also, FedEx expanded its health benefits plan to have four different levels of coverage, so that employees can choose a benefits package that fits their needs and their personal budgets.

But FedEx does not just provide health-care benefits; it also has established services to help employees improve their overall health. Many FedEx locations have wellness centers. Because many FedEx employees lift boxes and packages, the firm established a lower-back pain program to help reduce back injuries. For employees with chronic health problems such as arthritis, asthma, and diabetes, there is a disease management program to give them guidance, which also reduces their use of health-care services. A telephone hotline staffed by

nurses is available around the clock for employees to call with health-related questions.

FedEx uses a variety of means to communicate benefits information, including an internal TV network that features a variety of health-related programs. Employees can also access information electronically or contact a benefits call center.

Overall, FedEx employees have responded positively to these health-related efforts, despite increases in their payroll deductions for health benefits. It is likely that FedEx will have to keep making changes in its benefits because of increasing health-care costs. But through planning, continuing communication, and education, FedEx will likely continue delivering its healthcare benefits to meet both the company's and the employees' needs.[59]

Questions

1. Why is having multiple health-care plans important for FedEx in slowing down increases in the cost of benefits?

2. Discuss how the availability of disease management, training programs, and a nursing hotline might help with health benefits costs.

SUPPLEMENTAL CASE: Benefiting Connie

This case describes the problems that can occur when trying to coordinate time-off leaves for employees. (For the case, go to **http://mathis.swlearning.com/**)

Learning Review Answers: 1. a 2. d 3. b 4. b

NOTES

1. *Employee Benefits Study* (Washington, DC: U.S. Chamber of Commerce, 2003); and *SHRM/CNNFN Job Satisfaction Series: Job Benefits Survey*, 2003, www.shrm.org.
2. Joseph J. Martocchio, *Employee Benefits: A Primer for Human Resource Professionals*, (New York: McGraw-Hill/Irwin, 2003), Chap. 1.
3. Kevin Sweeney, "Around the Benefits World," *Employee Benefit News*, October 2003, 35–36.
4. U.S. Bureau of Labor Statistics, *www.bls.gov*.
5. Elayne Robertson Demby, "Nothing Partial About These Benefits," *HR Magazine*, August 2003, 72–81.
6. Examples of metrics for benefits can be found in Jim Simon, "Weighing the Cost of Employee Benefits," *Workspan*, March 2003, 56–57; and Jac Fitz-Enz and Barbara Davidson, *How to Measure Human Resources Management*, 3rd ed. (New York: McGraw-Hill, 2002), 141–156.
7. U.S. Bureau of Labor Statistics, *www.bls.gov*.
8. U.S. Census Bureau, *www.census.gov*.
9. *Public Employees Retirement System of Ohio v. Betts*, 109 S. Ct. 256 (1989).
10. Kathy Kristof, "Firms' Pension Fund Shortages," *Denver Post*, May 5, 2003, 2C; and Janice Revell, "GM's Slow Leak," *Fortune*, October 28, 2002, 105–106.
11. *EBRI 2004 Retirement Confidence Study*, www.ebri.org.
12. George B. Kozol, "Defined-Benefit Plans Emerge as Better Choice for Held Businesses," *Journal of Financial Service Professionals*, March 2003, 41–48.

13. Maureen Minehan, "Employer-Sponsored Pensions," *Workplace Visions,* 1 (2003).

14. Dallas L. Salisbury, "Will Cash Balance Plans Survive?" *Employee Benefit News,* April 15, 2004, 50–51.

15. *Arizona Governing Committee v. Norris,* 103 S. Ct. 3492, 32 FEP Cases 233 (1983).

16. John Nownes, "What Every Plan Administrator Needs to Know About QDROs," *HRAM Highlights,* October 2003, 8.

17. Carol Patton, "Peer Persuasion," *Human Resource Executive,* May 16, 2004, 25–29.

18. J. N. Hall, "Building Smart 401(k) Plans," *Compensation & Benefits Review,* August 2003, 27–35.

19. Leah Carlson, "Eye to Eye on Vision," *Employee Benefit News,* April 15, 2004.

20. *www.uschamber.com* or *www.benefit-study.com.*

21. Jim Hopkins, "Health Costs, More than Taxes, Drain Small Businesses," *USA Today,* April 21, 2003, 1A.

22. "Retiree Health-Care Costs Climb to $63.4 Billion at GM," *Omaha World-Herald,* March 12, 2004, B1.

23. Dale Buss, "Shouldering the Burden," *HR Magazine,* April 2003, 48–52.

24. Sheila Anne Feeney, "Battle Over Benefits," *Workforce Management,* November 2003, 28–34.

25. Bill Leonard, "Huge Increase Forecast for Consumer-Directed Health Plans," *HR News,* March 19, 2004; and "Putting CDH Plans into Perspective," *Employee Benefit Adviser,* January/February 2004, 9.

26. Adapted from F. Akinci and T. Sinay, "Perceived Access in a Managed Care Environment: Determinants of Satisfaction," *Health Services Management Research,* 16 (2003), 85–96.

27. A concise review of the provisions of each type is available at Haneefa T. Saleem, "Health Spending Accounts," *Compensation and Working Conditions Online,* December 19, 2003, *www.bls.gov.*

28. Jay Greene, "Assessing the Health Savings Option," *HR Magazine,* April 2004, 103–108; and Jay Garriss, "Forging an Ideal HRA," *Workspan,* May 2004, 18–25.

29. "Majority Says a Significant Reduction in Health Benefits Is Worse than No Pay Increase," *Wall Street Journal,* October 24, 2003, *www.wsj.com/health.*

30. Shari Caudron, "Delivering the Tough Benefit News," *Workforce,* September 2002, 32–36.

31. "Gap Emerges Between Employer/Employee Views on Workplace Satisfaction," December 9, 2003, *www.metlife.com/research-center.*

32. Jennifer L. Gatewood, "The Honesty Policy," *Human Resource Executive,* July 2002, 26–30.

33. For details on HIPAA, see *www.hhs.gov/ocr/hipaa.*

34. Annette L. Halpin and Thomas M. Brinker Jr., "Tax Relief Through Cafeteria Plans and Flexible Spending Accounts," *Journal of Financial Services Professionals,* 57 (2003), 14.

35. Andrea Kagan, "Can You Hear Me Now? The Importance of Communicating Employee Share Plans," *Workspan,* February 2004, 36–39.

36. Andy Meister, "A Matter of Degrees," *Workforce Management,* May 2004, 32–38.

37. D. D. Grant, "Managing Employee Leaves: A Legal Primer," *Compensation and Benefits Review,* August 2003, 36–46.

38. Gregory M. Davis, "The Family and Medical Leave Act: 10 Years Later," *SHRM Legal Report,* July/August, 2003, 1–8.

39. *Ragsdale v. Wolverine Worldwide,* 122 S. Ct. 1155 (2002).

40. Tom Klett, "Challenges Loom from California's Paid Family Leave," *Employee Benefit News,* July 2003, 35.

41. Maryann Hammers, "Family-Friendly Benefits Prompt Non-Parent Backlash," *Workforce Management,* August 2003, 77–79.

42. Garry Drantz, "Successful Adoption Programs Cost Little, but Enhance Loyalty," *Workforce Management,* April 2004, 60–61.

43. Nancy R. Lockwood, "The Aging Workforce: The Reality of the Impact of Older Workers and Eldercare in the Workplace," *SHRM Research Quarterly,* December 2003, *www.shrm.org/research.*

44. Barbara Parus, "Who's Watching Grandma?" *Workspan,* January, 20, 2004, 40–43.

45. Reagan Baughman, Daniela DiNardi, and Douglas Holtz-Eakin, "Productivity and Wage Effects of 'Family Friendly' Fringe Benefits," *International Journal of Manpower* 24 (2003), 247.

46. Patrick J. Kiger, "A Case for Child Care," *Workforce Management,* April 2004, 34–40.

47. Elayne Robertson Demby, "Do Your Family-Friendly Programs Make Cents?" *HR Magazine,* January 2004, 75–78.

48. Kelly Blassingame, "Domestic Partner Mandate Complicates Decision Making," *Employee Benefit News,* March 2004, 1, 15.

49. "Domestic Partner Benefits: Facts and Background," *Facts from EBRI,* March 2004, *www.ebri.org.*

50. Gillian Flynn, "No Relaxation for Your Vacation Policies," *Workforce,* August 2002, 78–79.

51. Jackie Reinberg, "It's About Time: PTOs Gain Popularity," *Workspan,* February 2002, 53–56.

52. Lucky R. Ford and Karen Locke, "Paid Time Off as a Vehicle for Self-Definition and Sensemaking," *Journal of Organizational Behavior,* 23 (2002), 489.

53. Lynn Gresham, "Pet-Insurance Posts Ready Gain in Benefit Offering," *Employee Benefit News,* September 15, 2003, 63–64.

54. For information see Professional Association of Diving Instructors, *www.padi.com.*

55. Kelly M. Blassingame, "The Ship's Come In," *Employee Benefit News,* March 2004, 1+.

56. "Employees Prefer to Enroll for Benefits Online," *SHRM Online,* February 27, 2003, *www.shrm.org/hrnews.*

57. Based on Laura Landro, "Online Data for Health Plans," *Wall Street Journal,* June 20, 2002, D4; and Jennifer L. Gatewood, "Luring the Liabilities," *Human Resource Executive,* March 20, 2002, 23–28.

58. Martin Levy, "C's of Cafeteria Plans," *Workspan,* June 2002, 43–46.

59. Based on "Choice Offsets Cost for FedEx Workers," *Workforce Management,* S4–S5.

Employee Relations

CHAPTER 15

Health, Safety, and Security

After you have read this chapter, you should be able to:

◆ Define health, safety, and security and explain three legal areas of concern.

◆ Identify the basic provisions of the Occupational Safety and Health Act of 1970 and recordkeeping and inspection requirements.

◆ Discuss the activities that constitute effective safety management.

◆ Describe three workplace health issues and how employers are responding to them.

◆ Explain workplace violence as a security issue and describe some components of an effective security program.

◆ Specify several global health, safety, and security concerns.

World-Class Safety in a Small Company

The American Society of Safety Engineers (ASSE) has identified several companies that define "world-class" safety. The companies ranged in size from the Johnson & Johnson company in 57 countries (109,100 employees) to the Quincy Compressor facility in Bay Minette, Alabama (141 employees). All the companies shared one factor in common: they treat safety as a business value, not a program that has been added. Perhaps focusing on the smallest of the companies—Quincy Compressor—will pinpoint some good ideas for dealing with worker safety.

Quincy keeps all 141 employees involved in safety. The company uses behavior-based safety programs, reporting of near-miss incidents, root cause analysis for accidents, continuing training, and employee recognition. Employees have the authority to change situations they feel are unsafe. They earn points for doing safety audits of other areas, correcting hazards, providing ideas, and conducting mini safety meetings with their teams.

Near-miss incidents are reported, videotaped, and shown to every employee for input. The intent is *not* to place blame but to make sure the condition does not happen again. Every month, a member of each team audits another team. These audits bring a new set of eyes to an area and helps educate the auditors about what safety issues exist elsewhere. Team leaders present seven-minute safety training topics each month and incentive programs reward safe behavior, participation, and safety improvements.

These efforts have worked, as injuries have been reduced by 91% since 1996. The plant manager notes that machining and assembly work are accompanied by numerous hazards—so "this is a race with no finish." But clearly, this small company is running it very well.[1]

"If only it weren't for the people always getting tangled up with the machinery . . . Earth would be an engineer's paradise."

—*Kurt Vonnegut*

Today, employers are expected to provide work environments that are safe, secure, and healthy. However, at one time, employers viewed accidents and occupational diseases as unavoidable by-products of work. This idea may still be prevalent in some less-developed countries. Fortunately, in the United States and most developed nations, it has been replaced with the concept of using prevention and control to minimize or eliminate risks in workplaces.

Employers in a variety of industries have found that emphasizing health and safety pays off in a number of ways. Lower employee benefits costs for health care, fewer work-related accidents, lower workers' compensation costs, and more productive employees are all results of employers' stressing health and safety.

▮▮ HEALTH, SAFETY, AND SECURITY

A number of laws and regulations have established requirements for U.S. employers. As highlighted by safety leaders Johnson & Johnson and Quincy Compressor, employers have recognized that addressing health, safety, and security issues is part of effective HR management.

Nature of Health, Safety, and Security

Health General state of physical, mental, and emotional well-being.

The terms *health, safety,* and *security* are closely related. The broader and somewhat more nebulous term is **health,** which refers to a general state of physical, mental, and emotional well-being. A healthy person is free from illness, injury, or mental and emotional problems that impair normal human activity. Health management practices in organizations strive to maintain the overall well-being of individuals.

Safety Condition in which the physical well-being of people is protected.

Security Protection of employees and organizational facilities.

Typically, **safety** refers to a condition in which the physical well-being of people is protected. The main purpose of effective safety programs in organizations is to prevent work-related injuries and accidents. The purpose of **security** is protecting employees and organizational facilities. With the growth of workplace violence, security at work has become an even greater concern for employers and employees alike.

Health, Safety, and Security Responsibilities

The general goal of providing a safe, secure, and healthy workplace is reached by operating managers and HR working together. As Figure 15-1 indicates, the primary health, safety, and security responsibilities in an organization usually fall on supervisors and managers. An HR manager or safety specialist can help coordinate health and safety programs, investigate accidents, produce safety program materials, and conduct formal safety training. However, department supervisors and managers play key roles in maintaining safe working conditions and a healthy workforce. For example, a supervisor in a warehouse has several health and safety responsibilities: reminding employees to wear safety hats; checking on the cleanliness of the work area; observing employees for any alcohol, drug, or emotional problems that may affect their work behavior; and recommending equipment changes (such as screens, railings, or other safety devices) to engineering specialists in the organization.

A position that is becoming more common in many companies is that of safety, health, and environment officer. This combination may make sense where danger results from chemical or other sources of pollution that may be hazardous to both employees and the public or the environment. Because both safety and environ-

Figure 15-1 *Typical Division of HR Responsibilities: Health, Safety, and Security*

HR Unit	Managers
◆ Coordinates health and safety programs ◆ Develops safety reporting system ◆ Provides accident investigation expertise ◆ Provides technical expertise on accident prevention ◆ Develops restricted-access procedures and employee identification systems ◆ Trains managers to recognize and handle difficult employee situations	◆ Monitor the health and safety of employees daily ◆ Coach employees to be safety conscious ◆ Investigate accidents ◆ Observe the health and safety behavior of employees ◆ Monitor workplace for security problems ◆ Communicate with employees to identify potentially difficult employees ◆ Follow security procedures and recommend changes as needed

mental responsibilities require working with different government agencies, a good choice is to fill this job with someone who has the skills to ensure compliance with a wide range of regulatory issues.[2]

Security affects everyone in an organization and is often an HR responsibility. Since 9/11, the security issues that an employer might worry about have grown in number and scope. Certainly, workplace violence, computer security, and theft at work have been and continue to be concerns. But now, for some employers, security issues include protecting employees from terrorist attacks, loss of electric service, bomb threats, and hostage situations. Perhaps more correctly labeled "crisis management planning" at its most extreme, dealing with such issues provides an opportunity for HR to create value in the organization and to help mitigate some risks to the company.[3]

Managing *risk* to the company can take the form of avoiding negligent hiring or negligent retention by keeping workers who should have been terminated. In either case, HR is well situated to be of assistance.[4]

Current State of Health, Safety, and Security

About 4.7 million non-fatal injuries and illnesses occur at work annually, which gives an average injury rate of 5.3 cases per 100 employees. Specific rates vary depending on the industry, job, etc., with 1.7 cases per 100 employees in the finance industry and 7.2 cases per 100 in manufacturing.[5]

The three major causes of injury (overextending, falling, and bodily reaction) were responsible for over half of the direct costs of injury. Accident *costs* have gone up faster than inflation because of the rapid increase in medical costs, even though the number of accidents has been decreasing for some time.[6] The main safety enforcement agency of the federal government, the Occupational Safety and Health Administration (OSHA), gave 8% more citations (83,760) to employers in one recent year and focused on repeat offenders, while the *rate* of injuries and fatalities at work reached the lowest point ever.[7]

Research on health and safety continues to show that poorly managed companies have higher losses from accidents, but well-managed companies have lower

Research on the Self-Employed and Accidents

Many individuals in the U.S. do not work for anyone else, but are self-employed. In an article in the *Monthly Labor Review,* Pegula noted that although they make up only 7.4% of the U.S. civilian workforce, self-employed workers had 20% of the workplace fatalities. When comparing self-employed workers to those working for someone else, the self-employed individuals were almost three times as likely to be killed.

The difference in fatalities was found to be attributable to several factors. The self-employed were more likely to work in industries and occupations with higher fatality rates, especially farming. Over 25% of the self-employed who died

on the job were farmers. In addition, the self-employed were more likely to:[8]

- Die while working in a retail store in a robbery
- Die as a result of homicide, accident, or a self-inflicted injury
- Spend more hours working, thus allowing more time for accidents to occur

The conclusion that can be drawn is that the self-employed are willing to work in more dangerous circumstances and therefore are more vulnerable to illnesses, injuries, and death. Those who are self-employed should be aware of the safety risks that they face.

losses from accidents.[9] An interesting phenomenon is that self-employed workers have higher accident rates than do those who work for others. See the HR Perspective for a discussion of this topic.

LEGAL REQUIREMENTS FOR SAFETY AND HEALTH

Employers must comply with a variety of federal and state laws when developing and maintaining healthy, safe, and secure workforces and working environments. Three major legal areas are workers' compensation legislation, the Americans with Disabilities Act, and child labor laws.

Workers' Compensation

First passed in the early 1900s, workers' compensation laws in some form are on the books in all states today. Under these laws, employers contribute to an insurance fund to compensate employees for injuries received while on the job. Premiums paid reflect the accident rates of the employers, with employers that have higher incident rates being assessed higher premiums. These laws usually provide payments to replace wages for injured workers, depending on the amount of lost time and the wage level. They also provide payments to cover medical bills, and for re-training if a worker cannot go back to the current job. Leading causes of worker injuries, which often result in workers' compensation claims, are overextension, falls, and losing balance.

Expanded Scope of Workers' Compensation Workers' compensation coverage has been expanded in many states to include emotional impairment that may have resulted from physical injury, as well as job-related strain, stress, anxiety, and pressure. Some cases of suicide have also been ruled to be job related, with payments due under workers' compensation.

A new twist on workers' compensation coverage relates to the increasing use of telecommuting by employees. However, in most situations, while working at home for employers, individuals are covered under workers' compensation laws. Therefore, if an employee is injured while doing employer-related work at home, the employer likely is liable for the injury. This aspect of workers' compensation liability is not widely known.

Controlling Workers' Compensation Costs Workers' compensation costs have increased for many employers and have become a major issue in many states. These costs represent from 2%–10% of payroll for most employers. The major contributors to the increases have been higher medical costs and litigation expenses.

Workers' compensation fraud is a fast-growing and expensive problem. It is estimated that 25% of the workers' compensation claims filed are fraudulent. False and exaggerated claims make up the bulk of the fraud—costing employers $5 billion annually.[10] Employers must continually monitor their workers' compensation expenditures. Efforts to reduce workplace injuries, illnesses, and fraud can reduce workers' compensation premiums and claims costs. Many of the safety and health management suggestions discussed later in this chapter can contribute to reducing workers' compensation costs.

FMLA and Workers' Compensation The Family and Medical Leave Act (FMLA) affects workers' compensation as well. Because the FMLA allows eligible employees to take up to 12 weeks of leave for their serious health conditions, injured employees may ask to use that leave time in addition to the leave time allowed under workers' comp, even if it is unpaid. Some employers have policies that state that FMLA runs concurrently with any workers' comp leave.

Americans with Disabilities Act and Safety Issues

Employers sometimes try to return injured workers to "light-duty" work in order to reduce workers' compensation costs. However, under the Americans with Disabilities Act, when making accommodations for injured employees through light-duty work, employers may undercut what are really essential job functions. Also, making such accommodations for injured employees for a period of time may require employers to make similar accommodations for job applicants with disabilities.

Additionally, health and safety recordkeeping practices have been affected by the following provision in the ADA:

> *Information from all medical examinations and inquiries must be kept apart from general personnel files as a separate confidential medical record available only under limited conditions specified in the ADA.*

As interpreted by attorneys and HR practitioners, this provision requires that all medical-related information be maintained separately from all other confidential files. Also, specific access restrictions and security procedures must be adopted for medical records of all types, including employee medical benefits claims and treatment records.

Child Labor Laws

Safety concerns are reflected in restrictions affecting younger workers, especially those under the age of 18. Child labor laws, found in Section XII of the

Figure 15-2

Selected Child Labor Hazardous Occupations (minimum age: 18 years)

Hazardous Work

- Manufacturing or storing explosives
- Driving a motor vehicle and being an outside helper
- Coal mining
- Logging and saw milling
- Using power-driven woodworking machines*
- Exposure to radioactive substances and to ionizing radiations
- Operating power-driven hoisting apparatus
- Operating power-driven, metal forming, punching, and shearing machines*
- Mining, other than coal mining

- Slaughtering or meatpacking, or rendering
- Using power-driven bakery machines
- Operating power-driven paper products machines*
- Manufacturing brick, tile, and related products
- Using power-driven circular saws, and guillotine shears*
- Wrecking, demolition, and shipbreaking operations
- Roofing operations*
- Excavation operations*

* In certain cases, the law provides exemptions for apprentices and student learners in these occupations.

Fair Labor Standards Act (FLSA), set the minimum age for most employment at 16 years. For "hazardous" occupations, 18 years is the minimum. Figure 15-2 lists 17 occupations that the federal government considers hazardous for children who work while attending school.

Two examples illustrate violations of these provisions. At a fast-food restaurant specializing in roast beef sandwiches, a teenage worker operated a meat slicer, which is a hazard covered by the FLSA. At a national discount retailer, teenage workers were found to have operated the mechanical box crushers. Both situations resulted in enforcement actions and fines for violating the FLSA.

In addition to complying with workers' compensation, ADA, and child labor laws, most employers must comply with the Occupational Safety and Health Act of 1970. This act has had a tremendous impact on the workplace. Therefore, any person interested in HR management must develop knowledge of the provisions and implications of the act, which is administered by the Occupational Safety and Health Administration.

OCCUPATIONAL SAFETY AND HEALTH ACT

The Occupational Safety and Health Act of 1970 was passed "to assure so far as possible every working man or woman in the Nation safe and healthful working conditions and to preserve our human resources." Every employer that is engaged in commerce and has one or more employees is covered by the act. Farmers having fewer than 10 employees are exempt. Employers in specific industries, such as coal mining, are covered under other health and safety acts. Federal, state, and local governments are covered by separate statutes and provisions.

The Occupational Safety and Health Act of 1970 established the Occupational Safety and Health Administration, known as OSHA, to administer its provisions. The act also established the National Institute for Occupational Safety and Health (NIOSH) as a supporting body to do research and develop standards. In addition, the Occupational Safety and Health Review Commission (OSHRC) has been established to review OSHA enforcement actions and to address disputes between OSHA and employers who have been cited by OSHA inspectors.

By making employers and employees more aware of safety and health considerations, OSHA has significantly affected organizations. It does appear that OSHA regulations have contributed to reductions in the number of accidents and injuries in some cases. But in other industries, OSHA has had little or no effect. Figure 15-3 indicates the percentage of workplace illnesses and injuries by industry. In the figure the health, legal, hospitality, education, and other services are grouped in the services category.

OSHA Enforcement Standards

To implement OSHA, specific standards were established regulating equipment and working environments. National standards developed by engineering and quality control groups are often used. OSHA rules and standards are frequently complicated and technical. Small-business owners and managers who do not have specialists on their staffs may find the standards difficult to read and understand. In addition, the presence of many minor standards has hurt the credibility of OSHA.

Figure 15-3

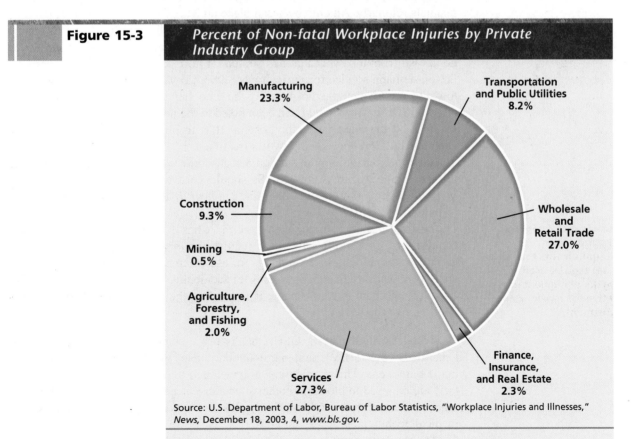

Percent of Non-fatal Workplace Injuries by Private Industry Group

Manufacturing 23.3%

Transportation and Public Utilities 8.2%

Construction 9.3%

Mining 0.5%

Agriculture, Forestry, and Fishing 2.0%

Services 27.3%

Wholesale and Retail Trade 27.0%

Finance, Insurance, and Real Estate 2.3%

Source: U.S. Department of Labor, Bureau of Labor Statistics, "Workplace Injuries and Illnesses," *News*, December 18, 2003, 4, *www.bls.gov.*

A number of provisions have been recognized as key to employers' efforts to comply with OSHA. Two basic ones are as follows:

- *General duty:* The act requires that the employer has a "general duty" to provide safe and healthy working conditions, even in areas where OSHA standards have not been set. Employers who know or reasonably should know of unsafe or unhealthy conditions can be cited for violating the general duty clause.
- *Notification and posters:* Employers are required to inform their employees of safety and health standards established by OSHA. Also, OSHA posters must be displayed in prominent locations in workplaces.

Hazard Communication OSHA has enforcement responsibilities for the federal Hazard Communication standard, which requires manufacturers, importers, distributors, and users of hazardous chemicals to evaluate, classify, and label these substances. Employers also must make available to employees, their representatives, and health professionals information about hazardous substances. This information is contained in material safety data sheets (MSDSs), which must be kept readily accessible to those who work with chemicals and other substances. The MSDSs also indicate antidotes or actions to be taken should someone come in contact with the substances.

Information technology allows employers to use the Internet to maintain MSDSs on chemicals and workplace substances. Using MSDS software, firms can update electronic MSDSs regularly rather than having to reissue printed manuals regularly. An employer can place all MSDSs on an intranet, through an Internet link, or access manufacturers' information sheets. Many MSDSs can be found on Web sites. For example, at a Maryland printing company, an employee got a rash from a solvent that had spilled on him. The company subscribed to a fax-on-demand service for retrieving MSDSs. Co-workers called the service and took the employee to the hospital. By the time they got there, the current version of the MSDS for the solvent had been faxed to the hospital, and a fax service person was on the phone with the hospital staff to provide information about the chemical and the injured employee's treatment.[11]

If the organization employs a number of workers for whom English is not the primary language, then the MSDSs should be available in the necessary languages. Also, workers should be trained in how to access and use the MSDS information.

Lock out / tag out regulations
Requirements that locks and tags be used to make equipment inoperative for repair or adjustment.

As part of hazard communications, OSHA has established **lock out / tag out regulations.** To comply with these regulations, firms must provide mechanics and tradespeople with locks and tags for use when they make equipment inoperative for repair or adjustment, to prevent accidental start-up of defective machinery. Only the person whose name is printed on the tag or engraved on the lock may remove the device.

Bloodborne Pathogens OSHA has issued a standard regarding exposure to hepatitis B virus (HBV), human immunodeficiency virus (HIV), and other bloodborne pathogens. This regulation was developed to protect employees who regularly are exposed to blood and other such substances from contracting AIDS and other serious diseases. Obviously, health-care laboratory workers, nurses, and medical technicians are at greatest risk. However, all employers covered by OSHA regulations must comply in workplaces where cuts and abrasions are common. Regulations require employers with the most pronounced risks to have written control and response plans and to train workers in following the proper procedures.

Personal Protective Equipment (PPE) One goal of OSHA has been to develop standards for personal protective equipment (PPE). These standards require that employers analyze job hazards, provide adequate PPE to employees in hazardous jobs, and train employees in the use of PPE items. Common PPE items include safety glasses, hard hats, and safety shoes. If the work environment presents hazards or if employees might have contact with hazardous chemicals and substances on the job, then employers are required to provide PPE to all those employees.

Ergonomics and OSHA

Ergonomics
Study and design of the work environment to address physiological and physical demands on individuals.

Cumulative trauma disorders (CTDs)
Muscle and skeletal injuries that occur when workers repetitively use the same muscles to perform tasks.

Ergonomics is the study and design of the work environment to address physiological and physical demands on individuals. In a work setting, ergonomic studies look at such factors as fatigue, lighting, tools, equipment layout, and placement of controls.

For a number of years, OSHA focused on the large number of work-related injuries due to repetitive stress, repetitive motion, cumulative trauma disorders, carpal tunnel syndrome, and other causes. **Cumulative trauma disorders (CTDs)** are muscle and skeletal injuries that occur when workers repetitively use the same muscles to perform tasks.

Carpal tunnel syndrome, a cumulative trauma disorder, is an injury common to people who put their hands through repetitive motions such as typing, playing certain musical instruments, cutting, and sewing. The motion irritates the tendons in the carpal tunnel area of the wrist. As the tendons swell, they squeeze the median nerve. The result is pain and numbness in the thumb, index finger, and middle finger. The hands of victims become clumsy and weak. Pain at night increases, and at advanced stages, not even surgery can cure the problem. Victims eventually lose feeling in their hands if they do not receive timely treatment.

Problems caused by repetitive and cumulative injuries occur in a variety of work settings. The meatpacking industry has the highest level of CTDs. Grocery cashiers experience CTDs from repetitively twisting their wrists when they scan bar codes on canned goods. Office workers experience CTDs too, primarily from doing extensive typing and data entry on computers and computer-related equipment. Most recently, attention has focused on the application of ergonomic principles to the design of work stations where computer operators work with personal computers and video display terminals for extended periods of time.

OSHA Ergonomics Standards In 2000, OSHA developed some ergonomics standards to address concerns about *musculoskeletal disorders,* which affect muscles, nerves, tendons, ligaments, joints, cartilage, blood vessels, and spinal disks. Employers and other groups reacted negatively, thinking the standards were onerous and too costly. As a result, the U.S. Congress repealed the standards.

Since then, OSHA has approached ergonomics concerns differently. It has adopted voluntary guidelines for specific problem industries and jobs, gone after industries with serious ergonomic problems, and given employers tools for identifying and controlling ergonomics hazards.[12] Among the industries receiving guidelines initially are nursing homes, poultry processors, and retail grocery stores.[13] The HR Perspective highlights ergonomics issues in nursing homes.

Nursing Homes and Ergonomics

In a national program aimed at notifying businesses when their employee injury rates are close to exceeding the national average, nursing homes have been highlighted by OSHA as one of the most dangerous work settings. Nurses and other employees in nursing homes spend considerable time lifting residents, because elderly residents are often unable to move themselves. When patients require help getting into and out of beds and wheelchairs, staff members are more likely to get muscle and back injuries. To reduce these injuries, more nursing homes are using more mechanized lifting equipment and teaching employees proper lifting techniques.

OSHA says its goal is to identify workplaces of concern and offer assistance to those businesses so that they can address hazards and reduce injuries and illnesses. For instance, OSHA recently reached an agreement with Beverly Enterprises, which operates 240 nursing homes nationwide. The company agreed to curb the back injuries happening to employees who lift residents, through the use of training and mechanical lifting equipment. Some others in the industry, with prodding from labor unions, are adapting or considering "no manual lift" policies. As one administrator notes, "Nursing is the only profession where they consider the lifting of 100 pounds to be light."[14]

Successful Ergonomics Programs There are several components of a successful ergonomics program. First, management must commit to reducing injuries caused by repetition and cumulative trauma, including providing financial and other resources to support the efforts. Involvement of employees is key to getting employee support. Other actions should include reviewing jobs where CTD problems could exist and ensuring that proper equipment, seating, lighting, and other engineering solutions are utilized. Also, supervisors and managers should be trained to observe signs of CTD and how to respond to employee complaints about musculoskeletal and repetitive motion problems.

Work Assignments and OSHA

The rights of employees regarding certain work assignments have been addressed as part of OSHA regulations. Two prominent areas where work assignments and concerns about safety and health meet are reproductive health and unsafe work.

Work Assignments and Reproductive Health Related to unsafe work is the issue of assigning employees to work in areas where their ability to have children may be affected by exposure to chemical hazards. Women who are able to bear children or who are pregnant have presented the primary concerns, but in some situations, the possibility that men might become sterile has also been a concern.[15]

In a court case involving reproductive health, the Supreme Court held that Johnson Controls violated the Civil Rights Act and the Pregnancy Discrimination Act through a policy of keeping women of childbearing capacity out of jobs that might expose them to lead.[16] Although employers have no *absolute* protection from liability, the following actions can help:

- Maintain a safe workplace for all by seeking the safest working methods.
- Comply with all state and federal safety laws.

THOMSON

WEST

EEOC FETAL PROTECTION GUIDELINES
Provides a discussion and checklist on fetal protection requirements.
Custom Search:
☑ ANALYSIS
Exact Phrase: Guidelines on fetal protection

- Inform employees of any known risks.
- Document employee acceptance of any risks.

Refusing Unsafe Work Both union and non-union workers have refused to work when they considered the work unsafe. In many court cases, that refusal has been found to be justified. The conditions for refusing work because of safety concerns include the following:

- The employee's fear is objectively reasonable.
- The employee has tried to have the dangerous condition corrected.
- Using normal procedures to solve the problem has not worked.

OSHA Recordkeeping Requirements

OSHA has established a standard national system for recording occupational injuries, accidents, and fatalities. Employers are generally required to maintain a detailed annual record of the various types of accidents, for inspection by OSHA representatives and for submission to the agency. Employers that have had good safety records in previous years and those with fewer than 10 employees are not required to keep detailed records. Because of revisions effective in 2002, many organizations must complete OSHA Form 300 to report workshop accidents and injuries. These organizations include firms having frequent hospitalizations, injuries, illnesses, or work-related deaths, and firms in a labor statistics survey conducted by OSHA each year.

No one knows how many industrial accidents go unreported. It may be many more than anyone suspects, despite increased surveillance of accident-reporting records by OSHA. OSHA guidelines state that facilities whose accident records are below the national average rarely need inspecting.

Reporting Injuries and Illnesses Four types of injuries or illnesses are defined by the Occupational Safety and Health Act. They are as follows:

- *Injury- or illness-related deaths*
- *Lost-time or disability injuries:* These include job-related injuries or disabling occurrences that cause an employee to miss regularly scheduled work on the day following the accident.
- *Medical care injuries:* These require treatment by a physician but do not cause an employee to miss a regularly scheduled work turn.
- *Minor injuries:* These require first aid treatment and do not cause an employee to miss the next regularly scheduled work turn.

The recordkeeping requirements for these injuries and illnesses are summarized in Figure 15-4 on the next page. Notice that only very minor injuries do not have to be recorded for OSHA. For example: As Brian was repairing a conveyor belt, his hand slipped and hit the sharp edge of a steel bar. His hand was cut, and he was rushed to the hospital. He received five stitches and was told by the doctor not to use his hand for three days. This injury is recorded in the OSHA 300 log because the stitches and restricted duty require that it be recorded.[17]

OSHA Inspections

The Occupational Safety and Health Act provides for on-the-spot inspections by OSHA representatives, called compliance officers or inspectors. In *Marshall v. Barlow's, Inc.,* the U.S. Supreme Court has held that safety inspectors must

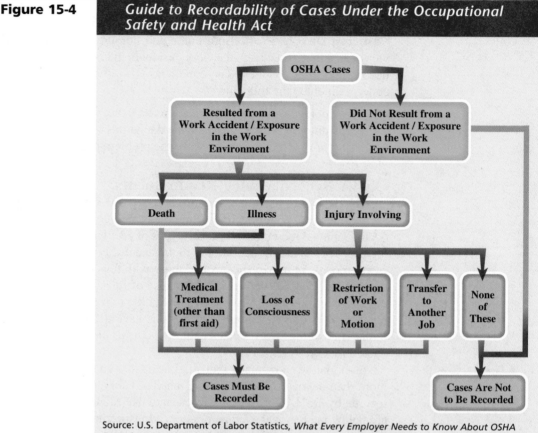

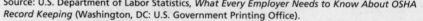

Source: U.S. Department of Labor Statistics, *What Every Employer Needs to Know About OSHA Record Keeping* (Washington, DC: U.S. Government Printing Office).

produce a search warrant if an employer refuses to allow an inspector into the plant voluntarily. The Court also ruled that an inspector does not have to show probable cause to obtain a search warrant. A warrant can easily be obtained if a search is part of a general enforcement plan.[18]

Dealing with an Inspection When an OSHA compliance officer arrives, managers should ask to see the inspector's credentials. Next, the HR representative for the employer should insist on an opening conference with the compliance officer. The compliance officer may request that a union representative, an employee, and a company representative be present while the inspection is conducted. In the inspection, the officer checks organizational records to see if they are being maintained and to determine the number of accidents that have occurred. Following this review of the safety records, the officer conducts an on-the-spot inspection and may use a wide variety of equipment to test compliance with standards. After the inspection, the compliance officer can issue citations for any violations of standards and provisions of the act.

Citations and Violations Although OSHA inspectors can issue citations for violations of the provisions of the act, whether or not a citation is issued depends on the severity and extent of the problems, and on the employer's knowledge of them. In addition, depending on the nature and number of violations, penalties

Figure 15-5

Figure 15-5 *Most Frequently Cited OSHA Violations (general industry, non-construction)*

1. Hazard communication program, training, labeling, and warnings
2. Inadequate machine guarding, including at point of operation
3. Lock out / tag out energy control program and procedures
4. Head protection: hard hats
5. Recordkeeping violation: unsatisfactory OSHA log of illnesses and injuries
6. Inadequate emergency drenching facilities
7. Non-complying guardrails or handrails on stairs or work platforms
8. Guard adjustment on abrasive wheel machinery
9. Non-complying electrical wire cabinet boxes
10. Pulley guards on power transmission belts

Source: U.S. Department of Labor, Occupational Safety and Health Administration, *www.osha.gov.*

can be assessed against employers. The nature and extent of the penalties depend on the type and severity of the violations as determined by OSHA officials. Figure 15-5 shows the most frequently cited violations for a recent year. Notice that a mixture of workplace and administrative violations are among those cited most often.

Five types of violations are cited by OSHA. Ranging from the most severe to minimal, including a special category for repeated violations, they are as follows:

♦ *Imminent danger:* When there is reasonable certainty that the condition will cause death or serious physical harm if it is not corrected immediately, an imminent-danger citation is issued and a notice posted by an inspector. Imminent-danger situations are handled on the highest-priority basis. They are reviewed by a regional OSHA director and must be corrected immediately. If the condition is serious enough and the employer does not cooperate, a representative of OSHA may obtain a federal injunction to close the company until the condition is corrected. The absence of guardrails to prevent employees from falling into heavy machinery is one example of an imminent danger.

♦ *Serious:* When a condition could probably cause death or serious physical harm, and the employer should know of the condition, OSHA issues a serious-violation citation. Examples of serious violations are the absence of a protective screen on a lathe and the lack of a blade guard on an electric saw.

♦ *Other than serious:* Violations that could impact employees' health or safety but probably would not cause death or serious harm are called "other than serious." Having loose ropes in a work area might be classified as an other-than-serious violation.

♦ *De minimis:* A *de minimis* condition is one not directly and immediately related to employees' safety or health. No citation is issued, but the condition is mentioned to the employer. Lack of doors on toilet stalls is a common example of a de minimis violation.

♦ *Willful and repeated:* Citations for willful and repeated violations are issued to employers who have been previously cited for violations. If an employer knows about a safety violation or has been warned of a violation and does

Figure 15-6

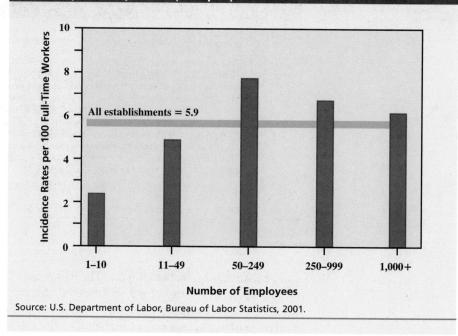

Workplace Injuries by Employer Size

Source: U.S. Department of Labor, Bureau of Labor Statistics, 2001.

not correct the problem, a second citation is issued. The penalty for a willful and repeated violation can be high. For example, if death results from an accident that involves such a safety violation, a jail term of six months can be imposed on responsible executives or managers.

For an example of fines, consider a case in which a West Virginia metal manufacturer instructed its employees to operate the machines differently than usual when OSHA conducted an inspection. It also hid pieces of equipment, and management lied about its usual practices. These actions led to a "willful" violation and $288,000 in fines for 23 violations, primarily because the firm tried to cover up its non-compliance.[19]

Critique of OSHA Inspection Efforts

OSHA has been criticized on several fronts. Because the agency has so many work sites to inspect, many employers have only a relatively small chance of being inspected. Some suggest that many employers pay little attention to OSHA enforcement efforts for this reason. Labor unions and others have criticized OSHA and Congress for not providing enough inspectors. For instance, it is common to find that many of the work sites at which workers suffered severe injuries or deaths had not been inspected in the previous five years.

Employers, especially smaller ones, continue to complain about the complexity of complying with OSHA standards and the costs associated with penalties and with making changes required to remedy problem areas. Very small employers point out that according to statistics from OSHA (see Figure 15-6), their businesses already have significantly lower work-related injury and illness rates than larger ones. Larger firms can afford to hire safety and health specialists and establish more pro-active programs.

Well-designed and well-managed safety programs can pay dividends in reduced accidents and associated costs, such as workers' compensation and possible fines. Further, accidents and other safety concerns usually decline as a result of management efforts emphasizing safety. Often, the difference between firms with good safety performance and firms that OSHA has targeted as being well below the industry average is that the former have effective safety management programs.

Successful safety management is not a mystery. The topic has been researched extensively.[20] A summary of what is known about managing to minimize accidents includes discussion of these issues:

- Organizational commitment
- Policies, discipline, and recordkeeping
- Training and communication
- Participation (safety committees)
- Inspection, investigation, and evaluation

Organizational Commitment and a Safety Culture

Three approaches are used by employers in managing safety. Figure 15-7 shows the organizational, engineering, and individual approaches and their components. Successful programs may use all three in dealing with safety issues.

At the heart of safety management is an organizational commitment to a comprehensive safety effort. This effort should be coordinated from the top level of management to include all members of the organization. It should also be reflected in managerial actions. If the president of a small electrical manufacturing firm does not wear a hard hat in the manufacturing shop, he can hardly expect to enforce a

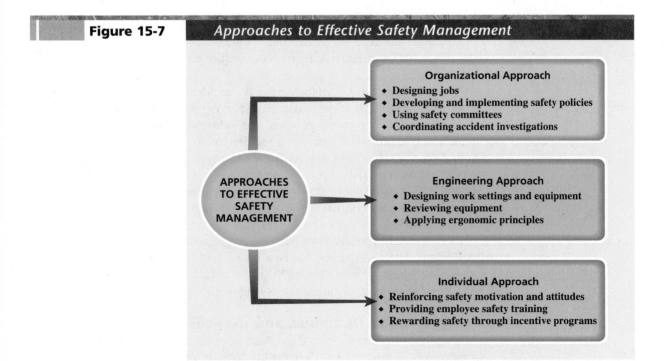

Figure 15-7 — *Approaches to Effective Safety Management*

APPROACHES TO EFFECTIVE SAFETY MANAGEMENT

Organizational Approach
- Designing jobs
- Developing and implementing safety policies
- Using safety committees
- Coordinating accident investigations

Engineering Approach
- Designing work settings and equipment
- Reviewing equipment
- Applying ergonomic principles

Individual Approach
- Reinforcing safety motivation and attitudes
- Providing employee safety training
- Rewarding safety through incentive programs

requirement that all employees wear hard hats in the shop. Unfortunately, sincere support by top management often is missing from safety programs.

One result of a strong commitment to safety is that a "safety culture" pervades the organization. Firms such as Johnson & Johnson, DuPont Chemical and Energy Operations, and Frito-Lay are well known for emphasizing safety as part of their organizational cultures.

Safety and Engineering Employers can prevent some accidents by having machines, equipment, and work areas designed so that workers who daydream periodically or who perform potentially dangerous jobs cannot injure themselves and others. Providing safety equipment and guards on machinery, installing emergency switches, installing safety rails, keeping aisles clear, and installing adequate ventilation, lighting, heating, and air-conditioning can all help make work environments safer.

Designing a job properly requires consideration of the physical setting of the job. The way the work space surrounding a job is utilized can influence the worker's performance of the job itself. Several factors that affect safety have been identified, including size of work area, kinds of materials used, sensory conditions, distance between work areas, and interference from noise and traffic flow.

Individual Considerations and Safety Engineers approach safety from the perspective of redesigning the machinery or the work area. Industrial psychologists and "human factors" experts see safety differently. They address the proper match of individuals to jobs and emphasize employee training in safety methods, fatigue reduction, and health awareness. Numerous field studies with thousands of employees, conducted by experts, have looked at the human factors in accidents. The results have shown a definite relationship between *emotional factors,* such as stress, and accidents. Other studies point to the importance of *individual differences, motivation, attitudes,* and *learning* as key factors in controlling the human element in safety.

Behavior-based safety (BBS) approaches are efforts to reduce *risky behavior* and increase safe behavior by defining unsafe behavior and attempting to change it.[21] While BBS is beneficial, it does not constitute a complete approach to dealing with safety.

Work schedules can be another cause for accidents. The relationship between work schedules and accidents can be explained as follows: Fatigue based on physical exertion sometimes exists in the industrial workplace of today. Boredom, which occurs when a person is required to do the same tasks for a long period of time, is rather common. As fatigue increases, motivation decreases; when motivation decreases, workers' attention wanders, and the likelihood of accidents increases.[22] A particular area of concern is *overtime* in work scheduling. Overtime work has been consistently related to accident incidence. Further, the more overtime worked, the more severe accidents appear to be.[23]

Another area of concern is the relationship of accident rates to *different shifts,* particularly late-night shifts. Because there tend to be fewer supervisors and managers working the "graveyard" shifts, workers tend to receive less training and supervision. Both of these factors lead to higher accident rates.

Safety Policies, Discipline, and Recordkeeping

Designing safety policies and rules and disciplining violators are important components of safety efforts. Frequently reinforcing the need for safe behavior and frequently supplying feedback on positive safety practices are also effective ways of improving worker safety. Such efforts must involve employees, supervisors, managers, safety specialists, and HR staff members.

For policies about safety to be effective, good recordkeeping about accidents, causes, and other details is necessary. Without records, an employer cannot benchmark its safety performance against other employers and may not realize there is a problem.[24]

Safety Training and Communication

Good safety training reduces accidents. Supervisors should receive the training first, and then employees should receive it as well, because untrained workers are more likely to have accidents. Safety training can be done in various ways. Regular sessions with supervisors, managers, and employees are often coordinated by HR staff members.

Communication of safety procedures, reasons why accidents occurred, and what to do in an emergency is critical. Without effective communication about safety, training is insufficient. To reinforce safety training, continuous communication to develop safety consciousness is necessary. Merely sending safety memos is not enough. Producing newsletters, changing safety posters, continually updating bulletin boards, and posting safety information in visible areas are also recommended.

Employers may need to communicate in a variety of media and languages to address the special needs of workers who have vision, speech, or hearing impairments; who are not proficient in English; or who are challenged in other ways.[25]

Safety Committees

Employees frequently participate in safety planning through safety committees, often composed of workers from a variety of levels and departments. A safety committee generally meets at regularly scheduled times, has specific responsibilities for conducting safety reviews, and makes recommendations for changes necessary to avoid future accidents. Usually, at least one member of the committee comes from the HR department.

Companies must take care to ensure that managers do not compose a majority on their safety committees. Otherwise, they may be in violation of provisions of the National Labor Relations Act, commonly known as the Wagner Act. That act, as explained in detail in Chapter 17, prohibits employers from "dominating a labor organization." Some safety committees have been ruled to be labor organizations because they deal with working conditions.

In approximately 32 states, all but the smallest employers may be required to establish safety committees. From time to time, legislation has been introduced at the federal level to require joint management/employee safety committees. But as yet, no federal provisions have been enacted.

Inspection, Investigation, and Evaluation

It is not necessary to wait for an OSHA inspector to check the work area for safety hazards. Inspections may be done by a safety committee or by a safety coordinator. They should be done regularly, and problem areas should be addressed immediately, to keep work productivity at the highest possible levels. Also,

THOMSON

WEST

SAFETY COMMITTEES
Discusses different types of safety committees and how they operate.
Custom Search:
☑ ANALYSIS
Exact Phrase: Safety steering committee

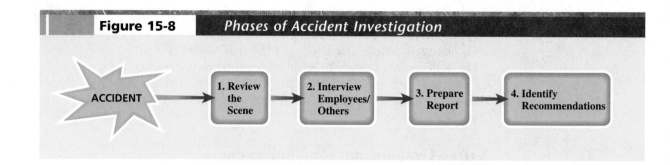

Figure 15-8   *Phases of Accident Investigation*

ACCIDENT → 1. Review the Scene → 2. Interview Employees/Others → 3. Prepare Report → 4. Identify Recommendations

OSHA inspects organizations with above-average rates of lost workdays more frequently.[26]

When accidents occur, they should be investigated by the employer's safety committee or safety coordinator. The phases of accident investigation are depicted in Figure 15-8. In investigating the scene of an accident, the inspector needs to determine which physical and environmental conditions contributed to the accident. Investigation at the scene should be done as soon as possible after an accident to ensure that the conditions under which the accident occurred have not changed significantly.

The second phase of the investigation is the interview of the injured employee, his or her supervisor, and witnesses to the accident. The interviewer attempts to determine what happened and what caused the accident. These interviews may also generate some suggestions on how to prevent similar accidents in the future.

In the third phase, using observations of the scene and interviews, the investigator completes an accident investigation report. This report provides the data required by OSHA.[27]

Finally, the investigator makes recommendations on how the accident could have been prevented, and on what changes are needed to avoid similar accidents. Identifying why an accident occurred is useful; taking steps to prevent similar accidents from occurring is also important.

Closely related to accident investigation is research to determine ways of preventing accidents. Employing safety engineers or having outside experts evaluate the safety of working conditions is useful. If many similar accidents seem to occur in an organizational unit, a safety training program may be necessary to emphasize safe working practices. As an example, a printing company reported a greater-than-average number of back injuries among employees who lifted heavy boxes. Safety training on the proper way to lift heavy objects was initiated to reduce the number of back injuries.

Organizations should monitor and evaluate their safety efforts. Just as organizational accounting records are audited, a firm's safety efforts should be audited periodically as well. Accident and injury statistics should be compared with previous accident patterns to identify any significant changes. This analysis should be designed to measure progress in safety management.

EMPLOYEE HEALTH

Employee health problems are varied—and somewhat inevitable. They can range from minor illnesses such as colds to serious illnesses related to the jobs performed. Some employees have emotional health problems; others have alcohol or drug problems. Some problems are chronic; others are transitory. All may affect organizational operations and individual employee productivity.

Workplace Health Issues

Employers face a variety of workplace health issues. Previously in this chapter, cumulative trauma injuries and exposure to hazardous chemicals have been discussed because OSHA has addressed these concerns through regulations or standards. There are other concerns associated with employee substance abuse, emotional/mental health, workplace air quality, smoking, and obesity.

Substance Abuse Use of illicit substances or misuse of controlled substances, alcohol, or other drugs is called **substance abuse.** The millions of substance abusers in the workforce cost global employers billions of dollars annually. In the U.S., the incidence of substance abuse is greatest among white men ages 19–23. At work, it is higher among men than women and higher among whites than other groups. Also, blue-collar workers are more likely than white-collar workers to abuse substances.[28]

Substance abuse
Use of illicit substances or misuse of controlled substances, alcohol, or other drugs.

Employers' concerns about substance abuse stem from the ways it alters work behaviors, causing increased tardiness, increased absenteeism, a slower work pace, a higher rate of mistakes, and less time spent at the work station. It can also cause an increase in withdrawal (physical and psychological) and antagonistic behaviors, which may lead to workplace violence.

Most large companies test applicants and employees for drug use. Many small companies do not. As a result, small companies may become havens for drug users—places they can get a job.[29] Alcohol testing and drug testing are used by many employers, especially following an accident or some other reasonable cause. Some employers also institute a random testing program. The U.S. Department of Transportation requires drug testing for aviation workers, commercial freight carrier employees, railroad workers, mass transit employees, pipeline employees, and commercial vessel operators.[30]

People abuse drugs and alcohol for many reasons;[31] employers prefer that employees *not* use drugs for an equally large number of reasons. Employees generally see drug testing as fair.[32] But it is expensive, and there are enough difficulties with it that some management teams wonder what a cost-benefit analysis might reveal.[33]

Figure 15-9 shows common signs of substance abuse. However, not all signs are present in any one case. A pattern that includes some of these behaviors should be a reason to pay closer attention.

| **Figure 15-9** | *Common Signs of Substance Abuse* |

- ◆ Fatigue
- ◆ Slurred speech
- ◆ Flushed cheeks
- ◆ Difficulty walking
- ◆ Inconsistency
- ◆ Difficulty remembering details
- ◆ Argumentative behavior
- ◆ Missed deadlines

- ◆ Many unscheduled absenses (especially on Mondays and Fridays)
- ◆ Depression
- ◆ Irritability
- ◆ Emotionalism
- ◆ Overreacting
- ◆ Violence
- ◆ Frequently borrowing money

Types of Drug Tests The most common tests for drug use are urinalysis, radioimmunoassay of hair, and fitness-for-duty testing. *Urinalysis* is used most frequently. It requires a urine sample, which must be tested at a lab. Despite concerns about sample switching and the ability of the test to detect drug use only over the past few days, urinalysis is generally accurate and well accepted.

Radioimmunoassay of hair requires a strand of an employee's hair, which is analyzed for traces of illegal substances. This test indicates a relationship between drug dosage and the concentration of drugs in the hair. A 1-inch hair sample provides a 90-day profile. Sample swapping generally proves more difficult in this test than in urinalysis, and the longer time period covered offers testing advantages. However, the testing remains somewhat controversial and is not recommended following accidents, because it cannot detect how recent the drug use was.

Fitness-for-duty tests can be used alone or in conjunction with drug testing. These tests can distinguish individuals under the influence of alcohol or prescription drugs to the extent that their abilities to perform their jobs are impaired. Some firms use fitness-for-duty tests to detect work performance safety problems before putting a person behind dangerous equipment. As an example, in one firm, when a crew of delivery truck drivers comes to work, they are asked to "play" a video game—with serious consequences. Unless the machine presents a receipt saying they passed the test, they are not allowed to drive their trucks that day. The computer has already established a baseline for each employee. Subsequent testing measures the employees against their baselines. Interestingly, most test failures are not drug or alcohol related. Rather, fatigue, illness, and personal problems more frequently render a person unfit to perform a sensitive job.[34]

Handling Substance Abuse Cases The Americans with Disabilities Act (ADA) affects how management can handle substance abuse cases. Current users of illegal drugs are specifically excluded from the definition of *disabled* under the act. However, those addicted to legal substances (alcohol, for example) and prescription drugs are considered disabled under the ADA. Also, recovering substance abusers are considered disabled under the ADA.

To encourage employees to seek help for their substance abuse problems, a *firm-choice option* is usually recommended and has been endorsed legally. In this procedure, a supervisor or a manager confronts the employee privately about unsatisfactory work-related behaviors. Then, in keeping with the disciplinary system, the employee is offered a choice between help and discipline. Treatment options and consequences of further unsatisfactory performance are clearly discussed, including what the employer will do. Confidentiality and follow-up are critical when employers use the firm-choice option.

Emotional/Mental Health Many individuals today are facing work, family, and personal life pressures. Although most people manage these pressures successfully, some individuals have difficulties handling the demands. Also, specific events, such as death of a spouse, divorce, or medical problems, can affect individuals who otherwise have been coping successfully with life pressures. A variety of emotional/mental health issues arise at work that must be addressed by employers. It is important to note that emotional/mental illnesses such as schizophrenia and depression are considered disabilities under the ADA. Employers should be cautious when using disciplinary policies if employees diagnosed with such illnesses have work-related problems.

Stress that keeps individuals from successfully handling the multiple demands they face is one concern. All people encounter stress; when "stress overload" hits, work-related consequences can result. HR professionals, managers, and supervisors all must be prepared to handle employee stress; otherwise, employees may "burn out" or exhibit unhealthy behaviors, such as drinking too much alcohol, misusing prescription drugs, and bursting out in anger.[35] Beyond trying to communicate with the employee and relieving some workload pressures, it is generally recommended that supervisors and managers contact the HR staff, who may intervene and may refer affected employees to outside resources through employee assistance programs.

Depression is another common emotional/mental health concern. Estimates are that 20% of individuals in workplaces suffer from depression. One indicator of the extent of clinical depression is that sales of prescription drugs covered by employee benefits plans to treat depression, such as Prozac and Zoloft, have risen significantly in the past several years.[36]

The effects of depression are seen at all organizational levels, from warehouses and accounting offices to executive suites. Carried to extreme, depression can result in an employee suicide. The subsequent guilt and sorrow felt by those who worked with the dead individuals becomes an issue for HR staff, who may be aided by crisis counselors. To deal with depression, it is recommended that HR professionals, managers, and supervisors be trained in the symptoms of depression and what to do when symptoms are noticed. Often, employees who appear to be depressed are then guided to employee assistance programs and helped with obtaining medical treatment.

Workplace Air Quality A number of employees work in settings where air quality is a health issue. Poor air quality may occur in "sealed" buildings (where windows cannot be opened) and when airflow is reduced to save energy and cut operating costs. Also, inadequate ventilation, as well as airborne contamination from carpets, molds, copy machines, adhesives, and fungi, can cause poor air quality and employee illnesses. In industrial settings, the presence of various chemicals and substances also can lead to poor air quality.

Air quality concerns prompted the U.S. Environmental Protection Agency (EPA) to define *sick building syndrome* as a situation in which occupants experience acute health problems and discomfort that appear to be linked to time spent in a building. Also, OSHA has investigated workplace illnesses caused by poor air quality. One major contributor to air quality problems is smoking in workplaces.

Smoking at Work Arguments and rebuttals characterize the smoking-at-work controversy, and statistics abound. A multitude of state and local laws deal with smoking in the workplace and in public places. In response to health studies, complaints by non-smokers, and state laws, many employers have instituted no-smoking policies throughout their workplaces. Although employees who smoke tend to complain initially when a smoking ban is instituted, they seem to have little difficulty adjusting within a few weeks, and many quit smoking or reduce the number of cigarettes they inhale and exhale each workday. Some employers also offer smoking cessation workshops as part of health promotion efforts.

Obesity Nearly one-third of U.S. adults are obese. Even people of healthy weight put on a pound or two each year as they approach middle age unless they exercise more and eat less. Obesity is a fact of modern life and a concern to employers, and a movement to involve employers in employee weight management is apparently gaining momentum. The reason employers are concerned is cost. The economic costs of obesity include doctor visits, diabetes, high blood pressure, higher health-care premiums, and lost workdays. The Institute on the Costs and Health Effects of Obesity was formed to address the increasing problem of obese employees. Companies in the Institute include such multi-nationals as Fidelity Investments, Ford, General Mills, Honeywell, IBM, Morgan Stanley, and PepsiCo.[37]

Health Promotion

Health promotion
Supportive approach of facilitating and encouraging healthy actions and lifestyles among employees.

Employers concerned about maintaining a healthy workforce must move beyond simply providing healthy working conditions and begin promoting employee health and wellness in other ways. **Health promotion** is a supportive approach of facilitating and encouraging healthy actions and lifestyles among employees. Health promotion efforts can range from providing information and increasing employee awareness of health issues, to creating an organizational culture supportive of employee health enhancements, as Figure 15-10 indicates. Going beyond just compliance with workplace safety and health regulations, organizations engage in health promotion by encouraging employees to make physiological, mental, and social choices that improve their health.

The first level of health promotion leaves much to individual initiatives for following through and making changes in actions and behaviors. Employers provide information on such topics as weight control, stress management, nutrition, exercise, and smoking cessation. Even though such efforts may be beneficial for some employees, employers who wish to impact employees' health must offer second-level efforts, such as more comprehensive programs and actions that focus on the lifestyle "wellness" of employees. The third level requires a commitment to wellness that is seldom seen in employers.

Wellness programs
Programs designed to maintain or improve employee health before problems arise.

Wellness Programs Employers' desires to improve productivity, decrease absenteeism, and control health-care costs have come together in the "wellness" movement. **Wellness programs** are designed to maintain or improve employee health before problems arise, by encouraging self-directed lifestyle changes.

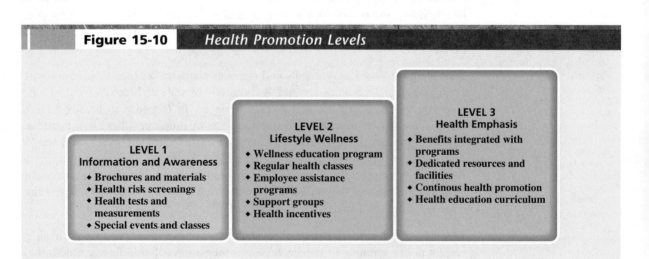

Figure 15-10 *Health Promotion Levels*

LEVEL 1
Information and Awareness
- Brochures and materials
- Health risk screenings
- Health tests and measurements
- Special events and classes

LEVEL 2
Lifestyle Wellness
- Wellness education program
- Regular health classes
- Employee assistance programs
- Support groups
- Health incentives

LEVEL 3
Health Emphasis
- Benefits integrated with programs
- Dedicated resources and facilities
- Continous health promotion
- Health education curriculum

Technology Transforming HR

On-line Health?

Web-based wellness programs seem almost impossible. Doesn't a physician need to examine a patient in order to prescribe a wellness plan? Employees can't exercise on-line, can they? But compared with traditional wellness programs, on-line wellness programs do a good job of providing information at a reasonable cost. Administrative, printing, and mailing expenses are not nearly as high with on-line programs as with typical on-site programs.

Ford, Microsoft, Chevron, and Watson Wyatt, Worldwide, are just a few of the companies that offer on-line wellness programs. These programs use information and subtle psychology to motivate people to live healthier lifestyles. They typically focus on exercise, nutrition, sleep, and stress and life balance.

In one on-line wellness program, each day participants answer a series of questions about their behavior in the last 24 hours: How much food and water did you consume? How much exercise and sleep did you get? and so on. The program then computes life practice indexes from the information, to show the participants how well they are doing. A key to the program is an "on-line coach" who monitors each participant and sends e-mails of praise or nudges the person to follow healthier behaviors.

Such services can be delivered for $5–$15 per employee, compared with $25–$50 per employee for a more conventional service. Employees seem to like it—a study revealed that 92% found the service helpful, and 48% went on-line rather than calling or going in face-to-face, because the on-line program offers immediate access and information. Most individuals logged on to get information on specific subjects of interest.[38]

Early wellness programs were aimed primarily at reducing the cost and risk of disease. Newer programs emphasize healthy lifestyles and environment, including reduced cholesterol and heart disease risks and individualized exercise programs and follow-up. Employer-sponsored support groups have been established for individuals dealing with health issues such as weight loss, nutrition, and smoking cessation.

The top-rated topics for wellness programs are stress management, exercise/fitness, screenings/checkups, health insurance education, disease management (heart disease, diabetes, etc.), nutrition and diet, and smoking cessation. The Technology Transforming HR deals with a recent innovation in this area—on-line wellness programs.

Organizations can assess the effectiveness of their wellness programs in a number of ways. Looking at participation rates by employees is one way. Studies have found that participation rates vary by age and type of activity, but generally, over half of employees participate in the different activities in a wellness program.[39] Although more participation would be beneficial, the programs have resulted in healthier lifestyles for more employees. Cost-benefit analyses by organizations also tend to support the continuation of wellness programs.

Employee assistance program (EAP)
Program that provides counseling and other help to employees having emotional, physical, or other personal problems.

Employee Assistance Programs (EAPs) One method organizations use as a broad-based response to health issues is an **employee assistance program (EAP),** which provides counseling and other help to employees having emotional, physical, or other personal problems. In such a program, an employer contracts with a counseling agency. Employees who have problems may then contact the agency, either voluntarily or by employer referral, for assistance with a broad range of problems. Counseling costs are paid for by the employer, either in total or up to a pre-established limit.

EAPs commonly provide help with troubled employees, problem identification, short-term intervention, and referral services. For example, an administrative assistant in New York had dizzy spells, endured a loud ringing in her ears, and felt that life and work were overwhelming her. She was also upset and weepy. She talked to someone in the company who referred her to the company EAP, which helped her find an appropriate counselor. She learned that she suffered from anxiety and clinical depression, and that her mental health problems were the basis of her physical problems. She received appropriate treatment and her employer paid for most of the expenses.[40]

EAPs help employees with a variety of problems. The most common employee issues dealt with are: (1) depression and anxiety, (2) marital and relationship problems, (3) legal difficulties, and (4) family and children concerns. Other areas commonly addressed as part of an EAP include substance abuse, financial counseling, and career advice. Critical to employee usage of an EAP is preserving confidentiality. For that reason, employers outsource EAPs to trained professionals, who usually report only the numbers of employees and services provided, rather than details on individuals using an EAP. The effectiveness of EAPs depends on how well employers integrate and support them in the workplace.[41]

SECURITY CONCERNS AT WORK

Traditionally, when employers have addressed worker health, safety, and security, they have been concerned about reducing workplace accidents, improving workers' safety practices, and reducing health hazards at work. Over the past decade, providing security for employees has grown in importance. Top security concerns at work are as follows:

- Workplace violence
- Internet/intranet security
- Business interruption/disaster recovery
- Fraud/white-collar crime
- Employee selection/screening concerns

Notice that virtually all of these areas have significant HR implications. Heading the list of security concerns is workplace violence.

Workplace Violence

The National Institute for Occupational Safety and Health (NIOSH) estimates that 10–15 workplace homicides occur every week. It also estimates that an additional 1 million people are attacked at work each year.[42] About 70% of workplace fatalities involve attacks against workers such as police officers, taxi drivers, and convenience store clerks. Often, these deaths occur during armed robbery attempts.

Almost 80% of workplace killings occur when a stranger comes on the premises. In the remaining 20%, the killer has some relationship with the workplace— as a former employee, customer, etc.[43] What has shocked many employers in a variety of industries has been the number of disgruntled employees or former

LOGGING ON...

The National Institute for the Prevention of Workplace Violence
This institute provides research, information, and training on workplace violence.
*www.
workplaceviolence911.com*

Figure 15-11

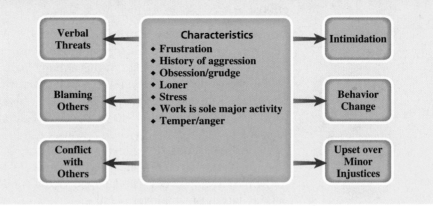

Profile of a Potentially Violent Employee

employees who have resorted to homicide in the workplace to deal with their anger and grievances.

There are a number of warning signs and characteristics of a potentially violent person at work. Individuals who have committed the most violent acts have had the relatively common profile depicted in Figure 15-11. A person with some of these signs may cope for years until a trauma pushes the individual over the edge. A profound humiliation or rejection, the end of a marriage, the loss of a lawsuit, or termination from a job may make a difficult employee turn violent.

Management of Workplace Violence The increase in workplace violence has led many employers to develop policies and practices for preventing and responding to workplace violence. As a first step, employers need to conduct a risk assessment of the organization and its employees. Unfortunately, few employers have conducted such a study. After completing a study, an organization can establish HR policies to identify how workplace violence is to be dealt with in conjunction with disciplinary actions and referrals to employee assistance programs.

One aspect of these policies is a violence response team. Composed of security personnel, key managers, HR staff members, and selected employees, this team functions much like a safety committee but with a different focus. Such teams conduct analyses, respond to and investigate employee threats, and may even help calm angry, volatile employees.

Employers must be careful, because they may face legal action for discrimination if they discharge employees for behaviors that often precede violent acts. For example, in several cases, employees who were terminated or suspended for making threats or even engaging in physical actions against their co-workers have sued their employers, claiming they had mental disabilities covered under the Americans with Disabilities Act (ADA).

Post-violence response is another part of managing workplace violence. Whether the violence results in physical injuries or deaths, or just intense interpersonal conflicts, it is important that employers have plans to respond afterward. Their response must reassure employees who may be fearful of returning to work or who experience anxiety and sleeplessness, among other reactions. Providing

THOMSON

⁕

WEST

WORKPLACE VIOLENCE
Identifies steps to take to minimize workplace violence and gives a sample policy.
Custom Search:
☑ ANALYSIS
Exact Phrase: Causes of workplace violence

referrals to EAP resources, allowing employees time to meet with HR staff, and arranging for trained counselors on-site are all part of post-violence response efforts.

Domestic Causes of Workplace Violence Women are much more likely than men to experience violence committed as a result of a personal relationship. Too often, violence that begins at home with family or "friends" can spill over to the workplace. One in five homicides of women at work are perpetrated by current or former husbands or boyfriends. Also, many abused women report being harassed frequently at work, by telephone, or in person by abusing partners.

The worse reaction by employers is to ignore obvious signs of domestic violence. In fact, some employers have been sued and found liable for ignoring pleas for help from employees who later are victims of domestic violence in company parking lots or on employer premises.

Workplace violence is a difficult concern, and guarantees for eliminating it do not exist. However, the following are suggestions that may help combat violence at work.

- Zero-tolerance policies (immediate termination for violent acts or threats)
- Referral of both violent employees and victims to EAPs
- Employee/supervisor training in conflict resolution and stress recognition
- Access to legal counseling
- Use of restraining orders against aggressors
- Training to identify potential victims, bullies, or aggressors
- Self-defense training for employees
- Careful screening for violent predictors in the employee selection process
- Limited access to the facility
- Profiling of potentially violent workers
- Formation of a violence response team

Training on Dealing with Workplace Violence Managers, HR staff members, supervisors, and employees should be trained on how to recognize the signs of a potentially violent employee and what to do when violence occurs. During training at many firms, participants learn the typical profile of potentially violent employees and are trained to notify the HR department and to refer employees to outside counseling professionals. Specific suggestions addressed in training for dealing with potentially violent employees include the following:

- Notice verbal and non-verbal reactions by individuals that may indicate anger or hostility.
- Listen to individuals exhibiting such reactions, and pay attention to the words, actions, and unspoken "messages."
- Ask questions requiring explanations and longer answers that allow individuals to "vent."
- Respond calmly and non-threatingly to individuals' emotions, and acknowledge concerns and understanding about how the individuals feel.
- Get assistance from others, particularly HR staff members or another manager not directly affected by the situation being discussed.
- Indicate the need for time to respond to the concerns voiced, and then set up another time for follow-up.

◆ Notify security personnel and HR staff members whenever employees' behaviors change dramatically or when job disciplinary action may provoke significant reactions by employees.

Security Management

An overall approach to security management is needed to address a wide range of issues, including workplace violence. Often, HR managers have responsibility for security programs, or they work closely with security managers or consultants to address employee security issues.

Security audit
Comprehensive review of organizational security.

Security Audit In a **security audit,** HR staff conduct a comprehensive review of organizational security. Sometimes called a *vulnerability analysis,* such an audit uses managers inside the organization (such as the HR manager and the facilities manager) and outsiders (such as security consultants, police officers, fire officials, and computer security experts) to assess security issues.

Typically, a security audit begins with a survey of the area around the facility. Such factors as lighting in parking lots, traffic flow, location of emergency response services, crime in the surrounding neighborhood, and the layout of the buildings and grounds are evaluated.[44] The audit also may include a review of the security available within the firm, including the capabilities of guards. Another part of the security audit reviews disaster plans, which address how to deal with events such as earthquakes, floods, tornados, hurricanes, and fires. Efforts to prepare for catastrophes like these have become even more prominent since 9/11.

Controlled Access A key part of security involves controlling access to the physical facilities of the organization. As mentioned earlier, many workplace homicides occur during robberies. Therefore, employees who are most vulnerable, such as taxi drivers and convenience store clerks, often are provided bulletproof partitions and restricted access areas.

Many organizations limit access to facilities and work areas by using electronic access or keycard systems. Although not foolproof, these systems can make it more difficult for an unauthorized person, such as an estranged husband or a disgruntled ex-employee, to enter the premises. Access controls can also be used in elevators and stairwells to prevent unauthorized persons from entering designated areas within a facility.[45]

Computer Security Yet another part of security centers on controlling access to computer systems. With so many transactions and records being handled by computers, adequate security provisions are crucial to prevent unauthorized access to computer information systems. Growth of the Internet and of e-mail systems has made computer security issues an even greater concern. This concern is magnified when individuals are terminated or leave an organization. HR staff must coordinate with information technology staff to change passwords, delete access codes, and otherwise protect company information systems.[46]

Employee Screening and Selection

A key facet of providing security is screening job applicants. Regulations somewhat limit what can be done, particularly regarding the use of psychological tests and checking of references. However, firms that do not screen employees adequately may be subject to liability if an employee commits crimes later. For instance, an individual with a criminal record for assault was hired by a firm to maintain sound equipment in clients' homes. The employee used a passkey to enter a home and assault the owner, and the employer was ruled liable. Of course, when selecting employees, employers must be careful to use only valid, job-related screening means and to avoid violating federal EEO laws and the Americans with Disabilities Act.

Security Personnel

Providing adequately trained security personnel in sufficient numbers is a critical part of security management. Many employers contract for these personnel with firms specializing in security. If security is handled in-house, security personnel must be selected and trained to handle a variety of workplace security problems, ranging from dealing with violent behavior by an employee to taking charge in natural disasters.

██ GLOBAL HEALTH, SAFETY, AND SECURITY

Safety and health laws and regulations vary from country to country, ranging from virtually non-existent to more stringent than those in the United States. The importance placed on workplace safety relates somewhat to the level of regulation in each country.

International Emergency Health Services

With more and more expatriates working internationally, especially in some less-developed countries, significant health and safety issues require attention. Addressing these issues is part of the HR role. One consideration is provision of emergency evacuation services. For instance, how to evacuate and care for an expatriate employee who sustains internal injuries in a car accident in the Ukraine or Sierra Leone may be a major issue. Many global firms purchase coverage for their international employees from an organization that provides emergency services, such as International SOS, Global Assistance & Healthcare, or U.S. Assist. If an emergency arises, the emergency services company dispatches physicians or even transports employees by chartered aircraft. If adequate medical assistance can be obtained locally, the emergency services company maintains a referral list and arranges for the expatriate to receive treatment. Emergency services firms may also provide legal counsel in foreign countries, emergency cash for medical expenses, and assistance in reissuing lost documents. Some large multi-nationals have begun to expand their EAP coverage to include international employees as well.[47]

International Security and Terrorism

As more U.S. firms operate internationally, the threat of terrorist actions against those firms and the employees working for them increases. The extent to which employees are likely to experience security problems and violence depends on the country. It is crucial that the HR staff regularly check the security conditions in countries where expatriates are traveling and working.

Global firms take a variety of actions to address security concerns.[48] For example, one U.S. firm removed signs identifying its offices and facilities in a Latin American country in order to reduce the visibility of the firm and thus reduce its potential as a target for terrorist acts. Many international firms screen entry by all employees, and many use metal detectors to scan all packages, briefcases, and

LOGGING ON...

Travel Warnings
Current travel warnings and consular advisories by country are available from the U.S. State Department.
http://travel.state.gov

other items. Firms commonly use physical barriers such as iron security fences, concrete barricades, bulletproof glass, and electronic surveillance devices in offices as part of their security efforts.

Kidnapping

Not all violence occurs at work. Kidnapping, murder, home invasion, robberies, and carjackings happen relatively frequently in some cities, such as Mexico City. In a number of countries throughout the world, U.S. citizens are especially vulnerable to extortion, kidnapping, bombing, physical harassment, and other terrorist activities.

To counter such threats, many global firms have *kidnap and ransom insurance*. This insurance covers the costs of paying ransoms to obtain releases of kidnapped employees and family members, pay for the bodily injuries suffered by kidnap victims, and deal with negotiation and other expenses.

Individual employees and their family members working and living abroad must constantly be aware of security concerns. Both pre-departure and ongoing security training should be given to all expatriates, their dependents, and employees of global firms working internationally, especially if located in high-risk areas.

SUMMARY

- Health is a general state of physical, mental, and emotional well-being. Safety is a condition in which the physical well-being of people is protected. Security is the protection of employees and organizational facilities.
- Workers' compensation coverage is provided by employers to protect employees who suffer job-related injuries and illnesses.
- Both the Family and Medical Leave Act (FMLA) and the Americans with Disabilities Act (ADA) affect employer health and safety policies and practices.
- The Fair Labor Standards Act (FLSA) limits the types of work that younger employees, especially those under the age of 18, can perform.
- The Occupational Safety and Health Act states that employers have a general duty to provide safe and healthy working conditions.
- The Occupational Safety and Health Administration (OSHA) has established enforcement standards to aid in a number of areas, including hazard communication.
- Ergonomics looks at the physiological and physical demands of work.
- OSHA addresses employee work assignments, requires employers to keep records on occupa-

tional illnesses and injuries, inspects workplaces, and can issue citations for several levels of violations.
- Effective safety management requires integrating three approaches: organizational, engineering, and individual.
- Developing safety policies, disciplining violators, keeping safety records, conducting safety training, communicating on safety issues, establishing safety committees, inspecting work areas for safety concerns, investigating accidents, and evaluating safety efforts are all part of comprehensive safety management.
- Substance abuse, emotional/mental health, workplace air quality, smoking at work, and obesity, among other common health issues, are growing concerns for organizations and employees.
- Employers promote employee health at several levels to improve organizational operations and individual employee productivity.
- Employers have responded to health problems by establishing and supporting wellness programs and employee assistance programs (EAPs).
- Establishing and maintaining an organizational culture of health continues to pay off for a number of employers.

- Security of workplaces has grown in importance, particularly as the frequency of workplace violence increases.
- Employers can enhance security by conducting a security audit, controlling access to workplaces and computer systems, screening employees ad-equately, during the selection process, and providing security personnel.
- Global security relates somewhat to the varying levels of regulation in different countries. Security problems around the world are well documented but do not always get enough attention.

REVIEW AND APPLICATION QUESTIONS

1. How does one go about controlling workers' compensation costs, and why is that important?
2. What should an employer do when facing an OSHA inspection?
3. As the HR manager of a distribution and warehouse firm with 600 employees, you plan to discuss a company wellness program at an executive staff meeting next week. The topics to cover include what a wellness program is, how it can benefit the company and employees, and the process for establishing it. To aid in developing your presentation to the executives, consult the following Web site: *www.welcoa.org* and other Web sites you locate.

LEARNING REVIEW

To check your knowledge of the chapter, review the following. (Answers after the supplemental case.) For more questions, see the Study Guide.

1. Who is responsible for workers' compensation costs?
   a. Employers
   b. Employees
   c. Employees and employers jointly
   d. State and local governments
2. The general duty clause of the Occupational Safety and Health Act refers to _____.
   a. areas in which no OSHA standards have been adopted
   b. the philosophy and ideas of safe management
   c. strictly following all established standards
   d. investigating all organizational accidents

3. What can happen if an employer has been warned of a safety violation but does not correct the situation, and a death occurs?
   a. The business may be shut down for up to one year.
   b. The employer can be fined 25% of its yearly gross income.
   c. Workers' compensation insurance will not pay, leaving the employer liable for civil litigation on the ground of gross negligence.
   d. A jail term of six months can be imposed on responsible executives or managers.
4. The most common cause of homicides at work are _____.
   a. attacks by disgruntled employees
   b. armed robbery attempts
   c. attacks by former employees
   d. confrontations resulting from abusive domestic relationships

CASE

ANHEUSER-BUSCH BREWS EMPLOYEE WELLNESS

Anheuser-Busch (A-B) is best known for its Budweiser, Bud Lite, and Michelob beers. To get those products brewed and to market takes a large number of employees in a number of brewing plants in the U.S. In addition to producing beer, A-B has also worked to produce healthy employees. One prime example of the health and wellness efforts at A-B can be seen at its Jacksonville, Florida, brewery. Many of the workers at the Jacksonville plant have considerable years of experience, with the average age of the workforce being 48 years. As the workforce has grown older, employee health and wellness has become a higher priority.

Beginning several years ago an annual health appraisal on employees was conducted by occupational nurses. This extensive appraisal obtained employees' details on personal and family health history, nutrition habits, blood pressure, cholesterol, and other health measures. Once all of the data on each employee were compiled, "health report cards" were provided to the employees and their primary care physicians. Then employees were encouraged to participate in wellness programs relevant to their individual needs. Also, an employee wellness committee met regularly to plan wellness programs and events, including a month-long wellness fair. Spouses, children, and family members, as well as employees, were invited to participate in the fair.

These efforts have resulted in healthier employees for A-B, fewer medical care costs for employees and their dependents, and fewer workplace illnesses and injuries. Because of all of these health initiatives, the Jacksonville plant has been awarded a "gold star" designation by the Wellness Council of America. While brewing beer, Anheuser-Busch has also produced employee wellness.[49]

Questions

1. Identify how A-B has incorporated elements from each of the levels of health promotion described in the chapter.
2. How could wellness and health promotion efforts be justified to senior managers at A-B corporate headquarters?

SUPPLEMENTAL CASE: "What's Happened to Bob?"

This case concerns some of the warning signs of possible alcohol abuse and the consequences at work. (For the case, go to http://mathis.swlearning.com/)

Learning Review Answers: 1. a 2. a 3. d 4. b

NOTES

1. Based on "World Class Safety," *Occupational Hazards,* September 2003, 71–72; and "A Small Company with a Mighty Safety Record," *Occupational Hazards,* September 2003, 77–78.
2. Allan Rickmann and Andrew Ellis, "Must SHE Be Obeyed?" *Safety and Health Practitioner,* September 2003, 42–50.
3. Philip S. Deming, "Crisis Management Planning: A Human Resource Challenge," *SHRM White Paper,* April 2002, 1–5.
4. "Finding the Good Egg: Risk Management Begins with Hiring the Right People," *Commercial Carrier Journal,* June 2003, 41–47.
5. "Work Injuries and Illnesses 2002," *Monthly Labor Review,* January 2004, 1.
6. "Injury Costs Skyrocket Study Finds," *National Underwriter Property and Casualty,* May 12, 2003, 30–33.
7. "OSHA Inspections Increased in Fiscal '03," *Industrial Safety and Hygiene News,* January 2004, 8–9.

8. Stephen M. Pegula, "Occupational Fatalities: Self Employed Workers and Wages and Salary Workers," *Monthly Labor Review,* March 2004, 30–40.

9. "Delivering a One-Two Combination to Fatten the Cost of L.O.S.S.," *Occupational Hazards,* October 2003, 46–51; Paul D. Allison et al., "Corporate Health Revisited: Illness and Organizational Dynamics," *Journal of Applied Behavioral Science,* 38 (2002), 177–190; and Amparo Oliver et al., "The Effects of Organizational and Individual Factors on Occupational Accidents," *Journal of Occupational and Organizational Psychology,* 75 (2002), 473–488.

10. Jerry Landsma, "Red Flags to Spot Possible Comp Fraud," *Business Insurance,* November 24, 2003, 11–14.

11. "Electronic MSDS," *Industrial Safety and Hygiene News,* September 2003, 42–43; and "Office Ergo Solutions: Low Cost Tactics to Improve Ergonomics on a Tight Budget," *Industrial Safety and Hygiene News,* December 2003, 17–20.

12. "OSHA's New Ergo Plan: Guidelines Favored Over Rules," *Industrial Safety and Hygiene News,* June 2002, 14–15.

13. Bernie Knill, "Ergonomics Gets a Boost," *Material Handling Management*, August 2003, 54–56.

14. Jake Thompson, "Taking Aim at Injuries," *Omaha World-Herald,* April 1, 2002, B1; and "The Business Case for OSHA's Nursing Home Ergonomics Guidelines," *Occupational Hazards*, June 2003, 35–41.

15. Stephanie Armour, "Workers Take Employers to Court over Birth Defects," *USA Today,* February 26, 2002, 1.

16. *United Autoworkers v. Johnson Controls, Inc.,* 111 S. Ct. 1196 (1991).

17. Bob Brown, "Paper Trail," *Industrial Safety and Hygiene News,* December 2003, 19–21.

18. *Marshall v. Barlow's, Inc.,* 98 S. Ct. 1816 (1978).

19. "Labor Department Official Warns Companies Against Trying to Thwart OSHA Inspections," *Safety Director's Report No. 2-10,* October 2002, 1.

20. J. Craig Wallace, "Can Accidents and Industrial Mishaps Be Predicted?" *Journal of Business and Psychology,* 17 (2003), 503–514; and Lovisa Olafsdottir, "Prevention Health and Safety Programs in Companies Provide a More Successful and Healthier Workplace," *Work,* 22 (2004), 27–30.

21. Don J. Eckenfelder, "Why We Need an Antidote for Behavior-Based Safety," *Occupational Hazards,* September 2003, 98–105; and Steve Roberts, "How to Play It Safe," *Safety Management,* July 2003, 57–62.

22. Denny Holland and Joe Luetzinger, "Fatigue Management: A Literature Review," *Journal of Employee Assistance*, 33 (2003), 24–35.

23. Philip Tucker, "The Impact of Rest Breaks upon Accident Risk, Fatigue and Performance," *Work and Stress,* 17 (2003), 123–137.

24. "Use This Information to Show Management Why You Need an OTS Injury Prevention Plan," *Safety Director's Report,* November 2003, 1–2.

25. Justin Pritchard, "Immigrants Dying to Work," *The Denver Post,* March 14, 2004, 4A.

26. "Inspections, Maintenance Are Keys to Smooth Operations," *Hotel and Motel Management,* March 15, 2004, 50–52.

27. Joel Bennett, "Using Evidence-Based Workplace Training," *Journal of Employee Assistance*, 33 (2003), 12–16.

28. G. Shaon Reynolds and W. E. K. Lehman, "Levels of Substance Use and Willingness to Use Employee Assistance Programs," *Journal of Behavioral Health Services and Research,* 30 (2003), 238–248; and Royer Cook and William Schlenger, "Prevention of Substance Abuse in the Workplace: Review of Research on the Delivery of Services," *Journal of Primary Prevention,* 23 (2002), 115–128.

29. "Drug Abusers Find Jobs in Small Companies," *Contractor,* September 2003, 7–8.

30. Ernie Huelke, "Drug Testing: Your Role in Safety Guarantees Involvement at Some Point," *Industrial Safety and Hygiene News,* April 2003, 35–40.

31. Samuel B. Bacharach et al., "Driven to Drink," *Academy of Management Journal,* 45 (2002), 637–658.

32. Matthew E. Paronto et al., "Drug Testing, Drug Treatment and Marijuana Use: A Fairness Perspective," *Journal of Applied Psychology,* 87 (2002), 1159–1166.

33. Ron J. Ozminkowski et al., "Relationships Between Urinalysis Testing for Substance Abuse and the Occurrence of Injuries at a Large Manufacturing Firm," *American Journal of Drug and Alcohol Abuse,* 29 (2003), 151–167; Andy Meisler, "Negative Results," *Workforce Management,* October 2003, 35–41; and "Are You Spending Too Much on Drug Prevention Testing?" *Safety Director's Report,* September 2002, 2–6.

34. Evelyn Beck, "Is the Time Right for Impairment Testing?" *Workforce,* February 2001, 68–71.

35. Joseph F. Mangan, "Stress Wounds," *Human Resource Executive,* November 2003, 72; and Christopher Stewart, "Prescription for Disaster," *Sales and Marketing Management,* November 2003, 49–53.

36. Barbara Morris, "Stress Test 2004," *Human Resource Executive,* January 2004, 38–43; and Cora Daniels, "The Last Taboo," *Fortune,* October 28, 2002, 137.

37. "Obesity Weighs on Employers' Minds," *Omaha World-Herald,* December 1, 2003, D1; and Maureen Minehan, "Global Obesity Epidemic Drives Up Employment Costs," *Global Perspectives, www.SHRM.org/global.*

38. Traci Purdim, "Healthy, Wealthy, Wise and Web Based," *Industry Week,* May 2004, 52–53; and Michael Prince, "Altering Lifestyles Through Internet Fitness Monitoring," *Business Insurance,* April 8, 2002 1G; and "Ceridian Makes Online EAPS and Work Life Services a Real Possibility," *Managing Benefit Plans,* September 2002, 1–2.

39. "How to Transform a Wellness Program into a Retention Tool," *Safety Director's Report,* September 2003, 5–10.

40. Kathryn Tyler, "Mind Matters," *HR Magazine,* August 2003, 1–4.

41. Linda Sutton, "Setting a Two-Year Plan," *Journal of Employee Assistance,* April 2003, 16–19.

42. Marlene Piturro, "Workplace Violence," *Strategic Finance,* May 2001, 35–38.

43. Robert Grossman, "Bulletproof Practices," *HR Magazine,* November 2002, 7–11.

44. "Workplace Security," *Wall Street Journal Reports,* September 29, 2003, R1–R8.
45. "On Guard," *Wall Street Journal Reports,* March 11, 2002, R1–R16.
46. Will Strother, "A Security Primer," *SHRM White Paper,* *www.shrm.org/hrtx*

47. John Pompe et al., "EAP Type Services for International Employees and Families," *WorldatWork Journal,* Second Quarter 2004, 69–78.
48. "Bechtel: Striving to Be the Best," *Occupational Hazards,* September 2003, 72–75.

49. Based on "Brewery's Aging Workforce Is Given a Shot of Wellness," *Bulletin to Management,* May 4, 2000, 147.

CHAPTER 16

Employee Rights and Discipline

After you have read this chapter, you should be able to:

- Explain the difference between statutory rights and contractual rights.

- Define employment-at-will and discuss how wrongful discharge, just cause, and due process are interrelated.

- Identify employee rights associated with access to employee records and free speech.

- Discuss issues associated with workplace monitoring, employer investigations, and drug testing.

- List elements to consider when developing an employee handbook.

- Differentiate between the positive approach and progressive approach to discipline.

Tracking Employees with Technology

The use of technology has expanded the extent of conflicts over employer and employee rights. Technology has blurred the line between company time and private time. For instance, many employees feel that it is acceptable to use their company computers for personal matters. So when the company monitors e-mail, voice mail, and Internet use by employees, conflicts arise. Employers have disciplined or fired employees who used company computers to access pornographic Web sites, or who wasted work time by browsing eBay, downloading music files, or playing games.

The battle over the use of technology is also expanding in other areas. Police officers can be tracked using GPS systems, and their logbooks can be compared against what the tracking system shows. In a number of cities, officers have been disciplined or fired for falsifying logbooks to show them as being on duty, when they really were parked, sleeping, or in a local coffee shop or bar. Trucking firms use GPS systems to track locations, schedules, and routes of drivers. Other firms track the keystrokes of data-entry processors or length of call time of customer service representatives.

Generally, court decisions have supported employers' rights to track and monitor employees when the employees are using company facilities, company computer systems, and on-the-job time. But employers should inform employees that monitoring can occur and get signed permissions from them. Undoubtedly, these efforts help clarify employer and employee rights, but despite them, conflicts are likely to grow as employers use more advanced technology to track the employees' performance.[1]

"The right to be left alone—the most comprehensive of rights and the most valued by civilized men."

—*Louis Brandeis*

This chapter considers three related and important issues in managing human resources: employee rights, HR policies and rules, and discipline. These areas may seem separate, but they definitely are not. The policies and rules that an organization enacts help to define employees' rights at that employer, as well as constrain those rights (sometimes inappropriately or illegally). Similarly, discipline for those who fail to follow policies and rules is often seen as a fundamental right of employers. Employees who feel that their employers have taken inappropriate action can challenge that action—both inside and outside the organization—using an internal dispute resolution process or through a variety of external legal means.

▉ RIGHTS AND RESPONSIBILITIES ISSUES

Rights Powers, privileges, or interests that belong to a person by law, nature, or tradition.

Rights generally do not exist in the abstract. Instead, they exist only when someone is successful in demanding their application. **Rights** are powers, privileges, or interests that belong to a person by law, nature, or tradition. Of course, defining a right presents considerable potential for disagreement. For example, does an employee have a right to privacy of communication in personal matters when using the employer's computer on company time? Moreover, *legal rights* may or may not correspond to certain *moral rights,* and the reverse is true as well—a situation that opens "rights" up to controversy and lawsuits.

Responsibilities Obligations to perform certain tasks and duties.

Rights are offset by **responsibilities,** which are obligations to perform certain tasks and duties. Employment is a reciprocal relationship (both sides have rights and obligations). For example, if an employee has the right to a safe working environment, then the employer must have an obligation to provide a safe workplace. If the employer has a right to expect uninterrupted, high-quality work from the employee, then the worker has the responsibility to be on the job and to meet job performance standards. The reciprocal nature of rights and responsibilities suggests that both parties to an employment relationship should regard the other as having rights and should treat the other with respect.

Statutory Rights

Statutory rights Rights based on laws or statutes.

Employees' **statutory rights** are the result of specific laws or statutes passed by federal, state, or local governments. Various federal, state, and local laws have granted employees certain rights at work, such as equal employment opportunity, collective bargaining, and workplace safety. These laws and their interpretations also have been the subjects of a considerable number of court cases.

Contractual Rights

Contractual rights Rights based on a specific contract between an employer and an employee.

An employee's **contractual rights** are based on a specific contract with an employer. For instance, a union and an employer may agree on a labor contract that specifies certain terms, conditions, and rights that employees represented by the union have with the employer.

Contracts formalize the employment relationship. For instance, when hiring an independent contractor or a consultant, an employer should use a contract to spell out the work to be performed, expected time lines, parameters, and costs and fees to be incurred. Contractual rights can be spelled out formally in written employment contracts or implied in employer handbooks and policies disseminated to employees.

Employment contract Agreement that formally outlines the details of employment.

Non-compete agreements Agreements that prohibit individuals who leave the organization from competing with an employer in the same line of business for a specified period of time.

Employment Contracts A formal **employment contract** is an agreement that outlines the details of employment. Written employment contracts are often very detailed. Traditionally, employment contracts have been used mostly for executives and senior managers, but the use of employment contracts is filtering down the organization to include highly specialized professional and technical employees who have scarce skills.

Depending on the organization and individuals involved, employment agreements may contain a number of provisions, as Figure 16-1 depicts. Some key ones are highlighted next.

Typically, an *identification section* lists the parties to the contract, and the general nature of the employee's job duties. The level of compensation and types of benefits are often addressed, including any special compensation, benefits, incentives, or perquisites to be provided by the employer. The employment contract may also note whether the employment relationship is to be for an indeterminate time, or whether it can be renewed automatically after a specified period of time. The contract may spell out a severance agreement, continuation of benefits, and other factors related to the employee's leaving the employer.[2]

Commonly, employment contracts include **non-compete agreements,** which prohibit individuals who leave the organization from working with an employer in the same line of business for a specified period of time. A non-compete agreement may be presented as a separate contract or as a clause in an employment

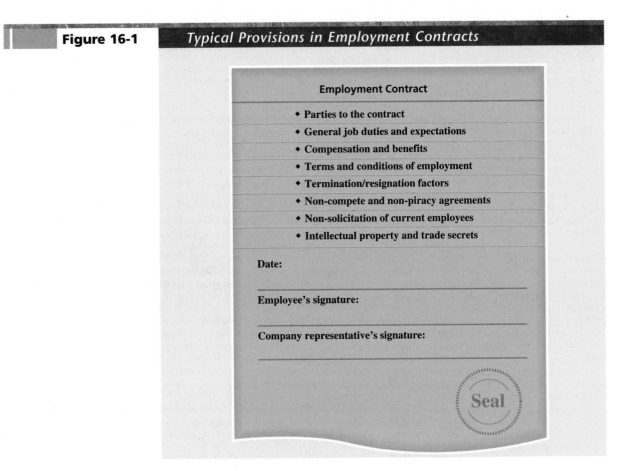

Figure 16-1   *Typical Provisions in Employment Contracts*

Employment Contract

- ◆ Parties to the contract
- ◆ General job duties and expectations
- ◆ Compensation and benefits
- ◆ Terms and conditions of employment
- ◆ Termination/resignation factors
- ◆ Non-compete and non-piracy agreements
- ◆ Non-solicitation of current employees
- ◆ Intellectual property and trade secrets

Date:

Employee's signature:

Company representative's signature:

Seal

contract. Though primarily used with newly hired employees, some firms have required existing employees to sign non-compete agreements. Different court decisions have ruled for or against employers that have fired employees who refused to sign the agreements.[3]

Overly restrictive agreements that severely affect an individual's right to find other employment have often been ruled unenforceable by state courts. For example, a New York court ruled that 12 months was too long to restrict an Internet technician from working for a competitor.[4]

Employment contracts also may contain *non-piracy agreements,* which bar former employees from soliciting business from former customers and clients for a specified period of time. For instance, a company was able to enforce an agreement when two ex-employees started a competing firm and attempted to provide services to a major customer of their former company.[5] Also, clauses requiring *non-solicitation of current employees* can be incorporated into employment agreements. These clauses are written to prevent a former employee from contacting or encouraging co-workers at the former firm to join a different company, often a competitor.

An additional area covered in employment contracts is protection of *intellectual property* and *trade secrets*. A 1996 federal law made the theft of trade secrets a federal crime punishable by fines up to $5 million and 15 years in jail. Employer rights include the following:[6]

- The right to keep trade secrets confidential
- The right to have employees bring business opportunities to the employer first before pursuing them elsewhere
- A common-law copyright for works and documents prepared by employees for their employers

LOGGING ON...

Human Resources Law Index
This Web site on workplace legal information discusses such issues as employment contracts and other issues.
www.hrlawindex.com

Implied Contracts

The idea that a contract (even an implied or unwritten one) exists between individuals and their employers affects the employment relationship. The rights and responsibilities of the employee may be spelled out in a job description, in an employment contract, in HR policies, or in a handbook, but often are not. The rights and responsibilities of the employee may also exist *only* as unwritten employer expectations about what is acceptable behavior or performance on the part of the employee. For instance, a number of court decisions have held that if an employer hires someone for an indefinite period or promises job security, the employer has created an implied contract. Such promises establish employee expectations, especially if there has been a long-term business relationship.[7] When the employer fails to follow up on the implied promises, the employee may pursue remedies in court. Numerous federal and state court decisions have held that such implied promises, especially when contained in an employee handbook, constitute a contract between an employer and its employees, even without a signed document.

Employment Practices Liability Insurance (EPLI)

Workplace litigation has reached epidemic proportion as employees who feel that their rights have been violated sue their employers. As a result, some employers have purchased insurance to try to cover their risks from numerous lawsuits. Employment practices liability insurance (EPLI) policies typically cover employer costs for legal fees, settlements, and judgments associated with employment actions. For example, at one telecommunications firm, an EPLI policy covered virtually all of a $10 million judgment against the company for racial discrimination.[8]

To determine the level of risk and premiums to be charged to employers wanting EPLI, most insurance carriers review the employers' HR policies and practices.[9] The review may include a detailed look at an employer's HR policy manuals, employee handbooks, employment forms, and other items. It may also involve an examination of the employer's history of employment-related charges and complaints over the past three to five years.

RIGHTS AFFECTING THE EMPLOYMENT RELATIONSHIP

As employees increasingly regard themselves as free agents in the workplace—and as the power of unions declines—the struggle between individual employee and employer "rights" is heightening. Employers frequently do not fare well in court. Further, not only the employer is liable in many cases. Individual managers and supervisors have been found liable when hiring or promotion decisions have been based on discriminatory factors, or when they have had knowledge of such conduct and have not taken steps to stop it. Several concepts from law and psychology influence the employment relationship: employment-at-will, just cause, due process, and distributive and procedural justice.

Employment-at-Will (EAW)

Employment-at-will (EAW) Common-law doctrine stating that employers have the right to hire, fire, demote, or promote whomever they choose, unless there is a law or a contract to the contrary.

Employment-at-will (EAW) is a common-law doctrine stating that employers have the right to hire, fire, demote, or promote whomever they choose, unless there is a law or a contract to the contrary. Conversely, employees can quit whenever they want and go to another job under the same constraints. An employment-at-will statement usually contains wording such as the following:

> *This handbook is not a contract, express or implied, guaranteeing employment for any specific duration. Although we hope that your employment relationship with us will be long-term, either you or the Employer may terminate this relationship at any time, for any reason, with or without cause or notice.*

In the past three decades, numerous state courts have questioned the *fairness* of an employer's decision to fire an employee without just cause and due process. Many suits have stressed that employees' job rights must be checked against EAW to balance legal and ethical concerns.[10]

EAW and the Courts In general, the courts have recognized three rationales for hearing EAW cases. They are as follows:

- *Public policy exception:* This exception to EAW holds that an employee can sue if he or she was fired for a reason that violates public policy. For example, if an employee refused to commit perjury and was fired, he or she can sue the employer.
- *Implied contract exception:* This exception to EAW holds that an employee should not be fired as long as he or she does the job. Long service, promises of continued employment, and lack of criticism of job performance imply continuing employment.

◆ *Good-faith and fair-dealing exception:* This exception to EAW suggests that a covenant of good faith and fair dealing exists between the employer and the at-will employee. If the employer breaks this covenant by unreasonable behavior, the employee may seek legal recourse.

Nearly all states have enacted one or more statutes to limit an employer's right to discharge employees. National restrictions include prohibitions against the use of race, age, sex, national origin, religion, and disabilities as bases for termination. Restrictions on other areas vary from state to state.[11]

Wrongful Discharge

Wrongful discharge Termination of an individual's employment for reasons that are improper or illegal.

Employers who run afoul of EAW restrictions may be guilty of **wrongful discharge,** which is the termination of an individual's employment for reasons that are illegal or improper. Some state courts have recognized certain non-statutory grounds for wrongful-discharge suits. Additionally, courts generally have held that unionized workers cannot pursue EAW actions as at-will employees because they are covered by the grievance arbitration process.

A landmark court case in wrongful discharge was *Fortune v. National Cash Register Company.* The case involved the firing of a salesperson (Mr. Fortune) who had been with National Cash Register (NCR) for 25 years.[12] The employee's termination came shortly after he got a large customer order that would have earned him a big commission. Based on the evidence, the court concluded that he was wrongfully discharged because NCR dismissed him to avoid paying the commission, thus violating the covenant of good faith and fair dealing.

Constructive discharge Deliberately making conditions intolerable to get an employee to quit.

Employers should take several precautions to reduce wrongful discharge liabilities. Having a well-written employee handbook, training managers, and maintaining adequate documentation are key.[13] Figure 16-2 offers suggestions for preparing a defense against wrongful-discharge lawsuits.

Closely related to wrongful discharge is **constructive discharge,** which is deliberately making conditions intolerable to get an employee to quit. Under nor-

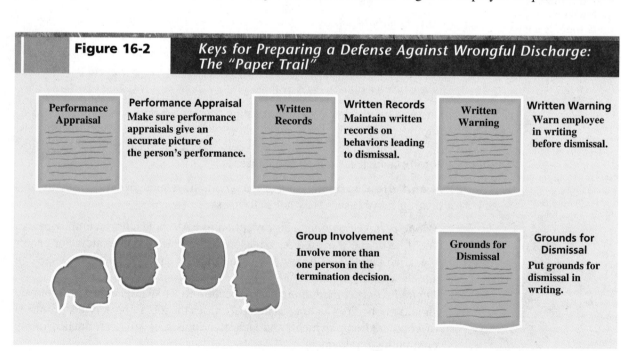

Figure 16-2 | *Keys for Preparing a Defense Against Wrongful Discharge: The "Paper Trail"*

Performance Appraisal
Make sure performance appraisals give an accurate picture of the person's performance.

Written Records
Maintain written records on behaviors leading to dismissal.

Written Warning
Warn employee in writing before dismissal.

Group Involvement
Involve more than one person in the termination decision.

Grounds for Dismissal
Put grounds for dismissal in writing.

Figure 16-3 | *Criteria for Evaluating Just Cause and Due Process*

Just-Cause Determinants

- Was the employee warned of the consequences of the conduct?
- Was the employer's rule reasonable?
- Did management investigate before disciplining?
- Was the investigation fair and impartial?
- Was there evidence of guilt?
- Were the rules and penalties applied evenhandedly?
- Was the penalty reasonable, given the offense?

Due Process Considerations

- How have precedents been handled?
- Is a complaint process available?
- Was the complaint process used?
- Was retaliation used against the employee?
- Was the decision based on facts?
- Were the actions and processes viewed as fair by outside entities?

mal circumstances, an employee who resigns rather than being dismissed cannot later collect damages for violation of legal rights. An exception to this rule occurs when the courts find that the working conditions were made so intolerable as to *force* a reasonable employee to resign.[14] Then, the resignation is considered a discharge. For example, an employee was told he should resign but refused. He was then given lesser assignments, publicly ridiculed by his supervisor, and threatened each day with dismissal. He finally resigned, sued his employer, and won the lawsuit because he had been "constructively discharged."

Just Cause

> **Just cause** Reasonable justification for taking employment-related action.

Just cause is reasonable justification for taking employment-related action. A "good reason" or just cause for disciplinary actions such as dismissal can usually be found in union contracts, but not in at-will situations. The U.S. has different just-cause rules than do some other countries.[15] Even though definitions of *just cause* vary, the overall concern is fairness. To be viewed by others as *just,* any disciplinary action must be based on facts in the individual case.

One case involving a female employee with three years' experience illustrates how just cause can be interpreted. After taking most of her maternity leave, she was told two weeks before her return that she was being terminated due to a business slowdown. The company said she was among 23 employees fired because of poor performance. Yet the employee had received pay increases and a promotion, had never had any performance problems documented, and was replaced by a full-time employee. Pointing to these facts, the court ruled that the employee could sue the company.[16]

Due Process

> **Due process** Requirement that the employer use fair means to determine employee wrongdoing and/or disciplinary measures, and that the employee have an opportunity to explain and defend his or her actions.

Due process, like just cause, is about fairness. **Due process** is the requirement that the employer use fair means to determine employee wrongdoing and/or disciplinary measures, and that the employee have an opportunity to explain and defend his or her actions. Figure 16-3 shows some factors to be considered when evaluating just cause and due process. How HR managers and their employers address these factors figures prominently in whether the courts perceive employers' actions as fair.

Employees' perceptions of fairness or justice in their treatment depend on at least two other factors. First, people obviously prefer *favorable outcomes* for themselves. They decide the favorability of their outcomes by comparing them with the outcomes of others, given their relative situations. This decision involves the concept of **distributive justice,** which deals with the question, Were outcomes distributed fairly? Fairness would not include disciplinary action based on favoritism when some are punished and others are not. Therefore, often fairness is dependent on employee perceptions.[17]

Distributive justice
Perceived fairness in the distribution of outcomes.

The second factor, procedural justice, focuses on whether the *procedures* that led to an action were appropriate, were clear, and provided an opportunity for employee input. **Procedural justice** deals with the question, Was the decision-making process fair? Due process is a key part of procedural justice when making promotion, pay, discipline, and other HR decisions.[18] If organizations provide procedural justice, employees tend to respond with positive behaviors that benefit the organization in return. For instance, one study found that procedural justice was a key factor in the level of trust subordinates had in their managers.[19]

Procedural justice
Perceived fairness of the processes used to make decisions about employees.

Complaint Procedures and Due Process In most cases, the complaint procedures used to provide due process for unionized employees differ from those for non-union employees. For unionized employees, due process usually refers to the right to use the grievance procedure specified in the union contract. Due process may involve including specific steps in the grievance process, imposing time limits, following arbitration procedures, and providing knowledge of disciplinary penalties. More discussion of the grievance process and procedures in unions can be found in Chapter 17.

Due process procedures for at-will employees are more varied and may address a broader range of issues. Many organizations, especially smaller ones, use an "open door" policy. This policy means that anyone with a complaint can talk with a manager, an HR representative, or an executive. Often, however, the door is not really open, especially if criticisms or conflicts are part of the complaint. Therefore, non-union organizations generally benefit from having formal complaint procedures that provide due process for their employees.[20] Just the presence of such a formal complaint mechanism provides one indicator that an employee has been given due process. Further, if employees view a due process procedure as fair and available for use, they may be less likely to sue their employers or quit their jobs. The HR Perspective discusses research that supports this view.

ALTERNATIVE DISPUTE RESOLUTION (ADR) AS DUE PROCESS

Disputes between management and employees over different work issues are normal and inevitable. How the parties resolve their disputes becomes important. Formal grievance procedures and lawsuits provide two resolution methods. However, more and more companies look to alternative means of ensuring that due process occurs in cases involving employee rights. Employers that handle disputes effectively have lower legal costs and faster resolution times.[21] Dissatisfaction with the expenses and delays that are common in the court system when lawsuits are filed explains the growth in alternative dispute resolution (ADR) methods such as arbitration, peer review panels, and ombudsmen.

Workplace Effects of Employees' Perceived Mistreatment

The effects of employee perceptions of workplace treatment have been widely discussed. A study by Boswell and Olson-Buchanan published in the *Academy of Management Journal* provided some interesting insights.

The researchers received over 400 surveys from staff employees at a university. Those surveyed were asked if they had experienced unfair treatment at work in the previous year, and if so, they were asked how they had responded. Information about their lengths of service, supervisory relationships, and loyalty was assessed.

Analyses revealed that the filing of grievances was related to both perceived and actual workplace mistreatment. It was found that individuals who felt mistreated were more likely to leave the university than those who had not been treated unfairly. Those with longer tenure, more loyalty, and greater supervisory support were less likely to leave. Those who had filed grievances were no more likely to leave than those who felt mistreated but had not filed a grievance. However, those who perceived personal mistreatment who said things such as, "The supervisor did not like me," "Everything I did was wrong," "She would embarrass me," or "I was told I was not sick when I took sick leave," were much more likely to withdraw from work.

The authors of the study concluded that grievance systems are supposed to provide an outlet for voicing concerns about mistreatment. However, filing a grievance does not seem to change the rate at which people who perceive that they were mistreated choose to leave the organization. If a grievance system is supposed to help an organization retain workers, it is not as effective as expected.[22]

Arbitration

Disagreements between employers and employees often mean lawsuits and large legal bills for settlement. One study found that most employees who believe they have experienced unfair discrimination do not get legal counsel.[23] However, their discontent and complaints are likely to continue. Consequently, to settle disputes, a growing number of employers are using arbitration in non-union situations.

Arbitration is a process that uses a neutral third party to make a decision, thereby eliminating the necessity of using the court system. Arbitration has been a common feature in union contracts. However, it must be set up carefully if the employers want to use it in non-union situations.[24]

Some firms use *compulsory arbitration,* which requires employees to sign a pre-employment agreement stating that all disputes will be submitted to arbitration, and that employees waive their rights to pursue legal action until the completion of the arbitration process.

Because employers often select the arbitrators, and because arbitrators may not be required to issue written decisions and opinions, many critics see the use of arbitration in employment-related situations as unfair.[25]

Continuing pressure from state courts, federal employment regulatory commissions, and additional cases have challenged the fairness of compulsory arbitration in some situations. A U.S. Supreme Court decision in *Circuit City v. Adams* held that requiring arbitration as a condition of employment is legal. However, in a later case, *EEOC v. Waffle House,* the Supreme Court ruled that the EEOC could intervene despite an arbitration ruling.[26]

Arbitration
Process that uses a neutral third party to make a decision.

LOGGING ON...

American Arbitration Association
Information and resources on arbitration can be found at this Web site.
www.adr.org

Peer Review Panels

Some employers allow their employees to appeal disciplinary actions to an internal committee of employees. This panel reviews the actions and makes recommendations or decisions. Panel members are specially trained volunteers who sign confidentiality agreements, after which the company empowers them to hear appeals. Eastman Kodak uses peer review panels as part of its Resolution Support Services Program. Employees from all parts of the company serve as panel members.[27]

Peer review panels can serve as the last stage of a formal complaint process for non-union employees, and their use has reduced the likelihood of unhappy employees' filing lawsuits. If an employee does file a lawsuit, the employer presents a stronger case if a group of the employee's peers previously reviewed the employer's decision and found it to be appropriate. In general, these panels reverse management decisions much less often than might be expected.

Ombuds

Some organizations ensure process fairness through ombuds, who are individuals outside the normal chain of command that act as problem solvers for both management and employees. At Shell Oil, Coors Brewing, and other firms, ombuds have effectively addressed complaints about unfair treatment, employee/supervisor conflicts, and other workplace behavior issues.[28] Ombuds address employees' complaints and operate with a high degree of confidentiality. Any follow-up to resolve problems is often handled informally, except when situations include unusual or significant illegal actions.

▌▌ BALANCING EMPLOYER SECURITY CONCERNS AND EMPLOYEE RIGHTS

LOGGING ON...

Privacy and American Business
This nonprofit organization is a leading resource for information on new and existing business privacy issues.
www.pandab.org

Right to privacy
An individual's freedom from unauthorized and unreasonable intrusion into their personal affairs.

Employees join organizations in the U.S. and some other countries with certain rights, including *freedom of speech, due process,* and *protection against unreasonable search and seizure.* Although the U.S. Constitution grants these and other rights to citizens, over the years, laws and court decisions have identified limits on them in the workplace. For example, an employee who voices threats against other employees may face disciplinary action by the employer without the employee's freedom of speech being violated.

But balancing employer and employee rights is becoming more difficult. On one side, employers have a legitimate need to ensure that employees are performing their jobs properly in a secure environment. On the other side, employees expect the rights that they have both at work and away from work to be protected.

The **right to privacy** is defined in legal terms as an individual's freedom from unauthorized and unreasonable intrusion into personal affairs. Although the right to privacy is not specifically identified in the U.S. Constitution, a number of past Supreme Court cases have established that such a right must be considered. Also, several states have enacted right-to-privacy statutes. A scope of privacy concerns exists in other countries as well, as the HR Globally discussion explains. HR policies and priorities in organizations are specifically affected by such issues as access to employee records, employees' freedom of speech, workplace monitoring, employer investigations, and substance abuse and drug testing.

European Union Data-Protection Directive

The European Union (EU) has been a leader in addressing privacy concerns of its citizens. In 1998, the EU Data-Protection Directive was enacted to require organizations to protect personal data. The directive has wide-ranging consequences for government entities, Internet providers, health-care providers, and employers. The directive goes so far as to forbid the transfer of personal data to countries outside the EU if data-privacy safeguards and guarantees do not exist. The directive is affecting multi-national firms in both business and employee matters. The EU has investigated and/or filed complaints against United Airlines, Microsoft, Ford, Marriott, and numerous other global firms for violating the provisions of the directive. As it affects employee data and records, the directive states the following:

♦ Personal data can be gathered only for identified reasons.

♦ Individuals must receive information about who receives and processes their data and why the data are being gathered.

♦ Persons have the right to access the data collected about them and to change, delete, or correct these details.

♦ Legal actions may be taken by individuals for misuse of their personal data.

These four provisions have significant implications for employer recordkeeping processes, including who accesses data, what data is collected, and how it is used. As the directive is implemented in all EU countries, including the 10 new members admitted in 2004, HR recordkeeping systems and procedures in many companies worldwide will be affected.[29]

Privacy Rights and Employee Records

As a result of concerns about protecting individual privacy rights in the U.S., the Privacy Act of 1974 was passed. It includes provisions affecting HR record-keeping systems. This law applies *only* to federal agencies and to organizations supplying services to the federal government; but similar state laws, somewhat broader in scope, have also been passed. For the most part, state rather than federal law regulates private employers on this issue. In most states, public-sector employees are permitted greater access to their files than are private-sector employees.

Employee Medical Records Recordkeeping and retention practices have been affected by the following provision in the Americans with Disabilities Act:

> *Information from all medical examinations and inquiries must be kept apart from general personnel files as a separate confidential medical record available only under limited conditions specified in the ADA.*

As interpreted by attorneys and HR practitioners, this provision requires that all medical-related information be maintained separately from all other confidential files. The Health Insurance Portability and Accountability Act also contains regulations designed to protect the privacy of employee medical records. As a result of all the legal restrictions, many employers have established several separate files on each employee, as illustrated in Figure 16-4 on the next page.

Security of Employee Records It is important that specific access restrictions and security procedures for employee records be established. These restric-

Figure 16-4 *Employee Record Files*

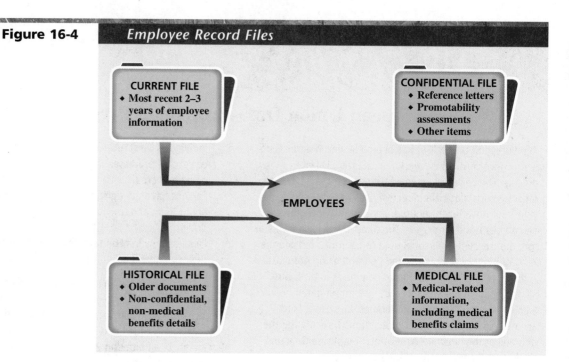

tions and procedures are designed to protect the privacy of employees and to protect employers from potential liability for improper disclosure of personal information. The following guidelines are offered regarding employer access and storage of employee records:

- Restrict access to records to a limited number of individuals.
- Use confidential passwords for accessing employee records in various HRIS databases.
- Set up separate files and restricted databases for especially sensitive employee information.
- Inform employees what types of data are retained.
- Purge employee records of outdated data.
- Release employee information only with employee consent.

Personnel files and records should usually be maintained for three years. However, different types of records should be maintained for shorter or longer periods of time because of various legal and regulatory standards.[30]

Employees' Free Speech Rights

The right of individuals to freedom of speech is protected by the U.S. Constitution. However, that freedom is *not* an unrestricted one in the workplace. Three areas in which employees' freedom of speech have collided with employers' restrictions are controversial views, whistle-blowing, and monitoring of e-mail and voice mail.

Employee Advocacy of Controversial Views Questions of free speech arise over the right of employees to advocate controversial viewpoints at work. Numerous examples can be cited. For instance: Can an employee of a tobacco company join in anti-smoking demonstrations outside of work? and Can a disgruntled employee at a non-union employer wear a union badge on his cap at work? In one U.S. case, a court decision ruled against a white worker who displayed Confederate flags on his toolbox, which offended some African American employees.[31] The court said that the worker's free speech right was not violated when the employer fired him for refusing to remove the flags. In situations such as these, employers must follow due process procedures and demonstrate that disciplinary actions taken against employees can be justified by job-related reasons.

Whistle-Blowing Individuals who report real or perceived wrongs committed by their employers are called **whistle-blowers.** The reasons why people report actions that they question vary, and are often individual in nature.[32] Many well-known whistle-blowing incidents have occurred in the past several years at companies such as Enron, Adelphia Communications, and WorldCom. For instance, a former employee of Warner-Lambert reported that the pharmaceutical firm used illegal means to market an epilepsy drug. The employee won a lawsuit that cost the firm millions of dollars.[33]

The culture of the organization often affects the degree to which employees report inappropriate or illegal actions internally or resort to using outside contacts.[34] Employers need to address two key questions in regard to whistle-blowing: (1) When do employees have the right to speak out with protection from retribution? and (2) When do employees violate the confidentiality of their jobs by speaking out? Even though the answers may be difficult to determine, retaliation against whistle-blowers clearly is not allowed, according to numerous court decisions.

Whistle-blowers are less likely to lose their jobs in public employment than in private employment, because most civil service systems follow rules protecting whistle-blowers. However, no comprehensive whistle-blowing law fully protects the right to free speech of both public and private employees.

Monitoring of E-mail and Voice Mail Employers increasingly have a right to monitor what is said and transmitted through their e-mail and voice-mail systems, despite employees' concerns about free speech. Advances in information and telecommunications technology have become a major issue for employers regarding employee privacy.[35] The use of e-mail and voice mail increases every day, along with employers' liability if they improperly monitor or inspect employees' electronic communications. Many employers have specialized software that can retrieve deleted e-mail, and even record each keystroke made on their computers.

There are recommended actions for employers to take when monitoring e-mail and voice mail. Those actions include creating an *electronic communications policy* and getting employees to sign a *permission form.* With those steps in place, employers should monitor only for business purposes and should strictly enforce the policy.

One problem with both e-mail and voice mail is that most people express themselves more casually than they would in formal memos. This tendency can create sloppy, racist, sexist, or otherwise defamatory messages. For example, Chevron settled out of court with some female employees for $2.2 million over a widely circulated internal e-mail that listed reasons why beer is better than women.[36] Other cases have been brought over jokes that were forwarded that had profanity or racial undertones. Another problem is that e-mail messages can be

THOMSON
WEST

E-MAIL COMMUNICATIONS POLICY
Provides sample e-mail and electronic communications policy.
Custom Search:
☑ FORMS AND POLICIES
Exact Phrase: E-mail and communications

Figure 16-5 | *Recommended Employer Actions on E-mail and Voice Mail*

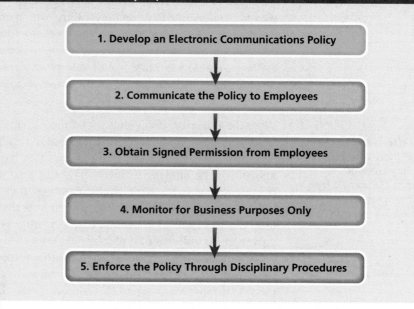

1. Develop an Electronic Communications Policy

2. Communicate the Policy to Employees

3. Obtain Signed Permission from Employees

4. Monitor for Business Purposes Only

5. Enforce the Policy Through Disciplinary Procedures

sent rapidly to multiple (sometimes unintended) recipients. Also, both e-mail and voice mail can be stored, and often legal cases hinge on retrieval of those messages. Figure 16-5 depicts recommended actions.

To address the various concerns regarding monitoring of e-mail and voice mail, many employers have established policies with four elements. Those elements are as follows:

- Voice mail, e-mail, and computer files are provided by the employer and are for business use only.
- Use of these media for personal reasons is restricted and subject to employer review.
- All computer passwords and codes must be available to the employer.
- The employer reserves the right to monitor or search any of the media, without notice, for business purposes.

Workplace Monitoring

The monitoring of e-mail and voice mail is only one illustration of how employers watch the workplace. In the U.S., the right of protection from unreasonable search and seizure protects an individual against activities of the government only. Thus, employees of both private sector and governmental employers can be monitored, observed, and searched at work by representatives of the employer. Several court decisions have reaffirmed the principle that both private-sector and government employers may search desks, files, lockers, and computer files without search warrants if they believe that work rules were violated.

Several forces have led to a growth in workplace monitoring. One major force is the expansion in available technology, ranging from the Internet to global tracking devices to enhanced video capabilities and improved information systems software. Second, the events of 9/11 in 2001 led to passage of the USA Patriot Act, which expanded legislation to allow government investigators to engage in broader monitoring of individuals, including in workplaces, in order to protect national security.[37]

The growing use of technology in organizations is making it more difficult to balance employer security rights with employee privacy concerns.[38] While computers, cameras, and telecommunications systems are transforming many workplaces, the use of these items by employers to monitor employee actions is amplifying concerns that the privacy rights of employees are being threatened.[39] Critics of the Patriot Act have raised specific concerns. Despite the privacy conflicts, many employers are checking on employees by tracking Internet use, monitoring performance, conducting video surveillance, etc.

Tracking Internet Use Many employers have developed and disseminated Internet use policies. Communicating these policies to employees, enforcing them by monitoring employee Internet use, and disciplining offenders are the ways employers ensure that the Internet is used appropriately. These efforts are necessary because about 90% of employees admit to visiting non-work Web sites during work hours and many companies are watching them do it: The numbers vary, but as many as 74% of firms always or sometimes monitor employees' Internet use.[40]

Through such monitoring, employers attempt to guard against some employees' accessing pornographic or other Web sites that could create problems for the employers. If law enforcement investigations find evidence of such access, the employer could be accused of aiding and abetting illegal behavior. Therefore, many employers have purchased software that tracks the Web sites accessed by employees. Also, some employers use software programs for blocking certain categories and Web sites that are inappropriate for business use.

Monitoring Employee Performance Employee activity may be monitored to measure performance, ensure performance quality and customer service,

"Oh, can't complain."

check for theft, or enforce company rules or laws. The common concerns in a monitored workplace usually center not on whether or not monitoring should be used, but on how it should be conducted, how the information should be used, and how feedback should be communicated to employees.[41]

At a minimum, employers should obtain a signed employee consent form that indicates that performance will be monitored regularly and phone calls will be taped regularly. Also, it is recommended that employers provide employees with feedback on monitoring results to help employees improve their performance and to commend them for good performance. For example, one major hotel reservation center allows employees to listen to their customer service calls and rate their own performance. Then, the employees meet with their supervisors to discuss both positive and negative performance issues.

Conducting Video Surveillance at Work Numerous employers have installed video surveillance systems in workplaces. Some employers use these systems to ensure employee security, such as in parking lots, garages, and dimly lit exterior areas. Other employers have installed them on retail sales floors and in production areas, parts and inventory rooms, and lobbies. When video surveillance is extended into employee restrooms, changing rooms, and other more private areas, employer rights and employee privacy collide. As with other forms of monitoring, it is important that employers develop a video surveillance policy, inform employees about the policy, perform the surveillance only for legitimate business purposes, and strictly limit those who view the surveillance results.

Employer Investigations

Another area of concern regarding employee rights involves workplace investigations. The U.S. Constitution protects public-sector employees in the areas of due process, search and seizure, and privacy at work, but private-sector employees are not protected. Whether on or off the job, unethical or illegal employee behavior can be a serious problem for organizations. Employee misconduct may include illegal drug use, falsification of documents, misuse of company funds, disclosure of organizational secrets, workplace violence, employment harassment, and theft.

Another problem faced by employers is *employee theft* of property and vital company secrets. Retailers are estimated to lose over $12 billion a year to employee theft. White-collar theft through embezzlement, accepting bribes, and stealing company property is a growing concern.[42] If the organizational culture encourages or allows questionable behavior, then employees are more likely to see theft as acceptable.[43]

Employee theft and other workplace misconduct can be addressed using a number of methods, as Figure 16-6 indicates. Besides watching current employees through the various types of surveillance and monitoring, firms may screen applicants through means such as honesty testing and background checks, in order to avoid hiring individuals who are more likely to violate workplace standards of conduct.

Honesty and Polygraph Tests Pencil-and-paper honesty tests are alternatives to polygraph testing. These tests are widely used, particularly in the retail industry and in other selected industries, and more than two dozen variations of them are available. However, their use has been challenged successfully in some court decisions.

THOMSON

WEST

INVESTIGATING MISCONDUCT
Provides guidelines for investigating charges of employee misconduct.
Custom Search:
☑ ANALYSIS
Exact Phrase: Investigating employee misconduct

Figure 16-6	Means Used to Reduce Employee Theft and Misconduct	
Before Hire		**After Hire**
◆ Applicant screening		◆ Workplace monitoring
◆ Honesty testing		◆ Review of unusual behavior changes
◆ Background investigation		◆ Selective use of polygraph testing

For current employees, polygraph testing (performed with lie detectors) is used by some organizations. The Employee Polygraph Protection Act prohibits the use of polygraphs for most pre-employment screening. The act also requires that employees must:

◆ Be advised of their rights to refuse to take a polygraph exam
◆ Be allowed to stop the exam at any time
◆ Not be terminated because they refuse to take a polygraph test or solely because of the exam results

Reviewing Unusual Behavior Another method of addressing workplace conduct is to review unusual behavior on and off the job. For instance, if an employee is suddenly wearing many new clothes and spending lavishly, inquiries as to the reasons why and the resources used might be warranted. In one case, inquiries at a county government office revealed that the county clerk had "borrowed" over $50,000 to purchase numerous items and take several trips to gambling destinations. In such situations, care should be taken during the review.

Conducting Work-Related Investigations Workplace investigations are frequently conducted using technology. Technological advances allow employers to review e-mails, access computer logs, conduct video surveillance, and use other investigative tactics. When using audiotaping, wiretapping, and other electronic methods, care should be taken to avoid violating privacy and legal regulations.[44]

Workplace investigations can be conducted internally or externally. Often, HR staff and company security personnel lead internal investigations. Until recently, the use of outside investigators—the police, private investigators, attorneys, or others—was restricted by the Fair Credit Reporting Act. However, passage of the Fair and Accurate Credit Transactions (FACT) Act changed the situation. Under FACT, employers can hire outside investigators without first notifying the individuals under investigation or getting their permission.[45]

Substance Abuse and Drug Testing

Employee substance abuse and drug testing have received a great deal of attention. Concern about substance abuse at work is appropriate given that absenteeism, accident/damage rates, health-care expenses, and theft/fraud are higher for workers using illegal substances or misusing legal substances such as drugs and alcohol. Figure 16-7 identifies some of the financial effects of substance abuse. Ways to address substance abuse problems were discussed in Chapter 15; employee rights concerns of those means are discussed in the following sections.

Drug-Free Workplace Act of 1988 The U.S. Supreme Court has ruled that certain drug-testing plans do not violate the Constitution. Private-employer programs are governed mainly by state laws, which can be a confusing hodgepodge.

Figure 16-7

How Substance Abuse Affects Employers Financially

Increased Absenteeism	♦ Pay for absent person ♦ Pay for fill-in staff
Increased Accidents/Damage	♦ Downtime ♦ Medical expenses ♦ Wages of temporary employees ♦ Replacement of damaged equipment ♦ Legal/investigation fees
Increased Health-Care Needs	♦ Increased insurance costs ♦ Employee time lost ♦ Administrative costs
Increased Theft/Fraud	♦ Unproductive hours ♦ Replacement of stolen items ♦ Fees for hiring of security services ♦ Legal fees and investigative costs

The Drug-Free Workplace Act of 1988 requires government contractors to take steps to eliminate employee drug use. Failure to do so can lead to contract termination. Tobacco and alcohol do not qualify as controlled substances under the act, and off-the-job drug use is not included. Additionally, the U.S. Department of Transportation (DOT) requires regular testing of truck and bus drivers, train crews, mass-transit employees, airline pilots and mechanics, pipeline workers, and licensed sailors.

Drug Testing and Employee Rights Unless state or local law prohibits testing, employers have a right to require applicants or employees to submit to a drug test. Pre-employment drug testing is widely used.

Where employers conduct drug testing of current employees, they use one of three policies: (1) random testing of everyone at periodic intervals, (2) testing only in cases of probable cause, or (3) testing after accidents.

If testing is done for probable cause, it needs to be based on performance-related consequences, such as excessive absenteeism or reduced productivity, not just the substance usage itself. From a policy standpoint, it is most appropriate to test for drugs when the following conditions exist:

♦ Job-related consequences of the abuse are severe enough that they outweigh privacy concerns.
♦ Accurate test procedures are available.
♦ Written consent of the employee is obtained.
♦ Results are treated confidentially, as are any medical records.
♦ Employer has a complete drug program, including an employee assistance program (EAP).

Employee Rights and Personal Behavior

An additional area in which employer and employee rights may conflict concerns personal behavior off the job. Employers encounter special difficulty in es-

LOGGING ON...

Institute for a Drug-Free Workplace
This Web site provides employers with information on maintaining a drug-free workplace, including the state and federal laws regarding drug testing.
www.drugfreeworkplace.org

tablishing "just cause" for disciplining employees for their off-the-job behavior. Most people believe an employer should not control the lives of its employees off the job except in the case of clear job-related consequences. For example, what should an employer do if an employee is an acknowledged transvestite, a member of an activist environmental group, a leader in a racist group, or an exotic dancer on weekends? These are just a few cases in which employee rights and personal behaviors can conflict with employer expectations.

Numerous legal issues have been addressed in various lawsuits by employees.[46] If an employer investigates deeply into an employee's personal life, an "invasion-of-privacy" claim can result. However, failure to investigate could jeopardize necessary and legal disciplinary actions that should be taken by employers.

HR POLICIES, PROCEDURES, AND RULES

Policies General guidelines that focus organizational actions.

Procedures Customary methods of handling activities.

Rules Specific guidelines that regulate and restrict the behavior of individuals.

HR policies, procedures, and rules greatly affect employee rights (just discussed) and discipline (discussed next). Where there is a choice among actions, **policies** act as general guidelines that focus organizational actions. Policies are general in nature, whereas procedures and rules are specific to the situation. The important role of policies requires that they be reviewed regularly.

Procedures provide customary methods of handling activities and are more specific than policies. For example, a policy may state that employees will be given vacations according to years of service, and a procedure establishes a specific method for authorizing vacation time without disrupting work.

Rules are specific guidelines that regulate and restrict the behavior of individuals. They are similar to procedures in that they guide action and typically allow no discretion in their application. Rules reflect a management decision that action be taken—or not taken—in a given situation, and they provide more specific behavioral guidelines than do policies.

Responsibilities for HR Policies, Procedures, and Rules

For HR policies, procedures, and rules to be effective, coordination between the HR unit and operating managers is vital. As Figure 16-8 shows, managers are the main users and enforcers of rules, procedures, and policies, and they should receive some training and explanation in how to carry them out. The HR unit

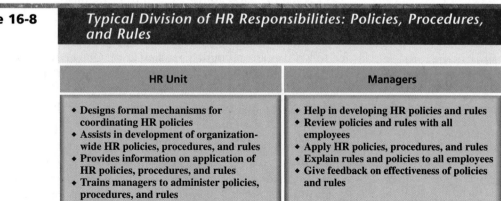

Figure 16-8   *Typical Division of HR Responsibilities: Policies, Procedures, and Rules*

HR Unit	Managers
• Designs formal mechanisms for coordinating HR policies • Assists in development of organization-wide HR policies, procedures, and rules • Provides information on application of HR policies, procedures, and rules • Trains managers to administer policies, procedures, and rules	• Help in developing HR policies and rules • Review policies and rules with all employees • Apply HR policies, procedures, and rules • Explain rules and policies to all employees • Give feedback on effectiveness of policies and rules

supports managers, reviews policies and disciplinary rules, and trains managers to use them. Often policies, procedures, and rules are provided in employee handbooks.

Employee Handbooks

Employee handbooks give employees a reference source for company policies and rules and can be a positive tool for effective management of human resources. Even small organizations can prepare handbooks relatively easily using available computer software. When preparing handbooks, management should consider legal issues, readability, and use.

Legal Review of Language As mentioned earlier, there is a current trend of using employee handbooks against employers in lawsuits charging a broken "implied" contract. This tendency should not eliminate the use of employee handbooks as a way of communicating policies to employees. In fact, not having an employee handbook with HR policies spelled out can leave an organization open to costly litigation and out-of-court settlements. A more sensible approach is to first develop sound HR policies and employee handbooks to communicate them, and then have legal counsel review the language contained in them. Recommendations include the following:

- *Eliminate controversial phrases.* For example, the phrase "permanent employee" may be used to describe a person who has passed a probationary period. This wording can lead to disagreement over what the parties meant by "permanent." A more appropriate phrase is "regular employee."
- *Use disclaimers.* Courts generally uphold disclaimers, but only if they are prominently shown in the handbook. To ensure that disclaimers do not negate the positive image presented by the handbook, they should not be overused. A disclaimer in the handbook can read as follows:

    This employee handbook is not intended to be a contract or any part of a contractual agreement between the employer and the employee. The employer reserves the right to modify, delete, or add to any policies set forth herein without notice and reserves the right to terminate an employee at any time with or without cause.

- *Keep the handbook current.* Many employers simply add new material to handbooks rather than deleting old, inapplicable rules. Those old rules can become the bases for new lawsuits. Consequently, handbooks and HR policies should be reviewed periodically and revised every few years.

Readability The HR specialists who prepare employee handbooks sometimes fail to write at an appropriate reading level. One review of some company handbooks revealed that on average, they were written at the third-year college level, which is much higher than the typical reading level of employees in most organizations. One solution is to test the readability of the handbook on a sample of employees before publishing it.

Use Another important factor to be considered in preparing an employee handbook is how it will be used. In addition to distributing policies and rules in an employee handbook, employers must communicate freely about HR issues, policies, and rules, and disseminate organizational information widely.[47]

To communicate and discuss HR information, a growing number of firms are distributing employee handbooks electronically using an intranet, which enables

THOMSON

WEST

EMPLOYEE HANDBOOKS
Discusses reasons for and problems with having employee handbooks.
Custom Search:
☑ ANALYSIS
Exact Phrase: Employee handbooks: pros and cons

Electronic HR Communications

As electronic and telecommunications systems have developed, many employers have added more technological methods of communicating with employees. With the growth of information systems in organizations and more use of e-mail systems, communications through organizations can be immediate. These operate worldwide through networks. For example, Musicland, a national retailer, provides its store managers weekly newsletters that are printed out for distribution to store employees. Additional news and store project tasks also are sent electronically on a regular basis to store managers and employees.

These systems often result in the bypassing of the formal organizational structure and channels to communicate with employees. The retailer Ikea uses its intranet to disseminate new product details, review company policies, identify job postings, and provide on-line training materials. In break rooms and training rooms at Ikea, there are intranet terminals for employees to use.

Some organizations also communicate using Web-based communication, which links facilities and groups in various locations. This way, technology allows the same message to be delivered simultaneously to various audiences. One retailing company using electronic communications is Limited Brands, whose stores include Victoria's Secret, The Limited, and Bath & Body Works. The Limited's regional and district managers all have laptops and wireless equipment for receiving operational and policy updates. The Limited's system even allows text messages to be sent directly to stores through its cash register system.

Another aspect of HR technology is expanded use of electronic "message boards" on company Web sites. Message boards allow communication among management, employees, and others on issues of concern. They can be useful, but are sometimes problematic if the communication becomes negative, insulting, or even filled with profanity. Thus, technology provides many advantages for HR communications, but some drawbacks as well.[48]

employees to access policies in employee handbooks at any time. It also allows changes in policies to be made electronically rather than distributed as paper copies.

Communicating HR Information

HR communication focuses on the receipt and dissemination of HR data and information throughout the organization. *Downward communication* flows from top management to the rest of the organization, informing employees about what is and will be happening in the organization, and what are the expectations and goals of top management. *Upward communication* enables managers to know about the ideas, concerns, and information needs of employees. Various methods are used to facilitate both types of communication.

Organizations communicate with employees through internal publications and media, including newspapers, company magazines, organizational newsletters, videotapes, Internet postings, and e-mail announcements. Whatever the formal means used, managers should make an honest attempt to communicate information employees need to know. The spread of electronic communications allows for more timely and widespread dissemination of HR information, as the Technology Transforming HR discussion indicates.

Figure 16-9 | *Typical Division of HR Responsibilities: Discipline*

HR Unit	Managers
◆ Designs HR procedures that consider employees' rights ◆ Designs a progressive discipline process in non-union organizations ◆ Trains managers to use the discipline process ◆ Helps managers administer discipline	◆ Are knowledgeable about organizational policies and rules ◆ Make disciplinary decisions ◆ Notify employees who violate policies and rules ◆ Discuss discipline follow-up with employees

EMPLOYEE DISCIPLINE

Discipline Form of training that enforces organizational rules.

The earlier discussion about employee rights provides an appropriate introduction to the topic of employee discipline, because employee rights often are a key issue in disciplinary cases. **Discipline** is a form of training that enforces organizational rules. Those most often affected by the discipline systems are problem employees. Fortunately, problem employees comprise a small number of employees, but they often are the ones who cause the most disciplinary situations. If employers fail to deal with problem employees, negative effects on other employees and work groups often result. Common disciplinary issues caused by problem employees include absenteeism, tardiness, productivity deficiencies, alcoholism, and insubordination.

Figure 16-9 shows a possible division of responsibilities for discipline between the HR unit and operating managers. Notice that managers and supervisors are the ones to make disciplinary decisions and administer the discipline. HR specialists are often consulted before disciplinary action is instituted, and they may assist managers in administering the disciplinary action.

Approaches to Discipline

The disciplinary system can be viewed as an application of behavior modification to problem or unproductive employees. The best discipline is clearly self-discipline. Most people can usually be counted on to do their jobs effectively when they understand what is required at work. Yet some find that the prospect of external discipline helps their self-discipline. One approach is use of positive discipline approach.

Positive Discipline Approach The positive discipline approach builds on the philosophy that violations are actions that can usually be corrected constructively without penalty. In this approach, managers focus on using fact-finding and guidance to encourage desirable behaviors, rather than using penalties to discourage undesirable behaviors. The four steps to positive discipline are as follows:

1. *Counseling:* The goal of this phase is to heighten employee awareness of organizational policies and rules. Often, people simply need to be made aware of rules, and knowledge of possible disciplinary actions may prevent violations.
2. *Written documentation:* If the employee fails to correct her or his behavior, then a second conference becomes necessary. Whereas the first stage took

place as a conversation between supervisor and employee, this stage is documented in written form, and written solutions are identified to prevent further problems from occurring.

3. *Final warning:* If the employee does not follow the written solutions noted in the second step, a final warning conference is held. In that conference, the supervisor emphasizes to the employee the importance of correcting the inappropriate actions. Some firms incorporate a decision day off, in which the employee is given a day off with pay to develop a firm, written action plan to remedy the problem behaviors. The decision day off is used to emphasize the seriousness of the problem and the manager's determination to see that the behavior is changed.

4. *Discharge:* If the employee fails to follow the action plan that was developed, and further problems exist, then the supervisor can discharge the employee.

The advantage of this positive approach to discipline is that it focuses on problem solving. The greatest difficulty with the positive approach to discipline is the extensive amount of training required for supervisors and managers to become effective counselors, and the need for more supervisory time with this approach than with the progressive discipline, which is discussed next.

Progressive Discipline Approach Progressive discipline incorporates steps that become progressively more stringent and are designed to change the employee's inappropriate behavior. Figure 16-10 shows a typical progressive discipline process; most progressive discipline procedures use verbal and written reprimands and suspension before resorting to dismissal. At one manufacturing firm, an employee's failure to call in when he or she will be absent from work may lead to a suspension after the third offense in a year. Suspension sends the

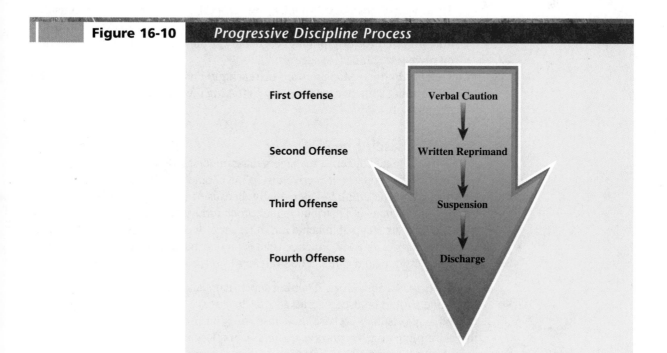

Figure 16-10 *Progressive Discipline Process*

First Offense — Verbal Caution

Second Offense — Written Reprimand

Third Offense — Suspension

Fourth Offense — Discharge

employees a strong message that undesirable job behaviors must change, or termination is likely to follow.

While appearing similar to positive discipline, progressive discipline is more administrative and process-oriented. Following the progressive sequence ensures that both the nature and the seriousness of the problem are clearly communicated to the employee. Not all steps in the progressive discipline procedure are followed in every case. Certain serious offenses are exempted from the progressive procedure and may result in immediate termination. Typical offenses leading to immediate termination include intoxication at work, alcohol or drug use at work, fighting, and theft. However, if a firm has a progressive discipline policy, it should be followed. Several court decisions have ruled that failure to follow written policies for progressive discipline can invalidate an employee's dismissal.[49]

Reasons Why Discipline Might Not Be Used

For a number of reasons, managers may be reluctant to use discipline. Some of the main ones include the following:

- *Organizational culture of avoiding discipline:* If the organizational "norm" is to avoid penalizing problem employees, then managers are less likely to use discipline or to dismiss problem employees.
- *Lack of support:* Many managers do not want to use discipline because they fear that their decisions will not be supported by higher management. The degree of support is also a function of the organizational culture.
- *Guilt:* Some managers realize that before they became managers, they committed the same violations as their employees, and feel that they cannot discipline others for doing something they used to do.
- *Fear of loss of friendship:* Managers may fear losing friendships or damaging personal relationships if they discipline employees.
- *Avoidance of time loss:* When applied properly, discipline requires considerable time and effort. Sometimes, it is easier for managers to avoid taking the time required for disciplining, especially if their actions may be overturned on review by higher management.
- *Fear of lawsuits:* Managers are increasingly concerned about being sued for disciplining someone, particularly for taking the ultimate disciplinary step of termination.

Effective Discipline

Because of legal concerns, managers must understand discipline and know how to administer it properly. Effective discipline should be aimed at the problem behaviors, not at the employee personally, because the reason for discipline is to improve performance. Distributive and procedural justice suggest that if a manager tolerates unacceptable behavior, other employees may resent the unfairness of that tolerance. The HR Practice relates an old management analogy about effective discipline, and offers a helpful way to remember the essentials.

Training of Supervisors Training supervisors and managers in when and how discipline should be used is crucial. Employees see disciplinary action given by trained supervisors who base their responses on procedural justice as more fair than discipline done by untrained supervisors. Regardless of the disciplinary approach used, training in counseling and in communications skills provides su-

Hot-Stove Rule

For many years, the Hot-Stove Rule has been a part of successful training programs designed to teach supervisors about discipline. Good discipline is like a hot stove in these ways:

♦ *It provides a warning.* A hot stove sends a warning in the form of heat that you can feel, and you know that if you touch it, you will be burned. Employees need a warning too before discipline occurs.

♦ *It is consistent.* A hot stove burns every time. Good discipline addresses the same offense under the same circumstances every time it occurs.

♦ *It is immediate.* A hot stove burns immediately if it is touched. The longer after an offense the discipline occurs, the less effective it is in changing behavior.

♦ *It is impersonal.* A hot stove burns anyone who touches it. Good discipline is not emotional or random, and it affects each violator the same.

pervisors and managers with the tools necessary to deal with employee performance problems.

Discharge: The Final Disciplinary Step

The final stage in the disciplinary process is termination. Both the positive and the progressive approaches to discipline clearly provide employees with warnings about the seriousness of their performance problems before dismissal occurs. Terminating workers because they do not keep their own promises is more likely to appear equitable and defensible to a jury.

Termination Process When terminating an employee, it is important to use a well-defined process. The following process, used by one large firm, is typical:[50]

1. *Coordinate manager and HR review:* The disciplining manager, that manager's superior, and an HR representative should review the documentation and make the final determination that the employee will be terminated.

2. *Select a neutral location:* It is generally recommended that termination occur in the HR department or a conference room, not the supervisor/manager's office. This location is not in the department where other employees can observe and is where needed HR documentation is available.

3. *Conduct the termination meeting:* The manager arranges for the employee to go to the termination location, where the HR representative and the manager are. The HR representative or the manager informs the employee of the reason for the termination. Any discussion with the employee should be based on facts and is not subject to change. Throughout the termination discussion, the supervisor and the HR representative should remain professional and calm, rather than becoming emotional or apologetic or making demeaning remarks.

4. *Have HR discuss termination benefits:* The HR representative explains the employee's benefits rights, answers any payroll-related questions, discusses any vacation or accumulated leave, and identifies the amount of the employee's final paycheck. At the same time, the HR representative should re-

"You're Fired—Get Out"

One difficult phase of employee termination is removal of ex-employees and their personal possessions from the company facilities. Both ethical and fairness issues arise in this action.

The standard advice from legal experts is to physically remove the employee as quickly as possible. This is often done by having the employee escorted by security guards out of the building. Some firms allow terminated employees to return to their desks, offices, or lockers to retrieve personal items under the observation of security personnel and the department supervisor/manager. But this means the ex-employee may be seen by and may talk with co-workers while still upset or angry.

Another approach used is that after the HR representative has explained the termination to the employee, the HR representative asks the employee if there is anything immediately needed from a desk or a locker—such as keys, a wallet, a purse, or a coat. The employee is not allowed back into the department; instead, at the same time, their supervisor/manager is excused to go and get the personal effects requested by the employee. The remaining items will be inventoried by the department manager and some

witnesses within 24 hours and boxed up, and then may be picked up from security by the employee or sent directly to the employee's home address.

These methods sound prudent. But what happens if employees are being terminated, not for cause but because jobs are being cut? At one university, employees with 15–20 years' service were told they had to be escorted by security officers back to their offices, get their personal possessions, and be off-campus in one hour. At a large company, employees were given a box and told that they had 30 minutes to get their personal items under the view of security personnel, and that their computer access had been eliminated while they were in the termination meeting. In both situations, the reactions of the ex-employees and the remaining employees were very negative. To them, the removal process showed a lack of trust in long-time employees with satisfactory performance records, who, as one remaining employee said, "were treated like criminals."

How do you view the need to balance legal rights, security, employee morale, and HR policies when removing terminated employees?

trieve the security badge, credit cards, and other company property. Many employers provide a specific letter or memo, which can serve as evidence that the employee was notified of the termination decision and details of benefits rights.

5. *Escort the employee from the building:* This phase is controversial, as the HR Perspective describes. The goal is to ensure that the employee, who is likely to be upset, angry, or emotional, is removed from the premises quickly without obvious conflicts and to prevent any possible concerns about computer or physical security.

6. *Notify the department staff:* The supervisor or manager returns to the department and notifies the department staff that the individual is no longer employed. No details or explanations should be provided, to avoid any long discussions and possible legal ramifications. Also, employees should be informed that if the ex-employee contacts them at work, the person should be referred to the HR department. However, the company cannot control contacts outside of work hours or locations.

Separation Agreements In some termination situations, formal contracts may be used. One type is a **separation agreement,** in which an employee who

Separation agreement Agreement in which a terminated employee agrees not to sue the employer, in exchange for specified benefits.

is being terminated agrees not to sue the employer, in exchange for specified benefits, such as additional severance pay or other "considerations."

For such agreements to be legally enforceable, the considerations usually should be additional items not part of normal termination benefits. For international employees, different legal requirements may exist in various countries, including certain requirements for severance pay and benefits.[51] When using separation agreements, care must be taken to avoid the appearance of constructive discharge of employees. Use of such agreements should be reviewed by a legal counsel.[52]

SUMMARY

- The employment relationship is a reciprocal one in which both employers and employees have statutory and contractual rights, as well as responsibilities.
- Contractual rights can be spelled out in an employment contract or be implied as a result of employer promises.
- Employment-at-will allows employers the right to hire or terminate employees with or without notice or cause.
- Courts are changing aspects of employment-at-will relationships through exceptions for violations of public policy, an implied contract, and good faith and fair dealing.
- Wrongful discharge occurs when an employer improperly or illegally terminates an individual's employment.
- Just cause for employment-related actions should exist. When just cause is absent, constructive discharge may occur, in which the employee is forced to "voluntarily" quit the job.
- Although due process is not guaranteed for the at-will employees, the courts expect to see evidence of due process in employment-related cases.
- Due process is important for both unionized and non-union employees. In non-union situations,

alternative dispute resolution (ADR) means may be used.
- Balancing employer security concerns and employee rights becomes an issue when dealing with access to employee records, free speech, workplace monitoring, employer investigations, and substance abuse and drug testing.
- Employers increasingly are facing privacy and free speech issues in areas such as whistle-blowing and monitoring of e-mail and voice mail.
- Employer investigations must be done to protect both employer and employee rights.
- Drug testing provides a widely used and legal method for employers to deal with increasing drug problems at work.
- To be effective, HR policies, procedures, and rules should be consistent, necessary, applicable, understandable, reasonable, and communicated.
- Courts sometimes view employee handbooks as implied contracts.
- Although employee self-discipline is the goal, positive or progressive discipline is sometimes necessary to encourage self-discipline.
- Managers may fail to discipline for a variety of reasons. However, effective discipline can have positive effects on the productivity of employees.

REVIEW AND APPLICATION QUESTIONS

1. Identify how the issues of due process and just cause are linked to employer disciplinary actions.
2. Discuss the following statement: "Even though efforts to restrict employees' free speech at work may be permissible, such efforts raise troubling questions affecting individual rights."

3. Assume that as the HR Manager, you have decided to prepare some guidelines for supervisors to use when they have to discipline employees. Gather the information needed, using Internet resources, such as *http://hr.blr.com,* and prepare a guide for supervisors on both positive and progressive discipline.

To check your knowledge of the chapter, review the following. (Answers after the supplemental case.) For more questions, see the Study Guide.

1. Employment-at-will is a common-law doctrine stating that employers have the right to hire, fire, demote, or promote whomever they choose unless _____.
   a. the employer is a federal government contractor
   b. there is a law or a contract to the contrary
   c. the employee has seniority over other employees
   d. the employer's action is viewed as unfair by all employees
2. _____ is deliberately making conditions intolerable to get an employee to quit.
   a. Involuntary quit
   b. Mandatory termination
   c. Voluntary resignation
   d. Constructive discharge
3. The concept of _____ focuses on the perceived fairness of the process used to make decisions about employees.
   a. arbitration
   b. distributive justice
   c. procedural justice
   d. constructive discharge
4. A _____ is composed of employees who hear appeals from disciplined employees and make recommendations or decisions.
   a. co-worker resolution panel
   b. discipline committee
   c. employee arbitration jury
   d. peer review panel

CASE
MANAGER ON CAMERA

A retail store was losing cash, but *only* when the surveillance system was turned off. The surveillance system could be turned off only from the manager's office. When the manager went on vacation, a video camera with no audio pickup was placed in his office to see how the system was being deactivated. When he returned from vacation, he noticed the camera and discussed it with the HR department but made no effort to have it removed.

The employer decided to transfer the manager to the same position at a nearby store because he had risen quickly through the ranks at the current store and was experiencing difficulty managing his former co-workers. The employer explained to the manager that the transfer decision was made to give him an opportunity to develop further with the company. The employer offered to give the manager its standard relocation package, or a raise to offset the increased commuting costs.

The manager rejected the transfer and resigned. Then he sued the employer, claiming it had wrongfully monitored his communications and that the transfer was in retaliation for his having raised the issue of his right to privacy. The employer argued that the firm's surveillance practices were legal and that the transfer was in no way an adverse employment action against the manager.

Both the federal and state wiretap laws in this case are clear. They block the secret interception of the transfer of a human voice.[53]

You be the judge.

Questions
1. Do you believe that the company was guilty of an illegal wiretap?
2. Was the company guilty of violating the manager's rights? Why or why not?

(Your instructor can provide the actual decision.)

SUPPLEMENTAL CASE: George Faces Challenges

This case describes the problems facing a new department supervisor when HR policies and discipline have been handled poorly in the past. (For the case, go to http://mathis.swlearning.com/)

Learning Review Answers: 1. b 2. d 3. c 4. d

NOTES

1. Charles Forelle, "On the Road Again, But Now the Boss Is Sitting Beside You," *Wall Street Journal,* May 14, 2004, A1; and "Results from SHRM/Wall Street Journal Workplace Privacy Poll," *www.shrm.org.*

2. Yale D. Tauber and Carol S. Silverman, "Employment Contracts Get the Employers in the Game," *Workspan,* August 2002, 38–42.

3. Michael J. Garrison and Charles D. Stevens, "Sign This Agreement Not to Compete or You're Fired," *Employee Responsibilities and Rights Journal,* September 2003, 103.

4. *Doubleclick v. Henderson,* 1997 WL 731413 (N.Y. Supp.).

5. "Court Affirms Duty-of-Loyalty Injunction Against Two Former Sales Representatives," *Bulletin to Management,* May 15, 2003, 155.

6. Michael Barrier, "Protecting Trade Secrets," *HR Magazine,* May 2004, 53–57.

7. Debbie Harrison, "Is a Long-Term Business Relationship an Implied Contract?" *Journal of Management Studies,* 41 (2004), 107.

8. Dave Lenckus, "EPLI Policy Pays Off for Verizon," *Business Insurance,* April 7, 2003, 28.

9. Jon G. Miller, "Analyzing Employment Practices Liability Insurance," *Compensation and Benefits Review,* November/December 2003, 38.

10. Mark V. Roehling, "The Employment-at-Will Doctrine, Second Level Ethical Issues and Analysis," *Journal of Business Ethics,* 47 (2003), 115–124.

11. Qiang Lin and Brian H. Kleiner, "New Developments Concerning Termination in Violation of Public Policy," *Management Research News,* 26 (2003), 239–247.

12. *Fortune v. National Cash Register Co.,* 373 Mass. 96, 36 N.E.2d 1251 (1977).

13. Carrie Brodzinski, "Avoiding Wrongful Termination Suits," *National Underwriter,* October 13, 2003, 38–39.

14. Robert J. Paul and Kathryn Seeberger, "Constructive Discharge: When Quitting Constitutes Illegal Termination," *Review of Business,* Spring 2002, 23–30.

15. John J. McCall, "A Defense of Just Cause Dismissal Rules," *Business Ethics Quarterly,* April 2003, 151.

16. *Batka v. Prime Charter, Ltd.,* SDNY, No. 2 Civ. 6265 (February 4, 2004), as described in *Workforce Management,* May 2004, 20.

17. Kelly Mollica, "Perceptions of Fairness," *HR Magazine,* June 2004, 169–170.

18. Richard A. Posthuma, "Procedural Due Process and Procedural Justice in the Workplace," *Public Personnel Management,* 32 (2003), 181–195.

19. Julia Connell, Natalie Ferrs, and Tony Travaglione, "Engendering Trust in Manager-Subordinate Relationships: Predictors and Outcomes," *Personnel Review,* 32 (2003), 569–580.

20. Corinne Bendersky, "Organizational Dispute Resolute Systems," *Academy of Management Review,* 28 (2003), 643–656.

21. Richard Nimark, "Getting Dispute-Wise," *Dispute Resolution Journal,* February/April 2004, 56–57.

22. Based on Wendy R. Boswell and Julie B. Olson-Buchanan, "Experiencing Mistreatment at Work," *Academy of Management Journal,* 47 (2004), 129–139.

23. *Fair Play* (Washington, DC: American Arbitration Association, 2003), 2–3.

24. Stella M. Swift, Catherine Jones-Riker, and James Sanford, "Legal and Procedural Strategies for Employees Utilizing Arbitration for Statutory Disputes," *Employee Responsibilities and Rights Journal,* March 2004, 37–47.

25. Stephanie Armour, "Arbitration's Rise Raises Fairness Issue," *USA Today,* June 12, 2001, B1.

26. Gillian Flynn, "Mandatory Arbitration Takes a Hit—but Lives," *Workforce,* May 2002, 70–71.

27. Margaret M. Clark, "A Jury of Your Peers," *HR Magazine,* January 2004, 54–59.

28. Carolyn Hirschman, "Someone to Listen To," *HR Magazine,* January 2003, 47–51.

29. For details, see John D. Woodward Jr. and Gary Roethenbaugh, "Fact Sheet on the European Union Privacy Directive," *www.dss.state.ct.us/digital/eupriv.html;* and Drew Robb, "Restricting Data Flow," *HR Magazine,* April 2003, 97–99.

30. Jonathan A. Segal, "Is It Shredding Time Yet?" *HR Magazine,* February 2003, 109–113.

31. *Dixon v. Coburg Dairy Inc.,* No. 02-1266 (4th Cir. May 30, 2003).

32. Michael J. Gundlach, Scott C. Douglas, and Mark J. Mantinko, "The Decision to Blow the Whistle: A Social Information Processing Framework," *Academy of Management Review,* 28 (2003), 107–123.

33. Jayne O'Donnell, "$26.6M Won't Change Me, Whistle-Blower Says," *USA Today,* May 14, 2004, 2B.

34. Benisa Berry, "Organizational Culture: A Framework and Strategies for Facilitating Employee Whistleblowing," *Employee Responsibilities and Rights Journal,* March 2004, 1.

35. Joan T. A. Gabel and Nancy R. Mansfield, "The Information Revolution and Its Impact on the Employment Relationship," *American Business Law Journal,* 40 (2003), 301–353.

36. Patricia S. Eyres, "Importance High: Employee E-Mail Policies," *Workspan,* December 2002, 52–56.

37. Nancy J. King, "Electronic Monitoring to Promote National Security Impacts Workplace Privacy," *Employee Responsibilities and Rights Journal,* September 2003, 127.

38. Anthony M. Townsend and James T. Bennett, "Privacy, Technology, and Conflict: Emerging Issues and Action in Workplace Privacy," *Journal of Labor Research,* 24 (2003), 195–205.

39. Kirsten Martin and R. Edward Freeman, "Some Problems with Employee Monitoring," *Journal of Business Ethics,* April 2003, 353.

40. "HR Professionals and Privacy Issues," *Workplace Visions,* 1 (2001), 2.

41. Robert H. Moorman and Deborah L. Wells, "Can Electronic Performance Monitoring Be Fair?" *Journal of Leadership and Organizational Studies,* 10 (2003), 2.

42. John M. Ivancevich et al., "Deterring White-Collar Crime," *Academy of Management Executive,* May 2003, 114–127.

43. Robert B. Cialdini, Peta K. Petrova, and Noah J. Goldstein, "The Hidden Costs of Organizational Dishonesty," *MIT Sloan Management Review,* Spring 2004, 67.

44. Louis K. Obdyke, "Investigating Security Breaches, Workplace Theft, and Employee Fraud," *SHRM Legal Report, www.shrm.org.*

45. Gregory M. Davis, "Just the FACT Act, Please," *HR Magazine,* April 2004, 131–138.

46. Stephen D. Sugarman, "Lifestyle Discrimination in Employment," *Berkeley Journal of Employment and Labor Law,* 24 (2003), 377.

47. Ronni M. Travers, "By the Book: The Whys and Hows of Employee Handbooks," *Government Finance Review,* December 2003, 50.

48. Based on Pamela Babcock, "Sending the Message," *HR Magazine,* November 2003, 66–70.

49. Stuart R. Buttrick, "NLRB Punishes Employer for Failing to Follow Progressive Discipline Policy," *Indiana Employment Letter,* January 2004.

50. Provided by Nicholas Dayan, SPHR, and Saralee Ryan.

51. Miguel A. Malo and Joaquin Perez, "Individual Dismissals in Europe and the United States: A Model on the Influence of the Legal Framework on Firing Costs," *European Journal of Law and Economics,* 14 (2003), 47.

52. Jonathan A. Segal, "Get Quid Pro Quo When They Go," *HR Magazine,* December 2003, 121–125.

53. Based on "Life in Front of Camera Does Not Suit Manager," *Bulletin to Management,* July 6, 2000, 216.

CHAPTER 17

Union/Management Relations

After you have read this chapter, you should be able to:

- Describe what a union is and explain why employees join unions.

- Identify several reasons for the decline in union membership.

- Explain the acts that compose the National Labor Code.

- Discuss the stages of the unionization process.

- Describe the typical collective bargaining process.

- Define grievance and explain why a grievance procedure is important for employers.

Offshoring of White-Collar Jobs Gives Unions Traction

Offshoring jobs from the U.S. has given labor unions a new issue to use when attempting to organize workers in some U.S. firms. For example, when Stephen Gentry was laid off from his job located in the U.S. after training his replacement located in India, he became convinced American workers need to band together to fight the offshore loss of jobs. The computer programmer joined a Seattle-based union trying to organize tech industry workers around the country. He felt no loyalty to his employer and that his job was taken by corporate greed.

Such employees may present good opportunities for unions to recruit members because the unions tell employees that they have no employment rights at work unless there is a collective bargaining agreement.

San Antonio–based SBC Communications settled a strike with its unionized employees, and part of the agreement was to work with the union to bring 3,000 company jobs back from the Philippines. That was important for the Communication Workers of America, which, like other unions, had been losing members, clout, and prestige. Fewer than 10% of the private-sector workers in the U.S. are union members today, down from 37% in 1960.

Estimates are that about 830,000 jobs will be sent overseas by the end of 2005 and 3.4 million jobs by 2015. Gentry says that before his layoff, he had a deep aversion to unions. Now, he thinks the union is trying to do what is right. If there are enough examples of winning on the outsourcing issue, a union organizer notes, "why wouldn't people turn to unions? It can be the one issue that will revitalize the labor movement."[1]

"Unions have a place, and as long as management doesn't manage well, you are going to have unions."

—Steve Darien

Union Formal association of workers that promotes the interests of its members through collective action.

A **union** is a formal association of workers that promotes the interests of its members through collective action. The state and nature of union/management relations vary among countries. In the United States, a complex system of laws, regulations, court decisions, and administrative rulings have clearly stated that workers may join unions when they wish to do so. Although fewer workers choose to do so today than before, the mechanisms remain for a union resurgence if employees feel that they need formal representation to deal with management.

▌▌ NATURE OF UNIONS

Employers usually would rather not have to deal with unions because unions constrain what managers can and cannot do in a number of areas. Generally, union workers receive higher wages and benefits than do non-union workers.[2] In turn, unions *can* be associated with higher productivity, although management must find labor-saving ways of doing work to offset the higher labor costs.[3]

Some employers pursue a strategy of good relations with unions. Others may choose an aggressive, adversarial approach. Regardless of the type of employer, several common factors explain why employees unionize.

Why Employees Unionize

As Figure 17-1 shows, the major factors that can trigger unionization are issues of compensation, working environment, management style, and employee treatment. Whether a union targets a group of employees or the employees request union assistance, the union must win support from the employees to become their legal representative. Research over the years has consistently shown that employees join unions for two primary reasons: (1) they are dissatisfied with how they are treated by their employers and (2) they believe that unions can improve

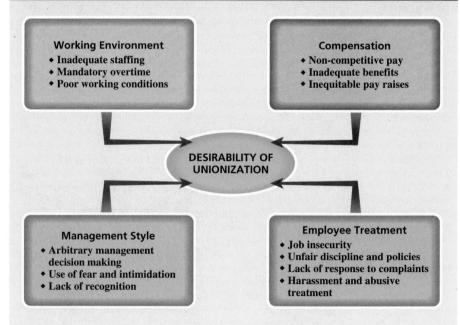

Figure 17-1   *Factors Leading to Employee Unionization*

Working Environment
♦ Inadequate staffing
♦ Mandatory overtime
♦ Poor working conditions

Compensation
♦ Non-competitive pay
♦ Inadequate benefits
♦ Inequitable pay raises

DESIRABILITY OF UNIONIZATION

Management Style
♦ Arbitrary management decision making
♦ Use of fear and intimidation
♦ Lack of recognition

Employee Treatment
♦ Job insecurity
♦ Unfair discipline and policies
♦ Lack of response to complaints
♦ Harassment and abusive treatment

Figure 17-2

Typical Division of HR Responsibilities: Labor Relations

HR Unit	Managers
• Deals with union organizing attempts at the company level • Monitors "climate" for unionization and union relationships • Helps negotiate labor agreements • Provides detailed knowledge of labor legislation as needed	• Promote conditions conducive to positive relationships with employees • Avoid unfair labor practices during organizing efforts • Administer the labor agreement on a daily basis • Resolve grievances and problems between management and employees

their work situations. If employees do not receive what they perceive as fair from their employers, they may turn to unions for help obtaining what they believe is equitable.

When unions leaders are asked by non-union workers, "Why should I join a union?" they respond with a list of reasons. Unions offer employees respect, effective complaint procedures, better wages and benefits, job stability, and security.

The primary determinant of whether employees unionize is management. Reasonably competitive compensation, a good working environment, effective management and supervision, and fair and responsive treatment of workers all act as antidotes to unionization efforts. Unionization results when employees feel disrespected, unsafe, underpaid, and unappreciated, and see a union as a viable option. Once unionization occurs, the union's ability to foster commitment from members and to remain as their bargaining agent depends on how well the union succeeds in providing services that its members want. To prevent unionization, as well as to work effectively with unions already representing employees, both HR professionals and operating managers must be attentive and responsive to employees.

HR Responsibilities with Unions

The pattern of dealing with unionized employees varies among organizations. In some organizations, operating management handles labor relations and HR is minimally involved. In other organizations, the HR unit takes primary responsibility for labor relations. A typical division of responsibilities between the HR unit and operating managers in dealing with unions falls somewhere between these extremes, as shown in Figure 17-2.

Global Labor Union Issues

In some countries, unions either do not exist at all or are relatively weak. Such is the case in China and a number of African countries. In other countries, unions are extremely strong and are closely tied to political parties. For instance, in Italy and France, national strikes occur regularly to protest proposed changes in government policy on retirement, pension programs, and regulations regarding dismissal of employees. The strength of unions in several countries is illustrated in Figure 17-3 on the next page.[4]

Figure 17-3

Union Membership as a Percentage of the Workforce for Selected Countries

Union membership is falling in many advanced countries, but collective bargaining is set in law as the way wages are determined in Europe. In many European countries, artificially high wages and generous benefits have kept the unemployment rate high as well; however, the pressures for change are increasing.[5] The range of labor problems is quite wide and varies from country to country. Child labor is an issue in some countries, whereas changes in participatory employment practices are issues in others.[6]

Co-determination
Practice whereby union or worker representatives are given positions on a company's board of directors.

Some countries require that firms have union or worker representatives on their boards of directors. This practice, called **co-determination,** is common in European countries. Differences from country to country in how collective bargaining occurs also are quite noticeable. In the United States, local unions bargain with individual employers to set wages and working conditions. In Australia, unions argue their cases before arbitration tribunals. In Scandinavia, national agreements with associations of employers are the norm. In France and Germany, industry-wide or regional agreements are common. In Japan, local unions bargain but combine at some point to determine national wage patterns.

Global labor relations standards are being addressed by several organizations. The International Labour Organization, based in Switzerland, coordinates the efforts of labor unions worldwide and has issued some principles and rights at work. Such coordination is increasingly occurring as unions deal with multinational firms having operations in multiple countries.

UNIONS IN THE U.S.

The union movement in the United States has been characterized by some approaches different from those used in other countries. In the United States, the key emphases have been the following:

♦ *Economic issues:* In the United States, unions have typically focused on improving the "bread-and-butter" issues for their members—wages, benefits, job security, and working conditions. In some other countries, political power and activism are equal concerns along with economic issues.

- *Organization by kind of job and employer:* In the United States, carpenters often belong to the carpenters' union, truck drivers to the Teamsters, teachers to the American Federation of Teachers or the National Education Association, etc. Also, unionization can be done on a company-by-company basis. In other countries, national unions bargain with the government or with employer groups.
- *Collective agreements as "contracts":* In the United States, collective bargaining contracts usually spell out compensation, work rules, and the conditions of employment for several years. In other countries, the agreements are made with the government and employers, sometimes for only one year because of political and social issues.
- *Competitive relations:* In the United States, management and labor traditionally take the roles of competing adversaries who often "clash" to reach agreement. In many other countries, "tripartite" bargaining occurs between the national government, employers' associations, and national labor federations.

Union Structure

American labor is represented by many kinds of unions. But regardless of size and geographic scope, two basic types of unions developed over time. In a **craft union,** members do one type of work, often using specialized skills and training. Examples are the International Association of Bridge, Structural, Ornamental and Reinforcing Iron Workers, and the American Federation of Television and Radio Artists. An **industrial union** includes many persons working in the same industry or company, regardless of jobs held. The United Food and Commercial Workers, the United Auto Workers, and the American Federation of State, County, and Municipal Employees are examples of industrial unions.

Labor organizations have developed complex organizational structures with multiple levels. The broadest level is the **federation,** which is a group of autonomous national and international unions. A federation allows individual unions to work together and present a more unified front to the public, legislators, and members. The most prominent federation in the United States is the AFL-CIO, which is a confederation of national and international unions.

National and International Unions National and international unions are not governed by a federation even if they are affiliated with it. They collect dues and have their own boards, specialized publications, and separate constitutions and bylaws. Such national-international unions as the United Steelworkers of America and the American Federation of State, County and Municipal Employees determine broad union policy and offer services to local union units. They also help maintain financial records and provide a base from which additional organizing drives may take place. Political infighting and corruption sometimes pose problems for national unions, as when the federal government stepped in and overturned the results of an election held by the Teamsters Union.

Local Unions Local unions may be centered around a particular employer organization or around a particular geographic location. The membership of local unions elect officers who are subject to removal if they do not perform satisfactorily. For this reason, local union officers tend to be concerned with how they

Craft union One whose members do one type of work, often using specialized skills and training.

Industrial union One that includes many persons working in the same industry or company, regardless of jobs held.

Federation Group of autonomous national and international unions.

are perceived by the union members. They often react to situations as politicians do because their positions depend on obtaining votes. The local unions are the focus and the heart of labor/management relations in most U.S. companies.

Local unions typically have business agents and union stewards. A **business agent** is a full-time union official who operates the union office and assists union members. The agent runs the local headquarters, helps negotiate contracts with management, and becomes involved in attempts to unionize employees in other organizations. A **union steward** is an employee who is elected to serve as the first-line representative of unionized workers. Stewards address grievances with supervisors and generally represent employees at the worksite.

Union Mergers

Like companies, unions find strength in size. In the past several years, about 40 mergers of unions have occurred, and a number of other unions have considered merging. For smaller unions, these mergers provide financial and union-organizing resources. Larger unions can add new members to cover managerial and administrative costs without spending funds to organize non-union workers to become members.[7]

UNION MEMBERSHIP IN THE UNITED STATES

The statistics on union membership tell a disheartening story for organized labor in the United States over the past several decades. As shown in Figure 17-4, unions represented over 30% of the workforce from 1945 to 1960. But by 2004, unions in the United States represented less than 14% of all civilian workers and

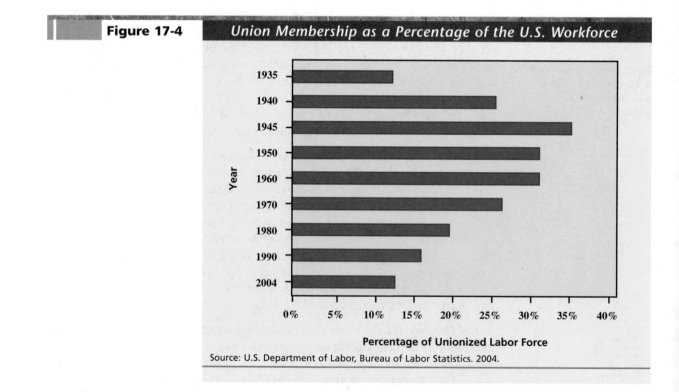

Figure 17-4   *Union Membership as a Percentage of the U.S. Workforce*

Source: U.S. Department of Labor, Bureau of Labor Statistics. 2004.

only 9.5% of the private-sector workforce. Even more disheartening for the unions, the actual number of members has declined in most years even though more people are employed than previously. Of the approximately 120 million U.S. workers, only about 16 million belong to a union.[8]

But within those averages, some unions have prospered. In the past several years, a few unions have organized thousands of janitors, health-care workers, cleaners, and other low paid workers using publicity, pickets, boycotts, and strikes.[9]

Public-Sector Unionism

Unions have had some measure of success with public-sector employees, particularly with state and local government workers. The government sector (federal, state, and local) is the most highly unionized part of the U.S. workforce.

Unionization of state and local government employees presents some unique problems and challenges. First, some employees work in critical service areas. Allowing police officers, firefighters, and sanitation workers to strike endangers public health and safety. Consequently, more than 30 states have laws prohibiting work stoppages by public employees. These laws also identify a variety of ways to resolve negotiation impasses, including arbitration. But unions still give employees in these areas greater security and better ability to influence decisions on wages and benefits.

Although unions in the federal government hold the same basic philosophy as unions in the private sector, they do differ somewhat. Previous Executive Orders and laws established methods of labor/management relations that consider the special circumstances present in the federal government. In the United States, the governmental sector is the only one to see recent growth in union membership.

Reasons for U.S. Union Membership Decline

It is speculated that several issues have contributed to the decline of unions: deregulation, foreign competition, a larger number of people looking for jobs, and a general perception by firms that dealing with unions is expensive compared with non-union alternatives. Also, management at many employers has taken a much more activist stance against unions than during the previous years of union growth.

To some extent, unions may be a victim of their own successes. Unions have emphasized helping workers obtain higher wages, shorter working hours, job security, and safe working conditions from their employers. Some experts and union leaders believe that one cause for the decline of unions has been their success in getting those important issues passed into law for everyone. Therefore, unions are not as necessary for many workers, even though those workers enjoy the results of past union efforts to influence legislation.

Geographic Changes Over the past decade, job growth in the United States has been the greatest in states located in the South, the Southwest, and the Rocky Mountains. Most of these states have "employer-friendly" laws, little tradition of unions, and relatively small percentages of unionized workers.

Another issue involves the movement of many low-skill jobs outside the United States. Primarily to take advantage of cheaper labor, many manufacturers with heavily unionized U.S. workforces have moved a significant number of low-skill jobs to the Philippines, China, Thailand, and Mexico. The passage of the North

American Free Trade Agreement provided a major impetus for moving low-skill, low-wage jobs to Mexico. It removed tariffs and restrictions affecting the flow of goods and services among the United States, Canada, and Mexico. Because of significantly lower wage rates in Mexico, a number of jobs previously suscepti-ble to unionization in the U.S. have been moved there.[10]

Workforce Changes Many of the workforce and economic changes discussed in Chapter 1 have contributed to the decline in union representation of the labor force.[11] The primary growth in jobs in the U.S. economy has been in technology, financial, and other service industries. There are growing numbers of white-collar employees including clerical workers, insurance claims representatives, data input processors, nurses, teachers, mental health aides, computer technicians, loan offi-cers, auditors, and retail sales workers. Unions have increased efforts to organize white-collar workers as advances in technology have boosted their numbers in the workforce. However, unions face a major difficulty in organizing these workers. Many white-collar workers see unions as resistant to change and not in touch with the concerns of the more educated workers in technical and professional jobs. In addition, many white-collar workers exhibit a mentality and set of preferences quite different from those held by blue-collar union members.

The growing percentage of women in the U.S. workforce presents another challenge to unions. In the past, unions have not been as successful in organiz-ing women workers as they have been in organizing men workers. Some unions are trying to focus more on recruiting women members, and unions have been in the forefront in the push for legislation on such family-related goals as child care, maternity and paternity leave, pay equity, and flexible work arrangements. Women in "pink-collar" low-skill service jobs have been somewhat more likely to join unions than women working in white-collar jobs.

Industrial Changes Another cause for the decline of unions is the shift in U.S. jobs from industries such as manufacturing, construction, and mining to service industries. There is a small percentage of union members in the financial services and wholesale/retail industries, the sectors in which many new jobs have been added, whereas the number of industrial jobs continues to shrink. In summary, union membership is primarily concentrated in the shrinking part of the econ-omy, and unions are not making inroads into the fastest-growing segments in the U.S. economy.

A look at Figure 17-5 reveals that non-governmental union members are heav-ily concentrated in transportation, utilities, and other "industrial" jobs. Unions have also targeted workers in the technology industry, specifically those in the dot.coms such as Amazon.com and Webvan. However, the bankruptcies of many dot.coms has made unionization more difficult.

Union Targets for Membership Growth

To attempt to counteract the overall decline in union membership, unions are focusing on a number of industries and types of workers. Some frequently tar-geted groups are professionals, contingent and part-time workers, and low-skill workers.

Professionals Traditionally, professionals in many occupations have been skeptical of the advantages of unionization.[12] However, professionals who have turned to unionization include engineers, physicians, nurses, and teachers. The

Figure 17-5

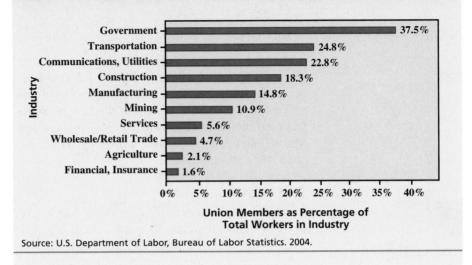

Union Membership by Industry

Union Members as Percentage of
Total Workers in Industry

Source: U.S. Department of Labor, Bureau of Labor Statistics. 2004.

health-care industry has been a specific focus for unionization, and over 50,000 doctors have joined unions. As the number of physicians who were salaried employees (perhaps with HMOs) increased from less than 25% to almost 50%, these professionals joined unions. Another area of union growth in the past few years has been nursing. The primary reason health-care employees consider unions is the growth of managed care and HMOs. A frequent complaint of health-care professionals is that they have lost control of patient-care decisions as a result of managed care and the spreading drive to reduce health-care costs. These complaints have led health-care employees to join unions.

Contingent and Part-Time Workers As many employers have added contingent workers instead of full-time employees, unions have tried to unionize part-time, temporary, and other employees. A decision by the National Labor Relations Board (NLRB) allows temporary workers to be included in firms to be represented by unions. Time will tell if the efforts to unionize part-time workers and other groups will halt the decline of union membership in the United States. When unions are present, collective bargaining agreements frequently limit the amount of contingent labor that may be used.

Low-Skill Workers On the other end of the labor scale, unions have targeted low-skill workers, many of whom have lower-paying, less desirable jobs. Janitors, building cleaners, nursing home aides, and meatpacking workers are examples of groups targeted by unions. For instance, in the health-care industry, workers in nursing homes dealing with the elderly are a fast-growing segment of the workforce. Many employees in this industry are relatively dissatisfied. The industry is often noted for its low pay and hard work, and many employees are women who work as nurse's aides, cooks, and launderers and in other low-wage jobs. Many of these individuals are also immigrants, and unions are targeting immigrant workers in low-skill jobs. Although these efforts are not always successful, unions are likely to continue pursuing industries and employers with numerous low-skill jobs and workers. The advantages of unionization are especially strong for these employees.[13]

HISTORY OF U.S. UNIONS

The evolution of the union movement in the United States began with early collective efforts by workers to address job concerns and counteract management power. As early as 1794, shoemakers organized a union, picketed, and conducted strikes. In those days, unions in the United States received very little support from the courts. In 1806, when the shoemakers' union struck for higher wages, a Philadelphia court found union members guilty of engaging in a "criminal conspiracy" to raise wages.

AFL-CIO

In 1886, the *American Federation of Labor (AFL)* united a number of independent national unions. Its aims were to organize skilled craft workers and to emphasize economic issues and working conditions.

As industrialization increased in the U.S., many factories used semiskilled and unskilled workers. However, it was not until the *Congress of Industrial Organizations (CIO)* was founded in 1938 that a labor union organization focused on semiskilled and unskilled workers. Years later, the AFL and the CIO merged to form a federation, the AFL-CIO. That federation is the major organization coordinating union efforts in the United States today.

LOGGING ON...

AFL-CIO
The AFL-CIO's homepage provides union movement information.
www.aflcio.org

Early Labor Legislation

The right to organize workers and engage in collective bargaining offers little value if workers cannot freely exercise it. Historical evidence shows that management has consistently developed practices calculated to prevent workers from using this right. Over a period of many years, the federal government has taken action to both hamper unions and protect them.

Railway Labor Act (RLA) The Railway Labor Act of 1926 (RLA) represented a shift in government regulation of unions. As a result of a joint effort between railroad management and unions to reduce transportation strikes, this act gave railroad employees "the right to organize and bargain collectively through representatives of their own choosing." In 1936, airlines and their employees were added to those covered by the act. Both railroads and airlines are still covered by this act rather than by other acts passed later.

Some experts believe that some of the labor relations problems in the airline industry stem from the provisions of the RLA, and that those problems would be more easily resolved if the airlines fell within the labor laws covering most other industries.

The RLA mandates a complex and cumbersome dispute resolution process. This process allows either the unions or the management to use the NLRB, a multi-stage dispute resolution process, and even the ability of the President of the U.S. to appoint an emergency board. The end result of having a prolonged process that is subject to political interference has been that unions work for two or more years after the expiration of their old contracts because the process takes so long.

Norris-LaGuardia Act The crash of the stock market and the onset of the Great Depression in 1929 led to massive cutbacks by employers. In some industries,

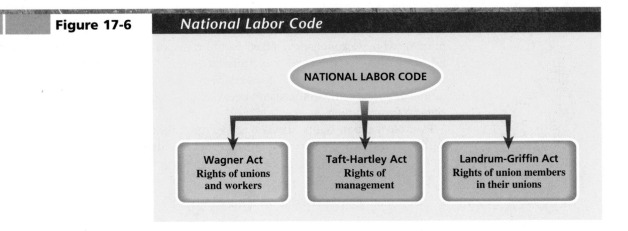

Figure 17-6 *National Labor Code*

the resistance by employees led to strikes and violence. Under laws at that time, employers could go to court and have a federal judge issue injunctions ordering workers to return to work. In 1932, Congress passed the Norris-LaGuardia Act, which guaranteed workers some rights to organize and restricted the issuance of court injunctions in labor disputes.

BASIC LABOR LAW: "NATIONAL LABOR CODE"

The economic crises of the early 1930s and the restrictions on workers' ability to organize into unions led to the passage of landmark labor legislation. Later acts reflected other pressures and issues that required legislative attention.

Three acts, passed over a period of almost 25 years, constitute what has been labeled the "National Labor Code": (1) the Wagner Act, (2) the Taft-Hartley Act, and (3) the Landrum-Griffin Act. Each act was passed to focus on some facet of the relations between unions and management. Figure 17-6 indicates the primary focus of each act. Two other pieces of legislation, the Civil Service Reform Act and the Postal Reorganization Act, also affect various aspects of union/management relations.

Wagner Act (National Labor Relations Act)

The National Labor Relations Act, more commonly referred to as the Wagner Act, has been called the Magna Carta of labor and was, by anyone's standards, pro-union. Passed in 1935, the Wagner Act was an outgrowth of the Great Depression. With employers having to close or cut back their operations, workers were left with little job security. Unions stepped in to provide a feeling of solidarity and strength for many workers. The Wagner Act declared, in effect, that the official policy of the U.S. government was to encourage collective bargaining. Specifically, it established the right of workers to organize unhampered by management interference.

Unfair Labor Practices Unfair labor practices may take many forms, but the filing of complaints about these particular practices has increased for many reasons.[14] For example: Bowling Transportation fired two employees as the result of a situation with AK Steel, which was Bowling's only customer. AK paid its contractors, including Bowling, a bonus of $1.00 for each injury-free hour worked, and encouraged its contractors to pass the bonus along to their employees. Bowling paid its employees only $.50 of each bonus dollar. The two Bowling employees who were unhappy talked to the transportation manager at AK, who asked Bowling to remove the two from the premises of AK. Bowling decided to terminate the two workers and accused them of trying to start a union. The NLRB ultimately ordered them reinstated because the Wagner Act gives employees the right to form a union.[15]

To protect union rights, the Wagner Act prohibited employers from utilizing unfair labor practices. Five of those practices are identified as follows:

- Interfering with, restraining, or coercing employees in the exercise of their right to organize or to bargain collectively
- Dominating or interfering with the formation or administration of any labor organization
- Encouraging or discouraging membership in any labor organization by discriminating with regard to hiring, tenure, or conditions of employment
- Discharging or otherwise discriminating against an employee because he or she filed charges or gave testimony under the act
- Refusing to bargain collectively with representatives of the employees

National Labor Relations Board (NLRB) The Wagner Act established the National Labor Relations Board as an independent entity to enforce the provisions of the act. The NLRB administers all provisions of the Wagner Act and of subsequent labor relations acts. The primary functions of the NLRB include conducting unionization elections, investigating complaints by employers or unions through its fact-finding process, issuing opinions on its findings, and prosecuting violations in court. The five members of the NLRB are appointed by the President of the United States and confirmed by the U.S. Senate.

Taft-Hartley Act (Labor-Management Relations Act)

The passage in 1947 of the Labor-Management Relations Act, better known as the Taft-Hartley Act, addressed the concerns of many who felt that unions had become too strong. As an attempt to balance the collective bargaining equation, this act was designed to offset the pro-union Wagner Act by limiting union actions; therefore, it was considered to be pro-management and became the second part of the National Labor Code.

The new law amended or qualified in some respect all the major provisions of the Wagner Act and established an entirely new code of conduct for unions. The Taft-Hartley Act forbade unions from engaging in a series of unfair labor practices, much like those management was prohibited from engaging in. Coercion, discrimination against non-members, refusing to bargain, excessive membership fees, and other practices were not allowed by unions. A 1974 amendment extended coverage of the Taft-Hartley Act to private, non-profit hospitals and nursing homes.

The Taft-Hartley Act also established the Federal Mediation and Conciliation Service (FMCS) as an agency to help management and labor settle labor contract disputes. The act required that the FMCS be notified of disputes over contract renewals or modifications if they were not settled within 30 days after the designated date.

National Emergency Strikes The Taft-Hartley Act allows the President of the United States to declare that a strike presents a national emergency. A

National Emergency Strike: The West Coast Dock Strike

An interesting strike marked the first time in 25 years that the national emergency provisions of the Taft-Hartley Act had been invoked. The strike was initiated by the International Longshore and Warehouse Union when a labor agreement between the union and the Pacific Maritime Association ended. The union represented 42,000 workers in California, Oregon, Washington, Alaska, and Hawaii. Its members unload a large portion of the materials shipped to the U.S.: four-fifths of the food and merchandise that goes to Hawaii comes by ship, and about 40% of the imports into the entire country come through West Coast docks.

The issues of the dispute were wages and benefits (longshore workers averaged $80,000 a year and supervisors $167,000 a year at the time) and, most importantly, the control of technology and work assignments on the docks. With proposed new technology that was already in use in Europe, trucks would pass under a scanner, bar codes would be read, a cargo list would be printed out, and shippers would be notified of where the shipment was located. The union noted, "Everything is a robot; there won't be any human beings out there." Indeed, use of the new technology had the potential of replacing many of the highly paid union members.

When the contract between the union and the association expired, work continued, with management accusing the union of "slowdown tactics" that eventually led to a "lockout" by management for 36 hours. Estimates were that without the movement of goods, the American economy would lose between $1 billion and $2 billion each day.

The government tried using a mediator to work with the two sides, but negotiations broke down as the union accused the mediator of bringing "armed thugs" into the meeting. The bargaining process deteriorated further, and eventually, President George W. Bush invoked the Taft-Hartley Act and its 80-day "cooling off period." Work resumed, with the union members being unhappy about being forced to work, and management alleging that the union workers were "sluggish"; productivity was very low.

A month and a half later, the sides reached agreement on a new contract paying the average longshore worker $100,000 a year. The six-year contract gave neither side all it wanted on the technology issue, but management was able to begin automating parts of the work.[16]

National emergency strike Strike that would impact the national economy significantly.

Right-to-work laws State laws that prohibit requiring employees to join unions as a condition of obtaining or continuing employment.

Closed shop Firm that requires individuals to join a union before they can be hired.

Open shop Workers are not required to join or pay dues to a union.

national emergency strike is one that would impact an industry or a major part of it in such a way that the national economy would be significantly affected. See the HR Perspective for an example.

Right-to-Work Provision One specific provision of the Taft-Hartley Act, Section 14(b), deserves special explanation. This section allows states to pass laws that restrict compulsory union membership. Accordingly, some states have passed **right-to-work laws,** which prohibit requiring employees to join unions as a condition of obtaining or continuing employment. The laws were so named because they allow a person the right to work without having to join a union.

The nature of union/management relations is affected by the right-to-work provisions. The Taft-Hartley Act generally prohibits the **closed shop,** which is a firm that requires individuals to join a union before they can be hired. Because of concerns that a closed shop allows a union to "control" who may be considered for employment and who must be hired by an employer, Section 14(b) prohibits the closed shop except in construction-related occupations.

In states with right-to-work laws, employers may have an **open shop,** which indicates workers cannot be required to join or pay dues to a union. The states that

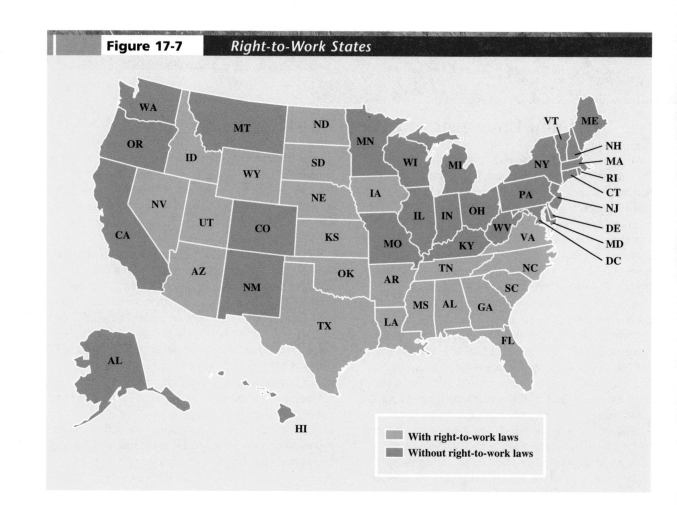

Figure 17-7   *Right-to-Work States*

Legend:
- With right-to-work laws
- Without right-to-work laws

LOGGING ON...

Right-to-Work
This Web site contains information from the National Right to Work Legal Defense Foundation.
www.nrtw.org

have enacted these laws are shown in Figure 17-7. In states that do not have right-to-work laws, the following types of arrangements exist:

- *Union shop:* Requires that individuals join the union, usually 30–60 days after being hired.
- *Agency shop:* Requires employees who refuse to join the union to pay amounts equal to union dues and fees in return for the representation services of the union.
- *Maintenance-of-membership shop:* Requires workers to remain members of the union for the period of the labor contract.

Landrum-Griffin Act (Labor-Management Reporting and Disclosure Act)

The third segment of the National Labor Code, the Landrum-Griffin Act, was passed in 1959. Because a union is supposed to be a democratic institution in which union members vote on and elect officers and approve labor contracts, the Landrum-Griffin Act was passed in part to ensure that the federal government protects the democratic rights of those members. Under the Landrum-Griffin Act, unions are required to establish bylaws, make financial reports, and provide union members with a bill of rights. The law appointed the Secretary of Labor to act as a watchdog of union conduct.

In a few instances, union officers have attempted to maintain their jobs by physically harassing or attacking individuals who have tried to oust them from office. In other cases, union officials have "milked" pension fund monies for their own use. Such instances are not typical of most unions, but illustrate the need for legislative oversight to protect individual union members.

Civil Service Reform Act of 1978

Passed as part of the Civil Service Reform Act of 1978, the Federal Service Labor-Management Relations statute made major changes in how the federal government deals with unions. The act also identified areas subject to bargaining and established the Federal Labor Relations Authority (FLRA) as an independent agency similar to the NLRB. The FLRA, a three-member body, was given the authority to oversee and administer union/management relations in the federal government and to investigate unfair practices in union organizing efforts.

In a somewhat related area, the Postal Reorganization Act of 1970 established the U.S. Postal Service as an independent entity. Part of the 1970 act prohibited postal workers from striking and established a dispute resolution process for them to follow.

UNIONIZATION PROCESS

The typical union organizing process is outlined in Figure 17-8. The process of unionizing an employer may begin in one of two primary ways: (1) a union tar-

Figure 17-8 | *Typical Unionization Process*

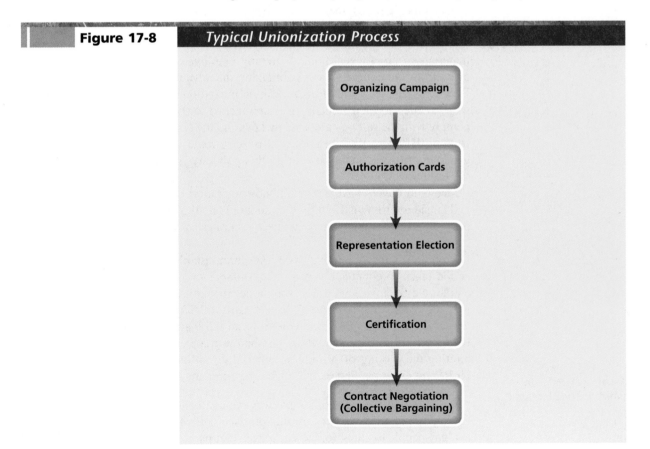

geting an industry or a company, or (2) employees requesting union representation. In the first case, the local or national union identifies a firm or an industry in which it believes unionization can succeed. The logic for targeting is that if the union succeeds in one firm or a portion of the industry, then many other workers in the industry will be more willing to consider unionizing.

In the second case, the impetus for union organizing occurs when individual workers in an employer contact a union and express a desire to unionize. The employees themselves—or the union—may then begin to campaign to win support among the other employees.

Employers may make strategic decisions and take aggressive steps to remain non-union. Such a choice is perfectly rational, but may require some specific HR policies and philosophies. For example, "preventive" employee relations may emphasize good morale and loyalty based on concern for employees, competitive wages and benefits, a fair system for dealing with employee complaints, and safe working conditions. Other issues may also play a part in employees' decisions to stay non-union, but if employers adequately address the points just listed, fewer workers are likely to feel the need for a union to represent them.

Once unionizing efforts begin, all activities must conform to the requirements established by applicable labor laws. Both management and the union must adhere to those requirements, or the results of the effort can be appealed to the NLRB and overturned.

Organizing Campaign

Like other entities seeking members, a union usually mounts an organized campaign to persuade individuals to support its efforts. The persuasion takes many forms, including personally contacting employees outside work, mailing materials to employees' homes, inviting employees to attend special meetings away from the company, and publicizing the advantages of union membership. Brochures, leaflets, and circulars can be passed out to employees as they leave work, mailed to their homes, or even attached to their vehicles, as long as they comply with the rules established by laws and the NLRB. The Technology Transforming HR describes how unions use electronic communications in their organizing efforts. The purpose of all this publicity is to encourage employees to sign authorization cards.

Many employers have a written "no-solicitation" policy to restrict employees and outsiders from distributing literature or soliciting union membership on company premises. Employers without such a policy may be unable to prevent those acts.[17]

A policy against solicitation is a long-term, established approach, not a single action taken to counter a specific and immediate unionization attempt. For example: the Steelworkers union sought certification by the NLRB to be the bargaining agent for the Canton, Ohio, facility of Schuler Engineering. After the union lost the election by one vote, it protested that the company had interfered with the right to organize when, just before the election, it adopted a rule prohibiting the posting of pro-union material on an employee bulletin board. The NLRB set aside the first election, and the company lost the second election.[18]

"Salting" Unions sometimes pay organizers to infiltrate a targeted employer and try to organize workers. In this practice, known as **salting,** the unions hire and pay people to apply for jobs at certain companies; when the people are hired,

Salting Practice in which unions hire and pay people to apply for jobs at certain companies.

Technology Transforming HR

Electronic Organizing Aids Unions

Historically, unions have resisted technology innovations that would displace their members. However, for organizing attempts unions have been quite willing to adopt electronic means, such as establishing Web sites where interested workers can read about benefits of unionization. For instance: The Service Employees International Union has Web sites and chat rooms where nurses at non-union hospitals can exchange information with unionized nurses. The American Federation of Teachers links its publications on educational topics to an on-line wire service for teachers, and provides union information on-line.

E-mail has also changed union organizing efforts. The United Food and Commercial Workers union receives over 100 e-mails in a typical day from workers wanting information on unionization and their rights to union representation. Other unions have gathered the home e-mail addresses of workers who are targets for unionization and sent those workers union solicitation information.

Employers with e-mail restrictions may enforce them when union solicitation e-mails are received, sent, or forwarded using employer-provided systems. But if they do so, they must also restrict all personal, non-business messages for everyone in the organization. For instance, if employees can send a blanket e-mail offering a free dog or advertise a car for sale, then they must be allowed to solicit other employees for union support, according to employment law experts. Thus, e-mail is protected by the NLRB as a "concerted activity." This ruling means that employees using e-mail to protest or comment on employers' actions or the desirability of unionization may be protected unless employers have clear, established, and enforced policies to the contrary.[19]

they begin organizing efforts. The U.S. Supreme Court has ruled that refusing to hire otherwise qualified applicants, even if they are also paid by a union, violates the Wagner Act. However, employers may refuse to hire "salts" for job-related and non-discriminatory reasons.[20]

Authorization Cards

Union authorization card Card signed by an employee to designate a union as her or his collective bargaining agent.

A **union authorization card** is signed by an employee to designate a union as her or his collective bargaining agent. At least 30% of the employees in the targeted group must sign authorization cards before an election can be called.

In reality, the fact that an employee signs an authorization card does not mean that the employee is in favor of a union; it means only that the employee would like the opportunity to vote on having a union. Employees who do not want a union might sign authorization cards because they want management to know they are disgruntled.

Representation Election

An election to determine if a union will represent the employees is supervised by the NLRB for private-sector organizations and by other legal bodies for public-sector organizations. If two unions are attempting to represent employees, the employees will have three choices: union A, union B, and no union.

Bargaining unit Employees eligible to select a single union to represent and bargain collectively for them.

Bargaining Unit Before any election, the appropriate bargaining unit must be determined. A **bargaining unit** is composed of all employees eligible to select a single union to represent and bargain collectively for them. If management and the union do not agree on who is and who is not included in the unit, the regional office of the NLRB must make the determination. A major criterion in deciding the composition of a bargaining unit is what the NLRB calls a "community of interest." At a warehouse distribution firm, delivery drivers, accounting clerks, computer programmers, and mechanics would probably not be included in the same bargaining unit; these employees have widely varying jobs, areas of work, physical locations, and other differences that would likely negate a community of interest. Employees who constitute a bargaining unit have mutual interests in the following areas:

- Wages, hours, and working conditions
- Traditional industry groupings for bargaining purposes
- Physical location and amount of interaction and working relationships between employee groups
- Supervision by similar levels of management

Supervisors and Bargaining Units Provisions of the National Labor Relations Act exclude supervisors from protection when attempting to vote for or join unions. As a result, supervisors cannot be included in bargaining units for unionization purposes, except in industries covered by the Railway Labor Act.

But who qualifies as a supervisor is not always clear. The NLRB uses a detailed definition that identifies a supervisor as any individual with authority to hire, transfer, discharge, discipline, and use independent judgment with employees. Numerous NLRB and court decisions have been rendered on specific situations. A major case decided by the U.S. Supreme Court found that charge nurses with RN degrees were supervisors because they exercised independent judgment.[21] This case and others have provided employers and unions with some guidance about who should be considered supervisors and thus excluded from bargaining units.

Unfair Labor Practices Employers and unions engage in a number of activities before an election. Both the Wagner Act and the Taft-Hartley Act place restrictions on these activities.

Management representatives may use various tactics to defeat a unionization effort. Such tactics often begin when union publicity appears or during the distribution of authorization cards. Some employers hire experts who specialize in combating unionization efforts. Using these "union busters," as they are called by unions, appears to enhance employers' chances of winning the representation election.

Wal-Mart is one company that works hard to avoid unionization. The company says it does not have unions because it takes care of its employees. It surveys employees regularly, and many workers have been promoted from cashier and stocker jobs to management jobs. A company-wide stock ownership program has generated significant long-term returns for employees.

Unions counter that Wal-Mart uses aggressive and even unfair labor practices to prevent unionization. When a union tries to organize workers, the company often reacts with a coordinated "union prevention" program. Mandatory employee meetings are held in stores, where managers and supervisors read prepared scripts explaining the consequences of unionizing and show videos emphasizing the negatives of unionization.

Election Process If an election is held, the union need receive only a *majority of the votes.* For example, if a group of 200 employees is the identified bargain-

Figure 17-9 | *Legal Do's and Don'ts for Managers During the Unionization*

Do (legal)	Don't (illegal)
◆ Tell employees about current wages and benefits and how they compare with those in other firms ◆ Tell employees that the employer opposes unionization ◆ Tell employees the disadvantages of having a union (especially cost of dues, assessments, and requirements of membership) ◆ Show employees articles about unions and relate negative experiences elsewhere ◆ Explain the unionization process to employees accurately ◆ Forbid distribution of union literature during work hours in work areas ◆ Enforce disciplinary policies and rules consistently and appropriately	◆ Promise employees pay increases or promotions if they vote against the union ◆ Threaten employees with termination or discriminate when disciplining employees ◆ Threaten to close down or move the company if a union is voted on ◆ Spy on or have someone spy on union meetings ◆ Make a speech to employees or groups at work within 24 hours of the election (before that, it is allowed) ◆ Ask employees how they plan to vote or if they have signed authorization cards ◆ Encourage employees to persuade others to vote against the union (such persuasion must be initiated solely by employees)

THOMSON

WEST

DECERTIFICATION
Describes what an employer should know about the decertification process.
Custom Search:
☑ ANALYSIS
Exact Phrase: Role in decertification

Decertification
Process whereby a union is removed as the representative of a group of employees.

ing unit, and only 50 people vote, only 26 (50% of those voting plus 1) need to vote yes for the union to be named as the representative of all 200 employees. Typically, the smaller the number of employees in the bargaining unit, the higher the likelihood that the union will win.

If either side believes that the other side used unfair labor practices, the election results can be appealed to the NLRB. If the NLRB finds evidence of unfair practices, it can order a new election. Figure 17-9 lists some common tactics management can use legally and some tactics it cannot use. If no unfair practices were used and the union obtains a majority in the election, the union then petitions the NLRB for certification.

Certification and Decertification

Official certification of a union as the legal representative for designated private-sector employees is given by the NLRB, or for public-sector employees by an equivalent body. Once certified, the union attempts to negotiate a contract with the employer. The employer *must* bargain; refusing to bargain with a certified union constitutes an unfair labor practice.

When members no longer wish to be represented by the union, they can use the election process to sever the relationship between themselves and the union. Similar to the unionization process, **decertification** is a process whereby a union is removed as the representative of a group of employees. Employees attempting to oust a union must obtain decertification authorization cards signed by at least 30% of the employees in the bargaining unit before an election may be called. If a majority of those voting in the election want to remove the union, the decertification effort succeeds. Some reasons that employees decide to vote out a union are that the treatment provided by employers has improved, the union has been unable to address the changing needs of the organizational workforce, or the image of unions has declined. Current regulations prohibit employers from initiating or supporting decertification because it is a matter between employees and unions, and employers must stay out of the process.

Contract Negotiation (Collective Bargaining)

Collective bargaining, the last step in unionization, is the process whereby representatives of management and workers negotiate over wages, hours, and other terms and conditions of employment. This give-and-take process between representatives of the two organizations attempts to establish conditions beneficial to both. It is also a relationship based on relative power.

The power relationship in collective bargaining involves conflict, and the threat of conflict seems necessary to maintain the relationship. But perhaps the most significant aspect of collective bargaining is that it is a continuing relationship that does not end immediately after agreement is reached. Instead, it continues for the life of the labor agreement and beyond. Therefore, the more cooperative management is, the less hostility and conflict with unionized employees carries over to the workplace. However, this cooperation does not mean that the employer should give in to all union demands.

Management/union relations in collective bargaining can follow one of several patterns. Figure 17-10 depicts them as a continuum, ranging from conflict to collusion. On the left side of the continuum, management and the union see each other as enemies. On the right side, the two entities join together in collusion, which is relatively rare in U.S. labor history and is illegal. Most positions fall between these two extremes.

▌ COLLECTIVE BARGAINING ISSUES

A number of issues can be addressed during collective bargaining. Although not often listed as such in the contract, management rights and union security are two important issues subject to collective bargaining. These and other issues may be classified in several ways as discussed next.

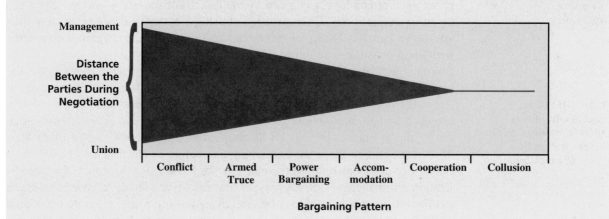

Figure 17-10 Continuum of Collective Bargaining Relations

Management Rights

Virtually all labor contracts include **management rights,** which are rights reserved so that the employer can manage, direct, and control its business. Such a provision might read as follows:

The employer retains all rights to manage, direct, and control its business in all particulars, except as such rights are expressly and specifically modified by the terms of this or any subsequent agreement.

By including such a provision, management attempts to preserve its unilateral right to make changes in areas not identified in a labor contract.

Union Security

A major concern of union representatives when bargaining is the negotiation of **union security provisions,** which are contract clauses to help the union obtain and retain members. One union security provision is the *dues checkoff,* which provides for the automatic deduction of union dues from the payroll checks of union members. The dues checkoff makes it much easier for the union to collect its funds; without it, the union must collect dues by billing each member separately.

Another form of union security results from *requiring union membership* of all employees, subject to state right-to-work laws. As mentioned earlier, a closed shop is illegal except in limited situations within the construction industry. But other types of arrangements can be developed, including *union shops, agency shops,* and *maintenance-of-membership shops.*

A growing type of union security in labor contracts is the *no-layoff policy,* or *job security guarantee.* Such a provision is especially important to many union workers because of all the mergers, downsizings, and job reductions taking place in many industries.

Classification of Bargaining Issues

The NLRB has defined collective bargaining issues in three ways. The categories it has used are: mandatory, permissive, and illegal.

Mandatory Issues Issues identified specifically by labor laws or court decisions as subject to bargaining are **mandatory issues.** If either party demands that issues in this category be subject to bargaining, then that must occur. Generally, mandatory issues relate to wages, benefits, nature of jobs, and other work-related subjects. Mandatory subjects for bargaining include the following:

- Discharge of employees
- Grievances
- Work schedules
- Union security and dues checkoff
- Retirement and pension coverage
- Vacations
- Christmas bonuses
- Rest- and lunch-break rules
- Safety rules
- Profit-sharing plans
- Required physical exam

Permissive Issues Issues that are not mandatory and that relate to certain jobs are **permissive issues.** For example, the following issues can be bargained over if both parties agree: benefits for retired employees, product prices for employees, or performance bonds.

Illegal Issues A final category, **illegal issues,** includes those issues that would require either party to take illegal action. Examples would be giving preference to union members when hiring employees or demanding a closed shop provision in the contract. If one side wants to bargain over an illegal issue, the other side can refuse.

COLLECTIVE BARGAINING PROCESS

The collective bargaining process consists of a number of stages: preparation and initial demands, negotiations, settlement or impasse, and strikes and lock-outs. Throughout the process, management and labor deal with the terms of their relationship.

Preparation and Initial Demands

Both labor and management representatives spend much time preparing for negotiations. Employer and industry data concerning wages, benefits, working conditions, management and union rights, productivity, and absenteeism are gathered. If the organization argues that it cannot afford to pay what the union is asking, the employer's financial situation and accompanying data become all the more relevant. However, the union must request such information before the employer is obligated to provide it. Typical bargaining includes initial proposals of expectations by both sides. The amount of rancor or calmness exhibited may set the tone for future negotiations between the parties.

The costs of wages and benefits are a concern in many industries. For example: In the unionized American companies building cars (the GM, Ford, and Chrysler group), labor costs average $7,655 per car. In the non-unionized Japanese companies building cars in the U.S. (Toyota, Nissan, and Honda), labor costs average $6,052 per vehicle.[22] This example illustrates that it is common for wages and benefits to be higher in unionized firms.[23]

Continuing Negotiations

After taking initial positions, each side attempts to determine what the other side values highly so that the best bargain can be struck. For example, the union may be asking the employer to pay for dental benefits as part of a package that also includes wage increases and retirement benefits. However, the union may be most interested in the retirement benefits, and may be willing to trade the dental payments for better retirement benefits. Management must determine what the union has as a priority and decide exactly what to give up.

Good Faith Provisions in federal law require that both employers and union bargaining representatives negotiate in good faith. In good-faith negotiations, the parties agree to send negotiators who can bargain and make decisions, rather than people who do not have the authority to commit either group to a decision. Meetings between the parties cannot be scheduled at absurdly inconvenient hours. Some give-and-take discussions also must occur.

Settlement and Contract Agreement

After reaching an initial agreement, the bargaining parties usually return to their respective constituencies to determine if the informal agreement is acceptable. A particularly crucial stage is **ratification** of the labor agreement, which occurs when union members vote to accept the terms of a negotiated agreement. Before ratification, the union negotiating team explains the agreement to the

LOGGING ON...

Labornet
This site describes unions, news, legislation, and upcoming union events.
www.labornet.org

THOMSON
WEST™

REFUSAL TO BARGAIN
Describes conditions relating to refusal to bargain as an unfair labor practice.
Custom Search:
☑ ANALYSIS
Exact Phrase: Refusing to recognize

Ratification Process by which union members vote to accept the terms of a negotiated labor agreement.

Figure 17-11

Typical Items in a Labor Agreement

Labor Agreement	
1. Purpose of agreement 2. Non-discrimination clause 3. Management rights 4. Recognition of the union 5. Wages 6. Incentives 7. Hours of work 8. Vacations 9. Sick leave and leaves of absence 10. Discipline	11. Separation allowance 12. Seniority 13. Bulletin boards 14. Pension and insurance 15. Safety 16. Grievance procedure 17. No-strike or lockout clause 18. Definitions 19. Terms of contract (dates) 20. Appendices

union members and presents it for a vote. If the members approve the agreement, it is then formalized into a contract. Figure 17-11 lists typical items in labor agreements.

Bargaining Impasse

Regardless of the structure of the bargaining process, labor and management do not always reach agreement on the issues. If they reach an impasse, then the disputes can be taken to conciliation, mediation, or arbitration.

Conciliation Process by which a third party attempts to keep union and management negotiators talking so that they can reach a voluntary settlement.

Conciliation and Mediation When an impasse occurs, an outside party such as the Federal Mediation and Conciliation Service may help the two deadlocked parties to continue negotiations and arrive at a solution. In **conciliation,** the third party attempts to keep union and management negotiators talking so that they can reach a voluntary settlement, but makes no proposals for solutions. In **mediation,** the third party helps the negotiators reach a settlement.[24] In neither conciliation nor mediation does the third party attempt to impose a solution. Sometimes, *fact-finding* helps to clarify the issues of disagreement as an intermediate step between mediation and arbitration.

Mediation Process by which a third party helps the negotiators reach a settlement.

Arbitration Process that uses a neutral third party to make a decision.

Arbitration In **arbitration,** a neutral third party makes a decision. Arbitration can be conducted by an individual or a panel of individuals. "Interest" arbitration attempts to solve bargaining impasses, primarily in the public sector. This type of arbitration is not frequently used in the private sector because companies generally do not want an outside party making decisions about their rights, wages, benefits, and other issues. However, grievance, or "rights," arbitration is used extensively in the private sector. Fortunately, in many situations, agreements are reached through negotiations without the need for arbitration.[25] When disagreements continue, strikes or lockouts may occur.

Strikes and Lockouts

Strike Work stoppage in which union members refuse to work in order to put pressure on an employer.

If a deadlock cannot be resolved, then an employer may revert to a lockout—or a union may revert to a strike. During a **strike,** union members refuse to work in order to put pressure on an employer. Often, the striking union members picket

Lockout Shutdown of company operations undertaken by management to prevent union members from working.

or demonstrate against the employer outside the place of business by carrying placards and signs. In a **lockout,** management shuts down company operations to prevent union members from working. This action may avert possible damage or sabotage to company facilities or injury to employees who continue to work. It also gives management leverage as in the NHL strike in 2004.

Types of Strikes Five types of strikes can occur. They are as follows:

◆ *Economic strikes* happen when the parties fail to reach agreement during collective bargaining.

◆ *Unfair labor practices strikes* occur when union members walk away from their jobs over what they feel are illegal employer actions, such as refusal to bargain.

◆ *Wildcat strikes* occur during the life of the collective bargaining agreement without approval of union leadership and violate a no-strike clause in a labor contract. Strikers can be discharged or disciplined.

◆ *Jurisdictional strikes* exist when members of one union walkout to force the employer to assign work to them instead of to members of another union.

◆ *Sympathy strikes* take place when one union chooses to express support for another union involved in a dispute, even though the first union has no disagreement with the employer.

As a result of the decline in union power, work stoppages due to strikes and lockouts are relatively rare. Many unions are reluctant to go on strike because of the financial losses their members would incur, or the fear that a strike would cause the employer to go bankrupt. In addition, management has shown its willingness to hire replacements, and some strikes have ended with union workers losing their jobs.

Replacement of Workers on Strike Management retains and sometimes uses its ability to simply replace workers who strike. Workers' rights vary depending on the type of strike that occurs. For example, in an economic strike, an employer is free to replace the striking workers. But with an unfair labor practices strike, the workers who want their jobs back at the end of the strike must be reinstated.

UNION/MANAGEMENT COOPERATION

LOGGING ON...

National Labor Management Association
This Web site contains information and articles geared towards helping management and organized labor work together effectively.
www.nlma.org

The adversarial relationship that naturally exists between unions and management may lead to strikes and lockouts. However, such conflicts are relatively rare. Even more encouraging is the growing recognition on the part of union leaders and employer representatives that cooperation between management and labor unions offers the most sensible route if organizations are to compete effectively in a global economy.[26]

Over the past decade, numerous firms have engaged in organizational and workplace restructuring in response to competitive pressures in their industries. Restructurings have had significant effects, such as lost jobs, changed work rules, and altered job responsibilities. When restructurings occur, unions can take different approaches, ranging from resistance to cooperation. Specifically, when unions have been able to obtain information and share that information with their members in order to work constructively with the company management at various levels, then organizational restructurings have been handled more successfully.

Cooperation and Joint Efforts

There are a number of notable examples of successful union/management co-operation.[27] One frequently cited example is at Saturn, a part of General Motors. There, union/management cooperation was established when the Tennessee plant was built, and it has survived a number of challenges and changes for more than a decade. Other firms with successful union/management cooperation include Ford and Boeing, despite occasional conflicts that arise.

Employee Involvement Programs

Suggesting that union/management cooperation or involving employees in making suggestions and decisions could be bad seems a little illogical. Yet, some decisions by the NLRB appear to have done just that. Some historical perspective is required to understand the issues that surrounded the decisions.

In the 1930s, when the Wagner Act was written, certain employers would form sham "company unions," coercing workers into joining them in order to keep legitimate unions from organizing the employees. As a result, the Wagner Act contained prohibitions against employer-dominated labor organizations. These prohibitions were enforced, and company unions disappeared. But the use of employee involvement programs in organizations today have raised new concerns.

Because of the Wagner Act, many employee involvement programs set up in recent years may be illegal, according to an NLRB decision dealing with Electromation, an Elkhart, Indiana, firm. Electromation used teams of employees to solicit other employees' views about such issues as wages and working conditions. The NLRB labeled these teams "labor organizations," in line with requirements of the Wagner Act. It further found that the teams were "dominated" by management, which had formed them, set their goals, and decided how they would operate. The result of this and other decisions forced many employers to re-think and re-structure their employee involvement efforts.

Federal court decisions have upheld the NLRB position in some cases and reversed it in others. One key to decisions allowing employee involvement committees and programs seems to be that these entities not deal directly with traditional collective bargaining issues such as wages, hours, and working conditions. Other keys are that the committees be composed primarily of workers and that they have broad authority to make operational suggestions and decisions. For instance, at Crown Cork & Seal, employee teams include just one member of management, and the teams address production, safety, training, and attendance issues. Recommendations from the teams are rarely, if ever, ignored by the plant manager.[28]

Unions and Employee Ownership

Unions in some situations have encouraged workers to become partial or complete owners of the companies that employ them. These efforts were spurred by concerns that firms were preparing to shut down, merge, or be bought out, resulting in a cut in the number of union jobs and workers.[29]

Unions have been active in helping members put together employee stock ownership plans to purchase all or part of some firms. Such programs have been successful in some situations, but have caused problems in others. Some in the labor movement fear that such programs may undermine union support by creating a closer identification with the concerns and goals of employers, instead of "union solidarity."

GRIEVANCE MANAGEMENT

Complaint Indication of employee dissatisfaction.

Unions know that employee dissatisfaction is a potential source of trouble for employers, whether it is expressed or not. Hidden dissatisfaction grows and creates reactions that may be completely out of proportion to the original concerns. Therefore, it is important that dissatisfaction be given an outlet. A **complaint,** which is merely an indication of employee dissatisfaction, is one outlet. Complaints often are made by employees who are not represented by unions.

Grievance Complaint formally stated in writing.

If an employee is represented by a union, and the employee says, "I should have received the job transfer because I have more seniority, which is what the union contract states," and she submits it in writing, then that complaint becomes a grievance. A **grievance** is a complaint formally stated in writing.

Management should be concerned with both complaints and grievances, because both indicate potential problems within the workforce. Without a grievance procedure, management may be unable to respond to employee concerns because managers are unaware of them. Therefore, a formal grievance procedure provides a valuable communication tool for the organization, which also is beneficial for maintaining and improving employee relations.

Grievance Responsibilities

The typical division of responsibilities between the HR unit and operating managers for handling grievances is shown in Figure 17-12. These responsibilities vary considerably from one organization to another, even between unionized firms. But the HR unit usually has more general responsibilities. Managers must accept the grievance procedure as a possible constraint on some of their decisions.

Grievance Procedures

Grievance procedures Formal channels of communication used to resolve grievances.

Grievance procedures are formal channels of communication designed to settle grievances as soon as possible after problems arise. First-line supervisors are usually closest to a problem. However, these supervisors are concerned with many other matters besides one employee's grievance, and may even be the subject of an employee's grievance. To receive the appropriate attention, grievances go through a specific process for resolution.

Figure 17-12	*Typical Division of HR Responsibilities: Grievance Management*

HR Unit	Managers
◆ Assists in designing the grievance procedure ◆ Monitors trends in grievance rates for the organization ◆ May assist in preparing grievance cases for arbitration ◆ May have responsibility for settling grievances	◆ Operate within provisions of the grievance procedure ◆ Attempt to resolve grievances where possible ◆ Document grievance cases for the grievance procedure ◆ Engage in grievance prevention efforts

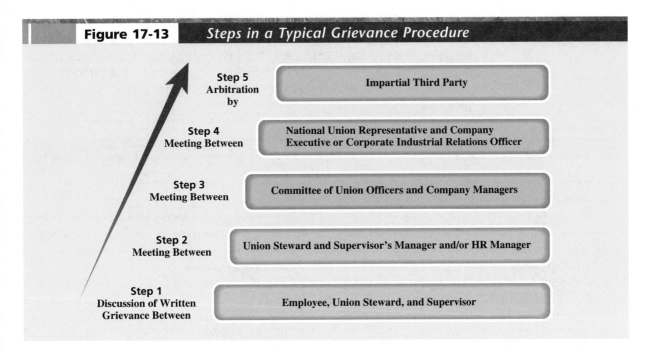

Figure 17-13 *Steps in a Typical Grievance Procedure*

Step 5
Arbitration by — Impartial Third Party

Step 4
Meeting Between — National Union Representative and Company Executive or Corporate Industrial Relations Officer

Step 3
Meeting Between — Committee of Union Officers and Company Managers

Step 2
Meeting Between — Union Steward and Supervisor's Manager and/or HR Manager

Step 1
Discussion of Written Grievance Between — Employee, Union Steward, and Supervisor

Union Representation in Grievance Procedures A unionized employee generally has a right to union representation if he or she is being questioned by management and if discipline may result. If these so-called *Weingarten rights* (named after the court case that established them) are violated and the employee is dismissed, he or she usually will be reinstated with back pay. A recent case concerns an NLRB decision to extend these rights to non-union employees involved in disciplinary grievance situations. A lower court decision ruled that non-union employees may request that a co-worker be present during disciplinary meetings.[30] That decision has been appealed to higher courts and will likely be decided ultimately by the U.S. Supreme Court.

THOMSON
——★——
WEST

GRIEVANCE PROCEDURES
Discusses how grievance procedures typically operate.
Custom Search:
☑ ANALYSIS
Exact Phrase: Good grievance procedures

Grievance arbitration Means by which a third party settles disputes arising from different interpretations of a labor contract.

Steps in a Grievance Procedure

Grievance procedures can vary in the number of steps they include. Figure 17-13 shows a typical grievance procedure, which consists of the following steps:

1. The employee discusses the grievance with the union steward (the representative of the union on the job) and the supervisor.
2. The union steward discusses the grievance with the supervisor's manager and/or the HR manager.
3. A committee of union officers discusses the grievance with appropriate company managers.
4. The representative of the national union discusses the grievance with designated company executives or the corporate industrial relations officer.
5. If the grievance is not solved at this stage, it goes to arbitration.[31] An impartial third party may ultimately dispose the grievance.

Grievance arbitration is a means by which a third party settles disputes arising from different interpretations of a labor contract. This process should not be confused with contract or issues arbitration, discussed earlier, in which arbitration is used to determine how a contract will be written. The U.S. Supreme Court has ruled that grievance arbitration decisions issued under labor contract provisions are enforceable. Grievance arbitration includes more than 50 topic areas, with discipline and discharge, safety and health, and security issues being most prevalent.

SUMMARY

- A union is a formal association of workers that promotes the interests of its members through collective action.
- Workers join unions primarily because of management's failure to address organizational and job-related concerns.
- The structural levels of U.S. unions include federations, national and international unions, and local unions. Business agents and union stewards work at local levels.
- In the United States, current union membership as a percentage of the workforce is down dramatically, to compose less than 14% of the civilian workforce.
- While public-sector unions have grown, unions in general have experienced a decline in membership due to geographic, workforce, and industrial changes.
- In attempts to grow, unions are targeting professionals, contingent and part-time workers, and low-skill workers.
- The history of unions in the U.S. indicates that they primarily focus on wages, hours, and working conditions.
- The "National Labor Code" is composed of three laws that provide the legal basis for labor relations today: the Wagner Act, the Taft-Hartley Act, and the Landrum-Griffin Act.
- The Wagner Act was designed to protect unions and workers; the Taft-Hartley Act restored some powers to management; and the Landrum-Griffin

Act was passed to protect individual union members.
- The unionization process includes an organizing campaign, authorization cards, a representation election, certification and decertification, and collective bargaining.
- Collective bargaining occurs when management negotiates with representatives of workers over wages, hours, and working conditions.
- The issues subject to collective bargaining fall into three categories: mandatory, permissive, and illegal.
- The collective bargaining process includes preparation and initial demands, negotiations, and settlement and contract agreement.
- Once an agreement (contract) is signed between labor and management, it becomes the document governing what each party can and cannot do.
- When impasse occurs, work stoppages through strikes or lockouts can be used to pressure the other party.
- Union-management cooperation has been beneficial in a number of situations, although care must be taken to avoid violations of NLRB provisions.
- Grievances express workers' written dissatisfactions or differences in contract interpretations. Grievances usually follow a formal process to resolution.
- A grievance procedure begins with the first-level supervisor and may end—if the grievance is not resolved along the way—with arbitration.

REVIEW AND APPLICATION QUESTIONS

1. Discuss the following statement: "If management gets a union, it deserves one."
2. Suppose a co-worker just brought you a union leaflet urging employees to sign an authorization card. What do you expect to happen from this point on?
3. As the HR manager, you have heard rumors about potential efforts to unionize your warehouse employees. Use the following Web site (*www.genelevine.com*) to develop a set of guidelines for supervisors if they are asked questions by employees about unionization.

To check your knowledge of the chapter, review the following. (Answers after the supplemental case.) For more questions, see the Study Guide.

1. What is the primary determinant of whether or not employees unionize?
   a. Management
   b. Government
   c. Co-workers
   d. Union organizers
2. Unions have attempted to counteract the overall decline in membership by _____.
   a. reducing membership dues and initiation fees
   b. organizing manufacturing workers in less-developed countries
   c. boycotting states with "employer-friendly" laws
   d. attempting to unionize contingent and part-time workers
3. What is the purpose of right-to-work laws?
   a. To encourage full employment
   b. To prohibit closed shops and union shops
   c. To require that employers bargain in good faith with union representatives
   d. To prohibit unions from organizing in a particular state
4. Which of the following bargaining issues would require either party to take illegal action?
   a. Requiring employees to take annual physical exams
   b. Giving preference to union members when hiring employees
   c. Management and unions negotiating before setting product prices
   d. Requiring management to deduct union dues from employee payroll checks

CASE
LABOR'S NEW SHARP SWORD

Several dozen union members rallied in Cincinnati to protest Kroger Company's proposal to cut health benefits for southern California workers on strike. They were not Kroger employees, but construction union members who were there at the request of a group of construction labor officials who were trustees of union pension funds. These funds owned 5 million shares of Kroger stock. As stockholders the construction unions were there to help their grocery store employee brethren.

Unions have $350 *billion* in pension funds, most of it invested in stock. That money represents much negotiating power with boards of directors on behalf of labor. Using this approach and combining it with old-fashioned tactics such as picketing, unions are challenging employers on health-care benefits, outsourcing, corporate reform, independent boards, and curbs on CEO pay. The unions are clearly becoming more comfortable wielding the clout of big shareholders.

Some union officials worry that if the Securities and Exchange Commission thinks that this is an inappropriate use of shareholder votes, it might use its regulation power to call it to a halt. However, an AFL-CIO official argues that paying good benefits and respecting employee rights does not stand in conflict with the ideas of maximizing shareholder value, but actually encourages it.

In another example of union shareholder power, the Service Employees International Union (SEIU) has signed up hundreds of office-building janitors by pressuring state and local pension funds of their members who work in the public sector. Many of those funds invest in large office buildings—frequently owning a majority share. About a dozen of these funds have adopted "responsible contractor" policies that require real estate companies managing the buildings to hire janitorial companies that pay "fair" wages and benefits. In practice, that usually means the contractor must be union or allow the SEIU to try to organize employees in the building.[32]

Questions
1. How do you view allowing unions to pressure boards of directors through their pension plans?
2. Draw distinctions between these tactics and those of secondary boycotts outlawed by the Taft-Hartley Act.

SUPPLEMENTAL CASE: The Wilson County Hospital

The case deals with labor disputes in a unionized hospital. (For the case, go to **http://mathis.swlearning.com/**)

Learning Review Answers: 1. a   2. d   3. b   4. b

NOTES

1. T. A. Badger, "White Collar Off-shoring a Growth Issue for Unions," *Laramie Boomerang,* June 8, 2004, 11.

2. Thomas C. Buckmuller et al., "Union Effects on Health Insurance Provision and Coverage in the United States," *Industrial and Labor Relations Review,* 55 (2002), 610-628; and Daniel B. Klaff and Ronald G. Ehrenberg, "Collective Bargaining and Staff Salaries in American Colleges and Universities," *Industrial and Labor Relations Review,* 57 (2003), 92–104.

3. Barry T. Hirsch, "What Do Unions Do for Economic Performance?" *Discussion Paper Series IZA DP No. 892,* Institute for the Study of Labor, October 2003.

4. International Labor Organization, *www.ilo.org.*

5. Neal E. Boudette, "Strategic Shift," *Wall Street Journal,* March 11, 2004, A1; "A Plan to Put Germans Back into Jobs," *The Economist,* August 24, 2002, 41; and "Déjà Vu?" *The Economist,* June 7, 2003, 59.

6. Thomas Palley, "The Child Labor Problem," *Journal of Economic Issues,* 36 (2002), 601–615; Takao Kato and Motohiro Morishima, "The Productivity Effects of Participatory Employment Practices," *Industrial Relations,* 41 (2002), 487–519.

7. "Here, Unite Latest Duo to Tie Knot," *Nation's Restaurant News,* March 22, 2004, 30.

8. "Union Rolls Hold Steady as Employment Declines," *Bulletin to Management,* February 21, 2002, 61.

9. "Some Workers Gain with New Union Tactics," *Wall Street Journal,* January 31, 2002, A2.

10. Huberto J. Nunez, "Maquila Workers in Mexico," *Labor History,* 43 (2002), 440–449.

11. Susan N. Houseman, "Why Employers Use Flexible Staffing Arrange-ments," *Industrial and Labor Relations Review,* 55 (October 2001), 149.

12. Maureen Hannay, "The Unionization of Professionals," *Journal of Labor Research,* 23 (2002), 487–499.

13. Roderick D. Iverson and D. B. Currwan, "Union Participation, Job Satisfaction and Employee Turnover," *Industrial Relations,* 42 (2003), 101–105; and Rosemary Batt et al., "Employee Voice, Human Resource Practices and Quit Rates," *Industrial and Labor Relations Review,* 55 (2002), 573–595.

14. Holly J. McCammon, "Labor's Legal Mobilization," *Work and Occupations,* 28 (2001), 143–175.

15. *Bowling Transportation, Inc. v. NLRB,* (6th Cir. No. 01-2386/2588 December 12, 2003).

16. The vignette is composed of information gleaned from various newspaper accounts of the incident from June 10, 2002, to November 24, 2002; the *Seattle-Times* was the main source.

17. Camille A. Olson and Michael J. Rybick, "Spotlight on Union Organizing: No Solicitation, No Distribution," *Legal Report SHRM,* May/June 2002, 5–7.

18. Maria Greco Danaher, "Inconsistent Bulletin Board Rule Tanks an Employer's Election Win," *www.SHRM.org/hrnews.*

19. Jack Fiorito and William Bass, "The Use of Information Technology by National Unions: An Exploratory Analysis," *Industrial Relations,* 41 (2002), 34–47.

20. Margaret M. Clark, "When the Union Knocks on the Recruiters Door: Legal Rules on the Hiring of Union 'Salts,'" *SHRM Legal Report,* October 2003, 7–8.

21. *NLRB v. Kentucky River Community Care, Inc.,* 121 S. Ct. 1861 (2001).

22. David Kiley, "Foreign Companies Cast Long Shadows on Van Negotiations," *USA Today,* August 6, 2003, B1.

23. Bruce E. Kaufman, "Models of Union Wage Determination," *Industrial Relations,* 41 (2002), 110–157.

24. Richard A. Posthuma et al., "Mediator Tactics and Sources of Conflict," *Industrial Relations,* 41 (2002), 94–109.

25. Corinne Bendersky, "Organizational Dispute Resolution Systems: A Complementaries Model," *Academy of Management Review,* 28 (2003), 643–656.

26. Sarah Oxenbridge and William Brown, "The Two Faces of Partnership?" *Employee Relations,* 24 (2002), 262–276.

27. Miguel Martinez Lucio and Mark Stewart, "Assessing the Principles of Partnership," *Employee Relations,* 24 (2002), 305–320.

28. G. Roger King, "New Guidelines from the NLRB on Participative Management Initiatives and Employee Committees," *SHRM Legal Report,* November/December 2001, 1–4.

29. Douglas M. McCabe, "Administering the Employment Relationship: The Ethics of Conflict Resolution in Relation to Justice in the Workplace," *Journal of Business Ethics,* 36 (2002), 33–48.

30. "Non-Union Employees Are Entitled to Have a Co-worker Present at Investigatory Interviews," *www.lawmemo.com.*

31. William M. Haraway III, "Rediscovering Process Values in Employee Grievance Procedures," *Administration and Society,* 34 (2002), 499–521.

32. Aaron Bernstein, Amy Borrus, and Christopher Palmeri, "Labor Sharpens Its Pension Sword," *Business Week,* November 24, 2003, 62–64.

▮▮ HUMAN RESOURCE CERTIFICATION INSTITUTE TEST SPECIFICATIONS*

There are two levels of certification, the Professional in Human Resources (PHR) and the Senior Professional in Human Resources (SPHR). Two different exams are used for certification testing. PHR questions tend to be at an operational/technical level, whereas SPHR questions tend to be more at the strategic and/or policy level.

Examination questions for both levels cover a wide range of topics. Each multiple choice exam consists of 200 scored questions plus 25 pretest questions for a total of 225 questions. Pretest questions are not counted in the scoring of the examination and are used for statistical purposes only. Each question lists *four possible answers,* only one of which is correct.

Item Classification Scheme

The test specifications identify six functional areas. After each major functional area are the weightings for that area. **The first number in the parentheses is the PHR percentage weighting, and the second number is the SPHR percentage weighting.** Within each area *responsibilities* and *knowledge* topics are specified.

FUNCTIONAL AREA:

01 STRATEGIC MANAGEMENT (12%, 26%)

The processes and activities used to formulate HR objectives, practices, and policies to meet the short- and long-range organizational needs and opportunities, to guide and lead the change process, and to evaluate HR's contributions to organizational effectiveness.

Responsibilities:

01 Interpret information related to the organization's operations from internal sources, including financial/accounting, marketing, operations, information technology, and individual employees, in order to participate in strategic planning and policy making.

02 Interpret information related to the general business environment, industry practices and developments, and technological developments from external sources (for example, publications, government documents, media, and trade organizations), in order to participate in strategic planning and policy making.

03 Participate as a partner in the organization's strategic planning process.

04 Establish strategic relationships with individuals in the organization, to influence organizational decision-making.

05 Establish relationships/alliances with key individuals in the community and in professional capacities to assist in meeting the organization's strategic needs.

06 Evaluate HR's contribution to organizational effectiveness, including assessment, design, implementation, and evaluation of activities with respect to strategic and organizational measurement in HR objectives. (** *06 refers to participation in change management*)

07 Provide direction and guidance during changes in organizational processes, operations, planning, intervention, leadership training and culture that balance the expectations and needs of the organization, its em-

ployees, and other stakeholders (including customers). (** *07 refers to participation in change management*)

08 Develop and shape organizational policy related to the organization's management of its human resources.

09 Cultivate leadership and ethical values in self and others through modeling and teaching.

10 Provide information for the organizational budgeting process, including budget development and review.

11 Monitor legislative environment for proposed changes in law and take appropriate action to support, modify, or stop the proposed action (for example, write to a member of Congress, provide expert testimony at a public hearing, lobby legislators).

Knowledge Of:

01 lawmaking and administrative regulatory processes

02 internal and external environmental scanning techniques

03 strategic planning process and implementation

04 organizational social responsibility (for example, welfare to work, philanthropy, alliances with community-based organizations)

05 management functions, including planning, organizing, directing, and controlling

06 techniques to sustain creativity and innovation

FUNCTIONAL AREA:

02 WORKFORCE PLANNING AND EMPLOYMENT (26%, 16%)

The processes of planning, developing, implementing, administering, and performing ongoing evaluation of recruiting, hiring, orientation, and organizational exit to ensure that the workforce will meet the organization's goals and objectives.

Responsibilities:

01 Identify staffing requirements to meet the goals and objectives of the organization.

02 Conduct job analyses to write job descriptions and develop job competencies.

03 Identify and document the essential job functions for positions.

04 Establish hiring criteria based on the competencies needed.

05 Assess internal workforce, labor market, and recruitment agencies to determine the availability of qualified applicants.

06 Identify internal and external recruitment methods and implement them within the context of the organization's goals and objectives.

07 Develop strategies to market the organization to potential applicants.

08 Establish selection procedures, including interviewing, testing, and reference and background checking.

09 Implement selection procedures, including interviewing, testing, and reference and background checking.

10 Develop and/or extend employment offers.

11 Perform or administer post-offer employment activities (for example, employment agreements, completion of I-9 verification form, relocation agreements, and medical examinations).

12 Facilitate and/or administer the process by which non-US citizens can legally work in the United States.

13 Design, facilitate, and/or conduct the orientation process, including review of performance standards for new hires and transfers.

14 Evaluate selection and employment processes for effectiveness and implement changes if indicated (for example, employee retention).

15 Develop a succession planning process.

16 Develop and implement the organizational exit process, including unemployment insurance claim responses. (*includes severance, turnover and outplacement*)

17 Develop, implement, manage, and evaluate affirmative action program(s), as may be required.

Knowledge of:

07 federal/state/local employment-related laws (for example, Title VII, ADA, ADEA, Vietnam Veterans, WARN) and regulations (for example, EEOC Uniform Guidelines on Employee Selection Procedures)

08 immigration law (for example, visas, I-9)

09 quantitative analyses required to assess past and future staffing (for example, cost benefit analysis, costs-per-hire, selection ratios, adverse impact)

10 recruitment methods and sources

11 staffing alternatives (for example, telecommuting, outsourcing)

12 planning techniques (for example, succession planning, forecasting)

13 reliability and validity of selection tests/tools/methods

14 use and interpretation of selection tests (for example, psychological/personality, cognitive, and motor/physical assessments)

15 interviewing techniques

16 relocation practices

17 impact of compensation and benefits plans on recruitment and retention

18 international HR and implications of international workforce for workforce planning and employment

19 downsizing and outplacement

20 internal workforce planning and employment policies, practices, and procedures

FUNCTIONAL AREA:

03 HUMAN RESOURCE DEVELOPMENT (15%, 13%)

The processes of ensuring that the skills, knowledge, abilities, and performance of the workforce meet the current and future organizational and individual needs through developing, implementing, and evaluating activities and programs addressing employee training and development, change and performance management, and the unique needs of particular employee groups.

Responsibilities:

01 Conduct needs analyses to identify and establish priorities regarding human resource development activities.

02 Develop training programs.

03 Implement training programs.

04 Evaluate training programs.

05 Develop programs to assess employees' potential for growth and development in the organization.

06 Implement programs to assess employees' potential for growth and development in the organization.

07 Evaluate programs to assess employees' potential for growth and development in the organization.

08 Develop change management programs and activities.

09 Implement change management programs and activities.

10 Evaluate change management programs and activities.

11 Develop performance management programs and procedures.

12 Implement performance management programs and procedures.

13 Evaluate performance management programs and procedures.

14 Develop programs to meet the unique needs of particular employees (for example, work-family programs, diversity programs, outplacement programs, repatriation programs, and fast-track programs).

15 Implement programs to meet the unique needs of particular employees (for example, work-family programs, diversity programs, outplacement programs, repatriation programs, and fast-track programs).

16 Evaluate programs to meet the unique needs of particular employees (for example, work-family programs, diversity programs, outplacement programs, repatriation programs, and fast-track programs).

Knowledge of:

21 applicable international, federal, state, and local laws and regulations regarding copyrights and patents

22 human resource development theories and applications (including career development and leadership development)

23 organizational development theories and applications

24 training methods, programs, and techniques (design, objectives, methods, etc.)

25 employee involvement strategies

26 task/process analysis

27 performance appraisal and performance management methods

28 applicable international issues (for example, culture, local management approaches/practices, societal norms)

29 instructional methods and program delivery (content, building modules of program, selection of presentation/delivery mechanism)

30 techniques to assess HRD program effectiveness (for example, satisfaction, learning and job performance of program participants, and organizational outcomes such as turnover and productivity)

FUNCTIONAL AREA:

04 COMPENSATION AND BENEFITS (20%, 16%)

The processes of analyzing, developing, implementing, administering, and performing ongoing evaluation of a total compensation and benefits system for all employee groups consistent with human resource management goals.

Responsibilities:

01 Ensure the compliance of compensation and benefits with applicable federal, state, and local laws. *(includes IRS Rulings, strict definitions of which tend to go more with K-31; applications/calculations/ interpretations of those rulings tend to go more with K-32)*

02 Analyze, develop, implement, and maintain compensation policies and a pay structure consistent with the organization's strategic objectives. *(includes broad definitions and designs)*

03 Analyze and evaluate pay rates based on internal worth and external market conditions. *(includes wage and salary surveys)*

04 Develop/select and implement a payroll system.

05 Administer payroll functions.

06 Evaluate compensation policies to ensure that they are positioning the organization internally and externally according to the organization's strategic objectives. *(0406 refers to 'tweaking,' 'refinement,' or 'alterations;' turnover issues related to compensation also belong under this responsibility)*

07 Conduct a benefit plan needs assessment and determine/select the plans to be offered, considering the organization's strategic objectives. *(0407 addresses more specific definitions and plan design issues; includes 401K; tends to go more with K-38)*

08 Implement and administer benefit plans. *(addresses more the carrying out of the objectives of the benefit plan; tends to go more with K-39)*

09 Evaluate benefits program to ensure that it is positioning the organization internally and externally according to the organization's strategic objectives. *(refers more to evaluation and tweaking of the benefit plan; tends to go more with K-38)*

10 Analyze, select, implement, maintain, and administer executive compensation, stock purchase, stock options, and incentive, and bonus programs. *(includes profit-sharing)*

11 Analyze, develop, select, maintain, and implement expatriate and foreign national compensation and benefit programs.

12 Communicate the compensation and benefits plan and policies to the workforce.

Knowledge of:

31 federal, state, and local compensation and benefit laws (for example, FLSA, ERISA, COBRA)

32 accounting practices related to compensation and benefits (for example, excess group term life, compensatory time)

33 job evaluation methods

34 job pricing and pay structures

35 incentive and variable pay methods

36 executive compensation

37 non-cash compensation methods (for example, stock option plans)

38 benefits needs analysis

39 benefit plans (for example, health insurance, life insurance, pension, education, health club)

40 international compensation laws and practices (for example, expatriate compensation, socialized medicine, mandated retirement)

FUNCTIONAL AREA:

05 EMPLOYEE AND LABOR RELATIONS (21%, 24%)

The processes of analyzing, developing, implementing, administering, and performing ongoing evaluation of the workplace relationship between employer and employee (including the collective bargaining process and union relations), in order to maintain effective relationships and working conditions that balance the employer's needs with the employees' rights in support of the organization's strategic objectives.

Responsibilities:

01 Ensure compliance with all applicable federal, state, and local laws and regulations. *(catch-all responsibility, including NLRB, ADA, FMLA)*

02 Develop and implement employee relations programs that will create a positive organizational culture. *(most of the legal definitions and general definitions)*

03 Promote, monitor, and measure the effectiveness of employee relations activities.

04 Assist in establishing work rules and monitor their application and enforcement to ensure fairness and consistency (for union and non-union environments).

05 Communicate and ensure understanding by employees of laws, regulations, and organizational policies.

06 Resolve employee complaints filed with federal, state, and local agencies involving employment practices. *(formal, legal complaints)*

07 Develop grievance and disciplinary policies and procedures to ensure fairness and consistency.

08 Implement and monitor grievance and disciplinary policies and procedures to ensure fairness and consistency. *(includes investigation)*

09 Respond to union organizing activity.

10 Participate in collective bargaining activities, including contract negotiation and administration.

Knowledge of:

41 applicable federal, state, and local laws affecting employment in union and non-union environments, such as anti-discrimination, sexual harassment, labor relations, and privacy

42 techniques for facilitating positive employee relations (for example, small group facilitation, dispute resolution, and labor/management cooperative strategies and programs)

43 employee involvement strategies (for example, alternate work schedules, work teams)

44 individual employment rights issues and practices (for example, employment at will, negligent hiring, defamation, employees' rights to bargain collectively)

45 workplace behavior issues/practices (for example, absenteeism, discipline)

46 methods for assessment of employee attitudes, opinions, and satisfaction (for example, opinion surveys, attitude surveys, focus panels)

47 unfair labor practices

48 the collective bargaining process, strategies, and concepts *(up to and after contract)*

49 public sector labor relations issues and practices

50 expatriation and repatriation issues and practices

51 employee and labor relations for local nationals (i.e., labor relations in other countries)

FUNCTIONAL AREA:

06 OCCUPATIONAL HEALTH, SAFETY, AND SECURITY (6%, 5%)

The processes of analyzing, developing, implementing, administering, and performing ongoing evaluation of programs, practices, and services to promote the physical and mental well-being of individuals in the workplace, and to protect individuals and the workplace from unsafe acts, unsafe working conditions, and violence.

Responsibilities:

01 Ensure compliance with all applicable federal, state, and local workplace health and safety laws and regulations.

02 Determine safety programs needed for the organization.

03 Develop and/or select injury/occupational illness prevention programs.

04 Implement injury/occupational illness prevention programs.

05 Develop and/or select safety training and incentive programs.

06 Implement safety training and incentive programs.

07 Evaluate the effectiveness of safety prevention, training, and incentive programs.

08 Implement workplace injury/occupational illness procedures (for example, worker's compensation, OSHA).

09 Determine health and wellness programs needed for the organization.

10 Develop/select, implement, and evaluate (or make available) health and wellness programs.

11 Develop/select, implement, and evaluate security plans to protect the company from liability.

12 Develop/select, implement, and evaluate security plans to protect employees (for example, injuries resulting from workplace violence).

13 Develop/select, implement, and evaluate incident and emergency response plans (for example, natural disasters, workplace safety threats, evacuation).

Knowledge of:

52 federal, state, and local workplace health and safety laws and regulations (for example, OSHA, Drug-Free Workplace Act, ADA)

53 workplace injury and occupational illness compensation laws and programs (for example, worker's compensation)

54 investigation procedures of workplace safety, health, and security enforcement agencies (for example, OSHA)

55 workplace safety risks

56 workplace security risks (for example, theft, corporate espionage, information systems/technology, and vandalism)

57 potential violent behavior and workplace violence conditions

58 general health and safety practices (for example, fire evacuation, HAZCOM, ergonomic evaluations)

59 incident and emergency response plans

60 internal investigation and surveillance techniques

61 Employee Assistance Programs

62 employee wellness programs

63 issues related to chemical use and dependency (for example, identification of symptoms, drug testing, discipline)

CORE Knowledge Required by HR Professionals

64 needs assessment and analysis

65 third-party contract management, including development of requests for proposals (RFPs)

66 communication strategies

67 documentation requirements

68 adult learning processes

69 motivation concepts and applications

70 training methods

71 leadership concepts and applications

72 project management concepts and applications

73 diversity concepts and applications

74 human relations concepts and applications (for example, interpersonal and organizational behavior)

75 HR ethics and professional standards

76 technology and human resource information systems (HRIS) to support HR activities

77 qualitative and quantitative methods and tools for analysis, interpretation, and decision-making purposes

78 change management

79 liability and risk management

80 job analysis and job description methods

81 employee records management (for example, retention, disposal)

82 the interrelationships among HR activities and programs across functional areas

CURRENT LITERATURE IN HR MANAGEMENT

Students are expected to be familiar with the professional resources and literature in their fields of study. Five groups of resources are listed below.

A. Research-Oriented Journals

In HR management, the professional journals are the most immediate and direct communication link between researchers and the practicing managers. These journals contain articles that report on original research. Normally, these journals contain either sophisticated writing and quantitative verifications of the author's findings, or conceptual models and literature reviews of previous research.

Academy of Management Journal
Academy of Management Review
Administrative Science Quarterly
American Behavioral Scientist
American Journal of Health Promotion
American Journal of Psychology
American Journal of Sociology
American Psychological Measurement
American Psychologist
American Sociological Review
Annual Review of Psychology
Applied Psychology: An International Review
Behavioral Science
British Journal of Industrial Relations
British Journal of Management
Business Ethics
Cognitive Studies
Decision Sciences
Dispute Resolution Quarterly
Employee Responsibilities and Rights Journal
Entrepreneurship Theory and Practice
Ethics and Critical Thinking Journal
Group and Organization Studies
Human Organization
Human Relations

Human Resource Development Review
Human Resource Management Journal
Human Resource Management Review
Human Resources Abstracts
Industrial & Labor Relations Review
Industrial Relations
Industrial Relations Journal
Industrial Relations Law Journal
Interfaces
International Journal of Entrepreneurial Behavior and Research
International Journal of Human Resource Management Education
International Journal of Management Reviews
International Journal of Training and Development
International Journal of Selection and Assessment
Journal of Abnormal Psychology
Journal of Applied Behavioral Science
Journal of Applied Business Research
Journal of Applied Psychology
Journal of Business
Journal of Business Communications
Journal of Business and Industrial Marketing
Journal of Business and Psychology
Journal of Business Ethics

Journal of Business Research
Journal of Business Strategy
Journal of Collective Negotiations
Journal of Communication
Journal of Comparative International Management
Journal of Compensation & Benefits
Journal of Counseling Psychology
Journal of Experimental Social Psychology
Journal of Human Resources
Journal of Individual Employment Rights
Journal of Industrial Relations
Journal of International Business Studies
Journal of International Management
Journal of Knowledge Management
Journal of Labor Economics
Journal of Labor Research
Journal of Leadership and Organizational Studies
Journal of Management
Journal of Management Development
Journal of Management Education
Journal of Management Studies
Journal of Managerial Psychology
Journal of Occupation and Organization Psychology
Journal of Organizational Behavior
Journal of Organizational Change Management
Journal of Organizational Excellence
Journal of Pension Planning
Journal of Personality and Social Psychology
Journal of Quality & Participation
Journal of Quality Management
Journal of Social Issues
Journal of Social Psychology
Journal of Social Policy
Journal of Social Psychology
Journal of Vocational Behavior
Journal of Workplace Learning
Labor History
Labor Relations Yearbook
Labour
Management Science
New Technology, Work, and Employment
Occupational Psychology
Organization Behavior and Human Decision
    Processes
Personnel Monographs
Personnel Psychology
Personnel Review
Psychological Bulletin

Psychological Review
Public Personnel Management
Quarterly Review of Distance Education
Social Forces
Social Science Research
Sociology Perspective
Sociometry
Work and Occupations

B. Selected Professional/ Managerial Journals

These journals generally cover a wide range of subjects. Articles in these publications normally are aimed at HR professionals and managers. Most articles in these publications are written to interpret, summarize, or discuss the implications of research. They also provide operational and administrative ideas.

Academy of Management Executive
Across the Board
Administrative Management
Arbitration Journal
Australian Journal of Management
Benefits and Compensation Solutions
Berkeley Journal of Employment and Labor Law
Business
Business Horizons
Business Management
Business Monthly
Business Quarterly
Business and Social Review
Business Week
California Management Review
Canadian Manager
Columbia Journal of World Business
Compensation and Benefits Management
Compensation and Benefits Review
Corporate Governance
Directors and Boards
Economist
Employee Benefit Plan Review
Employee Benefits News
Employee Relations
Employee Relations Law Journal
Employment Practices Decisions
Employment Relations
Employment Relations Today

Forbes
Fortune
Global HR
Harvard Business Review
Hospital and Health Services Administration
HR Magazine
Human Behavior
Human Capital Management
Human Resource Development International
Human Resource Executive
Human Resource Management
Human Resource Management International Digest
Human Resource Planning
IHRIM Link
INC.
Incentive
Industrial Management
Industry Week
International Management
Journal of Systems Management
Labor Law Journal
Long Range Planning
Manage
Management Consulting
Management Planning
Management Research News
Management Review
Management Solutions
Management Today
Management World
Managers Magazine
Michigan State University Business Topics
Monthly Labor Review
Nation's Business
Occupational Health & Safety
Occupational Outlook Quarterly
Organizational Dynamics
Pension World
Personnel Management
Personnel Management Abstracts
Psychology Today
Public Administration Review
Public Manager
Public Opinion Quarterly
Recruiting Today
Research Management
SAM Advanced Management Journal
Security Management

Sloan Management Review
Supervision
Supervisory Management
Training
Training and Development
Workforce
Workforce Management
Working Woman
Workplace Ergonomics
Workplace Visions
Workspan
WorldatWork Journal

C. Selected HR-Related Internet Links

American Arbitration Association
  http://www.adr.org
Academy of Management
  http://www.aom.pace.edu
American Federation of Labor/Congress of
  Industrial Organizations (AFL-CIO)
  http://www.aflcio.org
American Institute for Managing Diversity
  http://www.aimd.org
American Psychological Association
  http://www.apa.org
American Society for Industrial Security
  http://www.asisonline.org
American Society for Payroll Management
  http://www.aspm.org
American Society for Training and Development
  http://www.astd.org
Australian Human Resource Institute
  http://www.ahri.com.au
CPR Institute for Dispute Resolution
  http://www.cpradr.org
Employee Benefit Research Institute
  http://www.ebri.org
Employment Management Association
  http://www.shrm.org/ema
Foundation for Enterprise Development
  http://www.fed.org
Hong Kong Institute of Human Resource
  Management
  http://www.hkihrm.org
Human Resource Certification Institute
  http://www.hrci.org
Industrial Relations Research Association
  http://www.irra.uiuc.edu

Institute for International Human Resources
http://www.shrm.org/docs/IIHR.html
Institute of Personnel and Development (UK)
http://www.ipd.co.uk
International Association for Human Resource Information Management
http://ihrim.org
International Association of Industrial Accident Boards and Commissions
http://www.iaiabc.org
International Foundation of Employee Benefit Plans (IFEBP)
http://www.ifebp.org
International Personnel Management Association
http://www.ipma-hr.org
International Personnel Management Association Assessment Council
http://ipmaac.org
National Center for Employee Ownership
http://www.nceo.org
National Health Information Research Center
http://www.nhirc.org
Society for Human Resource Management
http://www.shrm.org
Union Resource Network
http://www.unions.org
World at Work
http://www.worldatwork.org

D. Selected Government Internet Links
Bureau of Labor Statistics
http://stats.bls.gov
Census Bureau
http://www.census.gov
Department of Labor
http://www.dol.gov
Economic Statistics Briefing Room
http://www.whitehouse.gov/fsbr/esbr.html
Employment and Training Administration
http://www.doleta.gov
Equal Employment Opportunity Commission
http://www.eeoc.gov
FedStats
http://www.fedstats.gov
National Institute of Environmental Health Sciences
http://www.niehs.nih.gov

National Institute for Safety and Health (NIOSH)
http://www.cdc.gov/niosh/homepage.html
National Labor Relations Board
http://www.nlrb.gov
Occupational Safety and Health Administration
http://www.osha.gov
Office of Personnel Management
http://www.opm.gov
Pension and Welfare Benefits Administration
http://www.dol.gov/ebsa/welcome.html
Pension Benefit Guaranty Corporation
http://www.pbgc.gov
Small Business Administration
http://www.sba.gov
Social Security Administration
http://www.ssa.gov
Training Technology Resource Center
http://www.ttrc.doleta.gov
U. S. House of Representatives
http://www.house.gov
U. S. Senate
http://www.senate.gov

E. Abstracts, Indices, and Databases
ABI Inform Global
ACM Digital
ArticleFirst
Arts & Humanities Search
Book Review Digest
Books in Print
Business and Company ASAP
ComAbstracts
ContentsFirst
Criminal Justice Abstracts
Dissertation Abstracts
Ebsco Masterfile Premier
Ebsco Online Citations
ECO: Electronic Collections Online
EconLit
Education
ERIC
Essay and General Literature Index
Expanded Academic Index
Government Periodicals
GPO Monthly Catalog
Health Reference Center
HRAF: Human Relations Area

Human Resource Abstracts
Index to Legal Periodicals and Books
Internet and Personal Computing Abstracts
NCJRS Justice Information Center
NetFirst
Newspaper Source from Ebsco

PAIS: Public Affairs Information Service
PapersFirst
PsycInfo
Readers Guide Abstracts
Sociological Abstracts

Glossary

A

Acceptance rate   Percent of applicants hired divided by total number of applicants.

Active practice   Performance of job-related tasks and duties by trainees during training.

Adverse selection   Situation in which only higher-risk employees select and use certain benefits.

Affirmative action   Employers are urged to hire groups of people based on their race, age, gender, or national origin, to make up for historical discrimination.

Affirmative action plan (AAP)   Formal document that an employer compiles annually for submission to enforcement agencies.

Applicant pool   All persons who are actually evaluated for selection.

Applicant population   A subset of the labor force population that is available for selection using a particular recruiting approach.

Arbitration   Process that uses a neutral third party to make a decision.

Assessment centers   Collections of instruments and exercises designed to diagnose individuals' development needs.

Attitude survey   A survey that focuses on employees' feelings and beliefs about their jobs and the organization.

Autonomy   Extent of individual freedom and discretion in the work and its scheduling.

Availability analysis   Identifies the number of protected-class members available to work in the appropriate labor markets for given jobs.

B

Balance-sheet approach   Compensation plan that equalizes cost differences between identical international and home-country assignments.

Bargaining unit   Employees eligible to select a single union to represent and bargain collectively for them.

Base pay   Basic compensation that an employee receives, usually as a wage or a salary.

Behavior modeling   Copying someone else's behavior.

Behavioral interview   Interview in which applicants give specific examples of how they have performed a certain task or handled a problem in the past.

Benchmark jobs   Jobs found in many organizations and performed by several individuals who have similar duties that are relatively stable and require similar KSAs.

Benchmarking   Comparing specific measures of performance against data on those measures in other organizations.

Benefit   Indirect reward given to an employee or a group of employees for organizational membership.

Blind to differences   Differences among people should be ignored and everyone should be treated equally.

Bona fide occupational qualifications (BFOQ)   Characteristic providing a legitimate reason why an employer can exclude persons on otherwise illegal bases of consideration.

Bonus   One-time payment that does not become part of the employee's base pay.

Broadbanding   Practice of using fewer pay grades with much broader ranges than in traditional compensation systems.

Burden of proof   What individuals who file suit against employers must prove in order to establish that illegal discrimination has occurred.

Business agent   Full-time union official who operates the union office and assists union members.

Business necessity   Practice necessary for safe and efficient organizational operations.

Business process re-engineering (BPR)   Measures for improving such activities as product development, customer service, and service delivery.

C

Career   Series of work-related positions a person occupies throughout life.

Career paths   Represent employee's movements through opportunities over time.

Cash balance plan   Retirement program in which benefits are based on an accumulation of annual company contributions, expressed as a percentage of pay, plus interest credited each year.

Central tendency error   Occurs when a rater gives all employees a score within a narrow range in the middle of the scale.

Closed shop   Firms that require individuals to join a union before they can be hired.

Coaching   Training and feedback given to employees by immediate supervisors.

Co-determination   Practice whereby union or worker representatives are given positions on a company's board of directors.

Co-payment   Strategy requiring employees to pay a portion of the cost of insurance premiums, medical care, and prescription drugs.

Cognitive ability tests   Tests that measure an individual's thinking, memory, reasoning, verbal, and mathematical abilities.

Collaborative HR   The process of HR professionals from several different organizations working jointly to address shared business problems.

Collective bargaining   Process whereby representatives of management and workers negotiate over wages, hours, and other terms and conditions of employment.

Commission   Compensation computed as a percentage of sales in units or dollars.

Compa-ratio   Pay level divided by the midpoint of the payrange.

Compensable factor   Factor that identifies a job value commonly present throughout a group of jobs.

Compensation committee   Subgroup of the board of directors, composed of directors who are not officers of the firm.

Compensatory time off   Hours given to an employee in lieu of payment for extra time worked.

Competencies   Individual capabilities that can be linked to enhanced performance by individuals or teams.

Competency-based pay   Rewards individuals for the capabilities they demonstrate and acquire.

Complaint   Indication of employee dissatisfaction.

Compressed workweek   Schedule in which a full week's work is accomplished in fewer than five 8-hour days.

Conciliation   Process by which a third party attempts to keep union and management negotiators talking so that they can reach a voluntary settlement.

Concurrent validity   Measured when an employer tests current employees and correlates the scores with their performance ratings.

Constructive discharge   Deliberately making conditions intolerable to get an employee to quit.

Consumer-driven health (CDH) plan   One that provides employer financial contributions to employees to cover their own health-related expenses.

Content validity   Validity measured by a logical, non-statistical method to identify the KSAs and other characteristics necessary to perform a job.

Contractual rights   Rights based on a specific contract between an employer and an employee.

Contrast error   Tendency to rate people relative to others rather than against performance standards.

Contributory plan   Pension plan in which the money for pension benefits is paid in by both employees and employers.

Core competency   A unique capability that creates high value and differentiates an organization from its competition.

Correlation coefficient   Index number giving the relationship between a predictor and a criterion variable.

Cost-benefit analysis   Comparison of costs and benefits associated with training.

Craft union   One whose members do one type of work, often using specialized skills and training.

Criterion-related validity   Validity measured by a procedure that uses a test as the predictor of how well an individual will perform on the job.

Cross training   Training people to do more than one job.

Culture   Societal forces affecting the values, beliefs, and actions of a distinct group of people.

Cumulative trauma disorders (CTDs)   Muscle and skeletal injuries that occur when workers repetitively use the same muscles to perform tasks.

D

Decertification   Process whereby a union is removed as the representative of a group of employees.

Defined-benefit plan   Retirement program in which an employee is promised a pension amount based on age and service.

Defined-contribution plan   Retirement program in which the employers makes an annual payment to an employee's pension account.

Development   Efforts to improve employees' abilities to handle a variety of assignments and to cultivate employees' capabilities beyond those required by the current job.

Disabled person   Someone who has a physical or mental impairment that substantially limits life activities, who has a record of such impairment, or who is regarded as having such an impairment.

Discipline   Form of training that enforces organizational rules.

Disparate impact   Occurs when members of a protected class are substantially underrepresented as a result of employment decisions that work to their disadvantage.

Disparate treatment Occurs when members of a protected class are treated differently from others.

Distributive justice Perceived fairness in the distribution of outcomes.

Draw Amount advanced from and repaid to future commissions earned by the employee.

Dual-career ladder System that allows a person to advance up either the management ladder or a corresponding ladder on the technical/professional side of a career.

Due process Requirement that the employer use fair means to determine employee wrongdoing and/or disciplinary measures, and that the employee have an opportunity to explain and defend his or her actions.

Duty Larger work segment composed of several tasks that are performed by an individual.

E

Economic value added (EVA) Net operating profit of a firm after the cost of capital is deducted.

Effectiveness The extent to which goals have been met.

Efficiency The degree to which operations are done in an economical manner.

E-learning Use of the Internet or an organizational Intranet to conduct training on-line.

Employee assistance program (EAP) Program that provides counseling and other help to employees having emotional, physical, or other personal problems.

Employee stock ownership plan (ESOP) Plan whereby employees have significant stock ownership in their employers.

Employment contract Agreement that formally outlines the details of employment.

Employment "test" Any employment procedure used as the basis for making an employment-related decision.

Employment-at-will (EAW) Common-law doctrine stating that employers have the right to hire, fire, demote, or promote whomever they choose, unless there is a law or a contract to the contrary.

Encapsulated development Situation in which an individual learns new methods and ideas in a development course and returns to a work unit that is still bound by old attitudes and methods.

Entitlement philosophy Assumes that individuals who have worked another year are entitled to pay increases, with little regard for performance differences.

Environmental scanning Process of studying the environment of the organization to pinpoint opportunities and threats.

Equal employment Employment that is not affected by illegal discrimination.

Equity Perceived fairness between what a person does and what the person receives.

Ergonomics Study and design of the work environment to address physiological and physical demands on individuals.

Essential job functions Fundamental duties of a job.

Exempt employees Employees to whom employers are not required to pay overtime under the Fair Labor Standards Act.

Exit interview An interview in which individuals are asked to give their reasons for leaving the organization.

Expatriate Citizen of one country who is working in a second country and employed by an organization headquartered in the first country.

F

Federation Group of autonomous national and international unions.

Feedback Amount of information employees receive about how well or how poorly they have performed.

Flexible benefits plan Program that allows employees to select the benefits they prefer from groups of benefits established by the employers.

Flexible spending accounts Benefits plans that allow employees to contribute pre-tax dollars to buy certain additional benefits.

Flexible staffing Use of workers who are not traditional employees.

Flextime Scheduling arrangement in which employees work a set number of hours a day but vary starting and ending times.

Forced distribution Performance appraisal method in which ratings of employees' performance are distributed along a bell-shaped curve.

Forecasting Using information from the past and the present to identify expected future conditions.

4/5ths rule Discrimination exists if the selection rate for a protected group is less than 80% (4/5ths) of the selection rate for the majority group or less than 80% of the majority group's representation in the relevant labor market.

401(k) plan Agreement in which a percentage of an employee's pay is withheld and invested in a tax-deferred account.

G

Gainsharing System of sharing with employees greater-than-expected gains in profits and/or productivity.

Garnishment A court action in which a portion of an employee's wages is set aside to pay a debt owed a creditor.

Glass ceiling Discriminatory practices that have prevented women and other protected-class members from advancing to executive-level jobs.

Global market approach Compensation plan that attempts to be more comprehensive in providing base pay, incentives, benefits, and relocation expenses regardless of the country to which the employee is assigned.

Global organization Firm that has corporate units in a number of countries that are integrated to operate worldwide.

Grapic rating scale Scale that allows the rater to mark an employee's performance on a continuum.

Green-circled employee Incumbent who is paid below the range set for the job.

Grievance Complaint formally stated in writing.

Grievance arbitration Means by which a third party settles disputes arising from different interpretations of a labor contract.

Grievance procedures Formal channels of communication used to resolve grievances.

H

Halo effect Occurs when a rater scores an employee high on all job criteria because of performance in one area.

Health General state of physical, mental, and emotional well-being.

Health maintenance organization (HMO) Plan that provides services for a fixed period on a pre-paid basis.

Health promotion Supportive approach of facilitating and encouraging health actions and lifestyles among employees.

Host-country national Citizen of one country who is working in that country and employed by an organization headquartered in a second country.

Hostile environment Sexual harassment in which an individual's work performance or psychological well-being is unreasonably affected by intimidating or offensive working conditions.

HR audit Formal research effort that evaluates the current state of HR management in an organization.

HR Generalist A person who has responsibility for performing a variety of HR activities.

HR metrics Specific measure tied to HR performance indicators.

HR Specialist A person who has in-depth knowledge and expertise in a limited area of HR.

HR strategies Means used to anticipate and manage the supply of and demand for human resources.

Human capital The collective value of the capabilities, knowledge, skills, life experiences, and motivation of an organizational workforce.

Human Resource (HR) management The direction of organizational systems to ensure that human talent is used effectively and efficiently to accomplish organization goals.

Human resource (HR) planning Process of analyzing and identifying the need for and availability of human resources so that the organization can meet its objectives.

Human resource management system (HRMS) An integrated system providing information used by HR management in decision making.

I

Illegal issues Collective bargaining issues that would require either party to take illegal action.

Immediate confirmation Based on the idea that people learn best if reinforcement and feedback are given after training.

Importing and exporting Buying and selling goods and services with organizations in other countries.

Independent contractors Workers who perform specific service on a contract basis.

Individual retirement account (IRA) Special account in which an employee can set aside funds that will not be taxed until the employee retires.

Individual-centered career planning Career planning that focuses on an individual career rather than on organizational needs.

Individualism Dimension of culture that refers to the extent to which people in a country prefer to act as individuals instead of members of groups.

Industrial union One that includes many persons working in the same industry or company, regardless of jobs held.

Informal training Training that occurs through interactions and feedback among employees.

J

Job Grouping of tasks, duties, and responsibilities that constitutes the total work assignment for employees.

Job analysis Systematic way of gathering and analyzing information about the content, context, and human requirements of jobs.

Job criteria Important elements in a given job.

Job description Indentification of the task, duties, and responsibilities of a job.

Job design Organizing tasks, duties, and responsibilities into a productive unit of work.

Job enlargement Broadening the scope of a job by expanding the number of different tasks to be performed.

Job enrichment Increasing the depth of a job by adding responsibility for planning, organizing, controlling, or evaluating the job.

Job evaluation Formal, systematic means to identify the relative worth of jobs within an organization.

Job family Group of jobs having common organizational characteristics.

Job posting System in which the employer provides notices of job openings and employees respond by applying.

Job rotation Process of shifting a person from job to job.

Job satisfaction A positive emotional state resulting from evaluating one's job experiences.

Job sharing Scheduling arrangement in which two employees perform the work of one full-time job.

Job specifications The knowledge, skills, and abilities (KSAs) an individual needs to perform a job satisfactorily.

Just cause Reasonable justification for taking employment-related action.

K

Keogh plan Special type of individualized pension plan for self-employed persons.

Knowledge management The way an organization identifies and leverages knowledge in order to be competitive.

L

Labor force population All individuals who are available for selection if all possible recruitment strategies are used.

Labor markets External supply pool from which organizations attract employees.

Leniency error Occurs when ratings of all employees fall at the high end of the scale.

Living wage One that is supposed to met the basic needs of a worker's family.

Lock out / tag out regulations Requirements that locks and tags be used to make equipment inoperative for repair or adjustment.

Lockout Shutdown of company operations undertaken by management to prevent union members from working.

Long-term orientation Dimension of culture that refers to the preference of people in a country for long-term values as opposed to short-term values.

Lump-sum increase (LSI) One-time payment of all or part of a yearly pay increase.

M

Managed care Approaches that monitor and reduce medical costs through restrictions and market system alternatives.

Management by objectives (MBO) Performance appraisal method that specifies the performance goals that an individual and manager mutually identify.

Management mentoring Relationship in which experienced managers aid individuals in the earlier stages of their careers.

Management rights Rights reserved so that the employer can manage, direct, and control its business.

Mandatory issues Collective bargaining issues identified specifically by labor laws or court decisions as subject to bargaining.

Marginal job functions Duties that are part of a job but are incidental or ancillary to the purpose and nature of the job.

Market banding Grouping jobs into pay grades based on similar market survey amounts.

Market line Graph line that shows the relationship between job value as determined by job evaluation points and job value as determined by pay survey rates.

Market pricing Use of survey data to identify the relative value of jobs based on what other employers pay for similar jobs.

Masculinity/femininity Dimension of culture that refers to the degree to which "masculine" values prevail over "feminine" values.

Massed practice Practice performed all at once.

Mediation Dispute resolution process by which a third party helps negotiators reach a settlement.

Mentoring Relationship in which experienced managers aid individuals in the earlier stages of their careers.

Motivation The desire within a person causing that person to act.

Multi-national enterprise (MNE) Organization that has operating units located in foreign countries.

N

National emergency strike Strike that would impact the national economy significantly.

Negligent hiring Occurs when an employer fails to check an employee's background and the employee injures someone.

Negligent retention Occurs when an employer becomes aware that an employee may be unfit for employment, continues to employ the person, and the person injures someone.

Nepotism Practice of allowing relatives to work for the same employer.

Non-compete agreements Agreements that prohibit individuals who leave the organization from competing with an employer in the same line of business for a specified period of time.

Non-contributory plan Pension plan in which all the funds for pension benefits are provided by the employer.

Non-directive interview Interview that uses questions developed from the answers to previous questions.

Non-exempt employees Employees who must be paid overtime under the Fair Labor Standards Act.

O

Open shop Workers are not required to join or pay dues to a union.

Organizational commitment The degree to which employees believe in and accept organizational goals and desire to remain with the organization.

Organizational culture The shared values and beliefs in an organization.

Organization-centered career planning Career planning that focuses on jobs and on identifying career paths that provide for the logical progression of people between jobs in an organization.

Orientation Planned introduction of new employees to their jobs, co-workers, and the organization.

P

Paid time-off (PTO) plans Plans that combine all sick leave, vacation time, and holidays into a total number of hours or days that employees can take off with pay.

Panel interview Interview in which several interviewers meet with the candidate at the same time.

Pay compression Occurs when the differences among individuals with different levels of experience and performance become small.

Pay equity Idea that pay for jobs requiring comparable levels of knowledge, skill, and ability should be similar, even if actual duties differ significantly.

Pay grades Groupings of individual jobs having approximately the same job worth.

Pay survey Collection of data on compensation rates for workers performing similar jobs in other organizations.

Pay-for-performance philosophy Requires that compensation changes reflect individual performance differences.

Pension plan Retirement program established and funded by the employer and employees.

Performance appraisal Process of evaluating how well employees perform their jobs and then communicating that information to the employees.

Performance consulting Process in which a trainer and the organizational client work together to determine what needs to be done to improve results.

Performance management Composed of the processes used to identify, measure, communicate, develop, and reward employee performance.

Performance standards Indicators of what the job accomplishes and how performance is measured in key areas of the job description.

Permissive issues Collective bargaining issues that are not mandatory and relate to certain jobs.

Perquisites (perks) Special benefits—usually non-cash items—for executives.

Person/job fit Matching the KSAs of people with characteristics of jobs.

Person-organization fit The congruence between individuals and organizational factors.

Phased retirement Approach in which employees gradually reduce their workloads and pay.

Physical ability tests Tests that measure an individual's abilities such as strength, endurance, and muscular movement.

Placement Fitting a person to the right job.

Policies General guidelines that focus organizational actions.

Portability Pension plan feature that allows employees to move their pension benefits from one employer to another.

Power distance Dimension of culture that refers to the inequality among the people of a nation.

Predictive validity Measured when test results of applicants are compared with subsequent job performances.

Predictors Measurable or visible indicators of a selection criterion.

Preferred provider organization (PPO) A health-care provider that contracts with an employer group to supply health-care services to employees at a competitive rater.

Primacy effect Occurs when a rater gives greater weight to information received first when appraising an individual's performance.

Procedural justice Perceived fairness of the processes used to make decisions about employees.

Procedures Customary methods of handling activities.

Productivity Measure of the quantity and quality of work done, considering the cost of the resources used.

Profit sharing System to distribute a portion of the profits of the organization to employees.

Protected class Individuals within a group identified for protection under equal employment laws and regulations.

Psychological contract The unwritten expectations employees and employers have about the nature of their work relationship.

Psychomotor tests Tests that measure dexterity, hand-eye coordination, arm-hand steadiness, and other factors.

Q

Quid pro quo Sexual harassment in which employment outcomes are linked to the individual granting sexual favors.

R

Ranking Performance appraisal method in which all employees are listed from highest to lowest in performance.

Rater bias Occurs when a rater's values or prejudices distort the rating.

Ratification Process by which union members vote to accept the terms of a negotiated labor agreement.

Realistic job preview (RJP) Process through which a job applicant receives an accurate picture of a job.

Reasonable accommodation A modification or adjustment to a job or work environment for a qualified individual with a disability.

Recency effect Occurs when a rater gives greater weight to recent events when appraising an individual's performance.

Recruiting Process of generating a pool of qualified applicants for organizational jobs.

Red-circled employee Incumbent who is paid above the range set for the job.

Reinforcement Based on the idea that people tend to repeat response that give them some type of positive reward and avoid actions associated with negative consequences.

Reliability Consistency with which a test measures an item.

Repatriation Planning, training, and reassignment of global employees to their home countries.

Responsibilities Obligations to perform certain tasks and duties.

Retaliation Punitive actions taken by employers against individuals who exercise their legal rights.

Return on investment (ROI) Calculation showing the value of expenditures for HR activities.

Reverse discrimination When a person is denied an opportunity because of preferences given to protected-class individuals who may be less qualified.

Right to privacy An individual's freedom from unauthorized and unreasonable intrusion into their personal affairs.

Rights Powers, privileges, or interests that belong to a person by law, nature, or tradition.

Right-to-sue letter Letter issued b the EEOC that notifies a complainant that he or she has 90 days to file a personal suit in federal court.

Right-to-work laws State laws that prohibit requiring employees to join unions as a condition of obtaining or continuing employment.

Rules Specific guidelines that regulate and restrict the behavior of individuals.

S

Sabbatical Paid time off the job to develop and rejuvenate oneself.

Safety Condition in which the physical well-being of people is protected.

Salaries Consistent payments made each period regardless of the number of hours worked.

Salting Practice in which unions hire and pay people to apply for jobs at certain companies.

Security Protection of employees and organizational facilities.

Security audit Comprehensive review of organizational security.

Selection Process of choosing individuals with qualifications needed to fill jobs in an organization.

Selection criterion Characteristic that a person must have to do a job successfully.

Selection rate Percentage hired from a given group of candidates.

Self-directed team Organizational team composed of individuals who are assigned a cluster of tasks, duties and responsibilities to be accomplished.

Self-efficacy Person's belief that he or she *can* successfully learn the training program content.

Seniority Time spend in the organization or on a particular job.

Separation agreement Agreement in which a terminated employee agrees not to sue the employer, in exchange for specified benefits.

Serious health condition Health condition requiring in-patient, hospital, hospice, or residential medical care or continuing physician care.

Severance pay Security benefit voluntarily offered by employers to employees who lose their jobs.

Sexual harassment Actions that are sexually directed, are unwanted, and subject the worker to adverse employment conditions or create a hostile work environment.

Simulation Technique that requires participants to analyze a situation and decide the best course of action according to the data given.

Situational interview Structured interview composed of questions about how applicants might handle specific job situations.

Situational judgment tests Tests that measure a person's judgment in work settings.

Skill variety Extent to which the work requires several different activities for successful completion.

Spaced practice Practice performed in several sessions spaced over a period of hours or days.

Special-purpose team Organizational team formed to address specific problems, improve work processes, and enhance product and service quality.

Statutory rights Rights based on laws or statutes.

Stock option plan Plan that gives the right to purchase a fixed number of shares in company stock at a specific price for a limited period of time.

Stock purchase plan Plan in which the corporation provides matching funds equal to the amount invested by the employee for the purchase of stock in the company.

Straight piece-rate system Pay system in which wages are determined by multiplying the number of units produced by the piece rate for one unit.

Strategic HR management Use of employees to gain or keep a competitive advantage, resulting in greater organizational effectiveness.

Stress interview Interview designed to create anxiety and put pressure on applicants to see how they respond.

Strictness error Occurs when ratings of all employees fall at the low end of the scale.

Strike Work stoppage in which union members refuse to work in order to put pressure on an employer.

Structured interview Interview that uses a set of standardized questions asked of all job applicants.

Substance abuse Use of illicit substances or misuse of controlled substances, alcohol, or other drugs.

Succession planning Process of identifying a longer-term plan for the orderly replacement of key employees.

T

Task Distinct, identifiable work activity composed of motions.

Task identity Extent to which the job includes a "whole" identifiable unit of work that is carried out from start to finish and that results in a visible outcome.

Task significance Impact the job has on other people.

Team interview Interview in which applicants are interviewed by the team members with whom they will work.

Tax equalization plan Compensation plan used to protect expatriates from negative tax consequences.

Telecommute To work via electronic computing and telecommunications equipment.

Third-country national Citizen of one country who is working in a second country and employed by an organization headquartered in a third country.

Training Process whereby people acquire capabilities to perform jobs.

Turnover The process in which employees leave an organization and have to be replaced.

U

Undue hardship Significant difficulty or expense imposed on an employer in making an accommodation for individuals with disabilities.

Uncertainty avoidance Dimension of culture that refers to the preference of people in a country for structured rather than unstructured situations.

Union Formal association of workers that promotes the interests of its members through collective action.

Union authorization card Card signed by an employee to designate a union as her or his collective bargaining agent.

Union security provisions Contract clauses to help the union obtain and retain members.

Union steward Employee selected to serve as the first-line representation of unionized workers.

Unit labor cost Computed by dividing the average cost of workers by their average levels of output.

Utilization analysis Identifies the number of protected-class members employed in the organization and the types of jobs they hold.

Utilization review Audit of the services and costs billed by health-care providers.

V

Validity Extent to which a test actually measures what it says it measures.

Variable pay Compensation linked directly to individual, team, or organizational performance.

Vesting Right of employees to receive certain benefits from their pension plans.

Virtual team Organizational team composed of individuals who are geographically separated but linked by communications technology.

W

Wages Payments directly calculated on the amount of time worked.

Wellness programs Programs designed to maintain or improve employee health before problems arise.

Well-pay Extra pay for not taking sick leave.

Whistle-blowers Individuals who report real or perceived wrongs committed by their employers.

Work Effort directed toward accomplishing results.

Work sample tests Tests that require an applicant to perform a simulated job task.

Workers' compensation Security benefits provided to persons injured on the job.

Workflow analysis Study of the way work (inputs, activities, and outputs) moves through an organization.

Wrongful discharge Termination of an individual's employment for reasons that are improper or illegal.

Y

Yield ratios Comparisons of the number of applicants at one stage of the recruiting process with the number at the next stage.

Author Index

Subject Index

Human resource planning, 43–47
See also Strategic human resource (HR) management and planning
Human Resource Planning (Lawler and Mohrman), 18
Human resource strategies, 46–47
Human resources audit, 61
Human Resources Law Index Web site, 496
Human resources metrics, 57–59
Human Rights Act in the United Kingdom, 99
Hy-Vee, 415

IBM, 167, 211, 304, 418, 436, 438, 480
Identity mismatches, 136
IGA. *See* Independent Grocers Association
IHRIM. *See* Association for Human Resource Information Management
Ikea, 513
Illegal discriminatory practices, 115
Illegal issues in collective bargaining, 545–546
Immediate confirmation in learning, 275
Immigrants, 13, 135–136
Immigration forms, 234
Immigration Reform and Control Acts (IRCA), 110, 136, 234
Implied contracts, 496
Importing, 35
Improshare, 413
Incentive magazine, 406, 421
Incentive programs, 6
Incentives for performance, 400–404
Independent contractor regulations, 379
Independent contractors, 12, 170, 202
Independent Grocers Association (IGA), 281
Independent work, 404
India
    call centers in, 74
    international outsourcing, 5, 10, 525
Indirect compensation, 364
Individual analyses for training needs, 271
Individual employee performance, 78–79
Individual incentives, 403–406

Individual pay, 390–391
Individual performance, 68, 404
Individual relations. *See* Organization/individual relations
Individual retirement accounts (IRAs), 437
Individual retirement options, 437
Individual vs. team rewards, 374
Individual-centered career planning, 297–299
Individualism, 37, 404
Industrial unions, 529
Informal performance appraisals, 338
Informal training, 278–279
Information falsification, 233
Information technology (IT), 11, 143, 159, 198, 215
Innovative training, 275
Insightlink, 90
Institute on the Costs and Health Effects of Obesity, 480
Institute for a Drug-Free Workplace Web site, 510
Institute of Management and Administration Web site, 385
Instructor-led classroom training, 284
Insurance benefits, 444
Intangible assets of organizations, 8
Intel, 35
Intellectual capital, 8–9
Intellectual property, 496
Intensive recruiting, 201
Inter-rater reliability, 241
Intercultural competence training, 288–289
Interests and careers, 299
Intermediate-range forecasts, 50
Internal equity, 375–376
Internal publications, 513
Internal Revenue Service (IRS), 202, 379, 436
Internal sources for recruiting, 205–209
Internal supply of human resources, 51–52
Internal training, 278–279
Internal workforce assessment, 48–49
International Association of Bridge, Structural, Ornamental and Reinforcing Iron Workers, 529

International emergency health services, 486
International employees, 104
International Foundation of Employee Benefits Plans, 27
International Journal of Selection and Assessment, 351
International Labour Organization, 528
International Longshore and Warehouse Union, 537
International outsourcing, 5, 10, 370
International Personnel Management Association (IPMA), 26
International Society for Performance Improvement, 27
    Web site, 267, 330
International SOS, 486
International Telework Association & Council (ITAC) Web site, 170
International unions, 529
Internet, 12
    electronic sexual harassment, 143
    on-line development, 315
    online training, 281–283
    tracking employee use, 493, 507
    and workflow, 162
Internet recruiting, 214–217
Internet-based pay surveys, 385–386
Internships, 210, 283
Interpersonal training, 275
Interviewing, 240–249
    effective interviewing, 245–248
    interviewers, 244–245
    in job analysis, 177–178
    non-directive interviews, 244
    in performance appraisal feedback, 354–355
    problems in, 248–249
    questions used, 246–247
    reliability and validity of, 241
    semistructured interviews, 244
    stress interviews, 244
    structured interviews, 241–243
    Web site, 245
Intra-rater reliability, 241
Intrinsic rewards, 364
Introductory employees, 338
Intuit, 43, 399
Inventory of organizational capabilities, 49

Organizational databases, recruiting in, 205–206
Organizational strategy
  in performance management and appraisal, 328
  in training, 267–269
Organizations
  analyses for training needs, 270
  assets of, 8
  capabilities inventory, 49
  commitment of, 70–71
  competitiveness and training in, 264–265
  cost pressures and restructuring in, 13–14
  cultural compatibility, 56
  division of responsibilities, 7–8, 45
    in benefits, 461
    in compensation, 365
    in employee discipline, 514
    in health, safety, and security, 460–461
    in job analysis, 174–175
    in performance appraisals, 338–339
    in recruiting, 199
    in selection, 226–227
    in union/management relations, 527
  effectiveness of, 39–43
  effectiveness and strategic HR management, 39–43
  efficiency of, 39
  ethics of, 22
  human resource (HR) management in, 6–8
  incentives of, 404, 413–415
  linkage of organizational and HR strategies, 35
  productivity, 40–41
Orientation of new employees, 5, 85, 275–277
OSHA. *See* Occupational Safety and Health Act of 1970
OSHRC. *See* Occupational Safety and Health Review Commission
Outdoor training, 317
Outplacement assistance, 432
Outplacement services, 55
Outplacing workers, 14
Outsider rating, 341
Outsourced recruiting, 199–200
Outsourcing, 525
  analyses and assistance, 41
  human resource administrative functions, 15–16

international, 5, 10, 370
  of training, 280
Overtime, 378, 474
OWBPA. *See* Older Workers Benefit Protection Act

Pacific Maritime Association, 537
Paid family leave, 446
Paid leave for new parents, 428
Paid-time-off (PTO) programs, 73, 449–450
Panel interviews, 245
Pappadeux Seafood Kitchen, 421
Pappas Pizza, 421
Pappas Restaurants, 421–422
PAQ. *See* Position Analysis Questionnaire
Parent with a serious health condition, 445
Parents, paid leave for, 428
Parmalat, 21
Part-time employees, 12, 84, 429, 533
Passports, 234
Paternity leave, 449
Pay adjustment matrix, 391–392
Pay compression, 390–391
Pay equity, 106, 380
Pay grades, 387–388
Pay increases, 391–393
Pay inequity, 139
Pay ranges, 388–390
Pay secrecy vs. openness, 376
Pay structures, 373, 386–391
Pay surveys, 384–386
  Web site, 385
Pay-for-performance, 399–402
Paychecks, plastic, 366
Payless ShoeSource, 328
Peer rating, 340–341
Peer review panels and ombudsmen, 500
Pension funds, 553
Pension plans, 425, 434–437
PEOs. *See* Professional employer organizations
PepsiCo, 313, 480
Perceived mistreatment, 501
Performance, 163
  ability/effort/support equals, 78
  and compensation, 86–87
  incentives, 400–404
  See also Individual employee performance
Performance Appraisal Problems Web site, 354
Performance awards, 406

Performance consulting, 266–267
Performance management, 6
  at Bristol-Myers Squibb (BMS), 358–359
  components of, 330
  cultural differences in, 331
  effective, 356–357
  executive commitment to, 330
  linkage to appraisal, 328–330
Performance management and appraisal, 326–360
  decisions about performance appraisal process, 337–339
    division of responsibilities for appraisal, 337–338
    informal vs. systematic appraisal processes, 338
    timing of appraisals, 338–339
  executive commitment to performance management, 330
  feedback on appraisals, 354–357
    effective performance management, 356–357
    feedback as a system, 355
    interviews, 354–355
    reactions of appraised employees, 356
    reactions of managers, 355–356
  identifying and measuring performance, 331–334
    elements of, 331
    job criteria, 331–332
    performance standards, 333–334
    relevance of performance criteria, 333
    types of performance information, 332–333
  legal concerns in performance appraisals, 334–335
  linkage of performance management and appraisal, 328–330
  methods for appraising performance, 343–351
    category scaling methods, 343, 345–347
    combination of methods, 350–351
    comparative methods, 347–349
    e-systems, 337
    management by objectives (MBO), 350
    narrative methods, 349–350

Removal of terminated employees and possessions from the company facilities, 518
Rent-A-Center, 240
Repatriate Career Planning Web site, 302
Repatriation, 301–302
Replacement of workers on strike, 548
Reproductive health and work, 468
Required training, 275
Resignations, 52
Responsibilities in employment, 494
    See also Employee rights and discipline
Responsibilities in jobs, 172
Restricted stock, 417
Restructuring, 13–14, 40, 56
    and retirements, 303–304
Results-based performance information, 332
Resumes as applications, 236
Retaliation, 103
Retention, 5, 67, 80–90
    career opportunities, 85
    employee relationships, 87
    employer characteristics, 80–82
    evaluation and follow-up, 90
    job design/work, 83–84
    managing retention, 87–90
    rewards, 85–87
Retirement, 52
    early retirement buyouts, 54–55, 433–434
    equity in pension plans, 436
    issues in, 302–303
    median age by gender, 344
    phased, 84, 146, 433
    U.S. government agencies, 53
Retirement benefits, 425, 428, 433–439
Return on investment (ROI), 41–42, 59, 399
    of training, 287
    of tuition aid, 445
Revenue sources, training as, 265
Reverse discrimination, 133
Rewards and retention, 85–87
Right-to-sue letter, 123
Right-to-work laws, 537
Right-to-work Web site, 538
Rights. *See* Employee rights and discipline
Rightsizing, 14, 54
Riverside County, California, 257
RJPs. *See* Realistic job previews

Rockresorts, 291
ROI. *See* Return on investment
Romance at work, 142
Rothchild Berry Farms, 413
Routinization in jobs, 160
Royal Caribbean International, 377
Runzheimer International Web site, 370

Sabbaticals, 317
Safe work environment, 84, 183
    See also Health, safety, and security
Safety committees Web site, 475
Safety management, 473–476
    See also Health, safety, and security
St. Peter's Hospital in Albany, New York, 169
Salaries, 365
    for executives, 416
Salary guide chart, 391
Salary-only sales compensation plan, 407
Salary-plus-commission sales compensation plan, 408
Sales compensation, 407–409
Salting, 540–541
Same-sex marriages, 448
Sampling error, 354
Sam's Club, 363
Sandwich generation, 84
SAP, 5
Sara Lee, 418
Saratoga Institute, 58
Sarbannes-Oxley Act of 2002, 418
SAT. *See* Scholastic Aptitude Test
Savings plans, 443
SBA. *See* Small Business Administration
SBC Communications, 125, 377, 438, 525
SBP. *See* Skill-based pay
Scanlon plan for gainsharing, 413
Scattergrams, 388
Scheduling, compressed, 84
Schizophrenia, 478
Scholastic Aptitude Test (SAT), 240
School recruiting, 210–211
"School to work" programs, 211
School-to-work transition, 283
Schuler Engineering, 540
Scorecard for Skills Web site, 287
Sea Island Shrimp House, 281
Securities and Exchange Commission, 553

Security audits, 485
Security benefits, 431–432
Security in the workplace. *See* Health, safety, and security
SEIU. *See* Service Employees International Union
Selecting human resources, 224–259
    background and definition, 226
    background investigations, 249–253
        legal constraints, 251–252
        medical examinations and inquiries, 252–253
        reference-checking methods, 250–251
        sources of, 250
        Web-based, 249
    criteria, 22–28
    division of responsibilities, 226–227
    global staffing assignments, 253–255
        legal issues, 254–255
        selection process, 254
        types of employees, 253–254
    in governmental agencies, 257
    interviewing, 240–249
        effective interviewing, 245–248
        interviewers, 244–245
        non-directive interviews, 244
        problems in, 248–249
        questions used, 246–247
        reliability and validity of, 241
        semistructured interviews, 244
        stress interviews, 244
        structured interviews, 241–243
    job offers, 253
    job performance, 228
    placement, 226–227
    predictors, 227–229
    process of selection, 5, 83, 229–236
        applicant job interest, 231
        application forms, 233–236
        flowchart, 230
        legal concerns, 229–231
        pre-employment screening, 231–233
    reliability, 229
    testing, 225, 233, 236–240
        ability tests, 236–238
        controversial and questionable tests, 240

United States Constitution, 504
amendments to, 98
United States Department of
Justice, 115
United States Department of
Labor, 104, 115, 140, 202,
214, 284
Bureau of Labor Statistics, 385
Employment and Training
Administration, 179–180
Wage and Hour Division, 376
United States Department of
Transportation, 477, 510
United States Office of Personnel
Management, 115
United States Postal Service, 539
United Steelworkers of America,
529
United Technologies, 418
University of Michigan, 24, 133
University recruiting, 209–210
UPS, 23
Upward communication, 513
Urinalysis drug testing, 478
U.S. Assist, 486
USA Patriot Act, 506–507
Use of incentives Web site, 401
USERRA. *See* Uniformed Services
Employment and
Reemployment Rights Act
(USERRA) of 1994
Utah Society for Healthcare
Human Resources
Administration, 386
Utilization analysis, 59, 136
Utilization review for health-care
providers, 439

Vacation pay, 449
Vacation time, 248
Validity, 117–118
and equal employment,
118–121
of interviews, 241
in selecting human resources,
228–229
Value and effectiveness of training,
263
Values, identifying, 299
Valuing jobs, 382–384
Variable pay, 364, 398–415
defined, 400
group/team incentives, 403–404,
410–413
design of, 410–411
problems with, 411

success and failures of,
411–412
types of, 412–413
incentives for performance,
400–404
fun and travel, 421–422
metrics for, 402–403
and motivational research, 402
pay-for-performance,
399–402
individual incentives, 403–406
bonuses, 405
piece-rate systems, 404–405
special incentive programs,
405–406
organizational incentives, 404,
413–415
employee stock plans, 415
profit sharing, 414–415
sales compensation, 407–409
challenges of, 408–409
effectiveness of, 409–410
ethical concerns and, 407
metrics in sales performance,
409
types of, 407–408
successes and failures of, 403
types of, 403–404
See also Benefits;
Compensation; Executive
compensation
Varying standards in rater error,
352
Verizon, 33, 43, 60
Vesting in pension plans, 436–437
Victoria's Secret, 513
Video interviewing, 245
Vietnam Era Veterans
Readjustment Assistance
Act of 1974, 112
Violence in the workplace,
482–485
Virtual employees, 12
Virtual job fairs, 213
Virtual Resource Center (VRC), 29
Virtual teams, 167
Visa, 366
Visas and documentation
requirements, 136
Vision insurance, 438
Visual learners, 273
Vocational/technical schools,
recruiting in, 210
Voice mail monitoring, 493,
505–506
Voluntary absences, 71

Voluntary benefits, 430–431
Voluntary separation programs,
54–55
Voluntary turnover, 74
VRC. *See* Virtual Resource Center
Vulnerability analysis, 485

Waffle House, 377
Wage curve, 388
Wage and Hour Division, United
States Department of
Labor, 376
Web site, 378
Wage and salary systems, 6
Wage/hour regulations, 183
Wages, 365
Wagner Act (National Labor
Relations Act (1935), 376,
475, 535–536
Wal-Mart, 14, 35, 48, 104–105,
110, 363, 377, 379, 395
Walgreen's, 44, 194
Walsh-Healy Public Contracts Act,
380
WARN Act. *See* Worker
Adjustment and Retraining
Notification (WARN) Act
Washington Mutual, 422
Watson Wyatt, 16
Weather Channel, 451
Web auction sites, 169
Webvan, 532
Wegman's Food Markets, 18, 429
Weighted application forms, 236
Weingarten rights, 551
Well-pay, 450
Wellness Council of America, 489
Wellness programs, 84, 441, 452,
480–481
Wendy's, 447
West coast dock strike, 537
Whistle-blowing, 505
White-collar jobs, 525, 532
Whites, demographics of, 130
Whole learning, 274
WIA. *See* Workforce Investment
Act
Wildcat strikes, 548
Wiretap laws, 520
Women
and careers, 303
with mentors, 321
pink-collar workers, 532
in the workforce, 13
workforce demographics,
137–138